AUGSBURG COLLEGE & SEMINARY
George Sverdrup Library
MINNEAPOLIS 4, MINNESOTA

THE HOLSTEIN PAPERS

THE MEMOIRS, DIARIES AND
CORRESPONDENCE OF
FRIEDRICH VON HOLSTEIN
1837–1909

III
CORRESPONDENCE
1861–1896

HOLSTEIN IN 1879
BY ANTON VON WERNER

THE
HOLSTEIN PAPERS

EDITED BY
NORMAN RICH & M. H. FISHER

VOLUME III

★

CORRESPONDENCE
1861–1896

CAMBRIDGE
AT THE UNIVERSITY PRESS
1961

PUBLISHED BY
THE SYNDICS OF THE CAMBRIDGE UNIVERSITY PRESS

Bentley House, 200 Euston Road, London, N.W.1
American Branch: 32 East 57th Street, New York 22, N.Y.
West African Office: P.O. Box 33, Ibadan, Nigeria

©
CAMBRIDGE UNIVERSITY PRESS
1961

The editors and publishers wish to record their gratitude to Michigan State University for a generous grant assisting the publication of the Holstein *Correspondence*

Printed in Great Britain by
Robert MacLehose and Company Limited
The University Press, Glasgow

CONTENTS

Introduction ix

CORRESPONDENCE

1861	*page* 3	1885	145
1868	24	1886	159
1869	27	1887	198
1871	29	1888	244
1874	31	1889	307
1876–7	40	1890	324
1878–9	46	1891	363
1880	48	1892	396
1881	50	1893	431
1882	59	1894	455
1883	77	1895	489
1884	101	1896	581

Volume IV of this series will
contain a general index

PLATES

Holstein in 1879, by Anton von Werner — *frontispiece*

Bismarck in 1888 — *facing page* ix

BISMARCK IN 1888

INTRODUCTION

LETTERS form the largest part of the Holstein document collection. As filed by the archivists of the German Foreign Ministry, they make up seventy of the ninety-one volumes of the Holstein Papers. Only three of the letters preserved by Holstein himself antedate 1880. Holstein had kept no diaries before this time for reasons of diplomatic discretion, and this may also be the explanation for his failure to preserve his personal letters. Why he suddenly began keeping his letters after 1880 is impossible to determine, but in 1881 he began to keep a diary as well, and in 1883 he even began to write his memoirs. Both diaries and memoirs were soon abandoned, but Holstein kept up the practice of preserving his letters until the end of his life. When he died in 1909, these personal papers were the only possessions of any value that he was able to leave to his friend Frau von Lebbin in his will.

In keeping his personal letters after 1880, Holstein did not entirely abandon his long-established habits of discretion. Suspicious about the security of his office and his own flat, he began sending his diary entries and a large number of his letters to his cousin Ida von Stülpnagel for safekeeping. In later years he sent many of his personal papers to Frau von Lebbin for the same purpose.

Of all the letters preserved in the Holstein Papers, only a few could be called personal in the strictest sense of the term. The great majority formed part of that vast private-political correspondence that Holstein conducted throughout his career with the knowledge and approval of the four Chancellors under whom he served. Letter-writing of this kind was by no means unusual among members of the German foreign service. Almost every German diplomat of this period corresponded widely and at length about political matters with other members of the service. Holstein was outstanding only in the extent of his correspondence. Even his famous right to send private letters and telegrams on official matters through official channels was a privilege he shared with many other members of the Foreign Ministry.

The letters Holstein kept after 1880 reveal an impressive range of friends and acquaintances. His most important correspondence at this time was with Herbert and Wilhelm von Bismarck, the sons of the Chancellor, and with Paul von Hatzfeldt, the Ambassador to Constantinople, who was soon to become head of the German Foreign Ministry and was then for many years Ambassador in London. Holstein was also maintaining an active correspondence with his old chief in Paris, Prince Hohenlohe, later Governor of Alsace-Lorraine and

German Chancellor; with Hohenlohe's First Secretary, Max von Thielmann; and with his Second Secretary, Bernhard von Bülow, who was also to become German Chancellor. In St Petersburg he was corresponding with the First Secretary, Wilhelm von Redern, and with the Second Secretary, Alfred von Kiderlen-Wächter. Then there was Otto von Bülow, the Foreign Ministry representative on the staff of the Kaiser, Wilhelm von Thielau in Budapest, Ludwig von Plessen in Madrid, Derenthall in Rome, Brincken in Weimar, Hirschfeld in Constantinople, Stumm in London, and many others. It was a list that was to be subject to many changes in years to come but the list itself was always a long one.

Correspondence with Holstein was a privilege much cherished by members of the diplomatic corps. Holstein kept his friends supplied with political information which supplemented and filled in the official despatches sent to the diplomatic missions. He indicated the type of information required from a particular mission to fill in the gaps in Berlin's knowledge, and took the trouble to criticise the political reports not only of neophytes but of experienced officials. When one of his friends had a disagreement with his superior officers or had fallen into disfavour in Berlin because of some misunderstanding, Holstein went to great lengths to clear up the matter. It was to Holstein that his correspondents first turned with requests for promotion or transfer. They could then be sure of an expert appraisal of their chances before risking an official application. Holstein did a good deal himself to sponsor the promotion of his friends or their transfer to better posts. Nor were his activities on behalf of his friends all official. He arranged business matters in Berlin for those stationed abroad, or met wives and children who might be passing through the capital. He would send birthday congratulations to a young attaché who had just been sent to a foreign post, or telegraph parents about the promotion of a son before it had been officially announced. Such acts of kindness transcended utilitarian relationships and were the more appreciated because kindness was not a prominent characteristic of the German civil service. Yet the primary objectives of Holstein's letter-writing were information and influence. When a friend retired from the service, Holstein might do his best to secure him the maximum pension, but active correspondence soon ceased.

Holstein's circle of acquaintances was not confined to the diplomatic world. He corresponded with members of other departments of the government, prominent journalists, members of the Reichstag, with officials at Court and with army leaders. It was no coincidence that these correspondents were men in key positions in their various spheres. During the Bismarck era they included at one time or another Gerson Bleichröder, Bismarck's banker and financial adviser; Pindter, the editor of the official *Norddeutsche Allgemeine Zeitung*; Rottenburg, one of Bismarck's most trusted officials in the Reich Chancellery; Götz von Seckendorff at the Court of the Crown Prince, and Adolf von Bülow, the Adjutant of Prince Wilhelm, the later Kaiser Wilhelm II.

With the fall of Bismarck in 1890, Holstein's correspondence with Bismarck's sons ceased, but in the meantime he had established a close relationship with Prince Philipp zu Eulenburg, the intimate friend and adviser of Kaiser Wilhelm II. In 1894 his old friend Prince Chlodwig zu Hohenlohe became Chancellor, and in 1900 the Chancellorship fell to his friend Bernhard von Bülow. He therefore remained in close touch with the direction of affairs. His influence also increased immeasurably. Whereas under Bismarck his role had been restricted—at least officially—to carrying out the Chancellor's policy, under Bismarck's successors Holstein himself became a formulator of policy. These successors were heavily dependent on his knowledge and experience, but above all they depended on him for ideas. The extent of this dependence was strikingly demonstrated by Bülow, who secretly engineered Holstein's dismissal in 1906 when he thought the old Counsellor had become a political liability. Only a few weeks after Holstein's dismissal, however, Bülow once again turned to him for advice, and from that time until Holstein's death in 1909 Bülow consulted him constantly.

Despite the great quantity of letters preserved by Holstein, there are numerous and serious gaps in his correspondence. Apart from the almost total absence of letters before 1880, there are sudden breaks in his correspondence with friends from whom he was receiving letters regularly, there is a very thin coverage of letters for entire years, and there are no letters at all from certain important figures with whom Holstein was known to have been in close contact. A number of these gaps can be explained. A break in a regular correspondence often occurred when Holstein's friend was in Berlin and letter-writing became unnecessary. There are many indications that Holstein destroyed numerous letters at the request of their writers—although he also preserved a good many he had been asked to destroy. Many of Holstein's personal letters on official matters were sent through official channels and were subsequently filed in the Foreign Ministry archive. A number of letters sent for safe-keeping to his cousin Ida von Stülpnagel were kept by her at the time of his death and were not handed over to Frau von Lebbin as Holstein's will had stipulated. In addition, whole sections of the Holstein archive were removed after Holstein's death. The historian Friedrich Thimme received permission from the owner of the Holstein Papers to take the Hatzfeldt letters for the years 1897–9 when working on a biography of Hatzfeldt. When the Holstein archive was confiscated by the Gestapo in 1935, Thimme did not hand these letters over to the German government. It is not known what became of them. Professor Thimme also seems to have removed the Radolin–Holstein letters from the period of the First Morocco Crisis, and these letters too have apparently been lost.

But apart from the gaps in the Holstein Correspondence that can be accounted for, there are a disconcerting number of gaps that have no satisfactory explanation. At the time of Bismarck's dismissal, for instance, Holstein was in close touch with General von Waldersee, who played a significant part in the events leading to the 1890 crisis. A publication of Waldersee's correspondence includes some highly suggestive letters from Holstein bearing on this problem, but the Holstein Papers contain only a handful of letters from Waldersee, and no important ones. The Holstein Papers contain no letters whatever from General von Schlieffen, who became Chief of the General Staff in 1891, although Holstein for years supplied Schlieffen with information on German foreign policy and the two men were in close touch with one another during the crucial months of the First Morocco Crisis.

It can now be established with certainty that Holstein himself destroyed a large number of his letters dealing with particular problems. Thanks to the efforts of Professor Frauendienst and the Musterschmidt-Verlag, the publishers of the German edition, the letters from Holstein to Prince Philipp zu Eulenburg-Hertefeld were made available to the editors through the kindness of the present Prince Eulenburg. In addition to preserving the letters Holstein had written to him, Prince Eulenburg also made copies of his letters to Holstein, and from these it can be seen that Holstein destroyed Eulenburg's letters dealing with the Bismarck crisis of 1890 and the Caprivi crisis of 1894, to name only two examples. On 11 December 1894 Holstein wrote to Eulenburg: 'Your letters have *all* been destroyed. In cleaning out my desk recently during the crisis, I did not let a single one escape.'

All this might lead to the assumption that Holstein not only destroyed many letters soon after he received them, but that he edited his entire document collection before his death, carefully eliminating all material that might injure his historical reputation. Such an assumption is not altogether valid, however. The Eulenburg Papers reveal that many of the letters Holstein destroyed were thoroughly innocuous, they do not establish him as playing a crucial part in the dismissal of Bismarck or Caprivi, and indeed numerous documents destroyed by Holstein show him in a highly favourable light. Furthermore it is extraordinary to find how many letters and private papers Holstein retained in his archive that might be considered compromising. In pursuing his secret and enormously dangerous personal policy during the last years of Bismarck's Chancellorship, he not only kept letters revealing this policy but recorded his activities in his diaries. Similarly, he kept the letters he received from the journalist Maximilian Harden, including copies of letters he wrote to Bülow on Harden's behalf. These letters reveal the extremely close relationship existing between Holstein and Harden and would have been all the proof many of Holstein's enemies needed to show that he was the guiding spirit behind Harden's journalistic campaign against Eulenburg and his friends, as these enemies contended. The existence of so much unfavourable material in the Holstein Papers makes it difficult to establish a rationale or system behind Holstein's destruction of documents. It is quite possible that there was none.

In an effort to fill in some of the gaps in the Holstein Papers, we have included in the present publication all Holstein documents of historical interest which we have found in the files of the German Foreign Ministry and in other collections deposited in the Foreign Ministry archive. Thus we have tried to fill in the gap caused by the removal of the Hatzfeldt letters with documents from the files of the German Embassy in London, and the gap in the Radolin letters from the Radolin Papers in the Foreign Ministry files. When the originals of documents were found of which there were only copies in the Holstein Papers, the text of the original has been printed, and any important textual differences have been indicated in footnotes. Whenever documents from other collections have been used, their origin has been noted.

In making use of the Foreign Ministry files, we were inevitably guided by a passage in the introduction to the catalogue of the Holstein Papers prepared by the official archivists of the German Foreign Ministry in 1941. '(1) Because of their close interconnection with the secret political documents of the Foreign Ministry, the Holstein Papers cannot in future be submitted in their entirety to the examination of private researchers any more than the secret files themselves. (2) Certain sections of the Papers can be submitted to private researchers, if at all, only if they form a unity in themselves and if their substantive and formal connection with other parts of the Papers as well as with other previously published literature can be established from the beginning.' Following up these statements, we have used the Holstein Papers to trace material in the official files that might not have been made available to researchers in the past. The results in most cases were far from sensational. Official archivists, by refusing to release documents to researchers, often confer on such documents far greater importance than they actually possess. Nevertheless, the effort to relate all documents on foreign policy in the Holstein Papers to the official files of the German Foreign Ministry has filled in many gaps on subjects covered lightly or not at all in official German document publications.

The Foreign Ministry itself added a number of documents to the Holstein collection which are especially interesting because they come from the pre-1880 period. These were letters written to Holstein while he was serving as Attaché in St Petersburg in 1861 and which were found in the archive of the St Petersburg Embassy after Holstein's death. In March 1910 the German Foreign Ministry gave these letters—most of them from Holstein's father—to Frau von Lebbin, the heiress of the Holstein Papers, and they were subsequently incorporated in the Holstein archive.

In addition to documents from the Foreign Ministry archive we have included a small number of Holstein letters we received in typescript from Baroness Vera von der Heydt, the present heiress of the Holstein Papers. These letters seem to have come from the archive of her father, the banker Paul von Schwabach, who received the Holstein Papers as a gift from Frau von Lebbin in 1913 and who had an extensive document collection in his own right. The most significant of Baroness von der Heydt's documents were typewritten copies of Holstein's letters to the British journalist Valentine Chirol. We have not been able to discover how these copies got into the Schwabach archive.

Also included among Baroness von der Heydt's typescript were a number of Holstein letters marked as coming from the Bernhard von Bülow Papers. It was only after these letters had been incorporated in the present edition that we learned they had originally been given to Dr Helmuth Rogge while he and Baroness von der Heydt were working together on an edition of the Holstein Papers before they were confiscated by the Gestapo. As Dr Rogge has indicated that he does not intend to publish all of these documents from the Bülow Papers himself, we are keeping some of the copies we received through Baroness von der Heydt in this edition.

Dr Rogge has also most graciously allowed us to see microfilm copies of Holstein's letters to Maximilian Harden which he has edited.[1] The opportunity to see both sides of this complicated correspondence has greatly aided us in our own task of editing the Harden–Holstein letters. Dr Rogge has been good enough to go over our edition for the years 1906–9, making numerous suggestions and correcting numerous errors. We wish to express our sincere appreciation to Dr Rogge for this kindness.

The editors have made every effort to include in the present volumes all letters of historical significance found in the Holstein Papers. We have printed the majority of the copies or drafts of letters written by Holstein himself not only for the sake of the Holstein record, but because it is evident that he considered letters of which he made a handwritten copy important.

By far the largest number of documents in the Holstein collection are letters written to Holstein. Most of these letters have not been included in this edition. For the most part the omitted letters were from friends in diplomatic posts outside the mainstream of policy, including the smaller German states, letters from people of little historical interest, or letters which add nothing further to our knowledge of the period. From the letters selected for publication, details of private life (when these did not affect policy) have usually been omitted, as well as material fully covered by other document publications such as *Die Grosse Politik*. All omissions have been marked thus: [...].

In editing the present volumes, we have refrained from any attempt to correct interpretations of Holstein's policy or character current in other historical literature. Wherever necessary we have elucidated the text by reference to the files of the German Foreign Ministry, to printed documents or memoir literature, or to works based on unpublished documents. We have tried to correct errors of fact, but apart

[1] *Holstein und Harden* (München 1959).

from that Holstein and his correspondents have been allowed to speak for themselves.

The correspondence has been arranged chronologically, and the date has been uniformly written at the head of each document for the sake of clarity. Spelling and punctuation have been standardised.

As in the previous volumes, the translation is intended to follow the original as closely as possible, but the many styles of the letters and the hasty nature of much of the writing posed numerous problems. We have tried to reproduce in some measure the flavour of the various writers, and have therefore followed faithfully the stilted phrases of Holstein's father, the involved subtleties of Hatzfeldt's diplomatic arguments, or the raw humour of Kiderlen-Wächter. In general, however, we have attempted to make the translation readable and intelligible, even when the German original left much to be desired on both counts. At the same time we have tried to avoid giving our own interpretation to points left vague or ambiguous by the writers.

We wish to express our thanks to Michigan State University for a series of All-University research grants which have materially aided in the preparation of these volumes; to Mrs Joan Spencer and Mr Ian F. D. Morrow for their work on the translation; and to Mrs Joan Rich for her help in making the index.

Once again we would like to thank Professor Werner Frauendienst for his co-operation in producing the German edition and for numerous suggestions for improvements that have been incorporated in both the English and German editions.

As was the case with the previous two volumes, we bear final responsibility for the selection of the material to be published, the textual accuracy of the documents, the translation, and the editorial work for both the German and English editions.

Microfilms of all the manuscripts in the Holstein collection, together with a corrected typewritten transcript of these documents, will be made available to scholars in the Public Record Office in London and the National Archives in Washington at the time of the publication of these volumes.

NORMAN RICH
M. H. FISHER

1960

CORRESPONDENCE

1861

In November 1860 Friedrich von Holstein was provisionally admitted to the Prussian diplomatic service. Before final admission to the service, he had to serve a period of probation without pay in one of Prussia's diplomatic missions abroad and to pass a series of examinations in Berlin.

On 6 December Holstein received his first appointment as Attaché at the Prussian Legation in St Petersburg, where at that time Otto von Bismarck[1] was Minister. He arrived at his post in January 1861. From this period of his career come the first letters in the present collection.

1. August von Holstein to his Son[2]

Karlstein,[3] 30 January 1861

My old darling boy,

I was terribly upset, and indeed all of us were, about your illness. May the good Lord grant that you are now better again. Write soon —quite briefly—to tell us how you are. Did you call in Herr Bismarck's doctor at once, and stay indoors? I expect you to do this immediately out of love and regard for me. Since the climate and the food are so different from here, and you are not used to them, you must take twice as much care of yourself at first. It will ease my mind if I can count on your doing this and doubtless you will do me this kindness! Write often until you are quite well—even if only a few lines to say how you are.

Your aunt[4] and Ida[5] send you their affectionate regards and their heartfelt sympathy. That you should welcome the period of mourning[6]

[1] Otto von Bismarck-Schönhausen, Count in 1865, Prince in 1871. Prussian Minister to the Federal Diet in Frankfurt, August 1851–9; Minister in St Petersburg, April 1859–62, in Paris, May–September 1862; Prussian Minister-President, 1862–72, 1873–90; Prussian Foreign Minister, 1862–90; Chancellor of the North German Confederation, 1867–71, of the German Reich, 1871–90.

[2] This letter is badly damaged.

[3] In March 1848, August von Holstein sold his estate at Trebenow and took his family to live at Karlstein near Zehden an der Oder, the home of his sister Minna von Holtzendorff. The Holstein family did not stay long at Karlstein, but lived for the most part in Berlin or abroad. It was only after the death of his wife on 24 July 1858, and particularly after his son had gone to St Petersburg, that August von Holstein spent the greater part of his time at Karlstein.

[4] Minna von Holtzendorff.

[5] Ida von Holtzendorff. Daughter of Minna von Holtzendorff and a cousin of Friedrich von Holstein. On 2 October 1866 she married Alfred von Stülpnagel-Dargitz.

[6] Friedrich Wilhelm IV, King of Prussia, had died on 2 January 1861.

because the respite from social activity causes less interference with your work is a point of view I cannot share. It is precisely the social life, getting to know people and their character, that in my opinion really makes diplomatic life in St Petersburg so instructive and interesting, and I believe that you ought to attach even greater importance to this than to purely academic studies; I mean true social life and interesting people, and not that of the casinos or at Kroll's. When you are *completely* recovered, you must display your diplomatic talents by seeking to overcome the difficulties in this sphere, too, and build up as large and interesting circle of acquaintances as possible. In many respects it will not be different from Berlin, but to attain your ends you will have to disregard this and always remember that this is seed-time and as you sow, so will you reap. I am very sorry that Herr Loen[1] will be away for about another three weeks and I only hope that he does not remain away for good. Since he is soon to be [ ][2] to the command of a regiment, [ ][2] this would not be impossible. In my opinion you had therefore better not count on his return. If I am not mistaken, I believe he told me that he frequented the salons of the Russian nobility as well as those of the diplomatic corps and the financiers. You should find out about this from Herr Schlözer[3] and act accordingly. Above all go as often as possible to Mme T's soirées where you will certainly find these three kinds of people together and will most easily make acquaintances. Social life will probably be liveliest in financial circles this year and also among the highest rank of business people, who in Russia are regarded as members of the nobility. If I were you, as soon as you are quite well again, I would ask Herr Schlözer to introduce you to his friends, unless you think that this would make you suspect in other circles. If Herr Loen is not back, talk frankly with Herr Bismarck about this. Since he has shown himself to be a kindly and well-disposed Chief to you in other matters, you can certainly speak to him quite frankly about this. Under no circumstances [before] you are well again, then do not neglect [ ].[2] As you say [nothing] about this perhaps it is not the case, yet the self-indulgence frequently shown by your colleagues from other countries might perhaps lead you to think that it is necessary only to do the one thing and neglect the other. I do not believe this of the son of your dear mother, yet everyone must watch over himself.

Now, my dear old fellow, when you are completely restored to health and quite in your usual *train*, tell us about your life and how you spend your days, for even the least important things are, as you can well imagine, of the greatest interest to me, old rascal. Have you made your bow to all the Imperial Family? And have you been pre-

---

[1] Leopold, Baron von Loen. Prussian Military Attaché in St Petersburg, 1858–65.

[2] Gap in the text.

[3] Kurd von Schlözer. Secretary of the Legation in St Petersburg, 1857–62; temporary Chargé d'Affaires in Copenhagen, 1863; Secretary of the Prussian Legation to the Holy See, 1864–9; Consul-General of the North German Federation in Mexico, 1869–71; German Minister in Washington, 1871–82, to the Holy See, 1882–92. (See his *Petersburger Briefe 1857–1862* (Stuttgart and Berlin, 1921).)

sented to Duke Georg?[1] [ ][2] Your other news greatly interested us. As [some people] have wondered why you didn't join the army, I hope you answered—what is, after all, the truth—that while you were out chamois-hunting [ ][2] and this affected the eyes [ ][2] only after the usual smallpox [ ][2] and are now completely recovered. If you have [not already done this] then do not forget to do so when the occasion calls for it, so that it should not be thought that you were a shirker[3] [ ][4]

2. August von Holstein to his Son

27 February–2 March 1861[5]

My dear boy,

God bless you! I send you this greeting from Berlin where we arrived to-day, Wednesday. [...]

Thursday night. [...] From there[6] I went to Herr Loen to commend you to him once again; he leaves on 15 March at the earliest, and I should think it will probably be later. He told me—do not let anybody know about this—that H. v. S[chlözer] had spoken very favourably of you in a letter; you spoke and wrote English and French very well, though in the conduct of affairs you were naturally lacking in experience and would have to acquire this in the course of time.[7] L. thinks that it would be useful for you to be on good terms with him. S[chlözer], like Hr B[ismarck], has little to do with Russian families; he, L., on the other hand, believes that one should associate with the people of the country in which one is living, and is therefore on friendly terms with many Russian families; he advises you to endeavour to establish similar friendships. But they are very suspicious of foreigners and one must be very cautious—you may therefore have been quite right in this—and especially cautious in one's manner of speaking and one's judgments. By a single ill-founded, ill-considered or erroneous utterance one could forfeit one's standing in society, and once lost it would be very difficult to regain. You must be specially careful about this and at the same time very polite to everybody [...]

Friday evening

I heard to-day—do not say anything about this since it is possibly not true—that H. v. Loen is to be replaced at St Petersburg by the commanding officer of the Eighth Hussar Regiment, Major von Rauch. For your sake I am very sorry. I am afraid that it will happen. However, by that time you will have learned the ropes anyway. Be sure

[1] Georg, Duke of Mecklenburg-Strelitz. Russian Lieutenant-General and Inspector General of the Army.
[2] Gap in the text.
[3] Holstein was rejected for military service because of a 'weak chest and general bodily weakness'. (From the Foreign Ministry personnel files.)
[4] The rest of the letter is damaged.
[5] This long letter was written in the course of several days. Only a small part is printed here.
[6] In the section of the letter omitted here, August von Holstein described his round of visits in Berlin.
[7] See Schlözer, *Petersburger Briefe*, pp. 187–8.

to follow his advice and that of Fallois carefully, and be on your guard against thoughtless remarks and witticisms. And another thing: your Chief cannot stand thoughtlessness, so think twice about what you say, even when you are with him *en famille* [...]

I have heard from Cohn[1] that you have withdrawn 500 roubles. Write down exactly what you spend, since otherwise I might suspect that other hands are dipping into your purse. Apart from this 500, an amount of over 3,400 Th[alers] has been paid either to you in cash or in settlement of your accounts since the day on which you left for Trieste.[2] I did not therefore expect that you would already be in need of money. Keep your accounts accurately and avoid senseless and extravagant tips. [...]

Since your bear-hunt gave you great pleasure, it was also a source of joy for us; it is obvious that every place has its own customs, for we should never sell even the pelt of a fox before we had caught it, whereas in St Petersburg one pays for the whole bear in advance.[3] Now goodnight and adieu, my dear boy. God guard and keep you.

Your very loving
Father
Berlin, 2 March 1861
(for it is already 12.30.)

Do you keep your money safely locked up? Otherwise I had better buy you a small cash-box with a reliable lock. [...]

3. August von Holstein to his Son

[23 March 1861]

My old darling boy,

Your dear letter of the 16th gave us all great pleasure; it was all the greater because yesterday morning Herr Meyer-Cohn played a clever trick by writing to ask whether he should forward a letter from you to me that he had received from the Foreign Ministry. I was so enraged by this joke that I was all the more delightfully surprised by your letter. I am so glad that you are well; and so—touch wood!—am I. I am very much pleased that you are gradually finding your way about in society, for I believe that nowhere else will you have a better opportunity of acquiring what you still lack in the way of social polish and elegance of manner. With your talents you will find this easy to achieve if you apply resolute determination and persistence. I believe it will be the same with your knowledge of your profession and its routine, although this will take longer. Do not lose heart, but strive on unceasingly with the resolution that is yours when you wish to use it to train yourself and to satisfy your Chief. A short time ago I heard it said that one of the best traits in his character was that he went to quite excep-

---

[1] *Geheimer Kommerzienrat* Meyer-Cohn. Banker to August von Holstein and subsequently to his son.

[2] Holstein made a trip to Italy in the autumn of 1860. (See *The Holstein Papers*, vol. I, *Memoirs*, p. 1.)

[3] For Holstein's description of a bear-hunt, see *Memoirs*, pp. 10–11.

tional lengths in championing and protecting, as well as commending, those among his subordinates who won his approval. If at times he can be violent and brutally outspoken, do not let yourself be drawn into opposition and ingratitude on that account, especially as he has your good at heart. How do you get on with his children? Do be careful with the governess; as a class such people are only too often as pretentious as they are touchy, and often they exercise great influence with the family, and therefore can easily do much harm. So be polite to her, yet at the same time avoid thereby any closer acquaintanceship. This —the closer acquaintanceship—as a rule leads very quickly to raillery and teasing, and they in turn give rise to wounded feelings and enmity. Your announcement that you will not dance more than is compatible with your health gave me much pleasure. Take good care of yourself in general, for the climate there makes this even more necessary than at home; and especially in spring when the mists rise from the marshes, you must be very careful not to catch cold. You must also do this for the sake of your appearance because a drawn face does not suit you and I am always hoping you will make a rich marriage—now don't go pulling such a long face that I can see it from here—resign from government service, live in the country, cut a figure in the Chamber in winter and keep a house. To put your mind at rest, I will add that although I mean a sensible marriage, I do not thereby mean a marriage contrary to inclination. I was also very glad to hear that you frequently visit the Consul-General[1] because you can certainly learn a lot from him, whether it be general information or practical advice for your future. But elderly gentlemen are often crotchety, so take care that you do not visit him more often than you think is agreeable to him. I am exceedingly pleased to hear that you are now being introduced more frequently into the society of the Russian aristocracy, because I am firmly of the opinion that this is far more useful for you and that you will enjoy yourself there far better than in purely diplomatic circles. Miss no opportunity of being very attentive to elderly ladies, because this will be of great assistance in opening doors and giving you a place in society; and also do not forget to pay the obligatory calls mentioned by Herr Loen. It was not in your own best interest to have written so cursorily to the Countess Veronika.[2] You want all the news from Berlin, yet she can hardly reply other than in the manner in which you wrote to her. Her reply can therefore only be very brief; if you want a lot of information, especially from women, then you must not write too briefly and casually to them since with the best will in the world they cannot reply otherwise. [...] You have not answered my question whether you read the *Kreuzzeitung* daily with all its news and announcements; I would advise you to do so, for in this way you will keep in touch with your own country. Today, Saturday the 23rd, that clever Cohn sent me your letter of 7/23 Febr. The incidental expenses appear to me to be enorm-

---

[1] Konstantin von Fehleisen. Consul-General of Baden in St Petersburg.

[2] Veronika von Hacke, *née* von Flemming. A daughter of the Hereditary Marshal of Pomerania, and an old friend of the Holstein family. On 20 July 1860 she married Count Edwin Hacke.

ously heavy; still I know you well enough to be certain that you avoid what is unnecessary; you will have to do whatever is unavoidable. Can you not buy a carriage from somebody who is going away? As you are now already better known I would think that this should not be difficult. But be most careful in dealing with Herr T; such people are no better than Jews. What did not please me in your letter was to see that you have up to now really avoided all social gatherings. I am wholly of Herr Bismarck's opinion in this matter. You are thereby losing one of the great advantages of your stay there; you will in consequence learn less of the world and people and how to get on with them, and you will be sorry later that you did not make better use of your opportunity. Your official work and your health are the first consideration, but when these do not suffer I think it only right and wise that you should take part as much as possible in social life, and by that I mean true social life, and not that of young men about town, but you know my views on this matter as well as I know yours. I was truly astonished that Herr Bismarck should have been so kind and thoughtful about rooms for you, and consequently I am more than ever convinced that you should pay as little heed to Hr S[chlözer] in this regard as in that of the prescribed calls. [...]

God keep you, my darling boy, and defend you. This is the heartfelt wish of your Father. [...]

Do you accompany Hr. and Fr. v. Bismarck[1] to communion? I think this would greatly please our beloved Mama.

4. August von Holstein to his Son

26 March 1861

My dear boy,

[...] Finally some remarks on your last two letters. On quiet reflection you will certainly agree with me that you are partly missing or not attaining the object of your present appointment by the solitary existence you have led for the past three months: for you particularly wanted to go to St P[etersburg] because there you would most quickly learn the ins and outs of diplomacy. This includes not only a knowledge of diplomatic practice, but in particular a knowledge of men and of the way to handle them and to get one's own way with them. But how can you learn this if you shut yourself up and make calls only now after nearly three months? I certainly advise you always to give priority to your official work, but then you should go into society as much as you can *without* injury to your health. In this connection also I share Herr Loen's opinion that the association with Russian families in particular will be as pleasant as it will be useful for you. Nor can I agree with you that you could not again visit F[ehleisen] for the reasons you give. Here I wholly share Mama's view; that you must look on this as time spent in study, not in amusement. You can easily move in such society without accepting what is distasteful to you or contrary to your prin-

---
[1] Johanna von Bismarck, *née* von Puttkamer. The wife of Otto von Bismarck.

ciples. In Herr Loen's company—please remember me to him—I hope you will by now have left a fair number of visiting-cards and that you are coming properly into circulation. Write to us very fully about all this because it is of such interest to us. As to your expenditure, you know that I [have] complete confidence in you in this respect also, and that distrust of you always was, and will be, foreign to me, but I do believe that with the best intentions you must often spend more than is necessary or than you get value for, partly through inexperience, ignorance of affairs or trickery. Try therefore to guard yourself as much as possible against these three, and especially against your servant. For since you cannot cover small incidental expenses with 50 roubles monthly—although Herr Loen put a high figure on everything—I think that your Leporello must look upon himself as part of you and feeds at your expense, etc, as, for example, in regard to the price of laundry and the number of articles for the laundry, etc. The local townspeople must certainly get these things more cheaply than you in the diplomatic corps. If I were you I would try to avoid such unnecessary expenses. On the other hand you know that I am never opposed to useful expenditures or to those that give real pleasure. For example—your hunt was enormously expensive yet despite this I am very glad that you had it. [...]

Don't upset your digestion with Easter eggs and similar heavy foods, though this will be hard to avoid!

Now an affectionate farewell, my dear boy, enjoy the holidays and write again soon. In his thoughts you are embraced by your very loving Father.

The flights of the wild ducks, etc., make a magnificent spectacle every evening now. If only you were here to set them in motion.

5. August von Holstein to his Son

Karlstein, 4 April 1861

My own darling boy,

[...] I cannot remember ever having known so early and warm a spring at home. The violets have been in bloom for the past eight days, most of the trees are putting out their leaves, peas and summer rye are already one inch high, while yesterday the sheep were already sent out to pasture, although burning is still going on and there is plenty of fodder. The day before yesterday we even had a thunderstorm. In St Petersburg it will certainly not be so warm. Watch out in the spring mornings and evenings that you do not catch cold. It is so easy to catch cold then. For this reason we have spent a very quiet Easter here; the main event and the cause of most joy was the arrival of your dear letters on the morning of the 1st. Early that morning I felt I ought to send a messenger for the post, and we were still drinking our coffee when we were most pleasantly surprised and overjoyed at the arrival of your letters of the 23rd and 26th. What concerned me most on your account was the news that your Chief is going on leave for several months, probably until late in the autumn, and will therefore be away at least four to five months. I am very sorry about this, first of all for social reasons and then because of your career. As regards the former, you will lose a great deal and the same holds true of your work. By reason of his keen intelligence and penetrating insight, his society and judgment are highly instructive for you. In him and his wife you will also lose most benevolent patrons. For the short time that he is away, try to do your work with all the more regularity and devotion in order to gain his approval. Will you try to speak to him about your examination before his departure?[1] This would be most useful to you in any event, so that you get the necessary testimonials from him and not later on from some secretary acting on his behalf. The judgment of the latter would not be rated so highly by the Ministry as that of the Chief; that is to say, praise from such a person would be of little value, whereas his censure would carry full weight. Hence you must now be doubly careful of what you do. Take an early opportunity therefore of speaking with Herr von Bismarck. Who will take his place? How do you like the non-diplomatic work in your office? By that I mean the type of work that is performed by a district magistrate and belongs properly to his sphere of activity? I think that in years to come, when you get married and life abroad as a Secretary of Legation no longer appeals to you, you should try to become a district magistrate. In that case, this work in St Petersburg will be most useful to you. For that reason, try to acquire practical knowledge and ability in this field, too. Here also Herr von B[ismarck]'s judgment is certainly of great importance for you. It seems doubtful to me in these circumstances whether your personal studies in St Petersburg are as useful to you as they were in Berlin. After your official work is done, you should study men and life itself; here you must follow your judgment and reason more than your inclinations. You will always have time for academic studies, but not for mingling with the St Petersburg *haute volée* and *beau monde*. I am very glad that you are still enjoying the life and society there. Do not cease to take an interest in everything, and do not let yourself be led astray by your colleagues and the blasé manner of most diplomats, whose tastes are jaded, and who find everything uninteresting and boring, and find fault with everything. You have always followed another path, and I can only advise you to continue on it and not to allow your judgment to be affected by such conduct. Follow your own judgment only and of course the advice of older men who wish you well, like Herr Bismarck and Herr Loen. If you want to get something which will be of use to you for the future out of St Petersburg, something which your stay there, if properly used, certainly will and must give you, then you must do everything you can to get to know people and therefore live more sociably than heretofore. I do believe that if you want to engage in studies other than those connected with your work and your examination, the study of the Russian language would be of the greatest advantage to you. It will be very easy for you, and even if you get no im-

---

[1] The final examination for entry into the diplomatic service.

mediate advantage from it and your colleagues do not regard it as essential, nevertheless one can never know whether it may not be useful in the future. The well-known Job Witzleben[1] chiefly owed his good fortune to it. It could easily happen in our unstable tragic times that we might fight as Russia's ally, and then diplomats would often be sent to join the staff at Headquarters. In such an event it would be an incalculable advantage for you if you spoke Russian, even without necessarily being a soldier. I am convinced that with your rapid grasp of things you would learn it very easily, and without a teacher, if you got hold of a Russian Ahn[2] and invariably talked Russian with your *Pani Kresling*.[3] Think this over; perhaps knowledge of the language might help you socially? Has Herr Loen been kind enough to send your cards around with his? Always show yourself upright and frank with him, and act as I have advised you towards him and Herr B[ismarck]. That reminds me of a question I meant to ask: Are you always diplomatically reserved in your judgments and properly discreet? A diplomat makes fewer enemies this way and also makes people think that there is more behind his reserve than is usually the case. So avoid emphatic opinions and instead always confine yourself as far as possible to generalities. What sort of colleagues have you got in the diplomatic corps? After the holidays social life in St Petersburg must certainly be lively? I hope that you are going out as much as you can without injury to your health, which you must always look after very carefully. And do not neglect dancing, since, as you know, great importance is attached to this in Berlin. Do not dance more than your health will stand, but not less, and do not avoid dancing with women who are bad dancers; for that is the best way of practicing and gives great assurance in guiding one's partner. But do not dance more than your health will stand. Have you tried the mazurka? You ought to. Is conversation with ladies in St Petersburg just the same as in Berlin? That is to say, are they only interested in such subjects as people in society, the theatre, concerts, balls and entertainments? If so, then be a proper gossip with the best of them in the spirit of the old saying: When one is among wolves one must howl with them. You will find then that conversation presents no difficulty. [...]

What is the weather like there? For the past ten or twelve days I have not had a fire. Look after your fur coat carefully so that the moths do not get at it. It would be best if you gave it to the furrier to take care of. What have you done with the second kamchatka beaver collar? Have you tried to buy a droshky from a departing diplomat? I would strongly advise you to do so. And also for obvious reasons that you do not get unnecessary summer clothes made. Since *all* your things are unworn, and therefore new to St Petersburg, you do not need anything and can certainly use the money you would thus spend in a more

[1] Prussian Minister of State and of War, 1834–7.
[2] Franz Ahn. Publisher of foreign language textbooks.
[3] The editors have transliterated August von Holstein's mixture of Roman and Greek characters.

pleasant and useful manner. Take care with the Prince;[1] people like that are touchy and easily take offence, which would be all the more awkward as he will probably deputise for Herr B[ismarck]. Strained relations of this kind between three people who must frequently be in each other's company are very unpleasant and oppressive, especially as the third takes sides, so that one is left isolated. So with both of them avoid everything that could give rise to trouble, and then go your own direct way as always without allowing them to influence you. So don't ask them for advice about anything of which you are doubtful, but always and only Herr Bism[arck] or Herr Loen. Now farewell for to-day, my old darling boy. Most affectionate greetings from Aunt and Ida and Adele;[2] the latter wrote a short while ago, all about household matters and women's fashions in Mecklenburg and therefore of no interest to you. I embrace you, my old dear rascal.

Your very loving Father.

[...]

6. August von Holstein to his Son

Karlstein, 9 April 1861

My old darling boy,

Since Itze[3] is writing to you to-day I am enclosing a few lines in order to tell you how glad I was to get your letter of the 2nd. Easter seems to have been very uneventful for you too; we saw nobody, for which I was thankful. I am very sorry about Herr Bismarck's illness.[4] It is so terribly painful, as, unhappily, we know so well from the cases of Aunt Luise[5] and Uncle August Bernstorff. Has Herr Bismarck by any chance consulted Frerichs?[6] He certainly should do so; he [Frerichs] has had so much experience with this type of illness. Uncle August Bernstorff is now quite well, apparently. Tell this to H[err] B[ismarck] to comfort him, and if you think that it would be of service to him, ask Uncle Bernstorff about it—he is now living in Strelitz. If you write to him, you must begin by congratulating him and assuring him of your great pleasure at learning of his appointment as Grand Master of the Horse, about which I have told you to-day. I am also very concerned about this illness for your sake. It is unfortunate that your appointment was so delayed.[7] Meanwhile one must accept the inevitable, and you must

---

[1] Georg, Prince von Croy-Dülmen. First Secretary in the Prussian Legation in St Petersburg, 1859–62.

[2] Adele von Holtzendorff. Daughter of Minna von Holtzendorff and a cousin of Friedrich von Holstein.

[3] Ida von Holtzendorff.

[4] On 21 April 1861 Johanna von Bismarck wrote to Keudell: 'Bismarck has repeatedly suffered small attacks of rheumatism that probably affected me more than they did him. In addition his nerves are always in such a shocking state that one can only look at him with anxiety.' (Robert von Keudell, *Fürst und Fürstin Bismarck* (Berlin and Stuttgart,1902), p. 84.)

[5] Luise von Holstein. August von Holstein's sister.

[6] Dr Friedrich Theodor Frerichs. From 1859 Director of the Medical Section at the Charité Hospital in Berlin.

[7] The Prussian Foreign Minister von Schleinitz had refused Holstein's first request for a transfer from the judiciary to the diplomatic service in June 1860. The transfer was finally granted only after an appeal to the Prince Regent. (See *Memoirs*, p. 4.)

try all the harder to gain his approval in all things, because his opinion of your work and abilities is of such great importance for your examination and your career. It would not be a bad thing if you, like Count Hatzfeldt,[1] were appointed Secretary on the basis of your service and also, should a vacancy occur at St Petersburg, if you could remain there in that capacity. Since Prince Croy has become engaged it is very possible that he will leave, and in that case it would not be a bad thing and no small promotion if you were to become Second Secretary. If you tell me that this is impossible, I can only say that nothing is impossible and that the attainment of one's ambition depends nearly always on perseverance and how one goes about it; especially so in the case of a diplomatic career, where the machinery is set in motion in so many ways in order to achieve its purpose. For this reason I cannot agree at all with your conduct in abstaining from social life. Unless you take some part in it, you can never become a good diplomat. In no other career are women, and especially older women, of greater help and assistance than in this one. I should think that this was particularly true of the two aristocratic ladies you mentioned, by reason of their position and influence. I believe that it is also of real importance for your position what Prince Gorchakov[2] and his deputy[3] think of you and that they show themselves as well-disposed towards you as possible. If this be the case, then I believe that you can speedily open the way to promotion. After quiet reflection and consideration I am sure that you will agree with me. If, however, you continue to avoid society, then you will be left behind and achieve nothing. Your belief that your entry into society is rendered difficult because your Chief does not entertain is one I cannot share. If you were a son of the house, then you might be right. Since, however, everyone knows that you are an attaché, I simply do not understand how you have got the idea that this could be harmful for you. I am in complete disagreement with your colleagues' opinion in this matter and I am surprised that you do not follow your own judgment rather than that of your colleagues. Your position depends solely upon yourself, for the higher and wealthier Russian aristocracy will not care whether or not Herr B[ismarck] entertains, and in no circumstances will they let this affect them in their relations with an attaché. It will not be at all difficult with your per-

[1] Paul, Count von Hatzfeldt-Wildenburg was provisionally admitted to the Prussian diplomatic service on 3 June 1859, and was sent as an Attaché to Paris. As a result of his outstanding work, he was admitted to the regular diplomatic service in November 1860 without first having to take the customary examinations, and was appointed Second (supernumerary) Secretary in Paris. Secretary in Paris, 1860–6; Secretary of Legation at The Hague, 1866–8; *Vortragender Rat* in the Foreign Ministry from 1868; on Bismarck's personal Foreign Ministry Staff, 1870–1; head of the French Section in the Foreign Ministry, 1872–4; Minister in Madrid, 1874–8; Ambassador in Constantinople, 1879–81; State Secretary in the Foreign Ministry, 1881–5; Ambassador in London, 1885–1901. Holstein made friends with Paul Hatzfeldt when they were both serving as legal aides at the law courts in Berlin. (See Arthur von Brauer, *Im Dienste Bismarcks* (Berlin, 1936), p. 108.)

[2] Alexander, Prince Gorchakov. Russian plenipotentiary at the German Federal Diet in Frankfurt, 1850–4; Minister in Vienna, 1854–6; Foreign Minister, April 1856–82; Chancellor, 1871–82.

[3] Count Ivan Tolstoy. Deputy to the Russian Foreign Minister.

sonality to find acceptance. Dance and gossip with the best of them, and you will soon see that I am right. At social as distinguished from purely diplomatic gatherings, talk in a lively and witty way and waste no time on intellectual profundities. Women love this and prefer indifferent witticisms and scandal to serious conversation. This has never been difficult for you; take advantage of this ability and you will soon be leading a more amusing life than heretofore. By wanting nothing more than to be a slave to work, you suppress your individuality and let your light—as our splendid Mama used to say—hide under a bushel. But this you could have done with much less trouble and expense in Gumbinnen, etc. Think all this over quietly and carefully and you will agree with me; but then make a firm resolve and carry it out, and do not put off making calls, and returning calls after each invitation, since the season is nearly over and you will have gained nothing from it. Your year as attaché will soon be at an end, and I cannot deny that I would be very hurt if this were to be the case. In that case it would also be contrary to my wish if you were to stay on longer. On the other hand, if you profit by it, and your desires and expectations are fulfilled, then I am of the opinion, as you know, that one must willingly make sacrifices. In that case, however, one must keep one's objective constantly in view and not allow oneself to be diverted from it by minor or imaginary difficulties, wounded self-esteem or exaggerated sensitivity. [...]

Farewell for to-day, my old darling boy. Ida has doubtless told you that Aunt Minna had to spend her birthday yesterday in bed where she still is to-day. I hope she will be up again tomorrow! With deepest love

Your Father
[...]

7. August von Holstein to his Son

Karlstein, 13 April 1861

My old dear darling boy,

I am putting this letter in the cash-box,[1] and even if that delays it, it will at any rate arrive safely and unread. I am going to write about several things that I would prefer should not be read, so burn this letter at once. The first is your attitude towards Herr Schlözer: I think it is not difficult to be on good terms with a man like him, even though it is not always pleasant and it is occasionally difficult to put up with his unwarranted pretensions. After all he seems to be a worthy person and since he is much older than you, and occupies an important post, you can without in any way lowering your own dignity subordinate yourself to him and carry out his official instructions. Never fail to treat him with a certain degree of respect, which you probably neglected to do at the outset, thereby laying, without your knowledge or desire, the

---

[1] The birthday present of a cash-box mentioned in August von Holstein's letter of 18 April 1861.

foundation of your strained relations. I gave you this advice even before your departure. But you thought that this was unnecessary in the diplomatic service and now you probably already have the proof that elderly men in important posts in that profession are just as vain as lawyers. Do what I say, because I am convinced that your situation will soon become quite tolerable, although an intimate [friendship] will never arise because of the difference in your characters. This is all the more important because Herr Bismarck is going on leave. It seems to me not improbable that when H. v S. sees that H. v B. is friendly to you and trusts you, he may well try to play you up for that reason, because his one desire is to be the only important man. You must therefore be all the more careful in your behaviour towards him. But do not be misled by his kindness and favours and words of praise into confiding in him more than you ought, and never be tempted into passing on confidential remarks to him. Such men do not respect these and in bad humour or annoyance may use them to create embarrassment. So always be diplomatic towards him and thus train yourself in small as in greater matters. As for the Prince,[1] it seems to me that because of his character it can only be pleasant and desirable for you that he remains in St Petersburg until you have passed your examination. If you still have Herr B's confidence and goodwill then (which I do not doubt), and have him as your intercessor in Berlin, and if by then you have put yourself in the good graces of Prince Gorchakov and Prince Tolstoy, the Under State Secretary, I believe it is not at all impossible that you will become Second Secretary there. But you must work from the outset with this in mind, working perpetually with the greatest energy and regularity, trying above all more and more to gain Herr Bismarck's confidence, and then, as far as your work and *your health* permit, entering into social life and trying to make yourself agreeable to these men and their wives. If you have this aim clearly and steadily in your mind's eye, I believe that it is not impossible, and indeed probable, that you will achieve your ambition. Do not therefore let yourself be tempted to strengthen P[rince] C[roy] in his resolve to resign, but on the contrary —when *nobody* is listening—try to persuade him to abandon it. You will not thereby do him a wrong, but only what every other young man who is not his intimate friend would also do. Once you have got your place in the budget, that is to say a Secretaryship with pay, then it will not be difficult for you to get yourself transferred elsewhere if you are tired of St Petersburg or it does not suit your health. Anyone with ambition, my dear old boy, must act according to principles, hold fast to them without making exceptions, and never alter them, only change ways and means according to circumstances. If he always rigorously tests and judges everything, and acts accordingly, he will with persistence usually achieve his ambition. Without this it is seldom that anyone attains his aim, but sways to and fro like a reed without ever getting anywhere—the unhappiest and least satisfying fate for anyone who is ambitious and asks a great deal of life, as most young people do.

[1] Prince Croy.

This is certainly the case with you : for when most of your social equals would definitely have preferred to live as independent country gentlemen on their estates, you did not like the idea and wanted much more to achieve something. In the normal easy life of the civil service this is not possible; and as for the army, you were too accustomed to good treatment and consideration to have liked the subordination and lack of regard for personal feelings that accompany the training of a very young second lieutenant; nor would active service have suited you better, for only the senior officers have a chance to gain honour. You yourself have recently learnt through your travels that the unintellectual life one leads travelling, if it is not motivated by interest in the natural sciences—an interest entirely lacking in you—soon palls, and mind and soul become a vacuum. So it is only in the diplomatic service that you have any chance of achieving your aim. I discussed with Herr von Loen whether you had any prospects of getting ahead without influential connections, and he replied : Nowhere better than there has he a chance to get ahead quickly, because nowhere else is there such a lack of competent people; he has no need for connections if only he distinguishes himself in some way or other. Think over all this and act accordingly. For this reason, although as you know your choice of a diplomatic career was not my wish, I was disappointed that you go out so seldom and in this way are making only a one-sided effort to get ahead. You are thus placing yourself behind your colleagues, to whom you can measure up in every way. You must have more self-confidence and not be so quick to feel yourself insulted and snubbed. One or the other was certainly the reason why you went out so little and shut yourself up. You must devote all your energies to combat and overcome such feelings. Otherwise you will never get anywhere and slight yourself. No wonder then if others do the same. Only through your appearance in the social world can you attain a position there, and not by your work, as you well know from society life in Berlin, where those who do not go about in society are treated disdainfully. If therefore you have ambitious plans, and allow yourself to imagine big things, you must also have the strength of will to apply the means which lead to the goal. The truly ambitious man does this; he shuns no discomfort and trouble; and he usually succeeds, whereas the man who acts through vanity takes it for granted that, due to his merits, his desires must be fulfilled without trouble; and he achieves nothing. I am not saying this with regard to yourself, my dear boy, but only to give you my ideas about the two classes of those who want to make something of themselves—ideas that throughout my life I have found proved true by experience. If therefore you wish to get something and do something exceptional, you must not shrink from any permissible means to achieve your end. Otherwise you will waste your efforts and tire yourself out before you reach the half-way mark. Under the prevailing circumstances I believe it is not at all impossible that if P[rince] C[roy] takes his departure next winter or spring, you will be given his post, if from now on you set your course towards it.

The second point about which I want to speak to you to-day is the money question. It is to be hoped that you are adhering to your intention of keeping accounts of your expenditure, since otherwise you cannot know how much you are being robbed and, above all, cannot have that comparative measure of your expenditure that is absolutely essential when one has such considerable expenses as yours. Do you also keep all your receipts in a drawer? You must not fail to do this to avoid having to pay bills twice. You must keep a close watch on your servant and give him little money at a time so that he does not cheat you too much. Herr Loen estimated everything at the highest and, since you have no heavy household expenses, your servant must be profiting at your expense, or perhaps you are spending more than is necessary when you have a guest. You say you only need what Herr Loen estimated was necessary, yet you are leaving out of account that the 5,570 roubles that you were supposed to require annually included 50 roubles for rent and 120 for food monthly, in all 170 roubles, which up to now you have not had to pay or at least the latter only occasionally. Now it will be necessary to pay both. Therefore you must watch carefully over your budget in order to avoid being cheated or having quite unnecessary expenses (unnecessary tips), by which a great deal of money can be simply wasted. Your news about the apartment you can rent from the Russians surprised me in so far as it seems that you must rent it for one year. Naturally I advise you above all to put out suitable feelers to find out whether Herr or Frau von Bismarck would object to your using their apartment while they are away—something you can probably best do through the governess. If they do object, then you must certainly rent an apartment; otherwise I see no reason why you should. In your place, I would see even less reason for doing so because your work is made so much easier if you live in the house, and you can thus make yourself much more useful and agreeable to your Chief. I hope that under no circumstances you will have rented the apartment for one year at 660 roubles, for since you only wanted to stay there for a year at the most until your examination, and have been there nearly 4 months already, you certainly cannot have rented it otherwise than by the month. Otherwise the budget of 50 roubles monthly would have been considerably exceeded. [...]

You have also not said anything to me about your reception by Duke Georg. Does he behave like a Russian or a Mecklenburg prince? Have you not visited Fehleisen again? I would advise you to do so; for one thing it is very useful for you to learn to mix in such company and to make yourself welcome by your behaviour; for another, bankers like him have many connexions everywhere and can therefore be very useful to you. This last you must always keep in mind if you are to get some compensation for your sojourn abroad; for however much you like it there, you must surely have moments of homesickness now and then, and for these one must reap the rewards in the future. Now, may Almighty God keep you, my dear old darling rascal. I still have three letters to write to-day, so now a heartfelt farewell. I have written to you to-day only about matters that I would not willingly write about in other letters. More tomorrow about other things. I embrace you in my thoughts.

Your little Papa [...]

8. August von Holstein to his Son

Karlstein, 18 April 1861

My old darling boy,

Since there are so many miles between us, I will to-day at least send you in writing my most heartfelt wishes for your birthday. May Almighty God watch over you, defend and bless you, and grant fulfilment to all the deepest wishes of our dearly loved Mama for you. Be always mindful of God and let us hope that our wishes for you will be fulfilled through His grace. My thoughts will be very very much with you on the 24th, when I would so gladly spend an hour with you in person, so that I might by word of mouth give you my heartfelt wishes. Unhappily this cannot be, and therefore I must be content to spend the day with you in imagination and *par distance*.

I am overjoyed that you are well. Now that it is spring take great care that you do not catch cold in the evenings and mornings, which is said to be so easy to do in St Petersburg, and is supposed to result often in a fever. Do be very careful because usually the liver is affected for years afterwards—to say nothing of the pains of the fever. I hope you never go out without having breakfasted? I would strongly advise you against this, because the pernicious mists that rise in the town in the morning are far more dangerous when one has an empty stomach. I am very pleased that you are going out more, and your account of your visit to the [ ][1] gave me great joy, because the way in which you were treated by [ ][1] allows me to conclude that it is known that your Chief is pleased with you and that you are useful. Try to preserve this good opinion by all means, and, without injury to your health (which must always take first place since once ruined it cannot be restored), seize every opportunity of going into society. The Austrian diplomats have the reputation of becoming good diplomats through mingling in society rather than by study, of which they are said to be no lovers, and yet they almost invariably overreach us, because through their experience of life and knowledge of the proper way of handling men with their various idiosyncrasies, they usually achieve far more important successes than the Prussians with their theoretical knowledge. You must therefore try as far as possible to unite these two things. And for this reason do not neglect to make the frequent and brief calls which are customary in St Petersburg. Your gun will follow this letter shortly. I would very gladly have sent other birthday presents with it but no matter how much Aunt, Ida, and I racked our brains we could think of nothing that would give you pleasure. The cash-box and a walking-stick are all, and I am afraid that while the former will certainly be very useful to you, it is nevertheless a very simple and ugly thing.[2] [...]

[1] A gap in the text.
[2] This may be the cash-box in which Holstein's St Petersburg correspondence was found. (See *Memoirs*, p. xvii.)

Once more may Almighty God grant you His protection and grace and the fulfilment of our dear Mama's wishes for you as also of your own cherished desires (excluding the extravagant and too extreme). Aunt and Ida wish you many happy returns and send you their love. If your ears ring on the 24th, then remember that you are in the thoughts of your far distant and everloving

little Papa.

Every one is very anxious here about the outcome of the Polish affair.[1] I fear a general war, touched off by Napoleon who feels the ground shaking under his feet in France and who would therefore like to divert the storm abroad. The brilliant success of the latest, and at last forceful, intervention by Prince Gorchakov in Warsaw has caused astonishment as well as rejoicing; but we have not heard the last of things there, and doubtless they take their orders from Paris.

9. August von Holstein to his Son

Karlstein, 24 April 1861[2]

My dear old boy,

[...] I was greatly pleased yesterday to get your letter, and thank you most heartily for it. To-day my thoughts are especially with you as you can well imagine. But duty and work always come first and hence our separation from each other on this day cannot be helped. Almighty God guard you and keep you, prosper you, and richly bless you. I would have much preferred to give you my most heartfelt wishes in person, as well as those of our dearest Mama, but for the above reasons this is impossible, and I console myself today with the thought of the long years that the all-bountiful God—thanks be to Him!—in His infinite mercy has given to us to live together with you in intimate and happy companionship, and I recall many a happy memory from the days of my greatest happiness. What did you do to-day? Did you celebrate? We have thought of you constantly, as you can imagine, and at dinner Aunt proposed your health. Once more best wishes and greetings from both of us, and also from Friedrich.[3]

10. August von Holstein to his Son

27 April 1861

My dear dear fellow!

[...] The news that you intend to come here this summer is, as you can imagine, a matter for rejoicing, yet nevertheless I would only

---

[1] On 27 February Polish patriots staged a great demonstration in Warsaw. Several people were killed or wounded by Russian troops. On 27 March Gorchakov placed virtual dictatorial powers in the hands of the Marquis Alexander Wielopolski, a Pole who hoped to restore Poland to its constitutional status of 1815, and who promised to work in close collaboration with the Tsarist Government.

[2] This is part of a letter begun on 22 April.

[3] The end of the letter is missing.

advise you to take this leave if your work permits it and you do not thereby lose the good opinion of your superiors and thus injure your prospects. You must be very sure of these two things and act accordingly. While Herr Bismarck is away you can perhaps not easily be spared, and after his return he may not approve of your absence from work. Make quite sure of this and do nothing that would cause doubts to arise about your eagerness for work and your staying powers. In this way younger people can do themselves great harm in the eyes of their seniors, for they take a stricter view of these matters. For this reason I <u>was</u> not at all pleased that you spoke to Herr B. about the Russian language. It is to be hoped that you at least did it indirectly, or at least in such a way that he cannot think that vacillation and lack of endurance lay behind your question; because if he did so the interest he has hitherto shown in you would certainly be lessened. I have given you my views on your future in the letter enclosed in the box,[1] and I would therefore be all the more upset if you had raised the question in a rash and undiplomatic manner. I firmly believe that you can only count on quick promotion and being advanced over the heads of many of the older attachés etc., if a change takes place there at a time when many of them cannot go out there, and many of the others may not be acceptable to the Chief. The indispensable requirement, however, is his complete confidence in your character, work and perseverance. It is often said that 'the heart's desire is the call of fate', and it is easily possible that your predilection for and great longing to go to St Petersburg, greatly displeasing as they were to me, have in this justified themselves, and you will succeed there and advance in your career more rapidly than in other places. Nowhere else would you have the same opportunity to develop yourself, and since you like the work and it interests you so much, I believe promotion is not impossible. That is why I deeply regret that you have gone out so little this winter. I would have said nothing more about it, since what is done is done, were I not convinced that your point of view is wrong and based on a self-deception from which—though unhappily nothing can be done about it now—I would gladly see you preserved on subsequent occasions. For you say that if Prince Croy or Herr Loen had been there sooner you would have been launched by them and could have led a much more active social life. This may be very true. Nevertheless you [could have] lived very sociably anyway, for Herr Bismarck introduced you to Princess Tolstoy[2] and she was kind enough to invite you to her receptions. If you had availed yourself of this, it would have fully sufficed to have extended your circle of acquaintances as widely as you wished. You yourself say that Russian families were friendly to you, and also that they constitute a very clever and elegant society. So you would have found everything there that would have pleased you and been useful to you, while your visits would probably have been welcome to the majority of families since young unmarried diplomats are welcome

[1] The letter of 13 April 1861.
[2] Countess Tolstoy, wife of Count Ivan Tolstoy.

everywhere. But you always only liked dances, and went only to them with pleasure; so you were happy to have the pretext—the absence of Prince Croy and Herr Loen—to make excuses to yourself for your failure to carry out your earlier resolve to go into society as much as possible in order to acquire a knowledge of men and their behaviour. Had you gone to parties like those you formerly went to at the Freisings, that is to say where you could learn something, and not merely to those that afforded you only amusement, you would probably have passed your time more agreeably and more usefully for your future than has been the case, since I imagine that many an evening has passed without affording you particular pleasure or interesting conversation. If you think it over carefully, you will probably find that the cause was not the absence of Prince Croy or Loen, but rather shyness and nervousness, etc.,—you never did like going to parties where you didn't think you would enjoy yourself—and that lack of will-power and energy deceived you into making excuses to yourself. I would not have mentioned or spoken of my views in this matter at all, my dear old fellow, if I had not been anxious to save you from more mistakes in the future, for I am convinced that afterwards nobody would be more angry about them than yourself. Do try therefore to get rid of this nervousness and lack of self-confidence, because these things make social life more disagreeable and will rob you of your pleasure. I don't quite understand what your colleagues—that is to say, the attachés—have told you about summer pastimes, for the Russian aristocracy leaves the city, and those who remain probably belong to financial and business circles, in which diplomats surely don't mingle regularly, although these are certainly quite useful as part of your training. I would therefore not advise you to buy a second horse for the summer until you see that you need it and can afford it. Since you never or hardly ever go out in the mornings, the horse can make all afternoon journeys—if you need it *only* in the afternoons—without becoming overtired, and in that case you definitely do not need a second horse. What has happened about the apartment? If only for the sake of your comfort I hope that you can live in the Legation as long as possible, for an apartment at any distance involves many discomforts. The Russians will now be celebrating Easter. I was much astonished that you took so little notice of ours; I noticed this from your letters you wrote on the first and second days of Easter and was not a little astonished by it, because I had imagined and hoped that you would have been to Holy Communion with your Chief and his wife beforehand. For if I am not mistaken I have heard that Frau von Bismarck is very pious and inclines to Lutheranism, and as we also take the Holy Communion according to the Lutheran rite (also at your confirmation) I hoped that you would partake together with them. We intended to do so here; unhappily Aunt's state of health did not permit it. She is quite well again now [...]

                                        Your very loving little Papa. [...]

11. August von Holstein to his Son

1 May 1861

[...] As I was placing this letter[1] in its envelope yesterday, I decided to wait until to-day before sending it, assuming that the letter from Adele or Fräulein Luise Gundlach, which Ida has been expecting daily, would arrive, and that I should then be able to send you the latest news from Mecklenburg. Instead I got your letter of the 24th which overjoyed me. The celebration of your birthday by your Chief and his wife astonished me as much as it pleased me. It is really friendlier and more generous of them than one had any right to expect. To me it is very welcome testimony that they are both well disposed towards you, and I hope you will preserve their good opinion. Knowing how you think both about your official and private life, I do not doubt that you will do so. But in such small groups as the staff of a Legation, such marks of goodwill are often regarded with hostility and jealousy. This could be the case there as well. You must therefore be doubly careful about how you behave; in your official work you must try more than ever to avoid the possibility that the slightest criticism could be levelled against you, so that it doesn't look as though the Chief were playing favourite; while off duty you must avoid letting others feel that, because of your favoured position, you were becoming overweening and were unwilling to accord them the *superiorité* to which they lay claim. Most men can be won by an appeal to their vanity; probably this is also the case with your people, if you take and handle them accordingly—that is to say, naturally, and of course only in such a way that you do not thereby lower yourself. With Herr Schlözer, who is much older, a very thorough, prudent and experienced man of affairs, and a distinguished man of letters, it will not be difficult for you to give him the respect his achievements command; with the Prince also it will not be difficult for you to be on a good footing, if my fear (which is perhaps wholly unfounded) should be momentarily realised and the friendly relationship thereby temporarily impaired. Act therefore with circumspection and tact towards these and others, and gradually everything will return to its former state, provided that you do not leave yourself open in some other way to the accusation of having done something unworthy. But this does not fit in with your character and so as time goes by the relationship among you will once again be quite agreeable. I can't blame your Chief for wanting to go on leave; but for your sake I am very sorry. As one can never tell how long he will be away—last year it must surely have been six to eight months—you must seriously consider whether you should still discuss your examination with him. As I know that you always like to get these things finished and done with as soon as possible, think over everything in this connection carefully. You will have seen from the letter enclosed in the cash box that I share your views about the examination, and what ideas I have on the subject; I think it can be done, and is the only thing to do in order to achieve most quickly what you desired. If

---

[1] This letter was begun on 30 April.

—as often happens—I do not express myself very clearly here, you surely always know what I mean. The behaviour of your Chief and Frau von Bismarck towards you really gives me quite extraordinary pleasure; see to it that this is not destroyed through negligence and insincerity [?] on your part and tale-bearing on the part of others. So take the greatest care with Schnablunsky.[1] On the other hand it pains me very much that you so often sit alone in the evening. Why do you not prefer to go out? You would surely find someone or other whom you know, or some ladies whom you could talk to with pleasure now and again. Do you still go to see the Consul-General sometimes? Boredom is a very poor form of amusement and I would rather try to avoid it. The tea you brewed for yourself caused great amusement here and made us all wish to see it done some time, especially myself as you can well imagine. How is your coffee holding out? Is there anything you want me to send you? [...]

The outcome of the Warsaw affair[2] was very surprising; what a pity that such an energetic move was not made at the outset. The old lesson that only soldiers are of any use against democrats was brilliantly borne out once again. [...]

Once again most affectionate greetings from Aunt and Ida. In my thoughts I embrace you, my dear old boy,

Your most loving Father.

[1] Probably Schlözer is meant.   [2] See p. 19, note 1.

1868

Holstein returned to Germany in April 1862 in order to take his final examinations for the diplomatic service. These were delayed by his own ill health and by the death of his father in April 1863. He passed the examinations in May 1863, and subsequently served in the diplomatic corps in a number of minor posts until 1868.[1]

At the beginning of 1868 Holstein asked for leave from the service in order to take part in a business venture to provide a mechanised towing-system for river and canal transport.[2]

12. Holstein to Karl von Eisendecher[3]

Brussels, 14 March 1868

Dear Eisendecher,

[...] I am still here. You will hardly suppose that I am having a madly gay time; rather the contrary. However I am still extremely anxious to keep an eye on the progress of my affairs and to give them a push in the right direction.

Can you imagine me standing for hours on a tug-boat, often in pouring rain, watching the machinery work? This is what happened in Liège in the first week of March, A.D. 1868. But you will not believe how much less boring a matter becomes when it is linked with the prospect of profit and loss.

I have already briefly explained our system to you. A vessel is fitted with a steam-engine which has a specially constructed fly-wheel. A steel cable that lies free on the bed of the river or canal, and is only secured at each end, is laid over the fly-wheel, which grasps it with curved iron teeth. The wheel turns and the cable, held by the teeth, makes a half turn with the wheel, and then falls back into the water behind. The distance that the vessel has travelled corresponds exactly to the length of cable that has passed over the wheel.

The difficulties connected with the system were:

First, the question: won't the cable slip off the wheel when the load is heavy and the opposing current strong? This question was answered

---

[1] See Holstein's letters to his aunt and cousin. (Helmuth Rogge, *Friedrich von Holstein. Lebensbekenntnis in Briefen an eine Frau* (Berlin, 1932), pp. 33–69.)

[2] See Helmuth Rogge, 'Friedrich von Holstein, Max Eyth und die Tau-Schleppschiffahrt', *Blätter für deutsche Landesgeschichte* (1952), pp. 169–276.

[3] From the Eisendecher Papers. Eisendecher was at this time a member of the Prussian Foreign Ministry staff in Berlin. Minister in Tokyo, December 1874–August 1881, in Washington, 1882–4, in Karlsruhe, 1884–1914.

by making the vessel fast and then starting the engine. The cable did not slip an inch and the engine, held between two fixed points—the cable and the vessel—stopped. Hence complete success.

Second, the question: Will the vessel answer the rudder? Splendidly. From one side of the canal to the other.

Most of the other difficulties—for example, bends and locks—have also been solved satisfactorily. But I will not bore you with too many details.

The great advantage of the new system lies in the fact that you get the same result with only half the horse-power, that is, you get as much with 12 horse-power as you now get with 24. You probably know better than I that under the most favourable circumstances a paddle-steamer today utilises only 60, a screw-driven steamer only 50 per cent of its applied power, because wheels and screw find no firm point of resistance in the water. Under certain circumstances the percentage falls to 25% or 15%, on canals for example.

Our machine pulls on the cable, hence on a firm point of resistance. That is the whole secret. The cable is the flexible and mobile iron rail on which our river railway runs. The sole loss of power—it is very insignificant—arises from the angle of inclination of the cable from below.

As you see the undertaking has everything to turn the head of a novice. Everything is there: the prospect of magnificent results, general utility, and last but not least the fascination of the unknown, the uncertain, the adventurous. Besides all this, the undertaking is like diplomacy, in that your vision spans the entire world. We are now negotiating about the Neva, the Nile, and the North American canals. Concessions have been applied for in Germany and France, and for that purpose my partner[1] has to-day left for The Hague.

The size of the steam-tug and of the cable naturally depend upon local conditions: depth, width, current, degree of slope. Trials that have been both exhaustive and satisfactory have been made with small machines. But nobody had the courage to order a bigger tug that can take seagoing vessels in tow at the mouths of rivers in a storm. This is what I have decided to do. 40 horse-power. The engineers are busy on the plans. John Fowler in Leeds, from whom we got our fly-wheel (clip-drum) will get the order.

If it succeeds I shall not only have substantially benefited the undertaking but also my own affairs. If it fails I shall have to face the consequences. Let us hope for the best. In any case it keeps my hands full, in pleasant contrast to the usual nerve-racking inactivity of diplomats. As I am a diplomat I cannot be too conspicuous and so I prefer to conduct correspondence in the name of my partner. Moreover I am accustoming myself to take decisions in important—important for me at least —matters. I already have a pretty strong conviction that unless I break my neck at once, I will in a short time be useful in a fairly significant way. Moreover, all this brings one into contact with a large number

[1] Oskar, Baron von Mesnil. (See Rogge, *Friedrich von Holstein*, p. 72.)

of people, and indeed mostly with the best business people. So I say to myself that perhaps in this way one can accumulate some experience of life outside diplomacy, which is in my opinion absolutely necessary in order not to be entirely remote from practical business life.

The one problem is that of my leave. I will ask for leave for a year either now or in some months when the tugs that have been ordered are ready. If I don't get the leave I will probably resign. But I imagine it will be granted.[1]

There you have my plans for the immediate future, old boy. Keep them to yourself. [...]

Farewell, keep your chin up, and do not forget

Your lonely friend
H.

Give my regards to the young Bismarcks,[2] if you get the chance. [...]

---

[1] On 3 April 1868 Holstein was granted a year's leave of absence. (From the Foreign Ministry personnel files.)

[2] Herbert and Wilhelm von Bismarck, the sons of Otto von Bismarck.

Herbert, Count von Bismarck. From 15 January 1874 in the Foreign Ministry; attached to several Legations, but principally employed as private secretary to his father; First Secretary in the German Embassy in London, November 1882–4; Acting First Secretary in St Petersburg, January 1884; Minister at The Hague, 11 May 1884–5; Under State Secretary in the Foreign Ministry, 10 May 1885–6; State Secretary, 1 May 1886–90; Prussian Minister of State, 1888–90.

Wilhelm, Count von Bismarck. In the Prussian Judiciary Service, 1874–9; temporarily attached to the office of the Governor of Alsace-Lorraine, September 1879–80; an official in the Reich Chancellery, 1881–2; *Regierungsrat*, mostly on the staff of the Chancellor, October 1882–4; *Vortragender Rat* in the Prussian Ministry of State, May 1884–5; *Landrat* in Hanau, August 1885–9; Head of the Administration of Hanover, March 1889–95, of the province of East Prussia, 1895–1901.

1869

13. Holstein to Karl von Eisendecher[1]

Homburg v.d.H., 20 July 1869

Dear E.

Since we parted faint symptoms of an attack of gout have become apparent. As a result I have been here for some weeks and am now going to Nauheim for a few more weeks. The cure here has taken it out of me, as you will see from my handwriting, otherwise I would have answered your letter much sooner.

Now for business. The meat tests[2] have so far turned out so well that the English Admiralty has ordered a further £2000 worth. The formation of the company will only take place when all the tests are completed; by then in my opinion at least another three months will have gone by. Probably more. When the time comes, and the situation is such that I see an almost certain profit from such an investment for you, you can rely upon my memory, old fellow. Simply leave the necessary instructions at home. By the way, Southwell[3] wrote some days ago that you were not going to China. Does that mean China only, or any foreign part at all? I would be glad for my own sake if the latter were true, although you are a funny stick and a lazy ruffian when it comes to writing. The boys[4] came to Brussels; they had a terrible time in Paris. In Brussels we made the excursion to Waterloo and the next day Moritz Lottum[5] gave a great dinner. Bill brought with him a frightful bull-dog—a present from Southwell. The brute ran away in Brussels, and Bill came close to fighting everybody in the hotel. Next day he found it again.

On my way here the two kept me company from Bonn to Bingen. But the outing was spoilt by rain. With all his harsh qualities Herbert has great conscientiousness that springs in his case from self-esteem; he will, I think, always do his duty no matter what happens, even when it costs him dear; he may be hard because of doubts about the presence of good qualities in others. His danger is that he will banish himself to a lonely pinnacle of proud misanthropy even before he has really tested wind and currents. Bill could sink to the level of a companionable egoist

[1] From the Eisendecher Papers.
[2] A cousin of Holstein's father, Oswald von Fabrice, Minister of Saxony to Brussels, was testing a method of preserving meat.
[3] Lord Southwell, who had accompanied Holstein on his journey to the American prairies in the autumn of 1866.
[4] Herbert and Wilhelm von Bismarck.
[5] Count Moritz Lottum. Attaché at the German Legation in Brussels. Holstein and Lottum had been Attachés together in Washington.

and *bon viveur* if he continues to be spoilt. At the same time the lively interest that he takes in most things, in contrast to Herbert, and his exceptionally quick grasp, do a lot to compensate.

I just cannot understand that their father does so little to influence them. In this way they have only the disadvantages of their father's position, the pampering, and the unjustified contempt for humanity that springs from it—Herbert especially—without the counterweight of their father's sound advice. The chief difficulty for other fathers—that their sons think themselves cleverer—is after all completely absent in this case.

There is nothing to be done about it, yet it makes me very sad. If the boys do not go to pieces from the start, especially inwardly—outwardly it matters less—then they may go far. Yesterday Herbert wrote that Bill had 'been out' once and he twice. Bill got a very small cut on the cheek. Herbert fought one duel without result, the second time he defeated his opponent. Yesterday they were to fight again and, as it seemed to me, with more skilful opponents. I therefore sent a reply paid telegram early this morning to ask how they are and will leave this letter open for a few hours in expectation of a reply.

I can write little about myself and this place. I am very bored. I am too done up to read serious books or to go hunting. I know no one, but a few days ago an elderly lady arrived, the wife of the Dutch Foreign Minister,[1] and her presence here has made my life much more agreeable.

The *tonnage* goes well. All trials have been successful. Now there only remains the demonstration. End of September or beginning of October.

Send me word of yourself to Nauheim.
Ever yours
Holstein.

The boys telegraph that they are well. So probably somebody else has been done for.

[1] T. M. Roest van Limburg. Dutch Foreign Minister from 1868.

1871

Holstein's leave of absence from the diplomatic service was renewed in 1869 and again in 1870, but immediately before the outbreak of the war with France he returned to the service.

A few days after the war began, Holstein was entrusted with a secret and highly delicate mission to Italy, a sign of Bismarck's continued confidence in his judgment and ability.[1] Upon his return, he served for a time in the Political Division of the Foreign Ministry in Berlin. Unable to stand the relative inactivity of office routine while so much was going on in France, he applied unsuccessfully for work in the front lines with the Order of the Knights of St John, and then early in January 1871 he appeared unsolicited at Bismarck's headquarters in Versailles. Somewhat to his surprise he was allowed to remain, and was later officially attached to Bismarck's personal staff. After the war Holstein stayed in France, first on the staff of General von Fabrice, the commander of the German occupation forces, and subsequently on the staff of Count von Waldersee,[2] the first post-war German representative to France. In November 1871 he was appointed Second Secretary at the new Imperial Legation in Paris.[3]

Throughout the war, Holstein never lost his interest in the towing project, in which he appears to have invested heavily. In a letter to Bismarck of December 1871, he reported that a Rhine Towing Company had been founded, and asked for permission to join the board of directors of the new organisation, a position, so Holstein assured his Chief, which would not interfere with his official duties.[4] Holstein's request was granted, but the towing company did not do well financially in its first two years of operation. In 1873 Holstein withdrew from his position on the board of directors.[5] His reason for doing so is not known, but it is possible that he had lost heavily on his investment in the towing project, and that the remainder of his fortune was lost in the great financial

[1] See *Memoirs*, pp. 43–6.
[2] Alfred, Count von Waldersee. Chargé d'Affaires in Paris, 1871; Chief of the General Staff of the Tenth Army Corps, 1871–81; Quartermaster-General and Vice-Chief of the Army General Staff, 1882–8; Chief of the General Staff, 1888–91; from 1891 General commanding the Ninth Army Corps in Altona; Inspector-General of the Third Army, 1898; General Field Marshal, 1900.
[3] Rogge, *Friedrich von Holstein*, p. 115.
[4] *Ibid.*, pp. 116–17.
[5] Rogge, *Blätter*, pp. 237–8.

crash in Germany in 1873. After 1873 Holstein seems to have lived on his official salary, and gradually fell into that frugal mode of life which was to characterise his later years.

14. Holstein to Karl von Eisendecher[1]

[Paris], 4 November 1871

Dear Eisendecher,

[...] You have not always had a smooth passage, old friend. Nor have I, so we are even. At present I am getting on very well with Arnim[2] who is an agreeable Chief as far as I have hitherto been able to judge. Living conditions otherwise are naturally most unpleasant and the cost of living is unequalled either in London or in Rio or anywhere. Socially we are treated like whores whom hotelkeepers either keep out altogether or only take in at a price. Moreover we are not even allowed to pay *in natura*, as they sometimes do.

Among ourselves we get along quite well. The Lynars,[3] where I am dining with Arnim to-day, and with whom one sometimes goes to the theatre, are an agreeable addition to our company. Princess Lynar[4] is loathed by our little friend *la* Hatzfeldt.[5] Why I do not know. Probably some old *jalousie*. H. has never called on L. L. is easygoing and less sharp-tongued than our little *belle Hélène*. Dönhoff[6] has got to know some Americans and occasionally organises cotillons. I associate with serious people from whom I learn something about the situation, as is only proper for the Political Secretary. I am specially charged with political affairs. Lynar and the others look after routine matters. I think I can pride myself on providing the Chief with very reliable sources and information. Only it costs money, since the French really only come to see you if you ask them to lunch.

Now *addio*, old boy. Kindest regards to Herbert and Bill.

Your sincere friend
Holstein.
[...]

[1] From the Eisendecher Papers.
[2] Harry, Count von Arnim-Suckow. Prussian Minister, then Minister of the North German Federation to the Holy See, 1864–71; Commissioner for the Franco-German peace negotiations, March 1871; Minister, then Ambassador in Paris, 1871–4.
[3] Alexander, Prince zu Lynar. Counsellor of Legation in Paris.
[4] Mary, Princess zu Lynar, *née* Parson (of Ohio).
[5] Helene, Countess von Hatzfeldt, *née* Moulton. Wife of Paul von Hatzfeldt.
[6] August, Count von Dönhoff-Friedrichstein. Attaché in Paris.

1874

15. Bernhard Ernst von Bülow[1] to [Carl Wilke][2]

Saturday evening, 31 October 1874

After closer consideration I ask you *not* to allow Herr von Holstein to read or look through our documents at tomorrow's conference,[3] but to put before him *ex actis*, and discuss with him only those individual matters on which he will be able to furnish information; specifically Count Arnim's relations with the Press, the alleged [instructions?] from Herr von H. from Varzin[4] (autumn 72) in the matter of the *Echo du Parlement*,[5] speculations on the stock exchange,[6] relations with members of the Embassy—the keeping of the archives.

If Herr von Treskow were to attend and take down the statements, it would be useful.

It would also be interesting to take this opportunity of enquiring in more detail about the relationship of the subordinate members of the Embassy to Count A. For example—is Herr von Scheven[7] wholly reliable? A Chief of this kind corrupts, and I have the impression that these men had closer relations with journalists than was desirable.

B. Bülow

16. Statement by Friedrich von Holstein[8]

Recorded in Berlin, 1 November 1874

In the course of the conference to-day, *Legationsrat* Herr von Holstein made the following statement:

---

[1] State Secretary in the German Foreign Ministry, 1873–9.

[2] *Geheimer Legationsrat*; Justiciar in the German Foreign Ministry. The document is from the Foreign Ministry files.

[3] Holstein had been recalled to Berlin to appear as a witness in the criminal proceedings instituted by the Imperial Government against the former German Ambassador in Paris. Count von Arnim had refused to return some documents which he had appropriated from the archives of the Paris Embassy. (See Norman Rich, 'Holstein and the Arnim Affair', *Journal of Modern History*, March 1956, pp. 35–54.)

[4] Prince Bismarck's estate in Pomerania.

[5] On 21 September 1872 a Belgian newspaper, the *Echo du Parlement*, published an article stating that Arnim intended to hand in his resignation because the position of Ambassador did not compensate for the unpleasantness he met with in Parisian society. On 25 September Holstein telegraphed from Varzin to Under State Secretary Thile in Berlin that the Imperial Chancellor wished the *Echo* article to be treated ironically by the German Press provided that Arnim had no objections. Thile in a telegram of 26 September passed on this information to Arnim in Paris. (From the Foreign Ministry files.)

[6] In the course of the investigation preceding the Arnim trial, Arnim was accused of having released the *Echo* article himself in order to take advantage of the resulting panic on the stock exchange for some private speculation. Arnim, after first denying the charge altogether, later admitted that he had inspired the article. (From the Foreign Ministry files.)

[7] Head of the Chancellery at the Paris Embassy. [8] From the Foreign Ministry files.

As far as my relations in general with Count Harry von Arnim during the time we were together in Paris are concerned, they were as follows:

When Count Arnim came to Paris he behaved towards the Secretaries on the staff of the Embassy in a friendly way without establishing closer relations with any one of them. At that time I did not know him well. His behaviour was peculiar in that he liked confidentially to inform first one person, then another, about some matter with the remark that it was not to be discussed; these were the ordinary political questions that occur in the course of business. He talked to me in this confidential way about his conception of the attitude which Germany should adopt towards President Thiers.[1] I remember that I did not conceal my disagreement, and repeatedly defended my opinion with all the arguments I could muster.[2] The confidences—if one can call them so—made to me in this connection arose naturally out of the fact that because I wrote quickly he often dictated to me drafts of dispatches on this subject, especially in the beginning when work was very heavy. When in October 1872 I returned from Varzin to Paris, we still had frequent discussions about Thiers in which our differences became still clearer. One day Count Arnim at last asked me if I corresponded with anyone in Berlin; I replied: 'Yes.'[3] He asked if politics were also touched upon in my letters. I replied that that was the case. He asked about the nature of my political remarks. I answered that they were my opinions, which differed from those of His Excellency. After this we did not have many more political conversations; our relations with each other were polite, but distant. In the autumn of 1873 Count Arnim let me know through Herr Lindau[4] that he had taken it amiss that I had not called upon him when I was passing through Berlin, where he was also staying. This communication was made to me here by Herr Lindau. On my return to Paris Count Arnim greeted me very coolly, and from that time—from the middle of October 1873—I believe we have not spoken a word to each other. As for my own feelings, in view of the state of affairs that was already taking shape, a transfer from Paris would not have been unwelcome to me, but, on the other hand, I saw no reason to take the initiative.

On the several points that have been put before me, I have this to say:

1. On the subject of Count Arnim's relations with the Press, the correspondents Levisohn, Landsberg and Beckmann[5] came to the Embassy and were always received by the Ambassador alone; that is to say, as far as I know, no member of the Embassy was present at their conversations. My personal opinion of the aforesaid correspondents, which I express here in strict confidence is as follows. First, as regards Beck-

---

[1] Louis Adolphe Thiers. President of the French Republic, 1871–3.

[2] Bismarck thought it was in Germany's interest to support Thiers and the French Republic, for as a republic France would remain weak and find difficulty in making alliances. Arnim, on the other hand, favoured an Orleanist restoration, in the belief that a republican France would weaken the monarchical principle everywhere.

[3] See below, p. 36, note 4.

[4] Dr Rudolf Lindau. Attached to the Paris Embassy for Press and commercial affairs, 1871–8; from 1878 *Legationsrat* in the German Foreign Ministry.

[5] German journalists in Paris.

mann. He likes to make money, but apart from that has a passion for his professional work as a journalist. Incredibly industrious, very useful as a scout to collect information. He has served under several flags and sometimes changed sides quickly. But I have not the slightest proof, and up to now not even a hint, to show that he simultaneously serves several parties with conflicting political aims. I have always kept Beckmann at a distance on account of his very intimate relations with Count Arnim, yet I must nevertheless say this for him, that at the time when he carried out the orders of the latter, in my opinion he did so in the conviction that the Ambassador represented German policy.

As far as Levisohn is concerned, he was correspondent of the *Kölnische Zeitung* and was soon transferred from Paris. In my opinion he was never on very intimate terms with Count Arnim. I remember clearly that in the autumn of 1872, or it may have been in the summer, Count Arnim dictated an article to me which dealt with Thiers' policy, and which, at my express desire, he later allowed to be copied in the Chancellery. Afterwards Count Arnim asked Dr Levisohn, who was in the Embassy, to have the article published in the *Kölnische Zeitung*. Dr Levisohn said he was willing to do so, but without showing any enthusiasm. The draft of the article laid before me here, which is said to have been confiscated from Count Arnim and which bears the date 27.5.72, is the one I have referred to above. I have no personal knowledge whether Count Arnim inspired other publications in the *Kölnische Zeitung*. I have never to my knowledge written down any further draft of any article which I could suspect Count Arnim might have made use of in the Press.

Finally, as regards Dr Landsberg, I gained a good impression of him from my sojourn in Paris. He did not seem to be on so intimate a footing with Count Arnim as was the case with Beckmann; he did not appear at the Embassy so often, and after the conversations he had with the Ambassador, he usually paid a visit to the Chancellery, where, as I believed, he passed on to the Secretaries who were present almost everything he had told the Ambassador. Consequently I was very much surprised when I learned that he was suspected of being responsible for the publications in the Vienna *Presse* in April of this year.[1]

From my own personal knowledge I cannot say anything whatever about whether or not Count Arnim was in touch with the editors of such Paris newspapers as the *Français, Gaulois* or *Journal de Paris*. Nevertheless, I myself repeatedly noticed, as did the other members of the Embassy, how completely the views expressed by these papers agreed with those of the correspondents Beckmann and Landsberg.

2. I was staying in Varzin when the report published by the *Echo du*

---

[1] On 2 April 1874 the Vienna newspaper *Presse* published confidential diplomatic documents about Arnim's policy during the Vatican Council. These documents showed that Arnim feared serious political difficulties in connection with the doctrine of Papal Infallibility, and had therefore advised that the Powers should make representations to the Council to exercise a moderating influence on papal policy. The publication of these documents was evidently designed to illustrate the superior wisdom of Arnim's ecclesiastical policy as compared with Bismarck's.

Parlement arrived there.[1] On the Prince's order I then wrote the note to his Excellency von Thile[2] that has been shown to me here (A. 2725) dated 24 September 1872, and drafted the telegram of the 25th (A. 2726).[3] I remember that I also wrote at that time to Count Arnim, but I do not know whether I also mentioned this matter; I think not.[4] I have no reason for thinking that he made use of this manipulation of the Press for speculations on the stock exchange, or that such was his intention.[5]

The enquiry was adjourned at this point.

Read, approved, signed.

Holstein
v. Bülow[6] II as witness
Wilke

Continued the same evening.

Herr *Legationsrat* von Holstein continued his statement as follows:

After my attention had been drawn to the passage on pages 4 and 5 in the letter of Count Arnim of 20 June of this year (A. 2427),[7] in which a letter is mentioned that I am said to have written from Varzin to Count Arnim, [I] now recall that I did at that time write this letter to Count Arnim.[4] The expression 'Supercargo' brings back to me a similar utterance of His Highness and I therefore assume that at least this portion was written by order of the Chancellor.[8] Otherwise I do not

---

[1] See above, p. 31, note 5.

[2] Hermann von Thile. Head of the Prussian/German Foreign Ministry, 1862–72.

[3] Holstein wrote on 24 September that Bismarck had no objection to the publication of the item in the Berlin newspapers, which had so far been prevented, but that Arnim should first be asked if he was in agreement. (From the Foreign Ministry files.)

[4] Holstein's letter to Arnim has not been found.

[5] Arnim was suspected of deliberately delaying the payment of the French war debts and the withdrawal of the German troops from France for purposes of speculation.

[6] Otto von Bülow. *Vortragender Rat* in the German Foreign Ministry, 1874–9; Minister in Bern, 1882–92. Frequently the Foreign Ministry representative in the Kaiser's retinue. He was referred to as Bülow II in official documents to distinguish him from State Secretary Bülow.

[7] In a letter of 28 May 1874 the Foreign Ministry confronted Arnim with the testimony of the journalist Albert Beckmann, who stated that he had released the *Echo* article on Arnim's instructions. In a letter to the Foreign Ministry of 20 June 1874, Arnim admitted having inspired the article: 'While I was in Pomerania on leave I sent a memorandum, which, however, was not signed by me, to the said Beckmann in order that it might be published in some manner. [...] I must, however, most emphatically deny that I gave him the order to go to Brussels and by his whole conduct to give it the importance which he mistakenly gave it in this way. I only wanted to bring about a certain effect in Paris through the publication of the report. I also recall quite definitely that Beckmann did not keep to the wording of the memorandum as I had written it out for him. I know that the manner in which he carried out his instructions made a very unpleasant impression on me.' (From the Foreign Ministry files.)

[8] In his letter of 20 June, quoted above, Arnim said: 'Herr von Holstein wrote to me from Varzin at the time when he was acting as private secretary to the Imperial Chancellor, and presumably at his orders, that a telegram had arrived there in duplicate asking whether publication in the Berlin papers should be permitted. Herr von Holstein wrote: "The duplicate was signed by Albert, presumably Beckmann." The Imperial Chancellor approved circulation and added: "There are situations in which seemingly civilised nations must be treated like wild animals. One then sends them a sort of supercargo. All this can still happen." ' (See also *Darstellung der in der Untersuchungssache wider den Wirklichen Geheimen Rath Grafen von Arnim vor dem Königlichen Stadtgericht zu Berlin im December 1874 stattgehabten öffentlichen Verhandlungen* (Berlin, 1875), p. 179.)

remember the content of this letter, but believe I can assume that the content, as given by Count Arnim, is correct. I immediately came to the conclusion from the signature Albert on the telegram—this is Beckmann's Christian name—that there was a connection with Count Arnim and was therefore somewhat astonished when Count Arnim after my return to Paris hinted to me that the paragraph in the newspaper might very well originate with some discontented German of the *Cercle de l'Union* like Kahlden.[1] This is all that I can remember about this question.

3. If I am asked what I know about Count Arnim's speculations on the stock exchange, I can say that in the spring of 1872 *The Times* correspondent Oliphant often told me that there was a rumour that Prince Bismarck was involved in the so-called Henckel[2] scheme for the redemption of war debts, that is to say, as I understood it, that he would directly benefit from the settlement of the business.[3] I particularly remember that Oliphant was supposed to have heard this in the salon of a Baroness Blaze de Bury[4] which was frequented by the circle around M Thiers. The reason for the rumour could easily be found in the endeavour to exercise pressure on the decisions of the French Government. The groundlessness of this rumour became obvious when all Henckel's schemes were rejected in Berlin one after the other. But I know nothing to show that Count Arnim was in any way implicated in the dissemination of this rumour. Apart from Count Henckel, Count Arnim at that time also associated a great deal with Senator Godefroy from Hamburg who had also placed a financial scheme before the French Government. In addition to Henckel and Godefroy, Count Arnim often saw Baron Emil Erlanger[5] and Herr Bamberger of the *Banque de Paris*. But I have no knowledge as to what money transactions these persons negotiated with Count Arnim. I know no more about the money matters which may have been arranged between Count Arnim and the Duc Decazes.[6] That the latter took a lively part in stock exchange activities was regarded in Paris as one of those notorious axioms for which proof is hard to find—at least it was not accessible to me.

4. When I was asked for my opinion of the subordinate staff of the Embassy, I must state that I believe all the members were thoroughly honourable and trustworthy. This applies also and especially to Herr

[1] On 1 October 1872 Arnim had written to the Foreign Ministry: 'One of the papers here is now suggesting that Herr von Kahlden, who is well known in Berlin, is responsible for the circulation of the false newspaper report that I have tendered my resignation. He is said to have put this report into circulation because of his anger at being excluded from the Jockey Club, which spoiled his game of whist. Be that as it may, the few lines which probably through some blunder have found their way to Brussels from some letter-box have given rise to unusual excitement.' (From the Foreign Ministry files.)

[2] Guido, Count von Henckel-Donnersmarck. A leading industrialist.

[3] See below. Holstein's memorandum of 13 January 1894.

[4] The wife of a French writer who promoted the appreciation of German music and poetry in France.

[5] A financier in Frankfurt-am-Main, subsequently in Paris.

[6] Louis Charles Amadieu, Duc de Decazes. Leader of the right Centre in the French National Assembly, 1871–2; French Ambassador in London, 1872–3; Foreign Minister, 1873–7.

von Scheven. It cannot really be said that he is always very amiable, and he has the urge to make himself important. Nevertheless he keeps the Chancellery in very good order, though not from time to time without friction with one official or another. I cannot believe either of him or of any of the other subordinate officials that they took the part of Count Arnim in the matter under discussion.

5. At no time did I have anything to do with the political Chancellery, not even during the time when, owing to Count Wesdehlen's[1] absence and the illness of *Hofrat* Taglioni,[2] I had to fulfill the functions both of Councillor of Embassy and Head of the Chancellery. The filing-cabinet in the Secretarial Chancellery, which holds the political archives, was under the charge of Herr Hammerdörfer, who was also responsible for the entries in the register. Besides the one in the Secretarial Chancellery, there was also a big cabinet in Count Arnim's bedroom and in this there were said to be a number of documents that were under the sole control of Count Arnim. I have myself seen him now and then take documents out of this cabinet. The majority of the documents which were in this last-named cabinet were as a rule only registered long after their arrival—if ever. Hammerdörfer, who thus found himself given the impossible task of keeping the political archives in order, often complained to me, especially in the recent past, that once again nothing had been registered for weeks on end.

Finally I will again mention that during my entire stay in Paris I did not find the smallest reason for assuming that any single one of the secretaries or attachés, civil or military, in the Embassy conducted himself in his official duties other than in a thoroughly patriotic and honourable way, or that he had anything else in mind than the best interests of the German Empire. The consequence was that Count Arnim, as regards official matters, stood completely isolated in the Embassy.

Read personally, approved, signed
Holstein
Wilke   von Treskow
as witnesses to the signature.

17. Bernhard Ernst von Bülow to Tessendorf[3]

B[erlin], 11 December 1874.

In connection with the allegation made today at the Arnim trial against *Legationsrat* von Holstein in Paris,[4] the Foreign Ministry requests you

[1] Ludwig, Count von Wesdehlen. First Secretary in the Prussian Legation in Florence and in Rome from 1868, in the German Embassy in Paris, 1873–80.

[2] Head of the Chancellery in the Embassy in Paris.

[3] Chief Public Prosecutor in Berlin. The document is from the Foreign Ministry files.

[4] Arnim's counsel, *Rechtsanwalt* Dockhorn, had stated: 'I must now, however painful it may be to me, make certain explanations concerning the attitude of Herr von Holstein to the accused. Herr von Holstein has admitted to the accused that he was assigned to Paris by the Foreign Ministry for the purposes of keeping watch over the accused and of sending regular reports to the Foreign Ministry or to another authority that I personally do not care to name. Herr von Holstein admitted this to the accused and promised that he would not do it

to bring to the notice of the Court before the impending examination of Baron von Holstein, who arrives here on Sunday, the following statement.

The Foreign Ministry declares it to be untrue that Herr von Holstein was ever instructed to keep watch upon his former Chief, Ambassador Count Arnim, and to furnish secret reports on his conduct of affairs.

The Foreign Ministry cannot, however, permit its right to make such an assignment to be contested in any way. The interests that are at stake for the Empire in the faithful and trustworthy conduct of his official duties by the Head of a Mission are too great to exclude the possibility of instructing a trustworthy subordinate to make such reports as a part of his duty when clarification seems called for in regard to such loyalty and trustworthiness.

Moreover, cases might well arise where some such subordinate might feel himself occasioned and indeed compelled by his oath of office to inform the Foreign Ministry when it appears to him that suspicions of the trustworthiness and fidelity of the Head of the Mission are well-founded.

B[ernhard] B[ülow]

18. Tessendorf to Carl Wilke[1]

Berlin, 12 December 1874

In the secret session to-day, the accused held to his former statements, and finally handed over the copy of a letter written by Herr von Holstein to him in April 1872,[2] which letter *heavily compromises* v.H. The ques-

---

again. Nevertheless there are cogent reasons for supposing that despite this assurance Herr von Holstein continued to play the role of informer against the accused.' (*Darstellung*, p. 161.) Immediately after Dockhorn's accusation, the Foreign Ministry summoned Holstein to Berlin to appear as a witness at the public Court proceedings. Hohenlohe telegraphed on 11 December that Holstein, although unwell, would go to Berlin on the following day. (From the Foreign Ministry files.) Just before Holstein appeared in the witness stand on Monday morning, December 13, *Rechtsanwalt* Dockhorn asked to make a statement. 'I see from the stenographic report', he said, 'that I am supposed to have submitted evidence to indicate that Herr von Holstein was assigned to keep watch on the accused. I don't know whether I said that, but I will not deny having done so. In any case it would have been based on incorrect information. The accused simply maintains that Herr von Holstein admitted to him that he had made reports about him behind his back to his official superiors, and that these had increased the ill-feeling between the Chancellor and the accused; that he had asked the pardon of the accused and promised not to do it again. That is the substance of the evidence.' Holstein replied on this point: 'At that time I wrote to various acquaintances, not only political but also others, about my opinions, and as I said, these were opposed to the political course of Count Arnim. I have already described the conversation with Count Arnim when he asked me about this correspondence, and when I told him I would request a transfer. In connection with this, I have been mistakenly accused of using the childish expression "that I would not do it again"; instead, I told Count Arnim that I would request a transfer if he wished. Count Arnim thereupon said: no, please don't, I can't hold that against you, etc.' (*Darstellung*, pp. 230–1, 234.)

[1] From the Foreign Ministry files.

[2] Not found. In describing his early relations with Arnim, Holstein stated at the trial: 'I can still remember that—I think it was in April 1872—when I was in Berlin and the Chancellor expressed the definite intention to retire, I was one of those who believed that if Bismarck decided to retire Count Arnim would be best as his successor. I even believe that at the time I wrote to Count Arnim in this sense.' (*Darstellung*, pp. 232–3.)

tion was also discussed as to who was responsible for the conflict between the Chancellor and the accused. In answer to my remark that nothing could be decided about this without interrogating the Chancellor and that the latter could furnish the most reliable information to reveal the true state of affairs, the defence said they did not wish to make application to this effect, and the Court after deliberating decided that since the questions awaiting decision had nothing to do with politics the interrogation of His Highness would be dispensed with.

Most obediently
Tessendorf

19. Bernhard Ernst von Bülow to Chlodwig zu Hohenlohe[1]

TELEGRAM

Berlin, 16 December 1874

Since Herr v. Holstein's testimony and the fact that Arnim's lawyer had to withdraw his allegation on Monday[2] have completely won over public opinion here to his [Holstein's] side, it is in every way desirable that his personal position in the matter be properly presented also in Paris and that the slander that was yesterday in part renewed should not gain credence. Please do everything possible to this end by having Lindau make use of his testimony, especially with regard to the slander that has found its way into the *Journal des Débats* of the 15th of this month.[3]

B[ernhard] B[ülow]

20. Bernhard Ernst von Bülow to Chlodwig zu Hohenlohe[4]

Berlin, 20 December 1874

Your Highness

I thank you very much for the kind letter of the 17th[5] and the enclosed cutting from the *Figaro*. It will not of course be possible to refute all the attacks and misrepresentations concerning Herr von Holstein or to prevent their recurrence, especially since his incriminating evidence has aroused the full fury of the Arnim party, so that we can expect more of the same in future. Meanwhile society and the Press here are fully satisfied with the statements of Herr von H.—I have heard nothing against him and His Majesty the Kaiser received him most graciously in special audience—always the decisive thing in Berlin. Tomorrow I will insert this in the Press together with a short comment

---

[1] Chlodwig, Prince zu Hohenlohe–Schillingsfürst. Ambassador in Paris, 1874–85; Governor of Alsace-Lorraine, 1885–94; Chancellor of the German Reich and Prussian Minister-President, 1894–1900. The document is from the Foreign Ministry files.

[2] See above, p. 36, note 4.

[3] A similar telegram was sent to Count Münster in London.

[4] From the Foreign Ministry files.

[5] Hohenlohe wrote to Bülow on 17 December that Lindau had inserted an article rehabilitating Holstein in the *Figaro* 'which left nothing to be desired'. (From the Foreign Ministry files. See also Hohenlohe's diary entries of 20, 22, and 25 December 1874 in Helmuth Rogge, *Holstein und Hohenlohe* (Stuttgart, 1957), pp. 58–60.)

on the unworthy procedure of Arnim's defence counsel.[1] The whole thing was done with the calculation that the cross-examination of witnesses would end on Saturday and that it would thus be too late for the victim of the slander to be called to the stand.

As to the verdict and the grounds on which it was based,[2] I will only say that we will not appeal against the sentence, which in itself is of no importance, but against the latter. These are sometimes childish, sometimes against the spirit of the law, as for example the treatment of the *Echo du Parlement*[3] and the disclosure question,[4] in which the evidence in the official statements was wholly ignored. The President[5] is a very insignificant, very weak-willed, paltry man; a lawyer, lately transferred here from Gleiwitz, a small town in Posen, overwhelmed by the importance of the case and the aura surrounding the accused and the defence counsel. If in spite of all this he was condemned to three months, one can say that he deserved three years. The rulings about diplomatic documents, etc, will indeed paralyse all conscientious and orderly government. *Enfin*—it is not a complete acquittal, the effect of which would have been deplorable, even though Arnim as a politician and state official had been completely uprooted and ruined. The renown in Europe *des juges à Berlin* will not be heightened by this unsavoury combination of absurdities and fallacies. If the Court of Appeal does not find a complete remedy, we must at all events alter the appropriate legislation: otherwise every archive would be *à la merci* of every official who had a passion for interesting documents. Meanwhile the feverish interest in this affair will now certainly subside and we will again be given time in which to hear and to talk about other things.

With all good wishes
Your most devoted
v. Bülow

[1] Arnim's counsel were *Rechtsanwalt* Munckel of Berlin, *Rechtsanwalt* Dockhorn from Posen, and Professor Dr Holtzendorff from Munich.
[2] On 19 December the Court decided that Count Harry von Arnim was not guilty of stealing documents or of official misdemeanours but of actions contrary to public order. He was sentenced to three months' imprisonment.
[3] See above, p. 31, note 5.
[4] The revelations in the Vienna *Presse*. See above, p. 33, note 1.
[5] *Stadtgerichtsdirektor* Reich.

1876-7

In April 1876 Holstein was recalled to Berlin to work in the Foreign Ministry. On 27 May he was appointed to the Political Division where he remained until the end of his career.

21. Holstein to Karl von Eisendecher[1]

Berlin, 15 July 1876

Dear Eisendecher,

You can be very certain that I have not forgotten you, nor will I. I have not written because for the most part I am not in the mood for writing. As one gets older and finds oneself more and more alone on the battlefield of life, one's spirits do not become more cheerful. I avoid passing on this mood to others as far as possible.

I miss you here quite extraordinarily. At the moment I am alone here without any close acquaintances; and I had few such as you.

The Bismarcks will probably return from Kissingen towards the end of the month. Bill is in Marienbad. He had swellings on the ankle again, both shortly before his departure and shortly after his arrival there.

They are a curious family; it strikes me every time that I see them again.

For the old man, I confess that I have an affection that will most likely always be with me. I believe that he has more feeling than one thinks, more than the rest of the family, only it is hidden deep down like Barbarossa in the Kyffhäuser mountain and does not come to the surface. Outwardly he is a figure of bronze—to his detriment, for this outward coldness and the cynicism he exhibits have little by little driven old friends away, so that now, at the summit of power and fame, he stands more isolated than anybody in a similar position ever has before. The salon is empty. Obernitz,[2] Lehndorff,[3] Maltzan,[4] Dietze,[5] Lucius.[6] Often nobody at all. He says nothing about it, but I believe nevertheless that he feels it.

---

[1] From the Eisendecher Papers.
[2] *Geheimer Regierungsrat*.
[3] Heinrich August, Count von Lehndorff. Adjutant-General to Wilhelm I.
[4] August, Count von Maltzan-Gültz. Hereditary Lord High Chamberlain.
[5] G. A. von Dietze-Barby. District Counsellor; Free-Conservative Member of the Reichstag.
[6] Robert Lucius, later Baron Lucius von Ballhausen. A leader of the Free-Conservatives in the Reichstag, 1870-9; Prussian Minister for Agriculture, Crown Lands and Forestry, 1879-90.

I believe this isolation is due far more to personal irritation than to political actions. Some of these actions might very well have seen the light of day in quite a different form if the Chief had not earlier lost contact with the Conservatives. The family's habit of abusive criticism, especially that of the Princess,[1] with which you are acquainted, has contributed more to this feeling than he himself. A man like him should be surrounded with calming influences. Instead, the others constantly stir him up. When he says that someone has made a mistake the choir choruses, yes, he is a blockhead, etc. The result of it all is that the man stands alone and feels himself deserted. It saddens me when I see him thus, but what can one do about it? With the Princess and her conduct I am, as you already know, not in agreement. She does not soothe him enough and she also neglects the constant little attentions. The fact that, when he does get seriously ill, she makes herself sick by foolish night-nursing, does not help matters. She and she alone could exercise a beneficial influence over his diet. She could, moreover, get him away from Varzin. Instead she shuns every expenditure—even the smallest —that would make Friedrichsruh more habitable. She told me this herself. Bismarck had wanted this and that done, but her fingers hurt her from paying out so much money. She herself admitted that ten days in the Sachsenwald forest did more to put him on his legs than four months in Varzin, 'but that is just coincidence, it is silly talk on the part of Struck[2] and Bucher[3] to maintain that Varzin is unhealthy.'

About the Countess[4] I have formed no proper opinion; I do not know her well enough for that. But I think that she has absolutely no heart, and regard her as absolutely egotistical. I certainly do not believe that she cared that much about Eulenburg.[5]

I think a lot of Herbert and Bill, especially of the former. He makes himself extraordinarily useful to his father and is becoming very serviceable. In the circumstances the continual pampering and clever flattery of which he is the object cannot fail to leave traces, and I think that he shows the effects at times. Nevertheless they are less apparent than might have been expected. It is said to be more obvious in mother and daughter.

La Arnim-Kröchlendorff[6] is playing a silly role *vis-à-vis* the Boitzenburgs.[7] Instead of contenting herself with the fact that through no merit of her own she has such a brother, she is very unhappy that since the trial[8] the Boitzenburg family have cut her; and she continues to give

---

[1] Johanna von Bismarck.
[2] Dr Heinrich Struck. *Geheimer Sanitätsrat*, later Director of the Office of Public Health.
[3] Lothar Bucher. *Vortragender Rat* in the Foreign Ministry, 1864–86.
[4] Marie, Countess von Bismarck, daughter of Otto von Bismarck. In November 1878 she married Kuno, Count zu Rantzau.
[5] Marie von Bismarck was engaged to Wendt, Count zu Eulenburg, who died before their marriage.
[6] Malwine von Arnim-Kröchlendorff, *née* von Bismarck. Sister of Otto von Bismarck.
[7] Sofie Adelheid, sister of Count Adolf von Arnim-Boitzenburg, was married to Harry, Count von Arnim-Suckow.
[8] The Arnim trial. The supporters of Arnim believed that Bismarck had pressed the case in order to destroy a potential rival for the Chancellorship.

them opportunities for 'snubbing' her. For instance, a Boitzenburg son recently married a Countess Schulenburg. Immediately *la* Arnim-Kröchlendorff was at hand with a wedding-present for the bride. Whereupon she (the bride) wrote to her that she thanked her very much, but regretted that since a wife must respect her husband's wishes she could not associate with Frau von Arnim.

Incidentally the Arnims agitate ceaselessly and probably we are far from having heard the last of all that.

Our old friend Southwell is deranged and is privately watched by keepers after having several times attempted suicide.

Otherwise I have little else to tell. My own existence is without interest. I would gladly have become First [Secretary] in Paris, but partly owing to the Chief's dislike of Wesdehlen, partly through the intrigues of people who wanted to get rid of me there, it came about that Wesdehlen was passed over when posts were being filled.[1] Since I did not want to go to St Petersburg or Constantinople, the Chief, who showed himself very considerate towards me, let me know that 'as a proof of particular confidence' he wanted to have me here. Hence I sit here, but have little to do, and also think that I am very unwelcome to the two Bülows[2] and Radowitz.[3] In short, the whole thing does not make one feel cheerful.[4]

Now, old fellow, write to me again soon. I will probably write to you again before the arrival of your reply. Be assured that you can always count on me, in all things. I visualise your future in two ways: either you will just come back, marry a pretty, sensitive girl—which will not be difficult for you with your gentleness and your dreamy eyes —and live quietly in Germany. Or else you see to it that in two years time or a little later you come to Europe, to Athens for example or to some similar post at first. If you do well there in Japan, which I do not doubt, this can certainly be pulled off. The Princess will be useful to you in this. You could also do both, marry and stay in the service. Only do not brutalise yourself in Japan, as so many do, with grog and Mussman [*sic*]—which does not mean that I am telling you to live like a monk. [...]

Frau von Lebbin, *née* Brandt,[5] sends her regards. She says that her uncle[6] is thoroughly wretched in China and regrets the change.

Faithfully yours
F Holstein.

Naturally treat this letter as *most private and confidential*.

[1] See also *Diaries*, p. 338, note 3.
[2] Bernhard Ernst von Bülow and Otto von Bülow.
[3] Joseph Maria von Radowitz. Minister in Athens, 1874–82, but frequently recalled for work in the Foreign Ministry in Berlin; Ambassador in Constantinople, 1882–92, in Madrid, 1892–1908.
[4] In a letter to Eisendecher of 12 September 1876, Herbert von Bismarck wrote: 'Holstein has been working in the Ministry in Berlin since May—Stumm has taken his place in Paris. He is *tolerably* content—as usual peeved that he has so little to do! If it's nothing worse than that!' (From the Eisendecher Papers.)
[5] Helene von Lebbin. Friend of Holstein for many years. (See *Memoirs*, pp. xvi–xxi.)
[6] Maximilian von Brandt. Minister in Peking, 1874–92.

22. Holstein to Karl von Eisendecher[1]

Berlin, 29 December 1876

Dear Eisendecher,

My New Year wishes from afar will not in fact reach you until February, nevertheless you will still belatedly see that you were not forgotten. There is really not so great a gulf between near and far, perhaps there are even some advantages in a foreign country. For example, on Christmas Eve you were probably with others in a situation similar to your own, and probably felt less lonely than I, who spent the evening alone. Here especially, where most people have relatives, one feels more alone on that evening than one would abroad. I was invited by the Chief but did not go. Over in the Wilhelmstrasse things are as before. The Chief is apparently well, touch wood! The impression that I had gained earlier that he has become milder in his general manner of thinking proves to be true. The political work seems to be as easy for him as ever—and there is not a little of it. It would be absurd to write to you about the course of events: in six weeks when this letter reaches you the telegraph will already have informed you of things that are to-day hidden from me. The Russians have little desire for war. Satisfactory terms which come anywhere close to the demands they have made hitherto, they will not get without war. The question is therefore: what is the main consideration for the Tsar and Gorchakov, satisfaction or peace? Here we do not yet know the answer. But it is to be feared that if peace is preserved at the expense of national aspirations, the dynastic sentiment in Russia will receive a heavy blow.[2] We are distrusted, and it is thought that we will take advantage of the disturbances in the East in order to attack somebody; but the two or three people who have influence here have not the slightest intention of doing so. Personally I would regret it if the Eastern Question did not now take a real step forward. I have already said that no one here wants war, and it may therefore this time be possible, by means of Bismarck's dexterity, to localise it. But if the question remains open, and the most crying abuses are not remedied, then there will certainly be a general conflict in the not too distant future.

Herbert is now working here in the Ministry. Perhaps he will still go to Vienna. For his age he is already remarkably useful. The old man takes great delight in him. I think that H. is engaged in a flirtation with Princess Carolath, *née* Hatzfeldt,[3] which, however, does not interfere with his work. Intellectually, Bill has developed quite remarkably, but physically he has become even stouter, and his rheumatism often keeps him in bed. This is the drawback in his case, the sole reason that prevents me from being sure of his career.

[1] From the Eisendecher Papers.
[2] Panslavic elements in Russia were putting pressure on the Tsarist government to go to the aid of Slavs and Orthodox Christians in the Balkans whose recent rebellions against Turkish rule had been decisively defeated.
[3] Elizabeth, Princess von Carolath, *née* Countess Hatzfeldt-Trachenberg. In April 1881 she was divorced from Prince Carolath-Beuthen in order to marry Herbert von Bismarck, but the marriage was prevented by Herbert's father.

Countess Marie has grown stouter. Little is now heard of former events. Moreover, as you know, I am not sufficiently close to the female members of the family to have any opinion in that quarter. Up to now the ladies have gone out little. Nor have the boys, more than is necessary.

1 January 1877

A happy New Year, old boy. May '77 bring you as little sorrow and as much joy as possible.

I will continue where I left off. The boys do not go out very much because conditions in society are not pleasant for them. The three groups hostile to the Imperial Chancellor which are socially of consequence—Ultramontanists, Arnim's supporters, and the Court clique—have a formidable number of adherents. The foreign diplomats are very cautious, none the less they prefer to associate with those circles. For this reason, quite apart from open enmities, the boys have been rendered very suspicious and believe that you never can tell whose hand you may be shaking. You know my passion for society. I never go out at all, because beyond what I have now, I want nothing and aspire to nothing, not even a wife. My daily companion is Thielau[1] who is working here temporarily. Unfortunately he will probably be going to Madrid soon. [...]

Hatzfeldt, who now has a great deal to do, is working most satisfactorily in Madrid; but, unfortunately, his wife stands between him and an embassy. What is more, her father is said to have lost a great part of his money recently.

I have something to tell you about K.[2]—you know whom I mean. In order to put an end to our affair he turned, as perhaps you know, to three ladies, one after the other: the Princess,[3] his wife,[4] and my cousin,[5] who lives in the country close to his wife's estate. I refused all overtures and simply said that if he did not want anything else from me, I did not want anything either, but I did not wish to have anything to do with him.

This autumn, shortly before he went to V[arzin], Radow[itz] came to me to inform me that he had been authorised by K. to arrange an interview, or discussion, with me. The Princess had written me that this was desirable. I said that I thought a discussion was superfluous, that I would stand by everything I had said, and, moreover, that I rejected a *tête-à-tête* if for no other reason than that I did not know if our conversation would subsequently be correctly reported. Rad. delivered this message and K. burst forth into the highest praise of me declaring that he demanded no sort of retraction, on the contrary, he was convinced

[1] Wilhelm Otto Florian von Thielau. Secretary of Legation in Brussels, 1874–5, in Madrid, 1877–8; Consul-General in Sofia, 1878–81, in Budapest, 1881–3; Prussian Minister in Oldenburg, 1883–4, in Weimar, 1884–6.
[2] Robert von Keudell. In charge of the Personnel Division in the Foreign Ministry, 1863–1872; Minister in Constantinople, 1872–3, in Rome, 1873–87 (Ambassador from 1876).
[3] Johanna von Bismarck.
[4] Hedwig von Keudell. Daughter of von Patow, the former Minister for Trade and Commerce and later for Finance.
[5] Ida von Stülpnagel.

that I had acted in everything with the best intentions, and he counted on time to heal the ravages of mistrust. He only wanted to shake my hand again after this unfortunate misunderstanding. The following day he visited me at the Ministry in the company of Rad. (as I had demanded). We shook hands, talked for five minutes in R's presence about trivialities and parted. K. was immediately at hand with a proposal that we should dine together which I rejected through R., who said I was right to do so.

What do you say to all that? It is scarcely probable that K. will have changed his nature. 'Vindictive as an Indian.'

I am not going to bother any more about him. The affair is finished as far as I am concerned. I forgot to say that already before the latest incident he had informed me through my cousin that he was ready to apologize. Rad. says that the whole affair gives him the impression that K. feels that he is decidedly in the wrong in his behaviour towards me (*as well he might*).

At all events this much is certain, that the whole business, with the annoyance it has caused me, and the absence from work caused by that annoyance, has had consequences affecting my whole life.[1]

Now about other things.

On New Year's Eve there were at the Chief's Frau von Arnim, the Spitzembergs,[2] Lehndorff, Rosenberg,[3] Obernitz, Thielau, Kurowski,[4] (the present Special Bureau), Kessel,[5] Stülpnagel (Military Attaché in Munich, where he became acquainted with Herbert). The [Christmas] tree was chopped up in the traditional way. The Chief was quite gay. Otherwise the circle, as always, is a narrow one. The Reichstag evenings are very interesting; the Chief seems to like them, as tournaments.

What the new Reichstag will be like is very doubtful. Perhaps the telegraph will take it upon itself to inform you about this before this letter arrives.

Let me hear from you. In the course of this year Europe will probably again see you on leave.

Your faithful friend
F Holstein. [...]

---

[1] On 7 March 1872 Holstein wrote to Karl von Eisendecher:

'As regards the K. affair: In answer to my letter—which you know—I received a note couched in threatening terms that ended with "eye for an eye" etc. I answered that I regretted his threats, but that I indeed intended, for example, to prove that he was responsible for an official set-back that conflicted with his avowed friendly feelings. I would regard all further demands for explanations on his part as indicating a wish to drive the affair to extremes. To this I have not received any answer.

'Since I had to put forward an official reason to avoid discovery of the real reason, I am to some extent in his power. He can damage me with the Chief by showing the letter. But in that case, I will throw discretion to the winds.' (From the Eisendecher Papers.) Apart from this letter and the letters published by Rogge (*Friedrich von Holstein*, pp. xxv, 115, xxvi, 117, 120), nothing further is known about Holstein's quarrel with Keudell.

[2] Karl Hugo, Baron von Spitzemberg. Württemberg Minister in Berlin; Hildegard von Spitzemberg, *née* Varnbüler.

[3] Heinrich von Rosenberg. From 1875 commanding officer of the Ziethen Hussar Regiment, No. 3.

[4] Assistant judge. *Vortragender Rat* in the Ministry of State.

[5] Bernhard von Kessel. Prussian General.

1878-9

23. Holstein to Christoph von Tiedemann[1]

Varzin, 2 January 1878

Dear Tiedemann,

Thanks for your kind letter. Many irons in the fire? On the contrary. Since I have been here I have written two things. This, to be sure, is due to the health, or rather the ill-health of the Prince. Bad bronchial catarrh. Struck has been here since the 30th of last month and is staying on until tomorrow. But it is getting better.

For the rest—snow, visits, wild boar hunts. I am almost the only person who goes for walks. As a result, when I visited the Prince for a moment yesterday he asked me: 'Can it be that you are training?'

Yesterday there were various New Year callers. Otherwise only Frau von Thadden is still here.

I leave with Bill, Saturday or Sunday.

There is nothing more to tell except that the Berlin doctor to-day upset a lamp over the Prince's papers. As a result there is hardly any blotting-paper left in the house.

Yours
H.

24. Herbert von Bismarck to Karl von Eisendecher[2]

Varzin, 7 November 1879

My dear Karl,

[...] The death of old Bülow[3] has greatly upset my father; it is a great, almost an irreplaceable, loss! You will probably have read the details in the newspapers! The choice of his successor is very difficult; my father at present knows of nobody, and until we are once more in Berlin nothing will be decided!

[...] You probably know that Bill is Manteuffel's[4] private secretary in Strasbourg. When my parents left Kissingen (where I did the work) for Gastein, he relieved me there, and then at the beginning of October he went to Strasbourg. He writes very cheerfully from there! Before

---

[1] *Vortragender Rat* in the Prussian Ministry of State from 1876; Head of the newly formed Reich Chancellery, 1878-81; Head of the Administration in Bromberg, 1881-99. The document is from the Tiedemann Papers.

[2] From the Eisendecher Papers.

[3] The State Secretary Bernhard Ernst von Bülow.

[4] Edwin, Baron von Manteuffel. Governor of Alsace-Lorraine, 1879-85.

my arrival Holstein was here for a fortnight as quill-driver. He has also made use of Kissingen, which has done him much good! […]
                       Faithfully as ever
                           Your
                                Herbert Bismarck.

1880

25. Holstein to Klemens Busch[1]

Berlin, 2 February 1880

Dear Busch,

The Chief asks me to tell you that he would like to speak to you in order to find out whether you would care to re-establish closer touch with him and with Berlin; and under what conditions? You are therefore asked to request by a telegram direct to the Chief a short leave for the purpose of attending to family affairs, and then to come here as quickly as possible.

So much for my instructions. It goes without saying that your new post would in every sense be better than the former; I am not empowered to say more about it in writing.

The State Secretary question is still quite undecided; all that is as yet certain is that Radowitz, Keudell and Solms[2] will not get it. I do not believe there will be a speedy decision, but an interim of several months.

At present the Chief is playing the role of State Secretary, corrects drafts, signs dispatches, etc., with extraordinary zeal. His health is, thank God, not bad. We have, after all, coddled him long enough. He was very ill in December, gall-bladder attack and swollen veins. Now he has a real passion for work, practically devours it; I do not need to tell you that he digests it. Moreover I can state in all conscience that working with him, even during days when he was ill and depressed, involved no kind of unpleasantness. In all I was with him for more than eleven weeks, first for three weeks in October, then from 29 November to 26 January.

He will not be able to carry on this present State Secretary activity for long in conjunction with parliamentary work. Who will be the temporary occupant—and I think of you as his eldest son[3]—I do not know. [...]

With the humility proper in a future victim of your despotic moods, I permit myself the suggestion that in punctilious satisfaction of the promptings of the official conscience, and also to avoid arousing any unpleasant conjectures, Your Excellency will be pleased to expedite the

[1] Consul-General in Budapest, 1879–80; temporary Head of the Political Division in the Foreign Ministry, 1880–1; Under State Secretary, March 1881–5; Minister in Bucharest, 1885–8, in Stockholm, 1888–92, in Berne, 1892–5. The document is from the Busch Papers.

[2] Eberhard, Count zu Solms-Sonnenwalde. Minister in Madrid, 1878–87; Ambassador in Rome, 1887–93.

[3] Holstein refers to the possibility of Busch becoming Under State Secretary in the Foreign Ministry.

desired telegram—*in re*: short leave for family business—within 59 minutes after the receipt of this letter.

Wherewith—and with respectful inclusion of greetings from Bucher and Rantzau[1]—I have the honour to sign myself as

Your Excellency's
Submissive
Holstein.

[...]

26. Wilhelm von Bismarck to Karl von Eisendecher[2]

Strasbourg, 12 December 1880

My dear Karl,

[...] The augurs in 76[3] feel very well under Stirum's[4] mild sceptre; whether Hatzfeldt will take it from him, and when, lies in the lap of the gods. He should arrive in Germany in the next few days in order to put his financial affairs in order. If he is not successful, he would naturally prefer to stay in Constantinople which he is not leaving with any enthusiasm anyway. It would be a pity, since he would unquestionably be the most suitable State Secretary. Mother Bolz[5] is very well and her salon is the one most frequented by Stirum and Holstein. The latter swims happily in the sea of work which he now has; passed the whole summer in Berlin and rejoices in the agreeable relations now prevailing in the Foreign Ministry. [...]

Farewell and a cordial Happy New Year
From your faithful
Bill B.

27. Herbert von Bismarck to Holstein

Friedrichsruh, 21 December 1880

Dear Holstein,

Together with my warmest congratulations, I am sending you by order of my father, who joins me in them, the enclosed patent as *Geheimer Legationsrat* with which he hopes to have fulfilled the wishes in your letter to Santa Claus.

Faithfully as ever
Your
H. Bismarck

---

[1] Kuno, Count zu Rantzau. *Vortragender Rat* in the Foreign Ministry, 1880–8; Prussian Minister in Munich, 1888–91. Married to Marie, the only daughter of Otto von Bismarck.

[2] From the Eisendecher Papers.

[3] No. 76 Wilhelmstrasse. The Foreign Ministry.

[4] Friedrich Wilhelm, Count zu Limburg-Stirum. Prussian Minister in Weimar, 1875–80; interim Head of the Foreign Ministry, 1880–1; in 1881 he was given indefinite leave of absence; Member of the Prussian Chamber of Deputies, 1871–1905 (from 1893 leader of the German Conservative Party); Member of the Reichstag, 1893–1906.

[5] Marie von Wallenberg, *née* von Rochow. Wife of the President of the Court Exchequer.

1881

28. Paul von Hatzfeldt to Holstein

Sommerberg, 15 September 1881

Dear Holstein,

[...] I leave it entirely to you to pass on to Varzin whatever of all this you consider necessary.[1] When he passed through Berlin the Prince did not let fall a single question about it,[2] and I was almost led to think that he had lost interest in it, all the more since he was altogether less friendly, indeed much cooler. If this supposition is right—and you of course will know this better—I need hardly say that I will very gladly return to Constantinople. Were I to remain in Berlin, it would be a great sacrifice in every way, and I would be making it principally for him. And if I cannot count on complete trust and complete good-will, the position would be quite insufferable and I would also be of little use.

We will talk about it again in Berlin and I shall then ask you to give me your frank opinion. By that time you should have been able to find out definitely what the Prince's plans and wishes are. My decision will depend—I can tell you this already—on whether or not the position is made tolerable for me both officially and personally. I must have the conviction that I can accomplish something and not be harassed and hunted like a young attaché.

Should I be confronted with the question after my return, as I imagine I will be, I would present my views to the Prince in some form—verbal or written—and would then have to await his decision on it, unless you know of some better way to an understanding. [...]

And now, dear friend, goodbye for to-day. Give my best regards to Busch and our other colleagues. I hear that the former is badly run down, which is very understandable in view of the absurd apportionment of work. I would also have to have a free hand in this if I am to take over the business. At present it is organised in such a way that in a short time the cleverest and strongest man is bound to become mentally dulled and physically ruined, and I personally want to stay fit for a few years yet.

Your truly devoted
P. Hatzfeldt.

[1] Hatzfeldt refers to his family and financial troubles which he had discussed in the first part of this letter.

[2] The post of State Secretary in the Foreign Ministry. Bismarck wanted to keep Hatzfeldt as permanent State Secretary—a post that had only been filled *ad interim* since Bülow's death in 1879.

29. Herbert von Bismarck to Holstein

Varzin, 20 September 1881

Dear Holstein,

Best thanks for your kind letter received yesterday. Unfortunately I can only give you a very gloomy answer, for since yesterday I have been in a state of the greatest anxiety about my father. [...]

It is too sad and embittering, it has *never* been so bad, and the old Kaiser should at least realise what he has done again![1] My father did not want to have Cohen,[2] because it was too far, but to have Zwingenberg instead, and now, according to Rantzau's telegram, he is coming tomorrow; if only his diagnosis is more hopeful than that of the local doctor—I am now completely shattered and feel incapable of any kind of writing; for the last 24 hours I have felt as if a living nerve had been cut, and, utterly worn out and run down as I am after all the labour and anxiety of the past year, I have only the one wish that at least I will be able to stay on my feet as long as my father will be dependent on my care here; I can no longer imagine the feeling of being without cares, and no amount of work helps one to get over them.

Now farewell. I know that your entire sympathy is with me. [...]

Ever faithfully
Your
HB. [...]

30. Herbert von Bismarck to Holstein

Varzin, 29 September 1881

Dear Holstein,

[...] I had hoped that my mother would be able to wait quietly for us in Berlin, because her way of preparing for a journey makes every one of them a hardship for her, and, since my father is resolutely determined not to remain here without a doctor, it can now only be a matter of days.

Since my mother, however, has herself written to my father that she still wanted so much to come here, he naturally agreed most readily; it is not obvious to him that for my mother this is an unnecessary strain. She has accustomed him throughout her whole life to look upon her health as indestructable and has energetically refused to discuss the matter; it is very difficult to bring my parents to an objective judgment on this point. [...]

Since we are now fortunately having perfect autumn weather here, and my father is also once again able to walk for two or three hours, I hope that the short visit will be rather stimulating and enjoyable for my mother than anything else. A time such as I have just gone through here will not only be frightfully depressing but positively dangerous for her—I was busy the whole day, or drove with my father for hours in a

---

[1] On 15 September Kaiser Wilhelm had sent a note to Bismarck complaining that he had not been informed of plans for resuming diplomatic relations with the Vatican and insisting that he be fully informed before anything further was done. (Bismarck, *Die gesammelten Werke*, (Berlin, 1923–35), vol. VIc, p. 224.)

[2] Dr Eduard Cohen. Bismarck's family doctor at Friedrichsruh, 1880–4.

jolting carriage; but apart from all that, it is gloomy here if one depends on company, as my mother does. This need has ceased for me, I have become accustomed through years of working with my father to be alone, and have thereby become narrow-minded and unfitted for social life; I have no illusions about this. I know that the human character is moulded precisely in those years of which I am now devoting the eighth to solitary secretarial work, and that it is cast for good into an unchangeable form. All that is immaterial after all, at least I have thereby made the lives of many others easier! I now simply let myself be 'shoved', and don't think that I am any longer 'shoving'. 'Let things take their course', as the Bavarians say. What will happen next we must see in Berlin; it is to be hoped that my father will not stay there long, for it must be glorious now in the Sachsenwald, and I hope so much that the air there will do him good. [...]

Faithfully as ever,
Your
H. Bismarck.

31. Herbert von Bismarck to Holstein

Varzin, 8 October 1881

Dear Holstein,

Many thanks for your two letters which I have received; I will now show the one from Hohenlohe[1] to my father; that H. will then be invited seems certain. [...]

My father is—thank goodness—much better and takes his pleasure here in the park and forest, where he amuses himself during his daily walks by cutting out branches with the pruning-saw: my mother, I am happy to say, is also definitely better than in the spring. As Zwingenberg, who leaves us tomorrow, guarantees there is no longer any danger of a return of the recent attack, it would certainly be the most sensible thing for my father to remain here as long as the autumn weather stays fine. The journey through Berlin will certainly take it out of him, and I hope that he will improve daily under the present regime.

Now good-bye.
Ever faithfully
Your
HB.

Enclosed is Hohenlohe's letter which my father has just read. He asks you to reply that he has wished for a talk as much as Hohenlohe and would be glad to see him. At the end of October, however, my father is not likely to be still in Varzin, he would then ask H. to visit him in Friedrichsruh, or possibly meet him in Berlin. In short: wherever it may be, Hohenlohe will be welcome.[2]

---

[1] In a letter of 2 October Hohenlohe had asked Holstein to find out whether his visiting Varzin towards the end of the month would be convenient.

[2] For Holstein's letter to Hohenlohe of 9 October, passing on this information, see Rogge, *Holstein und Hohenlohe*, p. 164.

32. Chlodwig zu Hohenlohe to Holstein

Alt Aussee, 12 October 1881

Dear Baron,

Your letter,[1] which I received yesterday, is yet another proof to me of your friendly solicitude, for which I am sincerely grateful to you. I am entirely of your opinion that a visit to Varzin or Fr[iedrichs]ruhe is better calculated to dispel the rumours of a quarrel than a meeting in Berlin. [...]

The report of a quarrel originated, in my opinion, in Progressive circles. In Bavaria, where the Ultramontanists are hostile to me, I must support the Liberals like Völk,[2] Schauss,[3] etc. The Progressive Party knows this very well. But they are now acting as though I had declared myself in support of the Progressive Party and against the Imperial Chancellor on account of my declaration in the Schillingsfürst constituency in favour of the Liberal Deputy, who is not a Progressive but a moderate Liberal, and they are drawing from this perfidious premise the corresponding conclusions.[4] The pan-German democratic editor of the *Augsburger Allgemeine Zeitung* has led the way in this matter.

With friendly greetings and hopes of an early meeting.

Your most devoted
C. Hohe nlohe.

33. Herbert von Bismarck to Holstein

Varzin, 15 October 1 881
(actually 16 October; it is 12:45 a.m.)

Dear Holstein,

In great haste I thank you for your letter and return Hohenlohe's;[5] to reply to it now is impossible and he must be content with a telegram if he will travel around in such a complicated fashion.[6] You know how it is with us! Nobody knows to-day whether we shall remain here for another four days or four weeks; it seems to me as if we will certainly still be here another eight to ten days—but who can tell?

I had already suspected that Hohenlohe had himself secretly instigated the whole uproar in the Press so as to win over the votes of the Progressives and advanced Liberals in his constituency; it is a sure way of gaining short-lived popularity, (*cf.* Eulenburg!),[7] to quarrel with the Chan-

---

[1] See p. 52, note 2.

[2] Dr Joseph Völk. A leader of the Bavarian Liberals, who supported the tariff system introduced by Bismarck in the Reichstag. A vote of censure passed by his former political friends forced him to leave the National Liberal Party. With Schauss and others he formed his own group, which was defeated in the election of 1881.

[3] Friedrich von Schauss. A Bavarian Deputy.

[4] Hohenlohe is referring to the approaching Reichstag elections, which took place on 27 October and 14 November.

[5] Of 12 October.

[6] In the unpublished portion of his letter, Hohenlohe described his travel itinerary.

[7] Botho, Count zu Eulenburg. Prussian Minister of the Interior in succession to his uncle Friedrich zu Eulenburg, March 1878–February 1881; subsequently Head of the Administration of Hesse-Nassau; Prussian Minister-President (under Caprivi as Chancellor), 1892–4. He resigned from the Ministry of the Interior as a result of a dispute with Bismarck over the jurisdiction of administrative authorities and the courts. (See Bismarck, *Die gesammelten Werke*, vol. VIc, no. 204, pp. 206–7.)

cellor over 'Liberalism'! Don't you yourself believe that the whole affair is an electioneering stunt mounted by Hohenlohe? That is why he does not want to see my father before the end of October so that the meeting will only become known after the 27th, and *then* naturally all the more widely, which is why he seized on your suggestion[1] so eagerly.

Faithfully yours

HB.

34. Herbert von Bismarck to Holstein

Varzin, 19 October 1881

Dear Holstein,

[...] You will vote of course?[2] My father says every Conservative is in duty bound to vote for the anti-Progressive candidate in his constituency. Perhaps Busch could tell the servants at the Chancellery that those who are on duty on election day can have time off to cast their ballot and also to use their influence with their acquaintances to make everyone vote against the Progressives. For all we know it may turn on a very few votes, at least to reach the final ballot.

Now good-bye
Ever faithfully
Your
HB.

35. Bernhard von Bülow[3] to Holstein

Paris, 21 October 1881

My dear Herr von Holstein,

Many thanks for your kind letter of the 19th, which I received yesterday. I still cannot obtain any real evidence for the suspicion that Gambetta[4] is trying to make contact with revolutionary elements abroad, but, being on the spot, I share the conviction that it is there that he will make his first attempt to drive in the wedge. The first thing he must say to himself if he takes over the Government is obviously that France was never so isolated. This isolation he would naturally prefer to bring to an end by holding out his right hand to Gladstone[5]-Dilke,[6] his left to Ignatiev.[7] Between Russia and France, however, Nihilism in the former and the Republic in the latter have driven a great wedge; between England and France lie Tunis and Egypt. It thus seems to me at this moment that little is left except the small consolation of a Latin

---

[1] See *Denkwürdigkeiten des Fürsten Chlodwig zu Hohenlohe-Schillingsfürst* (Stuttgart and Leipzig, 1906), vol. II, pp. 318–20.

[2] See p. 53, note 4.

[3] Second, then First Secretary in the Paris Embassy, 1878–84, in St Petersburg, 1884–8; Minister in Bucharest, 1888–94; Ambassador in Rome (Quirinal), 1894–7; State Secretary in the Foreign Ministry, 1897–1900; Chancellor of the German Reich and Prussian Minister-President, 1900–9.

[4] Léon Gambetta. French Minister-President, 1881–2.

[5] William Ewart Gladstone. British Prime Minister, 1868–74, 1880–5, January–July 1886, 1892–March 1894.

[6] Sir Charles W. Dilke. British Under Secretary of State for Foreign Affairs, 1880–2; President of the Local Government Board, 1882–5. A divorce case in which he was involved in 1885 put an end to his political career.

[7] Nikolai Pavlovich, Count Ignatiev. Russian Minister of the Interior, 1881–2.

Union. But since the monarchies in Rome and Madrid will always have more sympathy for the great Courts than for the neighbouring Republic, *and as this is very well known here*, the natural alliance with the radical parties in those countries will be sought. A proof of the correctness of this assumption is offered by the fears which Italian and Spanish diplomats in particular, in so far as they are Royalists, express about Gambetta. I shall keep an eye on this particular matter, and shall also watch the Press carefully to see, for example, what they will now publish about the Italian visit to Vienna and Berlin.[1]

I have wondered whether it would not be useful, in case Gambetta really takes over the Government, *to buy somebody close to him*. Among the rabble around him a suitable person could certainly be found. Although Gambetta is difficult to approach, he is all the more free and easy in the company of his intimates. Shall I talk this over, for example, with Landsberg? Naturally I would not take any step or let a word fall without your approval. [...]

In the extradition question[2] I have let the Russians take the initiative and confined myself to an entirely academic discussion with Barthélemy-Saint-Hilaire,[3] but am sufficiently in touch with Kapnist[4] to be able to keep an eye on the further development of this matter and especially upon Gambetta's attitude towards it. Our attitude in principle to this question is, of course, absolutely clear, but it seems to me that it would not be in our interest if France, and particularly Gambetta, found an opportunity to render Russia a great service. The present situation in which, according to Redern's[5] report, even Jomini[6] has come to under-

---

[1] The visit of the Italian King and Queen to the Imperial Court in Vienna, 27–31 October. They did not go to Berlin.

[2] After the assassination of Alexander II on 1/13 March 1881, Saburov, the Russian Ambassador in Berlin, raised the question with Bismarck of a joint protest by Germany and Russia to the Swiss Government because of the abuse of the right of asylum in Switzerland. Bismarck thought it politically useful, the Kaiser thought it desirable in principle, to support Russia in this question. Bismarck nevertheless wished to avoid any German initiative out of regard for Germany's relations with England and France. On 31 March Russia invited the Great Powers to a conference for the purpose of discussing measures against political criminals and especially the Russian proposal that in future these criminals should come under the normal extradition regulations for common criminals. England and France both refused to take part in such a conference. The French Government nevertheless declared its readiness to enter into negotiations with Russia concerning an extradition treaty. Bismarck's attitude to the Franco-Russian negotiations is revealed in the following letter from Herbert von Bismarck to Holstein of 25 October 1881. These negotiations, like the negotiations between the three Imperial Powers on the same question, produced no result It was not until January 1885 that an agreement was reached between Russia and Prussia according to which criminal acts against members of the reigning houses should come under the terms of the extradition treaty. (From the Foreign Ministry files.)

[3] Jules Barthélemy-Saint-Hilaire. Minister of Foreign Affairs in Ferry's Cabinet, September 1880–November 1881.

[4] Peter, Count Kapnist. Counsellor in the Russian Embassy in Paris; Minister at The Hague, 1884–92; Director of the Asiatic Department in the Foreign Ministry, 1892–5; Ambassador in Vienna, 1896–1904.

[5] Wilhelm, Count von Redern. First Secretary in the Embassy in St Petersburg, 1881–2. On 30 September Redern reported: 'Baron Jomini now seems to be free from all French sympathies. For example, he recently expressed himself to Count Kálnoky in the sense that no reliance could be placed on France and that a statesman could no longer take her into account in his political calculations.' (From the Foreign Ministry files.)

[6] Alexander, Baron Jomini. A member of the Russian Foreign Ministry.

stand that no reliance can be placed on France should be more to our advantage. [...]

Devotedly and affectionately
Yours very truly
Bernh. Bülow

36. Herbert von Bismarck to Holstein

Varzin, 25 October 1881

Dear Holstein,

With many thanks for your last letter I return herewith Bülow's,[1] which interested me greatly. I gave it to my father, who has read it through from beginning to end.

To the passage on page 7 (Russian extradition) my father observed that this was finessing. You might write that it would be in our interest to support[2] the Russians in *all* demands about extradition. It would be much worse than the eventuality suggested by Bülow should the Russians become distrustful of us, particularly on this point, and should they come to a *direct* agreement *with France* about anything, no matter how unimportant. In autocratic Russia all depends *entirely* on the Tsar; if it were suggested to him that we were lukewarm about this matter in Paris, he would gain the impression that we were indifferent to the safety of his skin, and like every mortal he would be deeply offended. Bülow should therefore take an opportunity of *saying* to his Russian colleague that he had instructions to join in everything the Russians may wish and suggest in this question, and to give it full support. The Russians must receive the impression that in this matter we are like Siamese twins with them, and that we will join in every move that they suggest since they are here the 'dominant twin'. It is important that *if* anything is achieved the *Russians* should have the impression that we have been absolutely reliable friends and seconds, and to see that Gambetta does not find 'an opportunity to render Russia a great service *without us or by our being passed over*'.

The underlined words are not in the relevant sentence of Bülow's letter, but they are in fact the main issue.

I leave it to your discretion to say something in this sense also to Prince Hohenlohe who, I think, will pass through Berlin in a couple of days. [...]

Adieu for to-day
Faithfully
Your
HB.

37. Chlodwig zu Hohenlohe to Holstein

Paris, 7 November 1881

My dear Baron,

[...] With reference to our discussion in Berlin. I recommend that you keep Bernhard Bülow in mind. I am becoming more and more

[1] Of 21 October.
[2] The word 'support' is underlined by Holstein with the remark: 'not to take the lead, then.'

convinced that politically I have in him a great support and that as First Secretary here he would give good service. It would be a pity if I lost him. And yet when his turn comes one cannot expect him to remain here as Second. Perhaps some arrangement can be made which will keep him here.

With friendly greetings
Your most devoted
CHohenlohe

38. Berhard von Bülow to Holstein

Paris, 7 November 1881

My dear Herr von Holstein,

I have received your friendly lines of the 28th of last month through the Ambassador, and ask to be allowed to express once again my best thanks for the kindly support which you have accorded to me during my interim. I will do my utmost to continue to earn your trust in the future. To-day's courier brings a number of—it seems to me—interesting reports from the Ambassador on the present situation. Gambetta's Ministry will certainly be formed before the end of the month. I am still of the opinion that, taken all in all, the moment at which Gambetta must make his entry upon the stage is not unfavourable. I mean this in the sense that I regard it as advantageous that the most important man they have available here should in due course wear himself out on domestic issues that will finally bring about the downfall of his Ministry. I too think this process will be slow, but I do not regard that as a misfortune. [...]

With esteem and devotion I am your
Bernh. Bülow

39. Klemens Busch to Holstein[1]

Rome, 9 December 1881

Dear H.

Even though our temperaments are so different that you often call me politically indolent, or are polite enough only to think so, nevertheless seldom has anything given me such pleasure as this mission.[2] As I spent my apprenticeship in negotiations with southern peoples, the exercise of this old skill gives me especial pleasure. And in manner of negotiation there is little difference between Byzantine Turks and prelates. You will see from my dispatches of today how the talks have gone up to the present.[3] In a practical sense not much has resulted from them

---

[1] From the Foreign Ministry files. This copy of the letter was made by Holstein for the official archives. The original has not been found.

[2] To negotiate with the Holy See about relaxing the anti-clerical legislation in Prussia (the *Kulturkampf*). (See *Memoirs*, pp. 63–4; *Diaries*, entry for 10 February 1882.)

[3] In a dispatch reporting his first detailed conversation with Cardinal Jacobini, the Papal Secretary of State, Busch wrote that he had informed Jacobini of the intention of the Prussian Government to ask the Landtag, which was to convene in January, for funds to establish a Legation at the Holy See. The Prussian Government also intended to demand an extension

up to now except some clarification of the points at issue. Perhaps that also has its value. [...]

Busch

40. Bernhard von Bülow to Holstein

Paris, 29 December 1881

My dear Herr von Holstein,

Permit me to take the opportunity of today's courier to add to my short letter of the 25th,[1] and especially to express to you once more my most humble thanks for your last friendly lines. I am greatly obliged to you, and for nothing so much as for all the hints you have given me concerning my work here. But my influence in the last one and a half years has been smaller than you suppose! The Ambassador is very kind to me and recently has again often allowed me to write political dispatches; but it is still above all with Thielmann[2] that he discusses affairs. It also lies in the nature of things that if the First Secretary has had a—usually lengthy—discussion, there is not much left for the Second. When Th. himself is in charge of affairs, I only very occasionally see the dispatches before they are sent off, learn little, and have still less opportunity for giving my own opinion. I should like, however, above all to repeat that I will certainly do what lies in my power to gain your approval, and will regard every observation that you accord me as a special proof of your kindness to me. [...]

It is, however, high time that I should close! Forgive my verbosity. In esteem and attachment I am your truly devoted

Bernh. Bülow

of its discretionary powers in ecclesiastical legislation. Jacobini replied that the Pope expected a modification of the May Laws (the Prussian anti-clerical legislation of May 1873). Busch emphasised that it was this *petitio principii* which was responsible for the fruitlessness of all previous discussions, and that to persist in this standpoint would condemn the negotiations to failure from the outset. Jacobini hinted at the hope 'that the permanent intercourse between the Royal Government and the Curia which would result from the accrediting of a Minister would lead to further negotiations and to an understanding'. Busch replied that this depended chiefly on the attitude of the Centre Party. (From the Foreign Ministry files.)

[1] Not found.

[2] Max von Thielmann. First Secretary in the Embassy in Paris, 1880–2, in Constantinople, 1882–6; Consul-General in Sofia, 1886–7; Prussian Minister in Darmstadt, 1887–90, in Hamburg, 1890–4; Ambassador in Washington, 1895–7; State Secretary of the Reich Treasury, 1897–1903.

1882

41. Klemens Busch to Anton von Saurma[1]

(Draft by Holstein)[2]

Berlin, 10 February 1882

The Chancellor thanks Your Excellency for dispatch No. 9[3] regarding the general situation in Egypt, which he has noted with interest, although he does not share your opinion on the urgency of intervention, least of all as regards the question of our own participation.[4]

The Chancellor finds it natural that Your Excellency should be concerned for the restoration of order in the country in which you live. We too wish the lot of humanity in Egypt and everywhere else to be improved, and that country to have a good government; but these considerations, based on an international point of view, should not make us forget that the furthering of this end is *not* one of the higher political tasks of Germany.

We will duly seek to prevent any complications which may arise in Egypt; but we would only be justified in intervening, to the prejudice of *our* peace and *our* own interests, if the sacrifices demanded by such an undertaking were not notably greater than the risks and losses which Germany would have at worst to expect. This condition will not have been fulfilled as long as it is only a question of the possible helplessness of the Egyptian government, and a few disturbances in the country.

The consciousness of being a major Great Power must not seduce us into pursuing a policy based on prestige in the French fashion. In reality our international and overall European interests are not sufficiently great to allow us to take the lead in Egyptian affairs.

For the moment we can only hold ourselves in readiness to support

---

[1] Anton von Saurma. Consul-General in Alexandria, 1876–November 1882; Minister in Bucharest, 1882–5, at The Hague, 1885–91; Prussian Minister in Stuttgart, 1891–3; Ambassador in Washington, 1893–5; in Constantinople, 1895–7; in Rome, 1897–9.

[2] From the Foreign Ministry files.

[3] In this dispatch of 27 January Saurma had reported that the Egyptian Government was no longer able to maintain order in the country, and that in his opinion European intervention would sooner or later be unavoidable. (From the Foreign Ministry files.)

[4] Egypt was nominally a part of the Turkish Empire, but since the beginning of the nineteenth century the rulers of Egypt had acted almost as independent sovereigns. The Khedives of Egypt had borrowed heavily from European investors and had plunged their country deeply into debt. In 1876 the British and French Governments, whose citizens had invested most heavily in Egypt, established a virtual condominium over Egypt, and reorganised the government in the interest of the foreign bondholders. The resulting situation aroused a powerful nationalist and anti-foreign movement in Egypt. A group of army officers led by Ahmed Arabi tried to overthrow foreign influence in the Egyptian Government, and on 5 February 1882 forced the Khedive to appoint a nationalist Ministry with Arabi as Minister for War.

whichever policy of the more interested Great Powers offers the greatest guarantee for European peace. Even the active intervention of the European Powers in the internal troubles of Egypt would not mean that we should take a leading part in the action. In case of possible individual action on the part of a single power, we should always cast our vote in accordance with rights established by European treaties. The question, however, as to whether this vote is to be implemented by participation in a military action depends for us on quite different considerations than what is *useful or desirable* for Egypt, the Near East, *or for other Great Powers*. If unilateral intervention on the part of the Western Powers were opposed by other Powers on the basis of European treaties, we would never evade our obligations to support a legitimate opposition *by diplomatic means*. But even if the *most extreme* decisions of the Gambetta Cabinet had been put into force in Egypt, the Chancellor would *even then* not have been concerned that there was any direct danger to German interests. Similarly, the threat to peace between England and France, or between these two and other Powers, would not, at least in the first instance, concern us.

Your Excellency will therefore be acting in accordance with the views of the Reich Chancellor, if you maintain the greatest reserve in your conduct, invariably remain in the background, and simply restrict yourself to accepting *ad referendum* all moves and proposals aimed at German participation in Egyptian questions.

B[usch]

42. Herbert von Bismarck to Holstein

London,[1] 26 April 1882

Dear Holstein,

Best thanks for your two letters which I received yesterday and today. Pursuant to yesterday's,[2] I had asked Count Münster[3] to ask Lord Granville[4] directly if he were negotiating with France. You will have seen the result before this letter. Münster says he had a frightful time drilling it out of him, and that finally Granville was only induced to speak when he said to him: 'Since you are always asking the Chancellor's advice, you must also place me in a position where I can keep him fully informed, and not maintain this affectation of mysteriousness.' Granville thereupon admitted that since the evening of Saturday, the 24th, when he and Tissot[5] were with the Queen at Windsor (audience to present letters of credence), he had been engaged in confidential dis-

[1] Herbert von Bismarck was assigned to the Embassy in London for temporary duty from November 1881 to June 1882.

[2] Marginal note by Holstein: 'in which I wrote that Bleichröder claimed to know of Anglo-French *pourparlers*.'

[3] Georg Herbert, Count zu Münster, Baron von Grothaus, from 1899 Prince Münster von Derneburg. Hanoverian Minister in St Petersburg, 1856–64; German Ambassador in London, 1873–85, in Paris, 1885–1900.

[4] George Leveson-Gower, second Earl of Granville. British Foreign Secretary, 1880–5; Secretary of State for Colonies, 1886.

[5] Charles Joseph Tissot. French Ambassador in Constantinople, 1880–2, in London, 1882–3.

cussions with France over a suitable démarche in Egypt. When I saw Granville last Friday things had not gone so far. Münster gained the impression that the proposal to send generals without troops to Egypt was Tissot's and was being pushed by him.[1] He considers Tissot *assez malin* to involve the English deliberately. For if the generals are actually sent, and, as can be foreseen, are insulted by the fanatical Egyptian Arabs, then 'the honour of the Western Powers' will be involved and the incentive furnished for armed intervention.

It is not improbable that the Sultan will refuse to send a Turkish general without troops, and that English and French colleagues for this general would also be extremely distasteful to him.

A concerted intervention by England and France is highly unpopular here and could easily bring about the downfall of the present Ministry. Granville is therefore swaying to and fro between fear of France and of a Cabinet crisis.

Dilke must for that reason be a cursedly uncomfortable Under-Secretary of State for him, because he is a most enthusiastic protagonist of the French alliance and possesses far more determination than his Chief.

I already suspect that there is some agreement, perhaps only in quite general terms, between England and France—either dating from the Salisbury[2]-Waddington[3] days, or only from the Radical era. The subservient role of England in this relationship is otherwise too incomprehensible. Granville's (he *now* positively distrusts the French and would prefer to work with us) oft-repeated phrase: 'We are only following the policy that our Cabinet found ready-made', and the memory of the obligations undertaken by Salisbury in the Tunis question,[4] which only became known more than two years after the Congress, have given me cause for thought. Against my first suspicion certainly is the fact that Beaconsfield[5] would never have entered into arrangements with France regarding Egypt—so Münster believes—and that Salisbury would not have been able to do so without his previous knowledge. Moreover Münster thinks that the present Cabinet would certainly make public

[1] Granville informed Münster that Freycinet would not view a concerted intervention by England and France unfavourably. The English Government wanted to avoid this. 'Lord Granville has therefore proposed the adoption of a middle course: that a proposal be made to the Porte to send a Turkish general to Egypt. If Paris desired, a French and an English general could be sent along to support him. It is hoped that the Turkish general would be successful in restoring discipline in the Egyptian Army and maintaining order. Monsieur Tissot had not expressed himself unfavourably on the subject of this proposal.' (Münster telegram of 25 April 1882. From the Foreign Ministry files.)

[2] Robert Gascoyne-Cecil, third Marquis of Salisbury. British Foreign Secretary, 1878–1880; second delegate at the Congress of Berlin; Prime Minister, 1885–6, 1886–92, 1895–1902; Foreign Secretary, 1885–6, 1887–92, 1895–1900.

[3] William Henry Waddington. French Foreign Minister, 1877–9; plenipotentiary at the Congress of Berlin; Minister-President and Foreign Minister, February–December, 1879; Ambassador in London, July 1883–93.

[4] This refers to the assurances given to the French at the Congress of Berlin that they might occupy Tunis when they saw fit. The French protectorate over Tunis was established in 1881. (See *Documents Diplomatiques Français (1871–1914)* (Paris), Première Série, vol. II, nos. 328 *et seq.*)

[5] Benjamin Disraeli, from 1876 Earl of Beaconsfield. British Prime Minister, 1868, January 1874–April 1880; first British plenipotentiary at the Congress of Berlin.

any secret agreement of Salisbury's, if it existed, in order to damage the latter in the opinion of the public. This does not seem to me so self-evident, since in the first place such a proceeding would be unheard-of and would forever destroy for England any possibility of concluding a secret agreement with any Power; and further the fear of embittering France (which could happen through such a publication) is still greater than the desire to damage Salisbury.

With the present Cabinet anything is possible and conceivable. Even if one rejects the suspicion of Salisbury as too improbable one can still believe Gladstone's ministry capable of anything.

All this is in a sense just thinking aloud. Since, however, you do it yourself from time to time, perhaps the reading of these hypothetical cases will while away an idle quarter of an hour.

Ever faithfully,
Your HB.

43. Herbert von Bismarck to Holstein

London, 3 May 1882

Dear Holstein,

I read your friendly letter of the 28th of last month with great interest and thank you most heartily for it.

I entirely share your opinion on the Italian affair.[1] Italy will never attack us directly if only because we have no common frontiers. For Austria, however, Italy is what France is for us—even though less dangerous because weaker.

Here, weakness is more and more the order of the day. Nothing has happened in the Egyptian affair since our last dispatches. The next thing we will hear will probably be some poltroonery on the part of the English Government!

In Ireland things will now get hotter than ever.[2] I recently wrote to you that the thoroughly insignificant Cowper[3] would have to serve as scapegoat, and at the same time asked you for a list of titles of the books desired by Forster.[4] And now he too has been driven out of the temple! Yesterday morning Forster had no thought of handing in his resignation; his request to me on Friday also shows that he thought he had still a long time to reign! Forster would take no part in the complete about-face which Gladstone decided on yesterday; it took him

[1] The negotiations which resulted in the Triple Alliance of 20 May 1882. In negotiating with Austria, Germany constantly emphasised that the chief object of the treaty was to secure Italian neutrality. (See *Die Grosse Politik der Europäischen Kabinette 1871–1914* (Berlin, 1922–7), vol. III, chap. XV.)

[2] On 2 May 1882 the Irish Nationalists under Parnell's leadership concluded the so-called Kilmainham Treaty with the Gladstone Government. By this treaty Parnell and other Irish leaders were liberated from Kilmainham Jail in return for their promise to collaborate with the British Government in the pacification of Ireland.

[3] Francis Thomas De Grey, seventh Earl Cowper. Lord-Lieutenant of Ireland, 1880–April 1882.

[4] William Edward Forster. Chief Secretary for Ireland. He resigned in protest against the Kilmainham Treaty, and never held office again. Forster had asked Herbert von Bismarck for books about peasant reform in Germany, i.e. the Stein-Hardenberg legislation and the redemption of annuity bonds in 1850.

completely unprepared. At the Cabinet meeting it nearly came to blows, so stormy was the debate.

Gladstone, Bright[1] and Chamberlain[2]—this triumvirate of revolutionaries—will now bring things to a greater state of anarchy, and it appears that the last-named will be Forster's successor. The Conservatives declare that with Forster the only decent and honourable man has left the Cabinet; they regard the Liberal lords in the Cabinet with justified contempt, for they allow themselves to be managed like puppets by the Birmingham calico-printer.[2] The consolidation of Chamberlain's rule and the virtually unopposed progress of radical republicanism is ominous for the old England. *Mutatis mutandis*—one could now almost make use of the lines from Heine's ballad about the Battle of Hastings: 'The lousiest lout from Normandy will be lord in the isle of the Britons. I saw a tailor from Bayeux who came riding with golden spurs.' Only now Bayeux=Birmingham.

The Duke of Bedford[3] with whom I dined here yesterday was very despondent. He said: '*This will be the beginning of much trouble*'—as if *trouble* were only to begin now! To-day's *Times* rightly says: '*In the House of Commons Parnell[4] is now the master of the situation.*' The object of the whole performance is to gain the votes of the *home ruler* [sic] in order to impose the *closure*, with the help of which Chamberlain will then be able to get some radicalising *bills* quickly through Parliament. Before his liberation Parnell is said to have been offered this *bargain* by Gladstone. If the former does not now abide by the pact, Gladstone is properly done. [...]

Ever faithfully
Your HB.

44. Herbert von Bismarck to Holstein

London, 20 May 1882

Dear Holstein,

Superflua non nocent. I have of course told Münster, with whom I dined yesterday at Granville's, everything that the latter and Dilke told me there, and he is now writing a report about it. But since I will only see his dispatch at the last moment, I do not know whether he will have said everything. Yesterday Granville was as pleased as if he had celebrated Christmas; he told me that he had been very anxious the day before yesterday and again yesterday morning because the Sultan had flown into a great rage over the despatch of the fleet.[5] But yesterday

---

[1] John Bright. Chancellor of the Duchy of Lancaster in Gladstone's Cabinet, 1873–4, 1880–2. He resigned because of British intervention in Egyptian affairs.

[2] Joseph Chamberlain. Mayor of Birmingham, 1873–6; President of the Board of Trade in Gladstone's second Cabinet, 1880–5; President of the Local Government Board in Gladstone's third Cabinet, February–March, 1886. He resigned from office on account of the introduction of the Home Rule Bill. Secretary of State for the Colonies in Salisbury's third Cabinet, and in Balfour's Cabinet, 1895–1903.

[3] Francis Russell, from 1872 ninth Duke of Bedford.

[4] Charles Stewart Parnell. Leader of the Irish Nationalist Party in the British House of Commons.

[5] On 20 May English and French squadrons appeared off Alexandria as a demonstration to support the Khedive against the Egyptian nationalists.

there was suddenly a complete about-face and a 'mild attitude' revealed itself in Constantinople, and this was specially due to the intervention of Prince Bismarck who had thereby rendered the English Government a great service. Mr Gladstone was also very grateful for it and had said: '*It is true that I do not always agree with Prince Bismarck, but that I must say: if he takes anything in hand, he does it wonderfully.*'[1]

I contented myself with smiling politely, because I knew nothing of any action on our part in Constantinople. According to a telegram from Hirschfeld[2] just received here nothing of the kind had taken place.[3] I believe the calming of the Sultan is probably the result of the communication made to him by Dufferin,[4] that in case of need France would permit Turkish intervention.

Dilke told me that according to Malet's[5] telegrams the Egyptian crisis would end with the removal of Arabi from the Ministry, and the other Ministers would remain in office. Dilke shared Malet's opinion.

I also forgot to write yesterday that Lobanov[6] not only in private conversations but also in remarks at the *Club* in the presence of Austrians and Frenchmen made fun of the *expédition navale*;[7] he called it '*un épouvantail*' because the ships had no troops on board. It was very well known in Egypt that consequently there could be no question of a landing[8] '*et ils se moquent de la démonstration: ils ne demandent pas mieux qu'Alexandrie soit bombardée, puisque c'est plutôt une ville Européenne qu'Orientale*'.[9]

---

[1] In English in the original.

[2] First Secretary of Embassy in Constantinople, 1881–2.

[3] Hirschfeld had reported by telegram on 19 May that the Sultan had informed the British and French Ambassadors of his desire for the withdrawal of the squadrons from Alexandria, but at the same time had expressed his willingness to enter into negotiations over Egypt. Germany had in fact taken no steps in Constantinople. (From the Foreign Ministry files.)

[4] Frederick Blackwood, from 1871 Earl, from 1888 Marquis of Dufferin and Ava. British Ambassador in St Petersburg, 1879–81, in Constantinople 1881–3; in the winter of 1882–3 he was sent to Egypt in order to lay the foundations of the new British administrative system; Governor-General of India, 1884–8; Ambassador in Rome, 1889–91, in Paris, 1891–6.

[5] Sir Edward Malet. British Agent and Consul-General in Egypt, 1879–83; Ambassador in Berlin, 1884–95.

[6] Prince Alexei Lobanov–Rostovski. Russian Ambassador in Constantinople, 1878–9, in London, 1879–82, in Vienna, 1882–94, in Berlin, January–March, 1895; Foreign Minister, 1895–6.

[7] Marginal comment by Bismarck: 'He would prefer Gambetta to F[reycinet]'.

[8] Bismarck: 'Dulcigno'. The reference is to the failure of a naval demonstration by the Powers to persuade the Sultan of Turkey to give up Dulcigno after the Congress of Berlin.

[9] Herbert von Bismarck wrote to Holstein on 19 May that he and Prince Lobanov had just been to lunch with the French Ambassador. 'Lobanov demanded to know what France thought of doing if a revolution broke out in Egypt or the lives and property of Europeans were threatened. Tissot replied: "The object of our policy is *de maintenir le status quo*." Lobanov answered: "You must nevertheless have kept in mind the possibility that you may not be successful and must have made decisions to meet that eventuality." Tissot denied this last point and remarked that such decisions were now superfluous because there were well-founded hopes that things would remain quiet in Egypt. Thereupon Lobanov declared that one never got anywhere merely by hoping. The Western Powers had now taken the lead and the others were indeed quite ready to follow them, only they demanded to know in what direction they were going to be led.'

I have just seen Münster's dispatch and will not now write the same thing over again.[1]

Rosebery[2] with whom I spoke yesterday evening, and who always talks to me pretty openly, said he did not understand his colleagues— the members of the Government—because they still regarded the future of England so hopefully. He thinks the situation is very serious, the Irish affair was badly handled, and the Radicals would bungle it still more; he called *the state of things 'very gloomy'*.[3] Let them stew in their own juice! The Conservatives' plan is to allow severe coercive measures against Ireland—which could not be passed by a Tory Government—to be put into force by Gladstone with their support, and afterwards to do everything in their power to overthrow Gladstone in order to govern in their turn with the coercive measures passed by the Liberals. Chaplin[4] has hatched this plan. You certainly know him; he is the son-in-law of the Duke of Sutherland. Naturally he does not speak of it openly.

Adieu for to-day.

Faithfully your HB. [...]

45. Herbert von Bismarck to Holstein

London, 31 May 1882

Dear Holstein,

[...] At the banquet yesterday I sat next to the Prince of Wales who took the opportunity afforded by our being together for so long to abuse the *'Gouvernement'*—as he called it—to his heart's content, especially its Egyptian policy. It was a scandal that things had come to such a pass that England played the second and France the first fiddle; this was the result of so much indecision, and now when matters had reached boiling-point, day after day was allowed to go by without anything being done. The sole possibility naturally was to requisition Turkish troops. Freycinet[5] led old Granville by the nose in an outrageous manner, and the most serious thing was that Freycinet, as H.R.H. well knew, was filled with a great hatred of England and allowed himself to be guided by this feeling. 'It is a pity that Gambetta is no longer at the helm, for he had rather a preference for England. Why did your father overthrow him—at least it is said everywhere that he did.' On this I permitted myself to explain to H.R.H. that this supposition was unfounded.

[1] Münster in a dispatch on 20 May said Granville had promised the Sultan to withdraw the fleet 'as soon as the position of the Khedive and above all the *status quo* in Egypt appeared assured'. (From the Foreign Ministry files.)

[2] Archibald Primrose, fifth Earl of Rosebery. Under Secretary of State at the Home Office, 1881–3; Lord Privy Seal, March–June, 1885; Foreign Secretary, February–August, 1886, August 1892–March 1894; Prime Minister, March 1894–June 1895.

[3] In English in the original,

[4] Henry Chaplin, later Viscount Chaplin. Conservative Member of Parliament. President of the Local Government Board in Salisbury's Cabinet, 1895–1900.

[5] Charles de Freycinet. French Prime Minister and Foreign Minister, December, 1879– September 1880, January–July 1882; Foreign Minister in Brisson's Cabinet, 1885–6; Prime Minister and Foreign Minister, January–December, 1886; Prime Minister and Minister for War, March 1890–February, 1892.

Münster has just come from Granville and you will get a telegram.[1]
It appears that Gr. is indeed permitting himself to be led 'by the nose'!

This letter must go, more soon. [...]

Always your HB.

46. Herbert von Bismarck to Holstein

London, 2 June 1882

Dear Holstein,

[...] You will see once more from Münster's report to-day summing up the situation how scatter-brained and flabby the politicians here are. The English and the French are both putting it out that they intend to use the conference as a means for loosening their relationship—if not entirely to dissolve it; they are now filled with mutual mistrust, but neither has the courage to take the next natural step—they want to leave this to the 'Concert of Europe'. [...]

I will express no opinion as to whether Granville expects very much to result from the conference. At the beginning of January, when I brought him my father's reply to his request for advice, I had already told him that my father thought that the Egyptian question could easily be made into a European one if England wanted this done; but that if he were an English Minister he would try to avoid it.[2] Granville then excitedly replied *'I think the Prince is quite right'*, and he was still protesting against the idea of a conference at the end of February when we received here (26.2.82) the instruction to signify our willingness to participate in case a conference were held.[3] Since he has not reached an independent decision during the last three months, he found himself obliged by the wishes of his colleagues to accept the proposal made by Freycinet. [...]

Ever faithfully
your HB.

47. Herbert von Bismarck to Holstein

London, 12 June 1882

Dear Holstein,

[...] This afternoon the Foreign Office was in a state of silly jubilation after Granville had wet his pants in the morning. Admiral Seymour[4] had sent a soothing telegram about the riots in Alexandria[5] and Ignatiev's resignation[6] has made the people here—curiously enough—

---

[1] Münster telegraphed to the Foreign Ministry on 3 May 1882: 'French Cabinet has proposed conference of ambassadors with inclusion of a representative of the Sultan for the settlement of the Egyptian affair. English Cabinet now in session has accepted the proposal.' (From the Foreign Ministry files.)

[2] See *Grosse Politik*, vol. IV, no. 724, pp. 26–30.

[3] See *Diaries*, entry for 11 March 1882.

[4] Sir Beauchamp Seymour. Commander of the British Fleet off Alexandria.

[5] On 12 June disturbances broke out in Alexandria in which some fifty Europeans were killed.

[6] On 12 June 1882.

drunk with joy. Bandy old Tenterden[1] almost danced round the room with pleasure. Ignatiev is nevertheless the embodiment of that Pan-Slavism which Gladstone so strongly champions, but Granville is always fearful that Ignatiev could somewhere or other promote complications that might lead to war, or else ally himself with the French, with whom he (Granville) is very much annoyed. It would be more in the spirit of Gladstone's policy if his colleagues were rather disturbed! I agree with your wish that the interim situation in the Foreign Ministry should finally turn into a *definitivum*; what you write about Hatzfeldt sounds very reassuring, only it seems to me that it will not be possible to arrange the rise of salary; my father *can* not accept such a thing, no matter from what quarter it might be suggested, *atque hic haeret!*[2] [...]

Farewell now and to our next meeting,

Ever faithfully
Your HB.

48. Ferdinand von Stumm[3] to Holstein

London, 4 July [1882]

Dear Herr von Holstein,

I hope you will allow me to resume our former relationship and as a trustworthy person is travelling to Cologne I am entrusting the dispatches to him. What a pity that Bismarck could not stay longer. I have never known that anyone could make himself so well known and so popular in so short a time, and in London it has never happened before. Men and women, old and young, united in singing his praises. It did my patriotic heart good to hear it. What is more, Bismarck worked quite unbelievably hard and could not have continued to keep

[1] Charles Abbott, third Baron Tenterden. Permanent Under Secretary of State at the Foreign Office, 1873–82.

[2] Since 3 July 1881 Hatzfeldt had been acting State Secretary in the Foreign Ministry. Owing to family and financial difficulties, Hatzfeldt hesitated to accept the position of State Secretary on a permanent basis. As State Secretary his income would be considerably less than it was as Ambassador in Constantinople. The situation was rendered still more difficult by Hatzfeldt's habit of taking frequent and lengthy leaves of absence on account of his health, and also by his demand to be appointed Prussian Minister of State—a position that had been held by the last permanent State Secretary, Bernhard Ernst von Bülow. Throughout the summer of 1882 Holstein played the part of intermediary between his friend Hatzfeldt, the Chancellor (through Herbert von Bismarck), and the Kaiser (through Otto von Bülow). On 16 August 1882 Herbert von Bismarck wrote: 'I have frequently and exhaustively discussed the matter with my father in the sense *que considérant* all the good and bad qualities of the possible candidates, H[atzfeldt] still remained by far the best. My chie. hesitations regarding H. are only the question of leave and his probable inability to make ends meet financially. If—and I would greatly regret it—nothing comes of H., my father will take Stirum. I do not consider him very suitable, but Schlözer is even less so, and my father would not have him. Radowitz is *completely* out of the question, my father is more than ever distrustful of him and his wife; he would sooner take the youngest Minister! Nor does Alvensleben suit him in any way. He said recently: "I am taking so much trouble to fill this post; yet when one looks at the other countries, nonentities or fools are Foreign Ministers, and still things go all right." From this point of view he may as a last resort fix upon Stirum!' Hatzfeldt's official appointment as permanent State Secretary in the Foreign Ministry and Prussian Minister of State was made on 9 October 1882.

[3] Ferdinand, Baron von Stumm. First Secretary to the Embassy in St Petersburg, 1878–1881, in London 1881–3; Prussian Minister in Darmstadt 1883–5; Minister in Copenhagen, 1885–7; Minister, later Ambassador, in Madrid, 1887–92.

up this *speed*.[1] The Prince of Wales above all was spell-bound by his charm. I have never seen such virtuosity—now talking profoundly with an elder statesman, now addressing a flattering remark to a gentle *lady*,[1] now in a hand's turn making an old friend of a young *swell*,[1] and infatuating elderly *duchesses*[1]—and all within ten minutes. I could never have believed that London society could have been capable of sincerely and universally regretting the departure of a foreigner, as it does now. And his stay here has done the splendid fellow no end of good. He had no time whatever to think about disagreeable things, and the sparkling eyes of the *ladies*,[1] which looked with great pleasure on the dashing son of the Chancellor, served to remind him that there are many good things in the world.

I have just spoken with Dilke for a moment. *Bad news are good news* :[1] now we are being firmly pushed ahead, and in the *immediate* future either the Sultan must go to Egypt or we must. And we are resolutely determined to take the latter course and indeed as soon as possible. Thus spoke Dilke. It could hardly be a question of occupying the Canal, but of an intervention in Egypt. England had little liking for the proposal that an adviser should be attached to the Turkish Military Commission. *Pure question of detail*.[1]—Ireland has disappeared completely into the background. Things that involve their money-bags always take precedence here. Do your utmost, please, to ensure that we receive very full political information. There is no need to fear indiscretions, and when one is oneself well informed it is easier to give information and to carry on conversations.

Münster wants to leave on the 15th.

Your sincerely devoted
Stumm

49. Herbert von Bismarck to Holstein

Varzin, 9 July 1882

Dear Holstein,

[...] My father says that Hatzfeldt could make things easier for him if he would write short letters on the situation several times each week, as old Bülow always did, and not forward the long dispatches. All this is naturally *for you alone*. Moreover it entirely accords with what you say in your letter received this morning and therefore you will be in agreement.

Send only a few things here. He who sends much gets many replies—and I have again developed a callouse on the forefinger through writing!

Saurma's sudden outburst of childishness has made my father both annoyed and depressed; he had thought better of him.[2] My father

[1] In English in the original.
[2] On 4 July Saurma telegraphed from Alexandria that the English Admiral had threatened the Egyptians with a declaration of war and an immediate bombardment if they sought to close the entrance to the harbour. He had also threatened to send a forceful note in the event of their setting up new coastal batteries. 'It seems urgently desirable to warn the irresponsible Admiral most earnestly to keep quiet', Saurma said. Bismarck replied to this telegram: 'Our task is not to warn the English Admiral but Saurma to keep quiet. It is not his business to interfere in the conduct of one of the European Powers or put forward *petita* if German interests do not demand it.' (From the Foreign Ministry files.)

would have been quite pleased if Seymour had bombarded the place, and Stumm wrote to me to-day that Dilke and some of our friends in Parliament greatly regret that Seymour omitted the bombardment. [...]

Ever faithfully
Your HB.

On 10 July Herbert von Bismarck wrote to Holstein: 'If only Seymour would really shoot tomorrow! It would be a pity if anything happened to prevent it, when everything is proceeding as one would wish despite Saurma. The telegram to him that you sent me was very good.'

The telegram to which Count Bismarck referred warned Saurma that he should hold himself strictly aloof 'and especially avoid all steps and utterances that could be interpreted as criticism of or opposition to England or any other Power'.[1]

Bismarck's own warning to Saurma struck a different note. 'Your Excellency is herewith once more instructed *under statutory accountability* to refrain from any action for which you have not received authority from Berlin. You possess no authority to engage in mediatory negotiations between England and its Admiral on the one side and Egypt on the other.'[2]

On 11 July Sir Beauchamp Seymour bombarded Alexandria in order to destroy the fortifications which the Egyptian nationalists were constructing. The French and the Italians rejected the request that they should participate in this action. On the same day Herbert von Bismarck wrote to Holstein: 'My father is decidedly pleased about the bombardment; he is also pleased that so much less came from Berlin to-day. As a result he is thank goodness somewhat better to-day—may it only continue!'

50. Herbert von Bismarck to Holstein

Varzin, 13 July 1882

Dear Holstein,

[...] I have just received a letter from Münster enclosing a private letter from Granville to him in which he (Granville) urgently asks for my father's advice; he is at his wits' end![3] My father will certainly only

[1] Hatzfeldt to Saurma, 9 July 1882. From the Foreign Ministry files.
[2] Telegram of 9 July 1882. From the Foreign Ministry files.
[3] Münster's letter to Herbert von Bismarck of 11 July 1882 was not filed in the Foreign Ministry. There is, however, a copy of Lord Granville's letter to Münster of the previous day. Granville asked to be informed of Bismarck's views on the Egyptian Question, and concluded: 'I should of course reserve full liberty of action, but the knowledge of what the Chancellor thought was practicable and desirable would be a most useful guide and probably prevent some unnecessary mistakes being made.' Bismarck replied with a dispatch to Münster of 14 July. He refused to adopt any standpoint in the matter 'since he was not in a position to endanger Germany's relations with the other Powers by making suggestions for English policy.' (See Wolfgang Windelband, *Bismarck und die europäischen Grossmächte* (Essen, 1940), pp. 343–6.)

reply *more solito* : 'We give our blessing to everything upon which you and France agree.' He says that the only good and honourable advice which he could give to England would be : 'Throw Gladstone out.' As long as the rudder is in the hands of that incalculable fellow who passes on everything to France like a sneak, one cannot talk openly with the English. 'If I were an English Minister I would now occupy the forts at Alexandria, then put money and ships at the Sultan's disposal, and bring Turkish troops to Egypt'—my father said.

Münster writes that England is arming on a colossal scale, mobilising the whole army, but has not the faintest notion of any plan or of what is to happen the next day!

Adieu for to-day
Faithfully your
HB.

51. Otto von Bülow[1] to Holstein

Gastein, 4 August 1882

Confidential

My dear Herr von Holstein,

[...] I thank you very much for the news you have sent me *quoad* Egypt,[2] dear Herr von Holstein; it was of great interest to me. Luckily light is again shining above the All Highest horizon here; the *point noir* about which I felt myself in duty bound to write to Count Hatzfeldt some fourteen days ago is disappearing more and more. It was an expression of the humane sentiments which His Majesty is disposed to allow to influence policy. A deeply seated dislike of the brutal English nevertheless still remains; however, the Kaiser no longer identifies himself with the opinions of his great-nephew in St Petersburg, but said that the instruction to Herr Onou[3] the day before yesterday ordering him to absent himself from the Conference[4] was 'regrettable hastiness' on the part of Tsar Alexander. [...]

Your very devoted
Otto v. Bülow

52. Holstein to Herbert von Bismarck

B[erlin], 5 November 1882

Dear Herbert,

Waldersee has just been here to express a threefold military anxiety :

1. Of all the Great Powers, apart from England, we have the worst artillery. We have progressed, but less than the others; our gun-

---

[1] At this time Bülow was the Foreign Ministry representative in the Kaiser's retinue.
[2] Not found in the Foreign Ministry files.
[3] Counsellor at the Russian Embassy in Constantinople.
[4] The Conference of Ambassadors which met in Constantinople on 23 June to discuss the situation in Egypt.

barrels are less good and the gun-carriages clumsier than elsewhere, and it is doubtful whether our more accurate shooting—which, incidentally, the others too may still attain—compensates for these two disadvantages. Waldersee has sought for an audience, and will see whether he can achieve anything with the Kaiser, but regards the All-Highest assent as doubtful, as always with anything new.

2. The Russian railway system is so superior to ours that they are able to place 20,000 more men on the frontier daily than we are. In order to surmount this unsatisfactory state of affairs we would hardly need to lay down new lines; double tracks and an increase in the number of sidings would suffice. The Russians by this latter method have enormously increased the efficiency of their single-track railway system.

In regard to (2) the General Staff has already for some time past put forward its views, and the Chancellor laid the matter aside for subsequent consideration. Since then, however, the development of the Russian strategical railway system has been proceeding uninterruptedly. The implementation of Count Waldersee's idea would[1] meet with formidable obstacles, because the participation not only of the Prussian Treasury but also of various private companies would be involved. The General believes nevertheless that failure to carry it out would be dangerous.

3. At present there is no middle course between a state of peace and general mobilisation. Consequently several military units detailed for the protection of threatened frontier positions must be on the move within an hour after the receipt of the mobilisation order—that is to say in a wholly unmobilised condition. The reserve troops and whatever else is necessary would follow them, and therefore for a part of the army there exists a situation that gravely resembles the *French* situation in 1870. This could be corrected if arrangements were made[2] to mobilise possibly two infantry divisions earlier than the rest of the army and send them to the Thorn District and Metz-Marsal respectively, the weakest points in the East and the West. By so doing and with a few battalions in the neighbourhood of Trakehnen[3] we should put an end to the whole 'Cavalry Scare'; the danger of our deployment being hindered by destruction of railways would be prevented, and the fear of a war beginning on German soil would be dispelled.

To my objection that the purchase of the first additional horse in a time of crisis would considerably increase the danger of war, Waldersee replied that this evil would still be a lesser one than a premature mobilisation of the whole army or an apathetic waiting while reliable information about enemy preparations was already coming in.

Count Waldersee said nothing nor did I question him about the reasons that caused him to confide strategical ideas to me. Count Hatzfeldt suspects that the General wishes to discuss the matter per-

[1] Marginal note by Chancellor Bismarck: 'could?'
[2] Bismarck: 'what arrangements?'
[3] Bismarck: 'I have proposed this for a long time without success.'

sonally with the Chancellor if at all possible. For this reason I am instructed to inform you of the foregoing.

Ever yours
FH.
[...]

53. Herbert von Bismarck to Holstein

Varzin, 7 November 1882

Dear Holstein,

Best thanks for yesterday's letter,[1] the more important part of which I am enclosing so that you can satisfy yourself that my father has read it. He also said with regard to it that the question of our artillery was a purely technical one which he was not able to judge. If our artillery is really so much worse than that of other nations this must naturally be remedied; in that case the matter must first be raised in the Press and discussed there so that the public and Parliament are prepared for it.

If one suddenly came before the Reichstag with a demand for a lot of money without any previous preparation or warning, one would meet with a cool reception.

As to the other two questions, my father went to the greatest trouble in 1879–80 to work on the Kaiser for the protection of our eastern frontier along the lines Waldersee suggested, and our archives contain plenty of material on the subject. He was unsuccessful with H.M. at that time because the General Staff let him down. If Moltke[2] had then given him enough support, the Kaiser would unquestionably have decided in favour of his demands. My father asked me to tell you that you should give the memoranda in question to Waldersee to read, and there he will find all the material that he may require to enable him to turn to account my father's own convictions in his discussion with H.M.

If my father is now to have a hand in a report Waldersee is preparing for the Kaiser, he must receive from Waldersee a direct and specific proposal to that purpose. But the matter is not urgent for the next few weeks, and within that time my father will surely return to Berlin. Waldersee's visit in itself would be very welcome; but as my father is not staying here much longer, the visit is not *officially* urgent, and my father thinks it would cause much excitement if Waldersee were now suddenly to come to Varzin immediately after the ambassadors have been here. Besides Waldersee would probably have made a direct enquiry if he had himself thought of coming here.

Lignitz[3]—who certainly had some interesting things to say, but who did not give my father any specially new or astounding information—pleaded for a strengthening of the infantry on the eastern frontier and the construction of three or four small defensive forts. These latter he considered urgently necessary. I said to my father that it would probably influence the Kaiser and render him more amenable if Schweinitz[4]

---

[1] Holstein's letter of 5 November.
[2] Helmuth von Moltke. Chief of the General Staff, 1858–88.
[3] Viktor von Lignitz. Military Attaché in St Petersburg.
[4] Hans Lothar von Schweinitz. Prussian General; Ambassador in St Petersburg, 1876–93.

were to write—as he has not yet done—detailed and urgent reports giving this view and Waldersee's. Inevitably the Ambassador has greater weight with H.M. than Lieut.-Col. Lignitz, and since Schweinitz is not only a General but also an Aide-de-Camp, the Kaiser attaches great importance to his judgment.

My father authorises me to write to you that it would perhaps be useful if Schweinitz were to talk to Waldersee, and also if Count Hatzfeldt were to ask the Ambassador to lay emphasis in his dispatches on the threatened position of our eastern frontier. Schweinitz will probably pass through Berlin in the course of this month on his return journey to St Petersburg.

Good-bye for the present

Yours ever HB.

54. Chlodwig zu Hohenlohe to Holstein

Paris, 14 November 1882

My dear Baron,

I have completed my journey according to plan, stopped for a day in Baden, travelled through for two nights, and arrived here yesterday. The Kaiserin was very gracious and told me much that was of interest. She mentioned that from an entirely reliable source she had heard that the Comte de Chambord[1] had used all his eloquence to keep the Duke of Cumberland[2] from coming to an agreement with the Prussian Government and the Reich. What struck me was that the Kaiserin spoke very unfavourably of the Orléans family. Formerly she sympathised very much with the family, and especially with the sons of her cousin[3] and friend, but has now ceased to do so. She fears their chauvinistic views and finds fault with their love of money. I found the Kaiserin exceptionally sensible on the Church question. She expressed herself very strongly against the Centre Party and accused them of working for political reasons against a peaceful settlement and of seeking to influence the Pope in this sense.[4]

I find here grave doubts about the duration of the Republic. The change of front made by Andrieux,[5] who is a sly fox, shows how much the place-hunters have already begun to look to a monarchical restoration. [...]

With best wishes

Your most devoted

C. Hohenlohe.

[1] Henri Charles Ferdinand Marie Dieudonné, Comte de Chambord. Bourbon Pretender to the French Throne.

[2] Ernst August, Duke of Cumberland and Brunswick. As Crown Prince of Hanover he was compelled to leave the country in 1866 after its annexation by Prussia. After the death of his father in 1878 he maintained his claim to the throne. On the death of Duke Wilhelm of Brunswick in 1884 he was unable to take over the government of the Duchy that was his by right of succession because he refused the Prussian demand that he should renounce his claims to Hanover.

[3] Helene von Mecklenburg married Ferdinand, a son of Louis Philippe, and their sons were Philippe, Comte de Paris and Robert, Duc de Chartres.

[4] See also Rogge, *Holstein und Hohenlohe*, p. 181.

[5] Louis Andrieux. Prefect of Police in Paris, 1879–81, and Deputy for Lyons. In the Chamber he proposed a revision of the French Constitution that would confer greater powers on the President and make Ministers independent of the Chamber.

55. Bernhard von Bülow to Holstein

Paris, 14 November 1882

My dear Herr von Holstein,

[...] I cannot fail to recognise that the danger of a monarchical restoration here has considerably increased since the summer when it was mentioned both in dispatches and conversations. I am afraid that when the public at large finally realises that France has lost her position in Egypt and that the beautiful days of the English alliance are also very likely over—a fact that is not yet clear to them—the republican stock will fall even further than it has already done as a consequence of the divisions in the republican party, disorganisation in the government of the country, in the administration of justice, and—it seems to me—in the army, and particularly as a result of socialist agitation. [...]

During the four years that I have spent here, my conviction has steadily increased that for the sake of our own safety we must support the Republic, for the very reasons—though with more justification—that have caused France since the time of Francis I to lend her support to particularism in Germany. Of all the possible forms that a restoration could take here, the Orléanist would in my opinion be by far the most dangerous for us. The Orléans family by their Coburg family connections in London and Vienna and by sharing the anti-German feelings and chauvinist aspirations of St Petersburg, have points of contact to an extent exceeding anything that would be open to the Bonapartes, much less to an upstart. It seems to me a matter of self-preservation to prevent their rise to power by every available means. We shall not be able to prevent the eventual demise of the Republic. But I believe we have it in our power to keep the Republic alive for many a year if on the one hand we keep our eyes open here for attempts at a restoration and plans for the overthrow of the government, and on the other hand let it be clearly known that a restoration, especially an Orléanist restoration, would mean war with us. The vast majority of the French nation fears such a war far more than it does collectivists and anarchists. When once it understands that an Orléanist restoration means war, it will be very difficult indeed for them (the Orléanists) to pose as the saviours of society. In my opinion it would be useful if our Press would from time to time sound a warning note along these lines, without, however, erecting a pedestal for the Orléans family by these attacks. Even before the Ambassador's return I thought I should *mea sponte* advise Stuht[1] verbally to reveal the plans of the Orléanists in his articles (ex-*Landsbergische Korrespondenz*). I enclose his article published yesterday. I do not think he has expressed himself very happily, and I myself would have written it differently, but I would like to know whether you approve of the line of thought and the outlook. In reply to Stuht's question as to the direction in which he was to throw light upon internal developments here, I told him that for the time being my personal view could be summed up by and large as follows: 1. The Republic is better than the Monarchy in the interests of peace. 2. Within the Republic

---
[1] German journalist in Paris.

itself the anti-Gambetta movement is better than Gambetta's supporters.

I have advised Stuht to criticise Gambetta less from the Conservative standpoint—this could make the politically ignorant German middle-class suspicious—than from the Liberal, and to suggest that Gambetta is not truly a man of the people; and also occasionally to reproduce an appropriate article from *Intransigeant* or *Lanterne* attacking his authoritarian ambitions. I regard Stuht as a somewhat unskilful but right-minded and thoroughly trustworthy journalist and his articles as worthy of attention because a large part of the German and Austrian public derive their views on France from them. [...]

In admiration and attachment I am your most obedient

Bernh. Bülow

56. Herbert von Bismarck to Holstein

Varzin, 17 November 1882

Dear Holstein,

Many thanks for your friendly lines and the two interesting letters from Paris.[1] My father read these through and I now return them. As regards the letter from Hohenlohe, he told me to write to you that Chambord's incitement of the Duke of Cumberland should be inserted in the Press—*Post* or *Kölnische Zeitung*.

My father said in regard to Bülow's letter, that at present Gambetta must not be attacked at all by the German Press and, in so far as we are capable of exerting an influence over it we must prevent it from happening. But we cannot praise him either, because to do so would only harm him; he must therefore as far as possible be left in peace. Gambetta would always be far more acceptable to Germany than any form of monarchical restoration because he is incapable of concluding an alliance.

My father wishes an article to be published by the *Kölnische Zeitung*—probably it would be best if it were to appear as a leader purporting to be written by a correspondent in Paris—it should be written more or less as follows:

In recent times rumours of a monarchical restoration and also movements directed from many quarters to that end have gained increased currency. It would not be in the interests of France that any such attempt—if it were to be made—should succeed, and since the vast majority of the French people are not only peace-loving but also need peace, it can hardly be supposed that they would consent to one of the Pretenders ascending the throne when that would mean war. France needs order, but not foreign entanglements, and on that account Gambetta's chances are far better than those of any of the Pretenders, because if he were to be called upon to be head of the French state he would not need a war in order to maintain himself or to gain prestige. The most certain way for France to be involved in war would be if the Orléans family were restored to the throne, since to-day they could not

---

[1] Of 14 November. (See above.)

rule as a traditional constitutional monarchy *à la Louis Philippe* or *à l'Anglaise*; they would therefore have to break with their whole past, and the setting-up of an Orléans Monarchy would fairly certainly have as its immediate result war between France and Germany. There is no doubt that the French people, opposed as they are to warlike adventures, are under no illusions about this state of affairs and therefore *as a Frenchman* one cannot denounce too strongly the ambitious plans of the Orléans Pretenders.

It would probably be best if Lindau were to insert in the *Kölnische Zeitung* an article along these lines, which you can perhaps find time to outline to him. My father also said that it would be going too far were our Press to 'sound a warning note' as suggested by Bülow on the next to last page of his letter. The 'warning' would sound schoolmasterly and arouse suspicion. It would be more practical and more in conformity with our aim to speak about the immediate future of France from the standpoint of the peace-loving *Frenchman* in the manner outlined above, and also perhaps at the same time to insinuate objectively that the situation was similarly regarded in Germany.

If you would instruct Bülow in this sense it might perhaps be of use.
[...]

Now farewell
Your faithful HB.

1883

57. Bernhard von Bülow to Holstein

Paris, 1 January 1883

My dear Herr von Holstein,

Since the day before yesterday when I received your kind lines of the 28th of last month, the old year has closed in a very dramatic manner: a few moments before the arrival of the new year Gambetta died. [...]

In this letter, which goes by post, I must refrain from any comment on the political effect of Gambetta's disappearance from the stage. Moreover it will only be possible with the passage of time to estimate accurately the significance of the event. If Gambetta's death unquestionably diminishes the desire for and the power to realise the ideal of *revanche*, it should on the other hand greatly accelerate the downfall of the Republic. It is only in so far as we succeed in arresting this latter process that in my opinion we can look upon Gambetta's premature demise as a gain. [...]

I cannot conclude without again thanking you specially for what you write to me about my personal future. You have always been so kind to me, dear Herr von Holstein, that I will be very outspoken with you, and not deny that—without mentioning it to others—*dans mon for intérieur* I had to some extent hoped for promotion. Although it has not turned out that way of course I shall not lose heart.[1] I will rather endeavour to carry out my duties at my post to the best of my ability. I enjoy being in Paris, which is still an interesting place politically, and particularly enjoy being under Hohenlohe. [...]

With the sincere wish that the year that began to-day will bring you only what is good and pleasant, I remain in constant respectful devotion your

Bernh. Bülow.

58. Bernhard von Bülow to Holstein

Paris, 27 January 1883

My dear Herr von Holstein,

Just a brief note to tell you that after the arrival of the telegram signed by the Chancellor with reference to the two-edged nature of our sympa-

---

[1] See Holstein's letter to Hohenlohe of 26 November 1882, in which Holstein had forecast that Bülow would probably be promoted to First Secretary on Thielmann's transfer. (Rogge, *Holstein und Hohenlohe*, pp. 181–2.)

thetic feelings for France,[1] I immediately advised those of the German correspondents here who take their instructions from us not to forget how our praise may be injurious[2] here and our censure of service.[3] Whenever they asked me I have always advised them to maintain the greatest possible caution and reserve in discussing the domestic affairs of France. In present circumstances I thought it would be useful if the Republicans were to learn through the voice of the German Press that their rule was beginning to be endangered, not so much by the extremely unpopular Prince Napoleon,[4] nor by the impotent Chambord, but by the Orléans. I have also noticed the zeal with which Blowitz,[5] who has gone over to the Orléanist camp, tries to represent the Republic as not endangered and the Orléanists as harmless in *The Times*. [...]

In my opinion the Republic has unquestionably lost ground, and for the first time in five years its rule is seriously threatened. Nevertheless it can maintain itself for many a year if the Republicans on the one hand keep a close watch on ambitious generals and on the other do not add too many new blunders to the many they have committed in the past; also if the conviction is maintained, which has prevailed here since the Arnim trial[6] and the XVI May,[7] that a restoration, and especially an Orléans Restoration—no matter under what banner—would bring war with us in its wake. If the hatred of us here has not greatly diminished in twelve years, the fear of us is happily the same as before. It seems to me that now that proof has been furnished here *in anima vili* of where republicanism on the European continent can lead a country in domestic and foreign affairs, this system should not be allowed to disappear here before it has weakened France still further, especially militarily, than is at present the case.

You know that I am specially thankful to you for every hint about reporting and the general situation. In admiration and devotion your

Bernh. Bülow

59. Bernhard von Bülow to Holstein

Paris, 27 April 1883

My dear Herr von Holstein,

[...] That I am now to be First[8] makes me extraordinarily happy.

[1] On 21 January Bismarck had telegraphed to Hohenlohe: 'I would like to advise that the German Press, in so far as it is dependent on us, should abstain from taking any stand on the situation there. Our sympathy after all still has a two-edged effect there if it takes sides publicly.' (From the Foreign Ministry files.)

[2] Marginal comment by Bismarck: 'Yes'.

[3] Bismarck: '?'.

[4] Prince Napoleon (Plon-Plon), son of Jerome, King of Westphalia, and Katerina, Princess of Württemberg.

[5] Heinrich Opper von Blowitz. For many years correspondent of *The Times* in Paris.

[6] The criminal proceedings against the former German Ambassador in Paris, Count Harry von Arnim. The evidence given at the public sessions of the trial revealed how consistently Bismarck had opposed Arnim's Orléanist policy.

[7] The crisis of 16 May 1877 arose over the question of whether Ministers were to continue to be responsible to the Chamber or whether the powers of the President should be extended. The former principle finally triumphed.

[8] First Secretary of Embassy.

I know that I owe this happiness above all to your goodwill, dear Herr von Holstein, of which you have afforded me many proofs. Be assured that I shall not forget it, and I hope that the future will give me opportunities for proving that this is no empty phrase. You will understand why I set such store on becoming First: for many reasons to stay on here as Second would have been extremely unwelcome! If my wishes were to be consulted in regard to the posts at which I would like to be First, I would much rather remain in Paris, partly through attachment to Hohenlohe, partly because I know the lie of the land here and therefore can perhaps render better service here than elsewhere. But if this cannot be done I will gladly go to Vienna or elsewhere *quo me fata vocant et numina deum*.

[...] The economic situation must now be considered as the most doubtful spot on the republican horizon. None the less, after surviving with our help the critical period that followed upon Gambetta's death, I hold that the Republic is not seriously endangered, as long as it is on guard against military manifestos and keeps an eye on ambitious intriguers *à la* Galliffet[1] and Billot.[2] It becomes more and more clear how right was the choice of Thibaudin,[3] who is inaccessible to Orléanist attempts at corruption, whereas it seems to me that he is slowly but surely disorganising the army. Tirard[4] performs the same service on the financial side. Since neither of them pushes things so far that a sudden reaction could be expected—which the unpopularity of the present Pretender as well as the conviction that the restoration would mean war with us render more difficult—it seems to me that it can only suit us if the Ferry[5] Cabinet remains in power for a time. The present Government also has the advantage over a Freycinet Government of pursuing a more active colonial policy. I hope that in the case of the Tonkin Expedition[6] as in Madagascar[7] some *farceur à la Brazza*[8] will shortly turn up to popularise the affair and make a retreat difficult. [...]

In admiration and loyalty as ever your
Bern. Bülow

---

[1] Gaston, Marquis de Galliffet. French General. Military Governor of Paris, 1880–2. As President of the Cavalry Committee he carried out a re-organisation of the French cavalry.

[2] Jean Baptiste Billot. French General; Minister for War, 1882–3, 1896–8. He resigned in 1883 to avoid signing the order by which the princes of the House of Orléans were placed on half-pay and relieved of their duties.

[3] Jean Thibaudin. French General. He succeeded Billot as Minister for War, but resigned in October 1883 after he had refused to be a party to the Government's apology to the King of Spain for the demonstrations in Paris against him.

[4] Pierre Emmanuel Tirard. French Minister for Finance in the Cabinets of Duclerc, 1882; of Fallières, 1883; of Ferry, 1883–5.

[5] Jules Ferry. French Prime Minister, September 1880–November 1881, February 1883–March 1885.

[6] For the purpose of suppressing the insurrection that had broken out in the French Protectorate of Tonkin.

[7] French demands in Madagascar led to war with the natives in June 1883.

[8] Savorgnan de Brazza. French explorer, who tried to open up a new route into the Congo from the Gulf of Guinea.

60. Lothar Bucher to Holstein

Berlin, 8 May 1883

Sir,

You have given an order to Krüger, the caretaker, to wall up the door between your office and mine and to have my room repapered. I do not contest your right, Sir, to have the door, which opened on my side, covered on the other side by a wall, and would indeed have welcomed an alteration which protected me from interruptions. I must, however, deny your right to unhinge the door and to have my room papered. I am not aware that the functions of the Councillor in charge of personnel or of the Under State Secretary have been delegated to you, and I do not doubt that I should have aroused your displeasure if I had taken it upon myself to order alterations in your room. In any case I respectfully request you, Sir, whenever in the future you have the intention of giving orders which concern my room, not to give the order before you have assured yourself of my consent, so that never again, as on this occasion, closed cupboards whose contents could not be known to the workmen are moved from their places, breakable objects contained in them smashed, and further damage done through the nature of their contents.

In highest esteem
Bucher.

61. Holstein to a Colleague

Berlin, 9 May 1883

Dear Colleague,

I found the attached letter[1] from *Herr Wirklicher Geheimer Legationsrat* Bucher here yesterday evening. It refers to the walling up of the communicating door between our offices. The existence of this door rendered it hitherto possible—indeed unavoidable—to hear the greater part of what was said in the adjoining room. Anyone who in the absence of *Geheimrat* Bucher sat on the sofa beside the door could not avoid hearing every word of the conversation that was being carried on in my room, and on the other hand I have often risen up from my sofa to avoid hearing what was being said in the neighbouring room.

I had arranged for the other communicating door in my room to be made sound-proof long ago. But on the side facing Bucher I did not want to take the initiative from an older colleague, and it was only when I saw that he was doing nothing that I finally expressed the wish to the caretaker some weeks ago that something should be done to make the door sound-proof. Any further steps, such as obtaining the authorisation of higher authorities, belong in my opinion to the competence of the caretaker. As you know he is the official to whom we Councillors regularly address ourselves on questions of minor alterations in our offices. The belief that I should have made application to authorities other than the caretaker seems to me no more worthy of

[1] Of 8 May. See above.

serious consideration than the idea of reaching a direct understanding with Herr Bucher, with whom I am no longer on speaking terms.

Moreover the question of correct procedure in this instance has only a purely formal importance since it would have been impossible for any authority which had been informed of the acoustic relationship between the rooms *not* to have authorised an *immediate* remedy. If occasion arises I will produce on this point the testimony of other colleagues such as Count Rantzau, who some days before the alteration convinced himself of the state of things by speaking to the caretaker through the closed door.

I ask you, dear Colleague, to bring the contents of this letter to the attention of Herr W. G. L. R. Bucher and to leave any further steps in the matter to his judgment.

With best wishes
Always yours truly
Holstein.

62. Bernhard von Bülow to Holstein

Paris, 30 May 1883

My dear Herr von Holstein,

To-day's courier brings you a dispatch from the Ambassador on the state of opinion in Russian circles here.[1] It seems that the agreement between Germany, Austria and Italy has again aroused in that quarter the desire for a Franco-Russian alliance, and that to pave the way for it they would like as a first step to see the present dispensation here replaced by a more stable regime. Of all the foreign missions in Paris, ours is the only one that really desires the maintenance of the Republic. All the other missions, besides sharing the prejudice against the republicans that is continually aired by society in the salons here, also hold the opinion that a monarchy on the Seine would better serve the interests of their respective countries. I have found this opinion most openly held by the Russians.

Meanwhile the brand of republicanism at present in power would hardly be averse to a rapprochement with Russia. The Government newspapers—*République Française* (Challemel),[2] *Réforme* (Waldeck),[3] *Paris* (young Gambettism)—have taken the opportunity of the Coronation in Moscow[4] to offer themselves to Russia as a wallflower offers herself to a rich suitor. This turning towards the East is strengthened by the growing bitterness against England, against whose 'egotism' and 'jealousy', as shown once more in the Tonkin question, the entire

---

[1] On 28 May Hohenlohe had reported that Russian circles in Paris were of the opinion that the Triple Alliance was directed against Russia. They deplored that no alliance was possible with the existing French Government. (From the Foreign Ministry files.)

[2] Paul Challemel-Lacour. A follower of Gambetta. French Minister in Bern, 1879; Ambassador in London, 1880–2; Minister for Foreign Affairs in Ferry's Cabinet, February–November 1883; President of the Senate, 1893–6.

[3] Pierre Waldeck-Rousseau. French Minister of the Interior in the Cabinet of Gambetta, November 1881–January 1882; of Ferry, February 1883–March 1885. Minister-President and Minister of the Interior, June 1899–May 1902.

[4] The coronation of Tsar Alexander III was celebrated in Moscow from 20 May to 9 June.

French Press from the extreme Right to the extreme Left is at present united in a common front. It will be significant in any assessment of the relationship between Russia and France to see whether Jaurès,[1] whom French acquaintances represent to me as incompetent and unpopular in St Petersburg, remains at his post or is replaced by another ambassador, for example General Billot. [...]

The dangers threatening the Republic from the subjection of the state to the private railways will only gradually become evident: the defeat suffered in Tonkin will now be exploited to the full by the monarchists as a proof that diplomatically, economically, and militarily *tout marche mal*. Nevertheless, so long as the Comte de Chambord and Prince Jérôme Napoléon do it the service of remaining alive, I have no fears for the Republic. As far as our interests are concerned, the Republic should, in my opinion, make use of the years I hope are still allotted to it, first by tying down French manpower and money in colonial enterprises, and then by setting in motion the struggle with the Church. As regards the former a Gambettist Ministry, despite its other drawbacks, would be by far the best; Say[2] would act with less assurance; Freycinet would probably use the axe everywhere. The present Cabinet by comparison acts so timidly towards the Curia that it could not be excelled by any other republican government in faint-heartedness. Waldeck-Rousseau in particular makes one advance after another to the clergy and recently said in the presence of one of my friends that he wanted to give posts only to clericals because *'ils sont bien élevés et propres à tout; avec les républicains il n'y a rien à faire'*. It seems to me that a fight with Rome would not merely tone down the pretensions of the Curia towards us but also deepen the Party differences here, and more than anything else have a diversionary and demoralising effect. If the German Press were to encourage the French in colonial undertakings and a more self-assured attitude towards the Papacy it would naturally arouse suspicion here. But it also serves no good purpose when—for example—the *Kölnische Zeitung* depicts in the crudest colours the consequences for France that could arise out of French hankerings after Syria, Tonkin, etc. And it would do no harm if the cowardly retreat of the Gambettists before Ultramontanism were, if not openly criticised in our Press, at least made widely known and thus somewhat more firmly impressed on the consciousness of the anti-clerical elements here.[3] [...]

In respect and devotion your
Bern. Bülow

63. Bernhard von Bülow to Holstein

Paris, 11 June 1883

My dear Herr von Holstein,

Forgive me that I have waited until today to express my gratitude

[1] Benjamin Jaurès. French Admiral. Ambassador to St Petersburg, 1882–3.
[2] Léon Say. French Finance Minister, 1872–3, 1875–9, 1882.
[3] Note by Holstein: 'Lindau-*Kölnische*.' Holstein means that this should be brought to the attention of Rudolf Lindau, the Foreign Ministry official in charge of Press affairs, for dealing with the *Kölnische Zeitung*.

for your very friendly and kind lines. I found them here on Saturday after my return from Dieppe where I had gone with my brother Alfred[1] for a few days. At the same time I received my appointment as First [Secretary] here. Let me tell you once more how earnestly I will endeavour to continue to prove myself worthy of your confidence, to which I am above all indebted for the fulfilment of my hopes.

I am particularly grateful to you for submitting my political letters [to Bismarck] only when it seems to you opportune.

With renewed thanks and the wish that all will go well for you, I am your truly devoted

Bernh. Bülow

64. Alfred von Kiderlen-Wächter[2] to Holstein

Peterhof, 20/8 June 1883

Dear *Herr Geheimer Legationsrat,*

It was particularly pleasant and gratifying to me to receive a letter from you, all the more so in that in all initiated circles the receipt of such a letter is looked upon as an extremely *rare* distinction. Unfortunately I cannot show my gratitude by replying to your questions. How could an unassuming little worm in the Embassy, who during the coronation was only now and then honoured by being allowed to make good the mistakes of superior personages—how could I know what went on in higher and the highest circles? But I will nevertheless make an attempt to give you a picture of the little that I know as I see it.

If I tell you what you already know, I can at least hope that what I write is to a certain extent correct.

It was obvious that certain sanguine hopes connected with the coronation—especially a momentary material improvement, rise in the value of the rouble, etc—could not be fulfilled. The *moral* effect of the coronation was at all events of very great benefit for the monarchical principle, the principle which is here favourable to us. At most the effect was perhaps somewhat lessened by the fact that at the beginning—the entry of the Tsar—the general feeling 'Pray God that all will go well' was too obvious. On the other hand the official proclamations were particularly gratifying, especially the one addressed to the peasant deputations (village elders) which frankly professed conservative ideas and once and for all dispelled the fear here of 'public opinion' which is dangerous only to us.

You know better than I if and to what extent official Russia will maintain good relations with us;—the eternal, often petty fear of the so-called 'national dynamism' is perhaps less frequently before your eyes than ours, and therefore you may perhaps judge many happenings in

[1] Alfred von Bülow. Secretary at the Prussian Legation in Stuttgart, 1882–4.
[2] Alfred von Kiderlen-Wächter. Secretary of Embassy in St Petersburg, 1881–5, in Paris, 1885–6, in Constantinople, 1886–8; *Vortragender Rat* in charge of Balkan and Near Eastern affairs in the Foreign Ministry, 1888–94; Prussian Minister in Hamburg, 1894–5; Minister in Copenhagen, 1895–9; in Bucharest, 1899–1910; temporary State Secretary in the Foreign Ministry, November 1908–March 1909; State Secretary, 1910–12.

another light. When, however, one sees daily, and especially in the law reports in the newspapers, etc., how great is the fear of offending ostensible public opinion, then one begins to doubt the power of the Government (I do not question its good intentions). Formerly the small man in Russia found it hard to obtain his rights; now it is the large proprietors, the members of the higher and wealthier classes (especially for example joint stock undertakings and similar important elements of social life), who no longer obtain their rights as against the obstinate small man who, even when in the wrong, always has deluded public opinion and the democratic 'independent' judicature on his side. The importance of the Imperial proclamation directed against hopes of further land partition—as regards this tendency which up to now nobody has dared to oppose—just cannot be underrated. [*sic*]

The same fear of public opinion, as it is envisaged here in governmental circles, was in my humble opinion (forgive me if I repeat something which is trite and well known) the reason why Ignatiev's fall was so long-delayed. After they had at last summoned up the *courage* to depose him, and had seen that this did not mean the end of the world, it is certain that under the present government he is out for good. As far as I could see he pushed himself to the fore at the coronation whenever possible; but I think without any success. Women who pique themselves upon a certain political *air*, and journalists whom he knows how to flatter, may see to it that he is heard of now and then; for the rest I believe to be true what a highly placed Russian recently said to me about him—'*c'est un homme mort*'. And this is certainly all the more true because he cannot speak in public and consequently plays no part in the Imperial Council. [...]

I will not entertain you with the disagreeable *interna* of our Embassy; but I can tell you that I will bless the day on which I get away from my Chief,[1] with whom everyone must daily expect an unpleasant *rencontre* that renders further intercourse impossible—and against superiors it is hard to obtain one's rights! I am at least cautious enough now to put unpleasant matters in writing; this was after my word had been doubted and I was only able to justify myself by means of a note which had been preserved *by chance*. We have not yet reached the stage of disavowing the signature!!!

May I entreat you—in view of the goodwill you have invariably displayed towards me—to regard this little outburst of anger as made in strictest confidence.

With most distinguished regard and in sincere admiration, your truly devoted

Kiderlen.

65. Otto von Bülow to Holstein

Gastein, 24 July 1883

Dear Herr von Holstein,

I have the honour to reply to your question of the 21st that His

[1] General von Schweinitz.

Majesty has not raised any objections to the form or content of the instructions to Schweinitz regarding what he is to say[1] in case Giers[2] mentions the strengthening of the Prussian frontier garrisons. The Kaiser listened to the reading of the instructions with interest, but did not make any observation on the content, so I saw no reason to make a report. On the contrary he spoke in his now familiar manner about the behaviour of the Russians, which he called 'frightful' (a very frequent expression) and 'incomprehensible'. He also told me, as he had once before, that in September '79 in Alexandrovo he had already expressed his surprise to Miliutin[3] at the enormous increase of troops on our frontier, and when the latter returned an evasive answer, had said to him that the Russians could not seriously think that we had cast an eye on Russian territory: *franchement: il n'y a rien qui pourrait nous tenter*— or words to that effect.

Your communication of the apprehensions of the General Staff was of great interest to me and I thank you very much for it.[4] [...]

Farewell! Most sincerely
Your very devoted
O. Bülow.

66. Herbert von Bismarck to Holstein

Kiss[ingen], 27 August 1883

Dear Holstein,

Challemel should not be 'prepared' for anything other than what was stated in the two telegrams of the day before yesterday;[5] the object is precisely to make clear to him now the necessity for our increased military demands, in order that later on he does not suddenly get panicky and shaky. Now he can gradually accustom himself, his colleagues, and also public opinion through the Press, to the idea.

We will neither expect nor demand anything of Challemel; nor *can* he do anything without making his own situation impossible. The real

[1] Bismarck's instructions to Schweinitz, dated 30 June, were dispatched without previously informing the Kaiser. Schweinitz was ordered to tell Giers, but only if Giers himself raised the question, that in view of the increased number of Russian troops on the German frontier, Germany must also reinforce her troops. This constituted no reason for Russia to fear a change in Germany's 'friendly, neighbourly and pacific attitude'. (From the Foreign Ministry files.)

[2] Nikolai Karlovich Giers. Russian Foreign Minister, 1882–95.

[3] Dmitri, Count Miliutin. Russian Minister for War, 1861–81.

[4] Not found. The communication may have been along the same lines as Holstein's letter to Wilhelm von Bismarck of 21 July 1883 in which he wrote: 'The strengthening of the armed forces on the Russian western frontier could not nowadays, as it occasionally was in the past, be represented as a means of calming the Press and "public opinion". Never has so little noise been made and so much been accomplished than within the space of the past year. The Imperial signature on the ukases issued for this purpose can be explained solely, if one is not to question the Imperial sincerity, by the assumption that the German-Austrian agreement has been represented to the Tsar as an alliance with essentially aggressive aims. But it is precisely in the *Russian* preparations that the aggressive intent is most obvious, notwithstanding their many fortifications.'

[5] In two telegrams of 25 August 1883 Bismarck asked that Hohenlohe be instructed to explain to Challemel that he (Bismarck) did not desire a Press campaign against France. The French attitude forced him to prepare German public opinion in advance for increased military estimates. '*Paramus bellum quia volumus pacem.*' (From the Foreign Ministry files.)

object of the whole *Press-manoeuvre* is simply to prepare *our* public opinion for an increase in the military estimates (magazine rifle).

My father said to-day that it would perhaps be useful to publish articles in our Press in about a week's time praising the Comte de Paris[1] and supporting him, in order to make him impossible in France as *'le candidat de l'Allemagne'*. Written more or less along these lines: 'A king in France would be a better guarantee for peace than the many-headed Republic; a king is always concerned for his throne, says to himself therefore that if things go badly he will be thrown out and for that reason will be more cautious. In a Republic nobody feels himself responsible as an individual, it is simply a matter of voting *per majoritatem* and *le cœur léger*, hence war can be waged with greater imprudence. Moreover the Comte de Paris in particular is a peace-loving man and by virtue of his German mother[2] more capable than a Frenchman of stable rule.'

What do you think of this? I am somewhat uneasy that it could be a two-edged affair and that because of the French people's dread of war the Republic would be damaged and the Orléanists aided by articles of this kind. Then we should have failed in our object; the latter [is, as][3] said, only to blacken the Comte de Paris and make him impossible.

If it succeeds it would be wonderful. Since the initiative and first idea came from my father himself, one should think that its execution would be the best thing—*but still* . . .? In any case this shot, which is intended to take effect 'round the corner' must be fired with great caution and exact calculation (i.e. phrasing). [...]

Ever your

HB.

67. Herbert von Bismarck to Holstein

Gastein, 2 September 1883

Dear Holstein,

[...] I wrote briefly to Busch yesterday about Bulgaria.[4] My father wants the Russians to make their attitude clear. He says that it is actually outrageous that they should treat Bulgaria, in which they have no more rights than Austria or England, as if it were a Russian province.[5] The situation must be cleared up there. We should leave them

[1] Philippe, Comte de Paris, grandson of Louis Philippe. He was the Orléanist candidate for the French throne and after the death of the Comte de Chambord the leading pretender.

[2] Helene von Mecklenburg.

[3] The letter is torn at this point.

[4] In the Foreign Ministry files there is only a letter of 6 September from Herbert von Bismarck to the Under State Secretary Busch in which he wrote that his father had decided, in agreement with Kálnoky, that Russian intervention in Bulgaria 'would not unpropitiously alter the whole European situation, without leading to hostilities between Germany-Austria and Russia'. A union of Eastern Rumelia with Bulgaria would increase Bulgaria's independence *vis-à-vis* Russia.

[5] Russia had freed Bulgaria from Turkish domination after the war of 1877–8, but Russia's hope of creating a large Bulgarian state as a Russian sphere of influence in the southern part of the Balkan peninsula was frustrated by the opposition of other Great Powers. At the Congress of Berlin of 1878 a smaller Bulgarian state was created, but even over this area Russia found difficulty in establishing her dominion, for neither the Bulgarian parliament

alone in Bulgaria. If they bring the boil to a head, they must then decide either to leave it alone or to annex it. [...]

His Highness [Bismarck] is quite angry with Radowitz. I have just had to write to Busch that Radowitz is to be sharply reprimanded for laziness and that it is to be reported to His Majesty that if Rad's reporting continues to be so scanty he cannot remain any longer in Constantinople.[1]

Have the letter shown to you. I cannot repeat everything. It will amuse you that Hatzfeldt should be rubbed under Radowitz's nose in a comparison of 'past and present'. [...]

Yours ever
HB.

68. Bernhard von Bülow to Holstein

8 September [1883]

Best thanks for kind letter. I am like you of the opinion that at this moment we should weaken the Republic as little as possible; on the one hand because of the rising monarchical flood, on the other because the Tonkin question could under favourable circumstances take on proportions akin to the Tunisian, which was so useful to us in its time.

As long as you permit me to continue operations, I will do my best to preserve the Republic as such—or at least as long as the Republicans stay clear of Antoine[2] and Zorilla.[3]

B.

69. Alfred von Kiderlen-Wächter to Holstein

St Petersburg, 20 September 1883

Dear *Herr Geheimrat*,

As the courier is going anyway, I did not want him to leave quite empty-handed, though at present nothing is happening here. Judge my *opuscula* leniently.

(the Sobranje) nor Alexander von Battenberg, who had been made Prince of Bulgaria under Russian auspices, were willing to accept the position of Bulgaria as a Russian satrapy. In 1882 the Russian Government sent Generals Sobolev and Kaulbars to Bulgaria to serve as Bulgarian cabinet ministers and to govern the country in Russia's interest. Sobolev was acting as Bulgarian Prime Minister and Minister of the Interior, while Kaulbars was Minister for War. The Russian effort to rule Bulgaria as a Russian province was meeting with steadily increasing resistance in the country, and it was believed that Russia might try to intervene directly in Bulgarian affairs.

[1] Herbert von Bismarck instructed Busch that Radowitz was to be told that 'we were far better informed about conditions in Turkey in Hatzfeldt's time'. The Kaiser was to be informed that Bismarck had first learnt of the latest events in Constantinople from Kálnoky. (From the Foreign Ministry files.)

[2] Jules Dominique Antoine. Deputy for Metz in the Reichstag, 1881–5. He made himself conspicuous by his pro-French attitude, was expelled from Germany in 1885, and finally settled in Paris in 1889.

[3] Manuel Ruiz Zorilla. President of the Spanish Cortes, 1870; Prime Minister, 1871, 1872–3. After the abdication of King Amadeo on 12 February 1873, he left Spain, became a republican, and later opposed the recall of the King to the throne. From Paris he conducted a vigorous republican propaganda campaign, and refused to return to Spain when authorised to do so by the Sagasta Cabinet.

Concerning the news from Bulgaria,[1] I would like to tell you a little more about a conversation with the Director of the Asiatic Department, which here includes the Balkan Peninsula. It seems to me that Herr Zinoviev's remarks are highly characteristic of the outlook here. As is the case now with all Russians, including the calmer and more reasonable ones, he became greatly excited when he spoke of Bulgaria. Naturally he was furious with the Prince[2] and brought forward the well-known charges against him: he is ungrateful, disingenuous (Herr Zinoviev claims to have discerned this especially during his conversations with the Prince in Moscow), he pursues his own interests and forgets that after the *coup d'état* he could not have stayed in the country twenty-four hours without the help of the Russian officers.[3] The Tsar is also very angry with the Prince as he (Zinoviev) saw from his marginal comments. '*Mais nous le tiendrons quand même*', Herr Zinoviev added, '*parce que l'Empéreur a en grippe tout ce qui sent la révolution et par égards pour la famille Impériale.*' I thought I could take Herr Zinoviev's words to mean that the government really has no reason to support Prince Alexander, and moreover that if the generals left he would certainly be thrown out. Certain people would undoubtedly see to it that the Prince's throne would not stay upright long if Russia's official protection were taken from him along with the generals, and Russia could then quietly divest herself of all the responsibility which she still has while the generals, acting as ministers, remained in office. It seems to me that a ray of light was cast on Zinoviev's personal views by the fact that among the good turns Russia had done the Prince, he reckoned the recall of Hitrovo[4] at the Prince's desire, despite the fact that he (Hitrovo) was '*un excellent agent*'.

The warning given to the anti-German newspapers does not appear to have done much good, judging by their latest articles, and it seems that all that has happened is that the comments on troop movements on the frontier, which the Government disliked, have ceased. Incidentally I think I can distinguish three stages through which the newspapers have passed.

Two years ago daily articles on the next war still laid chief emphasis on the alliance with France. This has ceased, probably as a result of the way things are going in France, which has also, as far as I can judge, distinctly cooled off that section of Russian society which annually goes to Paris. After the declamations about the alliance with France there followed in the newspapers an intermediate stage of examinations of

[1] At the opening of the Sobranje on 15 September, the rival Bulgarian parties united to persuade Prince Alexander to restore the Constitution of Tirnova, which he had changed in 1881 to give himself greater powers at the expense of the Sobranje. The concession made by Prince Alexander at this time represented a union of the Prince and the Bulgarian parties against the influence of Russia. On 19 September the Russian Generals Sobolev and Kaulbars offered their resignations, which were immediately accepted by the Prince. On 20 September Prince Alexander issued a proclamation by which he restored the Constitution of Tirnova and appointed a Cabinet composed of three Liberals and three Conservatives.

[2] Alexander of Battenberg, Prince of Bulgaria, 1879–86.

[3] At the time of the *coup d'état* in 1881 Prince Alexander had appointed a Ministry headed by Russian officers.

[4] Russian Consul-General in Sofia up to May 1882.

the colossal defensive power which Russia owed to its great distances and its population's willingness for sacrifice. After the speeches of people like Skobelev,[1] and after the movement of troops to the frontier finally became obvious even to the general public, the newspapers and the 'public opinion' influenced by them began to estimate the strength of opposing offensive forces. [...]

Ever in sincere respect
Your very devoted
Kiderlen.

70. Alfred von Kiderlen-Wächter to Holstein

St Petersburg, 28 September 1883

Dear *Herr Geheimrat*,

[...] Bulgaria is naturally the topic of the day. Governmental circles, Press, and politically-minded Society are equally excited about the development of things in Bulgaria and over what they call the 'ingratitude' of the Prince of Bulgaria.

Although he is not in agreement with the sharply-worded article in Tuesday's issue of the *Journal de St Pétersbourg* (No. 243 of 25/13 of this month), Herr von Giers openly expressed his displeasure with Prince Alexander. Assurances are indeed officially given that there would be agreement to any solution of the Bulgarian crisis if law and order were established in the country under its present Prince. At the same time the fear is always expressed—whether it is born of genuine conviction I do not know—that the Prince would not be able to maintain himself without the support of Russia and her generals.

That the attempt to influence the situation there has not been abandoned, despite the refusal to accept any further responsibility, is shown by the fact that Herr Jonin[2] is remaining there—as Herr von Giers said *'avec une mission aussi modératrice que possible'*, or as Herr Zinoviev more frankly said *'parce que nous n'avons aucune raison de le rappeler'*.[3] [...]

In great haste but as ever with deepest regard and respect

Your most devoted Kiderlen.

71. Paul von Hatzfeldt to Holstein

Sommerberg, 29 September 1883

Dear Holstein,

[...] I am writing to-day about my discussion with the King of Spain,[4] and a copy must be made for Prince Bismarck.[5] [...]

---

[1] Michael Skobelev. Russian General; national hero of the Russo-Turkish War, 1877–8, and ardent Pan-Slavist. His speeches were strongly anti-German.

[2] Russian Consul-General in Sofia, 1883–4.

[3] On 22 June 1883 the Tsar wrote to Prince Alexander that he had decided to send Privy Counsellor Jonin, who enjoyed his fullest confidence, to Bulgaria. 'I hope we shall have your co-operation in working out a clearly defined policy, from which all intrigues and personal misunderstandings will be excluded, and that we may in this way achieve our object. That is the purpose of Jonin's mission, which has a definite time limit.' (See Egon Corti, *Leben und Liebe Alexanders von Battenberg* (Graz, Salzburg, Vienna, 1949), p. 132. Also published in English translation under the title *Alexander von Battenberg* (London, 1954).)

[4] King Alfonso XII had come to Germany to take part in the imperial manoeuvres near Homburg, 20–26 September.

[5] The conversation concerned the possibility of a German-Spanish alliance. (See *Diaries*, p. 44, note 1.)

If the Prince has any sense of justice he must recognise that the King's offer is a brilliant vindication of my whole Spanish policy since Madrid. The only question is how to bring the matter to a conclusion. I must make it quite clear that up to now I have not said a word about the matter either to the Crown Prince (on account of England!) or Solms, and also urgently request you to prevent this for the present. We can think it over quietly, since the King does not demand an immediate reply. It is said that the Crown Prince is to go to Madrid in April and that would probably be the right moment.[1] It would be best if I could go as well. Think this over and perhaps discuss it with Herbert who could take the preliminary steps with his father.

As for myself—I state this emphatically—I have *no* personal desire to make such a journey. [...]

And now adieu—I am absolutely worn out and need some rest.

As ever your
Hatzfeldt.

In case it should be of interest there, I should mention that the King of Spain has conferred on me the Chain of Charles III—in other words the highest that he can give excepting the Fleece. [...]

72. Herbert von Bismarck to Holstein

Friedrichsruh, 29 September 1883

Dear Holstein,

Best thanks for your letter which I will submit [to Bismarck]. I would have shown it to him more gladly if Tiedemann had not been mentioned, because such an *argumentatio ad hominem* weakens the effect and involuntarily brings *homo et res* into a relationship from which *res* never profit. Moreover I think it is questionable whether Tiedemann is suitable for Strasbourg; he has determination and ability, but no tact whatever and not the best manners. I should recommend him without question to be Minister of the Interior but not to be Minister in Strasbourg. To be sure, I do not know the conditions there from personal observation, but I can picture them. At the Interior a ruthless Minister would be *very* much in the right place after the two flabby liberalising Eulenburgs[2] and the shallow Puttk,[3] with his cheap toadying. I can indeed believe that Manteuffel is not going about things in the right way, but it is a very difficult position, and at the moment I can think of no replacement, unless one were able to send Prince Wilhelm there—but the two men ahead of him[4] would never allow it. [...]

Ever Your
HB.

[1] The journey of the Crown Prince to Spain took place in December 1883. (See *Diaries*, entry for 3 January 1884.)

[2] Friedrich Albert, Count zu Eulenburg. Prussian Minister of the Interior, 1862–78. Botho, Count zu Eulenburg, who succeeded his uncle as Minister of the Interior, 1878–81.

[3] Robert von Puttkamer. Minister of the Interior, 1881–8.

[4] The Kaiser and the Crown Prince.

73. Herbert von Bismarck to Holstein

Fr[iedrichsruh], 30 September 1883

Dear Holstein,

I have informed my father of your letter. He said that since he is now cutting down on his work he cannot coach Manteuffel; besides, he is afraid of making him disgusted with it all, which he does not want to do because he has nobody better. If M. were to leave, a crowd of incapable minor princes would fall upon Strasbourg. Moreover M. had told him himself that Hofmann[1] had become quite useless and that he wanted to have him replaced by the Puttkamer who is Head of the Judicial Department.[2]

Goodnight
Your HB.

74. Paul von Hatzfeldt to Holstein

Sommerberg, 6 October, 1883

Dear friend,

It seems that I was again in the wrong *de faire du zêle*. After the whole business had gone through my hands in Homburg it would certainly have looked extremely peculiar if I had refused Benomar[3] (who was still in Homburg and had been told by his Government to deal with me) an interview and referred him to Berlin, despite the fact that the Chancellor is not there.[4] Ordinary common sense should suggest to them that I deserved thanks for giving myself this trouble during my leave—just as they should have recognised that nobody knows the Spaniards and the whole business as well as I do. But God forbid. Far from any question of thanks or recognition, it will end with insults.

If I were not ashamed *vis à vis* Benomar, I would simply wire to him that he must turn to Berlin. It is no pleasure for me to have to devote myself to this business. I have, moreover, a house full of guests, and I would be very glad to be rid of the whole affair. Unfortunately decency forbids me, now that I have through foolish zeal let myself get into it. Therefore, if Benomar, who is laid up in Frankfurt with influenza, cannot come here tomorrow, I will accede to his request to visit him early on the day after tomorrow, speak to him in accordance with my instructions, and then tell him that for the future he must address

---

[1] Karl von Hofmann. State Secretary for Alsace-Lorraine, 1880–7.

[2] Maximilian von Puttkamer. Head of the Judicial Department in the Ministry for Alsace-Lorraine, 1879–89; State Secretary for Alsace-Lorraine, 1889–1901.

[3] Spanish Minister in Berlin, 1875–88.

[4] On 4 October Count Benomar asked Count Hatzfeldt on behalf of his Government what attitude Germany contemplated taking in regard to the demonstrations by the Paris populace against King Alfonso, who had angered French public opinion by attending the German Imperial manoeuvres and by his acceptance of the appointment of Commandant of the 15th Uhlans. Bismarck ordered that the Spanish Ambassador be informed that he (Bismarck) regarded a Spanish protest in Paris as proper, but that he did not wish 'to weaken the expression of Spain's justifiable indignation by our participation'. In a letter to the Foreign Ministry Bismarck said that Berlin was the place for conducting official business, and that when he and the State Secretary were simultaneously absent, Ministers of foreign states should address themselves to the Under State Secretary. (From the Foreign Ministry files.)

himself to Berlin. I do not want to have trouble and boredom and insults, on top of everything else.

As far as the matter itself is concerned I entirely disagree with your views. In the first place it can be inferred from my telegram, which is naturally not as detailed as a report would be, that I did not offer any kind of encouragement and that I also very clearly emphasised our wish to avoid any quarrel. It is on the other hand my firm conviction that as things are at present we cannot allow ourselves simply to repulse the Spanish approach if we do not want to lose for the future all the fruits of our previous endeavours. The slightly greater chance this might give of maintaining the French Government—*if* it is greater—is certainly *not* worth that. I can only say that I would regard it as a first-class political blunder. We must in every respect be friendly to King Alfonso, also in this instance, without ourselves taking the initiative and without ourselves taking part in any action which they (the Spaniards) may wish to take. The utmost they can demand of us is that *if* they make a move that we can approve of and *if* the French discuss it with us in Berlin or Paris, we will then express our point of view.

There you have my opinion in the matter; it has been well thought over and therefore I cannot alter it. His Highness [Bismarck] can of course do what he wishes, and I have prudently reserved this to him quite expressly.

In addition there are two facts that must be obvious to anyone with his eyes open: 1. that the hatred for us in France, which has not lessened one iota, is at its height among the radicals; 2. that in Spain too the radicals are our enemies. Conclusion: it is a matter of indifference for us who is in power in France except for one thing—the present government finds it less easy to gain allies. Would this not turn out to be a chimera if we ever really came to blows with Russia?? We must not permit the monarchy to be overthrown in Spain and replaced by the radicals. But this can happen if the monarchy is forced to put up with humiliations. I am not going to prove this statement, and on this point simply state that I know the country and its people.

I do not need to say that I do not love the Orléans and do not wish to render them any service. But I cannot—as already pointed out—convince myself that their chances will be increased by a hair's breadth through the fact that *we* are friendly to Spain in this case. Moreover I think that we must reckon with the possibility of their success and that we must as far as possible assure ourselves of Spain for this eventuality also.

Dixi et salvavi animam meam.

And now one thing more. It would naturally please me to know what His Highness said on the subject of my last reports (secret) from Homburg and how the matter therein referred to, about which I allowed myself to make suggestions, is to be further dealt with.[1]

Ever your
P. Hatzfeldt.

[1] See above, Hatzfeldt's letter of 29 September and footnotes thereto.

75. Bernhard von Bülow to Holstein

Paris, 12 October 1883

Dear Herr von Holstein,

[...] If Hohenlohe comes to Berlin, let him gain the impression in the interests of the cause that people there are tolerably pleased with me. Much could happen in Paris this winter and I stand almost alone in my political views, with which you are acquainted. [...]

Please forgive pencil and haste, every faithfully yours

Bernh. Bülow.

76. Karl von Wedel[1] to Holstein

Vienna, 19 October 1883

My dear Herr von Holstein,

Accept my most hearty thanks for your kind letter of 8 October, which greatly interested me, and permit me to answer it by making a humble attempt to follow you along the path you have taken.

The first thing I did was to enquire of the Intelligence Bureau of the General Staff here about possible reports of the transfer of the 15th Russian Army Corps. The very well-informed Austrian Military Attaché in St Petersburg[2] left here ten days ago to return there, and promised that he would immediately telegraph in case the report should prove correct. No such telegram has as yet arrived, while the consular reports that have come from Kiev and Warsaw in the last few days say nothing about prospective troop movements or any preparations indicating such a purpose.

I think therefore that the measure under discussion, which is based purely on newspaper rumours, can be banished to the realm of tendentious fictions.

May I say in strict confidence that in my experience my worthy colleague in St Petersburg, Herr von L[ignitz], takes a certain pleasure in giving his reports on military happenings in Russia a sensational and alarming colour. I refrain from any judgment as to whether such chauvinist inclinations are always very expedient and useful. We have indeed every reason to be mistrustful of our eastern neighbour, considering the incalculable conditions there, but I think that for that very reason we should watch events there with redoubled objectivity and not nourish and sharpen our mistrust without compelling reasons. Perhaps this standpoint is justifiably open to attack. But does not the uncomfortable state of public opinion in Europe spring more from fear or timidity at the prospect of war than from definite belief in it? And is it not undeniable that the more the belief in the continuance of peace is undermined, the greater the danger of war becomes, because one gets used to the idea of war as an unavoidable calamity, and because public

---

[1] Karl, Count (later Prince) von Wedel. Military Attaché in Vienna, 1877–87; Aide-de-Camp to the Kaiser, 1889–94; Minister in Stockholm, 1892–4; Ambassador in Rome, 1899–1902, in Vienna, 1902–7; Governor of Alsace-Lorraine, 1907–14; also held several military commands.

[2] Colonel Klepsch.

opinion finally comes to prefer a final decision to an insupportable state of uncertainty?

Count Waldersee is certainly right to show anxiety lest a further massing of Russian troops on the Galician frontier should create a depressing moral influence upon the decisions of the Austrian High Command. Nonetheless I am firmly convinced from my knowledge of conditions here, and from what I know of the people who make the decisions, that *under all circumstances* they will hold fast to the deployment in Galicia, that is to an *offensive* conduct of any possible war, since deployment behind the Carpathians would be tantamount to a defensive war, and indeed to one which would make a shift to the offensive very difficult. Austria is forced for political reasons and simply to preserve her very existence to make every effort from the outset to join up with the German Army. A deployment behind the Carpathians, however, would deprive the Austrian Army of any such possibility.

I am convinced that at the outbreak of war Russia will at once attempt to march into Galicia and thus to assure herself of the initiative, but only in the event that she has to fight Austria alone, whose army, as I know, is not highly regarded in Russia.

The offensive spirit is not very strong in the Russian Army and it will, at least in my opinion, break down completely if our army is deployed on the Polish frontier. The Austro-German offensive is concentric, the Russian eccentric, demanding great initiative for its conduct, very much more than I would ascribe to the Russian High Command.

These are, however, personal opinions that unhappily I cannot vouch for. But I can vouch for the fact that here they hold firmly to the principle that the decision in a war with Russia can only be sought in Russian Poland and that for that reason also the deployment of the Austrian army can only take place in Galicia. [...]

Your most devoted
Count Wedel.

77. Götz von Seckendorff[1] to Holstein

Wiesbaden, 5 November 1883

Dear friend,

You do not need to be assured that in the last few days I have often felt the need to write to you, but since Som.[2] was on the point of leaving for Berlin—he left yesterday evening—I thought it wiser and more prudent to leave it to him to explain the situation. Arrange a rendezvous with him *soon*—not in the Palace.

The 'journey' to ...[3] and whether Her Imperial Highness should go

[1] Götz, Count von Seckendorff. Chamberlain, later High Steward, to Crown Princess Victoria.

[2] Colonel (later General) Gustav von Sommerfeld. Aide-de-Camp of Crown Prince Friedrich Wilhelm.

[3] Dots in text. Seckendorff refers to the projected journey to Spain of the Crown Prince, who wished to be accompanied by his wife and family. Bismarck opposed this on the grounds that an official journey should not be turned into a pleasure trip.

too seems to me *de facto* not to be of great importance. Referring again to our 'little one'[1] who seizes every opportunity of sowing discord between the High Personages and the Prince [Bismarck], I would again *draw attention* to him and advise you and all well-disposed persons to watch him well. Som. will explain everything to you. The little fellow is absolute poison to us. Naturally extraordinary things are happening here with St.[2]

Hatz[feldt] must not fail to keep the High Personage [the Crown Prince] *au courant* directly or via S[ommerfeld]. This may often seem petty, but petty things often matter. A failure to do so can always be 'exploited' by the other side. [...]

Frequently interrupted and in haste

Your
G.S.

78. Bernhard von Bülow to Holstein

Paris, 13 December 1883

Dear Herr von Holstein,

It is even more difficult to bring about a clash between the French and the Chinese[3] than it was at one time to get Beckmann and Landsberg to fight a duel. Moreover the situation changes each day. We are doing our utmost to ensure that events take a course favourable to us. You can certainly be assured that in this connection also much is achieved behind the scenes! In particular the impression is widespread here that for commercial reasons Germany desires to see the dispute settled without recourse to arms.

I am most afraid of an English mediation which would mean that the fire in Tonkin would be stamped out by giving Sontay to France and Bacninh to China. In the event of any such mediation my idea would be to spread abroad a rumour that England had obtained from China the promise of the island of Hainan as broker's commission. I would telegraph this rumour, along the lines of the enclosed draft,[4] to the *Augsburger Allgemeine Zeitung* and the *Breslauer Zeitung*, publish it shortly afterwards in the *Korrespondenz*, and according to its reception, subsequently spin it out in various forms, in which mention could be made of Cyprus. I cannot believe that it would be traced back to us; more especially if I do not let it appear in the supposedly official *Post*. If you do not agree with this idea, telegraph to me at

71 Avenue Montaigne simply: *Non Charlotte*.

If it is to be published at once then: *Oui Charlotte*.

---

[1] Probably Karl von Normann. Private Secretary to Crown Princess Victoria, subsequently Aide-de-Camp to Crown Prince Friedrich Wilhelm. (See *Diaries*, entry for 5 January 1884.)

[2] Probably Albrecht von Stosch. Prussian Minister of State and Head of the Admiralty, 1872–83. (See *Diaries*, p. 37, note 1.)

[3] France had become involved in an undeclared war with China by attempting to subjugate Tonkin, which was nominally under Chinese sovereignty.

[4] Not printed.

If I hear nothing from you, I will put the rumour into circulation whenever it seems to me that the right moment has come.

Shall I get you some chocolates for Christmas?

Ever faithfully your
B.

79. Chlodwig zu Hohenlohe to Holstein

Paris, 17 December 1883

Dear Baron,

Since it seemed to me useful to discover what impression the intensification of French military preparations had made upon the Chinese Legation, I to-day returned the Marquis'[1] recent call, and as the reason for my visit mentioned the rumours circulating here of revolutionary uprisings in China so as to make it appear as if it were inspired by *sollicitude pour le Céleste Empire*. The Minister was touched by this act and assured me that the reports of revolution in China were without foundation. He added, however, that there was unrest and discontent in China occasioned partly by the conduct of French missionaries, which had given rise to incidents, as well as by the protests and claims arising out of each incident. This situation and also the fear that the War Party might overthrow the present pacifically-minded Government was the reason why he feared an open conflict with France, which would most probably lead to changes in high places. The Minister also expressed his satisfaction with the agreement between the neutral Powers for the protection of Europeans living in China, since this would of itself ensure that measures would be taken for the preservation of law and order in the country. If the fat interpreter, who never stopped smiling, translated correctly, it appeared from the Marquis' remarks that he was afraid that he and his friends would lose their posts. I pursued this train of thought, and taking his desire for peace as a starting-point, remarked that France was also afraid of war because her domestic and financial situation did not make war with China appear as a desirable eventuality. The less disposed to war China showed herself, the more bellicose France would become. Hence it became a question of whether or not the French Government was convinced that China shrank from the possibility of war. The Marquis then entered into a lengthy discussion of the negotiations with Challemel-Lacour and Ferry, and said of the former that one was never in doubt as to what he wanted, whereas Ferry used fine words but was not to be trusted. He thus did not know whether or not Ferry had decided to go to war. He refused to be drawn any further, but fell silent, so I turned the conversation to other matters in order to avoid giving the impression that I was inciting to war. Soon afterwards I took my departure. Possibly the—to me—inexplicable indiscretion in the evening edition of the *National Zeitung* of the 12th of this month (Beckmann naturally did not hear anything whatever *from us* about the conversations with Tseng) had increased his reserve. It is becoming steadily clearer to me that domestic political

[1] Marquis Tseng. Chinese Minister in Paris.

reasons, party interests, and dread of change in the organisation and personnel of the Chinese bureaucracy, play a decisive role in the Marquis' thoughts. [...]

> With kindest regards,
> Your most devoted
> C. Hohenlohe.

80. Bernhard von Bülow to Holstein

Paris, 17 December 1883

Dear Herr von Holstein,

A withdrawal of French troops from Tonkin was not unthinkable up to the conclusion of the Tonkin debate exactly a week ago. Since then, however, notwithstanding the intense and universal uneasiness over the Tonkin affair, it appears to me impossible—in so far as that word is ever to be found in a French dictionary. Everything now depends on the Chinese standing firm. Unfortunately there is little to be done with Tseng, whose fortunes are bound up with the Manchu dynasty as a son of the general who crushed the Taiping rebellion, and who is afraid that a Franco-Chinese war could bring about *internal* revolutionary changes in China that would be more disagreeable for him than humiliation abroad. We are doing our utmost to prevent his personal feelings from doing too much real damage, while at the same time we keep an eye on the French, who would sooner be out of the Tonkin imbroglio to-day than tomorrow. Would it not be possible to administer to the Chinaman in Berlin suitable doses of the cordial that we will give to Tseng drop by drop? The moment English mediation becomes a reality, I am serving a dish of roast Hainan with Cyprus wine. I have not wanted anything so much for a long time as to see the Tonkin tree grow and flourish.

Nobody was more astonished than we were by the announcement that appeared in the *National Zeitung* on the thirteenth of this month. The Ambassador and I have both maintained *absolute* secrecy about our conversations with Tseng and towards nobody more than Beckmann. Where did this indiscretion originate? It is all the more regrettable because it will still further increase Tseng's reserve. [...]

With best wishes for a happy Christmas,

> Ever faithfully your
> B. [...]

81. Bernhard von Bülow to Holstein

Paris, Saturday [22 December 1883]

Dear Herr von Holstein,

You will see in the *Augsburger Allgemeine Zeitung*, *National Zeitung*, *Breslauer Zeitung*, *Post* that my seeds have come up. Since *The Times*, after having the day before yesterday represented a French advance on Sontay as a *casus belli*,[1] to-day has already half renounced Bacninh, I will

[1] The Chinese Minister in Paris had warned the French Government that Chinese troops had occupied Sontay and that a French attack upon Sontay would be regarded by the Chinese Government as an act of war.

now cautiously try to draw attention to Yunnan. The English can hardly wish to see the French gain control of the free trade between Tonkin and Yunnan, since they themselves want to exploit South China either via Burma or from Hongkong.

The Broglie speech,[1] reported by the Ambassador,[2] clearly reveals the way in which an Orléanist restoration would set to work to disengage France from her colonial enterprises in order to be able unhindered to devote herself to building up a European coalition against us. [...]

Once again best wishes for Christmas.
Your faithful and devoted
B.

82. Bernhard von Bülow to Holstein

Paris, 29 December 1883

Dear Herr von Holstein,

Yesterday I dined with two old acquaintances of whom the first, Pallain, is a member of the Council of State and a Director in the Ministry of Finance, while the second, Francis Charmes, is editor of the *Débats* and a Deputy, and was formerly Head of a Department in the Ministry of Foreign Affairs. At the outset of their careers both men belonged to the circle round Thiers, later stood close to Gambetta, and now stand on equally good terms with Ferry, Grévy,[3] and Léon Say and seem likely to have distinguished political careers.

Our conversation naturally turned on the Tonkin affair, in which they condemned England's attitude with a bitterness unequalled even by the Press here. Even after England had driven France from Canada and the East Indies, and acquired immense colonies in every part of the world, she still grudged France the smallest gain; everywhere France found herself confronted by England. My acquaintances described the occupation of Egypt by England as the heaviest blow that had fallen on France since 1871. Who would venture to prophesy that France would ever again establish herself on the Nile? England also added insult to injury. Mrs Gladstone had asked Madame Waddington[4] if she knew Clemenceau.[5] When Madame Waddington, who was somewhat annoyed by the question, replied that she did not receive red revolutionaries, Mrs Gladstone said that Mr Gladstone looked upon Clemenceau as the most outstanding and distinguished of present-day French statesmen. At this point Pallain interrupted to remark that while it was natural that the English should be grateful to Clemenceau for having helped to obtain

---

[1] Jacques, Duc de Broglie. Minister for Foreign Affairs, 1873–4; Prime Minister, May–November 1877.

[2] Hohenlohe reported on 22 December that the Duc de Broglie had sharply criticised the Republic and held it responsible for France's isolation in Europe. (From the Foreign Ministry files.)

[3] Jules Grévy. President of the French Republic, 1879–85; 1886–7.

[4] The wife of the French Ambassador in London.

[5] Georges Clemenceau. French Deputy. Leader of the Extreme Left. Prime Minister and Minister of the Interior, 1906–9.

Egypt for them, they did not need to say so with such naïveté. Pallain also took this opportunity to observe that he found it wholly incomprehensible that for decades France should have sought the alliance with England, which Talleyrand had already likened to that of a rider and his horse, only that England was the rider. On the other hand France and Germany were enemies simply because of a small strip of land, whereas in everything else their interests nowhere clashed. France was dissipating her energy by concentrating her thoughts and efforts exclusively on the achievement of *revanche*, instead of following Austria's example. Shortly after the last war an influential man who was Minister of the Interior, Picard, had said to him that the most sensible thing that France could do would be to seek an alliance with Germany. This was an idea that Gambetta entertained more often than was suspected. The Imperial Chancellor had had no greater admirer than Gambetta, who had studied nothing so zealously as the speeches and dispatches of Prince Bismarck, had quoted him at every opportunity, and had sought to disseminate as widely as possible his ideas, particularly in regard to economic and social problems, in the belief that the future belonged to them. Unfortunately Gambetta had feared that he would lose the halo he had acquired in 1870–1 if he ceased to appear before the ignorant masses as a man of the *revanche*; yet even on his sick-bed he had debated the question whether an offensive and defensive alliance between Germany and France on some such basis as the return of Lorraine might not be possible.

Charmes, in commenting on his friend's—Pallain's—remarks, said that Gambetta had been the only French statesman who had had sufficient authority to bring about a real rapprochement with Germany. Public opinion in France was not yet sufficiently prepared for it. If the French were to hear tomorrow that their Government had reached an understanding with Germany, they would feel like a man who had had a jug of cold water suddenly poured over him. On the other hand the great majority of people here had very little desire and spirit for a war with Germany. Even should war break out between Germany and Russia, France would certainly at first wait and see what happened; if Germany sustained defeats she would as a matter of course take up arms to regain Alsace-Lorraine—but only in that event. Charmes is of the opinion that the interests of France and Russia are even more incompatible than those of France and England. The sympathy for Russia that unquestionably exists here is the expression of a shortsighted rancour against us: for Germany could at the worst allow the Russians to become masters of Constantinople, whereas France as a Mediterranean Power cannot.

My two acquaintances were in agreement that it is becoming more and more clear here that the Imperial Chancellor's foreign policy in general, and in particular the understanding between Germany, Austria-Hungary, and Italy, has only the maintenance of peace as an aim. Naturally I strongly supported this opinion, although for the most part I had only been an attentive listener to their other remarks. If I may allow myself to add my own decided opinion, I would say that apart from its impracticability for other reasons, the retrocession of Lorraine would do little to alter our relations with France. France would thankfully accept Lorraine and official circles would be overflowing with goodwill towards us for a few weeks, until one fine morning Déroulède[1] would parade before the statue of Strasbourg with some hundreds of idlers from the Patriotic League and cry : *Vive l'Alsace quand même!*; the majority of the Press would join in; Pallain, Charmes and a few other sensible Frenchmen would be sorry without saying so aloud; the ministers would maintain that such demonstrations cannot be forbidden in a free country; and there matters would rest as they do to-day, only with the difference that without Metz we should have to augment the garrison in Alsace and spend money on fortifications. On the other hand the remarks of my acquaintances seem to me to be not uninteresting as affording fresh proof of how greatly a more active French colonial policy is capable of making the French aware of the disadvantages of the notion of *revanche*, of demonstrating to them that they have other rivals besides ourselves, and, above all, of improving their feelings towards us. In conclusion I would respectfully ask that the information that I am sending you in this manner at the desire of the Ambassador should be regarded as very confidential, so as to avoid compromising Frenchmen who are not only well-disposed towards us but also serve as useful sources of information.

Your most devoted
Bernh. Bülow

[1] Paul Déroulède. Founder and President of the French League of Patriots.

1884

83. Kuno zu Rantzau to Holstein

Seeburg, 6 January 1884

My dear Holstein,

I thank you most sincerely for your friendly and sympathetic words.[1] In the course of time it will perhaps be a consolation to me that my mother knew how much I loved her; but at present I am dominated by the feeling of how small my love was in comparison with hers and how small was the return I made for her indescribable tenderness and self-sacrifice.

I return to Friedrichsruh tomorrow evening.

With the very best wishes
I am
Your faithful friend
Rantzau.

84. Herbert von Bismarck to Holstein

St Petersburg, 22 January 1884

Dear Holstein,

Besides his wife, Saburov[2] shall take along a greeting to you from me. Otherwise I must admit that I still don't have much to say from here. I have put together a report[3] that goes off to-day, after I had finally persuaded Schweinitz to send the Jomini [letters].[4] He gave them to me to read, but was of the opinion that they were not suitable for submission. The final passage seems to me the most remarkable: *what* the Russians want at present is perhaps not clear to themselves, but there can be no doubt as to the ultimate object of their desires—that we should abandon Austria to them, by that I mean to the Pan-Slavists, not the

---

[1] On the occasion of the death of Rantzau's mother.

[2] Peter Saburov. Russian Ambassador in Berlin, 1880–4.

[3] By 'report' Herbert von Bismarck meant a private letter to his father of 21 January. According to a note in the Foreign Ministry files, it was submitted to the Kaiser and then returned to the Chancellor without a copy being left in the files.

[4] In his dispatch of 20 January, Schweinitz stated that in accordance with his instructions he had sent a letter to Giers to inform him of the German *gravamina* concerning Russian troop concentrations on her frontier and the Pan-Slavist speeches by high-ranking Russian officers. Schweinitz enclosed with his dispatch two letters which Jomini had addressed to him. In the first Jomini described the troop concentrations on Russia's western frontier as defensive precautions against Austria, and concluded by pointing out that the existing mistrust was not to be overcome by official visits but only by deeds. In the second letter Jomini stated that Schweinitz's letter to Giers had been submitted to the Tsar, who had read it carefully but without comment. (From the Foreign Ministry files. See also *Denkwürdigkeiten des Botschafters General von Schweinitz* (Berlin, 1927), vol. II, pp. 258-9,

Tsar, who wants peace at any price. Unfortunately the former are the stronger as a consequence of the apathy and other *shortcomings* of the Tsar.

Schweinitz is kindness itself. He offered me his children's rooms as a flat and I am moving in to-day. The other members of the Embassy staff are very companionable fellows and I am received with every distinction by society here. At first, however, it is always tiresome and boring. [...]

Now farewell, regards to Bill and Rottenburg.[1]

Ever your
HB.

85. Herbert von Bismarck to Holstein

St Petersburg, 27 January 1884

Dear Holstein,

[...] I only want to add that I trust Dolgoruki[2] more and more. He must be cultivated and well treated, he is one of the few with whom the Tsar talks intimately and to whom he will listen; he hates Saburov and is working for his removal. '*Si on l'envoye à Paris, il deviendra rédacteur-en-chef de* l'Antiprussien', he said to me. He also expressed the wish that I should become *Chargé d'Affaires* for a time because the Tsar would then talk to me personally about politics—or so he thinks. Schweinitz will go on leave on 23 March; three–four weeks, but that won't work either because *more solito* eight days later I leave for Berlin for the 1st of April.[3] Dolg. wants to work for a meeting in late summer between the three Emperors (in our case the Crown Prince) and will try to get Shuvalov[4] instead of Orlov[5] sent to Paris. All this *secretissime*. Perhaps you will get my letter to my father[6] to read.

Farewell for this time,
Ever faithfully
Your HB.

86. Herbert von Bismarck to Holstein

St Petersburg, 5 February 1884

Dear Holstein,

[...] I have recently written to you that Dolgoruki is a person of the utmost usefulness. His ambition is to be Ambassador in Berlin and for that purpose he naturally needs good connections. I have worked an invitation for him to Friedrichsruh, where he will arrive next week.

Please keep absolutely secret what I recently wrote to you about a meeting of the three monarchs. Dolgur. said to me yesterday that he is

[1] Dr Franz Johannes von Rottenburg. Member of the Reich Chancellery staff, 1881–90; Under State Secretary in the Ministry of the Interior, 1894–5.
[2] Nicholas, Prince Dolgoruki. Russian Military Plenipotentiary in Berlin, 1879–87.
[3] Otto von Bismarck's birthday.
[4] Peter, Count Shuvalov. Russian Ambassador in London, 1874–9.
[5] Nicholas, Prince Orlov. Russian Ambassador in Paris, 1872–84, in Berlin 1884–5.
[6] Of 27 January. (See *Grosse Politik*, vol. III, no. 617, pp. 315–18.)

speaking to nobody about it for the present, since the chief condition for its realisation is that nothing should leak out about it before the Tsar has come to a decision—and that takes a long time. I am now beginning to know my way about fairly well and to feel firm ground beneath my feet. It has happened more quickly than I had thought. Women here are very useful if one wants to get on, which was not at all the case in England. Here they are more interested in politics than the men on the average. [...]

Now farewell.
Ever your
HB.

87. Johanna von Bismarck to Holstein

Friedrichsruh, 7 February 1884

My heartfelt thanks, dear Herr von Holstein, first of all for your friendly sympathy, and then because in my own heart I was filled with many depressing thoughts in *that* regard, which I did not express for there is such a Schweninger[1]-worship in my family that they are almost prepared to stone or strangle anyone who does not regard the dear doctor as in every way infallible. I have of course great faith in him and owe him much gratitude, which I never forget—but I cannot help it if I am sometimes worried about Bill's treatment—and just now I am again badly worried by this sudden strange illness—of which I had no notion—was indeed terribly shocked when I heard about it—and now I find my darling boy so changed that I must take hold of myself to avoid crying whenever I look at him. So I thank you a hundred times more for your little note, which was a great comfort to me; God bless you for it, dear Herr von Holstein, and may He be gracious to us and grant that we may be able to help our dearly loved Bill so that he will *soon* be as he always was! I think and worry so much about my dearly loved boy.

Yesterday I got a cheerful, sensible letter from Herbert. God be thanked for it!—In old friendship

Your J.B.

88. Herbert von Bismarck to Holstein

St Petersburg, 8 February 1884

Dear Holstein,

[...] I am so glad that you have read my various letters.[2] But please tell any others who have read them that the proposed meeting of the three [Emperors] must be handled with special discretion. If anything were to leak out about it before the right time, it will come to nothing and personally I think it could do much good. I mean above all that nothing should leak out to the Crown Prince's Household, possibly

[1] Dr Ernst Schweninger. Prince Bismarck's doctor from 1881.
[2] Herbert von Bismarck means his letters to the Chancellor. (See *Grosse Politik*, vol. III, nos. 617, 618, 621, pp. 315–20, 323–4.)

during reports by Hatzf[eldt] or Busch, since it is unfortunately well known that *there* nothing is kept secret. H[ere],[1] and in the three-sided relationship in general, much—if not everything—can be [achieved][1] by *really* clever diplomacy as it is now conducted by us thanks to His Highness. Austrian policy is too crude; if ours were at any time to be con[ducted][1] in the same way, then nothing in my opinion could prevent the collision between Austria and Russia. We must work continually on this problem, as though [ ][1] were always present. At present, fear of us holds everything here—thanks to the enormous prestige of my father—but the day will come when the cry 'Will you come with me, lovely boy?' will be heard in more pressing tones—just like the prostitute who finally seizes an unwilling passer-by by the coat-tails even though he already has another girl on his arm. Perhaps it must always come to blows in such cases, and especially when 'Louis' is near at hand and ready for a fight. But so long as it is possible to promenade with one on each arm and put them off with sweet lies, one should do it. Long walks cool the desires—as you no doubt know from experience? —and perhaps the importunate party may get tired, sit down by the wayside, or get a touch of domestic colic.

I have thoroughly prepared Dolgoruki to be on his guard against Bleichröder,[2] he was at first pretty astonished, but in the end amused and laughing scornfully.[3]

It is certainly a good thing that Bill is going to Nice. God grant that he recovers quickly and has a good time on the wonderful Mediterranean, of which I always think with a certain longing!

Farewell.

Ever faithfully,

Your HB.

89. Herbert von Bismarck to Holstein

St Petersburg, 22 February 1884

Dear Holstein,

The courier leaves tomorrow and so I will entrust him with my thanks for your last letter of the 16th, which has been burnt as you wished.

I regret that the Bavarian financial affair[4] has got into Bleichröder's hands, because I look on the filthy Jew as an evil in himself and am sorry for anyone who is or will be forced to enter into business relations with him. Naturally I do not know what induced my father to prefer to deal with the matter through bankers rather than *per imperatorem*. From Friedrichsruh I hear virtually nothing of a business nature, and Rantzau only writes when a courier leaves, and then invariably just before the bag is closed, briefly and hurriedly.

[1] Pasted over in the original.
[2] Gerson Bleichröder. Head of the Berlin Bank of that name, and banker to Prince Bismarck.
[3] See *Diaries*, entry for 12 February 1884.
[4] The King of Bavaria needed a loan to meet his debts. (See *Diaries*, entries for February 1884.)

The motives that you mention obviously do not come into question; you yourself cannot seriously have thought that my father would undertake an affair of high political importance in order to obtain a title or an order for that stinking brute Bleichröder. If some of the other points in your letter had reached Friedrichsruh it would perhaps have been very useful. The intimate relationship between my father and the head of the Foreign Ministry is far too loose and unsatisfactory, and since Hatzfeldt simply does not write at all, it would be desirable that someone else should. When I was with my father in recent years, you for the most part kept me informed; you do not seem to be doing this with Rantzau. Thus only the regular incoming documents reach my father, and at best short numbered political reports, though even these are rare. In this way contact, not to mention an intimate acquaintance with affairs, cannot be maintained when he stays away for six or seven months. In Bülow's time my father was away from Berlin more than seven months, but Bülow's custom of conducting a confidential correspondence by daily private letters enabled my father to keep more closely in touch with everything that went on in Berlin above and below stairs than even by personal contact. Reticence in the end easily gives rise to distrust—old Bülow knew that well—and how is my father to form a correct estimate of certain situations, when it is often a question of the shading of specific points, if he only receives official communications? The countless nuances, which can be decisive, cannot be expressed in them, but they can be expressed in private letters and in correspondence with the acting secretary. [...]

                              Now farewell
                              Ever your
                              HB.

90. Johanna von Bismarck to Holstein

Friedrichsruh, 24 February 1884

[...] Dear Herr von Holstein, have you not yet the least desire to see Friedrichsruh in its new dress? How would it be if you would decide quickly to come here for a few days to see how comfortably we now live here? The weather is so inviting for the short journey, flowers are budding, larches singing, and if you are gracious enough to want news of me, it is really much simpler for you to convince yourself with your own eyes that I am exactly as I was at Christmas. I talk unwillingly of myself and my crustiness, it is far too boring a subject. Bismarck, thank God, is well—the five Rantzaus also, and above all Schweninger's letters and Bill's telegrams have a cheerful ring—as do Herbert's letters—for which I constantly thank God. If the health of my dear ones is good and satisfactory, it really does not matter whether my old stomach gives me more or less pain. At any rate for *me* it is a matter of complete indifference—and I have no time to think about it because I am too happy about Bill and all of my family. God help him still further to a complete, splendid recovery for all time, and bring him back to us in a few weeks, well and in good spirits!

God be with you, dear Herr von Holstein, and may I say: To a speedy meeting here?
We would really be overjoyed!
All good wishes from your devoted
J.B.

91. Bernhard von Bülow to Holstein

Paris, 1 March 1884

Dear Herr von Holstein,

[...] I am much gratified by your praise of my journalistic activity. In order that you may be able to direct and possibly to correct me, I enclose an anthology chosen from the articles which I have written in the last fortnight and have had published partly directly, partly through the *Korrespondenz*, in various newspapers.[1] I endeavoured to further French colonial policy, while at the same time taking care that the French situation should not exaggeratedly be admired—especially in Southern Germany and Austria. Finally it seemed useful to me to demonstrate in the *National Zeitung* (which is read in a high place) by a striking example that England and her ruling House are not so favourably judged in France as members of that House sometimes take for granted.[2] [...]

As ever faithfully your
B.

92. Johanna von Bismarck to Holstein

Friedrichsruh, 3 March 1884

[...] I have just had an affectionate cheerful letter from my dear Herbert, and before that a telegram from Bill *tout va bien, temps beau!*—that was preceded some days ago by a letter from Schwen[inger] which said that the dear boy was so well that he (Schw.) could cheerfully leave—which he did on 29 Feb.—to console his patients in Munich who were eagerly demanding him. God be praised for all the good done to my dear boy! I had asked Bill not to write to me if it took too much out of him, but only to telegraph—he is certainly sticking to that now—I think he could now write a letter without injuring himself—but if he doesn't want to, he need not bother—if only I know that he is well. How do you find Schweinitz? I am outraged about the old cry-baby, who keeps my beloved boy tied down in St Petersburg on account of his sentimental exaggerated love of his children in Wiesbaden, so that I cannot have him [Herbert] for my 60th birthday. I am absolutely furious—and as I probably won't be able to see Bill either—I have a great desire to spend the birthday here—also hope that we will do so.

It is a thousand times more beautiful here than in loathsome old

---
[1] Not printed.

[2] The article in the *National Zeitung* of 24 February criticised the tactless review by the French newspaper *République Française* of the recently published memoirs of Queen Victoria, *More Leaves from the Journal of a Life in the Highlands, from 1862 to 1882* (London, 1884).

Berlin. Farewell, dear Herr von Holstein, many thanks for your letters and please write again to

Your devoted
J.B.

93. Herbert von Bismarck to Holstein

St Petersburg, 3 March 1884

Dear Holstein,

[...] What you write to me about Bleichröder is not pleasant. At most it is possible to do something about the fellow and his intrigues if one is there, that is in Friedrichsruh. I am very sorry that Rantzau did not submit Rottenburg's letter, and think it a mistake.[1] My father on the whole knows that Bl. is a filthy swine, but it is absolutely necessary to remind him of the fact from time to time by obvious proofs, so that the impression is never temporarily erased. Bl., like most of his kind, is sometimes useful, but only if one treats them badly and keeps them in constant fear. I am afraid this does not happen often enough.

I think it would be positively lamentable if we were to float a big Russian loan; the money that the Russians would get would only be used for military, naval and propaganda purposes. The Tsar knows nothing at all about this, nor can one expect him to understand financial matters or to concern himself with them. The news about Orlov and Bleich.[2] seems to me hardly credible, it would be too foolish for a [ ][3] Ambassador thus to deliver himself [into][3] the hands of a banker. I would prefer to think that Orlov only wants to entice Bleichröder, and it would be perfectly natural for a Russian if Dolgoruki were to do the same the moment Bl. is prepared to make a loan; the Russians desperately need money, their strategical constructions are costing frightful sums; they will get nothing in London, probably nothing in Paris either, only Berlin remains, and why shouldn't a Russian descend to dirty tricks to achieve something useful for his country?

You will remember from our reports in the middle or end of January that the daughter of the Paris Rothschild,[4] Madame Ephrussi,[5] was invited to a Court Ball here, to the universal indignation of Society, because it had never happened to a Jewess before. Already at that time negotiations were going on with Ephrussi for a loan and, with Rothschild behind him, he probably put pressure on Bleichröder. It would indeed be depressing if still more German money were to be tied up in Russian paper—but there is nothing to be done about the fools who do so. In England nobody would dream of such a thing! Of course they make up for it by conducting an all the more stupid foreign policy, which also costs them a lot of good money!

[1] Rottenburg had informed Rantzau of a scandal in which Bleichröder was involved. (See *Diaries*, entries for 18 and 27 February 1884.)
[2] See *Diaries*, entry for 18 February 1884.
[3] The original letter is torn at this point.
[4] Meyer Alphonse von Rothschild.
[5] In a dispatch of 30 January Schweinitz had reported 'that a Jew from Odessa, Herr Ephrussi, and his wife, a Paris Rothschild, are being fêted in the most fashionable circles'. (From the Foreign Ministry files.)

I am indeed sorry that I will not be coming to Berlin at the end of March. Now it will probably not be until well into May, and it would be extremely useful if I could put in a word personally. Schweinitz is so anxious to get to his wife that he will be staying only half a day in Berlin, and even then he says nothing without being asked. It is a pity, by the way, that he has that wife and family; he would be ten times more useful without them, for he certainly has more understanding and knows more than the rest of our ambassadors—not that that is saying a great deal. His chief *shortcomings* are: cold egoism, secretive reserve, and a stiffness of manner, which he regards as 'dignity', and also a number of pet prejudices to which he holds fast, sometimes against his better knowledge. Nevertheless one can talk sensibly with him about politics and he reads and ponders over the incoming documents. If he had a wife as I should like to picture an ambassadress of the German Empire, and if he understood how to cut a fine figure, then everybody here, where so much importance is still attached to such things, would be at his feet. Ideals, however, are never realised!

Now farewell.

Ever your HB. [...]

94. Johanna von Bismarck to Holstein

Friedrichsruh, 5 March 1884

Please, dear Herr von Holstein, tell all the fools who are spreading childish stupid lies about Bismarck and Saburov, that they should keep their mouths shut because not a single word is true.[1] Bismarck does not dislike him at all, and I positively like him—to the fury and astonishment of all who cannot stand him—which, it seems to me, is the case with the majority of the Berliners. He alone has ruined himself by his intrigues against Giers—Bismarck has never tried to get rid of him either by praise or censure, and would be very glad if he came once again to Friedrichsruh. So would I; and I think he will come. [...]

Many thanks for your letter and best regards from all.

J.v.B.
[...]

95. Paul von Hatzfeldt to Holstein

10 March [1884]

The Kaiser told me that the Grand Duke[2] had said *nothing against* Herb., but spoke *equally well of Berchem*[3] *and Herbert*. He had written in this sense to the Prince, and now one must await developments.[4]

[1] See *Diaries*, entries for 26 January, 7–8 February, 9 March 1884.
[2] Friedrich I, Grand Duke of Baden, 1856–1907.
[3] Max, Count von Berchem. First Secretary in the St Petersburg Embassy, 1875–8, in Vienna, 1878–83; Chargé d'Affaires in Stockholm, 1884; Director of the Economic Policy Division of the Foreign Ministry, 1885–6; Under State Secretary, 1886–90.
[4] Hatzfeldt had asked the Kaiser if Herbert von Bismarck would be acceptable as Prussian Minister in Karlsruhe (Baden). (See *Diaries*, entry for 4 May 1884.)

Moreover he kept on repeating that it would be a great pity to take Herb. away from St Petersburg now. I told him that it had never been intended to leave him there for any length of time; he was only there provisionally and was not on the regular establishment. The Kaiser himself said that he was an outstanding diplomat who would certainly have to be given an important post soon. But he would not give him a greater post, even if one were to fall vacant, as long as he was still only a Councillor of Embassy. Perhaps it might be possible to make some changes by means of which Herb. would receive a better transitional post—Stuttgart or something similar; His Majesty then remarked that this would not be much better professionally than Karlsruhe, which at least had importance through Court and dynastic relationships.

The Kaiser realises perfectly well that something must be done and that it is of importance that it should be done. If one were able to make a definite proposal to him—which would be easy if Eisendecher were transferred and if he saw that Herb was not to remain much longer in St Petersburg anyway, he would certainly agree.

I have done my part to prepare the ground. I will probably not receive any thanks—at best unpleasantness.

PH.

96. Herbert von Bismarck to Holstein

10 March 1884

[...] Schweinitz' report about A[lexander] III is interesting;[1] he has never had such a long conversation with the Tsar before. It confirms all my observations: we alone are preventing the hatred of Austria from erupting. Franz Joseph and Kálnoky[2] should burn large candles to us. Ill-feeling towards Vienna is also being nourished by Austrian indolence in the matter of the extradition of political criminals.[3]

Vannovski[4] and Obrutshev[5] simply tell the Tsar a pack of lies and Werder[6] everywhere talks in the same sense that 'the massing of troops means nothing, the Russian was such a good fellow'. For this reason they all want to keep Werder here.

Lignitz, incidentally, would no longer be suitable to take his place, now that the Tsar is mistrustful. Both must be changed—that is to say not the Tsar and L., but W. and L.[7] [...]

HB.

[1] Of 9 March 1884. (See *Grosse Politik*, vol. III, no. 628, pp. 331–2.)
[2] Gustav, Count Kálnoky von Köröspatak. Austro-Hungarian Ambassador in St Petersburg, 1880–1; Foreign Minister, 1881–95.
[3] See above, p. 55, note 2.
[4] General Peter Vannovski. Russian War Minister, 1881–97.
[5] General Nicholas Obrutshev. Chief of the Russian General Staff, 1881–98.
[6] Bernhard von Werder. Prussian Lieutenant-General; Military Plenipotentiary in St Petersburg, 1869–86; Governor of Berlin, 1886–8; Ambassador in St Petersburg, 1892–5.
[7] See above, note 1. According to the portion of the report not printed in the *Grosse Politik*, the principal subject of the conversation was the concentration of Russian troops on Russia's western frontier and the tension to which this gave rise. The Tsar did not want to admit that Germany had any grounds for feeling herself threatened. He spoke sceptically about a possible joint action of the three Imperial Powers against the anarchists, praised General Werder, and allowed it to be seen that he entertained a certain mistrust of Lignitz. (From the Foreign Ministry files.)

97. Holstein to Hugo von Radolinski[1]

Berlin, [31 March 1884]

Dear Radolinski,

I think Seckendorff's plan[2] is splendid and have given the advice to go straight ahead. But we will say *nothing* to our mutual friend.[3] He himself will be sincerely glad, but she[4] will boil over with rage at the thought that you, and more especially the little hot-tempered Mrs T.,[5] will come here again. Yes, I would like to see the face that the said *she* will make when she hears this news.

I can assure you in advance that the Big Chief[6] will be pleased by the change in this important post; besides I am prepared to present the matter to him at the right moment. Seckendorff does not wish it at present, and I must leave the choice of the time to him since it is *facenda sua*.

For myself I can only say that the prospect of having you both here again was one of the most joyful bits of news that I can remember receiving for a long time.

For *you* the change is perhaps a beckoning of fate to get you out of a position from which there was no recognisable way out. I am somewhat superstitious in these matters.

For Doudouce[7] the climate of Berlin at all events proved itself better than that of Weimar.

Ever yours
Holstein.

You are keeping the matter completely secret?

98. Bernhard von Bülow to Holstein

Algiers, 18 April 1884

Dear Herr von Holstein,

You have always been so kind to me and I feel not only politically but also personally so attached to you that I venture to ask for your advice and help in a matter that is decisive for my future.

My situation is as follows: exactly eight years ago, in the spring of

---

[1] Hugo Leszczyc, Count von Radolin-Radolinski; from 1888 Prince von Radolin. Prussian Minister in Weimar, October 1882–May 1884; High Chamberlain of Crown Prince Friedrich Wilhelm, 1884–8; Ambassador in Constantinople, 1892–5, in St Petersburg, 1895–1900, in Paris, 1900–10. The document is from the Radolin Papers.

[2] To make Radolin High Chamberlain to the Crown Prince. (See Friedrich Thimme, 'Aus dem Nachlass des Fürsten Radolin. Fürst Radolin, Holstein und Friedrich Rosen, *Berliner Monatshefte*, vol. XV, p. 733.)

[3] Paul von Hatzfeldt.

[4] Countess Helene von Hatzfeldt.

[5] Mrs Julia Tyrrell, the younger sister of Radolin's deceased wife, Lucy *née* Wakefield. Mrs Tyrrell was the mother of Sir Edward Grey's Private Secretary, Sir William (later Lord) Tyrrell, who subsequently became Permanent Under Secretary of State in the Foreign Office and finally British Ambassador in Paris. Mrs Tyrrell looked after Radolin's household affairs after the death of Countess Lucy in March 1880.

[6] Otto von Bismarck.

[7] Nickname for Lucy Josephine Julie, Radolin's daughter, who was married to Karl, Count von Moy de Sons on 23 January 1899.

1876, I became acquainted in Vienna with Countess Marie Dönhoff,[1] née Princess Camporeale, and fell in love with her. My relations with Count Dönhoff soon became embarrassing. Consequently I got myself transferred to Athens in the autumn of 1876 with the resolve, however, never to give up Countess Dönhoff and to set her free from her unhappy situation as soon as possible. Ever since I have always kept in touch with her by letter, have often seen her, without anyone noticing anything. In the summer of 1881 I induced Countess D. to start obtaining a divorce from Count D. Although the marriage had been a failure from the outset and for ten years neither of them had spoken a friendly word to the other—much less shaken each other's hand—Count D. energetically opposed a divorce. It was only after endless negotiations back and forth that D. was brought to the point at which in 1882 he sued for a divorce because of 'wilful desertion'. The divorce decree was issued on 18 June 1883. Countess D. had finally left Dresden in the spring of 1881. The proceedings were carried through in a decent manner without *de part et d'autre* bringing forward any recriminations or reproaches. The public paid no attention to the divorce proceedings. Count D. moreover had and has no idea that the divorce was on my account and was conducted by me behind the scenes. Nobody knows this with the exception of the very few people whom we were compelled to take into our confidence. I have kept that secret so well that last winter the stupid rumour went round that Countess D. had married the painter Lenbach or wanted to marry him. Nobody has any notion that I am the person in question. I will never let the world know that the divorce was on my account or reveal the true course of events. I will act as if I had met Countess D. for the first time after a long interval when I meet her this summer as if by accident. I plan to become engaged in the late autumn and to marry in December.

It would be a relief for the Catholic relatives of Countess D., especially her only brother Prince Camporeale and her stepfather Minghetti,[2] if her marriage with Count D. were annulled by the Church. An annulment could probably be obtained in Rome. On the one hand, however, Countess D. in the event of a second marriage would have to promise to allow her children to be brought up as Catholics and on the other a canonical divorce customarily costs two or three hundred thousand francs. Since we are neither wealthy enough to raise this sum nor I myself in particular am willing to allow even any possible daughters to be brought up as Catholics, it seems to me better if Countess D. were to become a Protestant, which in any case accords with her way of thinking. I take this opportunity of remarking that you must not think that Countess D. is politically unreliable because she is friendly with the Crown Princess. To tell the truth, up to now she understands very little of politics, but of course she will never have any political views other than my own. As to property, Countess D. receives an assured

[1] Divorced from Count Karl Dönhoff on 31 March 1883; born 6 February 1848, the daughter of Prince Domenico Camporeale and Donna Laura Minghetti, whose second husband was Marco Minghetti.

[2] Marco Minghetti. Italian Prime Minister, 1862–4; 1873–6.

income of 18,000 Fr. from her Sicilian estates which Minghetti manages for her, so that we will be able to manage. She naturally took nothing from Count D. as a result of the divorce. Dear Herr von Holstein, I am very conscious of the importance of the step I intend to take, even as I have also for a long time borne in mind the many and weighty reasons against it. I know that it is precisely those whose judgment I most value who will deplore my action, and that is very painful to me. But I can do nothing else. If I were to give up this—intellectually and emotionally—exceptionally gifted woman, who is life itself to me, who has afforded me so many proofs of love and loyalty and wholly entrusted herself to me, I would not know another happy moment and would be a broken man. I have regarded it as my duty to do what I could to preserve the *dehors*. By means of patience and caution I have succeeded in achieving in this regard whatever was at all possible. But nothing will prevent me from carrying through what I have been striving for for eight years. I will never leave Countess D., not even if my marriage to her were to oblige me to resign.

You know how devoted I am to the Service. You will give me my due that the difficulties of the situation in which I have found myself since 1876, and especially the anxieties and efforts associated with the divorce proceedings, never prevented me from carrying out my duties. I would very much like to continue in the Service, when at last peace after so many battles will strengthen my powers of work and make me more competent than I have been up to now. If, however, after the announcement of my engagement I do not receive official consent to my marriage, I will proffer my resignation. In that eventuality I think of settling in Heidelberg.

If you however think that it is possible for me to stay on, I ask you kindly to advise me how I can best act. I have no doubts whatever that as a married man I cannot be in Paris. There is no divorce in France, society is clerical in sympathies, even the official world has lately revealed Catholic leanings. Society and government circles alike would take pleasure in seizing the opportunity of ill-treating a Catholic turned Protestant, half Italian, half German. I am too proud to expose myself to such a situation, and in such circumstances would also be unable to carry on with my duties in Paris. In my opinion I would in comparison encounter far fewer difficulties in St Petersburg; it would also probably be possible in Sofia, Alexandria, Tangiers or Belgrade. I would not like to serve with Radowitz. If one is able and willing to keep me in the Service, it would naturally greatly ease my position if I were transferred from Paris to another post before my projected marriage became known.

Now that my decision is unalterable, it would not seem right to me to delay my marriage beyond Christmas. On the one hand it could gradually become known that the divorce was on my account, and this would worsen my situation, and on the other it is really necessary for the sake of my health for me to be finally freed from years of uncertainty. But I intend to announce my engagement only a very short time—two to three weeks—before the marriage. You will appreciate how tremendously important it is for me that until that time nothing is found out about my intentions.

I would like to say one thing more: you will have heard that Countess D. is an intimate friend of the Crown Princess, who even received her in Potsdam and Italy after the divorce, knows about our affair, and would certainly be willing at the decisive moment energetically to put in a good word for us. I would, however, rather not have to rely for support solely on this quarter. I am a Bismarck supporter and will remain so *usque ad mortem*, even if the Chancellor throws me out. The Crown Prince does not know that the divorce was on my account; it is probably better for me that he shouldn't. His feelings for Countess D. are most friendly. Seckendorff is *au courant* of the affair, as he is of everything that interests the Crown Princess.

In Berlin nobody knows of my situation and plans. I have informed my brother Adolf[1] of them at the same time as you. It would be very kind if you would allow him to speak to you about them. I know that you will look upon my news as a deep secret for the present from all quarters. I want to talk to Herbert when I have heard what you have to say. Perhaps it would be better if I spoke to him myself about the matter, so that he, who like you has always been a true friend of mine, should not think I do not trust him. As far as Hohenlohe is concerned, it would probably be better if I told him later on.

I am writing to you from Algiers partly because I have quiet here, whereas in Paris I will certainly find a great deal of work waiting for me, partly because I do not like to delay any longer in putting my situation before you. However my fate may be decided in due course, I will always be in gratitude, admiration and loyalty your

Bernh. Bülow

I have only registered the letter in order that it may arrive safely. There is no money with it. On the 26th of this month I will be back in Paris.

99. Herbert von Bismarck to Holstein

St Petersburg, 26 April 1884, at night

Dear Holstein,

Most hearty thanks for your kind letter and the postscript of the day before yesterday. That Schweinitz has had enough of me I could see from the various long talks I was obliged to have with him since his return. From his personal standpoint one cannot blame him, since during his absence my personal position here has grown too important for his liking, as he has learned partly from letters and partly from personal observations in the last twenty-four hours. In general I am at a disadvantage in my personal relationship with him because I am straightforward if brusque, whereas he has the manners of the Russian people. Nevertheless my method has the advantage in that at times, and against

---

[1] Adolf von Bülow. From 1879 Aide-de-Camp to Prince Wilhelm of Prussia.

his will, his innate violence forces him to speak out frankly: thus, for example, he let slip to-day that he had proved to His Majesty that to remove me from here would no longer be of any importance. *Tant mieux*, even though it was not intended in the way it will work out.

Posts like my present one are indeed always difficult and delicate for me. I must force myself into too small a bed, for a secretary's position can only be combined with the importance of my name by a very great display of pliability, and even then not for any length of time. With Münster it was different; in the first place he was after all a finer character and quite content if the work was done for him, and then he was alone, while Schweinitz is burdened with the enormous *drawback* of the stupid Werder, who has more influence over him than one might think and is for that reason injurious; it is a scandalous shame that he is here!

As for 'fooling around', I cannot help it, and the work is nevertheless more conscientiously done than under Schweinitz alone. I have re-organised the entire filing system; formerly nothing could be found, now everything goes like clockwork. If I were to sleep the night away while I am here, I would hear and see nothing. I acted no differently in London and consequently learnt more in a year and a quarter than sleepyheads in ten times that time.

It is an exaggeration that I always stay up until 4 o'clock. Now—for example—it is only 2:45 and I will shortly go to bed. To be sure, I have already been at a *souper-soirée*, but that is all in the way of duty here and you can believe me when I say that I have not operated in vain. [...]

The way in which you have written about my mother has shocked and much depressed me. I am deeply concerned about her weakness and suffering and ask you to write to me frankly how things are. Schweninger will be back in Berlin before this letter and he will tell you everything. If it is as bad as it unhappily seems to be from your letter, I will come to Berlin, for I would have no peace here; my heart aches too much, I long to see my mother again and to help her.

Now farewell. In three and a half weeks at the latest we will see each other again, even if I carry on here to the last moment, and then I will be able to tell you much which would be too long to write or that is too full of delicate nuances.

Ever your
HB.

100. Bernhard von Bülow to Holstein

Paris, 8 May 1884

Dear Herr von Holstein,

I was deeply moved by your kind letter of the 28th of last month. I do not want for words in dealing with people who mean nothing to me; but when I am warmly attached to someone, as I am to you, I become anxious lest the expression of my true feelings be taken for mere rhetoric. I can only say that I will never forget how you helped me in a serious crisis in my life.

Your advice is very valuable to me. You are right when you write that a life without any true vocation, even that of an independent scholar, would not satisfy me. If official consent is in due course refused me, I will obviously be forced to resign. In such a case I will do what you have hinted to me and what has already for some time been in my mind: as soon as I learn that permission is refused me, I will resign on some other pretext—for example, for reasons of health—and only marry after my resignation takes effect. I am in myself prepared for every eventuality, but would look on it as a great good fortune if I could remain in the Service. I realise that the pre-conditions for this are on the one hand that I do not delay until rumours arise; on the other that I give time to those who can and wish to support me to choose the right moment in which to bring the matter before the Chancellor. As regards the former I will continue for the future to be as cautious and discreet as possible. Rest assured that my heart will not run away with my head; moreover nobody is pressing me, least of all the one for whom I would be prepared and desire to make every sacrifice, as she, who is unselfishness personified, has sacrificed everything for me. Until now the world has not noticed anything whatever of my intentions. I will do everything to avoid attracting its attention to me. I will particularly write to my brother Adolf and Seckendorff to ask them to exercise the most scrupulous discretion: then, even if this or that society fox should tell tales about Countess D. being divorced on my account or that we want to get married, the public still will not know whether the allegation is true. So much nonsense is talked! If, however, my case is discussed in the New Palace[1] or Adolf allows his displeasure and annoyance to be seen, everyone will guess that there is something in it. People would begin to watch me, to talk about my intentions, and I would gradually be brought into a most unpleasant situation. Nothing seems to me to be of greater importance than that my plans do not become known until I myself make them known by my betrothal.

It was my wish to become engaged at the end of November and to marry before Christmas. However, if you think that it would render my staying on in the Service easier if I wait until next spring, I will not precipitate matters. If you have nothing against it, I will confide in Herbert when I see him here or elsewhere in the course of the summer. From the way he has always acted towards me and from what I know of his character, I do not think that he will leave me in the lurch. Otherwise I would prefer not to confide in anyone. Not even in Hohenlohe. If I may be permitted to express my opinion as to the way in which my destiny will shape itself, I think that my situation, official, social, and financial, will be rendered immeasurably easier for me if I were to be given, before my intentions are known, and if possible before the Chancellor knows of them, a small oriental post such as Sofia, Tangiers, or preferably Alexandria. Against St Petersburg, which I thought of for a moment, there is this to be said that even were it feasible, of which I can form no judgment, there is the expense and Schweinitz's

[1] Residence of the Crown Prince.

outlook on life; to Radowitz I would go most unwillingly; as a married man Paris is impossible for me. At the posts mentioned above my subsequent marriage would cause less sensation, I would have fewer social difficulties, and even my family would reconcile itself more easily to my decisions.

I cannot close without again expressing my most cordial thanks to you. It would have greatly pained me if I had not met with understanding from you. The fact that I can count on the continuance of your friendly sentiments does me more good than you yourself perhaps believe.

Ever faithfully your B. [...]

101. Herbert von Bismarck to Holstein

St Petersburg, 9 May 1884

Dear Holstein,

Best thanks for your letter received yesterday, and for all your very successful efforts.[1] It is to be hoped that in this case also it will prove true that 'when God gives anyone a post, He also gives them brains'. The outcome is of course absolutely brilliant, pleasant and flattering, actually *too* much so, and it will therefore arouse much envy and abuse. [...]

Ever faithfully,
Your HB.

102. Herbert von Bismarck to Holstein

St Petersburg, 18 May 1884

Dear Holstein,

[...] Prince Wilhelm leaves on Wednesday.[2] Werder has spoiled the journey to Moscow, which would have been useful.[3] The Prince has made a brilliant impression here. Both sexes are enthusiastic about him. He has treated me with quite special distinction, and brings me into the foreground in such a manner that my subordinate situation *vis à vis* the old Generals S[chweinitz] and W[erder] becomes more untenable by the hour. More about this by word of mouth. *I can tell volumes!*[4]

Farewell and continued thanks for your vigorous support, which I hope will preserve me from impossible Weimar situations.[5]

Ever your
HB.

[1] In helping to secure Herbert von Bismarck's appointment as Minister at The Hague.

[2] Prince Wilhelm was in St Petersburg from 17–22 May for the proclamation of the coming of age of Grand Duke Nicholas, the heir to the Russian Throne, and to confer on him the Order of the Black Eagle. (See *Grosse Politik*, vol. III, nos. 631–4, pp. 339–42.)

[3] Prince Wilhelm did in fact go to Moscow on 23 May.

[4] In English in the original.

[5] See *Diaries*, entry for 17 May 1884.

103. Herbert von Bismarcktein to Holstein

St Petersburg, 20 May 1884

Dear Holstein,

A few lines in great haste before the post goes.

You will see from Schweinitz' short report that he is offended;[1] its sole object is to sneak about Prince Wilhelm to the Kaiser; although that in itself is sure to be ineffective, perhaps the dispatch should go first to my father before it is laid before His Majesty, or it should be stated that the Prince had previously talked with me about everything. Actually I had only to listen, because the Prince had evidently admirably grasped the instructions given to him by His Majesty and His Highness.

Schweinitz is, however, furious because the Prince only discusses politics with me—yet I think this is a good thing because Schweinitz might only have made the Prince unsure of himself. It would be better if you got Waldersee to tell you himself about the impression made on his [Prince Wilhelm's] suite by Werder and Schweinitz. He is cursing, and how.

Adieu, I arrive Sunday or Monday

Ever your

HB.

104. Colonel von Wehren to Holstein

Berlin, 23 May 1884

My dear Herr von Holstein,

In accordance with your desire I herewith give you a short report of my interview with Count Rantzau, so far as I remember it.[2]

I told Count Rantzau that you had called on me this morning and had asked that I should give you my assistance in the following matter.

I read to Count R. the following version of your instructions: 'Yesterday evening when we met in a salon, Count R. behaved in such an impolite and rude manner towards me—for example, when I left he replied to my greeting without so much as looking at me—as to arouse the suspicion that he wished to provoke a conflict. For this reason I beg you to ascertain *whether* Count R. intended to *offend* me, that is, to provoke a *conflict*, and to tell him that if this is the case, I would like to see the affair decided as *soon* as possible.'

Count R. replied to this more or less as follows: Formerly he was on very friendly terms with Herr von Holstein and he had taken an interest in Herr von H., if only because of the well-known deep attachment displayed by Herr von H. for the person of His Highness the Prince and his family.

Nevertheless he had received the impression after his (Count R's) return from Friedrichsruh that H.v.H. had not only become cold to-

---

[1] In his report of 20 May, Schweinitz wrote that Prince Wilhelm had had talks with Tsar Alexander and Giers, but that he had not previously discussed with Schweinitz what he was going to say. (See *Grosse Politik*, vol. III, no. 631, p. 339.)

[2] See *Diaries*, entry for 24 May 1884.

wards him but was avoiding him. He did not know the reasons for this conduct.

He had received a letter from H.v.H. on the occasion of his mother's death and believed that he had replied to it in as friendly a tone as that in which it was written.[1]

He had always endeavoured to greet H.v.H. first.

He had visited H.v.H. after his return (I think in the Foreign Ministry). Count R's impression of 'coldness' and 'reserve' on the part of H.v.H. still remained after this visit.

He admitted that his behaviour on the evening in question at the departure of H.v.H. was not exactly very polite, but that he returned his own 'adieu' after the fashion of H.v.H.'s curt 'Adio'. In general, Count R. did not wish to show either more or less reserve and coolness towards H.v.H. than H.v.H. displayed towards him, Count R. He supposed that H.v.H. had felt himself insulted by him, Count R., but *how* he does not know. Count R. had expected as a consequence of their earlier close acquaintanceship that H.v.H. would have addressed a question to him concerning this matter. Count R. had no intention of being insulting in his behaviour towards H.v.H.

Nor had he any thought of provoking a conflict.

After these explanations by Count R., I regarded my mission as fulfilled. In saying this to Count R., I added: whether Count R. desired to have an interview or mediation between the two parties brought about through me.

Count R. refused this.

Your sincerely devoted
Colonel von Wehren.

105. Wilhelm von Bismarck to Holstein[2]

Friedrichsruh, 25 May [1884]

Dear H.

I thank you for informing me and return the Wehren letter herewith. I assume that this is what you mean by 'the memorandum' because I have not received anything else with your three epistles. I am in general of the opinion that it is useful now and then to show one's teeth, and it is possible that this was a suitable opportunity. I can naturally form no judgment about it; to do so I would have to have seen the incident. I think that R. will now be careful and so the matter will have been formally concluded. [...]

Cordially
Your BB.

106. Herbert von Bismarck to Holstein

[London], 24 June 1884

Dear Holstein,

To-day I am again in such a rush that I can only give the courier a very hurried greeting to take to you. I have worked hard during the

[1] See above, Kuno zu Rantzau's letter of 6 January 1884.
[2] See *Diaries*, entry for 26 May 1884.

last eight or ten days, not without results, as you will have seen; now the high tide of the *season* is at my throat and yesterday evening B. Bülow came for two days, and I want to launch him.

I would advise you that we should now be somewhat friendlier towards the English in order that they may see that it is to their advantage to comply with our wishes.[1]

In the course of the coming years they will find themselves in a pickle on account of Egypt anyway, no matter what one does now.

The weather is wonderful, and I wish each day had 48 hours, both for work and pleasure; it is quite interesting here at the moment.

Ever yours
HB.

Pr. of Wales, somewhat downcast, said to me that Hatzfeldt had told him in Wiesbaden that my father was annoyed with England.

107. Herbert von Bismarck to Holstein

[London], 28 June 1884

Dear Holstein,

[...] There is no doubt that I will be worked to death in Berlin.[2] As to drinking I say with Rodenstein: 'One talks forever of much drinking but never of much thirst.' *I am not aware that I am above the average, Rottenburg for instance beats me.*[3]

I think it was family anxiety that was expressed in what my father said to you; it is true that for the moment I am really not *up to the work*[3] in Berlin; my mother has probably talked to Schweninger, perhaps also to Rottenburg. *That* however is all only *personal* concern for my well-being. Only Bleichröder could have *deceitfully* talked like that, and my father does not listen to him in such matters.

What you say about Bill pleases me greatly, so far as it concerns me, otherwise it distresses me. It would be splendid for him to find a good wife—but where?

To an early meeting—probably.
Ever your
HB.

108. Bernhard von Bülow to Holstein

Paris, 28 June 1884

Dear Herr von Holstein,

My warmest thanks for your friendly lines of the 22nd of this month, which I did not receive, however, until after my return from London because the courier was twenty-four hours late. In London I found Herbert badly overworked, but nevertheless found an opportunity of

---

[1] For some time Britain had blocked Germany's bid for overseas possessions. To demonstrate to the British the value of German friendship and the danger of German opposition, Bismarck had sided with Britain's opponents on a number of international issues.

[2] Herbert von Bismarck refers to the possibility that he would go to Berlin as Under State Secretary in the Foreign Ministry.

[3] In English in the original.

talking to him fully about my affairs. The general impression that I have taken away with me is this: Personally Herbert wishes me exceedingly well; during the four days that I spent in London his friendly feelings towards me were expressed with a vigour I shall never forget, while of my political capacity his opinion is such as almost to make me blush. On the other hand he unfortunately still has an entirely false idea of Countess D[önho]ff. I will gradually and cautiously try to portray the Countess to him in a true light, and hope that he will then, at the indicated moment, give me official support. We have agreed that until next spring Herbert will not speak to anyone, not even to his father, about my intentions. I have not told Herbert that I had already written to you about my plans, and will only do so with your express agreement. Before I confided my own affair to Herbert, he told me that the Chancellor wanted to transfer me either to St Petersburg or London. I could only reply that I would go wherever it seemed most useful, but that of the two posts I would prefer St Petersburg, if only because in my opinion I could be of greater use there. The communication of my personal plans did not alter in any way Herbert's ideas on this question but even seemed to strengthen him in them. On arrival here I find to my own astonishment a telegram already awaiting me that informs me of my transfer. The order with fuller details as to when I have to leave for St Petersburg has not yet arrived. I must leave this evening in order to be present on 1 July at my brother Adolf's wedding. Although I have only five days leave, I certainly hope to come to Berlin, probably on 3 July, even if only for a few hours, because I would so much like to see you. Prince Hohenlohe is sorry to part with me, as I from him after being together for so long. Herbert hinted to me that Rotenhan[1] would come here, which would probably also please the Prince best.

In haste, ever faithfully your
Bernh. Bülow

109. Herbert von Bismarck to Holstein

London, 8 July 1884

My dear Holstein,

Warmest thanks for your friendly letter. What you write to me about Hatzfeldt and myself—about the opposition to our possible collaboration—may very well be right. I can only say that I am convinced that, notwithstanding the difficulties for him arising out of my relationship with my father, Hatzfeldt would get along well with me, *et quant à moi je ne demanderais pas mieux que de servir sous lui à Berlin*; he is the cleverest of them all and he has always shown the same attitude towards me; why should that not continue? As you know, however, I am not in the least keen on going to Berlin; I must first see after some months of rest how I feel about it. You will see from my letter to Hatzfeldt[2]

[1] Wolfram, Baron von Rotenhan. First Secretary in the Embassy in Paris, 1884–5; Under State Secretary in the Foreign Ministry, June 1890–6; Minister in Bern, 1896–7, to the Holy See, 1897–1908.
[2] Not found.

what my immediate plans are. I am now terribly overworked and wish I had more time to write. I was an hour with Chamberlain to-day, who is far more furious with France than I thought, even spoke of the possibility of war (think of it, that Radical); he would like most of all to throw all bondholders[1] overboard. On the subject of the House of Lords and the *franchise bill*,[2] he talked with cool acerbity; it would be the political death of the Lords if they threw it out a second time. As *wirepuller* Chamberlain is still the most influential Minister. Many of my parliamentary friends—even Whigs—say: 'Only a great war can save us; otherwise we shall be victims of the Radical Moloch and that will be the end of our position as a Great Power. God send us a war that costs us money and stirs us up!'

Sur ce, adieu
Faithfully your
HB.

110. Herbert von Bismarck to Holstein

V[arzin], 28 July [1884]

Dear Holstein,

[...] According to what has arrived to-day about Angra,[3] the English really seem to want to annex everything north of Angra behind our backs. My father said: 'For the moment nothing can be done. I will think it over. The right thing would perhaps be that without saying a word beforehand we simply send warships to New Guinea and proclaim German sovereignty over all the hitherto ownerless coasts of these islands.'

After this remark, which could probably soon take on concrete form, I hold it as urgently desirable that the dispatches and drafts regarding the South Seas and the delimitation of spheres of influence there between England and ourselves, about which Count Hatzfeldt spoke to me in Berlin, should now be sent here right away. Count Hatzfeldt has already sent the documents here once before, but after consultation with me, decided to have them worked over so that the principal document would consist of a *short* dispatch to Münster, with a longer Promemoria enclosed.[4] [...]

Always your HB.

[1] The holders of Egyptian bonds.

[2] A Bill to extend the franchise in parliamentary elections. The House of Lords was holding up the Bill, which led to great public demonstrations against the Upper House.

[3] A telegram from the German Consul in Capetown which reported a telegram from Lord Derby to the Cape Government dated 14 July. 'The English Government assumes that the Cape Colony would wish that the coast north of the Lüderitz possession [Angra Pequena], which stretches up to the 26th parallel, should be placed under British protection.' Lord Derby stated further that the English Government was ready 'to place other points along the coast towards the south under English protection, provided the Cape Colony bore the cost'. (*Weissbuch, Vorgelegt dem Deutschen Reichstage in der I. Session der 6. Legislatur-Periode*, Erster Teil (Berlin, 1885), no. 35.)

[4] The dispatch and a Promemoria were sent to London on 2 August. (*Weissbuch*, Zweiter Teil, no. 20.)

111. Herbert von Bismarck to Holstein

V[arzin], 1 August 1884

Dear Holstein,

[...] We have just coded a long telegram to you about the conference.[1] It seems that Ferry is proving spineless; he wants to get us into a mess and afterwards tell Gladstone: 'Yes, this damned German Government.' My father had thought Ferry would accept our offer with great eagerness, but *rebus sic stantibus nous devons virer de bord*. These shortsighted people who always want to finesse! I should think that the postponement of the conference would be in Gladstone's interest. For then the Egyptian financial mess can *tant bien que mal* hang in the balance until October, Parliament and public opinion will have their mouths shut for two and a half months by an appeal to the 'European decision', and grounds for agitation will thus be removed as far as possible; and during this time the wild agitation against the Upper House, which is to prepare the way for a favourable next election for Gladstone, can go on undisturbed. [...]

Probably I shall be in Berlin on the evening of the day after tomorrow, and hope to dine with you at 7:40 p.m. at Borchard's.

Ev. yours
HB.

112. Herbert von Bismarck to Holstein

Königstein, 10 August [1884]

Dear Holstein,

Best thanks for your letter and the several interesting pieces of news. If the French *really* are annoyed with us, it is most unjustified. Either affectation or bad management of affairs must be the reason for it. Otherwise it would be exactly analogous to Russia after the Congress of Berlin. If we were supposed to support France more on points of detail, they should have indicated the particular points for which they wished it. That this did not occur may be due to Ferry's mistrust and dislike, or to Hohenlohe's sleepiness. I will not and cannot go into that here, but with that old nightcap Hohenlohe it is impossible to carry on real political actions, when all depends on keen, ceaseless observation and skilful personal initiative on the part of the ambassador. Hohenlohe has not enough contact; since Bülow left, virtually none. Already on the proposal for an adjournment, he should on his own initiative have

---

[1] An international conference on Egypt's financial situation was held in London from 28 June–2 August 1884. Towards the end of the conference, the French representative, Waddington, had expressed the wish that Germany might support a French proposal for an adjournment of the conference as opposed to its dissolution. Bismarck instructed Hohenlohe to inform Ferry that Germany was willing to do this. On 31 July Hohenlohe telegraphed that Ferry had told him that France would actually prefer an adjournment, and that he would empower Waddington to support a *German* proposal to this end. In the telegram to which Herbert von Bismarck refers, the Chancellor ordered Count Münster to maintain reserve in London, and to take action only in conjunction with Russia and Austria-Hungary. The conference was adjourned *sine die* on 2 August. Münster did not vote on a French proposal to put a time limit to the adjournment. (From the Foreign Ministry files. See below, Wilhelm von Bismarck's letter to Holstein of 16 October 1884.)

found out and reported three days earlier how the matter really lay. He is too passive. At least one should avoid creating legends *à la Russe*, and tell the French frankly that we must know what they themselves want and want to *stick to*.[1] The so-called new approach about a conference in Paris (at which, moreover, the English would hardly appear) affords an opportunity for this. The irritation of the French is apparently not universal. The *Kölnische Zeitung* of the day before yesterday and earlier made it clear that the *Temps* as well as the *Figaro* had expressed gratitude for our 'more than correct attitude'. Behind the renewed spitefulness of the *République Française* there stands perhaps indirectly the figure of an irritated Beckmann? I talked to my father in Varzin about him, his importance and the manner of his dismissal, and it seemed to me that His Highness would not be disinclined to leave Beckmann at least the greater part of his pension if this were to be strongly proposed by Berlin. You might first write once again to Bill about this.

First of all we, together with Austria and France, should firmly demand the Alexandria indemnities[2] with a time limit attached, and then take a stand with everyone against England the moment she wants to make a bankruptcy declaration. Then Gladstone will become amenable soon enough. I find the *Kölnische Zeitung* so stupid; in the first place it always thinks that Gladstone wants to annex Egypt, which *he* never thinks of doing, but *we* must wish for. Secondly it should not blow up the importance of the colonial affair so clumsily. Why pay attention to the boasting tone of the English papers, and especially of the miserable *Times* Correspondent in Berlin?[3] By doing so it makes the English suspicious *too soon*, and disturbs our plans. One should give them a hint; admittedly it is already perhaps too late.

Has Bülow told you that Wolkenstein[4] was going to be cut at the Imperial Ball at Peterhof? I nevertheless think that for the immediate future it is better that Wolk. should stay in St Petersburg. It is perhaps possible that the correctness of my opinion will be modified in Varzin on the 15th. If Kálnoky is then reasonable,[5] and if *both* Kaisers

[1] On 6 August, Bismarck wrote to the Foreign Ministry: 'I ask that Baron Courcel should be sounded as to what France intends to do now [after the failure of the Egyptian conference], bringing up cautiously whether the French Government did not find it indicated that it should now make proposals to the Powers who are in agreement with France and to bring about, so to speak, an understanding under French leadership on the attitude which the non-English Powers will have to adopt in the Egyptian Question. Instead of indulging in 'recriminations over the past, it would be useful to seek an understanding for the future'. (Quoted by Windelband, *Bismarck und die europäischen Grossmächte*, p. 595. See also *Grosse Politik*, vol. III, pp. 413–4, note **.) Count Hatzfeldt carried out this instruction on 11 August. (From the Foreign Ministry files.)

[2] The compensation for the bombardment of Alexandria by English warships in July 1882. Bismarck was of the opinion that England ought to make compensation for the damage. (See Windelband, *Bismarck und die europäischen Grossmächte*, p. 596.) An International Commission later decided that England should pay an indemnity of £4 million.

[3] Charles Lowe. *Times* Correspondent in Berlin, 1878–91.

[4] Anton, Count von Wolkenstein-Trostburg. Austro-Hungarian Ambassador in St Petersburg, 1882–94.

[5] Count Kálnoky visited Prince Bismarck in Varzin, 15–19 August. (See *Grosse Politik*, vol. III, no. 643, pp. 363–5.)

on the 15th of next month are also **reasonable**,[1] then the spheres of interest can be delimited,[2] and *then* I would send Khevenhüller[3] to St Petersburg. He is the *only* Austrian who is suited to St Petersburg—and he is very suitable. The prerequisite for this is, however, that our relationship with Austria should be regarded as unbreakable. If that is not the case, then a clumsy representative like Wolkenstein, who only exists by our grace, is better for us.

Farewell. I am just about to go for a drive with Diskau, on whom I called at your recommendation.

Ever your
HB.

113. Wilhelm von Bismarck to Holstein

Mars la Tour,[4] 16 August [1884]

[...] I have received the treaties.[5] About the metal box, *vedremo*. Kálnoky meritoriously again said nothing to-day. His Highness has the impression that he only came here *for sham and show*.[6] K. remains here tomorrow, and as the day after is the birthday of his Kaiser we shall probably also have to keep him for the day after tomorrow.[7] [...]

Your BB. [...]

114. Herbert von Bismarck to Holstein

Königstein, 19 August 1884

Dear Holstein,

[...] Whether Waldersee will suit the Kaiser for Strasbourg is in my opinion questionable. I had thought one could exchange Waldersee with Caprivi[8] and thus both sides would gain, the General Staff as well as the Admiralty, that is to say the latter in their relations with the Foreign Ministry, which are after all getting closer all the time and with Caprivi could lead to friction. The latter is accounted as *far the*

---

[1] A reference to the forthcoming meeting of the Kaiser with the Emperors of Russia and Austria-Hungary.

[2] A serious conflict broke out in the summer of 1884 between Serbia and Bulgaria over a disputed strip of frontier territory. Bismarck declared that the partition of the Balkans into an Austrian and a Russian sphere of influence was imperative. (See *Grosse Politik*, vol. III, nos. 637–42, pp. 347–63.)

[3] Rudolf, Count Khevenhüller-Metsch. Austro-Hungarian Minister in Belgrade, 1881–6.

[4] Refers to the anniversary of the battle of Mars la Tour.

[5] Wilhelm von Bismarck had written on 14 August: 'What will we need in the way of documents for the discussions with Kálnoky? We don't really know. Perhaps you do? In any case send the text of the secret treaties and put with them whatever else you think worth while. But not too bulky.'

[6] In English in the original.

[7] In a letter to Holstein of 20 August, Wilhelm von Bismarck wrote: 'Kálnoky said nothing. His aim was obviously the great public, and to prevent the possibility that in due course he would be served with an accomplished fact *à deux* with the motto: Now eat *à trois* or die. On this he has been reassured.' (See Windelband, *Bismarck und die europäischen Grossmächte*, pp. 607–8.)

[8] Leo, Count von Caprivi. Prussian General. Head of the Admiralty, 1883–8; General commanding the 10th Army Corps in Hanover, 1889–90; Chancellor of the German Reich, 1890–4; Prussian Minister President, 1890–2.

best general.[1] Did Moltke not take him because he was made of harder stuff than W., and was thus less pliable; or was it in order to be all the more regretted at the time of his own future retirement? That would not have been exactly patriotic, but more in accord with human vanity. Among our ambassadors, unfortunately not one is suitable for Strasbourg. Schweinitz, who would go there with delight, cannot now be replaced in St Petersburg and he is also probably too stiff to be able to germanize in Alsace and at the same time to arouse sympathies. [...]

            Farewell
             Ever your
               HB.

115. Herbert von Bismarck to Holstein

Königstein, 21 August 1884

Dear Holstein,

[...] As for Waldersee, the only thing to be done would be for my father to speak with old Moltke in person and in confidence, and to try to persuade him to advise the Kaiser and the Crown Prince as his last wish to take Caprivi instead of W.

In such purely military matters my father achieves nothing with H.M.; on the contrary, H.M. is convinced that he understands *this* better and, encouraged by the thick-skinned Albedyll,[2] would stand the more firmly by W. If Albedyll were removed it would also be all to the good; his system of patronage and the power of his 'military ring' are truly a scandal! *How* can one possibly get rid of Manteuffel?[3] He regards himself as first-rate and indispensable and the Kaiser will not simply dismiss him; but his departure is *urgently* necessary. [...]

            Farewell
             Ever your
               HB.

116. Wilhelm von Bismarck to Holstein

V[arzin], 21 August 1884

Dear H.

[...] With the 'second official' at the close of his report to the Kaiser,[4] His Highness had your humble servant in mind.[5] He thinks that he is doing me a favour by this and consequently I say nothing. To be sure, I had at first thought that I would go along, but I now see that Herb., with his knowledge of Russian personalities, would be far more useful because His Highness must have someone who can keep him informed. It would still be a pleasure for me and from a personal

---

[1] In English in the original.
[2] Emil von Albedyll. Prussian General; Chief of the Prussian Military Cabinet, 1872–88; General commanding the 7th Army Corps, 1888–93.
[3] As Governor of Alsace-Lorraine.
[4] Of 21 August. (See *Grosse Politik*, vol. III, no. 643, pp. 363–5.)
[5] Bismarck wished to be accompanied by his two sons to the meeting of the three Emperors at Skiernievice in September. (See below, Herbert von Bismarck's letter of 24 August.)

standpoint H's company would indeed be very agreeable to me. I am only afraid of the quiverful impression which His Highness will make and which embarrasses *me*. I am not *necessary*—why should there be so much writing to be done? In that case a cipher clerk who writes better than I do would be more useful. I am thinking of how I can get out of it without offending His Highness, which I wish to avoid at all costs. It is to be hoped that the place is too small. Perhaps I will also be successful in drawing His Highness' attention to the comic element in the situation. [...]

Your BB.

117. Wilhelm von Bismarck to Holstein

24 August [1884]

Dear H.

[...] I am entirely of your opinion regarding Caprivi, but also agree with Herbert as regards the execution. *We* cannot do anything in the matter. Moltke himself proposed Waldersee, so far as I know. He must therefore himself withdraw the appointment. His Highness called Caprivi a crank (Zanzibar)[1]—but without anger. I think C. was right in this question. It is damnably ticklish, and he must after all know how far he can go. *Now* he is *au courant*. You will be interested in a correspondence with C. that you will find in the Reich Chancellery. I have had it filed there so that Kusserow[2] does not see it. In this, too, C. was right. Damn it all, one can't create a full-fledged Navy in ten years, especially under that swine St[osch]. We have worked at our land army for fifty or a hundred years. I too am in doubt about how Waldersee would manage the matter. I will propose W. as Ambassador in London, for Münster is tottering. What do you think about that? [...]

Goodnight. Your BB.

118. Herbert von Bismarck to Holstein

Königstein, 24 August 1884

Dear Holstein,

[...] The day before yesterday Bill wrote to me that it would be too much if my father were accompanied to Poland by both of us, and he would therefore not go along. This would greatly distress me; the whole thing is certainly a most interesting affair and I most heartily wish Bill to take part in it, would indeed be ready to make what is a great sacrifice for me and give it up myself—if my father agrees—so that he does not lose the chance. But I do not see why we should not both go. One reason given by Bill—that 'the house in Skiernievice is too small'—can easily be overcome by one of us staying the night in

[1] Caprivi had refused to send a warship to Zanzibar to protect German interests there. (See *Diaries*, entry for 19 September 1884.)
[2] Heinrich von Kusserow. *Vortragender Rat* in the Foreign Ministry, 1874–84; Specialist for Colonial Affairs.

Warsaw or in a farm-house. The other reason, that 'it would seem too pretentious if my father brought two sons with him', I refuse to accept as valid. We will not go as such, but as officials, and everyone knows that for years we have burdened ourselves with more work with my father than anyone else. Giers and Kálnoky will certainly bring at least two officials and there will be plenty of work for them to do, and if Bill and I go, then lame Bülow[1] does not need to go with the Kaiser, which would certainly simplify the matter. I am writing you all this because I know that you would prefer that Bill and I went than lame B., who has already lounged around with the Kaiser all summer, and to ask you to help in pushing Bülow aside and to see that Bill and I go along.

You can well understand how much it means to me to be present at the meeting for which I have worked in St Petersburg throughout the whole winter, but the fun would be spoilt for me if Bill stayed at home and the cripple came. I have written in this sense to Bill, naturally on the—for me obvious—assumption that it would be a pleasure for him. If he does not think so, and would prefer to do something else that week, then everything said above ceases to have any meaning.

But I can hardly believe it.

That Münster has not come to Varzin is due—so Bill writes—to aversion on my father's part. I also think it is better this way. My father after all is always too polite in his own country house, so that Münster with his thick skin would have noticed nothing, but only have felt himself more important. Now he has for the present a *levis nota* because he counted on an invitation. I have come to the irrevocable opinion as a result of careful reflection in my solitude that for Münster to be left any longer in London is, as things now are, almost inexcusable from a political standpoint. He ruins everything there; it would be *far* better not to have any ambassador there. To embroil oneself with a Power *unnecessarily* is a great mistake. But Münster will bring it to that, whereas I can judge the situation in England sufficiently well to know that through skilful representation we can attain everything we wish in London *without* embroilment. Couldn't there be some kind of switch that would bring Münster to Vienna? At the moment, in consequence of the present constellation, we can put up with an incompetent there best of all, and even Reuss[2] is after all nothing more than a demobilised corporal made postman. But then I think Münster will resign if he is sent to Vienna and that would indeed be the best conceivable solution.

I consider Waldersee very incapable as a diplomat. Moreover you were of the same opinion when you were with him in Paris.[3] Nevertheless he is as such certainly less risky than as Chief of the General Staff. With his tendency to indiscretion he could perhaps create unpleasant situations even at the Quirinal. Keudell, whom I consider even more stupid than Münster, at least holds his tongue. Nevertheless I will

[1] Otto von Bülow.
[2] Prince Heinrich VII Reuss. Ambassador in Vienna, 1878–94.
[3] Waldersee was temporary representative of the Reich with the French Government in 1871.

drink an extra bottle of champagne on the day on which Keudell leaves the Service.

Do you not think it would be wise to hold the elections *soon*—about the end of September?[1] Everything is now bubbling over on account of colonial policy, Skiernievice will add to it, but *then* in my opinion *carpe diem*. The Government can never compete with the Progressive Party in agitation; each further day that is given for *that purpose* is only a gain for the radicals, that is as certain as $2 \times 2 = 4$, let Puttkamer and his miserable Press advisers drivel about it as much as they like. Nobody knows what can happen before the end of October—time is precious. [...]

Now farewell
Ever your
HB.

119. Herbert von Bismarck to Holstein

Königstein, 26 August 1884

Dear Holstein,

Warmest thanks for your letter of the 23rd which crossed with my last to you. I am presumably also indebted to you for the telegram about Ampthill's[2] death. In all events it was very kind of Hatzfeldt to think of me. I would like as successor Dufferin or Lumley,[3] but above all avoidance of the dangerous Morier,[4] and have already written about this to Bill. The day before yesterday I also sent Bill a satisfactory letter from Granville[5] which you will doubtless get from Varzin. Gr. simply says in it *pater peccavi* and asks for friendly treatment. I must answer it and am very anxious as to what will be Varzin's decision.[6]

Whatever had His Majesty to write to Bleichröder about? I never thought that such a relationship existed!

For London I think Waldersee too unsuitable; if at all, then preferably Rome or Vienna; in my opinion he is *diplomatically* a complete *non valeur*, but as the price for filling the General Staff [post] better, one must after all take him. Obviously *I* can form no judgment as to his unfitness for the General Staff, but can only say what a few others have said. It is a matter for the *soldiers*, the divisional Heads in the General Staff, to express their opinion to Moltke, since he and they are responsible for it. Waldersee should be given an Army Corps—that would be the best. It is a pity that Wartensleben[7] has just got the 3rd Corps. But with that damned Albedyll there is also little to be done; he

[1] The elections for the Reichstag, which took place at the end of October 1884.
[2] Lord Odo Russell, from 1881 Baron Ampthill. British Ambassador in Berlin, 1871–84. Ampthill died on 25 August.
[3] Sir John Savile Lumley. British Ambassador in Rome, 1883–9.
[4] Sir Robert Morier. British Ambassador in St Petersburg, 1884–93.
[5] Of 20 August. (*Grosse Politik*, vol. IV, no. 751, pp. 79–80. See also Windelband, *Bismarck und die europäischen Grossmächte*, pp. 599–600.)
[6] See the following letter from Wilhelm von Bismarck. The reply to Granville of 30 August 1884 is printed in *Grosse Politik*, vol. IV, no. 752, pp. 80–3.
[7] Hermann Wilhelm, Count von Wartensleben. Prussian General; Commander of the 3rd Army Corps, 1884–8.

has long wanted to have the embassies as dumping ground for high-ranking military men who are useless as officers; watch out, if Waldersee now gets an embassy, then afterwards Lehndorff and Alten[1] and finally Albedyll himself will also want one as a matter of course! And one can hardly blame them if they think they are fitted for it, after they have seen Münster and Keudell occupying embassies for years!

Farewell for to-day.

Ever your

HB.

120. Wilhelm von Bismarck to Holstein

27 August [1884]

Mon cher,

What emerged in the talks with Courcel, I do not know in detail.[2] His Highness [Bismarck] only told me C. was satisfied, and he also gives that impression. H.H. thinks he noticed that Courcel was anxious lest the French might compromise themselves with us, especially with regard to their own fellow-countrymen. H.H. said only that we demanded nothing whatever from F., and only needed her for the purpose of taking up an attitude towards Engl. He also regarded U. States participation as undesirable, but it is not to be rejected if F. proposes it. H.H. suspects U. St. will refuse participation, I don't.[3]

Granville wrote to Herbert, figures of speech, we were always such nice people, etc. Asked for favourable treatment. He has received a lengthy draft of an answer,[4] reproaches about English dirty tricks, materially analogous to the *Norddeutsche Allgemeine Zeitung* article, but more courteous. General tone: we will only be friendly if you are more decent in colonial matters. H.H. wants to avoid an open row with E. But that will only be possible—if at the same time we intend to safeguard our own interests—if we always clench our fist. As long as we are friendly with Fr., they will be decent, and they will cease being so the moment we are again at loggerheads with F. I have also written this point of view to Herb., and cannot believe that he fancies he can muzzle the wily dogs with kindness. H.H. seems to be of my opinion now. Whether it lasts remains to be seen. See if you can get something

---

[1] Karl von Alten. Aide-de-Camp.

[2] Courcel was in Varzin from 26–7 August for talks with Bismarck. (See *Diaries*, entries for 27 and 30 August 1884.) In a letter to Wilhelm von Bismarck of 18 August, Holstein expressed the opinion that Germany's support for French policy in Egypt and Morocco would suffice to bring about a definite change of front in France's attitude towards Germany. (Windelband, *Bismarck und die europäischen Grossmächte*, p. 602.)

[3] Bismarck and Courcel agreed to propose an international conference for the regulation of the river traffic on the Congo and Niger. After an official exchange of notes between Berlin and Paris, invitations were sent to all the European Powers, with the exception of Switzerland, and also to the United States. (See *Grosse Politik*, vol. III, no. 688, pp. 424–6.) The conference met from 15 November 1884 to 26 February 1885. The United States took part.

[4] See above p. 128, note 6. Herbert von Bismarck wrote to Holstein on 8 September: 'I am glad that you had no objections to my letter to Granville; the contents, with a few exceptions, entirely corresponded with the Varzin draft.'

out of Courcel. I had no opportunity of being alone with him for any length of time; I either had something to do or *he* was with H.H. Also did not want to pump him. If *you* pump him, it will be easier. [...]

Goodnight

Your BB.

121. Wilhelm von Bismarck to Holstein

1 September [1884]

Dear H.

The whole situation should now be clear to you from His Highness' memorandum![1] H.H. is enthusiastic about the conference[2] for election reasons, would like to have it soon, and so I suspect that he will want to accomplish something. That will scarcely be achieved, however, without taking an attitude *opposed* to England. What the French now offer seems to me completely sufficient; the only question is whether at the decisive moment in the conference they will make their offer conditional upon our support in Egyptian affairs, which H.H. will then not want to [...].[3] But in my opinion the French can be quite content if we maintain *benevolent* neutrality and support their initiative against E., or even if we do not oppose it. They can then regulate their action, fast and slow as it pleases them. I look at the affair in a rosier light now that I realise that H.H. intends to make use of the Congo for purposes of internal policy. That means he will really do something about it; the English note that has just arrived about the Cameroons seems to me very opportune;[4] perhaps H.H. will thereby be pinned down. Herbert incidentally has agreed with my opinion that we will only gain England's goodwill—if only a goodwill accompanied by gnashing of teeth —by way of an alliance with France. Granville has again had the alternative put to him by H. which Münster failed to put to him in the spring:[5] in colonial matters *with* us through thick and thin; or you cannot reckon upon our friendship. I think the G's[6] will not go as far as that. The note about the Cameroons is a pretty beginning after Granville's assurances of friendship to Herbert. [...]

I was also pleased about a letter to Puttkamer in which H.H. scolded

[1] Of 30 August, concerning Bismarck's conversation with Courcel. (*Grosse Politik*, vol. III, no, 688, pp. 424–6.)

[2] See above p. 129, note 3.

[3] One word illegible.

[4] In a Note to Under State Secretary Busch of 29 August 1884, Sir Charles Scott informed the German Government that already in 1879 a number of the chieftains in the Cameroons had urgently requested England to take them under her protection, and that in succeeding years there had been many requests in this sense. In May 1884 an English Consul had been sent to the Cameroons. 'He went with instructions to accept the cession of the Cameroons, and at the same time to place the territory of Ambas Bay, where a British settlement has existed for a long time, under the protection and care of the British Crown.' (*Weissbuch, Vorgelegt dem Deutschen Reichstage in der I. Session der 6. Legislatur-Periode*, Erster Teil, no. 2.)

[5] Wilhelm von Bismarck refers to the instructions to Münster of 5 May 1884. (*Grosse Politik*, vol. IV, no. 738, pp. 50–2. See also *Diaries*, entry for 14 March 1885.) Herbert von Bismarck presented this alternative to Granville in a letter of 30 August 1884. (See above, p. 128, note 6.)

[6] Granville and Gladstone.

him about the Conservative electoral manifesto and protested against the introduction of *anything* positive in the electoral manifesto. *No* grain duties, *no* Stock Exchange or any other kind of taxes, *no* novelties, in short wholly negative. Only complaints about high court fees and other abuses, without indicating any method for improvement. *J'y suis pour quelque chose.* If I can now succeed in securing that the *Norddeutsche Allgemeine Zeitung* only rides the colonial horse in the election and gives up all *personal* pin-pricks I will be very glad. *Vedremo.*

You may well be right that I am the least passionate of the family. But that arises out of a circumstance that is not very gratifying to me. I simply don't care about *anything*. I have no private interests and I have made it a principle not to intrigue, not even against people who have offended me. That is incidentally also a very Christian standpoint. If I considered anyone a serious danger to the community, I would gladly remove him; but a principle that I have always observed—not to meddle with things which are none of my business—has now become more sharply accentuated. 'Gentle understanding', as Erkert says, but it does not spring from good nature, although this is the basis of my character, in so far as it is possible to speak of a basis in simmering mutable circumstances. Yes, yes—*au moral* I wind up with an increasingly bad balance. [...]

Goodnight.
Your BB.

122. Herbert von Bismarck to Holstein

Königstein, 3 September 1884

Dear Holstein,

Warmest thanks for your letter of Sunday;[1] what you write about our relations with France and the state of opinion there interested me very much; I am entirely of your opinion and hope that our policy *will avail itself of this most favourable moment* to squash Gladstone against the wall, so that he can yap no more. He *must* be driven *ad absurdum* in the general interest, but first he must ride the English deeper into the mire so that his prestige will vanish even among the masses of the stupid English electorate. The long letter that I wrote to Granville some days ago,[2] a copy of which will certainly be accessible to you, seemed to me almost too friendly, but will have the good effect of stiffening England's attitude towards France; the Chinese conflict[3] is *very* disagreeable to the English.

I would regard it as a misfortune to have the United States at the

[1] Holstein wrote on 1 September: 'If the French do not become convinced within the next three months that we have made fools of them, they will—not perchance love us—but give vent to their hatred for England in a manner which will for the moment render Gladstone and *his* Republic innocuous [...]. The effect it can have in France if they see that we *really* support them in something may perhaps be very great.' (Windelband, *Bismarck und die europäischen Grossmächte*, pp. 602–3.)

[2] See above p. 128, note 6.

[3] The war between France and China over Tonkin. The French maritime blockade of the Chinese coasts interfered with British commerce.

Congo Conference; the fact that the French could even conceive such an idea shows how ignorant they really are, and how incapable their foreign policy!

Since you remain in Berlin until the 15th, I will see you there. I will be there early on the 12th at the latest. Then, however, you should for once take a couple of weeks to get some fresh air in the mountains in order to fill yourself up with oxygen.

Adieu for to-day.
Ever your HB.

123. Wilhelm von Bismarck to Holstein

Varzin, 5 September [1884]

Dear H.,

Owing to all the annoyance and the scribbling which the carelessness of the Foreign Ministry has caused me, I have forgotten to answer your question about the memorandum. I had thought that I had made myself clear to Busch, but am now afraid that I am mistaken. His Highness wants a yardstick to which the discussions[1] could be related, and thinks that conclusions might be drawn from the texts of *former* treaties, which, if translated into practical terms, would be useful in bringing about greater clarity than has hitherto existed between Russia and Austria. A *partition of Turkey* will not come out of it, but perhaps a delimitation of the spheres of interest. H.H. has repeatedly touched upon the question with Kálnoky, but has found him hard of hearing, as you will see from H.H.'s report to the Kaiser.[2] H.H. now hopes that by means of the treaties it may be possible to find a line which will assign Serbia to the Austrians, Bulgaria to the Russians, without necessitating new mutual assurances.

Both will probably indulge in recriminations that the other has not observed the terms of the treaty. For this purpose H.H. wants a register of crimes to be drawn up, showing what both have hitherto done in contradiction to their assurances, so that if occasion arises he can hold the balance as arbitrator.[3] [...]

Goodnight
Your BB.

124. Herbert von Bismarck to Holstein

Königstein, 5 September 1884

Dear Holstein,

[...] Yesterday evening Barrère,[4] coming from Paris, telegraphed me that he wanted to visit me here. I expect him at any moment and

---

[1] The approaching conversations in Skiernievice.

[2] Of 21 August 1884. (*Grosse Politik*, vol. III, no. 643, pp. 363–5.)

[3] See Bucher's memorandum of 5 September 1884. (*Grosse Politik*, vol. III, no. 644, pp. 365–9.)

[4] Camille Barrère. French Diplomatic Agent and Consul-General in Cairo, 1883–5; Minister in Stockholm, 1885–8; Chargé d'Affaires in Munich, 1888–94; Ambassador in Bern, 1894–7, in Rome, 1897–1924.

will be glad to see him.[1] What a pity that I am not fully informed; but I will nevertheless try to stimulate his anti-English passions, and in addition deal with him in the sense of your letter:[2] 'he spared no seduction to woo the shy maid for his lusts'. I am entirely *de votre avis*, we must *for the moment at all events* make common cause with France and against Gladstone, until he is brought down.

Adieu.
Ever your HB.

125. Wilhelm von Bismarck to Holstein

7 September [1884]

Dear H.

[...] I am supposed not to be forebearing with people? Only recently I explained to you that to my regret that is exactly what I am to a high degree, so much so in fact that I am inclined to excuse a good deal of nastiness, or at least to understand it. Gradually this affects one's standards; it is bound to do so, even though up to now I have successfully fought against this consequence. I am only afraid of the pitilessness of logic, which in the long run can scarcely be overcome, at least in the case of someone like myself with a mathematical disposition and little feeling.

I foresee that I will never become anything outstanding, perhaps a good average; and I don't care for that one bit. I am now 32 years old and as I have always judged myself with honesty, I am more or less able to see how I will turn out, *pourvu que cela dure*. I have therefore made it my rule not to think of any future, to live for the day, and only to think of tomorrow and what directly concerns me. In this way I am quite happy and gay. As soon as I start to think, things turn sour. I am therefore happy that I have a lot to do and have no time left for myself. I would also be perfectly happy to loaf, but in that case it would have to be thorough and absorb me completely. Just a little has no effect whatever. [...]

Goodnight. Your BB.

126. Wilhelm von Bismarck to Holstein

8 September [1884]

Dear H.

[...] Herbert should not build himself castles in the air in Rome.

---

[1] For Barrère's conversation with Herbert von Bismarck, see *Grosse Politik*, vol. III, no. 689, p. 427. Only a small part of Count Bismarck's memorandum is printed there. Barrère spoke with particular harshness of the members of the Liberal Government in England. Herbert von Bismarck arrived at the following conclusion: 'I do not have the impression that Barrère was directly instructed by higher authorities to visit me: it seemed to me that before returning to Egypt he wanted above all to find out, confidentially but with certainty, whether the Franco-German understanding initiated in London had made progress and promised to be lasting. I thought that I should convince him that this was the case. The connection with Barrère, who in my opinion is a *rising man*, can perhaps prove useful; he himself told me that within one and a half years he would probably be given *la direction politique* in Paris, as the successor of Billot. Barrère will not hear of collaboration with England. The memory of the *joint dual control* [in Egypt] fills him with disgust.' (From the Foreign Ministry files.)

[2] See above p. 131, note 1.

His Highness is already completely taken up with the idea of shutting him up in Berlin. It will be difficult for us to get him away from that idea. H.H. is very indifferent to the fulfilment of other people's wishes; if they do not agree with his own, he simply does not understand them. [...]

Your BB.

127. Wilhelm von Bismarck to Holstein

9 September [1884]

[...] Whether I will go along to Poland is doubtful. His Highness said to-day that it would be hard for Her Highness if everyone left at the same time, and perhaps useful therefore if I stayed behind as a consolation. He is disposed to regard the matter as dangerous, and thinks that one should not [ ][1] anybody to a dangerous place if his duty does not require it. I have gathered from this that my going is of no importance to him, and this substantiates the opinion that I recently confided to you. *Puisqu'elle fait mon jeu* I wait calmly. It is all the same to me, and as you know the impression made by the appearance of the family —Hildebrand with two Hadubrands—is not to my liking. I do not think there is any danger. If there were a chance of being blown up, I would go with enthusiasm. [...]

Adio

Your BB.

128. Wilhelm von Bismarck to Holstein

V[arzin], 9 September [1884]

No, my little treasure, I will not have anything to do with it. I do nothing whatever on my own initiative. I am satisfied with what I have. I know that my work here gives satisfaction and—what is decisive for me—gives *me* satisfaction. It is also, as I have already said, not unduly heavy. I would simply make a mess of things as Congress Secretary; believe me, I know exactly what I can do. Some time ago His Highness spoke to me about taking me into the Foreign Ministry as *Vortragender Rat*, possibly as Councillor of Embassy, only this latter would not correspond with my rank. I replied coolly that in the spring I had already for my part brought up the question of the Counsellor of Embassy, but he had rejected it. That was all right with me, as was anything else, and rank a matter of indifference. Independence, my ideal, I will never attain. Perhaps when all energy has left me. The colonial desk does not attract me. If it is entrusted to me I will attempt it. My bad English will stand in my way, but will not be *impedim. dirimens*. The prospects you sketch for me with department and ministry, etc., leave me cold. You seem to think that what I have written to you during the past weeks arose from momentary ill-humour. That is a mistake. It is the result of long reflection and development. I watch myself more

[1] Word missing in the original.

carefully than anyone else and regard myself with the most extreme frankness, and I have on looking back remarked that—I cannot give the exact time but sometime in the past twelve or eighteen months—my outlook on life and the world has totally altered. To my detriment, undoubtedly; but I cannot honestly blame anyone for this fact. The most varied circumstances have played their part; to a great extent my urge to finish off everything immediately and thoroughly, and always to keep a level head. I have achieved that, and so protect my nerves, but everything that has to do with emotion and feeling goes to the devil. I am gay and do not worry about anything apart from slight passing irritations like saddle sores and choking. One can only accomplish that by killing all interests, as I only confirmed empirically. Had I known this *beforehand*, I might still have abandoned this course. Now it is too late; I would have to start again from the beginning, and that I would prefer to keep in reserve until I am completely out of the present circumstances *quovis modo*. [...]

Ad vocem Poland, His Highness said to me to-day: 'If it means a great deal to you, it will be all right, Mama won't die of anxiety during those two or three days.' I answered: 'I would be just as glad to stay in Berlin.' Whereupon he said: 'Think it over, we can talk about it in Berlin.' I will say nothing more about it and when H.H. mentions it again, I will simply say that he should do whatever would be most convenient to *him*, take me or leave me. I don't quite understand what was behind H.H.'s remarks—expression of a passing mood or what. The sudden pretence of anxiety on Mama's part, when she herself told me that she would worry if we did not *both* go, can not be seriously meant, and cannot be based on H.H.'s observations, as he claims. I will not, however, let myself be a shuttlecock, and as a loafer—or even if I am only described as such—I will *not* go along. Either I belong to H.H.'s suite on official grounds or not. I have already told you that Willisch[1] would be more suitable. I now know something of the trickiness of H.H., and always pin him down ruthlessly. To-day he obviously wanted me to express my wishes, and that he will not get.

I expect of you that you will not out of mistaken friendship go into action and spoil my game.

Goodnight.
Your BB.

129. Leo von Caprivi to Holstein

On board H.M. tender *Blitz*, 17 September 1884

My dear Herr *Geheimrat*!

Many thanks for your friendly lines,[2] which reached me yesterday on the Baltic by torpedo-boat. Simultaneously there came a report by the Chancellor to the Kaiser[3] in which complaints[4] were made of my

---

[1] *Geheimer Hofrat*. Inspector in the Cipher Bureau of the Foreign Ministry.
[2] See *Diaries*, entry for 19 September 1884.
[3] Not found. [4] See p. 126, note 1.

obstinacy in regard to recruitment for King Lüderitz[1] and Princess Rüte.[2] This latter surprised me in so far as on the 6th of this month I had a long discussion with the Under State Secretary Dr Busch, after which I believed myself to be in complete agreement with him. I cannot act on your friendly advice regarding a discussion with *Jupiter tonans*, since for military reasons my presence here is indispensable until Monday. Moreover, I do not think highly enough of my capacity for such a discussion to promise myself any success from it. Once the great man is angry with one, it is probably wisest to get out of his way in time; it will be my endeavour to do so.

Once again hearty thanks for your kindness and the assurance of the sincere regard with which I remain.

Your very devoted
Caprivi.

130. Wilhelm von Bismarck to Holstein

24 September [1884]

Dear H.,

[...] His Highness' interview with Caprivi[3] on the one hand pleases me. On the other I fear that the disdain for colonial activities and the explanation of them as electoral manoeuvres will gradually leak out to the general public, and will hardly contribute to the carnival atmosphere. There are still five weeks before the elections. Many indiscretions can occur in that time. 'I don't give a curse, curse, curse, all that plagues me is my thirst, thirst, thirst. My thirst, my thirst for knowledge.' As you see I am now almost fitted to be a courtier. [...]

I can find no reason for His Highness' love for England. Just at the moment when the danger with His Imperial Highness[4] is specially to be taken into consideration.

Goodnight
Your BB. [...]

131. Wilhelm von Bismarck to Holstein

26 September [1844]

Dear H.,

[...] Letter from Herbert from Mar Lodge; met Chamberlain on the train,[5] told him of letter to Granville.[6] Chamberlain, furious, will

[1] Adolf Lüderitz. A wholesale merchant in Bremen. In 1883 he bought the port of Angra Pequena and the adjoining coastland. His African properties formed the basis of Germany's South-west African colony.

[2] Sister of the Sultan of Zanzibar. Widow of a German merchant.

[3] See *Diaries*, entry for 23 September 1884.

[4] The Crown Prince.

[5] According to a memorandum by Herbert von Bismarck of 24 September (this is the letter mentioned by Wilhelm von Bismarck), he met Joseph Chamberlain on a train journey from Queensborough to London. See *Grosse Politik*, vol. IV, no. 753, pp. 83–5, where only a small part of the memorandum is printed. The omitted section was chiefly an account of Chamberlain's remarks about the internal political situation in England. (From the Foreign Ministry files.)

[6] See p. 128, note 6.

demand to see the letter. Granville has telegraphed to H. and asked him to come. H. replied: Already at Fife, *did not stop at London*.[1] H. told the whole story of our *claims* to Wales. W. again inveighed against Derby;[2] so it goes on, one insults the other. Herb. will go to Paris with instructions. His Highness will give orders about what is to be sent to him. Do take a look to see if there is not something to be added. The courier does not need to be in London before the 4th, that is, he has to leave Berlin on the 2nd. [...]

If Bl[eichröder] has stirred up His Highness against H[erbert], he has done H. a service since Herbert does not want to come to Berlin at all. Bl's influence is thus proved once again, but it no longer astonishes me. I know that it exists, but to quarrel with existing forces is useless; one must reckon with them. But I do think it worth while to expose dirty tricks by Bl. as often as possible. It is always a cold douche.

Caprivi will not bring the fleet up to par with mere thoroughness; too little initiative. Why doesn't he demand subsidies for the fisheries? H.H. would be quite ready, I think. The matter recently came under discussion. Caprivi really ought continually to curse and swear, disclaiming with his arms and legs in the air that too little is done for the navy.

Adio. All is in order here. Loneliness is a matter of indifference to me. And yet I find that I have less spare time here than in V[arzin]. The devil knows why, but not

Your BB.

132. Herbert von Bismarck to Holstein

Friedr[ichsruh], 11 October [1884]

Dear Holstein,

Many thanks for your letter which I found here to-day; that you agreed with my reports pleased me greatly. Probably Bill will send you two long reports from Scotland[3] that were sent directly here, and were not uninteresting.

Something can definitely be done with Ferry;[4] but he is not easy to handle and that worn out Hohenlohe is probably no longer capable of filling the Paris post—which is now particularly slippery and difficult, but rewarding for hard work—in the way the interests of our policy demand. This suspicion that was already stirring in me solely on the basis of my knowledge of the documents has now, after a completed autopsy, become an absolute certainty.

[1] Herbert von Bismarck did not visit Granville because Granville had not replied to his letter of 30 August. (See *Grosse Politik*, vol. IV, p. 83, note **; vol. IV, no. 754, pp. 85–7; see also *Diaries*, entry for 19 September 1884.)

[2] Edward Stanley, 15th Earl of Derby. Secretary of State for the Colonies in Gladstone's Cabinet, 1882–5.

[3] See p. 136, note 5. Only a short extract from the second report of 26 September was found in the Foreign Ministry files. It concerns a conversation Herbert von Bismarck had with the Private Secretary of the Prince of Wales regarding Sir Robert Morier.

[4] Herbert von Bismarck was in Paris from 5–7 October for conversations with the men in charge of French policy on the subject of the Franco-German understanding. (See *Grosse Politik*, vol. III, no. 694, pp. 431–7.)

We simply don't have the kind of ambassador that we now need in Paris. What a pity that one cannot duplicate Hatzfeldt; he is unique, really capable; but since he is indivisible, he is more valuable in Berlin

Rotenhan is good, but as he says himself, a beginner, and somewhat *slow and heavy*.[1] Nevertheless he can do good if he cautiously widens with a delicate hand the breach that I have opened. An opportunity for this is already afforded by the use of Plessen's[2] report of the 8th, which is being returned to-day and on the margin of which my father, at my suggestion, has written the explicit statement of his instruction: 'to be passed on for information, with general validity'.[3] I would only recommend that Rotenhan does *not* say anything to Ferry about the final lines of the closing marginalia on England's overwhelming seapower, because it weakens the impression made by what precedes it. Please write in that sense to Rotenhan, otherwise he will carry it out too conscientiously and repeat every word; I know this habit. The ambassadors mostly say too little, the chargé d'affaires as a rule too much.

Personal acquaintance and conversation with Ferry are very useful to me. I now have a much clearer view of possibilities there. But it makes me sad to think that they will not be exploited because of Hohenlohe's inadequacy. *C'est au delà de ses moyens.* If rightly handled, Ferry *would* come to have complete confidence in us; naturally it would take a long time, and handling him would require more dexterity than Prometheus and more patience than Sisyphus possessed.

My father thinks that we must without fail keep the promises made through me to the French, and squeeze and isolate England still more, until it becomes so bad that even the most stupid of the English Liberals will become alive to the folly of Gladstone's silly policy.

It is along this line that our policy will be directed for the present.

As to myself I will again propose to my father tomorrow that I now remain at The Hague until Christmas, and then place myself at his disposal. I think that will suit him.

Adieu. Ever your

HB. [...]

133. Herbert von Bismarck to Holstein

Fr[iedrichsruh], 12 October 1884

Dear Holstein,

[...] I certainly do not judge Hohenlohe too harshly; I think he should be ashamed as *archiramolli* to claim this important post for his incapacity. When you last saw him at work (it must have been in Berlin

---

[1] In English in the original.

[2] Ludwig, Baron von Scheel-Plessen, from 1898 Count von Plessen-Cronstern. First Secretary in the Embassy in Constantinople from June 1883, in St Petersburg from August 1883, in London, 1884–8; Minister in Athens, 1894–1902.

[3] The report records a conversation between Plessen and the Councillor of the French Embassy, Count Florian, about Egypt. The Chancellor wrote on the margin of this document: 'We will gladly support France [in her demands on England]; we have identical interests, since England has misused her superiority at sea.' (From the Foreign Ministry files.)

in 1881) he showed himself to be totally incompetent. Since then, however, his abilities have fallen off enormously, as I have been assured from the most diverse sources.

Hoping to see you soon
Ever your HB.

134. Wilhelm von Bismarck to Holstein

Fr[iedrichsruh], 16 October 1884

Dear Holstein,

The conversation turned to-day on Münster's vote on the question of the adjournment of the Conference, and Ferry's *ulcération* over it.[1]

His Highness would like to review the whole thing again, and asks you as the official in charge of this matter for a *brief* presentation of the facts.[2] It really turns only on that *one* telegram from Hohenlohe.[3]

H.H. had promised France support, and I think instructed Münster in that sense; then came Hohenlohe's telegram, according to which Ferry understood that in this matter the French 'would be happy to support us'. H.H. thereupon telegraphed to Münster that Ferry's reception of the matter was so cool and reserved that we must be cautious. Münster should support them, but reach agreement beforehand with Russia and Austria. Now Münster made his mistake; he did not discuss the matter with R. and A., but in the Conference waited to see what they would do. R. and A. waited to see what Münster did, and so all three of them did nothing.

I agree with Herb. that Hohenlohe's telegram was misleading. Ferry really *could* not have expressed himself in such a way.

I am writing all this in such detail so that you will know what it is all about and leave aside *all irrelevancies*. The hygiene question[4] also played a role in it, but in my opinion was of little importance. If you are of a different opinion from knowledge of the documents, and think that our pulling back in the hygiene question affected Ferry, then mention it. Refrain from comments; they could do damage. It is merely a question of the arrangement.[5]

Adio. Your BB.

[1] The London Conference on Egyptian finances. See above p. 122, note 1; *Grosse Politik*, vol. III, p. 413, note **; vol. III, no. 682, p. 418.

[2] This was drawn up by Holstein on the following day.

[3] Of 31 July 1884. See above, p. 122, note 1.

[4] The fact that England had encouraged the Cape Government to go ahead in South-west Africa caused Bismarck to take the French side in the Conference on Egypt with greater resolution and frankness. In order to make England's weakness clearly apparent at the Conference, Bismarck instructed Münster to raise the question of Egypt's health administration. This was a painful subject for England in view of the inadequate measures taken by English officials against the danger of cholera. Granville tried to remove this subject from the agenda, but the other Powers supported Germany. (Windelband, *Bismarck und die europäischen Grossmächte*, p. 591.)

[5] On 18 October Wilhelm von Bismarck wrote to Holstein: 'Abstract from the documents was satisfactory. I have written to Busch about it, to prevent the distrust regarding Hohenlohe from getting into the files. H.H. has it too, and I cannot resist having it myself. I still remember that telegram. It was clumsily worded.'

135. Wolfram von Rotenhan to Holstein

Paris, 18 October 1884

My dear *Herr Geheimrat*!

Owing to the shortness of time I can only send a brief report[1] and these two words by to-day's courier.

In making my communication to F[erry], I changed the passage in question as you suggested.[2]

The visit of Count Herbert was very enjoyable and interesting. He got on well, also personally, with the French. Ferry characterised him as *un homme sympathique*. It is to be hoped that the Minister believed everything that Count Bismarck told him. Up to now I have the feeling that he trusts us. But he does not dare to let his compatriots see this.

He also anxiously avoids being unfriendly to England.

In the highest respect.

Your most devoted
Rotenhan

136. Wilhelm von Bismarck to Holstein

19 October [1884]

Mon cher,

[...] Nothing has been telegraphed to Rotenhan from here. The instruction that leaves tomorrow has nothing to do with the Congo Conference.[3] Simply intended to remove *old* misunderstandings. Nobody sneaked on Hohenlohe. It is simply our common judgment based on the political situation that either his telegram was muddled or the approach to Ferry maladroit. We will soon see what F. *now* says to Rotenhan. From that we can then make further judgments. My 'bad taste' was only a joke.[4] But I am no longer offended by anything His Highness does. It is astonishing that after all his worries, he is still as he is. The only thing that depresses me now and again is the result. But he is seventy, and has passed the years in sorrow, irritation and work. Who knows what we would be like at seventy. I hope I don't live so long. I would not like to.

Goodnight.

Your BB.

137. Herbert von Bismarck to Holstein

The Hague, 1 November 1884

Dear Holstein,

Warmest thanks for your kind lines of the 30th of last month, with

---

[1] Not found.
[2] See Herbert von Bismarck's letter of 11 October.
[3] The instruction ordered Rotenhan to bring up again with Ferry at some suitable opportunity the question of the adjournment of the Egyptian Conference in order to dissipate any remaining mistrust that Ferry might still entertain. (From the Foreign Ministry files.)
[4] Wilhelm von Bismarck wrote on 18 October that his father had described one of his suggestions as being in 'bad taste'.

Rotenhan's letter[1] which I again enclose; the latter gives me pleasure, but even more so does his dispatch no. 276 of the 24th of last month.[2] If Rotenh. really said only the half of what he writes in comprehensible terms to Ferry *so that this one has digested it inwardly*,[3] then I think it was very useful. But this dispatch confirms again what I have always said, that Hohenlohe completely muffed the business at the beginning of August and that more blame rests on him than on Münster, from whom one did not expect anything better.

The material in the way of ambassadors with which my father has to work is really too deplorable. I often see Reuss here now; *c'est tout simplement un homme éteint!*

If Kapnist[4]—surely the one here is meant, and not his wooden brother in the Ministry in St Petersburg[5]—really came to the conference in Berlin, it would greatly please me. I see a lot of him, he is frequently—also *à deux*—my guest and I have spoken with him very thoroughly and confidentially; he is wholly *dans la bonne voie*, inspired by healthy self-confident ambition, and by virtue of his own capability convinced that everything is open to him, and in my opinion is the most capable Russian diplomat in office that I know. If he had the opportunity of developing his first European activity in Berlin, of becoming known there and of informing himself, it would be of great value for the future.

Thank you very much for your congratulations on my election;[6] it pleases me especially on account of my father, who set great store upon it, and in any case a Progressive vote is thus removed. It is to be hoped that in Berlin VI the Conservatives will vote for the Social Democrats, and the other way round in the other districts. It is a shame that so many Radicals were elected, I would prefer one hundred Social Democrats to a single one of those miserable creatures.

Vale!
Ever your
HB.

138. Bernhard von Bülow to Holstein

St Petersburg, 13 November 1884

Dear Herr von Holstein,

At last I can thank you more fully for your two kind and interesting letters. I have thought a lot about what you wrote about our good old Hohenlohe. My *ceterum censeo* is that his secretaries must be gingered up. Hohenlohe's weakness is that, although in general too indolent,

---

[1] Of 18 October.
[2] Rotenhan reported that in accordance with his instructions (see p. 140, note 3) he had spoken to Ferry and that the latter had ended the conversation with the following words: '*Eh bien, ce sont des malentendus qui sont passés. L'essentiel est à present de marcher ensemble côté à côté dans la question égyptienne.*' (From the Foreign Ministry files.)
[3] In English in the original.
[4] Peter, Count Kapnist. Russian Minister at The Hague, 1884–92.
[5] Dmitri, Count Kapnist. Director of the Asiatic Department in the Russian Foreign Ministry.
[6] As Deputy to the Reichstag.

he can now and then be incautious through exaggerated impressionability. This should be prevented by those under him, which is relatively easy with a man of Hohenlohe's docile nature. The situation in Paris at the present time obviously requires great attention. The English will naturally do all they can to draw the French away from us. For this purpose they will try to keep alive the notion of *revanche*, if necessary by bribing a few journalists and deputies; they will depict the dangers of overseas expeditions in an exaggerated light, and for this purpose set afoot false Stock Exchange rumours, which it is not difficult to do owing to the dependence of the Paris Bourse on the London Stock Exchange; they will arouse Freycinet's envy, the hatred of the Reds, and Grévy's *sourde rancune* against Ferry; and perhaps they will also slander us to Ferry, who is suspicious by nature. This must be countered by contacts with and the influencing of influential Frenchmen like Charmes, Pallain, etc., etc., keeping watch on Ferry and Grévy, inspiration of our Press through the *Korrespondenz*, which in turn influences the French Press. Do you not think that it would also be useful in present circumstances to warn Hoh. against Blowitz and Freycinet? I was always of the opinion that the fat Opper must be kept as an often good source of information; but I am convinced Blo[witz] is doing what he can to restore the Anglo-French understanding *qui est sa raison d'être*; he is very wily and Hoh. often very feckless. As for Freycinet, he, like the Reds in general, is a force which could be made use of in certain circumstances. But Hoh. should take care that Freycinet does not use him as a battering-ram against Ferry, whose fall now would certainly mean that France would turn towards England. Freycinet's real support is Clemenceau, who is Gladstone's man. In my opinion, as long as Gladstone remains in power, we had better not let the Reds take over in France. I know that the *haute finance* is opposed to Hoh., and just a year ago I warded off the blow which Bleichröder wanted to direct against him. You can rely upon it that I will always do what lies in my power for Hoh.

Well, Schweinitz has returned with wife and seven children. Schw. said nothing about you; all he said was that Hatzfeldt, you, Sommerfeld and Redern[1]—whom he hates like the devil—were always putting your heads together. Schw. has great qualities—intellect, an assured manner, tact, historical and literary knowledge, great experience—but his unpleasant qualities predominate. I have rarely encountered such a naively egoistical man. He looks on everything that affects himself and his family through a magnifying glass, so that it seems to him of immeasurable importance; whereas other people, their interests and desires, only exist for him in microscopic proportions. In addition his exaggeratedly narrow-minded outlook upon all aspects of life is somewhat irritating. You know the story of the woman, who, when asked by the assistant whether she wanted a Russian (fat) or a French (long) *bienfaiteur*, answered: A Frenchman who has lived in Russia. Schw. thinks or speaks like a Spanish Carlist who has served for some years with the

---

[1] Wilhelm, Count von Redern. First Secretary in the Embassy in St Petersburg, 1881–2.

First Guards Regiment and then married a very prudish Quaker. What is more, Schw. understands little of official routine. [...]

Ever yours
B.

139. Herbert von Bismarck to Holstein

The Hague, 6 December 1884

Dear Holstein,

I was very sorry not to have seen you again the day before yesterday; before twelve Kapnist was with me for a long time, and afterwards I had to waste nearly three hours in the Reichstag listening to silly speeches before I could make my own little *speech* in support of the lower-ranking officials, about which I spoke with you the day before. Well, in a fortnight, I think, we shall see each other again and then *pour tout de bon*. You know that I do not come to Berlin with much pleasure but solely because my father wishes it.[1] The whole way of life there is distasteful to me and does not suit me; this time again I did not feel at all well there, without exactly knowing why.

The chief cause may perhaps be the fact that my parents enjoy so little good health. It worries me and depresses my spirits that I have to look on helplessly while my parents—who, if there were any justice in the world, should have a better time than any one else—have really so little joy in life and live such lonely lives on account of their ill-health and on other grounds. They both *feel* lonely, as no one knows better than I, and it pains me, especially as I cannot alter it. If I now come to Berlin I shall have so much to do that I cannot be much at home and cannot even devote the customary hours from six until half-past nine to them. The mere thought of all the *faux frais* of professional, parliamentary and widely ramified personal relations oppresses me. 'I am weary of the rush and hurry, what means all joy and pain.' During the fortnight that remains to me here I shall get as much rest as possible, afterwards all that will be at an end, and I must drag out all that is within me even when I feel tired and old. Where will the energy come from? *I am so heartily sick of this!*[2] Yesterday I went straight to the beloved seashore; it was high tide with the waves breaking, and I hear with much joy the fresh sharp sound that wind and tide bring to one, and forget the worries and miseries of the world in contemplation of nature's grandeur. I shall miss that too very much in Berlin, where I find the dreary Tiergarten—the sole resource available—so horrible that I cannot bear to look at it. In London I was only an hour and a quarter from the sea, and in St Petersburg I could even race across the snowfields of the islands to the Gulf in three quarters of an hour, and every time I felt

---

[1] Herbert von Bismarck was being groomed for the post of Under State Secretary in the Foreign Ministry. On 3 January 1885 Bismarck issued the following instruction: 'All documents for signature by the Under State Secretary, in so far as they are concerned with political and colonial questions, as well as all matters entered under Ib [personnel, etc.], are in future to be presented for counter-signature to the Imperial Minister, Count H. von Bismarck-Schönhausen.' (From the Foreign Ministry files.)

[2] In English in the original.

depressed[1] I hurried over those short distances and was filled with renewed vigour. But in Berlin I can only look at myself in the ink-stand.

Even though I am determined to lead a contemplative life here, I still like to read something interesting, and would be grateful if a dispatch bag could again be sent to me every few days. Perhaps you will tell Busch to keep me supplied.

Now adieu. I hope that you contemplate the remainder of life with more equanimity than I am able to do.

Hic et ubique
Ever your
HB.

140. Chlodwig zu Hohenlohe to Holstein

Paris, 17 December 1884

My dear Baron,

As far as I can see here, there is as yet no question of any approach by France to England or of an understanding between the two regarding the Egyptian Question. Ferry does not yet know what he should do. He would like to speak out more decisively if he did not need England to bring the war with China to a close and if he knew what counter-proposals would receive the approval of Prince Bismarck. He told me to-day that he intended to propose a counter-project to the Powers. [...]

With friendly greetings,
Your most devoted
C. Hohenlohe[2]

[1] In English in the original.
[2] See Rogge, *Holstein und Hohenlohe*, p. 224.

1885

141. Bernhard von Bülow to Holstein

St Petersburg, 28 May 1885

Dear Herr von Holstein,

May I ask you to be so kind as to forward the enclosed letter to Herbert as quickly as possible, since he tells me he will be at The Hague until the 1st of next month.

Since my return I have been having almost daily altercations with my Big Chief over politics and dispatch-writing in general, and in particular over the present situation, which will not exactly increase his liking for me. If you had been there you would have been much amused. Thus Schweinitz, angered by certain sarcastic remarks about the 'Trio of Honourable Men', recently said in so many words: 'The sins of the last twenty years that you admire so much will one day be punished by God in the same way as the filthy deeds of Frederick the Great.' When I remarked that Jena seemed to me to be more in the nature of atonement for the indolence and incompetence that prevailed after the death of the great king and asked whether Bischoffwerder, Lichtenau and Haugwitz[1] were his ideals, his only answer was a peevish muttering. Objective arguments ricochet without effect from the armour of a man who regards things solely from the subjective standpoint of his own convenience and his fads.

I have steadily pointed out how necessary it is that Giers at least should not give up Merutshak.[2] This excellent Minister, whose continuance in office is so very much in our interest, is himself cutting off the bough on which he sits by his tractability towards England.

One of the first questions Schweinitz put to me after my return was: 'In the New Palace they are naturally very pleased that peace has been preserved?' When I answered that on the contrary the Crown Prince favoured forcible action by England, Schw. seemed very disappointed and displeased.

Do not let Berchem see that I am writing to Herbert about politics.

---

[1] General Johann Rudolph von Bischoffwerder, spiritualist and mystic, who exercised a dominant influence over King Friedrich Wilhelm II of Prussia; Wilhelmine Enke, later Countess Lichtenau, the King's mistress; and Christian, Count von Haugwitz, who directed Prussian foreign policy from 1792 to 1804, and (with Hardenberg) from 1805–6, and whose vacillating policy contributed to Prussia's collapse in 1806.

[2] A dispute over frontier territory in Afghanistan brought about a serious crisis in Anglo-Russian relations during the early months of 1885. Bülow refers to the negotiations over the contested territory that resulted on 10 September 1885 in a peaceful compromise.

B. writes to Schweinitz; if he were to put a flea in his ear, I wouldn't be able to accomplish anything more with the old gentleman.[1] [...]

With best wishes that all goes well with you,

Your faithful
B.

142. Paul von Hatzfeldt to Holstein

Sommerberg, 26 June 1885

Dear friend,

Many thanks for letters and *avis*.[2] I will accordingly probably be back there again by the 2nd, although as yet I cannot quite see what I am to do there. It would be absolutely unheard-of if I were to be disposed of without even being consulted. If—like so many other unheard-of happenings—it is to be done, then my arrival will not change anything.

To-day you can see of how little use it has been that during these four years I have been infinitely considerate and so careful about everything! Two things are quite incomprehensible to me: how can they already think of disposing of the post in Berlin in the desired manner, because it would really mean a slap in the face for everyone—and further, if they do intend to do so, why do they need an ambassador to fill it? In that case it would certainly be simpler—and more decent—if the post in Str[asbourg] were offered to *me*.[3] What Schwein[itz], Hohenl[ohe], Münster, or even Reuss can do there, I can do also.

And now good-bye, until we see each other on the 2nd in Berlin, where everything will fall into place. One thing I am already resolved upon: I will not sacrifice what is left of my health, and so I shall not allow myself to be sent to some place with a bad climate.

Goodbye, Ever your
PH.

143. Chlodwig zu Hohenlohe to Holstein[4]

Munich, 11 July 1885

My dear Baron,

Your kind letter of congratulation[5] was forwarded to me to Schillingsfürst from Ems, because I was unable to go there, and I thank you very much for it. I had to abandon my journey there because the Prince, with whom I have been in frequent correspondence in recent days, advised me to go first to Strasbourg for two days without attracting any attention in order to meet the heads of the administration and to

---

[1] See *Diaries*, entry for 4 June 1885.

[2] Holstein had written to Hatzfeldt that he would soon be pushed into an ambassadorial post in order to make room for Herbert von Bismarck as State Secretary. He advised Hatzfeldt to be in Berlin when Bismarck passed through on 2 July. (See *Diaries*, entry for 28 June 1885.)

[3] Edwin von Manteuffel, the Governor of Alsace-Lorraine, had died on 17 June 1885. See *Diaries*, entry for 13 July 1885.

Hohenlohe had just been appointed Governor of Alsace-Lorraine, a post he held until 1894. (For Holstein's letter of 7 July 1885, see Rogge, *Holstein und Hohenlohe*, p. 241.)

collect the information I needed.[1] For that reason I shall go to Baden this evening, travel from there for the day to Strasbourg so that my name will not appear in any hotel register, and at the same time report to the Kaiser who will probably receive me in the Mainau. Since the Prince advised me not to go to Berlin because there is nobody there from whom I could get any information, I shall return to Paris to await the final decision after having reported to the Kaiser. It is true that I have not run after this post. When one has been Ambassador in Paris for eleven years, one only goes to Strasbourg as a matter of patriotic duty. I admit that I would rather have remained a few years longer in Paris, and that it will be hard for me to leave it, even though I fully appreciate the distinction of the new post.

With friendly greetings
Your most devoted
CHohenlohe.

144. Gustav von Sommerfeld to Holstein[2]

Kissingen, 12 July 1885

Dear Holstein,

Best thanks for your kind lines. Her[3] behaviour, which at first sight seems peculiar, is very understandable to me. By temperament she is timidly self-conscious, moreover she is afraid of the guest who comes on the 7th.[4] She herself explained this to me with the unmistakable air of truth, and I am not gullible! Moreover, according to the impressions brought back by the husband[5] from Ems, the situation was no longer *tendue*, for the state of health[6] there has improved considerably. The chief preoccupation is naturally the marriage![7] She will not hear of it; is she afraid that this subject could be brought into the discussion? One piece of news entirely *entre nous*—the letters of which I spoke to you *have* been sent! This means that she has in no way given up her intentions, desires an understanding for the future.[8] On what basis? With what in view? Actuated by what motive? To explain my opinion about this in writing would be too lengthy. I am, as the present situation demands, most suspicious. But I do not share S[eckendorff]'s opinion which is summed up in the one word 'farce'. This catch-word, moreover, means nothing. One must have one's reasons even for indulging in farce. Furthermore, we are far too calculating to attempt 'indulging' with such great personages without good reason. S[eckendorff]'s judgment is not wholly objective; more about this by word of mouth; here one must go on handling the situation *correctly* on the basis of cool, calm, factual and quite impersonal reflection—we will, I think,

---

[1] See Hohenlohe, *Denkwürdigkeiten*, vol. II, pp. 359–61.
[2] See *Diaries*, entry for 13 July 1885.   [3] Crown Princess Victoria.
[4] Bismarck.   [5] The Crown Prince.   [6] Of the Kaiser.
[7] The projected marriage of Victoria, second daughter of the Crown Princess, with Carlos, Crown Prince of Portugal.
[8] An understanding about a marriage between Princess Victoria and Prince Alexander of Bulgaria.

together see to it that this is done, in so far as it rests with *us*. Moreover it seems to me that in spite of everything something has been gained!

Most faithfully yours
Sommerfeld

145. Herbert von Bismarck to Holstein

K[önigstein], 17 July [1885]

Dear Holstein,

Best thanks for your letter and telegram; as a result of the latter I enclose a letter for Bülow which you will perhaps be kind enough to seal up and hand to the Central Bureau to be forwarded. I have not exchanged a word with him for more than a year about his *matrimonial suit*.[1] The whole thing revolts me. The passion for matchmaking of the high-born protectress,[2] and the idea of seeing our friend saddled with this shrivelled-up lemon-skin, which he himself has squeezed utterly dry, in so far as others have left anything, disgust me. I take it that you are not fond of a second-hand marriage either.

That you exploded Lumsden's[3] *appreciation of the Zulfikar*[1] was a very good thing.[4] The Russians naturally want to gain time and, as we know from Salisbury's letter,[5] the English do too. Hence the worm will certainly not die so quickly.

Before my departure I spoke to A. Bülow in the same sense; he of course knows Prince Wilhelm better than anyone since the latter as he is now is his creation.[6] Nonetheless I would have liked to have had the Prince for a year to eighteen months in Berlin before he takes over the First Guard Regiment, which will again chain him to Potsdam for another two years. The sole condition is that Bülow should once again serve as aide-de-camp, and that he will not yet do.

Goodbye. Ever your
HB.

146. Herbert von Bismarck to Holstein

K[önigstein], 21 July [1885]

Dear Holstein,

Best thanks for your letter. So the long letter which my father on his

[1] In English in the original.
[2] The Crown Princess.
[3] General Sir Peter Lumsden, the English member of a commission for the delimitation of the frontiers of Afghanistan. (See above p. 145, note 2.)
[4] The Zulfikar Pass continued to be a serious cause of contention between England and Russia in Afghanistan. On 8 July Count Münster reported from London a conversation with Sir Peter Lumsden. The latter declared that in his opinion the strength of Russia in Central Asia was overrated and that England by acting forcibly in November or December 1884 could have driven Russia from the Afghanistan frontier for many years. The contents of this report were communicated on 16 July to the Russian Ambassador in Berlin by Bismarck's order. On the same day Schweinitz telegraphed from St Petersburg that Giers had told the English Ambassador that Russia had strengthened her troops at the Zulfikar Pass but did not intend to act aggressively. (From the Foreign Ministry files.)
[5] Salisbury's letter to Bismarck of 2 July 1885. (*Grosse Politik*, vol. IV, no. 782, pp. 132–3.)
[6] Adolf von Bülow had been Aide-de-Camp to Prince Wilhelm since 1879.

last day in Berlin wrote in his own hand to His Majesty about Portugal has been fruitless![1] My father informed him about everything in it, and expected H.M. would in consequence write direct to His Imperial Highness [the Crown Prince] and intervene as head of the family; that would have been the proper thing to do. This aversion to acting in the most important matters according to lower middle-class principles and this anxious avoidance of involvement in alleged affairs of the heart is truly deplorable. Now the reply has naturally been drafted verbatim according to the *bon plaisir* of Her Imperial Highness.[2] [...]

Ever your H.B.

147. Chlodwig zu Hohenlohe to Holstein

Paris, 20 August 1885

My dear Baron,

[...] The way in which the Chancellor envisages policy in Alsace-Lorraine—as formulated by you[3]—is certainly the only right way. The people have been told so much about healing of wounds and reconciliation that they all end by feeling injured and wanting to be healed anew each day. At the same time it is so often emphasised that 'one cannot change one's feelings as one changes one's coat' and that attachment to the old country is only natural, that finally everyone talks *honoris causa* of their unalterable feelings and their attachment to the old country. Since Manteuffel at the same time showed the protestant notables all possible kindnesses as soon as they made the concession to him of asking him personally, the autonomists finally found that they gained nothing by allowing themselves to be called *'renégat'* by the French and 'Swabians' by the Alsace-Lorrainers. Such is the opinion of an observer there. [...]

With friendly greetings
Your most devoted
C. Hohenlohe.

148. Karl von Wedel to Holstein[4]

Vienna, 2 September 1885

Most confidential

My dear Herr von Holstein,

As you know, His Highness the Prince of Bulgaria was invited by His Majesty Kaiser Franz Joseph to this year's big manoeuvres at Pilsen from 28 August to 1 September. During the whole of this time the Prince associated with us, that is to say the Prussian officers, most closely and spent every evening with us in confidential comradely inter-

---

[1] See *Diaries*, p. 214, note 1.
[2] See *Diaries*, p. 225, note 1.
[3] See Holstein's letter to Hohenlohe of 17 August 1885. (Rogge, *Holstein und Hohenlohe*, pp. 242–3.)
[4] See *Diaries*, entry for 9 September 1885.

course. You can imagine that with such opportunities the conversation often turned on conditions in Bulgaria, and that the Prince talked pretty openly about the difficulties that he encountered there, etc.

At the end of one such evening which we had spent in his apartment, the Prince asked me whether he could meet me next morning—on Sunday, 30 August—because he wished to discuss several matters with me. Since I was bound by several engagements and therefore could not fix a definite time, I proposed that I should visit him, and consequently the following morning towards 11 o'clock I went to see him. ⟨Prince Alexander⟩[1] was already awaiting me, and ⟨opened the conversation with the remark that it was a necessity for him to unburden himself for once to an older compatriot. I should therefore permit him to talk politics and possibly be so kind as to make some of his remarks known in Berlin. Upon this last remark I at once declared that I was not empowered to act as official intermediary in political matters of this kind⟩ and that I must therefore reserve to myself whether and to what extent I could take cognisance of his disclosures. At all events I was at the most in a position to make an attempt to bring his wishes and his opinions to the knowledge of His Highness Prince Bismarck through private channels.

⟨I have now hesitated for several days whether I should make use at all of this conversation with the Prince and only the thought that perhaps one or other point might be of interest to His Highness the Reich Chancellor induces me, my dear Herr von Holstein, to give you a short summary of the Prince's remarks.⟩ At the outset I intended to direct this communication to Count Herbert Bismarck but feared by doing so to give an official colour to the affair, whereas I wished to preserve its private character for obvious reasons connected with my position and the lack of political competence associated with it. For these reasons I of course leave it wholly and exclusively to your sympathetic judgment whether what I have written is at all suitable to be passed on.

⟨I might here make the preliminary observations that Prince Alexander took every opportunity of exhibiting and giving unreserved expression to his German sentiments, and that he himself frequently declared that his greatest failure was that he could not learn to cease to be a German and to become a Bulgarian.[2]

Of His Majesty the Kaiser, our most gracious Lord, Prince Alexander invariably[3] spoke with feelings of deepest reverence and repeatedly emphasised that he was fully prepared to obey the all-Highest commands and would count himself lucky if His Majesty would relieve him of his present thorny and thankless position.[4]

In the course of our aforementioned conversation the Prince came to speak of his relations with Her Royal Highness Princess Victoria. He assured me that he had not exchanged a single confidential word with

---

[1] The portions of the letter enclosed in brackets were copied and submitted to Bismarck.
[2] Marginal comment by Bismarck: 'Empty talk, get married!'
[3] Bismarck: 'How long.'
[4] Bismarck: 'and take [him] into the Imp[erial] family.'

the Princess[1] when he saw her at his brother's wedding in Darmstadt,[2] and that the thought of marrying her—even though it would be the greatest honour for him and he could not aspire to anything more distinguished—had never occurred to him.[3] How the rumour of his betrothal arose he himself could not say since he was not informed about the events that had occurred in Berlin over this matter. But the cold reception that His Majesty the Kaiser had accorded him at the time in Berlin[4] had deeply pained him, as had the harsh remarks of His Highness the Reich Chancellor,[5] which had caused him infinite pain, even though he was bound to recognise that they were thoroughly justified from a German standpoint. Prince Alexander also said that he was particularly distressed that now, when he had spent nearly four weeks in Germany, he had not been allowed to come to Berlin.[6] He then went on to say that when in the spring of this year a formal renunciation of the hand of Princess Victoria had been demanded of him, he had immediately complied,[7] because His Majesty the Kaiser's command was paramount in his eyes and because his dearest wish was to earn and to obtain His Majesty's satisfaction.[8] For this reason he had made this renunciation, notwithstanding the fact that no engagement or anything approaching it had ever taken place, and had also accepted a similar declaration by Princess Victoria.

In this connection, Prince Alexander went on to speak of the difficulties of the position in which he found himself as a result of these circumstances. Queen Victoria, with whom he had recently discussed his position, had proposed a marriage to him that would be in every respect and in the highest degree honourable for him. He could not, however, entertain this proposal since the person in question—he did not wish to mention any name for reasons of discretion—was a Catholic, while he was himself a Protestant, and his children would have to be Greek Orthodox. Moreover it was not this circumstance alone that dictated his refusal, but also another sentiment which he felt I would certainly be able to appreciate. As he had already told me, Princess Victoria and he—although never engaged—were now completely free[9] by reason of their exchange of declarations, yet it was repugnant to him to use this freedom immediately to make another marriage. He would therefore prefer that Princess Victoria should marry first,[10] which would certainly be much easier than for him, in order in this way to

[1] Bismarck: '??'.
[2] The marriage of Prince Henry of Battenberg on 23 July 1885 to Princess Beatrice, the youngest daughter of Queen Victoria.
[3] Marginal comment by Bismarck: 'Impudent lie. See his letter to H.M.' (Bismarck refers to Prince Alexander's letter to the Kaiser of 8 April 1885. See *Diaries*, entry for 7 March 1885; also Corti, *Alexander von Battenberg*, p. 219.)
[4] In May 1884.
[5] See *Diaries*, entry for 12 May 1884.
[6] Marginal comment by Bismarck: '!'.
[7] Bismarck: 'Not candidly, however, but ambiguously.' (See *Diaries*, entry for 7 March 1885.)
[8] Bismarck: 'as line of retreat.'
[9] Bismarck: 'So they weren't before after all?'
[10] Bismarck: 'If there was nothing, why these scruples?'

avoid giving the impression that he was bent on making the speediest possible use of his freedom.[1]

Although I believed that I should restrict myself in general merely to playing the part of a listener to the Prince's remarks, I could not refrain from a reply on this occasion. I of course emphasised that I could respect his feelings to a certain degree so far as the man himself was in question, but I could not in any way approve them in his role as Prince and politician. If there was nothing in the whole affair, then his scruples were totally without foundation, but if there was, then every knowledgeable and thinking person would not impute to him any such motives.[2] If he delayed making another marriage, the suspicion would seem only too justified that he was gambling on the death of our most gracious Sovereign,[3] in order then, perhaps, again to pursue his intentions with regard to Princess Victoria with more success; on the other hand, if he married someone else, he would by doing so remove any such suspicion and incidentally make his position in Bulgaria more stable.

This objection seemed to make an impression on the Prince, who in consequence returned to the Queen of England's proposal and the difficulty arising out of the difference in religion. He at once admitted the justice of my opinion, but emphasised the obstacles standing in the way of a suitable marriage, since he must marry a rich wife but did not wish to marry a Russian under any circumstances.[4]

Prince Alexander subsequently spoke of his situation with regard to Russia, and of the reproach levelled at him by His Majesty our Kaiser for his inconsiderate behaviour towards the Tsar, as also of the advice given to him by the former to put himself on a better footing with the latter. The reproach from the former was indeed hard, since whenever he had written to the Tsar of Russia in his capacity as Prince of Bulgaria, he had always acted according to protocol, while certain franker letters were not addressed to the Tsar but to his cousin[5] Alexander.[6] Nevertheless he could only accept His Majesty's reproaches as fully justified, and therefore had to accept with gratitude the gracious offer of all-Highest mediation[7] between himself and Russia, not only because the Kaiser, whom he honoured above everything, would take upon himself this role of intermediary, but also because in the general political situation and in view of Germany's position with regard to Russia, no Power was better suited than the former to free him from the straits to which he was reduced.[8] He had therefore written in this sense in April of this year to the Kaiser our most gracious master[9] and gratefully

[1] Bismarck: 'So he was previously engaged then.'
[2] Bismarck: 'Naturally.'
[3] Bismarck: 'Very true.'
[4] Bismarck: 'Why ever not?'
[5] Bismarck: '!'.
[6] Tsar Alexander III of Russia was a cousin of Alexander von Battenberg.
[7] Marginal comment by Bismarck: 'There is no question of that. Support if *he* seeks Russia's favour, which he does not do.'
[8] Bismarck: 'What would we gain by it? The German nation has no interest in the person of Battenberg.'
[9] See *Diaries*, entry for 7 March 1885.

accepted his gracious mediation, although with the reservation[1] that the Tsar would be moved to take into benevolent consideration reasonable objections raised by him, based on knowledge of local conditions, and not treat him as the responsible viceroy of an irresponsible autocrat.[2] Up to the present he had not received from Berlin any answer to this statement, yet he was extremely anxious to have one so that he might know how he stood with Russia. In this connection he could now only confirm that but three months ago he had received proofs of unfriendly sentiments on the Tsar's part. The Prince at this point added that Count Kálnoky had told him that in Kremsier[3] Tsar Alexander had at all events spoken of him less sharply than last year in Skiernievice.⟩

Prince Alexander later also spoke of his intention of possibly going to Franzensbad to visit Herr von Giers, and thus to make an attempt with him to pave the way to a better relationship with Russia, although he did not believe that this Minister's influence with the Tsar and Russian circles was very great. He had therefore on the same day as I was with him sent his adjutant to Franzensbad to ask Herr von Giers if his visit would be welcome to him. When he received an affirmative reply, Prince Alexander left Pilsen for Franzensbad yesterday afternoon after the end of the manoeuvres, and returned here early this morning. I spoke to the Prince to-day at breakfast and ⟨he was completely satisfied with the way in which his visit had passed off.[4] Herr von Giers had received him at the station and afterwards he conferred with the Minister in his house for one and a half hours, in the course of which the latter behaved in a very friendly manner and promised to report to the Tsar on the conversation. Subsequently Herr von Giers had visited him and accompanied him back to the station. In the course of the conversation the Minister made an attempt to discuss the past, but the Prince besought him to refrain from any such discussion as fruitless,[5] and to confine the conversation to the future. Prince Alexander, who told me he had never been the candidate of Tsar Alexander III because the latter had wanted to see a Russian on the Bulgarian throne, visited Count Kálnoky this morning at his [Kálnoky's] request and told him the result of his visit to Franzensbad. The Prince will leave Vienna the day after tomorrow to return to Bulgaria.

I hardly need tell you,⟩ my dear Herr von Holstein, ⟨that Prince Alexander also mentioned the troublesome affair of the decorations,[6] yet I do not consider it either opportune or of interest to go into this

---

[1] Marginal comment by Bismarck: '!'.

[2] Bismarck: 'He is nothing more.'

[3] Kaiser Franz Joseph and Tsar Alexander had met at Kremsier on 25 August 1885.

[4] In the version of the document submitted to the Chancellor, Holstein altered this passage to read: 'The Prince was completely satisfied ... his visit to Giers had passed off.'

[5] Marginal comment by Bismarck: '!! An arrogant *parvenu*.'

[6] Although he was not a sovereign prince, Alexander von Battenberg had arrogated to himself the right to confer Bulgarian orders. The Sultan of Turkey, the nominal sovereign of Bulgaria, had protested, and Bismarck had informed Prince Alexander in June 1883 that he should not give Kaiser Wilhelm any Bulgarian order. (See Schweinitz, *Denkwürdigkeiten*, vol. II, p. 236; Corti, *Alexander von Battenberg*, p. 125.)

matter and therefore content myself with saying that the Prince seems in part to perceive the grave mistake he made in this matter.⟩[1]

In asking you, my dear Herr von Holstein, to pardon the disconnectedness of my remarks on the ground of the present pressure of work on me arising out of the manoeuvres, and in also adding that I held myself in duty bound to communicate the contents of this letter to Count Goltz,[2] I sign with the expression of my most distinguished esteem

Your most devoted
Ct. Wedel.

149. Eberhard zu Solms to Paul von Hatzfeldt

Madrid, 16 September 1885

Dear Hatzfeldt,

[...] I have written very detailed dispatches about the excited state of public feeling.[3] It was neither stirred up from abroad nor in any way artificially incited. The idea that a foreign Power wanted to take from Spain part of its territory was enough to set the entire nation ablaze. The Ultramontanes and Republicans only gradually took over the affair, which finally took on a thoroughly revolutionary character. The King and Morphy[4] are the only ones who kept their heads; all the others went mad. The Infantas Isabel and Eulalia[5] I also except. It is only because of the King that the craziest decisions, planned even by the Ministers, were frustrated. Canovas[6] was still relatively calm. Respect for the King has also increased greatly. The army gives no cause for mistrust.

The King and the Ministers are however certainly very thankful for the moderation shown by our Government, and I personally have been thanked from all quarters for the composure I showed; naturally by Sagasta's[7] supporters with the ulterior motive of gaining my sympathy. These people, Sagasta, Vega Armijo, Martinez Campos, Jovelles, Venonzio Gonzales, etc., have revealed themselves as even more stupid than the Conservatives. Spain does not have a single statesman. The King has it in him to govern the country if he stuck to the job; but he only intervenes in crises.

To give advice as to how the affair is to be brought nearer to a

[1] At the Chancellor's request, Holstein on 7 September asked Wedel if he would agree to allow an extract of this letter to be submitted to the Kaiser and possibly to the Crown Prince. Count Wedel telegraphed his consent on the same day. Herbert von Bismarck read an extract of the letter to the Kaiser and then to the Crown Prince. (From the Foreign Ministry files.)

[2] Karl August, Count von der Goltz. First Secretary in the Embassy in Vienna, 1884–6, in Rome, 1886–90.

[3] Over the intended occupation by Germany of the Caroline Islands, which Spain claimed had been Spanish possessions since 1543. (See *Diaries*, entry for 23 August 1885 et seq.)

[4] The King's Private Secretary.

[5] Sisters of King Alphonso XII.

[6] Antonio Canovas de Castillo. Leader of the Conservative Party in Spain; Minister-President, 1883–5, 1890–2, 1895–7.

[7] Praxides Mateo Sagasta. Leader of the Liberal Party in Spain; Minister-President, 1881–3, 1885–6, 1886–90, 1892–5, 1897–9, 1901–2.

solution without having been asked by the Foreign Ministry for it is a risky business. But I think I have left nothing undone that could contribute to keeping the govt. informed about the situation.

    Farewell and again hearty thanks

          Yours in devoted friendship

                 Solms

150. Paul von Hatzfeldt to Holstein

Sommerberg, 18 October 1885

Dear Holstein,

Although you are certainly very busy, perhaps you can spare me a few minutes.

Herb[ert] has asked me when I wished for my appointment[1] and when I 'eventually' intend to return. At the same time I have heard confidentially that it is not desired that I should again take over affairs, which I could have imagined for myself.

If possible, have my letter to Herb. shown to you. I have told him I was ready to do anything the Prince desired. If he did not attach importance to my going immediately to London, it would naturally suit me much better on account of my cure. To take charge of affairs again for a short time did not seem advisable to me. But neither could I stay long in Berlin without a post. (It should be easy to understand that I definitely do *not* want that.) Nor would I want to be with Münster in London for any length of time. *If* his father shared my opinion on this subject, I would prefer to stay here until everything was ready.

Do me the favour of using your influence in this sense so far as you can.

I have also once again brought up the two questions (title and order).[2] I hope that the matter will be handled decently. [...]

Please send me news soon.

            In friendship as ever

                Your

                PH.

151. Hugo von Radolinski to Holstein[3]

Friday evening, [23 October 1885]

My dear friend,

Her Imperial Highness[4] has just told me that Their Highnesses attach *great importance* to seeing Count Hatzfeldt *here* before he leaves for London. H.I.H. has *much* to tell him about his new post and other matters.[5] She has authorised me to tell you of her wishes and hopes that *this consideration* will be shown to Their Highnesses, and that

---

[1] As Ambassador in London.   [2] See Hatzfeldt's letter of 25 October.
[3] See *Diaries*, entry for 24 October 1885.   [4] The Crown Princess.
[5] Marginal comment by Holstein: 'Oho!'.

Count H. will not be sent to London before he has seen Their Highnesses here. Will you let this be known in the proper place, and also advise Count H. that Their Highnesses, that is to say the Princess, urgently wish to speak to him before he goes there for good. [...]

Your faithful friend
Rado.

152. Paul von Hatzfeldt to Holstein[1]

Sommerberg, 25 October 1885

Dear Holstein,

Many thanks for your letters; I only delayed my answer until I could see things more clearly. This has come about to-day, as a result of the letter from H. Bismarck in which it is said that in general the Kaiser wanted me to go to London soon, and that Herb. thereupon informed him that I would come to Berlin at the end of the month to settle up my household affairs, which would only take a few days.

Finally the Kaiser then expressed the wish that I should reach London within ten days to a fortnight.

According to this, there is no question of an order from the Kaiser to go directly from here to London; nor have I been informed of a desire of this nature on the part of the Prince. If this were the case, I would naturally do so at once, no matter what serious objections I must have against it. I will not even mention the fact that it would hardly be decent to have anyone, who had been a Minister for four years, disappear like a thief in the night without any farewell—nor will I mention that it is pretty steep to expect someone simply to abandon his belongings and servants. These are considerations unknown in Berlin. But in addition there are two things that cannot be taken so lightly. First and above all I need information and instructions after hearing nothing for two months. Secondly, it would quite rightly be looked on as very strange if the new representative in London did not report beforehand to the Crown Prince and Crown Princess and enquire whether they had any orders for England. At least I would not like to take that upon myself without more ado.

I am writing to-day to H. Bismarck and telling him, 1. that although I am tormented with sciatica I am ready at *any* moment to go to London if His Majesty or his father order it; 2. that if this does not happen, I will give effect to the suggestions in his letter by coming to Berlin for some days to dissolve my household, pack my things and uniform, get instructions, say good-bye—all of which can be done in a few days; 3. that Count Münster has written to me that he will not leave before the 9th or 10th and proposed to me that I should arrive there on the 7th or 8th. If Münster gets permission for this everything will fit in, because I will arrive at the given time, which would correspond with the time indicated by H.M.

I think I can assume that Berlin will agree to this arrangement.

[1] See *Diaries,* entry for 27 October 1885.

Should it be desired nevertheless that I go immediately and directly to London, an official intimation that H.M. or the Prince desires it will suffice. [...]

I will confine myself to a few words about the question of a decoration. I am convinced that you have worked in my interest and thank you very much for it. But I cannot share your opinion. If they do not want to treat me particularly badly, it is self-evident that after four years and on the occasion of a change of this nature, I should be given a decoration, and that it should be the *customary*, that is the *indicated* Hohenzollern Order, which was given to Maybach,[1] Eulenburg,[2] etc. Since it is a matter of importance in this case to show the world that there is no question of disgrace, I very wisely put up the Red Eagle *as a condition*.[3] Maybach and A[ugust Eulenburg] could not take exception, because diplomats are treated differently, as, for example, Münster was, who has had it for a long time. In my humble opinion what is decisive, however, is the given promise. Moreover you know how little I care about such things. Only do not ask me to consider this behaviour correct.

And now goodbye for to-day. To our next meeting, unless I get instructions to go directly to London.

Your sincerely devoted
PHatzfeldt.

153. Paul von Hatzfeldt to Holstein

[London], 25 November 1885

Dear friend,

Many thanks for your letters. When I got the last I was just about to ask you for your private address!

The way business is conducted here is very remarkable. No Minister for days on end and nothing can be done. Once again I cannot see Salis[bury] at all before Monday, nor his deputy—who tells one nothing anyway.

From my standpoint everything has gone quite satisfactorily up to now. The question is only whether my point of view is shared there, for I hear nothing about it. Was my long private letter to Herb[ert] shown at the time to His Highness, and what did he say to it?[4] It would have been very valuable for me to know.

Nobody knows how the elections will turn out—only that there will probably only be a small majority, hence a weak Government will come

---

[1] Albert von Maybach. Prussian Minister of Public Works, 1878–91.

[2] August, Count zu Eulenburg. Chamberlain and Court Marshal to the Crown Prince, 1868–83; Chief Master of Ceremonies from 1883; Chief Court and House Marshal to Kaiser Wilhelm II from 1890.

[3] For exchanging the post of State Secretary for that of Ambassador in London.

[4] In this letter of 14 November Hatzfeldt had reported that he was pressing in London to bring about an agreement at the Conference of Ambassadors in Constantinople since a serious Eastern crisis could not be in Germany's interests. The letter was submitted to the Chancellor without Hatzfeldt being informed of the fact. (From the Foreign Ministry files.) The Conference of Ambassadors had been convened as a result of the revolution in Eastern Rumelia in September 1885. See note below.

in. It is still always *possible* that Salisb. will stay on. I stand *well* with him and can tell him *everything*.

In my opinion the principal thing now is to see that the Sub-Commision gets in by the back-door and that an armistice is concluded.[1] Russia and Austria made a démarche here yesterday in that sense. Why not we?

I would not look on it as a misfortune if the Greeks were to attack. The Turks will certainly still be able to do that much, and it would help to raise their prestige. They would then be busy there, would not be able to advance into Eastern Rumelia, and that again would be a good thing.

My impression that the people here would not drop the Bulg[arian] was, as you see, right. The interest in him at Windsor is as keen as ever.

Goodbye for to-day, dear friend, and please do not leave me without news.

Recently I asked you for some information on financial matters. The necessary installations here, state-carriage, etc., are really ruining me!

Ever your
PH.

[1] A revolution had broken out in Philippopolis on 18 September with the object of uniting Eastern Rumelia with Bulgaria. Prince Alexander was forced by strong nationalist pressure to assume the leadership of the movement, Serbia demanded compensation for the resulting increase in Bulgarian territory, and on 13 November 1885 declared war on Bulgaria. The Serbians were defeated at Slivnitsa (17–19 November) and Pirot (26–7 November). Austria intervened on behalf of Serbia, and on 3 March 1886 a peace treaty between Serbia and Bulgaria was signed at Bucharest on the basis of the *status quo*.

1886

154. Alfred von Kiderlen-Wächter to Holstein

Strictly Personal

Paris, 2 March 1886

My dear *Herr Geheimrat*,

My heartfelt thanks for the new proof of goodwill and sincere friendship which you gave me in your last letter. You will understand that it has both impressed and depressed me; but at least I was able to perceive from it that you are prepared to bear even with my limited ability and take into consideration the difficulty of my position *vis-à-vis* the extremely suspicious Ambassador.[1] A comparison with Bülow must naturally always be to my disadvantage; Bülow is in the first place known everywhere as an uncommonly capable diplomat, and in the second, if I may so express myself, he had in his Chief[2] at least a support and a valuable collaborator whereas I, *entre nous soit dit*, have only a ball and chain in mine. I will at all events do my utmost to fulfil the demands made upon me.

In any case, once again my most hearty thanks to you. I would be very grateful to you if in the near future you would be so kind, in so far as your own work permits, as to draw my attention in a word or two to mistakes and inadequacies in my reports.

I hope and wish with all my heart that you are again completely restored to health.

As ever in sincere respect and unalterable gratitude

Your obedient and devoted

Kiderlen.

155. Holstein to Hugo von Radolinski[3]

Wednesday evening, [April 1886]

Dear Rado,

If the Chancellor demands that you withdraw your resignation,[4] say: 'If Gen. Albedyll can produce a declaration by a *court of honour* to the effect that the letter of resignation contains a reflection on Sommerfeld's honour, then you will be prepared to withdraw or explain the indicated

---

[1] The German Ambassador in Paris was now Count Münster.
[2] Prince Hohenlohe.
[3] From the Radolin Papers.
[4] Radolin had handed in his resignation as Court Marshal to the Crown Prince on the grounds that he could no longer work with the personal adjutant of the Crown Prince, Colonel von Sommerfeld.

passage; but you make this dependent upon the declaration of the court of honour.'[1]

I leave it to you whether to retreat still further; I would hardly do so. Draw the Chancellor's attention to the fact that owing to the untrustworthiness hitherto shown by the opposite side, especially by Albedyll, it is for practical reasons not advisable for you to disarm by withdrawing your resignation.[2] We would then have no guarantee that after his leave Sommerfeld will not simply return.[3] The reason for his departure disappears if your resignation is withdrawn.

While observing every courtesy, be short and decisive in your statements to His Highness.

I will wait for you here until 12:15, then I must leave.

Your
H.

156. Holstein to Hugo von Radolinski[4]

Thursday morning, [April 1886]

Dear Rado,

I have thought over the business overnight and have arrived at the following:

Let it be felt that you, not His Highness [Bismarck], are the person to whom an obligation is due.

If H.H. demands that you should withdraw further than the court of honour demands, then simply say: 'No. First years of annoyance and then in addition retreat, no thanks. In that case Sommerfeld can be Court Marshal.' H.H. knows what that would mean for him. He will then get a move on. If H.H. wants to put you in touch with Rottenburg to talk over the wording of some kind of letter, then *refuse* by remarking: 'I request Your Highness to send the draft to my house where I will think it over at my leisure.'

As I said, I will be in the office until 12:15. I am writing this at home.

Your
H.

If H.H. tells you that the Crown Prince's word guarantees you your position, then say: 'I am not primarily concerned about that, but about being expected to retreat at Sommerfeld's orders. *That* I do not want.'[5]

---

[1] On the subject of Albedyll's part in the affair, Holstein wrote on 2 May to his cousin Ida von Stülpnagel: 'In order to intimidate the Crown Prince and Princess, who were anxious to keep Rado, Albedyll told them that Radolinski's statement that he did not want to serve with Sommerfeld any longer constituted a reflection on his honour that Sommerfeld could not ignore. The latter would challenge Rado, and he, Albedyll, could do nothing to prevent it.' (Rogge, *Friedrich von Holstein*, pp. 138–40.)

[2] Bismarck was trying to settle these personnel problems at the Crown Prince's Court.

[3] It was provisionally arranged that Sommerfeld should take a long leave of absence, after which he would not return to the Crown Prince's Court.

[4] From the Radolin Papers.

[5] On 22 April Radolinski sent Holstein the text of Sommerfeld's letter of resignation, which contained the assurance that he would not seek to return to the Crown Prince's service.

157. Holstein to Hugo von Radolinski[1]

Berlin, 5 May 1886

Hugo dear,

To-day K[essel][2] came to say goodbye; he left this evening for Homburg. He says that Som[merfeld], who handed everything over to him yesterday and to-day, is stiff and reserved, like a person who has by no means given up his case as lost. K. believes 'the affair is not yet over'.

Meanwhile *beati possidentes*. The other party is for the moment out of the picture. The *Neue Freie Presse* hints that Som. was unwelcome to the Chancellor on account of his liberalism. Will Som. now place himself on that side? That would be very funny.

On taking over, K. asked at the end whether there were still any secret matters of any kind whatever? Som. answered: 'Absolutely none.' The dirty linen has thus been washed. I suspect that the lie came from Seck[endorff] and was more or less deliberately disseminated by Alb[edyll].

Today I met our friend Fri[edberg].[3] He strongly disapproved of the post[4] being occupied again by a *soldier* and is trying hard to get His Imperial Highness to take an *assistant judge* on a permanent basis. Fri. probably feels that with the present combination H.I.H. is slipping through *his* fingers.

August Eul[enburg] visited me to-day and voiced proper sentiments. Very bitter against Alb[edyll].

Incidentally, I told K. to-day in some detail that the chief difficulty for you was not in getting Som. out, but getting him, K., in. He did not know about all this.

K. will try at first to get on well with Seck[endorff]. I told him that he would probably only put himself in a false position by this. [...]

Ever yours
H.

158. Herbert von Bismarck to Holstein

Homburg, 24 June 1886.

Dear Holstein,

[...] As for Waldersee, really, no thank you. In Vienna we need an active and persuasive man, for in the course of the next eight to ten months our whole future will pivot on Vienna. What a pity that I myself cannot go there for half a year! Reuss at least has tradition, and as we have none *better*, he will have to do for the time being. I hope that His Highness will settle the main problems with Franz Joseph in Gastein.[5] *A bon entendeur salut.* We have enough lazy camels like W. and

---

[1] From the Radolin Papers.
[2] Major Gustav von Kessel. Provisional successor to Sommerfeld as Aide-de-Camp to the Crown Prince.
[3] Heinrich von Friedberg. Prussian Minister of Justice, 1879–89.
[4] The post of personal Aide-de-Camp to the Crown Prince.
[5] A meeting took place on 8–9 August at Bad Gastein between the German and the Austrian Kaiser, at which Bismarck and Kálnoky were present. There are no detailed memoranda of these conversations. (See *Grosse Politik*, vol. V, p. 55, note ***.)

the personnel of the General Staff is not *our* affair but that of the ruler, who is most closely concerned with it. *Ne sutor ultra crepidam.* The Crown Prince will take Verdy[1] immediately anyway, and *after all* he is the most capable of them all. [...]

Ever your
HB.

159. Hugo von Radolinski to Holstein

26 June 1886

My dear friend,

By yesterday evening *everything* had already been sent *there*[2] via L.[3] by telegraph and to-day the person in question[4] is already fully informed. What was written about Mac[edonia][5] is just as distorted as the earlier incident;[6] for quite recently the person in question spoke about M. and said that this question must not under any circumstances be touched upon in any way, for it would have regrettable consequences. Also he would as before do everything to suppress a possible rising there, or rather to hinder it. After this statement L. very definitely denies that he could have said anything of a chauvinistic nature to C.v.R.[7] Moreover L. was with the person in question during the visit to Rum. There must quite definitely be some distortion of the truth. I have seen the original telegram which definitely denied any knowledge of the Sob[ranje] Dep[utation]. Since, moreover, Bratianu[8] is stone-deaf it is possible that he might not have heard rightly.

So poor Al[exander] is really innocent and is honestly following all the advice he has been given. Until Monday; we will probably dine at 6 o'clock in the Kaiserhof?

Your truly devoted
Rd.

---

[1] Julius von Verdy du Vernois. Prussian General. Head of a Division of the General Staff, 1870–1; Director of the general War Department in the Ministry of War; Divisional Commander, 1883; Governor of Strasbourg, 1887; Minister for War, April 1889–October 1890.

[2] To Sofia.

[3] Prof. Langenbuch, doctor of medicine, who acted as intermediary between Prince Alexander of Bulgaria and the Crown Prince's Court. (See Corti, *Alexander von Battenberg*, pp. 318, 355–7, 359–61.)

[4] Prince Alexander of Bulgaria.

[5] It was said that Prince Alexander had offered King Carol of Rumania a portion of the Dobruja and had even asked the Rumanian King for support in case he himself should advance into Macedonia. (See *Aufzeichnungen und Erinnerungen aus dem Leben des Botschafters Joseph Maria von Radowitz*, edited by Hajo Holborn (Berlin and Leipzig, 1925), vol. II, p. 264; Corti, *Alexander von Battenberg*, pp. 296–7; *Diaries*, entry for 22 July 1886.)

[6] Radolinski probably refers to the rumours circulating in May that Prince Alexander contemplated a visit to the Sultan in Constantinople. Prince Alexander denied this. (From the Foreign Ministry files.)

[7] King Carol of Rumania.

[8] Joan Bratianu, Rumanian Minister-President, 1876–81, 1881–8, with whom the information about Prince Alexander's offer to King Carol originated.

160. Philipp zu Eulenburg[1] to Holstein[2]

Munich, 16 July 1886

My dear Baron,

[...] The more the question of a new appointment to the Munich post was discussed[3] the clearer it became to me, as I lay on my sick bed in Liebenberg, how important this post was. An unwise choice could do us great damage.

Of the many dangers, let me take for example the possibility that the new Minister should lose the sympathy of the German Nationalists, as could happen through rudeness—indeed even through the noisy Prussian manner. He would find himself from that time on in a vacuum, and lacking all political support, because he could never establish a real connection with the ultramontane nobility. I myself—after four years—have finally 'sung my way into' these circles and have gained valuable political friendships, but I indulge in no illusions and know that *nevertheless* an abyss separates me from these people, even if they have permitted me to invite myself regularly to breakfast or luncheon with them.[4]

The Bavarian Ministry, whether it be of the colour of the present one or ultramontane, is equally sensitive to a certain type of north German behaviour and manner. This susceptibility in regard to us causes these people when they feel insulted to become *more accessible* to the insinuations of those elements whose *sole* task it is to combat Prussian influence in Bavaria. These are: the Nuncio, the French and Russian Ministers, our ally, the Austrian, and the Saxon[5]—that goes without saying. And all these people have their supporters among the Ultramontanes, behind whom the Wittelsbachs are dozing.

In quiet times, an unsympathetic personality in the post of Prussian Minister would in my opinion provide involuntary help for anti-German undermining activities, and the skirmishing that arises from political and official relations between Prussia and Bavaria would culminate in unpleasantness in the Bundesrat.

As soon, however, as a great political catastrophe should confront Germany with a time of crisis: misfortune in war, dangerous enemy alliances, etc., an ill-chosen personality as Prussian Minister would

---

[1] Philipp, Count zu Eulenburg-Hertefeld, since 1900 Prince. Secretary of Legation in Munich, 1881–7; Minister in Oldenburg, 1888–90, in Stuttgart, 1890–1, in Munich, 1891–4; Ambassador in Vienna, 1894–1902. Frequently the Foreign Ministry representative in the Kaiser's retinue. The correspondence between Holstein and Count Philipp zu Eulenburg was initiated by Holstein with a letter of 13 June 1886. (From the Eulenburg Papers.) The first letter from Eulenburg to Holstein in the Holstein Papers is dated 22 June 1886 and begins: 'For your good advice and your kindness in taking me under your wing, my warmest thanks.'

[2] This letter is printed in part and with minor variations under the date 13 July in Johannes Haller, *Aus dem Leben des Fürsten Philipp zu Eulenburg-Hertefeld* (Berlin and Leipzig, 1926), pp. 22–3.

[3] Georg, Baron von Werthern-Beichlingen, Prussian Minister in Munich, 1867–88, was due to retire shortly.

[4] Marginal comment by Holstein: 'So E. would like to get the job himself. Would not be bad.'

[5] Holstein: 'Fabrice.'

have a directly disintegrating effect—whereas a Minister supported by the sympathy of the Bavarian Government and the National Party would on the other hand be capable of assuming a most important role. I recall in this connection the importance of Werthern in the year 1870 before Bavaria's declaration of war upon France.

If we *want* to provoke Bavaria it will be easy to instruct a Prussian representative to this end. But the choice has to be made with great caution if we are striving for a peaceful fusion of all German provinces, if in the end we want the House of Wittelsbach to do no more than appear on the October meadow, drawn like the Merovingians by oxen (for which purpose some of the less gifted Princes might be used!), while the Hohenzollern Pepins inspect the Army and survey the administrative districts with the Heads of Government.

I am sending you, my dear Baron, the preceding reflections without any particular person in mind[1]—solely in the interests of the cause, which means much to me. 'Friendly activity' comes to my mind as a Prussian slogan for a workable German policy, and the men who are entrusted with the carrying out of this policy should correspond in their character and work with the meaning of this phrase.

With best greetings, in grateful devotion

Your
Philipp Eulenburg.

161. Otto von Bismarck to Hugo von Radolinski

Copy

K[issingen], 18 July [1886]

My dear Count,

Herewith I return with best thanks the enclosures[2] of your letter of the 3rd of this month.[3] The expressions used in the Darm[stadt] letters impressed me as being more rhetorical than political. Politics cannot be conducted with exaggerations, such as the idea that we have subordinated our policy to that of the Russians. A fundamental element in what is generally known as foreign policy is that friendly Great Powers show consideration to each other. If they do not do so, then the friendship simply ceases. Unlike in other states, the power of Russia is exclusively embodied in the person of the Tsar. Our policy necessarily takes into consideration not only R[ussia] but also Aus[tria], E[ngland], It[aly], indeed even Fr[ance], which, however, does not prevent us from upholding the interests of the German Reich against R[ussia] as well as against the others. But these are not present in *Bu[lgaria]*. I have given orders that further correspondence regarding the Prince of B[ulgaria] should be brought to your attention and I request you, my dear Count, fully to inform the high personages[4] as to the state of affairs.

[1] Holstein: '?'.
[2] Letters from Prince Alexander of Hesse and the Grand-Duke of Hesse. (See *Diaries* entry for 22 July 1886.)
[3] Not found.
[4] The Crown Prince and Crown Princess.

The bitterness with which Prince A[lexander] expresses himself, and his demand that his statements should be telegraphed to me word for word, reveal more egoism and less political understanding than I had given this gentleman credit for. His Highness possesses, as he has shown on other occasions, sufficient diplomatic cleverness to be able to realise that in the present case he expressly, and in a very dictatorial manner, demands that I should sacrifice the relations between the German Reich and Russia to his *personal* wishes and interests, and, indeed, for the entirely trivial question as to whether or not H.H. has a star on his epaulettes.[1]

With friendly regards
Yours

162. Paul von Hatzfeldt to Holstein

23 July 1886

Dear friend,

[...] The whole future development of things, also in the East, will depend very greatly on the attitude that Sal[isbury] will and can adopt.[2] Nobody can foresee what this will be, because his position in the House will be difficult. It is certain that Hart[ington][3] will not join the government, that he cannot in fact do so because only a few of his supporters would follow him. It is perhaps better this way, for he will continue to dispute the leadership of the Liberals in the House with Gladst[one] and by doing so will ease Sal.'s position. But it depends above all upon an agreement between them on a common programme in Ireland, and the next few days will show whether that can be achieved. Only then will one be able to say that Sal's position is assured and firm. And that is the indispensable preliminary for a resolute foreign policy.

As you know he was formerly very frank with me. But now it is questionable whether Bat[um] and the assumption that we permitted it[4] has not made him timid. We will soon see. Another obstacle here, with which you are familiar, is the general conviction—from which not even he is wholly free—that we, like Austria, cannot and will not in our

---

[1] Prince Alexander of Bulgaria wanted to be made a Prussian Lieutenant-General, an automatic promotion according to seniority to which the Prince thought he had a claim as a member of the Prussian Army. The promotion was refused on the grounds that Alexander, as Prince of a foreign Power, was only an honorary officer in the Army and had no claim to automatic promotion.

[2] Salisbury's second Cabinet took office on 26 July.

[3] Spencer Compton Cavendish, Marquis of Hartington, since 1891 Duke of Devonshire. As leader of the Liberal Unionists Hartington controlled the decisive votes in the existing Parliament. He was Lord President of the Council in Salisbury's and Balfour's Cabinets, 1895–1903.

[4] Giers informed Schweinitz on 23 June of the Tsar's decision to abolish the status of Batum as a free port and to occupy the territory. Giers had reminded the Tsar of Russia's treaty obligations to Germany and Austria, and had sought permission to obtain Bismarck's consent, and, in so far as Bismarck had no objections, to inform Austria also. Bismarck's marginal comments on Schweinitz's dispatch show that he approved of Russia's action. (*Grosse Politik*, vol. V, no. 973, pp. 41–3.) England, however, regarded the situation much more seriously. Rosebery told the Russian Ambassador that if Gladstone's Government were overthrown at the coming elections, the responsibility would rest on Russia and the Batum affair. (*Grosse Politik*, vol. V, no. 976, p. 45.)

own interest suffer certain encroachments. I have already fought many battles against this notion, but cannot make use of the most telling arguments.

You know from experience what I think about Herb[ert]'s theory of the division of the spheres of interest.¹ My opinion is unchanged. What you say about the feeling prevailing in Austria is what I myself feel. I have always thought that ultimately they could never agree and accept. It is also for me an article of faith that we must never allow Austria to collapse. The conclusion is obvious to anyone who recognises this principle. Which does not in any way exclude temporising, exerting a calming influence in Vienna, and, if occasion arises, also for once creating anxiety in order to keep him, K[álnoky], on the straight and narrow. Only one must not play out the trumps in one's hand that would be useful later on.

Permit me in this connection to repeat that in my opinion Pet[ersburg] is being overestimated if it is thought that a systematic policy is now being pursued there. It has not come to that yet. Irritation, bad temper, *coups de tête* on the part of a single person on whom, nevertheless, everything depends—that *can* go further if no opposition is in sight. But if a strong force stands in the way, like Sal[isbury] last year, then the talons are drawn in again.

A propos, what does Her Imperial Highness say about Bat[tenberg]? According to something her brother let fall, I must take it that she has written to him in a *real* rage on the subject which concerns us. *Faire attention à cela!*² [—...]

Addio.

163. Paul von Hatzfeldt to Holstein

S[ommerberg], 28 July [1886]

Dear friend,

[...] To-day I want to emphasise one thing. I *completely* agree that we should not *start a fight* with R[ussia]—who could wish it?—only we must not in my humble opinion drop the trumps that will be needed later and must not *discourage* the *others*. This last is the greatest difficulty in our situation. Batum is an example. The belief that we agreed also paralysed the others. The difficulty therefore is this: not to irritate the one and not to deprive the other of hope. The whole thing is in my opinion unfortunately only a question of time. In the long run all our consideration will not help—and then we will need the above-mentioned trumps very badly. His Highness knows that very well.

Unhappily it seems that things are once again not going well with Her Imperial Highness. Why? He³ did a bad bit of business when he did not keep me there!⁴ [...]

Addio

---

[1] The idea of dividing up the Balkans into spheres of interest between Russia and Austria-Hungary.
[2] See *Diaries*, entry for 22 July 1886.
[3] Bismarck.   [4] In Berlin.

164. Paul von Hatzfeldt to Holstein

30 July 1886

Dear friend,

[...] His Highness—whom I did not, as B[erchem] thinks, believe to be three y[ears] younger—is quite right to want to maintain a certain degree of detachment towards the Russians. That, however, does not solve the question of how we handle things here in case advances are made to us. It must not be overlooked that between Sal[isbury] and me it is not a matter of a new subject never hitherto touched upon, but of the continuation of earlier confidential exchanges of views. To act in this case in a negative and reserved manner would have a much more far-reaching significance and would be tantamount to saying: formerly I did indeed have confidence in you, but now I have it no longer—therefore leave me out of the game. At least there would be a very great danger that it would be interpreted in this way and have the same result as an attempt at pacification.

If we do not want this we must be clear about the attitude that is to be adopted. If H.H. will give me a free hand, I know very well what I have to do. I would hold fast to this standpoint: you know that we mean well by you. But you also know our situation, which can bring us between two fires. Your interest is very clear, but you must recognise it yourselves. As things are until now, no guarantee for others can be found in your conduct. Whoever wants to have friends must first of all show his willingness to act in order to inspire others with confidence. We have no special interest, but there are others who have.

This is all very simple, especially when one knows *que c'est le ton qui fait la chanson*. Only do not let us forget in this connection that this is a very critical moment, can at least be the forerunner of a very critical period, and that therefore the song which I am singing here is an exceedingly responsible one. Hence should a change have taken place, should H.H. have finally resolved to give the R[ussians] a free hand, and also to order Austria to keep quiet (division of the spheres of interest), then this song is no longer suitable to the occasion and I must be informed in order that I can act accordingly.[1]

I was annoyed over the dispatch from Bucharest.[2] Sturdza[3] perhaps exaggerated in order to beat upon the bush (not ours)[4] but there is probably something in it. Tell the Prince of Bulgaria through Hugo

---

[1] In a letter to Holstein on 2 August Hatzfeldt wrote: 'I can only understand the comments in this way: do not compromise me but keep the door open. Exactly what I think, although not easy to carry out. I also agree with letting Salisbury make the first approach. It will therefore probably be some time before we get together.' The comments to which Hatzfeldt referred were Bismarck's marginal notes on a letter from Hatzfeldt to Berchem in which he had asked whether he was 'to foster Lord Salisbury's confidence and to encourage a rapprochement from him' or to adopt an attitude of reserve. (From the Foreign Ministry files.)

[2] See p. 162, note 5.

[3] Demeter Sturdza. Rumanian Foreign Minister, 1883–8. Radowitz had been informed by Sturdza of the alleged remarks made by Alexander of Bulgaria to the King of Rumania. (Radowitz, *Aufzeichnungen*, vol. II, p. 264.)

[4] A pun on the name of the German official, Klemens Busch.

von Rad[olinski] that if he plays the fool like that one would have to drop him. I will also—if I can do so without doing damage—have this pointed out to him from here.

Best wishes. [...]

165. Hugo von Radolinski to Otto von Bismarck[1]

[31 July 1886]

Most Serene Prince,

My most respectful thanks to Your Highness for your gracious letter of July.[2]

I have read it to Her Imperial Highness and am instructed by Her Highness to tell Your Highness that she fully shares the political views set forth in the letter. Permit me, Your Highness, to take this opportunity of mentioning a remark which X[3] recently made to me in the course of a conversation and that may be of interest to Your Highness. X spoke to me of the youngest brother of the T[4] in most friendly terms and let it appear that she would be pleased if he sought a union with P.S.[5] She emphasised that the young Herr X would be of a far more suitable age for this P[rincess] than the eldest son of the T,[6] for whom her youngest daughter[7] would be more suitable from the point of view of age—though naturally not for some time—as a wife. It seemed to me that a double wedding was what Her Highness desired, particularly since the sisters together would feel more at home in X. This random remark showed me how gladly Her Highness would welcome a marriage alliance with that House [Russia], if only for political reasons.

I must in this connection observe that His [Imperial Highness] (the husband) knows nothing of this and that in conformity with the wish of Her [Imperial Highness] it would also be better for the present not to inform him of it. Similarly Her [Imperial Highness] does not desire that (the old father)[8] should be informed of these vague ideas before they attain some prospect of fulfilment. The initiative must obviously come from R[ussia] alone. Her [Imperial Highness] has permitted me to submit this plan to Your Highness *in strictest confidence* for your kind consideration.

166. Philipp zu Eulenburg to Holstein

Munich, 3 August 1886

My dear *Herr Legationsrat*!

[...] Prince Wilhelm is to blame that I have not answered your last friendly letter sooner. He had invited me to Reichenhall, kept me with him for six days, and did not give me a minute for a letter. I have made

---

[1] Note by Holstein: 'Rad[olinski] to the Chancellor. After I approved the draft, the letter goes off tomorrow. 31.7.86.'
[2] Of 18 July. See above.   [3] The Crown Princess.
[4] Grand Duke Paul, youngest brother of Tsar Alexander III of Russia.
[5] Princess Sophie, the third daughter of the Crown Princess.
[6] Grand Duke Nicholas, later Tsar Nicholas II.
[7] Princess Margarethe.   [8] Kaiser Wilhelm I.

use of the friendship with which he has blessed me for the purpose of fighting like a lion against *his English antipathies*.[1] If he is not thoroughly worked upon in this sense it may become extremely unpleasant politically for us some day.

I hope the Prince reads him a lecture on this subject in Gastein.[2]

I remain, my dear *Legationsrat*, ever your grateful and very devoted

P. Eulenburg.

167. Otto von Bismarck to Crown Prince Friedrich Wilhelm[3]

17 August 1886

I have the honour to acknowledge the receipt of Your Royal Highness' gracious telegram of yesterday[4] and ask you to accept my most obedient thanks for the gracious offer to undertake the journey to Russia.[5] I have requested Count Berchem to place Your Imperial Highness' offer before His Majesty with a recommendation for its acceptance, and respectfully request to be allowed to make a verbal report when I return to Berlin before the end of this month. Meanwhile I hope on the journey between here and Berlin to have had a discussion with Herr von Giers which can be of value for the exchange of views with His Majesty Tsar Alexander.[6]

If under normal circumstances the presence of the Tsar of Russia near the frontier has as a rule furnished the occasion for a friendly meeting; this has in the present instance become a political necessity because of the exaggerations regarding the importance of the meeting here which are to be found in the German and foreign, especially English, newspapers. The question is in this case, however, not only one of customary courtesy, for it will be impossible to avoid an exchange of political views. The appearance of Tsar Alexander near the frontier should take place, according to reports, about 11 September; later reports indicate that it will perhaps be a week later. I may therefore hope that before that time I will have an opportunity to report to Your Imperial Highness on the aspects of the situation that result from the

[1] These words were underlined by Holstein with the marginal comment: 'Cunning fellow, he thinks I will let that be known in the New Palace.'

[2] Prince Wilhelm was to be present in Gastein at the meeting of the Austrian and German Kaisers.

[3] The copy of this letter found in Holstein's papers was sent to Holstein by Radolinski. The copy in the files of the Foreign Ministry bears a marginal comment in Herbert von Bismarck's handwriting: 'Read to His Majesty on the 19th in Babelsb[erg].' The somewhat fuller version from the Foreign Ministry files is printed here.

[4] The Crown Prince's telegram was drafted by Holstein and Radolin and is printed in the *Diaries*, entry for 16 August 1886.

[5] After the meeting of the German and Austrian Kaisers in Gastein on 8 and 9 August, Kaiser Wilhelm amd Bismarck considered it advisable to pay the Russian Tsar the courtesy of sending a member of the German Imperial family to meet him when he would be travelling in the neighbourhood of the German frontier in September. It was decided to send Prince Wilhelm, who on the occasion of his journey to Russia in May 1884 had made an extremely good impression on Tsar Alexander. The Crown Prince opposed this plan on the grounds that his son was too inexperienced for such a delicate mission, and offered to go himself in his place. (*Grosse Politik*, vol. V, nos. 982, 984, pp. 55–6, 57; *Diaries*, entry for 16 August.)

[6] Bismarck saw Giers in Franzensbad on 26–7 August and in Berlin on 2–4 September. (See *Diaries*, p. 390, n. 2.)

recent discussions and those that will take place in the next few days with His Majesty, the Kaiser of Austria.[1] The maintenance of peace in Europe is in the present world situation to a large extent dependent on the impressions received by Tsar Alexander, because it depends on the personal will and temper of this monarch whether the weight of the Russian nation with its hundred million people is thrown into the balance for a warlike or peaceful future for Europe. As Your Imperial Highness will have seen from the newspapers, public opinion in Russia is chauvinistic, that is to say favourable to warlike undertakings, and only the person of the Tsar maintains a counter-balance. A simple move on the part of the Tsar to the other side would awaken in the Russian nation a unanimous enthusiasm for war, be it against Bulgaria, against the Porte, or against Austria. In the first two instances it is probable, in the latter certain, that the war would be a general one, except for England, and that it would involve France and Germany. It is unquestionably true, as the French newspapers nowadays declare, that the *chassepots* would go off of their own accord the moment war broke out between ourselves and Russia. A war of that nature may end as it will; it remains a calamity for victors and vanquished alike, the after-effects of which are felt for generations. The ignition-point of this world conflagration lies solely in Russia and in the person of the Tsar, and the cautious handling of the latter is therefore of an importance that justifies my respectful request that Your Imperial Highness allow me to make a verbal report regarding the intended meeting with Tsar Alexander before it takes place.

It will in any case first be necessary to await the definitive settlement of the Russian travelling plans regarding place and time, and the answer to our formal query where and when Tsar Alexander would be prepared to receive the projected visit. Not until then can we be certain what place nearest our border the Tsar will visit. That it will be Skiernievice is probable; but no certain information about this has as yet come to hand. If Warsaw should be the place nearest the frontier to be visited by the Tsar, then the question arises whether the projected visit there would be indicated on the occasion of the manoeuvres in that area, a question which would in my most respectful opinion require closer consideration from our point of view as well as that of Russia.

Bismarck.[2]

168. Holstein to Hugo von Radolinski[3]

Sunday evening, [22 August 1886]

Yes, dear Rado, that is the end.[4] I knew nothing, but felt that things were not going well.

[1] A further interview with the Kaiser of Austria did not take place.

[2] On the same day Kaiser Wilhelm decided in favour of the original plan to send Prince Wilhelm and not the Crown Prince. 'On account of his liberalising tendencies, the Crown Prince is not liked by Tsar Alexander.' (*Grosse Politik*, vol. V, p. 57, note *; *Diaries*, entries for 17 and 19 August.)

[3] From the Radolin Papers.

[4] During the night of 20 to 21 August Prince Alexander of Bulgaria was kidnapped by a group of Bulgarian officers and forced to abdicate.

The Provisional Government has issued a proclamation in which it says that the Prince rendered great services in war, but did not govern in a sufficiently *Slav* way, for which reason his abdication had become necessary.

He is now sitting imprisoned in Lom Palanka[1] but will before long be set at liberty. Not a hand appears to have been raised for him.

Seckendorff will thus have one enemy the more in Germany.

Hearty greetings

H.

169. Paul von Hatzfeldt to Holstein

27 August 1886

Here people still know *nothing*—not even *where* the P.[2] is, and still less what he intends to do—and wait—in the secret hope that Austria will be drawn in. People are said to be very disturbed about Franzensbad.[3]

For me the question depends simply on whether the P. has returned or not. In the latter case everything will remain quiet for the present and negotiations will be carried on, to and fro, for weeks over a successor. But if he has returned, then the affair *can* become serious, but only if Austria opposes a possible Russian intervention. Here they would probably support [the Austrian move] and the end could not be foreseen.[4] But up to now I do not believe *at all* in Austria's opposition, even in *that* case! And then *nothing* will happen here, and so everything would then remain quiet. [...]

Best greetings.

170. Paul von Hatzfeldt to Holstein

31 August 1886

A word that I forgot in today's report[5]—and had perhaps better not say.

In the course of conversation I said to S[alisbury] with regard to our position: our eyes must be turned to the W[est] for I doubt if you would protect us if the eventuality were to arise.[6] He shrugged his shoulders and said: '*I doubt it too.*'

What do you say to that?

[1] Prince Alexander was not brought to Lom Palanka, but to a monastery in Buchow about 25 km. from Sofia. He was taken from there to Varna, Rashovo and then to Reni.

[2] Prince Alexander of Bulgaria.

[3] The meeting between Bismarck and Giers at Franzensbad, 26–7 August. (See *Diaries*, p. 390, note 2.)

[4] Holstein passed on this information to the Austrians. (Tavera's telegram no. 65 of 29 August 1886, cited by Helmut Krausnick, *Holsteins Geheimpolitik in der Ära Bismarck, 1886–1890* (Hamburg, 1942) p. 31.)

[5] In this dispatch Hatzfeldt had reported a confidential discussion with Lord Salisbury about the situation in Bulgaria. Lord Salisbury had expressed the hope that the return of Prince Alexander to Bulgaria would for the present preserve peace. Turkey had been informed 'that the maritime Powers would fulfil their duty in the Black Sea if Turkey encountered danger from this quarter'. Lord Salisbury could not, however, understand the reserve shown towards him by the Vienna Government. Thus despite his wish for a resolute foreign policy, he could only adopt a wait-and-see attitude as a consequence of the Austrian reserve and domestic difficulties. (From the Foreign Ministry files.)

[6] A war with France.

171. Paul von Hatzfeldt to Holstein

1 September [1886]

Just been with Idd[esleigh][1] to hear what he had to say about his private letter to-day.[2] He was very satisfied when I told him that the report about the intentions of the English Government could not have come from me since *they* never informed me of their intentions.

But *please* a bit more discretion in Vienna and towards Vienna. I must be able to count on that, otherwise *nothing* more will be said to me! Impose that as a duty upon R[euss]! [...]

Please send as much news as possible about what is happening, especially in P[etersburg].

Greetings

172. Holstein to Hugo von Radolinski[3]

[3 September 1886]

Sal[isbury] and Idd[esleigh] take up the position that England can do nothing against the *three* Kaisers.[4] Paul [Hatzfeldt] and also Malet have both pointed out that there is no question of *three*. Germany will do nothing, but will not hold anybody back either. As I said, the English are frightfully stupid, they cannot see the principal issue: that once the Sultan is a Russian vassal, 85 million Mohammedan Indians will be Russian vassals.

173. Paul von Hatzfeldt to Holstein[5]

4 September [1886]

Dear friend,

I would very much like to know what in your opinion I can *really*

---

[1] Sir Stafford Henry Northcote, since 1885 Earl of Iddesleigh. Secretary of State for Foreign Affairs in Salisbury's second Cabinet, July 1886–January 1887.

[2] Hatzfeldt telegraphed on 1 September: 'Lord Iddesleigh informs me in a confidential private letter that according to a private letter from the English Ambassador in Vienna, the Imperial Ambassador there [Reuss] had told him that he learnt *from London* that the English Government was ready to come to an understanding with Russia and to sacrifice Prince Alexander. Ld Iddesleigh then asked whether I could explain this "inexplicable" report. I replied that it was not possible for me to say anything since I did not know on what such a report could be based.' Bismarck wrote on the margin of this telegram: 'Nothing of the kind is known here, and Prince Reuss' dispatches contain no indication of that kind. Ask Vienna Embassy what may be in it.' On 2 September Reuss telegraphed: 'I spoke to Count Kálnoky about the feeling in the English Cabinet along the lines of Your Highness' telegram No. 6, according to which the English may be inclined to come to an agreement with Russia in the Balkans.' Reuss had passed on this information to the English Ambassador, but he had never said that England was prepared to sacrifice Alexander. (From the Foreign Ministry files.)

[3] From the Radolin Papers.

[4] Holstein wrote in his diary (entry for 14 September 1886) that the English did not dare to act alone because they were convinced that the three Imperial Powers had already settled the Eastern Question amongst themselves. 'It is therefore Austria's duty to give England privately to understand that this is not the case [...]. Tentative approaches between Vienna and London are taking place at this moment.'

[5] See *Diaries*, entry for 14 September 1886.

still do here. With the best will I cannot any longer see that my presence serves any purpose, unless at the most to make the R[ussians] suspicious.

Read to-day's *Standard* which I am sending you. *Do ut des* and *not* single-handed—that is the opinion here. In addition the conviction grows daily that everything has been arranged and irrevocably decided between ourselves and the other two,[1] and therefore that it would be entirely useless to try to alter or oppose it.

What shall I do in these circumstances? I am completely in the dark. [...]

Quite seriously, it seems to me that it would be a very good idea if I were allowed to go on leave at present.

Best greetings.

174. Paul von Hatzfeldt to Holstein

London, 7 September 1886

Dear Holstein,

[...] To-day I have nothing to report. The Cabinet will meet to-day, and tomorrow morning I hope to learn what went on. I am assured that the Queen is very dissatisfied and is exerting all her influence in favour of a more energetic policy. How far her influence will extend—provided that the report is true—it is impossible to say. In the meantime yesterday's statement about Bulgaria in the House was very feeble and holds out little hope of an active policy. [...]

It seems to me very questionable whether they will really pull themselves together here even if things get worse. They have been seriously discouraged. The argument that is always brought forward now for abstaining from action is that obviously everything has been firmly settled among the three Imperial Powers and that England, which might perhaps have opposed Russia alone, is unable to stand up against the three allied Powers in the East. The secret thought that can at times be discerned is that they would gladly make definite proposals to Austria if only they knew that these would be accepted. They will not risk the fiasco of a refusal of definite and far-reaching proposals, if only because it would be a frightful blow to the Cabinet and its standing in the country.

I am taking advantage of every opportunity to repeat that we are not interested in Bulgaria, not even if things in the East went still further; that here they must recognise their own interests and act accordingly.

Good-bye for to-day, dear Holstein. I was delighted to hear from you again. I naturally leave it to your discretion to make what use you like of this letter.[2]

In sincere devotion
Your
P. Hatzfeldt

[1] Russia and Austria.   [2] A copy of this letter is in the files of the Foreign Ministry.

175. Holstein to Hugo von Radolinski[1]

8 September 1886

Dear friend,

As you will see from the newspapers, Sandro[2] has gloriously retired.[3] One begins to doubt whether he really did speak in that way about Macedonia.[4] *Havas* is a lying rag and completely Russian.

The English are beginning to bestir themselves. They have talked in St Petersburg of the possibility of sending their fleet into the Black Sea if the Russians occupy Bulgaria. Moreover the telegram [to] Morier spoke of the possibility and usefulness of maintaining Sandro in Bulgaria. Morier, who for months past has done nothing else but abuse Sandro, was beside himself at receiving such an instruction, will certainly have delayed carrying it out and have watered it down. Meanwhile the threat with the fleet has produced an enormous effect in St Petersburg. The Russians say to *qui veut l'entendre*, that the Tsar does not contemplate any occupation except in the case of anarchy in Bulgaria.

This declaration six weeks ago would have saved Sandro. My opinion is as follows: In London, people who pay around 10 or 20,000 pounds into the central election fund of their party are made baronets or peers as soon as their party comes to power. In return for the prospect of such advancement, the *Queen* would certainly be able to collect quickly and easily 100,000 pounds from wealthy City people to form a *secret Bulgarian election fund.* I think that Sandro would have very good prospects of being elected *again*, especially if his remarks about Macedonia could be categorically denied. And even if he did not accept re-election, it would be an enormous defeat for Moscow. Bulgaria would then probably become an (anti-Russian) republic. Think over this matter quickly. It is to be hoped that White[5] will still be sent *immediately* to Istanbul?

Provisionally for the time being.

176. Holstein to Hugo von Radolinski[6]

Thursday morning, 9 September 1886

As I suspected, Morier waited to carry out his instruction regarding Sandro's remaining in Bulgaria until after the latter's departure.[7] Giers arrogantly replied: He could not again approach his Emperor in this matter after his telegram to Sandro,[8] but then added soothingly that

---

[1] From the Radolin Papers.   [2] Alexander von Battenberg.

[3] On 28 August Prince Alexander returned to Bulgaria after a counter-revolutionary movement had recalled him to the throne. But Russia's antagonism made his position impossible, and on 7 September he abdicated for good.

[4] See p. 162, note 5.

[5] Sir William White. British Minister Extraordinary in Constantinople, 1885-6; Ambassador, 1886-91.

[6] From the Radolin Papers.

[7] See above Holstein's letter of 8 September.

[8] Of 20 August/1 September 1886: 'I cannot countenance your return to Bulgaria as I foresee the disastrous results it entails for that sorely tried country.' (Quoted by Corti, *Alexander von Battenberg*, p. 335.)

Russia did not contemplate intervention. Rumours and anxiety about the English fleet have already been reported by telegraph from Odessa. If England only knew what she can do. The Russians know far better than the English themselves what England in conjunction with Turkey could do.

They are very dissatisfied in St Petersburg with the composition of the Bulgarian Regency (Stambulov,[1] Karavelov,[2] Mutkurov[3]) and also of the Cabinet. There is *not a single* supporter of Russia in the Regency, and only *one* in the Cabinet (the Minister of Finance, Gersov). The Russian Agent has telegraphed that if he were to demand anything more, he would run the risk of Prince Alexander's staying.

Paul [Hatzfeldt] writes that the Queen is very dissatisfied and is working with all her might for an energetic policy. They are very worried in St Petersburg lest Sandro be re-elected, and for that reason they want to send a Russian commissioner to Bulgaria—'in an advisory capacity'—as quickly as possible.[4]

The English representative in Sofia[5] must be instructed as soon as possible to advise the Regency there to inform the Russian and other representatives, and also the Press that: 'As soon as there was disorder in the country they would turn to Russia for advice and request that a Commissioner be sent. This contingency had not yet arisen.'

The Commissioner would naturally only work for the election of the Russian candidate. Three things, therefore:

(1) Instruction to Lascelles about blocking the *Russian Commissioner*.
(2) *Bulgarian Election Fund*.
(3) *Immediate* dispatch of White to Istanbul on a provisional basis, giving as reason that the search for a *definitive* successor to Thornton[6] *was in progress* and that White was only a makeshift. Fane, the present *Chargé d'Affaires*, is incompetent. If you have the cypher with you, write in the customary manner to Edward M[alet] so that he can as usual send it on quickly. *Haste is necessary.*

177. Holstein to Hugo von Radolinski[7]

10 September 1886

According to newspaper reports, Dolgoruki, the Russian Commissioner, is already arriving to-day. This haste shows how uncertain the situa-

[1] Stefan Stambulov, the Bulgarian nationalist leader who had recalled Alexander, was at the head of the Regency.

[2] Petko Karavelov. Formerly President of the Bulgarian National Assembly and Minister-President under Prince Alexander.

[3] Commander-in-Chief of the Bulgarian army.

[4] A rumour was circulating at this time that the Tsar would send Prince Dolgoruki to Bulgaria. On 25 September he sent General Kaulbars to Bulgaria as Commissioner Extraordinary. (See *Letters of Queen Victoria*, edited by George E. Buckle, (London), Third Series, vol. I, pp. 204–5.)

[5] Sir Frank Cavendish Lascelles. British Diplomatic Agent and Consul-General in Sofia, 1879–87; Minister in Bucharest, 1887–91; Ambassador in St Petersburg, 1894–5, in Berlin, 1895–1908.

[6] Sir Edward Thornton. British Ambassador in St Petersburg, 1881–4, in Constantinople, 1884–6.

[7] From the Radolin Papers.

tion appears to the Russians. If only the *Bulgarian Election Fund* could be got together in England quickly enough. The matter could be settled in three days. The Queen must let some millionaire in the City who is ambitious or wants a title be told: 'You will be made a peer if you provide for the election.' Or she could create two peers and four baronets, it would still be cheap for the important object that is at stake for England. But quickly, quickly, quickly. You can see from Dolgoruki how events are pressing.

And then White, also quickly. *On n'est pas aussie bête que ça.* I would have thought Salisb[ury] was more adroit. And Paul [Hatzfeldt] who writes me: 'Can *you* understand why the Turks do not want White?'[1] Probably his thoughts are in Sommerberg or the heat does not suit him. And the English fleet to Besika but without any threat of any kind.

These three things then :
Election Fund, White, Fleet to Besika.
The Commissioner is settled. *Trop tard.*
Let us hope that will not always be said.

178. Paul von Hatzfeldt to Holstein[2]

Saturday, [11 September 1886]

Thanks for letters.

Have made two unsuccessful attempts to see S[alisbury], who only comes to town for an hour or two. Have just made another attempt and caught him as he was stepping into the street to go away. Only exchanged a couple of words—but not without importance.[3] He: 'Well, so you've killed our P[rince]?'[4] I: 'Not at all. It was you who allowed him to be killed.' He: 'What could we have done against the three Emperors?' I: 'There you are wrong. I always told you that we would do nothing but that we would stand in no one's way.' He: 'Yes, but what happens is this: It[aly] says she can do nothing without Aus[tria]—and when we turn to the latter, she says she can do nothing without you.' I: 'I don't think you have any idea what her attitude is.' This seemed to make a certain impression on him.

He gave me a rendez-vous for Tuesday afternoon because we could not go on talking on the street where people immediately began collecting. Unfortunately a lot of water can pass under the bridge by that time.

I also touched on two other matters during our short conversation:
1. Mor[ier] and his attitude. He said he could not understand it since his reports were quite correct—but then added: '*Il est vrai que c'est un gamin*'—he has thus after all become suspicious. 2. Malet.—he thought Malet would come to him, whereas Mal. thought he should wait to

[1] In a letter of 4 September. At the time of the revolution in Eastern Rumelia, Sir William White had supported the union of this province with Bulgaria, for which the Bulgarian Government had expressed their particular gratitude to him. When in September 1886 White was proposed as Ambassador to Turkey, the Turks refused to accept him, but finally agreed to his temporary appointment.

[2] See *Diaries*, entry for 14 September 1886.

[3] Hatzfeldt's report of the conversation is in French in the original.

[4] Alexander von Battenberg.

see if he was sent for. S. now intends to do so, which I regard as very useful.

All this is not much—but the thread is not completely broken.

Best greetings and more shortly.[1]

179. Holstein to Hugo von Radolinski[2]

Saturday, [11 September 1886]

Dear friend,

You will see from the enclosure[3] that Sandro himself does not want to return.[4] For he certainly should realise that Europe will not *ask* him to do so. On the contrary, it is rather to be expected that Europe will not confirm him after re-election, but leave it to him to create a *fait accompli*. The latter would not be so difficult because of the superstitious fear that the Russians have of England. You will have seen from the *Moscow Gazette* that the bombastic Katkov[5] is advising against marching into Bulgaria, simply and solely because the phantom of the English fleet has made its appearance.

Despite all this, I think the Bulgarian Election Fund would be useful. For by the re-election of Sandro, or the non-election of the Russian candidate, Russia's position in regard to Bulgaria would be altered for all time—the liberator would become the oppressor—while secondly Sandro's future would be assured. In these changing times, who knows all that the future holds in store?

By the way, the English Government has to-day given fresh proof of cowardice. They deny officially that they ever proposed White for Constantinople!

180. Holstein to Hugo von Radolinski[6]

Sunday evening, 10 [o'clock, 12 September 1886]

Hitrovo[7] told someone in St Petersburg that it was a great mistake that Russia had not intervened immediately or threatened intervention or sent a commissioner. The Bulgarians thus realised that Russia was not inclined to pursue a forcible policy, and were therefore quite shameless, as was shown by the election of an *anti*-Russian Regency. Russia should now attempt to win over both the Government and the Army, but this was not easy. In the first place the Bulgarians were not as corruptible as was assumed, while to those who were corrupt, England would easily be able to pay far more than Russia.

So much for Hitrovo. The Russians now demand that the Sobranje should not for the present elect a Prince, but that instead, in preparation for the election of a Prince, they should elect a 'constitutional'

[1] Note by Holstein: 'Contents communicated confidentially to Tavera. 13.9.'
[2] From the Radolin Papers.
[3] Not found.
[4] See p. 174, n. 3.
[5] Michael Katkov. Russian publicist.
[6] From the Radolin Papers.
[7] Russian Minister in Bucharest, 1886–91.

Regency in place of the (anti-Russian) one appointed by Prince Alexander.

Here is a point where England could already intervene with money.

Malet told Iddesleigh that all rumours that Germany would play the role of 'schoolmaster' and restrain others from acting against Russia were nonsense. Germany would maintain complete neutrality.

Iddesleigh seems to be somewhat *ramolli*.

White must go to Istanbul and the fleet *must* go to Besika as quickly as possible, especially during the election fever. In addition, the election fund!

Even if Alexander does *not* return after the election, he would still be elected and Russia *discredited*.

181. Holstein to Hugo von Radolinski[1]

Monday evening, [13 September 1886]

When I read the enclosure I said to myself that the advice to Sandro to return from Cernovice to Sofia was not bad after all.[2] His standing in Bulgaria is thereby permanently assured, he has become a legend.

The stupidity of those in England who desire an active policy is incomprehensible to me. They should start the Press campaign with the slogan: Bulgaria doesn't matter. Bosphorus doesn't matter, but the Sultan *does* matter: for [...][3] as Caliph he is the head of 85 million Mohammedan Indians. The moment he becomes a Russian vassal, he will exert his influence upon the 85 millions in any way the Tsar of Russia demands. In other words, the moment the Caliphate is annexed to the Russian sphere of influence, England's rule over India is condemned to death with only a brief respite. For it was the Mohammedans alone who made possible a successful outcome to the great Mutiny of '57. If they too were to become hostile, England is finished.

How is it possible, how is it comprehensible, that all the great newspapers in England do not publish *daily* leading articles on *that* subject? That they do not do so is a symptom of demoralisation. Only the *Morning Post*, the old Palmerston paper, writes about it; and to-day it has little influence.

Prince Wilhelm—this is entirely secret—found the Tsar very pacific and annoyed about the Battenberg sympathies of the Bulgarians, and therefore disinclined to intervene because he could not expose Russian soldiers to be treated by the Bulgarians as enemies. The Tsar now hopes that the larger Sobranje will start by electing a Regency with *Russian* sympathies.[4]

[1] From the Radolin Papers.
[2] Prince Alexander's return to the Bulgarian capital after his kidnapping. (See Corti, *Alexander von Battenberg*, p. 319.)
[3] Word illegible.
[4] Prince Wilhelm arrived in Brest-Litovsk on 10 September to visit the Tsar during the grand manoeuvres. The above information was communicated on 13 September by Prince Wilhelm to the Chancellor. On the same day Herbert von Bismarck informed Reuss in a private letter. (From the Foreign Ministry files. See *Grosse Politik*, vol. V, nos. 987–8, pp. 62–5.)

182. Hugo von Radolinski to Holstein

T[rencsén] T[eplicz], 15 September 1886

My dear friend,

I have most tenaciously made use of everything, by code messages and in innumerable letters.[1]

I get an answer daily, and naturally they are in agreement with everything, and telegraph that everything has been passed on to Mama.[2] My code messages, by the way, go from here without any trouble and without signature, and also reach their destination without any fuss. Many thanks for your most welcome and extremely interesting information and *hints*.

I have just this moment received the letter forwarded on to me which was sent there by official courier. They were very astonished when he arrived with this letter in the *Alps*.

The letter reads: His Highness[3] to the C.[4] Ber[lin] 8/9/86. From information given to me by Herr von G[iers],[5] the relatives of Gr[and] D[uke] P.[6] and of Pr[ince]ss Alex. of G.,[7] as also the two young people themselves, regard their engagement as good as settled and there is even talk that the marriage will take place at the beginning of next year. Herr von G. further told me that next year the *successor*[8] will go abroad and visit different Courts, probably under the guidance of Ct. A. Ad.[9] who is quite friendly to Germany. At the Court (where Bernhard B[ülow] is),[10] moreover, the marriage of the eldest sons of the brothers of the father of the present one is under consideration; these are Nic. Nicol..tch[11] and Nic. Mich...tch.[12] No firm decision has as yet been taken in regard to them; the former is much praised.

(sig.)

I[13] received this letter just now from her[4] and *I* am to answer *him*,[3] and thank him for it, as she does not like to meddle in the matter and because she does not like to put anything in writing. She writes to me: 'No doubt it is very kindly meant by him and *please thank him*. There is a little mistake however in the Angabe [statement]. N. Nich. I know quite well, he is very ugly and not agreeable, has bad health and is not steady. About N. Mich...tch please make *strict* enquiries.' *She* is mortally afraid that the Chief[3] could say something about this, *as*

---

[1] Radolin here informs Holstein that he has forwarded the advice contained in Holstein's letters to the Crown Prince's Court, which was at that time in the Tyrol.
[2] Queen Victoria. [3] Prince Bismarck. [4] Crown Princess Victoria.
[5] Probably during Giers' stay in Berlin from 2–4 September.
[6] Grand Duke Paul of Russia, brother of Tsar Alexander III.
[7] Princess Alexandra of Greece.
[8] Grand Duke Nicholas, the Heir-Apparent to the Russian throne.
[9] Count Alexander Adlerberg. Minister of the Imperial Household.
[10] St Petersburg.
[11] Grand Duke Nicholas Nicholaievich, nephew of Alexander II and son of Grand Duke Nicholas and Alexandra of Oldenburg.
[12] Grand Duke Nicholas Michailovich, nephew of Alexander II and son of Grand Duke Michael and Olga of Baden.
[13] The following sentence by Radolinski, and the note from the Crown Princess, are in English in the original.

coming from her, to the husband[1] or his father.[2] Naturally the initiative must come from the East[3] and we must act as if we were astounded. She is terribly afraid of being compromised because she started everything without the previous knowledge of her husband. I am naturally taking the position that I committed an *indiscretion* in regard to the Chief by insinuating to him something which I had *accidentally heard spoken of* in the N[ew] Palace. I am also quite prepared to take that upon my shoulders and to be known as an indiscreet person who reports what he hears by chance. But how am I to get it into the Chief's head so that he understands it in this way and says nothing about the business to the *male* members of the family? She attaches great importance to its being impressed upon him again. Could that not be done through the son H.[4]? No, better *not* by way of the son, since I am instructed to write to the father. Shall I write confidentially to the latter, that is to say the father? As to the time when we would like to have the two visitors here, that would be May of next year; for both will be confirmed at Easter; in June we all cross the sea to where Paul H[atzfeldt] is. It would also be desirable if both announced their visit *at the same time*. If the visit takes place, it must be the result of entirely free initiative on their part, and no sort of obligation for '*us*' must be involved or inferred from it. For God's sake, if only the *Grandfather*[5] does not learn of the part that *we*, that is to say the mistress[6] and the servant,[7] have played in it. If you are in agreement, I will frame my answer to the father along the lines indicated below. If you think it is all right and not too detailed, then telegraph only 'Yes, Good', and I will send the letter through you, that is, I will send it to you to B[erlin]. If you think changes are necessary, please point them out to me.

[Most] S[erene] P[rince]!

The C[rown Princess] instructs me to thank Your Highness very much for your letter of the 8th and also to express the hope that Your Highness' health has really improved. Her Imperial Highness was sincerely concerned about your recent illness. The immediate departure of H.I.H. at the time of the arrival of Your Highness' letter prevented her from at once replying herself. Moreover I assume that Her Highness did not like directly to touch upon the matter in question since *outwardly* she does not want to—and must not—know anything of the whole affair, especially as up to now she has not spoken of the matter either to her husband or to her parents-in-law. She also attaches the very greatest importance to the fact that nothing of what I mentioned to Your Highness at the time as a confidential communication, to be ascribed to '*my* indiscretion', should come to the knowledge of His Imperial Highness[1] or Their Imperial Majesties[8] as emanating from here. Her Imperial Highness counts in this matter on the friendly feelings of Your Highness for herself. The initiative must come entirely

[1] Crown Prince Friedrich Wilhelm. [2] Kaiser Wilhelm I. [3] From Russia.
[4] Herbert von Bismarck. [5] Kaiser Wilhelm I.
[6] Crown Princess Victoria. [7] Radolinski.
[8] Kaiser Wilhelm I and Kaiserin Augusta.

from R[ussia]. H.I.H. confidentially tells me that she knows Gr. D. N.N.[1] very well but does not find him especially attractive and he is supposed to have a weak constitution. She hardly knows G.N.*M.*[2] and must therefore find out more about him beforehand. If a visit should be planned for next year, I think the month of May would be the best time since *before* and *after* there will be all sorts of engagements and journeys. In my humble opinion it would also be desirable if the visit of both Gr. D[ukes] took place *simultaneously*, and naturally it should not bind or obligate either party in any way. It would be a simple courtesy visit. The religious question certainly need not be immediately touched upon, but I do not think that the parents would ever consent to a conversion that did not take place *wholly voluntarily* on the part of the daughter in question.

sig.

I would like to add the following concluding sentence; if you think it *inopportune*, or even harmful, then provided the rest satisfies you, telegraph only 'without final sentence'.

'In conclusion may I permit myself to add the supposition that the so willing readiness to enter into this alliance is not wholly without conditions and arises out of regard for the wishes of the eldest daughter.'[3] (sig.) Wouldn't this make the Capo[4] mad and would he, in fury, inform the old gentleman[5] about the whole affair? On the other hand it would be a good thing for him to be informed of the *real* intention in good time. This is her wish, too.

I am putting a piece of string round the letter so that when you get it you will be able to tell whether it has been opened or not.

Your faithful and devoted

183. Holstein to Hugo von Radolinski[6]

17 September [1886]

Dear friend,

I find the draft of the letter good, at most instead of 'to be ascribed to my indiscretion' I would have said: to be traced back to an indiscretion on my part. Without putting indiscretion in quotation marks. It is a nuance. But it will do as it is. [...]

I am in almost daily touch with Paul.[7] He has come to life and is working skilfully. I also see Tavera[8] daily.

Paul is also of the opinion that the election question is a money question and said so to Malet when he left for Balmoral.

---

[1] Grand Duke Nicholas Nicholaievich.
[2] Grand Duke Nicholas Michailovich.
[3] In other words, that Bismarck should permit the marriage of Princess Victoria to Alexander von Battenberg.
[4] Bismarck.
[5] Kaiser Wilhelm I.
[6] From the Radolin Papers.
[7] Paul von Hatzfeldt.
[8] Schmit, Ritter von Tavera. Austro-Hungarian Secretary of Embassy in Berlin.

Good-bye for to-day. It was a hot day in regard to business, especially callers.

The French are coming to life, seem to want to start a diplomatic action against the English in Egypt.

Ever yours
H.

184. Hugo von Radolinski to Holstein

19 September [1886]

My dear friend,

Here is the letter.[1] Should you have any further hesitation of any kind whatsoever, then do not send it off; but I should think there cannot be anything objectionable in it. But as I said. I follow you in this as in everything blindly, because I have infinite trust in you and your judgment. In case you want to read it through again, I enclose a second envelope with a stamp (official) since you would otherwise have to seal it and you have not got my seal. [...]

Lyncker[2] by the way arrives in Bornstedt on *Thursday*. It might interest you to know something about His Majesty. He must have been very ill after all. I am glad that Paul [Hatzfeldt] has now come to life and that you are keeping him *awake*. I wrote to him recently. It seems that 'Mama'[3] is furious and very bitter. What could be done to create an election fund has been done. I write lengthy letters daily and sent some code messages. I have been told in reply that everything has been immediately dispatched across the water.[4] [...]

Your faithful
R. [...]

185. Holstein to Hugo von Radolinski[5]

21 September 1886

Dear Rado,

Letter received and sent, since I could not think of any improvements. I think it is doubtful however whether it will meet with a friendly reception by Kuno[6] and his father-in-law. Kuno will ask why she[7] did not write herself.[8] [...]

I now have definite knowledge that A[ustria] would be prepared to come to an understanding with E[ngland] in regard to certain even-

---

[1] Radolinski's letter to Bismarck. (See above, Radolinski's letter of 15 September.)

[2] Moritz, Baron von Lyncker. Aide-de-Camp to Crown Prince Friedrich Wilhelm and subsequently Marshal of the Court to Kaiser Wilhelm II.

[3] Queen Victoria of England.

[4] That is, Radolinski's messages have been forwarded from the Crown Prince's Court to England.

[5] From the Radolin Papers.   [6] Kuno zu Rantzau.   [7] The Crown Princess.

[8] Radolinski wrote to Holstein on 23 September: 'I thought that Kuno would probably express himself in that way, and therefore explained in the letter—as though it were my idea—the reason why she did not write herself. Besides, the moment I got the letter I implored her to write him a few words without touching upon the chief subject. I do not know whether she has done so.'

tualities. But it must be achieved quickly since otherwise A. must safeguard its existence by other agreements. You can say this.[1] [...]

186. Anton von Monts[2] to Holstein

Riva, 24 September 1886

My dear Herr von Holstein,

I have allowed myself to send you as an enclosure a report on my farewell audience with the Pope, since some of his statements may not be without interest. [...]

The Pope is momentarily in a most conciliatory mood; de Freycinet pressed him hard, and offended him personally quite unnecessarily. Naturally the Pontifex seeks consolation and support elsewhere. We might now perhaps put through many things by making skilful use of these circumstances. Why, for example, should not the Holy See, now that the Pope has to some extent disavowed both himself and canon law with regard to little Belgium (Prohibition of divorce to Catholic judges), make some concession to us as well on the question of mixed marriages or at least restore the situation existing before the *Kulturkampf* and before the ordinance of that splendid Bishop Herzog.[3] [...]

With the renewed expression of my esteem and attachment, may I be permitted to sign as

Your most obedient
Anton Monts

ENCLOSURE

Memorandum by Anton von Monts

Riva, 24 September 1886

On 19 September I had the honour of being received by His Holiness for an audience that lasted about an hour.

After some introductory personal remarks concerning myself, the Pope began with some reflections on his role as mediator in the Carolines affair.[4] He would never forget the proof of confidence that Prince Bismarck gave him at that time.

As his relations with Germany had improved during the past years, so his relations with France had grown worse. The fact that a break had not yet occurred was only due to his extreme compliance in the

[1] In his letter of 23 September Radolin wrote: 'I have *immediately made use* of the other [information] regarding A. and E.'

[2] Anton, Count von Monts. Secretary of the Prussian Legation to the Holy See, 1884–6; First Secretary in the Embassy in Vienna, 1886–90; Consul-General in Budapest, 1890 4; Prussian Minister in Oldenburg, 1894–5, in Munich, 1895–1902; Ambassador in Rome, 1902–9.

[3] Eduard Herzog. From 1876 Bishop of the Old Catholic Church in Switzerland. In 1870–1, as Professor of Exegesis at the Theological College in Lucerne, he published a weekly paper *Katholische Stimmen* directed against the dogma of papal infallibility and supreme papal power.

[4] In September 1885 a request was made to Leo XIII to act as arbitrator in a dispute between Spain and Germany over the Caroline Islands. On 22 October the Pope gave a decision in favour of Spain. (See *Diaries*, entry for 23 August 1885 *et seq.*)

Chinese Question.[1] But he had only postponed Agliardi's[2] departure, and had by no means given up the idea of his mission.

There followed bitter complaints about France. He, Leo XIII, fully understood that this wholly incalculable country should be the object of continuous anxiety for German policy. Although he disliked Russia very much, and had great personal sympathy for Prince Alexander whom he had received when he passed through Rome seven years ago, he nevertheless saw that Germany could not have acted differently in the Bulgarian troubles. In this connection the Pope let fall a remark about England that was hardly flattering.

His Holiness went on to say that he could well imagine the Chancellor's problems, and that he would at present have little time left for ecclesiastical affairs. There was no need whatever for haste in further revising the May Laws,[3] and he had entire confidence in Prince Bismarck, who was already giving more than he had promised. As Supreme Pontiff, he had been much pleased by the recent amnesty accorded to all the priests in the diocese of Posen.

I did not think it inopportune at this stage to emphasise for my part that the Government of our most gracious Sovereign continuously made the greatest sacrifices in order to avoid disturbing the work of pacification. Members of the German College[4] were admitted to Prussia, although no illusions were entertained in Berlin about the dangerous nature of their activities. His Holiness replied that heretofore certainly everything but German thought and moderation had been taught in the German College. But since his accession to the Throne he had ceaselessly endeavoured behind the scenes to initiate a reform.[5] It was already possible to see some results of these endeavours in the College. Nevertheless he wanted to do even more, and the Government had only to express its wishes in regard to the extent to which the teaching programme should be altered, and which of the intransigent teachers should still be removed. His ideal was to make the German College into a school of nationally-minded priests who as a result of their thorough knowledge of conditions in Rome would subsequently be able in their priestly activities to play a conciliatory role.[6]

He was also ready at any time to confer the Cardinal's hat on a German Bishop nominated by His Majesty's Government. Among the existing Cardinals of German nationality none were willing or able to

[1] In a Note of 4 May 1886 the French Government protested to the Vatican against the proposal to send a permanent representative of the Holy See to the Chinese Government. The French considered this to be an encroachment on France's century-old right of protection over Catholics in China. The Pope rejected the French protest, but nevertheless decided in the middle of September, after negotiations with France had reached deadlock, to postpone sending a representative to China.

[2] Antonio Agliardi. Italian Cardinal. In 1884 he was appointed Apostolic Envoy to India; from 1887 Secretary of the Congregation for Extraordinary Ecclesiastical Affairs; Nuncio in Munich, 1889, in Vienna, 1892.

[3] The laws of May 1873 at the time of the *Kulturkampf*. After 1879 these laws were gradually repealed.

[4] The German College in Rome.

[5] Marginal comment by Holstein: '?'.

[6] Holstein: '?'.

look after German interests at the Holy See or to support him, the Pope, in his work for peace.

The conversation now turned to the Centre Party, and I seized the opportunity of making use of some ideas contained in the article of issue No. 422 of the *Norddeutsche Allgemeine Zeitung* of the 10th of this month. His Holiness said that the Centre Party only had a *raison d'être* during the *Kulturkampf*. But now there was no longer any question of a struggle; if the Centre wanted to carry on the struggle on its own account, then it would encounter his opposition. The teaching of the Catholic religion was to render unto Caesar, even when he was a heathen, the things that were Caesar's. All true Catholics should do everything for such a truly Christian and benign ruler as our Kaiser, his friend and ally; they should support his paternal Government in every way and in case of need be prepared to sacrifice their lives and possessions. This was his, the Pope's, view and in the course of time he hoped to inculcate it into all true German Catholics.

The Pope dismissed me in the most gracious manner by expressing the hope that he had convinced me of his sincere friendship for my exalted Sovereign and the new Germany.

Monts.

187. Hugo von Radolinski to Holstein

en route, Oderberg–Breslau
in the train, 25 September [1886], evening.

My dear friend,

On the journey from Trencsén to Breslau, where I am to stay tonight, going on to Jarotschin[1] early tomorrow morning, I am writing you a line to say that this morning I received a letter from *her*[2] with a friendly enclosure[3] for the Capo.[4] She says: 'I do it because you asked me to do so.'[5] I will send you the letter to the Capo tomorrow evening from Jarotschin and will enclose a short cover-letter since *she* asks me to forward the letter to him. She writes very nicely to him without touching upon the subject. She tells me *confidentially* that possibly the *youngest*[6] will *later* stay in the country where she is now.[7] There are people who are working for this. It would not be such a bad idea. But then what about the double arrangement?[8] [...]

Your faithful
Hugo

188. Hugo von Radolinski to Holstein

Jarotschin, 27 September 1886

My dear friend,

Here is Her Highness's letter with a cover-letter to His Highness.

---

[1] Count Radolinski's estate.   [2] Crown Princess Victoria.
[3] See enclosure to Radolinski's letter of 27 September 1886.   [4] Otto von Bismarck.
[5] In English in the original.   [6] Princess Margarethe.   [7] In Italy.
[8] The double marriage between the Russian Grand Dukes and the Prussian Princesses.

I am enclosing a copy of each for you.[1] If you should find something or other unsuitable, please tell me. [...]

I have received a letter from Buch[2] who has had a letter from our friend 'Carl',[3] according to which he is very happy to be back in his native land after the hard times he has been through. At the same time he is grateful that he was pressed to return *there*[4] at least *pro forma*. This had also given him a different standing at home. Please read the telegram dated 'Vienna, 26 Sept.' in issue No. 264 of the *Post* for the 27th, first column, right at the top. Has the Three E[mperor] friendship really become so shaky? I can understand why the Austrians and Hungarians are so angry with us, and I ask myself whether it has really gone so far that we face the alternative of having to choose between R[ussia] and Aus[tria]. I would like to have a hint from you, because I do not understand the present situation. I would also like to *pass on* your opinion.

It seems to me as if greater danger threatened us from one of our two friends than from the known enemy[5] who certainly does not seriously think of attacking us. That is, unless we sought a quarrel with him. Did you get my letter in pencil, written in the train from Oderberg to Breslau,[6] and what do you think of what was said in it about the 'youngest'? Does it appear to you desirable and advantageous?

Goodbye for to-day. Has the person in question[7] really been passed over for promotion, or will he, now that he is no longer a political figure, again be treated as a Prussian officer and promoted as such?[8] Please tell me what you think or hear about this. [...]

ENCLOSURE I
Crown Princess Victoria to Prince Otto von Bismarck
22 September 1886

Most esteemed Prince,

Accept again in writing my thanks for the letter which I received by courier in the Tyrol.[9] At that time I could only acknowledge receipt of the letter by telegram.

It is to be hoped that you are now free from the troublesome rheumatism which, as I learnt to my sincere regret, has again tormented you recently.

We hope to enjoy another four weeks and some baths here before we return again to Potsdam.

Hoping that the Princess is well

Your

[1] See Enclosures. [2] Dr Langenbuch. [3] Alexander von Battenberg.
[4] To Sofia. [5] France. [6] Of 25 September. See above. [7] Alexander von Battenberg.
[8] See p. 165, note 1. On 23 September Radolin wrote: 'They think it is very hard and unjust, now that Al[exander] was no longer an active political figure, that he should nevertheless have been passed over militarily. I could not refrain from replying that I ascribed that to Alb[edyll], since political reasons could not have had anything to do with the internal promotion of a Prussian officer who was nothing more than a *Prussian officer* and *not a political figure*. Whether that is correct is of course another question. But it is an opinion like any other, and Alb. will certainly have done his part in contributing to it.'
[9] See above, Radolinski's letter to Holstein of 15 September 1886.

ENCLOSURE II

Hugo von Radolin to Otto von Bismarck

Most Serene Prince!

By the exalted command of Her Imperial and Royal Highness the Crown Princess, I have the honour most obediently to send Your Highness the enclosed letter.

With profoundest respect

Your Highness'
most obedient

189. Hugo von Radolinski to Holstein

Jaro[tschin], 27 September 1886

My dear friend,

I have just received the following letter:

My dear Count,

I have received your letter[1] with best thanks. That discretion should be exercised in regard to the affair in question I consider to be a matter of course. The need for it also prevents me from entering into details in this letter, and I will refrain from doing so until such time as I shall have the pleasure of speaking to you personally. I hope to be in Berlin before the end of October, and will certainly pass through on my way to Friedrichsruh. Perhaps you will be there at that time, but I would like it even better if you would honour me with a visit in Friedrichsruh.

Yours
B[ismarck][2]

What do you think of this? I would be quite willing to go there later on. Adio.

Your faithful

190. Holstein to Hugo von Radolinski[3]

28 September [1886]

Dear Rado,

So far as I know the understanding between the Three still exists, if only because there is nothing else to be had.[4]

England does everything possible to make Austria *take the lead*, but at the same time *The Times* writes that England should not, will not, cannot bother herself about Bulgaria. I do not know if another Austrian Minister would have been more successful in rousing the English. As I told you, Kálnoky allowed himself to be influenced by Wolkenstein and drew back completely almost as soon as he had started. But at the same time he demands of Germany that as Austria's sole ally we should go to war for the Hungarian programme against Russia, Italy and France,

---

[1] See above, Radolinski's letter of 15 September 1886.
[2] Radolinski wrote on the margin: 'Probably written by Kuno [Rantzau].'
[3] From the Radolin Papers.
[4] See above. Radolinski's letter of 27 September.

not to mention Montenegro and Denmark. The angry tone of our Press is partly to be explained by this.

The French would like to win over Germany to an anti-English policy with regard to Egypt. But I have just drawn up a report to His Majesty, in accordance with instructions from His Highness, in which approval is requested for our treating the expected French proposals coolly.[1] As long as the French do not have a formal statement from us —which we will *not* give—that we give them a free hand against England, they will not move a muscle, England may do what she will.

I must close. Much to do, but no annoyances.

Yours
H.

191. Holstein to Hugo von Radolinski[2]

Wednesday, [29 September 1886]

I am very depressed. From some quarter or other His Highness is being continuously roused against the Bulgarian.[3]

After a long argument with Herbert, I have just succeeded in persuading him to try to put an end to this personal campaign.

Best wishes. I will write tomorrow. Paul [Hatzfeldt] goes on leave to-day with my approval, on condition that he is back again in three weeks at the same time as Sal[isbury].

Wolkenstein has vigorously warned Kálnoky against taking the initiative for a rapprochement with Eng. Wolk[enstein] seems to be absolutely Russian.

192. Hugo von Radolinski to Holstein[4]

J[arotschin], 2 October 1886

My dear friend,

From what I hear, E[ngland] will be armed and ready for all eventualities in about three weeks. They are determined after all to face any eventuality if R[ussia] goes too far. Wh[ite] will definitely stay there[5] as representative. He arrives on the 10th.

It seems that A.[6] is not at all conciliatory and absolutely refuses to influence the old gentleman[7] to show more sympathy for the arrangement in question[8] and the plans of the young lady.[9] *Il ménage la chèvre et les choux*, but finds that it is more in his interest at present to take the side of the old man.[7] It would be splendid if you, who have induced the son[10] to change his opinion so far, could influence him still further and persuade him to get the father[11] to talk his master[7] out of any further opposition, which in the long run cannot be maintained and will be use-

---

[1] See *Grosse Politik*, vol. VI, no. 1227, pp. 137–8. The Foreign Ministry files show that this document was drafted by Holstein.
[2] From the Radolin Papers.   [3] Alexander von Battenberg.
[4] See *Diaries*, entry for 5 October 1886.   [5] In Constantinople.   [6] General von Albedyll.
[7] Kaiser Wilhelm I.   [8] The Battenberg marriage.   [9] Princess Victoria.
[10] Herbert von Bismarck. See above, Holstein's letter to Radolinski of 29 September 1886.
[11] Otto von Bismarck.

less. If you could insinuate to the son how grateful the interested parents[1] would be to him, how highly he would stand in their, the parents', estimation, and that he will after all have to reckon with them for a long time to come—perhaps, believing in this assurance, he would show himself more sympathetic, especially if he were told that in any event it will be done *coûte que coûte* as soon as the great master[2] is no longer alive. For it is absolutely decided upon. Why should not the 'son' get the credit with them for having made this possible? He is after all also open to flattery and the recognition of his power and influence. Would you think it opportune if I were to write to him confidentially in this sense and ask for his help with the father? So many *mésalliances* are after all concluded; if the two sisters are dealt with in the desired fashion,[3] it would in the long run be a matter of indifference if, in order to achieve that end, the eldest were to marry according to inclination. By making such an arrangement the 'son' would win a colossal position with 'my people'[4] for himself and *undermine* A[lbedyll] who is now getting on his hind legs and saying that it is impossible to change the mind of the *old* gentleman. A word from the 'father'[5] would be sufficient to achieve this, and only think of the triumph for us if the Foreign Ministry were to achieve what A[lbedyll] does not want to do. For there is no longer any question that the moment the old gentleman closes his eyes *it will be done*. In the long run therefore it cannot be prevented. But whoever arranges and puts it through *now* will gain the glory. After all it cannot be prevented for all time. The 'son' would appear to *her* as a chivalrous, generous knight if he changed his father's mind and induced him to persuade the old gentleman to give way, and later *he* would certainly be thanked for it. He[6] is *not* a political personage any longer, and therefore from a political standpoint it is without importance. A. has now once again been able to prevent [*sic*.] his being passed over for promotion. From a political standpoint that too is now a matter of indifference and he should certainly be entitled to further promotion like any other officer now that he is no longer there.[7] [...]

Shall I answer the old Capo *now* that I would gladly come to Friedrichsruh or shall I remain silent and only announce my arrival in F. later on? I think it would be the proper thing to write soon *now*. But I will not do it without your advice.

Your affectionately devoted
R.

193. Holstein to Hugo von Radolinski[8]

Monday morning, [4 October 1886]

Dear Rado,

I have dropped everything to keep you from taking a false step. Do

---

[1] The Crown Prince and Crown Princess. [2] Kaiser Wilhelm I.
[3] See above, Radolinski's letter of 15 September 1886.
[4] The Crown Prince and Crown Princess. [5] Otto von Bismarck.
[6] Alexander von Battenberg. [7] In Bulgaria. [8] From the Radolin Papers.

nothing whatever with the old Capo¹ along the line you were thinking of. The only result would be that personally *vous vous perdrez dans son estime*—and wholly.

In the Capo's present mood it is hopeless to try and do anything for 'Karl'.² *Quite* hopeless.³

I also advise you not to visit the Capo. Either you will find yourself in a false position or you will clash with him.

The Capo has been told that *your* Capo⁴ wishes to place Karl in the highest posts, first in Alsace, then here.⁵ As far as I could discover, Adolf Bülow has played a part in hawking round this rumour. As a supporter of Alb[edyll] he was naturally highly delighted to sow mischief between your Chief and my Chief.

I do not yet know what can be done *later*; but *now* the irritation will be increased by every move that is made and by every contact. Hence: neither letter nor visit, nothing. I am absolutely sure about this. [...]

P.S.

In addition to Wolkenstein, Károlyi,⁶ the Austrian Ambassador in London, urgently advised Kálnoky against an understanding with England, which only wants to drive Austria into the fight but does not want to get in it herself.

In the immediate future the French Government will make urgent proposals here regarding Egypt. We are to promise to remain neutral in the struggle with England which France will provoke as soon as she is assured of our neutrality. Herbette,⁷ Freycinet's *homme de confiance*, will be sent here solely on account of this one question.

France will be friends, forgive and forget, if we entertain the French proposal. If we do not entertain it, France will—this has already been hinted at unofficially to me personally,—have to take into consideration the offers of friendship from Russia which are ceaselessly being made in Paris.

I doubt if the French will be successful with their proposal. His Highness is more suspicious of them than he formerly was, and I do my utmost to increase that suspicion. (Memorandum to His Majesty advising against the coming French advances.)⁸ [...]

Malet is shaping up very well. Personally he is in favour of an English policy of action.

194. Hugo von Radolinski to Holstein

J[arotschin], 4 October 1886

My dear friend,

[...] To follow up the idea in my last letter,⁹ could you not tell the

---

¹ Otto von Bismarck.   ² Alexander von Battenberg.
³ See *Diaries*, entry for 3 October 1886.   ⁴ Crown Prince Friedrich Wilhelm.
⁵ That is, to make Alexander von Battenberg Governor of Alsace-Lorraine and then Chancellor.
⁶ Alois, Count Károlyi. Austro-Hungarian Ambassador in Berlin, 1871–8, in London, 1878–88.
⁷ Jules Herbette. French Ambassador in Berlin, 1886–96.
⁸ See above p. 188, note 1.   ⁹ Of 2 October, see above.

son[1] that A[lbedyll] will stand out as the *strong* man if he refuses to advocate the marriage question along the desired lines?

If, however, the son through the father obtains the consent of the old gentleman,[2] then he is the *great* man *for all time*, undermines the influence of A., and will establish an unshakeable position with the parents[3] of the young lady.[4] Since the matter *will* certainly be carried out later on, it would certainly be better for the son to get all the benefits deriving from it, and stand out as the person who induced the father to obtain the consent. It will surely flatter him if the mother is forever grateful to him for what he did in the matter. Otherwise the gulf between the 'son'[1] and 'my people'[3] will become steadily greater.

All here send you affectionate greetings.

Your faithful
R.[5]

195. Hugo von Radolinski to Holstein

5 October 1886

My dear friend,

I have just received your letter[6] and before the post goes will reply in great haste with best thanks.

All right. Then I will do nothing and will *not answer the last letter*[7] *at all.* Meanwhile we can wait and see. Do you think it is also out of the question to speak to the son in the way I wrote about yesterday? I have meanwhile written to Italy[8] that we must be patient, although I believe that one need not allow oneself to be kept in leading strings by one's parents[9] *in everything.* What can happen if the son and his wife frankly tell the parents that it will take place? We are no longer children and know what to do with our children. What can the parents do about it? To disinherit is surely impossible. At worst the son and his wife will retire somewhere and sulk. These are the ideas that they have there if they come up against the parents' obstinacy in everything. [...]

Your faithful
R.

I should therefore not answer the letter at all, not even express thanks for the invitation?

196. Holstein to Hugo von Radolinski[10]

6 October 1886

Whether I advise that you do not speak direct to the younger generation[11] of the matter?[12] And how! Quite hopeless. Can only do harm.

I do not believe that the matter will be consented to willingly either now or later. That reminds me that as early as last year I was told—I

---
[1] Herbert von Bismarck.   [2] Kaiser Wilhelm I.
[3] The Crown Prince and Princess.   [4] Princess Victoria.
[5] Holstein replied on 5 October: 'Letter of 4.10. just received. [...] The idea about "Karl" is quite hopeless. Give it up.' (From the Radolin Papers.)
[6] Of 4 October. See above.   [7] From Bismarck. See Radolinski's letter of 27 September.
[8] To the Crown Princess.   [9] The Kaiser and Kaiserin.
[10] From the Radolin Papers.   [11] Herbert von Bismarck.   [12] The Battenberg marriage.

think by Cocotte[1]—that an attempt would be made to secure binding promises for all time that the event should not take place.

Your question about the pros and cons of the possible creation of a *fait accompli* I would prefer not to answer. Put yourself in my position. I have sometimes gone beyond the intentions of the Big Capo, have occasionally even used *my* ways in reaching *his* goals. But I have never consciously gone directly counter to his intentions. And since I don't know in advance how my advice would turn out—in case I should sit myself down to think the matter through thoroughly—I prefer to keep my hands off!

I am afraid there will again be trouble if the Chancellor reads in the newspaper that the Crown Prince has gone to all sorts of lengths with the Comte de Paris; the latter has rented a place in the neighbourhood. I am astonished more at Her Imperial Highness than at His Imperial Highness that precisely at the moment when France appears to be on a bad footing with England so much fuss should be made of the Orléans. Or do the lady and gentleman perhaps think, like Wilhelm Redern, that we should ally ourselves with France? A completely purposeless demonstration. [...]

Affectionate greetings.

197. Holstein to Hugo von Radolinski[2]

Monday, [11 October 1886]

Dear Rado,

The following is very important. The Russian Government expects that Prince Alexander will be re-elected by the great Sobranje and that he will then return without waiting for recognition by Europe.

If that happens the Russians will march in. The Austrians will then perhaps enquire in London if England will join them in making war. After the English refusal they will come to an agreement with Russia. There is only one way to prevent this eventuality, which would bring disaster upon both Prince Alexander and Bulgaria. The great Sobranje, instead of proceeding immediately with the election, must address a declaration to the Congress Powers drawn up along these lines:

'The overwhelming majority of the Bulgarian people are attached to Prince Alexander, now as formerly. (Or better still: The Bulgarian people are devoted to Prince A.) If Bulgaria were strong enough to secure acceptance of its will, nobody but Prince A. would be considered for election. But Bulgaria does not possess the power necessary to do this. The Sobranje also desires that the election should be an act of pacification and not a source of conflict. The Sobranje therefore addresses itself to the Powers with the request that they should indicate several persons, or even a single person, whose election would gain the approval of the Powers and at the same time, in so far as [it] depended on Bulgaria, would strengthen the peace of Europe. Until the will of the Powers became known, the Sobranje and the Government it had

---

[1] Countess Helene von Hatzfeldt. [2] From the Radolin Papers.

provisionally placed in office would justify their right of existence by ensuring that the order which had been preserved throughout the entire country, despite all previous attempts at disturbance, would continue to be maintained.'

The Powers will obviously never agree on any one. The present Government will therefore remain in office, Prince Alexander's throne will remain vacant and—time will have been won.

Forward this quickly. As Sal[isbury] is away and Iddesleigh is an idiot, the matter can only reach its destination via Heinrich-Karl.[1] But quickly, time presses.

In my definite opinion this is all that can be done *now* for the Prince: to hold his throne vacant for him. And the Russians can hardly do anything *against* it.

Monday.

The letter is already closed. Hence I am writing a second to say that the following telegram from Sofia has just come in:

'The Bulgarian Government has resolved not to summon the great Sobranje but first of all—some time during the week—to request *the Powers* to designate a candidate for the princely throne. As soon as that happens the Government will do everything possible to secure the election of this candidate.'[2]

The established agreement of noble minds! How very clever.

It is right that the Bulgarians always address themselves only to the Congress Powers *collectively*.

My proposal is only a paraphrase of this notion.

198. Holstein to Paul von Hatzfeldt[3]

26 October 1886.

Herbette has given Herbert Bismarck his word of honour that the French Government has not negotiated recently with any other Power over Mediterranean questions, especially over the Egyptian Question.[4]

We know that is a lie. Freycinet offered Tripoli to the Italians if they would support him in Egypt against the English. At the same time France declared to the Sultan that she was ready to defend the *droits sacrés* of the Porte, especially on the North African coast. The two offers—the one to Italy, and the other to Turkey—are contradictory.

It is not known what the Cabinet in Paris may also offer to the Russians and the English, but in general they make too much use of lies in Paris; this method of stirring things up wears out too quickly.

The Chancellor talked superbly to Shuvalov, as in former days.[5] He told him:

---

[1] The reference may be to Heinrich von Battenberg and Alexander von Battenberg.
[2] This telegram, dated 11 October, is in the Foreign Ministry files.
[3] Note by Holstein: copy of a letter to Hatzfeldt.
[4] See *Grosse Politik*, vol. VI, no. 1202, pp. 95–6; *Documents Diplomatiques Français*, Première Série, vol. VI, no. 325, pp. 324–5.
[5] Bismarck's conversations with Shuvalov on 19 and 20 October. (See *Diaries*, p. 313, note 3.)

'It is easier for Russia not to go into Bulgaria than to get out of Bulgaria again with honour. Bulgaria's future is a matter of indifference to Germany. Not for Austria, because no Austrian Government can calmly watch a *permanent* Russian occupation of Bulgaria, on account of Hungarian public opinion.'

In answer to the direct question by the Ambassador as to whether Germany would guarantee the Russians any form of assistance against Austria:

'It is in Germany's interest that the number of Great Powers should not decrease. If the two Powers, Russia and Austria, which are on terms of friendship with us, were to engage in war, we could at best calmly look on and see a battle lost by one or the other. But we could not tolerate that one of them, no matter which, should be dismembered or otherwise so greatly weakened that it ceased to be a Great Power. Such an event we should have to prevent.'

The statement is distinguished and dignified. It will keep the peace for the time being, but it will promote the Franco-Russian understanding because the Russians see that with us they will not achieve their aim: the destruction of Austria. I would therefore compare the present stage with the time of day when the morning mists rise; for the time being it is fine but later on there will be bad weather.

Muraviev[1] told me yesterday: '*Voyez-vous, tout ce qu'on appelle ici Bulgarian troubles va s'apaiser. Je ne vois pas encore les symptômes de l'apaisement, mais j'ai mon instinct.*'

Yesterday the French Military Attaché, de Saucy, said the same to the Austrian Chargé d'Affaires:[2] '*Tout ça va s'aplanir, vous allez voir; puisque le Comte Shuvalov doit avoir emporté de Varzin une forte dose d'un narcotique très-puissant.*'

So: the French Embassy knows what Shuvalov brought back with him.

I have drawn up a memorandum on these two identical statements.[3]
[...]

Affectionate greetings.[4]

199. Holstein to Paul von Hatzfeldt[5]

10 November 1886

Bülow's reports from St Petersburg reveal themselves as positively dangerous; only comparable with Lucchesini's activity in 1805. For months past Bülow has written in the following style:

'The Mistress of the Robes, Princess Kotsubey, told me that the Tsar was looking for ways and means to give expression to the antipathy mingled with contempt which he entertains for the French Republic.' or 'The Mistress of the Robes, Princess Kotsubey, says the Tsar

---

[1] Michael, Count Muraviev. Russian Counsellor of Embassy in Berlin, 1884–93; Minister in Copenhagen, 1893–7; Foreign Minister, 1897–1900.
[2] Schmit, Ritter von Tavera, while Széchényi was on leave.
[3] Not found.
[4] Hatzfeldt's reply of 7 November is printed in the *Diaries*, entry for 9 November 1886.
[5] Note by Holstein: 'Copy of a letter to Hatzfeldt.'

cherishes a favourite plan for having all the monarchical Powers permanently represented in Paris simply by chargés d'affaires.' or

'While Alexander II was suspicious of Prince Bismarck, Alexander III on the contrary has the fullest confidence in the German Chancellor and places the highest value on learning his opinions.' etc. etc.

It has now become more and more obvious that this was political romancing.

Freycinet has told Münster that at the beginning of September a confidant of the Tsar had on his direct instructions made proposals of the most far-reaching kind, whose nature Münster could certainly guess. These proposals were at that time rejected by the Council of Ministers because it did not wish to pursue a *politique d'aventures*. A second move was made about twelve days ago from the Russian side, again by the Tsar's direct order, and on this occasion through a member of the Imperial family: the Tsar desired it to be stated that Baron Mohrenheim[1] would shortly return to Paris, and in that connection he had expressed the wish that a French ambassador, a career diplomat, should be proposed as speedily as possible for St Petersburg. The acceptance of Laboulaye,[2] who was proposed as a result of this suggestion, followed with startling swiftness.[3]

Freycinet's statements are undoubtedly correct because they are supported by several circumstantial proofs. The above-mentioned second Russian suggestion followed *shortly after* Shuvalov's return from Varzin. He had obtained for the Russians the certitude that they could not count upon our assistance in destroying Austria, and that on the contrary we intended to preserve Austria.

Since Schweinitz has returned to St Petersburg, the dispatches have taken on a much soberer tone than Bülow's, although Schweinitz once told me a long time ago: 'A Prussian representative who reports unpleasant things about the state of affairs at the Russian Court is always done for, because what he says always comes back to St Petersburg sooner or later.'

If then Schweinitz does not actually report unpleasant things, he at least does not paint a rosy picture as Bülow did.

One knows where one stands if Schweinitz, for example, reports: 'Tsar Alexander, who cannot free himself from the belief that he was not sufficiently supported by Austria during the Bulgarian troubles, is also under the false impression that your Highness' wishes cannot

[1] Arthur, Baron von Mohrenheim. Russian Ambassador in Paris, 1884–98.
[2] Antoine de Laboulaye. French Ambassador in St Petersburg, 1886–91.
[3] See *Documents Diplomatiques Français*, Première Série, vol. VI, nos. 333, 337, pp. 336, 339. See also Münster's letter to Herbert von Bismarck of 5 November. (*Grosse Politik*, vol. VI, no. 1203, pp. 96–8.) Münster wrote to Holstein on 12 November: 'I am glad that my dispatch and letter aroused interest. What does our Embassy in St Petersburg say to this? It seems to have had no notion whatever of all that went on here. I shall also in future be in a position to keep track of all the intrigues that are engaged in here by the Russians. The Russians have been clumsy in all this, for they have made the French very mistrustful. Freycinet does not lightly venture into anything with them, and what is good is that he cannot stand Mohrenheim. I only hope for our sake that that ass remains here for a long time.'

meet with any opposition in Vienna.'[1] In other words, the Tsar makes us responsible for Austria's attitude, about which he is furious.

After this there is no danger of one's being lulled into a sense of security by Shuvalov's assurance that the Tsar had again confirmed his determination to maintain good relations with Germany.

Schweinitz in conclusion expresses a doubt 'whether Shuvalov has achieved success with His Majesty in explaining to him the Varzin point of view'.[1]

In short Schweinitz is behaving pretty well.

But now Reuss yesterday made the following very interesting and entirely confidential communication: Grand Duke Vladimir,[2] the husband of his niece, had told him that 'the Tsar was filled with mistrust and rage against Bismarck. He expresses this in the harshest terms in marginal comments or otherwise whenever an opportunity offers.'

At H. Bismarck's desire, Reuss has put this into writing.

We shall not be so very astonished about all this, you and I; we were long ago at one in the feeling that the Russian alliance *a fait son temps*. The exaggerated expectations which the Russians appear to have entertained last winter and ever since of the practical utility of our friendship now contribute to aggravate the estrangement.

As an ally for the future I count more upon Italy than upon England.

I am not surprised that Vienna at the outset rejected the English proposals.[3] To judge by the speeches of the great Randolph,[4] the proposals may have been frivolous enough; he has in recent months done great damage to England's Eastern policy and lost her that modicum of confidence that she had slowly regained.[5]

200. Chlodwig zu Hohenlohe to Holstein

Strasbourg, 17 December 1886

My dear Baron,

The conviction among the generals here is that war will break out with France in the near future. The imminent strengthening of the army corps arouses warlike hopes. Heuduck[6] says that with this army we would be able to take the offensive, which hitherto we could not have done. He also thinks that two powerful armies facing each other acted on each other like a magnet; it would therefore soon come to blows. Possibly he is right.

As for me, I ask myself whether in the event of a victorious war we would be able to crush France so thoroughly that she would be rendered defenceless for all time. And further: whether Russia, who is interested in seeing that France remains a permanent threat to us, would watch the

---

[1] Quotation from a dispatch by Schweinitz of 6 November on Shuvalov's audience with the Tsar. (From the Foreign Ministry files.)

[2] Vladimir Alexandrovich, the oldest brother of Tsar Alexander III.

[3] To oppose possible Russian schemes in Bulgaria. (*Grosse Politik*, vol. IV, nos. 871–2, pp. 279–83.)

[4] Lord Randolph Churchill.

[5] Hatzfeldt's reply of 11 November is printed in the *Diaries*, entry for 14 November 1886.

[6] Wilhelm von Heuduck. General commanding the 15th Army Corps in Alsace.

progress of the war to its end as passively as she did in 1870. If there is certainty about this, then I have nothing more to say. If there is not, then I ask whether there are not other ways of rendering France harmless to us. One such consists in putting a halter on her that would hinder her movements. One such halter would be Egypt with the North African coast. Then she would have England and Italy as opponents, and would be compelled to consign ideas of *revanche* and Alsace-Lorraine to limbo. If we could set Russia on India and France on Egypt we would have peace on both sides, and could save both the money and men that war would cost us. These are the—perhaps—foolish ideas of an old retired diplomat.

With friendly greetings
Your most devoted
C. Hohenlohe.

In contrast to the above-mentioned remark of Heuduck's is the assertion of a high-ranking officer, who assures me that our leaders are too old and that it is only to be hoped that war does not break out just now under the Albedyll regimes; in spite of our superiority in armaments, we could not count on victory with certainty because of bad leadership.[1]

201. Schmit von Tavera to Holstein

Berlin, Sunday, [19 December 1886]

My dear Colleague!

[...] Count Széchényi arrives here in an hour's time.

I don't think I can conclude my period of service as Chargé d'Affaires more fittingly than by thanking you from the bottom of my heart for the services you have rendered to me personally and to my country. How much you have thereby aided us, I myself am probably unable to appreciate fully. But so far as I can judge, it is more than enough to make me forever grateful to you.

I must now hurry to the *Anhalter Bahnhof*, and remain with warmest Christmas greetings,

Your sincerely devoted
Tavera.

---

[1] See Hohenlohe's letter to Holstein of 16 December 1886. (Rogge, *Holstein und Hohenlohe*, pp. 264–5.)

1887

202. Heinrich VII Reuss to Holstein

Vienna, 1 January 1887

My dear Herr von Holstein,

A safe opportunity has just offered itself which affords me the welcome occasion for thanking you very much for your friendly letter of the 29th which was particularly valuable for me.

Dispatch no. 861[1] does not give me any instructions to speak about our attitude, but I assume that I am empowered to let it be known, in case Count Kálnoky brings up the subject, that we do not agree to the *'régions des balcans'*.[2]

But now, before I receive my instructions, I would like to ask you some questions.

If I tell Kálnoky that we cannot agree to the *'régions des balcans'* because we are unable to take upon ourselves an obligation to maintain the status quo in the Balkan Peninsula, he will answer that it was we who accepted and recommended the first—Robilant's[3]—draft of the treaty.[4] And the beginning of Article II runs: *'Les Hautes Parties contractantes n'ayant en vue que le maintien, autant que possible, du statu quo territorial en Orient, s'engagent à user de leur influence pour prévenir etc. etc. toute modification territoriale.'*

By accepting this proposal, we too had therefore at least wanted to hinder territorial modifications in the Ottoman Empire.

In the second paragraph of this Article, *only* an obligation on the part of Austria and Italy to each other is in question, Germany is entirely left out, and for the simple reason that Germany has no interest in the Balkan States. For this reason Kálnoky also spoke in his final clause only of Italy and not of Germany.

If we now declare that we hold fast to the principle of the demarcation line,[5] and are therefore opposed to the Austrian clause, we should

---

[1] *Grosse Politik*, vol. IV, no. 842, pp. 225–6.

[2] Reuss refers to the additional clause relating to the status quo *'dans la région des balcans'* which Austria had introduced into the Italian draft for the renewal of the Triple Alliance. (See *Grosse Politik*, vol. IV, no. 839, Enclosure, pp. 217–19.) In dispatch no. 861 of 28 December 1886, Berchem had informed Prince Reuss that Germany would not agree to the Austrian additional clause.

[3] Nicolis, Count di Robilant. Italian Minister and Ambassador in Vienna, 1871–85; Foreign Minister in the Depretis Cabinet, 1885–7.

[4] See *Grosse Politik*, vol. IV, no. 836, Enclosure I, pp. 204–6.

[5] Dispatch no. 861 stated: 'We hold firmly to the line of demarcation which we proposed between the spheres of interest of Austria and Russia, even though we unfortunately have not yet persuaded Vienna to accept it: holding fast to this principle, however, means that Russia should be allowed a free hand in the eastern part of the Balkan Peninsula.'

thereby admit that we would also consent to a *changement territorial* in the eastern half of the Balkan Peninsula; and thus not merely to letting things take their course and to a possible occupation of Bulgaria by Russia, but also to a possible seizure of this country which alone can be regarded as *changement territorial*.

Count Kálnoky would then tell me that this is in contradiction to our recommendation of the Italian Art. II which says: that the *hautes parties contractantes* desire to see the *status quo territorial* maintained in the Near East.

They will not concede here that the principal advantage of the Italian Alliance is on Austria's side. For the old Treaty[1] Art. II, second paragraph, assures Germany of Italy's assistance in the event that the former is the subject of an unprovoked attack by France.

Kálnoky has hitherto always stressed that by this article Germany has a great advantage over Austria and that therefore, by means of his additional clause to the new Italian proposal, he wants to place Austria in the same advantageous position in regard to a Russian attack that we already had in the old Treaty in regard to a French attack.

One must of course wait and see whether Italy will now make use of the additional Austrian clause to raise the price. I cannot help thinking that Italy should be very content that Article IV[2] has been conceded to her unaltered.

I think that here they will hold very firmly to the *'régions des balcans'*, and I only hope that we will succeed in inducing them here to abandon it by pointing to the importance of the Treaty as a whole and Robilant's active friendship.

With best wishes for the new year I am

Your very devoted
H. VII Reuss.

203. Heinrich VII Reuss to Holstein

Vienna, 9 January 1887

My dear Herr von Holstein,

Best thanks for your letter of the 5th. My telegram of the 7th[3] will have shown you that the opposition here was not as bad as you thought it would be. Up to this moment I have not yet received a conclusive answer, but I think I can take it that Kálnoky will agree to the draft,[4] as amended by himself and Robilant. He, and especially the Kaiser, attach great importance to binding the Italians more firmly, because here there are still doubts about their (not Robilant's) reliability.

---

[1] *Grosse Politik*, vol. III, no. 571, pp. 245–7.

[2] Italy was conceded the right to demand the support of her allies in case French expansion in North Africa should oblige Italy to go to war with France.

[3] Reuss had reported by telegram on 7 January: 'Enclosure in Dispatch No. 8 [*Grosse Politik*, vol. IV, no. 844, pp. 230–1] communicated to Count Kálnoky, who promised me a quick reply after audience with the Kaiser of Austria. I have gained the impression from our conversation that there is a disposition to accept the *new* Italian proposal, perhaps with verbal changes.' (From the Foreign Ministry files.)

[4] *Grosse Politik*, vol. IV, nos. 839, 843, pp. 213–19, 226–30.

This pinning down is so important to the Austrians that they are prepared in return to pay the price of allowing the Italians to play a part in Near Eastern affairs, something they have hitherto anxiously avoided.

As far as I can see, and as I have stated frequently, the 'ambitious Balkan policy' or the 'schemes' of Count Kálnoky, about which you people in Berlin are always talking, consist in the fact that the Austrians would feel themselves threatened if they were encircled by a Slav ring extending to Montenegro: it is *that* that they want to prevent. The Austrians may be mistaken in this and deceive themselves in thinking that their interests are thereby threatened: that is quite possible. But they are far too spineless to pursue ambitious schemes.

Because they now see that we will not help them to prevent the closing of this ring, they want to assure themselves of the Italians' help. Here they are not placing too much reliance on the support of Italy, but they are counting more on the fact that Russia, because of the conclusion of this alliance, will become more cautious and will content itself with the position it held in Bulgaria in '85, which is gladly conceded here.

Nigra[1] is being kept informed, but does not take part in the negotiations here. He told me that in Berlin they wanted to draw England in. That was news to me. In my opinion they would very gladly agree to that here. Naturally I do not discuss it. I have restricted myself according to my instructions to representing and recommending both drafts[2] as acceptable to us, but have very decidedly urged the Minister to make his decision and to act quickly while there was time. He has made all sorts of criticisms of the Italian *exposé* and described Robilant's statements as erroneous. This however is only of dialectical importance and is a matter of indifference if the affair itself is settled. A few changes in the wording that do not alter the meaning have been proposed to me. What was typical was that in reading to me the new Italian paragraph in II, K. asked whether perhaps a bit of Trentino was concealed in the words *compensations équitables*.[3] Bojanowski[4] will bring you these lines; I am writing almost the same things to the State Secretary, but meanwhile did not want to let Bojanowski leave without thanking you for your letter.

With sincere regard,
H. VII Reuss.

I have just remembered that K. asked me whether the Chancellor had said nothing about his remarks on the communication *'de tous les renseignements'*. I replied to him that His Highness attached no importance to this. He said: 'That is all right by me, but I do not really see how we—Germany and Austria—shall escape from the dilemma we are in with regard to our treaty with Russia. However Prince B. will take care of that.'

---

[1] Constantino, Count Nigra. Italian Ambassador in Vienna, 1885–1904.

[2] By Count Robilant. (*Grosse Politik*, vol. IV, no. 843, Enclosure, pp. 228–30.)

[3] See Reuss' dispatch to Bismarck of 16 January. (*Grosse Politik*, vol. IV, no. 845, pp. 231–7.)

[4] Consul-General in Budapest.

204. Heinrich VII Reuss to Holstein

Vienna, 17 January 1887

My dear Herr von Holstein,

Best thanks for your letter of the 11th. I had hoped to have been able to offer you something better in my answer than I can with to-day's bad news. The report that Kálnoky is putting on the brake will give you as little pleasure as it does me.[1]

I was so taken aback by his statement that I told him frankly: 'I no longer understand you; you reject an arrangement that assures peace and should profit Austria more than anyone.'

I do not in fact understand what could have caused the Minister to turn back so suddenly on the road along which he was already going.

I believe that the restricted vision of Kaiser Franz Joseph, with which we are familiar, was not capable of grasping this superb conception. I know that he had been alarmed by the Chancellor's statements on world policy in the Reichstag,[2] and takes it for granted that Russia will now throw off all restraint. (I must say in passing that I have argued against this assumption). The fear of a Russian war has therefore suddenly appeared more imminent to him, and he hesitates on that account to engage himself elsewhere.

It seems that Kálnoky was unable to combat this notion, and was therefore compelled to translate it for us into flowery diplomatic language. He is not as shortsighted as his master (for he has been convinced up to now of the justice of our opinion), but that he too was influenced by this great speech cannot be denied. He is especially concerned about the stimulus to public opinion in Russia and throughout the Slav world.

I have plainly told both him and Szögyéni[3] that this fateful decision would make the worst possible impression upon us, and I believe that in this I am not deceiving myself.

Szögyéni is opposed to it because from the first he recognized the utility of the matter for Austria.

Robilant will not accept a simple renewal of the old treaty nor be content with rhetorical phrases. If we alone conclude it with him, then we are certainly safeguarded, but the whole thing loses its useful completeness.

I can assure you that I was really shocked by this affair; during my long career I have never experienced such a disappointment as this.

With sincere regard,
Your devoted
H. VII Reuss.

[1] Reuss wrote in the above-cited report to Bismarck of 16 January 1887: 'To-day the Minister [Kálnoky] at last summoned me and explained to me [...] that, considering the way the situation in the Near East was now developing, it would be better, from the standpoint of Austro-Hungarian interests, simply to renew the former treaty.'

[2] In the debate that followed his speech of 11 January, Bismarck expressly emphasized that Germany and Austria each had interests for which neither the one state nor the other could be expected to risk everything. (Bismarck, *Die gesammelten Werke*, vol. XIII, pp. 207-33.)

[3] Ladislaus, Baron (later Count) von Szögyéni-Marich. First *Sektionschef* in the Austro-Hungarian Foreign Ministry, 1883-92; Ambassador in Berlin, 1892-1914.

P.S. The wish you expressed in regard to your letters I will of course fulfil.

As to Wedel, I think he is safe. At all events I can assure you that he has a *very* high opinion of you. He is certainly ambitious and also much spoilt, he is also perhaps filled with a sense of his own value, but I cannot say of him that he is an intriguer.

205. Heinrich VII Reuss to Holstein

1 February 1887

My dear Herr von Holstein,

I owe you thanks for two letters which were of very great value to me.

In the second (of the 29th of last month) you seek to discover the reasons why they did not want to enter into the Italian proposals here. You assume a calculation here that was bound to lead to a *mis*calculation.

I cannot share this opinion. The longer I have to deal with Austrians, the more firmly the conviction has grown in me that these people are not capable of devising far-reaching plans and combinations. Kálnoky at times shows more understanding, but he runs his head against a wall either with the Kaiser, who is timorous, or with the Hungarians, who bolt.

The first sentence of your supposition may be to the point, namely, that Austria prefers *us* as allies to Italy because we demand nothing, whereas Italy always has a hand held out for tips. But at this point calculation ceases, and there begins a policy of timidity, pessimism, and the fear of letting themselves in for something of which the end cannot be seen with certainty. Hence Kálnoky's endeavour—which in Haymerle's[1] case was still more insufferable—to conclude treaties to guard against all—even the most improbable—eventualities.

It is quite understandable that with this sort of policy, you in Berlin must presume all kinds of ambitious schemes. The sole ambition that I have so far observed is, so to speak, a negative or *passive* one.

As to the Italians, who are not liked here and are regarded as untrustworthy, one does not want to give them the run of a preserve in which up to now they were not permitted to hunt. One would perhaps permit Albania to go to a reliable friend; but hardly to one who is restless and ambitious. Montenegro, to be sure, lies between Albania and the Austrian coastal lands, towards which every Italian, even Robilant, casts furtive glances, but the Austrians shy away from the prospect of having the 'spaghetti eaters' established on both sides of the Adriatic.

This is a mainspring of Austrian policy, which is not one of greed, but is consistently concerned with guarding against intervention by others.

How long will the people here be able to hold on to the beautiful dream which also flitted before Count Andrássy[2] at the Congress of Berlin!

[1] Heinrich, Baron von Haymerle. Austro-Hungarian Ambassador in Rome, 1877–9; Plenipotentiary at the Congress of Berlin, 1878; Foreign Minister, 1879–81.

[2] Julius, Count Andrássy. Austro-Hungarian Foreign Minister, 1871–9.

A weak but guaranteed Turkey, which guards the Straits and thus prevents the Russians from playing a maritime role.

In addition a conglomeration of small, independent, but powerless states, which by their particularism and mutual jealousies hold up the Pan-Slav movement. The people here would like to engage undisturbed in commerce with these states, and with Turkey, and—this is the sole idea for the future—because of this situation, another route to the Levant would be left open for Austrian commerce besides the one through the Adriatic.

Not to be suddenly disturbed by the Russians in this peaceful existence —that is the dream, 'the secret ambition', of Austrian statesmen.

If, on the other hand, Macedonia went to Bulgaria, and then Montenegro speedily followed suit, and all this under the Russian flag, the people here would be afraid of being smothered. That is what is known here as 'the indisputable Austro-Hungarian interest'. To banish this danger by a delimitation of the spheres of interest, as the Chancellor has advised them to do here for the past two years, they first of all lack the courage, but also confidence in Russia's trustworthiness.

Try it for once! This is something I have said repeatedly, but in vain. Here they have but a poor opinion of Russia's passion for upholding treaties.

What you say about Russia being able in advance to determine the exact moment when Austria must resort to force is certainly correct. The only question is whether Bosnia can in fact once again be roused to rebellion. The majority of the Mohammedans who formed the insurrectionary elements in the population have left, and I hardly think that the Serbians in the country, who are prosperous, will once again be willing to follow the Russian Pied Piper.

If, however, St Petersburg were to let Montenegro take up arms, and make an incursion into Bosnia or Serbia, then the situation would be as you foresee. For this very reason Austria should have grasped at the Italian alliance with both hands.

In my opinion Austria is not in any position to pursue ambitious plans because she knows very well—at least Count Kálnoky and many other sensible politicians in this country know—that she is not powerful enough. And to decide to arrange matters in such a way as to be in a position to wage a successful war at the side of a reliable ally—a war that could only be a balm to her internal troubles—to do that, she lacks the spirit that Caprivi's captain recommended to the cadet.

As regards the rejection of the Italian proposals, this lack of spirit dismayed me more than I can say. The value of the Austrian alliance must in consequence be lowered for us.

I cannot hide from you that the magnificent dispatch no. 53[1] again roused my feelings of reverence for our great Chief. He had cause enough to be annoyed by the Austrian reply of the 16th,[2] and nobody could have blamed him if he had hurled thunderbolts instead of applying

---
[1] See *Grosse Politik*, vol. IV, no. 847, pp. 240–4.
[2] See *Grosse Politik*, vol. IV, no. 845, pp. 231–7.

balm. And now I receive instructions that are drawn up in a friendly, almost paternal, tone, yet so convincing and logical that Kálnoky and his Kaiser were convinced by them and not by my 'persuasive arts', to which the dispatch appealed.

A load has indeed dropped from my mind, because this affair oppressed me. And it seems to me that Kálnoky is specially grateful that the Prince afforded him an opportunity of making good a great blunder.

It should be possible to meet the two wishes of his Kaiser that he conveyed to me.

Without the deletion of Art. IV, which the Chancellor was able to accomplish for Austria's sake, the result would have been disastrous.

Moreover it seems to me as if Count Robilant attached much greater weight to Art. II than to Austria's help against France. The door into the Balkan Zoo has now been opened for him.

I am sending H. Bismarck a letter by to-day's courier, which is identical except for the omission of any references to your letter.

Are we really slipping into war with France? They are very worried here and continue to arm madly. The summoning of the Delegations could not be avoided.

With my best regards
Your very devoted
H. VII Reuss

206. Paul von Hatzfeldt to Holstein

2 February [1887], Evening.

Dear friend,

I fought like a lion to-day with S[alisbury].[1] He wants to very much, provided that nothing more is demanded of him in *form* and *phrasing* than he can now perform.[2] For the present no names must be mentioned and general phrases used. C.[3] is wholly of my opinion in this. What matters is that Ro[bilant] should empower him to act as quickly as possible. If in addition you could arrange to convince him here that Vienna also agrees, it would advance the matter greatly. Since I know nothing since [I was in] Berlin, I naturally cannot judge whether this is possible.

One thing I must tell *you*. In the middle of the conversation, when I had forced S[alisbury] into a corner he said to me: 'If you only knew what difficulties my mistress creates for me. She is furious that you and the French are so bellicose. I should prevent it and keep both from war!' What do you think of that?[4] [...]

Greetings.

[1] Hatzfeldt telegraphed to the Foreign Ministry on 31 January that Corti had now received instructions to make definite proposals in England for an Anglo-Italian alliance, and had asked Hatzfeldt to support him in his endeavours. (*Grosse Politik*, vol. IV, no. 879, p. 297.)

[2] See Hatzfeldt's telegram of 2 February. (*Grosse Politik*, vol. IV, no. 880, pp. 297–8.)

[3] Luigi, Count Corti. Italian Ambassador in London, 1886–7.

[4] Hatzfeldt wrote on 3 February: 'Could you not get Hugo [Radolinski] to persuade his mistress to see Her M[ajesty] and explain to her how things stand, so that she does not treat us like naughty boys. That would not and could not do any good, but would only make for bad blood.'

207. Paul von Hatzfeldt to Holstein

5 February [1887]

Dear friend,

I flatter myself with the hope that my telegram to-day gave you a not unpleasant hour.[1] You can believe me when I say that I had to work hard for it. Now I would ask *urgently* for one thing: *battons le fer tant qu'il est chaud!* Believe me. You see that I have judged the man correctly after all—now take care that no time is lost. In my opinion it is necessary to answer quickly and readily in order to nail the matter down.

What I would also like if possible is to be allowed to take a hand in the *drafting* with regard to the omission of No. 4. It is possible to say *the same thing* in a *different* way; S[alisbury] also knows that, but it will, I am afraid, *not* happen if I cannot have a hand in it, because the others do not attach much importance to it. But for us it is important. Think about it!

Naturally S. complains that in the other matter we can do virtually nothing for him, although he should understand why.[2] But one thing seems to me necessary if the whole is to be of any value: that at any rate our active support of the others should cease or be considerably restricted. I think you are of my opinion in this and will do your part.

Please send me information.

Greetings.

208. Heinrich VII Reuss to Holstein

Vienna, 13 February 1887

Dear Herr von Holstein,

Everything is splendidly arranged, but I am afraid that you are right after all; the Italian affair is in the ditch. Not much more can be done with Robilant.[3] His retraction[4] was significant. And even if he does stay on, he will have lost some of the courage necessary for the pursuit of an ambitious policy. The man thought too much of himself, his grandiose instructions[5] to Launay[6] sounded far too arrogant. I am sorry because he is an honest man.

---

[1] Hatzfeldt had telegraphed to the Foreign Ministry: 'Lord Salisbury has just told Count Corti that he could enter into the understanding if the condition were dropped whereby he should undertake to support Italy in a possible attack on France (Article 4 of the Italian memorandum delivered here).' For the Italian memorandum see *Grosse Politik*, vol. IV, no. 887, Enclosure II, pp. 308–9. For Hatzfeldt's telegram see *ibid.*, vol. IV, no. 884, p. 303.

[2] Hatzfeldt probably refers to the British desire for support for Sir Drummond Wolff, who had been in Constantinople since the summer of 1886 as British Special Envoy for the Egyptian Question. On 17 February 1887 Radowitz was instructed by Bismarck to adopt a more friendly attitude towards England, while on 2 March Bismarck telegraphed that he had desired 'that you [Radowitz] should have more strongly emphasised to Sir D. Wolff your support for English endeavours in Egypt'. (See *Grosse Politik*, vol. IV, no. 808, p. 165.)

[3] On 8 February Robilant handed in his resignation. See p. 206, note 2.

[4] Regarding certain sections of the Triple Alliance Treaty. (See *Grosse Politik*, vol. IV, no. 849, pp. 246–7.)

[5] See *Grosse Politik*, vol. IV, no. 847, pp. 240–4.

[6] Eduardo, Count di Launay. Italian Ambassador in Berlin, 1867–92.

It is undeniable that Kálnoky completely missed the opportunity. Actually he did not demand that Italy should make all the sacrifices; but since Robilant acted as if he wanted it that way, he naturally allowed him to do so.

With England matters still stand as I recently reported. Here they do not have much confidence in the Engl. Cabinet and therefore will not commit themselves to it in any way. If war should break out with Russia, it is considered not impossible that England will lend her support, but it is not *counted upon*.

Kálnoky said to me to-day. 'The Russians do have luck: first Randolph renders them a service by weakening the English Government,[1] and now Ras Alula achieves the downfall of the only man who put up an energetic opposition.'[2]

With sincere regard

H. VII Reuss.

209. Heinrich VII Reuss to Holstein

Vienna, 20 February 1887

My dear Herr von Holstein,

That really is a splendid coup! and Austria can certainly say that she has come well out of it.[3] Yes indeed—if it weren't for the Chancellor where would our friends be! Kálnoky, to whom I hinted at the matter on instructions from the State Secretary,[4] had already been informed by Széchényi, and, as you had insisted, by a secret private letter.[5] The communications from London and Rome arrived yesterday.

You will know that *contrary* to the instructions given to me by the State Secretary, I received yesterday by telegram the Prince's order to deny any knowledge of the matter even to Count Kálnoky![6] This last was now unhappily no longer possible, but I did not say that I was

[1] In December 1886 Lord Randolph Churchill resigned from the post of Chancellor of the Exchequer in Lord Salisbury's government and was succeeded by G. J. Goschen.

[2] On 26 January 1887 Ras Alula, Commander-in-Chief of the forces of the Negus of Abyssinia, defeated an Italian force at Dogali. Robilant was fiercely attacked in the Italian Chamber. On 8 February he resigned, as did the entire Cabinet. All attempts to form another Ministry proved unsuccessful, and on 3 March the King refused to accept the resignation.

[3] Bismarck had removed Austrian and Italian objections to the renewal of the Triple Alliance by the proposal that the old Triple Alliance Treaty should be renewed in its original form, but that its provisions should be supplemented by means of new German-Italian and Austrian-Italian agreements. (See Reuss' dispatch to Bismarck of 19 February. *Grosse Politik*, vol. IV, no. 857, pp. 255–7.) At the same time Germany helped to bring about an understanding between England and Italy.

[4] In a private letter of 16 February Herbert von Bismarck wrote to Reuss: 'In order to stimulate Count Kálnoky, Your Highness can give him to understand quite confidentially, and with a request for *strict* secrecy, that we have been successful in bringing about a written agreement between England and Italy in which both Powers undertake to take joint action with regard to the maintenance of the status quo in the Mediterranean and the Black Seas.' (*Grosse Politik*, vol. IV, no. 893, pp. 315–16.)

[5] See Krausnick's citations from the letters written by Széchényi to Kálnoky in *Holsteins Geheimpolitik*, p. 121.

[6] In Bismarck's telegram of 18 February to Vienna, Reuss was instructed to conceal from *everyone* his knowledge of the Anglo-Italian agreement of February 1887, and in reply to possible questions on the part of Count Kálnoky or others, to state 'that he had no knowledge whatsoever of an Anglo-Italian agreement'. (From the Foreign Ministry files.)

already in possession of the *pièces*, which he himself showed to me to-day.

What happened that I should have received this delayed *contre-ordre*? Has Count Herbert not said anything to his father about his instructions to me?

Moreover Kálnoky has kept the secret from the English with the result that *over there* the fiction exists that the English had spoken the *first* word.

It is to be hoped that the signing will take place to-day in Berlin.[1]

The Russians are now beautifully caught by the ears. This is a just reward for their friendly intentions with regard to a Franco-German war. But when they get wind of the fact that we had a hand in all this, they will be really furious. I have little trust in Italian discretion.

Kálnoky is very grateful to you for seeing Széchényi,[2] as otherwise the Aust. Embassy would be still more out of touch with things than hitherto.

I thank you very much for your letter of the 16th which was very valuable to me.

With sincere regard
H. VII Reuss.

210. Chlodwig zu Hohenlohe to Holstein[3]

Strasbourg, 22 February 1887

My dear Baron,

The elections here yesterday turned out just as badly as we had expected.[4] The question is now being discussed among higher German officials as to what is to be done to assuage German national feelings, wounded by this Francophil demonstration on the part of the *Reichsland*.[5] One says that the regional diet should be suspended; another that the inhabitants of Alsace-Lorraine should be deprived of the right to vote in Reichstag elections. I am not in sympathy with forcible measures and share the opinion, which the Chancellor expressed in a letter to me in the course of the winter, *that in Alsace-Lorraine one must avoid arbitrary action*.[6]

We will do better if we enforce the law justly but inexorably and carry out every measure for securing the country against French influence.

What is your impression of the matter?[7] [...]

With friendly greetings
Your most devoted
C Hohenlohe.

[1] Reuss refers to the second Triple Alliance Treaty of 20 February 1887. (*Grosse Politik*, vol. IV, no. 858, pp. 257–8.)

[2] Széchényi's house had been placed under quarantine on account of scarlet fever.

[3] See Hohenlohe, *Denkwürdigkeiten*, vol. II, p. 410; Rogge, *Holstein und Hohenlohe*, p. 273.

[4] Hohenlohe had urgently appealed to the electors in Alsace-Lorraine to support those candidates who approved of the septennial military budget for the Reich (*Septennatsvorlage*). (See *Diaries*, entry for 14 March 1887.)

[5] Alsace-Lorraine.

[6] In a letter of 8 November 1886 Bismarck wrote: 'Arbitrary action and unjust pressure on individuals must be refrained from in the Reichsland with even greater care than everywhere else.' (Bismarck, *Die gesammelten Werke*, vol. VIc, p. 346.)

[7] For Holstein's reply of 3 March 1887 see Rogge, *Holstein und Hohenlohe*, pp. 274–7.

211. Eberhard zu Solms to Holstein

Madrid, 24 February 1887

My dear friend,

[...] Moret[1] still firmly believes in war. We have not spoken any further about alliance questions. Spain cannot afford us any positive assistance because of the neglected organisation of her army. But if she were to ally herself with France, the latter would only have to supply the necessary wagons and convoys to bring out of Spain very speedily several army corps which could be used wherever wished, and for her part would not need to keep a watch on the Pyrenees. This appears to me to be so obvious a disadvantage that I cannot conceive why we do not immediately make use of Spain's friendly intentions.[2] You talk of 'resentment over the Carolines'.[3] I am of the opinion that resentment should not play any part in politics. The Italian Minister[4] is very embarrassed that the matter is not progressing. Here they think that we are holding back partly because we are afraid of frightening France out of possible aggressive intentions by too widespread alliances. For the more discerning people calculate that Germany would do better to fight at once, provided one is convinced (and they are here) that this war will break out sooner or later anyway. We are regarded as the more powerful now.

If we get through this crisis,[5] there is perhaps a hope that war will be avoided altogether. You in Berlin are certainly in the best position to judge of this. [...]

Good-bye and once again thanks for your letter. With sincere regards.

Your most devoted
Solms

212. Heinrich VII Reuss to Holstein

Vienna, 15 March 1887

My dear Herr von Holstein,

I still have to thank you for your letter of the 5th. The second business has since then been cleared up, and Austria joins the Eng.-Ital. agreement.[6] Now comes the third with Spain.[7] I think the draft very

---

[1] Segismundo Moret y Prendergast. Spanish Foreign Minister in the Sagasta Cabinet, November 1885–June 1890.

[2] To conclude an alliance with Germany. (See *Diaries*, p. 325, note 1.)

[3] The quarrel between Germany and Spain over the possession of the Caroline Islands, which were awarded to Spain by the Pope, who was called upon to act as arbitrator. (See *Diaries*, entry for 23 August 1885 *et seq.*)

[4] Alberto, Baron di Blanc. Secretary-General of the Italian Foreign Ministry, 1881–3; Minister in Madrid, 1884–7; Ambassador in Constantinople, April 1887–91; Foreign Minister in the Crispi Cabinet, 1893–6.

[5] The crisis between France and Germany that had developed as a result of nationalist agitation in France.

[6] On 23 March Austria joined the first Mediterranean Agreement between Italy and England. (See *Grosse Politik*, vol. IV, nos. 905–6, pp. 329–31.) The exchange of notes is printed by Pribram under the date 24 March. (A. F. Pribram, *The Secret Treaties of Austria-Hungary, 1879–1914* (Cambridge, 1920), vol. I, pp. 98–103.)

[7] Spain joined the first Mediterranean Agreement on 4 May by an exchange of Notes with Italy. Austria joined in the Italo-Spanish Agreement on 21 May. (See Pribram, *Secret Treaties*, vol. I, pp. 120–2.)

feeble. Kálnoky shares this opinion and votes in favour (without my having prompted him) of doing the thing in the manner in which it seems the Chancellor wishes it done. English Notes! That is enough for him, even though Robilant wanted something more pompous. Only a formula has still to be found by which the Central Powers can participate in this exchange of Notes without offending the Romance brother-nations. Despite their unreliability, the Spaniards could certainly stage a diversion for us. [...]

Respectfully,
Your most devoted
H. VII Reuss

213. Heinrich VII Reuss to Holstein

Vienna, 30 March 1887

My dear Herr von Holstein,

[...] I think that your idea of letting the Balkan group suspect that something has happened is first-rate. A few days ago I wrote[1] that Kálnoky had given the Turk (who was anxious about possible schemes with regard to Tripoli and had made enquiries) to understand that the closer association of the Central Powers with Italy, in which England was included, was animated by a conservative spirit and therefore could only be a matter of satisfaction to the Turks. He therefore has the same idea as you, and I would be glad *if I could be authorised* to hint at the matter here, possibly 'on my own responsibility', in the manner which you indicated, so that the other Balkan states would also be reassured. Hengelmüller's[2] complaints tally with what Bray[3] wrote, while Kállay,[4] who knows Serbia well, said the same to me only yesterday. He is of the opinion that one should let these unreliable neighbours know *in advance* that Austria wants to pursue a peaceful policy, but that if she were to be attacked by anyone, and if one of these states merely looked like falling upon Austria in the event of things going badly in Galicia, then that country would immediately be occupied. Kálnoky also spoke of the need in this eventuality of instilling fear there, and also in Montenegro. [...]

I am entirely in agreement with you that a *breaking* of the bond between Austria and ourselves is not probable. It was only necessary to witness the universal alarm here when the notion was spread abroad that *we* would let Austria go. Reliance on our support is not yet fully restored to the degree it had reached before our repeated declaration that Bulgaria and the Balkan Peninsula were no concern of ours. The *people* here (not Kálnoky) had been convinced that it was a case of 'arm in arm with you'. They were wrong, but that was what they

[1] In a dispatch of 26 March 1887. (From the Foreign Ministry files.)
[2] Ladislaus, Baron von Hengelmüller von Hengervár. Austro-Hungarian Minister in Belgrade, February 1887–9; Minister (later Ambassador) in Washington, 1894–1913.
[3] Hippolyt, Count von Bray-Steinburg. German Consul-General (later Minister) in Belgrade, 1879–91.
[4] Benjamin von Kállay. Austro-Hungarian Finance Minister, 1882–1903.

thought. When they saw that the German alliance did not extend so far that Germany would fight for this country's follies, they really sobered up and the confident dreams are a thing of the past.

Naturally this is, generally speaking, a good thing and consequently the Chancellor's speeches have brought about the sobering up that he expected. But—they do not think us as nice as formerly. *They*, that is to say the mass of the people, the bourgeoisie, etc.

For our enemies, the clerical High Tories, friendship with Germany has always been an abomination. They would perhaps even grasp at a French alliance to ruin us. But they have *had* to make the best of it because the army, influenced by its leader, the Archduke Albrecht,[1] supports the German alliance. Why? Because a pessimistic outlook still obtains and the army knows very well that *with* us it will be unconquerable. The story about this Archduke is therefore not true. And now that we have made peace with Rome, it seems to me that for him the last barb is also gradually being removed.

If the party which Duke Ludwig fears were to come to power, it would perhaps help only unwillingly to draw the German coach, but it could not jump over the traces. Neither the Kaiser nor his son would do that, and a Slav majority in the Reichsrat here would not prevail over the Magyars in questions of overall policy. I am convinced that at the worst we could count on the sympathy of the Kaiserin. She knows that I hold this conviction, and I have also been given to understand that I am not deceiving myself. If the need should arise, Duke Ludwig could therefore be used. But if she is here at the time, that is if she can be reached, then it can all be done more easily.

I will follow your hint to make use of the preceding ideas as opportunity offers, and to study the question more closely. [...]

With the highest regard
Your most devoted
H. VII Reuss

214. Klemens August Busch to Holstein

Bucharest, 25 April 1887

Dear Holstein,

[...] I am glad to find from what you say that your ideas on relations with Russia coincide with my own solitary speculations. I cannot rid myself of the fear that all attempts to maintain a tolerable relationship are fundamentally only akin to the renewal of a promissory note that is overdue. We will have to redeem this note sooner or later; would it not be better if the settlement were made while we still have the Chief in full possession of his powers? But as the Mohammedan says, God knows better. [...]

With best wishes,
Your devoted
Busch.

---

[1] Albrecht, Archduke of Austria. Field Marshal. Inspector-General of the Imperial and Royal Army.

215. Heinrich VII Reuss to Holstein

Vienna, 12 May 1887

My dear Herr von Holstein,

I read in the newspapers that Count Herbert is away, and therefore permit myself to write you a few lines to accompany my long dispatch.[1]

The refusal of the Government here to agree to the publication of all the documents relating to the Agreement of 1877 will displease the Chancellor. For in dispatch no. 244 of the 8th of this month[2] he said clearly enough that he might do so even without Austrian permission.

This would not make a good impression here because Kaiser Franz Joseph, as Kálnoky told me, expressly *refused* permission.

Here they are unable to accept our reasoning as correct, namely that we as non-participants should be allowed to publish a secret agreement between two others because *one* of the participants has consented.

Perhaps this is quite agreeable to the Russians for various reasons, among others in order to compromise Austria with the Porte. Here it is precisely this that they don't want.

Possibly people here would disregard most of their ostensible objections if they were quite certain of the success of our move, that is to say, if the Ignatievs and Katkovs were thereby really routed. But they are doubtful about this here. Even Lobanov does not believe it, although he has every interest in seeing these people, who are also his political enemies, destroyed.

The latest Press reports from Berlin, *Kölnische Zeitung* and *Politische Korrespondenz*, have given satisfaction here. I think we would have saved ourselves much annoyance and much ill-feeling if we had not been in such a hurry with our disclosures and had waited for the reply from here. Here they did not think this very considerate. And it was not a good thing that errors should also have crept in.

Once again one often has to listen here to the remark—not from Count Kálnoky but from other politicians: what is the real use of the German alliance to us? In economic matters Germany ignores us, and in political questions, the moment it is a matter of an Austrian interest in the Near East, it is hastily announced in Berlin that that is no concern of Germany's; this happened last autumn and now again through the vagueness of the utterances about Bosnia.

One can of course reply to these people: would you prefer not to have the alliance at all? and one would certainly receive an answer in the negative. Not from everyone, because we have recently been able to learn how many groups there are here to whom 'Prussia' is an abomination.

To pay too little regard to good form is certainly not good. I think

---

[1] In that part of his dispatch from Vienna of 11 May 1887 which is not printed in the *Grosse Politik* (vol. V, no. 1102, pp. 272–3), Prince Reuss once more gave the reasons which had caused Kaiser Franz Joseph to protest against further publication of the documents concerning the Austro-Russian negotiations in 1876–7. (From the Foreign Ministry files. See *Diaries*, entry for 8 May 1887.)

[2] See *Diaries*, p. 342, note 1; *Grosse Politik*, vol. V, no. 1101, pp. 271–2.

we should not expose the friendship of our sincere friends to such trials of strength too often. Among these I count the Kaiser.

With sincere regard

H. VII Reuss[1]

216. Heinrich VII Reuss to Holstein

Vienna, 26 May 1887

My dear Herr von Holstein,

Thank you very much for your letter of the 24th and for the news about the Crown Prince contained therein. Let us hope that the Scot[2] is not mistaken.

As to Széchényi, I would like to recall the fact that the campaign against him has for a long time been carried on from *Berlin*. For nearly two years the same cry has been sounded in the State Secretary's letters: Széchényi must go!

You can see from my correspondence that this question has often been raised here, and that I have made no secret of our views about this ambassador, who was considered unsatisfactory in Berlin, but, as I was instructed, without at any time starting a discussion of the question.

Kálnoky has discovered that Sz. is not the man to negotiate with the Chancellor, and he would have recalled him long ago if he had had a better one in stock.

This attitude has changed in the recent past. When there was scarlet fever in Széchényi's house, you were the only person with whom Sz. had any contact. Kálnoky has often spoken gratefully to me about the fact that you had been so kind to him.

Since that time he is said to be much more industrious, better informed, and to have stuck to his job. As a result, and precisely because nobody better is available, his recall is no longer thought of here.

Therefore you have saved him! If Berchem is still intriguing against Sz., it would seem that he does not yet know about the change in attitude. I admit I do not know whether there is a family feud. [...]

Very sincerely

H. VII Reuss

217. Wilhelm von Bismarck to Holstein

Hanau, 31 May 1887

Dear Holstein,

Many thanks for your 'scolding' of the 25th, which I have consigned to the fire. From the outset I saw with regret that His Highness

---

[1] Note by Holstein: 'I am entirely of Reuss' opinion. The Chancellor in his isolation is losing contact with the world. Presumably the motive for the publication-scandal was, I think, to cause a stir and at the same time to consign the inglorious Schnäbele affair [see below, p. 226, note 2] to oblivion; then also to strike a blow at Andrássy. On the other hand, I consider useful the now impending publication of *our* secret treaty with Austria, valid until 1889.'

[2] Dr, later Sir Morell Mackenzie, a British throat specialist who was called in to treat the Crown Prince. Mackenzie declared that the larynx displayed no symptoms of a cancerous tumour.

[Bismarck] did not like Berchem. B. is decidedly the most suitable, and with H.H. and Herb. as superiors, one cannot expect any particular initiative on the part of an Under State Secretary. Nevertheless I do not think that B. will be finished so quickly. During my last talk with H.H., of which I spoke to you, H.H. did not actually abuse B. but only said that Herbert had far more political sense than B. That is quite natural. Perhaps Derenthall[1] will be the best successor, better than Krauel,[2] who up to now has only tried his hand at colonial policy. But an Under State Secretary must be someone who can deputise for Herbert when he is on leave in *all* fields, *tant bien que mal*.

H.H.'s courting of Russian friendship goes too far for me, too, because I think it is entirely futile. All domestic measures in Russia, tariffs, etc., are solely inspired by a blind national hatred of *us*. They quite definitely injure the Russians themselves in their material welfare, and are only introduced in order to injure and annoy us. I completely subscribe to what recently appeared in the *Petersburger Herold* that no matter *what* we do, Russia will always be dissatisfied. The Pan-Slav Press has achieved this by years of agitation. Schweinitz also seems to share this opinion. Herbert was formerly of the opinion that the Russians would love us as soon as we ceased holding them back from Constantinople. That was at Christmas. In April he seemed to me to have modified his ideas, and thus it is to be hoped that he will influence H.H. in a beneficial way. You could also draw his attention to this.

According to Herbert, Mackenzie is regarded in England as a quack. That is pretty evident to me. But why is H.H. so excited about Absalom's state of health?[3] Schwen[inger] as well as Her Highness have repeatedly complained about it in their letters. I cannot understand it. Perhaps it was not even the case. Moreover His Imperial Highness would in my opinion attach us even more dangerously to an English tow-line than the son to a Russian. The worst aspect is that he does not know what he is doing. He would perhaps then get us into a fight with both. In all events we would have to pay the reckoning for the whole of Europe. That is my impression.

Affectionate greetings
Your
BB.

218. Wilhelm von Bismarck to Holstein

Hanau, 13 June 1887

Dear Holstein,

Yesterday I wrote an acknowledgement to you in haste, and now I thank you again for your two letters. God be praised that the Kaiser seems to be on the mend again, while as regards His Imperial Highness

---

[1] Eduard von Derenthall. Consul-General in Cairo, 1883–4, in Alexandria, 1884–7; Minister in Weimar, 1887–94, in Lisbon, 1894–7, in Stuttgart, 1897–1903.

[2] Dr Friedrich Krauel. Temporarily attached to the Foreign Ministry, 1884–5; official in charge of colonial affairs, May 1885–90; Director of the Colonial Division of the Foreign Ministry, April–July, 1890; Minister in Buenos Aires, 1890–4, in Rio de Janeiro, 1894–8.

[3] The health of the Crown Prince.

one remains in uncertainty. I do not believe in Mackenzie. I have recently written to Herbert about Russia. Actually I cannot *wholly* agree with you. We cannot pursue an avowedly anti-Russian policy based on reliance on the other Powers because they would leave us in the lurch at the first opportunity. Look at England and Italy with their insecure Governments. The firm of Gladstone, even if without G. himself, could very easily return to power, with its Russo-and-Francophil policy, to the detriment of its own interests! And with Crispi in Italy things are also not going too well. There remains therefore only a see-saw policy as in the Reichstag: to threaten one with the other. When in '84 we made common cause with France against England, it was also only a means to an end, and as we can see now, it would not have been suitable as a lasting arrangement. At the time I also wished to be more strongly pro-French and anti-English, but I see that I was wrong and now it is the same with England and Russia. Recently there appeared in the *Kölnische Zeitung*, I think in the morning issue of Friday, a very good article showing England's interest in Russo-German antagonism, and England's pleasure at the enmity between Germany and France arising out of the war of '70. Unfortunately we cannot involve ourselves too deeply with Austria, either. Only the Democrats there are German in sentiment. All the others are ultramontane or anti-German nationalists. With that, a strong inclination to fight Austria's wars with our troops. [...]

Affectionate greetings
your
BB.

219. Hugo von Radolinski to Holstein

Ems,[1] Monday [4 July 1887]

My dear friend,

[...] After dinner I went with Pr. W[ilhelm] *en tête à tête* to smoke. He then opened his heart to me regarding his mother and I saw that he hates her dreadfully. His bitterness knows no bounds. What will come of all this? He then again spoke of the Rudolf[2] affair, and said that the Crown Prince had endeavoured to secure his aid to break up the Three Emperors' League and had summoned him to make common cause against Russia. Thus yet another version, different from the one which B.[3] told me at the time. What can the truth be? [...]

Your faithful
Rado.

[1] Radolin had been summoned to Ems to report to the Kaiser on the visit of the Crown Prince to England on the occasion of Queen Victoria's Jubilee.

[2] The Crown Prince of Austria. In a letter of 23 March 1887, Prince Wilhelm had informed Herbert von Bismarck that Archduke Rudolf on the occasion of his visit to Berlin had been specially well treated by the Crown Princess. In conversation with Archduke Rudolf, the Crown Princess had spoken with extreme sharpness against Russia and had greatly praised Alexander von Battenberg. He—Prince Wilhelm—had told the Archduke that he must see in this an attempt to break up the Three Emperors' League and to incite Austria against Russia in England's interest. (From the Foreign Ministry files.)

[3] Presumably Herbert von Bismarck.

220. Hugo von Radolinski to Holstein

London, 13 July 1887

My dear friend,

I hope this letter will reach you while you are still in Berlin before your departure for Kissingen. What does that mean? Kissingen and not Switzerland. I had hoped so much we could meet there. Nothing will now come of it; for until the end of this month I will hardly be able to move from the Isle of Wight. An exceptional success has been achieved.[1] The hoarseness has lessened very much and the voice is already fairly strong. It is no longer an exertion for him to speak. Even Wegner[2] thinks that this is an enormous success, that is to say a decided *improvement*; he will not give Mackenzie the credit. Weg. also thinks that now there is more certainly justifiable hope of a complete cure. What has happened therefore is what Mackenzie apodictically promised from the beginning. My master and mistress were very satisfied with my mission to Their Majesties in Ems and Koblenz, and as a matter of fact I believe that it was very useful and good that I saw both Majesties. It perhaps helped to promote a rapprochement, against which the toadies delight to work. I certainly noticed that it was not agreeable to the latter (in Ems) that I came. But that makes no difference to me. I snubbed them pretty badly there, and consequently they were very obsequious.

H.M. spoke to me at length about A.v.Batt[enberg] and told me he had received a very reasonable letter from him two years ago,[3] which, however, he had not *shown* because the tide was running so strongly against him and he did not want to take up the cudgels for him. The last letter from A.v.B.[4] had influenced H.M. in his favour. This whole episode has definitely contributed to cause H.M. to regard my people with favour. [...]

In loyal friendship
Your Rad. [...]

221. Holstein to Hugo von Radolinski[5]

Kissingen, 18 July 1887

Dear Rado,

[...] Mother Wallenberg[6] is here—a fact that nearly prevented me from coming, since I knew from previous years what a *crampon* she is in Kissingen where everybody flies from her. To my joy though also to my *ébahissement* I found her—the friend of Mother Bismarck—hand and

---

[1] In regard to the Crown Prince's health.
[2] The Crown Prince's doctor.
[3] Of 8 April 1885. (See *Diaries*, p. 171, note 4; Corti, *Alexander von Battenberg*, pp. 219–21.)
[4] A letter from Alexander von Battenberg to Radolinski of 27 May 1887, in which he again declared that he did not intend to ask for the hand of Princess Victoria. The letter was submitted to the Kaiser on 1 June. (From the Foreign Ministry files.)
[5] From the Radolin Papers.
[6] Marie von Wallenberg. See Rogge, *Friedrich von Holstein*, pp. 144–6.

glove here with Hermann Arnim,¹ the protégé of Seckendorff and Sommerfeld. Despite the poor opinion which I have had in recent years of Mother Bolz,² I was certainly surprised by this intimacy. Hermann Arnim was the very person who wrecked the position of the Princess inside her own family by publishing in the *Reichsglocke* two years later quite secret personal matters which the Princess had told him in Varzin. Since then the Princess learns nothing from her sons and rarely anything from her husband. Ah well, Mother Bolz has risen above these considerations and is delighted with H.A., who probably imagines that he will get back into a diplomatic career through her. Thus I have a good excuse not to bother about her. [...]

Be nice and write again soon—especially about the conversation with Her Majesty.

Affectionate greetings
H.

222. Hugo von Radolinski to Holstein

Yacht Victoria and Albert,
20 July 1887

My dear Holst.

I had the luck recently to talk alone with 'Mama'³ for *over an hour*, almost exclusively about Fridolin.⁴ After I had thoroughly roused the two daughters (Chr.⁵ and Beatrice⁶). Mama told me quite frankly she would do everything in her power to get rid of this personage, his influence had been an anxiety to her for years, she did not understand what her daughter saw in him, he was a vulgar man who opened letters and compromised her. Mama was really splendid, and I cannot tell you how friendly to me. She told me her daughter was no judge of character and is now afraid of everyone. You can imagine how forcibly I put the case and told her all my grievances against S[eckendorff]. Naturally I presented the matter solely from the standpoint of the injury that he did to his mistress. It is very seldom that Mama talks to anyone for so long in an intimate way. I flattered her terribly and told her that she was the only person to whose wishes her daughter paid regard. She smiled sweetly like a blushing girl and was really completely charming. For three days in succession she invited me to dine with her with an intimate group in W[indsor] Cast[le], and in addition I had been invited to dinners when I was in the country, only the invitation had

---

[1] Hermann, Count von Arnim-Boitzenburg. *Legationsrat*; Free Conservative Member of the Reichstag; cousin and brother-in-law of Harry von Arnim-Suckow.

[2] Nickname for Marie von Wallenberg.

[3] Queen Victoria of England.

[4] Götz, Count von Seckendorff. A quarrel had broken out between Seckendorff and Radolin. (See *Denkwürdigkeiten des General-Feldmarschalls Alfred Grafen von Waldersee*, edited by Heinrich Otto Meisner (Stuttgart and Berlin, 1922–3), vol. I, p. 320; *Letters of the Empress Frederick*, edited by Sir Frederick Ponsonby (London, 1929), pp. 192, 243–5.)

[5] Princess Helena, third daughter of Queen Victoria and wife of Prince Christian of Schleswig-Holstein.

[6] Princess Beatrice, fifth daughter of Queen Victoria and wife of Prince Henry of Battenberg, the brother of Prince Alexander.

not been forwarded to me. I spoke my mind about this to the slow-moving court officials here. On the whole I snub the stand-offish people here, and I hear that they have said that I seemed to be quite independent. I have not the least intention of running after these people. Mama urged me to remain in Norris and not to yield the place to S[eckendorff]. In short, I am *very satisfied* with my campaign and both daughters (Chr. and Beat.) are exceptionally useful and energetic allies. You will be satisfied with me when you hear all the details that I will tell you about. [...]

Adio. In haste your faithful
Hu.

223. Holstein to Hugo von Radolinski[1]

Kissingen, 24 July [1887]

Dear Rado,

[...] From a trustworthy source I have heard the following: Mackenzie has said that the present growth was almost eliminated, but there was the imminent danger that in the same place either cancer would develop or a new non-malignant growth, which could cause the Prince to suffocate.

He will never get back his parade-ground voice. Moreover I am told that the Crown Prince looks ill, yellow.

When I heard the above yesterday I asked myself whether Her Imperial Highness has not known this for a long time and whether S[eckendorff]'s present more clearly defined position is not connected with it. Free and easy Bohemian life in Italy.

Quien sabe? [...]

As ever
H.

224. Hugo von Radolinski to Holstein[2]

Norris Castle, Cowes (Isle of Wight),
24 July 1887

My dear friend,

D[r] M[orell] M[ackenzie] is suddenly more anxious. The swelling seems to have grown again, and all at once he talks less assuredly than formerly. He observed this to-day, and although he does not admit any definite danger for the moment, he is not quite so certain that the future will not be serious. He stresses the *age* of the invalid. In three weeks he wants the invalid to go to the mountains in Tyrol or Switzerland, and will not hear of his staying in Berlin for the winter. He recommends the Riviera and will send his *best* assistant to accompany him. This gave me a bad fright. What will happen? Please tell this only to those who should know, if you like to H[erbert] B[ismarck], confidentially, so that it does not become public, since perhaps D.M.'s

---

[1] From the Radolin Papers.
[2] See Rogge, *Friedrich von Holstein*, p. 145.

fears will not be confirmed. He will come again very soon and will then say more. Perhaps the growth will not have increased as it appears to have done to-day. At all events he thinks it is non-malignant, but he says he cannot know whether it will not become malignant in the course of time. Naturally neither the patient nor the family know anything about this. Hatz[feldt] is also very unwell. He has a bad cold and cannot come to the Naval Review as he had intended. Adio. I wanted to inform you of this new change in the situation as speedily as possible. Write to me soon.

Your Hu. [...]

225.   Hedwig von Brühl[1] to Holstein

New Palace, 26 July 1887

Dear Herr von Holstein,

Best thanks for your letter whose contents I have communicated only to H. v. Lyncker.

Mackenzie's statements were not entirely new to me, at least one could gather from private talks with him that he did not regard subsequent serious growths, even cancer, as completely impossible, while not necessarily believing in their probability; his opinion was very cautious, the only thing that he definitely asserted was that the existing growth could be removed from the inside—and in that he proved right. Moreover the Crown Prince has written to me himself that for over a fortnight his voice has steadily returned; what will subsequently be done to strengthen his vocal cords is still a secret, at least to him. *She* writes: now it can only be a question of the local treatment of a local complaint; for the autumn some milder climate must be sought, to bring about a general strengthening of the system and to increase the power of resistance; that is to say, the sickness is made an excuse for 'artistic travels' in Italy.

Our good Rado, despite all his successes, seems also to suffer much annoyance and was again on the point of handing in his resignation. Kessel has calmed him as much as possible; please do the same! he *must* not go, for then everything is lost. His conversation with the Queen was very gratifying; she is the only one who can *perhaps* convince the Crown Prince of the necessity that the adoration of Götz[2] must be rooted out before peace can return here—but I do not believe absolutely in her effectual help; although the people concerned are afraid of her—the fear of Götz is still greater; he probably has a trump in his hand that will beat anything. But as long as life is in us, we must continue the struggle because it is for Right—and therefore Rado must not allow himself to be driven away by irritation. Winterfeld,[3] who is there at the moment, plays a miserable role as mediator; he belongs to the Albedyll school and thinks one must exploit inevitable evil in *majoram*

---

[1] Lady-in-Waiting to Crown Princess Victoria.
[2] Götz von Seckendorff.
[3] Hugo von Winterfeld. Aide-de-Camp to Crown Prince Friedrich Wilhelm.

Dei gloriam. What you have heard about English influences on Mackenzie's optimistic official pronouncements seems to me very credible—only they have done little over there to train a second Anglophil Kaiser for themselves. Pr. W[ilhelm] and the Princess[1] were received with exquisite coolness, with bare courtesy—he only saw his grandmother a couple of times, at Court functions; *she* was always placed behind the black Queen of Hawaii!! Both returned not in the best of tempers, and were in no doubt as to the quarter which had intrigued against them.

Lyncker sends you his best greetings and with me wishes you a pleasant, peaceful and satisfactory cure in Kissingen. I had thought you were going to Tarasp?

Come back well and continue to be a good ally of ours in the fight with the dragon!

H.v.Brühl.

226. Hugo von Radolinski to Holstein

[London], 2 August 1887

My dear Holstein,
I have just arrived here from the Isle of Wight with His Imperial Highness because Mack[enzie] wants to do some further cauterisation. But he is satisfied with his patient's condition. Wight is too enervating; hence it has been decided to send the Cr[own Prince] into the hills of Scotland. He is to travel there only with me and an aide-de-camp and *without* the ladies. The air is more invigorating. After our return Mack. will again cauterise and examine, and following that the Cr. will travel to the Tyrol in order to spend the late autumn in Bolzano or some other place. It is doubtful, *very* doubtful, whether the Cr. will spend the winter in Berlin. It would be most regrettable if he had to stay away for the winter. Mack. has not yet made up his mind. I am opposing it. Yesterday I had a long conversation with the Pr. of Wales about Seck[endorff]. He started on the subject. I impressed upon him the urgent necessity of dismissing the person in question and told him that the Queen must be induced to explain this matter to the *Crown Prince*. That seems to me the best way. Pr. of W. was wholly of my opinion and also cannot stand Seck. [...]

Adio, in haste, your faithful

Rad.

The day after tomorrow I return to the Isle of Wight.

227. Hugo von Radolinski to Holstein

Cow[es], 3 August 1887

My dear friend,
My telegr.[2] must have astonished you not a little. I wrote it and sent it in agreement with our friend.[3] The explanation for it is as follows:

[1] Auguste Victoria von Schleswig-Holstein. Wife of Prince Wilhelm and subsequently German Kaiserin and Queen of Prussia.
[2] Not found. [3] Paul von Hatzfeldt.

A serious change of front is taking place here towards the East and the intended sacrifice of the 'Sick Man'.[1] The object of the change of front towards the East is to isolate the 'western' neighbour[2] who has also become a nuisance *here*, by taking away his *eastern* friend.[3]

The whole affair is *strictly secret*. Our friend has written about it.[4] But he attaches great importance to discussing the matter with you confidentially in person in order to be able to deal with the affair accordingly. It is fairly urgent because the man in charge of the affair[5] goes away on the 20th, and it would be desirable to be able to negotiate with him until then without pressure. If possible, come as quickly as you can to London as a tourist with a return-ticket—why should you not make a trip here in order to visit your friends Paul and myself? [...][6]

Adio. P. sends affectionate greetings.

228. Hugo von Radolinski to Holstein

Braemar, 14 August 1887

My dear friend,

Enclosed I am sending you an exchange of letters[7] and ask you to reply by telegram 'Agreed' or 'No'. I cannot really understand the letter from 'her',[8] but I see in it extremely bitter reproaches against myself. I replied at once so as to avoid the appearance of having asked for advice from anyone. I was even on the point of declaring that I would resign since I no longer possessed her confidence. But I did not. There will still be time enough to do so if you advise this step. I ask you very particularly for a reply by telegram because I won't have any peace until I know your opinion.

I noticed during the last days of my stay there that *she* was embarrassed. [...]

I was terribly sorry only to have seen you for a single day.[9] How glad I would have been to have stayed the following day with you. [...]

Write to me and *please a telegram* with the single word.

K[essel] sends best regards. Your faithful

Hu. [...]

ENCLOSURE I

Crown Princess Victoria to Hugo von Radolinski[10]

Cowes, August 12, 1887

Dear Count,

I had no time at the very last moment of your departure to speak about a thing which has caused me great annoyance.

[1] Turkey. [2] France. [3] Russia.
[4] See Hatzfeldt's dispatch to Bismarck of 3 August. (*Grosse Politik*, vol. IV, no. 907, pp. 335–7.)
[5] Lord Salisbury.
[6] Holstein subsequently spent a short time in London. (See Rogge, *Friedrich von Holstein*, pp. 146–7.)
[7] See enclosures. [8] Crown Princess Victoria. [9] In London. [10] In English in the original.

I should really have taken no notice of this matter on which silence seems to me the best and only answer but that the security I felt that the C[rown] P[rince] would *not* be worried and disturbed, at a moment like this, when his health requires *every* precaution, by vexations and distressing questions. [*sic*] This security I repeat has been shaken by the fact that, incredible as it seems to me, the Queen, other members of my family and friends of mine have had their confidence undermined by various strange reports which I cannot but think, in all justice and honorableness and common prudence [should] have found their way first to *me*.—I have never, that I know of, been inaccessible to advice or reason but this indirect mode of proceeding, damaging as it is, much more to those who have adopted it, than to myself, may cause me to defend myself and above all take every measure, to prevent my husband being harassed! It seems indeed strange that I should have to take such precautions. I feel strongly disinclined to enter into any details as I might express myself more bitterly than in calmer moments I should wish about this indirect attack on me, at a moment when I am cut off from the power of redress.—Those who profess to have so much zeal in my cause might mistakenly suppose themselves justified in trying to influence my mother in this matter. But I do not see what end is served by spreading right and left, injurious and compromising reports to others besides.—I have long known of this cabal but it has only just struck me that my silence may have been misunderstood. I therefore write these few lines.—The game of hunting people down is one I have witnessed more than once at Berlin. I will not say with what feelings. To destroy the reputation of another man can always be accomplished if unscrupulous means are used, but it is *not* an admirable method of getting rid of people against whom one has grievances, especially when by doing so, deep injury is inflicted, perhaps *unwittingly* on those one may wish to serve with loyalty and devotion.

Yours most sincerely,
+.

ENCLOSURE II

Hugo von Radolinski to Crown Princess Victoria

Br[aemar], 14 August 1887

Reply
I have received your letter of the 12th and regret that you regard me as capable of troubling the C[rown Prince] in any way whatever with the regrettable matter to which you allude in your letter. For over a year I have never spoken to the C. of the existing difficulties with Count S[eckendorff] nor allowed his name to pass my lips. The incident you know about of last spring in the New Palace, I mentioned at that time *only* to yourself and never said a word about it to the C. Nevertheless, as you will remember, the C was brought into the matter *against my will*, and this by the opposite side, whereas I had expected that the affair would be settled simply between myself and S., as was fitting,

without his hiding behind the authority of the Cr. I must therefore for my part deny the apprehension that you have expressed to me that I ever, and especially since his illness, troubled the Cr. with this matter. You can be assured that not for all the world would I do so *now*. My sole endeavour here is to guard the Cr. from all unpleasantness.

You reproach me bitterly with having touched upon certain baneful circumstances in other quarters. If I said anything it was solely in reply to questions put to me, and in this I deemed it to be my duty to be frank and to tell the truth. Whatever I may have said it was only what I have often told you in still more unmistakable terms. As I never do anything behind your back, I am prepared to assume the full responsibility for all I do and for that reason I do not deserve the reproach—'to hunt people down and to destroy the reputation of another man'. I level this reproach far more at *him* who without having the courage to come into the open pursues his selfish aims. I can only give you the assurance that in everything I do I have only your interests in mind, even if I should have, to my deepest regret, lost your favour and trust.

ENCLOSURE III

Hugo von Radolinski to Queen Victoria

From myself to Her Majesty
14 August 1887

In accordance with Your Majesty's command I permit myself to make a short report about the state of health——

I had the honour to receive Your Majesty's gracious telegram in London. I have ceaselessly endeavoured to keep every worry from the C[rown Prince]. Under the present circumstances I would on no account mention to him the subject of the recent discussion. Moreover I never had any such intention. I do not consider myself as called upon to do so. I would like to take this opportunity of presuming to inform Your Majesty in confidence that to-day I received a letter from the Crown Princess who reproaches me for having made disclosures regarding that matter. I could not refrain from telling the Crown Princess in reply that I regarded it as my duty to tell the truth frankly in answering the questions addressed to me and to repeat only what I had on more than one occasion permitted myself to say to the Crown Princess. I have not mentioned Your Majesty's name in my letter. At all events I am prepared to stand by what I have said because I am conscious that in all that I do, I act solely in the Crown Princess' own interests.

229. Holstein to Hugo von Radolinski[1]

Pontresina, 22 August [1887]

Dear Rado,

The English campaign has ended in favour of Seck[endorff]. He has long had Mama's[2] entourage for him and, as the invitation of Seck. to dine shows, she is not her own mistress.

[1] From the Radolin Papers.   [2] Queen Victoria.

On no account resign. You will certainly find allies in Germany. If Her Imperial Highness is cold, be colder still, and treat her accordingly.

Do not under any circumstances behave in public as *l'homme liège du mari*; she stands bad treatment better than neglect. Witness Normann. But show her that you are *not at all cowed*; also to S.—but without nonsense or grumbling.

Best regards
H.

230. Holstein to Hugo von Radolinski[1]

Pontresina, 31 August 1887

Dear Rado,

Lyncker writes me that La Perpignan[2] is staying on.[3] This circumstance strengthens an impression that has grown upon me recently.

Namely, that S[eckendorff] represented his quarrel with you in England as a *matter concerning English influence*. You are Bismarck's man, he is the Anglophil. Hence the sudden change of front on the part of Mama and entourage, hence too the prolonged stay of La Perpignan, whom I regard not only as an English agent but also as a French spy. Lady Ampthill[4] of course did a good deal to help the matter along. We must also recognise that my presence in London was probably exploited for the above-mentioned purpose.

There can be no doubt that new conflicts are brewing. But the question whether the *present* moment—that is to say the period when Her Imperial Highness is away from Berlin—is propitious for a crisis, I would answer in the negative from your standpoint. With or without Perpignan, S. will keep the upper hand as long as the absence lasts.

For the same reason I would like you to consult your Berlin allies whether your accompanying them [the Crown Prince and Princess] to Toblach [in the Tyrol] or at any rate your remaining there would serve any useful purpose. You yourself will achieve nothing there. The question is whether the others will be able for their part to do anything against you if you are away. This is something I cannot judge.

It would be useful, although perhaps not of any immediate effect, if Liebenau[5] were to explain to Prince Wilhelm the new roles played by S. and Per. as English, respectively French, observers. You must not come into the foreground in this matter, let somebody else bring it to the notice of Prince Wilhelm. [...]

Best regards
H.

[1] From the Radolin Papers.
[2] Lady-in-Waiting to Crown Princess Victoria and governess to Princesses Victoria, Sophia and Margarethe.
[3] Lyncker wrote on 27 August: 'Countess Br[ühl] has been eased out for the Tyrol and Frl. von Perpignan is staying on until further notice—isn't that the very devil?'
[4] Lady Emily Ampthill. Widow of Lord Odo Russell, 1st Lord Ampthill.
[5] Eduard von Liebenau. Court Chamberlain to Prince Wilhelm.

231. Eberhard zu Solms[1] to Holstein

Rome, 14 October 1887

My dear friend,

[...] Herr Crispi[2] is still singing the praises of the members of Prince Bismarck's family and of his reception at Friedrichsruh. His satisfaction is all the more enduring because he continues to receive proofs that the public fully recognises the correctness of his decision to undertake the journey. The Italians create the impression upon me that up till now they felt they only had acting rank as a Great Power, and that it was at Friedrichsruh that Crispi first obtained for them the letters patent confirming their status.

A very good impression seems to have been made on Crispi by the fact that his journey met with such approbation in Vienna and that Baron Bruck[3] displays towards him marked friendship and great confidence. Moreover Baron Bruck is exceptionally pleased with Crispi's frank and loyal character.

The Russian Ambassador, Baron Üxküll,[4] was very ill-humoured when Baron Bruck visited him, and said: *'Le voyage de Crispi ne veut rien dire; c'est un vieux saltimbanque.'* [...]

Farewell

Your sincerely devoted

Solms

232. Wilhelm von Bismarck to Holstein

Hanau, 20 October 1887

Dear Holstein,

I have not yet thanked you for your letter of September, and can now thank you both for it and for yesterday's, which contained little to edify me. I hope that you are somewhat pessimistic, and am eager to speak to R[otten]b[ur]g, who lunches with us tomorrow, and who will naturally not be told about your letter. It is natural that Herbert should have a great number of enemies quite apart from those whom he does not need to have, and it is not surprising that they should seek to trip him up. He first of all inherits His Highness' opponents, that is Wilmowski and Albedyll, who were always first-class [...],[5] and then he also had his own, as, for example, *le pâle*.[6] They could concoct all sorts of things; particularly Alb., who since the Sommerfeld affair has naturally been absolutely furious with Herb. But I hope that Franz [Rottenburg] will not conceal from me tomorrow what 'clouds' are 'gathering over' Herbert. It is obvious that Herbert would rather be an

---

[1] Solms had recently succeeded Keudell as Ambassador in Rome.

[2] Francesco Crispi. Italian Minister of the Interior in Depretis' Cabinet, 1877–8, April–July 1887; Prime Minister and Minister for Foreign Affairs and the Interior, 1887–91, 1893–6. He visited Bismarck at Friedrichsruh from 1–3 October 1887. (See *Grosse Politik*, vol. IV, nos. 917, 921, pp. 351–2, 358–60; vol. VI, no. 1291, pp. 228–9; *The Memoirs of Francesco Crispi*, edited by Thomas Palamenghi-Crispi (London, 1912–14), vol. II, pp. 221 et seq.)

[3] Karl, Baron von Bruck. Austro-Hungarian Ambassador in Rome, 1886–95.

[4] Russian Ambassador in Rome, 1876–91.

[5] Illegible.   [6] Bleichröder.

Ambassador than State Secretary. I could wish it for *his* sake, and believe that then, in relative *otium*, he would at last get married. But for His Highness he would be *irreplaceable*; for even if *I* wished to do it, I could not do it. Herbert is a diplomat and courtier, and it is precisely as such that he relieves H.H. of the most unpleasant *faux frais* of the whole business by skilful intercourse with foreign Ministers, as also by his handling of the Kaiser with whom he now and then gets things settled more easily than does H.H. I learnt this last winter when H.H. spoke with astonishment of Herb's success with the Kaiser. *I* was never a courtier, have always shown myself as the opposite of servile, and probably am regarded at Court as a *frondeur*. They probably have no great opinion of my ability in that quarter, and being totally inexperienced in the handling of affairs, I would need at least as many years as Herbert before I acquired value in H.H.'s eyes. Do not forget that the official relationship between H.H. and Herbert has existed for very nearly ten years, almost since the '78 Congress. Herbert has repeatedly been acknowledged by H.H. as a sort of ambassador at large, and I myself have frequently read H.H.'s warmly written approval of Herbert's reports.

All this I lack, and I would need years to acquire it. Apart from that I would soon come into conflict with H.H., all the more so because I might not always be able to follow the direction of his policy. Let us assume that you were right, that Herbert's position was shaken, that he was 'finished' after barely two years; well, this would happen to me in six months, because I have far less adaptability than he, and what then? Then I should have given up a position in which I feel completely content and happy, made a fool of myself, and pleased nobody. I have witnessed too often how people were buttonholed in order to induce them by all sorts of flatteries to accept a responsible post, how complaints were made of their 'indolence' and their 'want of patriotism', until finally they accepted unwillingly, and then when it did not work there was a similar outcry about their 'stupidity and incapacity'. For example: Botho Eulenburg, Manteuffel, Hobrecht,[1] Hatzfeldt. Well, you will easily be able to enlarge the list. Afterwards it is said as in the case of Bernuth:[2] 'not nearly enough'. Before I walk on such bird-lime, quite different conditions from those existing at present must obtain and I must be convinced that I understand the job better than *anybody* else, and that could take a very long time. Many years ago H.H. once told me: 'If I had to give anybody a word of advice it would be never to have anything to do with politics, but to live quietly at home and never to leave it; for in politics there is no such thing as complete satisfaction, and even when successful one is always uncertain as to whether one has acted correctly.' I subscribe to that completely, and when it is said by someone like H.H., what must the *Dii minorum* say! But enough for to-day. [...] Best regards. It is now half-past one and I am going to bed.

Your
BB.

[1] Arthur von Hobrecht. Prussian Finance Minister, 1878-9.
[2] Former Head of the Berlin police.

233. Ferdinand von Stumm to Holstein

Madrid, 25 October 1887

Dear Herr von Holstein,

[...] Some days ago I had a long talk with Cambon.[1] [...]

Cambon says that nobody in France wants war with us. That had been clearly shown by the attitude of the Government and the Press during the last frontier incident.[2] Even Boulanger[3] had never really thought of war (I could not concede that to him in the light of the facts). A *modus vivendi* must be found between the two nations. We have a common enemy who must not be allowed to attack us individually— Russia. According to him a French statesman must say to Germany: Here are Alsace and Lorraine—a wound that has not been and cannot be healed; agreement is impossible on this subject but nevertheless we must live alongside and together with each other; therefore let us talk as little as possible about that matter and instead attempt to be useful and helpful to each other in other, non-European, spheres; there we would draw closer to each other and who knows but that some time in the future the old and open wound might not be healed by certain concessions. When I mentioned Ferry's fall, he said that Ferry only fell on account of Tonkin, not because he had solicited Germany's good offices.[4] Unhappily the firm conviction still existed universally in France that Germany would seize a favourable opportunity to pick a quarrel; he—Cambon—had never believed in war, was firmly convinced of Germany's pacific intentions, and even this spring was not shaken in this belief. There was no question of an alliance between France and Russia, notwithstanding the fact that French chauvinism obviously greatly inclined to this idea. If, however, France should some day find herself wholly isolated in Europe, and certain events in recent times seemed to be paving the way towards it more and more, then France would certainly be compelled by necessity to draw closer to Russia. Thus—more or less—Cambon; I shall not repeat my objections and counter-arguments. One notices everywhere that France is beginning to feel uncomfortable in her isolation; also in the *mamours* that were lately lavished by Paris on Spain and which caused M. Cambon to propose a partition of Morocco here, even though apparently merely as a passing observation. Here they do not let themselves be decoyed by such things; Moret is far too pleased with the policy he inaugurated, feels too much at home in *good* European society to be able to break loose. Moreover the Queen[5] has something to say in the matter and

[1] Paul Cambon. French Ambassador in Madrid, 1886–91, in Constantinople, 1891–8, in London, 1898–1920.

[2] The Schnäbele incident. Guillaume Schnäbele was a French frontier official who had misused his position for espionage in Alsace-Lorraine. He was arrested on 20 April but released on 28 April when it became clear that he had crossed the frontier at the invitation of a German colleague. (See *Grosse Politik*, vol. VI, nos. 1257–64, pp. 182–9.)

[3] Georges Boulanger. French General and champion of the idea of a war of revenge against Germany; Minister of War in the Cabinets of Freycinet and Goblet, 1886–7; General Commanding the 13th Army Corps (Clermont), 1887–8.

[4] See *Memoirs*, pp. 107–10.

[5] Maria Cristina, widow of Alfonso XII. Regent of Spain, 1885–1902.

may have more and more. She hates France and the French. As a woman, the memory of the injury done to her husband in Paris remains with her more firmly and deeply than with others.[1] [...]

Yours sincerely,
Stumm.

234. Hugo von Radolinski to Holstein

San Remo, Thursday, 10 November 1887

My dear friend,

When I arrived here, Rabe[2] met me with the news that all was lost. Mack[enzie] had been summoned by telegram. He summoned the other two doctors by telegram. M. himself recognised in a few days that the new swelling that had formed very quickly *under* the vocal cord was cancerous and did not want to assume the responsibility for further treatment without consulting other specialists. Drs Krause[3] (Berlin) and Schrötter[4] (Vienna) have arrived, have also diagnosed the growth as cancer, and suggest as the sole method of treatment (or as the sole admittedly *very slight* chance) the major operation of removing half or the whole of the larynx from the outside. They would then advise a return to Berlin. All this is to be told to the Royal patient. It has already been hinted to him and he took it with admirable calmness and courage. Whether we return to B. will be decided in a few days. The hope of keeping him alive for a year is very slight. I feel quite inexpressibly for him. He is pathetically good, patient. She is also very upset. He is, moreover, ceaselessly preoccupied with what will happen to his wife and daughter after his death. He has shed many tears at this thought, so *she* told me! So that is what he is being tortured with. Always the old story of last spring. She will go away afterwards. But the daughter. He told me today with deep sorrow that his son could hardly wait for his end. He was already behaving as though he were Cr[own Prince]. [...]

Your faithful
Hu.

Adio. I am utterly depressed. God grant only that his end will not be too full of suffering.

235. Wilhelm von Bismarck to Holstein

Hanau, 10 November 1887

Dear Holstein,

Thanks for your letter. Have written to Herbert. Your statements are contradictory. You quite rightly say: 'If the Tsar makes promises publicly we will have gained nothing whatever because he *cannot* keep them', and then you want me to write to Herbert saying that we must

---

[1] King Alfonso visited Germany in 1883 and was made honorary head of a Strasbourg Uhlan regiment by the Kaiser. On his return journey he was insulted in Paris by the crowd.
[2] Chamberlain to Crown Prince Friedrich Wilhelm.
[3] Dr Hermann Krause. Throat specialist.
[4] Dr Leopold Schrötter, Ritter von Kristelli. Throat specialist.

demand public promises. I have resolved this contradiction by representing to Herbert that candour is always better than secretiveness, and have then argued that publicity must be demanded, particularly because it will certainly *not* be granted. I still think it would be better if His Highness had no part in the affair.[1] I therefore sent Schweninger to Friedrichsruh yesterday in the hope that he might persuade H.H. not to make the trip. But I have just had a telegram from him that H.H. is well again. However much I rejoice at this, I would be quite pleased if H.H. were now to contract briefly one of the various illnesses that unfortunately he is sure to suffer from during the winter. His Majesty seems to desire H.H.'s presence very much, if only as second and mentor, which is indeed understandable. But since H.M. also is at present annoyed with the Russians it would be possible if one so desired —that is if H.H. did—to make him understand the expediency of staying away. If H.H. were present, the meeting would cause Russian bonds to rise and probably make Crispi and Kálnoky somewhat nervous. It is to be hoped that the latter feeling will die down again. [...]

Sincerely yours
BB.

236. Hugo von Radolinski to Holstein

S[an] Remo, 21 November 1887

Confidential
Excuse this hasty scrawl.
My dear friend,

Some (two) days ago H.I.H. the Crown Princess handed me an opened letter from the Chancellor with the request to keep it until she required it again because she had no safe place in which to keep it. I took a look at it and found that it contained the order and accompanying memorandum on deputising [for the Kaiser]. I at once asked the Crown Princess to bring the letter to the notice of the Crown Prince since it was addressed to him, even though it would annoy him. She categorically refused because on the advice of the doctors she was supposed to spare him every annoyance, and this would greatly anger him. At the Crown Prince's desire *she* opens all letters addressed to him, that is to say she selects them so as to prevent anything reaching him that would annoy him. Therefore nothing was left for me to do except to lock up the letter *with my things*, and say nothing more to the Crown Prince, since it was solemnly enjoined upon me to keep from him everything that could excite him. I had the misfortune, when Dr Bramann[2] came, to speak to the Crown Prince about his mission,[3] whereupon the Crown Prince got into such a fury and state of excitement at the thought that a doctor

---

[1] On his return from Denmark, where he had stayed longer than he had intended owing to the illness of his youngest children, the Tsar proposed to visit Berlin. On the morning of 18 November the Tsar arrived in Berlin and continued on his journey the same evening. He had a meeting with Bismarck. (See *Grosse Politik*, vol. V, chapter XXXVI.)

[2] Dr Fritz von Bramann. Surgeon; Assistant to Dr Ernst von Bergmann.

[3] Bramann was sent to San Remo at the Kaiser's orders to perform a tracheotomy in case it should suddenly become necessary. He did in fact perform it.

should have been sent to him *without his agreement having previously been obtained* that the doctors feared a worsening of his condition. At the time I thought it my duty to inform the Crown Prince of Bramann's mission because he would in any case certainly have heard of it, and I *had to prepare* him in case the man would suddenly be needed. Considering the effect that the communication of this unpleasant news had upon him, I could not act otherwise in the matter of the Chancellor's letter *than obey the order*, namely, to keep it and *for the present* to say nothing to the Crown Prince about it. I thought that during the ensuing days an opportunity of doing so would present itself and I wanted *to prepare* him for it *gradually*. Now today Prince Heinrich[1] arrived and brought a letter from Prince Wilhelm to the Crown Prince. In this letter Prince Wilhelm wrote that he had been called upon to deputise for the Kaiser this winter. Prince Heinrich confirmed this and asked if he [the Crown Prince] had not received the Order. Appalling outburst of fury and excitement on the part of the Crown Prince over the matter, over the lack of consideration, as if they thought he were already dead, [...][2] the doctors, it was unheard of to appoint Prince Wilhelm to deputise for the Kaiser without previous consultation with him, etc. The Crown Prince asked the Crown Princess about the alleged letter from the Chancellor with the Order. The Crown Princess, intimidated by the Crown Prince's dreadful state of excitement, told him that she knew *nothing* about the letter. Afterwards she hastily summoned me. She told me *en tête à tête* about the whole affair, and asked me to go to the Crown Prince and take the blame. Naturally I was prepared to do so and felt none of the fear that she apparently had of him. So I went to him and handed him the *opened* letter from the Chancellor, and, without directly telling him that I had opened the letter but also without compromising the Crown Princess, I told him that the letter had been withheld in order to avoid any emotional upset on his part. I had wanted to wait for a more favourable moment when he was better and calmer to give him the letter. In addition it was a communication that was not so urgent since it could not be altered. *Kind*, as he always is, I calmed him down very quickly; at first he wanted to travel at once to Berlin in order to prevent this deputising, etc. I told him that was useless, he would only make himself worse, and by doing so make the question of a deputy really urgent. For heaven's sake, he should not excite himself because any excitement would be fatal to him, as the doctors had told both him and me. This affair had upset him so much that he had had to take something to calm him and to prevent his condition from getting worse. In a word —every emotional disturbance must be spared him if a serious deterioration was not to set in. Actuated by this point of view the Crown Princess had refrained from showing him the Chancellor's letter at once. After I left the Crown Prince—thank heavens in a calmer state of mind—, I met Prince Heinrich. He asked me where the Imperial Order was and why the Crown Prince had not received it. I told him what had taken

[1] Heinrich, Prince of Prussia. Second son of Crown Prince Friedrich Wilhelm.
[2] One word illegible.

place and said that I had to follow the Crown Princess's order on this matter after she had told me that she held me responsible for seeing that nothing unpleasant was communicated to him. Whereupon the Prince told me—I must say to my astonishment—that it was *my duty* not to withhold such letters from the Crown Prince, and that I did not have to obey the Crown Princess on this point. I answered that I could not take upon myself the responsibility for exciting the Crown Prince and injuring his health. If the Crown Princess ordered me to keep a letter for her I had to obey. Moreover it did not affect the matter in the least if the Crown Prince were told about the deputy question a few days later and in a considerate manner; up till now the time had been very unfavourable because he was still excited over the Bramann affair. Prince Heinrich's reproof hurt me badly. At my age to be told my duty by a young man of twenty-three years[1] is a *propos* I cannot pass over without more ado. I have incidentally told Captain Seckendorff[2] that he can tell his Prince that I am exceedingly hurt by his remark, and would have left here at once if I did not consider it my duty not to leave the Crown Prince at this moment. I recognise the influence of Count Seck. over his cousin, the Captain, in Prince Heinrich's coolness towards me. He is probably undermining me in the eyes of the Prince in the same way as he is gossiping against Cap[rivi] to the young man. [...] I would also like to tell you in confidence that the Crown Princess has told me in the most decided manner that at the given time she will use all her influence with the Crown Prince to prevent his being talked into refusing the Crown—as some people seem to desire, she added. She herself (she said) set little value on the Crown (who really believes that!!) but she would not consent that her husband should be subject to another Kaiser during his lifetime, that is, after his father is dead, of course.

She also thinks that the Crown Prince can still survive for some years. She added that both the Chancellor and Count H[erbert] B[ismarck] would certainly prefer to work with a more accommodating master than with the still youthful and consequently impetuous son. This I also leave to your judgment to tell Count H.B. confidentially. The Crown Princess added that she was convinced that the Chancellor would not support the abdication of the Crown Prince. [...]

Now adio, dear friend. Write to me soon or perhaps telegraph me as to what I should do in the matter in question.

Your

Rado. [...]

237. Hugo von Radolinski to Holstein

S[an] Remo, Wednesday, 23 November 1887

Confidential
My dear friend,

The affair is settled. I complained to Capt. Seck[endorff] about the

[1] Prince Heinrich was twenty-five years old.
[2] Albert, Baron von Seckendorff. Captain in the German Navy; Aide-de-Camp to Prince Heinrich. Cousin to Count Götz von Seckendorff.

behaviour of the young man and told him that I could not put up with such reproofs from so young a man. The young man subsequently came to see me in the most affectionate manner and told me that he asked my forgiveness from the bottom of his heart if he had hurt my feelings. He had had no such intention, he knew how self-sacrificing and dutiful I was, and he again and again asked me to forgive him. He did it so nicely and so affectionately that the incident is ended. Moreover he had not known the actual circumstances and in his agitated state he had, without reflecting on their significance, let fall the words: it is the *duty* of the gentlemen in attendance to bring such matters immediately to the knowledge of the Crown Prince notwithstanding contrary orders.

The matter was thus brought to an end and I hope you got my telegram[1] telling you to throw my letter into the wastepaper basket and to say nothing more to anybody about it. The question of the deputy angered *him* (H.I.H.) terribly and I was unable to prevent him from writing a cutting letter to His Highness. All I managed to achieve was to tone down some expressions. In conclusion the poor man told the Chancellor: 'Because of the urgent desire that I entertain to fulfil my duties in every way, and in view of the trust that I have in you, I ask you no less urgently than sincerely on future occasions to pay regard to me despite my absence, and to consult me before such steps are taken.' *Before* this he said in his letter: 'It has touched me painfully, seeing that I am both in my right mind and in full possession of my faculties, that without informing me of the proposed action or asking my opinion, a weighty step affecting the rights of the heir to the throne was taken, especially since at the moment no reason existed for such precipitancy.' There then followed the above-mentioned conclusion.[2] In order to lessen the wound, Her Imperial Highness has written a very nice kindly letter to H.H. thanking him for his telegram. [...]

I am terribly sorry for the poor woman. She keeps up his morale, but when she is alone she gives way to tears. Only she should not smile so much in public. It does her harm and one cannot help thinking that she does not feel deeply. Which is not so. She is also absolutely resolved that he will eventually ascend to the throne. After waiting so long the poor man must have this satisfaction at least, and I will do all I can in the way of nursing and care to ensure that he survives to see that day and afterwards to remain on the throne as long as possible.

I really believe that for her the idea that subsequently she must roam the world without any definite position is horrifying. *Elle réalise peut-être ce qui l'attend avec son ami.* She has a horror of it. She is now behaving well and displaying energy. [...]

Adio, your R. [...]

[1] Not found.
[2] A copy of the Crown Prince's letter to Bismarck of 21 November was found in the Radolin Papers. See also Bismarck's letter to Crown Princess Victoria of 3 December and his letter to Radolinski of the same date. (Bismarck, *Die gesammelten Werke*, vol. VIc, nos. 372–3, pp. 371–3.)

238. Holstein to Hugo von Radolinski[1]

28 November 1887

Dear Rado,

Instinctively I was afraid that with your Don Quixotry—pardon—you would get yourself into hot water. And that has now happened:

First, the letters addressed to *you* that came by King's Messenger for His Imperial Highness, *you* had to hand to him. Since any objections to this course can only be of a medical nature, you must allow a doctor to decide the matter and not Her Imperial Highness.

Second, I am doubtful whether you should have accepted the custody of the letter opened by her.

Third, I have no doubts that you acted with the youthful illusions of a *jeune premier* of the romantic school when you made yourself responsible for the *supercherie* of your lady. There are indeed cases in which one does that sort of thing. [...]

But surely *that* was not your intention? Or do you want to recommend yourself as an associate deity [*Nebengötze*][2]?? Then certainly! Nevertheless it was precisely against that that I had most strongly warned you. But what good are warnings? Youth—and you are an *entresol* below me in age—wants to acquire wisdom in its own right instead of having it handed down by the aged. I can do nothing to alter this universal law.

The affair had no bad results for you *here*. Prince Wilhelm and Herbert do indeed feel that your behaviour was not quite correct, but regard you as an uncommonly honourable man. Herbert particularly impressed that on the Prince, who in any case from the outset of the affair was favourably disposed towards you.

In the 'highest' circles here you have only *one* irreconcilable enemy—*la jeune et charmante Meiningen*.[3] Only recently she really let fly at you. I tell you this deliberately because I think that the time has come for you 'to take notice' of this and other matters.

In the first place my advice to you is that when M. arrives you adopt an acid tone and drop an occasional polite but cutting remark before witnesses. That is precisely *your* best weapon. Why let it rust?

Secondly, if I were you I would now demand that Kessel *and* Lyncker be summoned here immediately. Otherwise *you* would leave, but settle your account with Götz beforehand. It is not worthy of you to allow yourself to be driven into a corner there among a lot of enemies while Dohme's[4] star is in the ascendant. Act for once as if you were an Englishman who insists on being treated properly, and not a Prussian who can be beaten on the head.

I can expect that some attention be paid to my advice, for you know how long it takes me to decide on action. Now the moment has most

---

[1] From the Radolin Papers.
[2] Holstein is punning here on the name of Götz von Seckendorff.
[3] Charlotte, Hereditary Princess of Sachsen-Meiningen. Daughter of Crown Prince Friedrich Wilhelm.
[4] Robert Dohme. Art Historian; Librarian to the Crown Prince.

certainly come. You are at the point of *d'être tourné en bourrique* like many a clever man before you.

I leave it to you how to make your plan of action known in the appropriate quarter. Can Rabe be used for this purpose? I think that a slight hint would suffice to make the god [den Götzen][1] compliant through fear. But it would perhaps be better and more certain to confront the goddess [die Götzin][2] with the alternative.

Best wishes.

In as much as I advise you to speak personally with the goddess [Götzin][2] I assume that you are armed against tears and the like. *Otherwise* it would be better quietly to put your tail between your legs and slip noiselessly away. For I already sense that now with la Meiningen's stay, a period of humiliation lies before you; for that reason I advise action.

Ever yours
H.

239. Heinrich VII Reuss to Holstein

Vienna, 8 December 1887

My dear Herr von Holstein,

Many thanks for your very interesting letter of the 6th. The Waldersee affair made no impression here.[3] Kálnoky said he had had some difficulty in explaining the various changes of mind on the part of our General Staff to Beck,[4] who had talked with Field Marshal Moltke about five years ago. Beck had not been able to follow the various changes in general policy and could not understand why *at one time* (France did not then come into the picture) the General Staff had organised everything on the basis of joint action with Austria against Russia *alone*. Then again the necessity of deploying all available forces against France had come under consideration because one was certain of Russia. Finally, there was the necessity for dividing up the available force against France and Russia.

And now, first the word went out that Russia would attack, therefore prepare yourselves.[5] Then again: R. will not attack *immediately*.[6]

---

[1] Holstein is punning here on the name of Götz von Seckendorff.

[2] Another pun on the name of Götz von Seckendorff. The reference is to the Crown Princess.

[3] Waldersee had discussed the question of a Russo-Austrian war with the Austrian Military Attaché, Colonel von Steininger, and with Ambassador von Széchényi. This caused Prince Bismarck to protest vigorously against such 'encroachments on the part of the military' in a letter to Count Waldersee of 7 December 1887. (Waldersee, *Denkwürdigkeiten*, vol. I, pp. 340–1, 419–23; *Grosse Politik*, vol. VI, no. 1181, pp. 57–8, note **; *Aus dem Briefwechsel des Generalfeldmarschalls Alfred Grafen von Waldersee*, edited by Heinrich Otto Meisner (Berlin and Leipzig, 1928), vol. I, pp. 127 *et seq.*)

[4] Friedrich, Baron von Beck-Rzikowsky. Austro-Hungarian General; Chief of the General Staff, 1881–96.

[5] Waldersee noted in his diary on 29 November: 'I was with Reuss who intends to go on to Vienna after coming from Friedrichsruh. He is to advise the Austrians to do whatever the General Staff deems necessary for their protection, and to tell Russia about it frankly.' (*Denkwürdigkeiten*, vol. I, p. 339.)

[6] Herbert von Bismarck wrote in a memorandum of 6 December: 'When Count Széchény visited me eight days ago for the first time since his return, he remarked that General Count

Beck said that he no longer knew what he should believe and had become completely confused.

Kálnoky has explained to him the interrelation of the whole affair. That now as formerly our General Staff is convinced that R. desires war but that the word has gone out from Friedrichsruh: no over-hasty action! That W[aldersee] had taken this as his guiding principle and toned things down. But he, Kálnoky, thinks that *au fond* all of us are convinced that it must come to war, and for that reason he for his part has now very cautiously agreed that preparations shall be made here accordingly.

You know the instructions which the Prince has given me.[1] Herbert writes that his father still holds to them.[2]

On the other hand he is so very annoyed that the Austrians told me on the very first day that they wished to wait and see,[3] that I have now given them free rein and have only warned them against making false diplomatic moves.

It was already obvious to me in Berlin that carrying out my instructions would be a delicate job. I was *not* to and yet I was to.

My arguments, which were recently countered by cautious assurances, have finally produced the opposite effect. They are seriously making preparations. How far this will go I cannot prophesy. It is hardly likely to go very far because they are certainly very much *opposed* to war here. But I am not holding them back.

You have acted wisely in toning things down. In the financial affair there was no question of a stock exchange speculation, but only a typical Austrian muddle.[4]

What effect did the memorandum have on the Kaiser?[5]

With best wishes and in haste

Yours very sincerely
H. VII Reuss.

Waldersee had told Colonel von Steininger that Austria did not need to hurry in strengthening her military establishment because there was no immediate prospect of an Austro-Russian war.' (Waldersee, *Denkwürdigkeiten*, vol. I, p. 419; see above, p. 233, note 3.)

[1] Bismarck informed Austria of his suspicion that ever since Russia had been informed of the terms of the Austro-German treaty, she was doing everything possible to provoke Austria to attack, and he expressed the hope that Austria would not yield to Russian provocation. (See *Grosse Politik*, vol. VI, no. 1157, p. 12.)

[2] In a dispatch of 6 December 1887 which was largely identical with his memorandum of the same day (see above, p. 233, note 6) Count Bismarck summarised the German attitude in the words: 'Austria should avoid every provocation, but at the same time energetically pursue the strengthening of its armaments and military resources.' (From the Foreign Ministry files.)

[3] The Austrians wanted to await further Russian moves before undertaking costly military preparations of their own. (See Reuss' report to Bismarck of 1 December 1887. *Grosse Politik*, vol. VI, no. 1159, pp. 13–17.)

[4] Prince Reuss refers to the 28 million gulden voted in the previous year's Austro-Hungarian military credits which had not been spent and which were not being used. (From the Foreign Ministry files.)

[5] Reuss probably refers to Waldersee's memorandum of November 1887 on the development of Russia's military strength since the beginning of the year which Moltke sent to Bismarck on 30 November accompanied by a detailed report. (See Waldersee, *Denkwürdigkeiten*, vol. I, p. 339; Count Moltke, *Die deutschen Aufmarschpläne, 1871–90*, edited by Ferdinand von Schmerfeld (Berlin, 1929), pp. 137–50; *Grosse Politik*, vol. VI, pp. 24–5, note **.)

240. Heinrich VII Reuss to Holstein

Vienna, 10 December 1887

My dear Herr von Holstein,

Many thanks for your two letters of yesterday which I have just received; I would like to send these lines in haste by Monts.

My opinion is that Waldersee's intervention in and influence upon decisions here is being exaggerated by us. As I have already written to Herbert B. or you,[1] Count Kálnoky does not attach much importance to it but judges the affair quite correctly.

The reason why they hesitated, and still hesitate, here is to be found elsewhere. Beck said so to Deines,[2] and I am today sending H. Bismarck the letter which Deines wrote to me about it.[3]

Namely: they are convinced that if the measures resolved on here for the defence of Galicia are carried into effect (displacement of battalions, etc.) things will begin to move. The General Staff is convinced of the necessity of this step, but would prefer to see it postponed for a couple of weeks because those measures for general mobilisation which are reviewed and brought up to date each year are not yet completed. If therefore an order for mobilisation were forced upon them tomorrow or in a fortnight, probably a state of complete confusion would result.

I can understand that the Austrian General Staff wishes to avoid this.

All pressure to do more *immediately* will therefore be useless and could also, in the already mentioned circumstances, be accompanied by unpleasant results.

The dispatch of the 8th, no. 684 regarding the *casus foederis*,[4] is *for me* alone; I am not yet permitted to tell the Austrians about it, but they will notice that this point of view now exists. But I *must* mention it if we engage in military discussions, which Kálnoky has suggested, and I think it would be prudent to do so soon. It would encourage them here. Kálnoky is not so fainthearted as you think. He is not in the least *wobbly*.

The notion of recalling Széchényi at this time would not be a good one. He does his job quite well. To send Wedel here would serve no real purpose. Deines spends all his time with Beck, who likes him very much and is also very frank with him; hence what is there for *still* another person to do? If officers of the General Staff were to be sent

---

[1] See above Reuss' letter of 8 December.

[2] Major Adolf von Deines. German Military Attaché in Vienna, 1886–93.

[3] Deines' letter to Reuss of 9 December reached the Foreign Ministry on the 11th. Deines wrote that Beck had countered his pressure for Austrian military preparedness by the arguments summarised by Reuss in the following paragraph. (From the Foreign Ministry files. See also *Grosse Politik*, vol. VI, p. 61, note *.)

[4] The dispatch, signed by Herbert von Bismarck, stated: 'With reference to your observation in Report No. 487 [*Grosse Politik*, vol. VI, no. 1159, pp. 13–17] that Count Kálnoky probably assumes that the *casus foederis* would not be taken too literally once it was clear that Russia had really decided to attack Austria, the Chancellor observed that this assumption was justified. But His Highness hesitated to allow this to be clearly expressed in Vienna, because he feared that the Austrians would then rely upon us more than ever and would not take sufficient precautionary military measures of their own.' (From the Foreign Ministry files.)

here for consultations, then Wedel would be useful and these preliminary discussions could be entrusted to him *and* Deines.

Here, however, they want the preliminary discussions to take place in Berlin, and they are right. Kálnoky hopes that the officers here would be facilitated in their task there.

Should it come to the precise determination of troop movements and the like, the dispatch of Prussian officers to the Austrian General Staff would in any case be necessary. For that purpose Wedel would be absolutely first-rate, particularly when matters started to move.

Perhaps, however, we would then prefer to send a higher-ranking general (Verdy?). But I would prefer Wedel for this purpose.

I have just hastily read over Moltke's memorandum.[1] It is superbly clear. I will communicate it to them here tomorrow.

Once again I wish to request what I explained at the outset: that the delay here should be rightly understood.

I have not noticed that the Hungarians are pressing for war. Now that the danger draws closer they will grow tamer.

With best wishes,
Your devoted,
H. VII Reuss

241. Bernhard von Bülow to Holstein[2]

St Petersburg, 10 December 1887

Dear Holstein,

Tomorrow's courier affords me the possibility of thanking you very much for your very interesting and friendly letter of the 2nd of this month. I ask your permission to reply by a dictated letter because I must refrain from writing for some days on account of a slight inflammation of the eyes.

During the last fortnight, feeling here with regard to Germany had outwardly calmed down a great deal, and the official world, society, and even the Press, are at present again speaking of us in friendly terms. In my opinion we should certainly not allow ourselves to be lulled into a feeling of security on this account, because the display of reasonableness towards Germany is accompanied by increasing enmity towards Austria. If you will allow me to express my humble opinion on the situation, I must first of all say that I must leave it to more competent soldiers than I am to judge the military aspects of such a situation: that is to say, the answer to the question as to what are our military prospects in event of war against Russia, or against Russia and France; whether postponement or hastening of the outbreak of war would be better for us militarily; how and where if the occasion arises the war could be begun most favourably from a military standpoint. From a purely political viewpoint the prospects of a war with Russia are not too brilliant. If we conclude peace speedily with the Russians, and if they emerge from the conflict with a black eye, we should be burdened for a very long time

---

[1] See above p. 234, note 5.   [2] From the Foreign Ministry files.

with their unassuageable thirst for revenge which could be even stronger than that of the French: the Russians are more fanatical, more capable of sacrifice, more patriotic than the French, they will in such a case think only of revenge, and in a few years it would start all over again. It is possible that defeat in war would bring about internal changes in Russia, but it is not certain, while it is also questionable whether such changes would necessarily weaken Russia, and especially weaken her in the long run. Many Russians believe that for the cleansing and reconditioning of Russia's Augean stables as well as for the development and stimulation of the quiescent latent forces here, nothing could be more effective than for Russia to suffer some reverses which would compel reforms. If we do go to war with Russia, we should not make peace until we have rendered her incapable of attacking us for at least a generation. *A small bullet excites a man, a strong one stops him*: that is a saying that applies particularly to the Russians. We would have to bleed the Russians to such an extent that, far from feeling relieved, they will be incapable of standing on their legs for twenty-five years.[1] We must stop up Russia's economic sources for years to come by devastating her black-earth provinces,[2] bombarding her coastal towns, destroying her industry and commerce to the greatest possible extent. Finally, we must drive Russia back from the two seas—the Baltic and Black Sea— which are the foundations of her great position in the world. I can only picture to myself a Russia truly and permanently weakened after the cession of those territories which lie to the west of a line from Onega Bay through the Valdai Hills to the Dnieper. Such a peace—unless there were a complete internal breakdown here in the event of war, which to that extent can hardly be foreseen—would only be enforceable if we stood on the banks of the Volga. I leave aside in this connection the question whether the restoration of Poland in any form whatever and the annexation of the Baltic provinces[3] by us would serve any useful political purpose. If we resurrect Poland we must certainly in all events organise it in such a way that the Catholic Poles and the Orthodox Little Russians[4] within its frontiers approximately balance one another so as to make it impossible for this resurrected Poland to pursue a hostile policy towards us or seek a reconciliation with Russia; while on the other hand we should seize the opportunity afforded us by war to drive the Poles *en masse* from our Polish provinces. On the other hand Russia might possibly be a more comfortable neighbour than a resurrected Poland, which would be the natural ally of France and Austria.[5] Apart from the fact that war with Russia is from the military standpoint such a serious matter, and one calling for very careful consideration, it would in itself from a political standpoint certainly be better if we could get along with the Russians.[6] It seems to me that when everything is taken into

[1] Marginal comment by Chancellor Bismarck: 'That is not so easy.'
[2] Bismarck: 'How?'
[3] Marginal comment by Herbert von Bismarck: 'Then preferably Poland.'
[4] Insertion by Herbert von Bismarck: 'with Baltic.'
[5] Marginal comment by Bismarck: 'Eccentric conjectures of this kind must not be set down on paper!'
[6] Bismarck: 'Yes.'

account, the situation created at Skiernievice is more advantageous for us than any possible outcome of a Russo-German war.[1] Our endeavours to achieve a *modus vivendi* with Russia were certainly politically justified; but have been rendered unavailing by the weakness and still more by the boundless stupidity of Russian governmental circles. As things are now, and notwithstanding that Russia is for the moment again speaking in friendlier tones, we must be ready for everything on Russia's part, and the distrust of her that obtains in Berlin is well-founded. We must above all not allow the Russians to separate us from the European Powers friendly to us. The great King said: *'Si je suis uni avec la Russie, tout le monde me laissera intact et je conserverai la paix.'* That was true so long as there was some likelihood that the ruling men in Russia were willing and able to give practical effect to their undertakings. Nevertheless if the Russians were today to offer us all the kingdoms of the world and their splendour in return for our abandoning our Central European allies, I would say: Get thee behind me, Satan.[2] During the past year Russian public opinion has been poisoned to its depths and excited against us; Katkov and his associates have so shaken the Government's authority, the Tsar reveals himself as so narrow-minded, cowardly and incalculable, that even if the Russian Government meant to behave honourably towards us it would hardly be in a position to act in an honourable way. If we were to stand alone without friends, the Russians would immediately join with the French against us; the Government might have promised anything they liked, but they would be swept away just the same. Our sole guarantees for peace with the Russians are our armed might and our alliances. I have the impression that now as formerly the Russians are everywhere seeking to break up these alliances, and for that very reason perhaps they are now flirting with us. The Russian newspapers which are designed for foreign readers (*Nord, Journal de St Petersbourg*) adopt a more friendly attitude to Germany than those intended to be read by the Russian public. Üxküll is likely to be replaced shortly by a cleverer man—Vlangaly[3] or Niky Dolgoruki or Fredericks.[4] I hear that great efforts are again being made by Russia to bring about a reconciliation with the Curia and that it is particularly hoped that the latter will at least concede one of Russia's two fundamental demands (use of the Russian language in the Catholic religious services in the Polish provinces and supervision of the correspondence between the Pope and the Russian Bishops by the Russian Ministry of the Interior). In this connection Lobanov is to press Galimberti[5] pretty strongly. As regards England, Morier takes care of Russian interests, reassures the Russians on the attitude of his Government whose unconditional neutrality and reserve he guarantees, and agitates against us in every possible way. During his approaching four

---

[1] Marginal comment by Herbert von Bismarck: 'Coals to Newcastle!'

[2] Marginal comment by Bismarck: 'Correct. It is in our interest not to lessen the number of Powers; Russia among them. Otherwise the struggle with Austria and the coalition against us would again come to life.'

[3] Assistant to the Russian Foreign Minister; Ambassador in Rome, 1891–7.

[4] Russian General. Military Attaché in Paris.

[5] Luigi Galimberti. Papal Nuncio in Vienna, 1887–92; Cardinal from 1893.

weeks' leave—he is going to London—Morier is not leaving the First or Second Secretary in charge of affairs, but the Third Secretary, Hardinge, who is his private secretary and *âme damnée*, merely to ensure that nobody else gets the chance of interfering with his Russophil-Germanophobe policy. The attitude of the Russians to Austria is somewhat complex. Giers at the moment would obviously like to intimidate Austria or provoke her to attack. This latter aim is based on the hope that if Austria were to be the aggressor we would leave her to fight it out alone. In so far as the Tsar thinks about it at all, it is possible that his thoughts are influenced by the idea that if the run-away horse of Pan-Slavism could no longer be held in check, it would be better for it to run its head against the Austrian rather than directly against the German wall. But there is no question of a real national hatred of Austria similar to that against us which is steadily and artificially propagated and which has produced—especially since last summer—luxuriant blooms. While Russian diplomacy would like to some extent to induce us with all sorts of blandishments and promises, and also with threats of French support, to abandon Austria, and while the majority of Russian officers would certainly much prefer to fight against Austria than against the far more dreaded Germany, the 'intelligentsia' here would gladly come to an understanding with Austria, if only to be able to vent their hatred on us. It seems unquestionable, precisely to those who live here amongst the Russians, that under no circumstances can we permit Austria to be overrun, weakened, or indeed destroyed, by the Russians[1]—we would in that case make the same mistake in regard to the Russians that our policy made with regard to France ninety-two years ago in the Peace of Basel.[2] The moment the Russians had dealt with Austria they would attack us, because by their very nature they cannot—especially in victory—show moderation. On the other hand it would appear to be politically preferable—now, as before, I leave the military standpoint out of consideration—if the Russians attacked Austria first rather than if they—or they and the French—directly attacked us. To judge by their diplomatic representatives here, the Austrians are not a little fearful of a conflict with Russia. The very people who four weeks ago declared that Austria could under no circumstances make concessions in regard to Bulgaria now say that Bulgaria is a matter of indifference to Austria.[3] At the same time they complain that Austria did not come to an understanding with Russia sooner, and they no longer display the joyful confidence and cheerfulness which inspired them while we were the chief object of Russian rancour, but a dejectedness that is particularly out of place in front of the Russians. Confronted with the Russian attempts to provoke a collision, the Austrian Embassy behaves like the Frenchman who on receiving a box on the ear glanced at his friend and said: '*Je crois que ce soufflet au fond ne me vise pas, mais mon ami que voici en sera profondément irrité.*' The

[1] Marginal comment by Bismarck: 'Correct.'
[2] Insertion by Herbert von Bismarck: 'and 1805.'
[3] Marginal comment by Bismarck: 'I have *always* assumed that.'

Austrians must not be given the opportunity in the event of a Russo-German conflict of slipping out at the last moment as they and the Italians did in 1870 in regard to France. 'Messieurs les Autrichiens, tirez les premiers!' As long as no shots have been exchanged between Russians and Germans, we would always be able at the eleventh hour to come to an arrangement with the Russians at the expense of Austria, and consequently we can control the latter. But the moment the first drop of Russian or German blood were shed, the national hatred here for the *nemez* would probably flare up immediately to such an extent that as far as one could foresee no understanding could any longer be reached with the Russians. In this event the Austrians on the other hand would probably only need to make a few concessions to the Russians in the Near East, or merely to increase the Slav character of the Cis-Leithanian Government by the elimination of the Poles and the more pronounced Germans, and the simultaneous replacement of Kálnoky by a man of peace *à tout prix* like Wolkenstein, or even an anti-German feudal magnate, for the Russians to build golden bridges over which the Vienna Government could retreat. I am horrified to see that I have already reached the fourth sheet and will not take up any more of your time. In so far as I may express an opinion, it is that the continuance of our present attitude towards Russia is for the moment the sole correct policy. We can hardly be mistrustful enough in regard to intentions and movements here and will only be able to achieve something with the Russians if we continue to speak to them in the cold and determined tones which we have hitherto used. Apart from that we must wait and see whether the Russian Press really remains more or less calm, what the attitude of Russian diplomacy in Paris will be, and especially and above all, whether the Russians cease or carry on with their military preparations. [...]

With best regards,
Your
Bernh. v. Bulow.

242. Heinrich VII Reuss to Holstein

Vienna, 18 December 1887

My dear Herr von Holstein,

I am extremely grateful to you for your letter of the 16th of this month and the very useful *avertissements*. Like you I say: God be thanked that the storm has passed over! I made a mistake in sending on Deines' letter;[1] that was imprudent. I may well have underestimated the matter because he told me of his conversation and informed me of the impressions he gained in the course of it. According to this it really did not appear as if he had wanted to promote war. It is very much to be regretted that this incident made such an impression that now we are

[1] See p. 235, note 3.

again marking time. I had to assume from Dispatch No. 686 (together with Memorandum)[1] and the accompanying notes that we had wanted to urge them on here. I did so—and now it seems to have been too much.

I am only very glad that I did not give any—not even the smallest—hint that, as you wrote to me at that time, the Chancellor had given up the *casus foederis*. That would have been an appalling mistake! Nevertheless I did not disillusion Kálnoky when he seemed to me to harbour the hope that we would perhaps not interpret the *casus foederis* too literally. I had told him often enough *when* the *c.f.* would apply—and let it rest there.

Dispatch No. 686 could not lead me to do anything else but *assume* that while the Chancellor did not want to hear anything of a war of aggression, he still believed the situation to be threatening, that is to say, believed in the deployment and attack of the Russian Army. I was indeed instructed to deny Waldersee's cautious utterances, draw attention to Klepsch's opinion, and, since the attack could come quite unexpectedly (as Yorck[2] thinks), counsel them here that they might at least do what is most necessary! All of which did not sound as if we were at ease.

In short, I made use of everything that was sent to me from Berlin to urge them on; if I had not done so matters would have continued to drag along here. But now no toning down! That would have a deplorable effect. And especially not after the brilliant reception accorded to our military estimates by the Reichstag.[3] For then the Stock Exchange speculators, with some appearance of justification, would again raise the cry that we made all this noise in order to get the estimate passed.

If we now intend to show ourselves very reserved in the General Staff conferences, as Count Bismarck writes me,[4] that will make a bad impression here. I think that here they would like to discuss the question objectively. Naturally the people here will say that if the *casus foederis* arises we propose to do this or that. But the second question, which is bound up with this is: what constitutes a *casus foederis*? Is it the first shot that is fired that decides it or does the alliance come into force as soon as it is established beyond all question that Russia *will* go to war?

But then the military immediately becomes a political question and the talks are doomed to failure in advance. That would be bad.

Please support me in asserting that *nobody* here wants war. I do not know how the contrary belief has come into existence with us.

---

[1] Dispatch No. 686 forwarded the memorandum about Russia's military preparations (see p. 234, note 5) to Vienna. (See *Grosse Politik*, vol. VI, p. 24, note **; the dispatch is printed in Waldersee, *Denkwürdigkeiten*, vol. I, pp. 421–3.)

[2] Maximilian, Count Yorck von Wartenburg. Prussian Major; attached to the Military Plenipotentiary in St Petersburg.

[3] After the Reichstag had passed the seven year military budget on 11 March 1887 (the Septennate), new military estimates were submitted to it before the close of the year. Under the influence of the threatening danger of a war on two fronts, the Reichstag passed the so called militia law to provide for an enlargement of the war strength of the German army.

[4] Not found, but see *Grosse Politik*, vol. VI, no. 1179, pp. 55–6.

I have made my report today as short as possible.[1] I would like to hear if I have hit the right tone.

As for the question of pressure, Kálnoky told me yesterday that you and Count Herbert kept driving spurs into the Ambassador and had asked when the first regiments were marching to Galicia? etc. On top of this came Deines' pressure, and that had heated the blood of the military men.

I will continue to advise them to carry on vigorously with defensive measures.

In this connection it would certainly be useful if our Press would cut down their exhortations, which often sound somewhat schoolmasterly. It only puts them in a bad humour here and produces the opposite of what is desired.

With best greetings,
Yours very sincerely
H. VII Reuss.

243. Heinrich VII Reuss to Holstein

Vienna, 23 December 1887

My dear Herr von Holstein,

Many thanks for your letter of the 18th. You will see from my dispatch that the laconic answer which Count Bismarck gave Széchényi about the military talks did not, as I foresaw, give much satisfaction here.[2] Count Kálnoky to be sure asked me to explain this reply to him, and when I did so he said he understood our point of view. Nonetheless Steininger's[3] instructions[4] would be sent.

I conclude from this that these latter will empower the Military Attaché to *discuss* something *more* than merely general views on a possible joint conduct of a war.

Kálnoky, however, accepts the situation. Is contenting himself with our reply, but obviously hopes that the talks will produce the desired clarification. I am convinced that were Moltke to say something about the possible numerical strength of our support, *they* would regard this here as a clarification of the situation. Soldiers on leave have not yet been recalled, this is to be done immediately, and to begin before the New Year.

I am entirely of your opinion that the tendency here to go to sleep must be hindered by the voice of the non-official Austrian Press. And up to now this has been done.

---

[1] In a short report of 18 December Reuss said that the instructions for Lieutenant-Colonel von Steininger for the military talks to be held in Berlin were already prepared, but that Kálnoky had not told him anything more about their contents. (From the Foreign Ministry files. See below, note 4.)

[2] Reuss wrote on 21 December that Széchényi had reported to Vienna that Count Bismarck had informed him that the military discussions would only be of a quite general nature. In a conversation with Kálnoky, Reuss confirmed that the talks could not deal with the setting up of a plan of operations. (From the Foreign Ministry files.)

[3] Karl, Baron von Steininger. Austro-Hungarian Military Attaché in Berlin, 1882–95.

[4] See *Grosse Politik*, vol. VI, no. 1185, Enclosure, pp. 65–6.

Kálnoky sets damned little value on St Petersburg's peace assurances, did not show himself very convinced to Lobanov, even though he took cognisance of them with *empressement*.[1]

H. VII Reuss

[1] See *Grosse Politik*, vol. VI, no. 1170, pp. 34–6.

1888

244. Eberhard zu Solms to Holstein

Rome, 2 January 1888

My dear friend,

[...] I know that neither H.M. the Kaiser, you, Count Bismarck, or our officers, would be displeased if war were to break out, but that His Highness [Bismarck] is strongly opposed to it. If therefore I report facts such as that Damiani[1] would gladly bring matters to a break over Tunis, that following my instructions I have advised that hostilities should break out elsewhere, and, finally, that I assured Crispi that it will start in Europe but not in Africa—then it might be assumed that everybody could find what he liked in my dispatches.[2]

In this I have been mistaken. I am abstaining from all attempts to influence matters in either a pacific or bellicose direction. But if I am not to report what is said to me in this connection by influential people simply because what the Italians say and do produces an opposite impression upon each of our highest personages, and unfailingly produces an expression of displeasure from one side or another not with the Italians but with the reporter, then I can easily expose myself to the risk that events suddenly occur without their having been reported from their inception. 'How can the Ambassador allow himself to be so completely taken by surprise without opening his eyes!?'—they will say then.

As I had written,[3] Crispi's position was not threatened because he cannot be replaced. But there are many currents in parliamentary life, and recently there have been some which are temporarily less favourable for the Minister. I could not pass this over in silence because here it is always possible, since it has often happened, that such a movement will quite unexpectedly result in a change of government, although it is not probable at present. One cannot leave out of account the fact that Signor Crispi does not get on with the King and is unpopular with the Court. The Minister for War[4] is also among his hidden opponents. In the last few days Crispi has overcome all difficulties brilliantly and for the first time the King, in his talks with myself and the Austrian Ambassador, has paid him the fullest tribute. The situation is thus once again very good; it is a fortunate change because a fortnight ago it was unfavourable, as you will have seen from the newspapers.

[1] Under State Secretary in the Italian Foreign Ministry.
[2] Not found.
[3] In a letter to Holstein of 14 December 1887. Not printed.
[4] Ettore Bertole-Viale. Italian War Minister, 1887–91.

Major von Engelbrecht's[1] dispatches nevertheless strike a pessimistic note. I have often remonstrated with him about it. But in the end he always proved everything by statistics. Engelbrecht is exceptionally well-informed; he gets his information from the generals in the War Ministry who place great confidence in him. The facts that he reports about armaments, mobilisation, etc., do not please me at all. Since, however, we count on Italy's co-operation, our General Staff must be in a position to know precisely what she can perform; only in this way can we avoid disappointment. Like you, I rely on our officers in judging military matters, and I do not want to take the responsibility for toning down the opinion, based on knowledge of the facts, of an experienced General Staff officer. I hear from Baron Bruck that the reports of his Military Attaché, Colonel von Forstner, are equally pessimistic. But it is encouraging that the Italians are working at a furious pace, so that with every day the Army and Fleet will be better prepared for battle.

But I will bore you no longer.

For the New Year I wish you all health and prosperity and everything your heart desires. Continue to give me your friendly assistance in the coming days, and to believe in the genuine friendly wishes of your most sincerely devoted

Solms

I have not yet been able to get hold of your friend Blaserna,[2] whom you commended to me. I will invite him to dine in the next few days.

E.S.

245. Heinrich VII Reuss to Holstein

Vienna, 2 January 1888

My dear Herr von Holstein,

Many thanks for your letter of the 29th. I cannot understand how it can be believed that the Austrians are less afraid of war than we are. I recently wrote to Herbert B.[3] that if he spent twenty-four hours here he would convince himself of the contrary.

Do you know what will be the immediate result of our playing things down? That the Austrian War Minister will do less than ever. Kálnoky is probably still keeping up the pressure, and much money has already been spent on horses for the batteries, completion of fortifications, munitions; and preliminary plans for mobilisation, which were not completed at the beginning of December (that is, by the Ministry), will be ready by 15 January. I do not dare to write this officially because I believe that the big misunderstanding is due in part to my writing[4] that Beck had said that his preliminary arrangements for mobilisation could only be completed in six weeks, that is to say on 15 January.

This referred to the mobilisation plans which are reviewed annually

[1] Karl von Engelbrecht. Military Attaché in Rome, 1882–95.
[2] Pietro Blaserna. Senator. Professor of Physics in Rome.
[3] This letter has not been found.
[4] In a letter of 11 December 1887 forwarding Deines' letter of 9 December. (See p. 235, note 3, and Reuss' letter of 18 December 1887.)

and brought up to date, about which Deines reported. It never occurred to them to want to *mobilise* on 15 January. The Kaiser most categorically told me he did not want any war, no winter campaign.

Kálnoky swallowed the explanation about our appearance in the arena without a murmur. But it is easy to understand that the definite knowledge that we will only come on the scene if Austria is already at war with R[ussia] will have a disheartening effect here.[1] Austrian pessimism can easily raise its head again and the modicum of courage which we have instilled into them will be lost.

We will wait and see; perhaps everything will be different.

With the best New Year's wishes
Your devoted
H. VII Reuss

Monts is very grateful for the friendly reception you and H[erbert] B[ismarck] accorded him.

246. Chlodwig zu Hohenlohe to Holstein

Strasbourg, 4 January 1888

My dear Baron,

Many thanks for your friendly wishes for the New Year,[2] which I warmly reciprocate.

Your action in the Curator affair was of real service to me and strengthened my position.[3] You have again shown yourself as the energetic forceful friend to whom I am already indebted for many a *coup d'épaule*. I would like to repay you for this in some way but fear that such a selfless ascetic as you are will afford me little opportunity. Hence you must content yourself with my friendly sentiments of gratitude with which I am

Your truly devoted
CHohenlohe.[4]

247. Bernhard von Bülow to Holstein

St Petersburg, 5 January 1888

Dear Holstein,

Many thanks for your very interesting letter of the 26th of last month. Official Russia continues to speak to us in the most pacific and friendliest way. Perhaps this attitude is to be partly ascribed to the

---

[1] See *Grosse Politik*, vol. VI, nos. 1186, 1188, pp. 66–9, 70–2.

[2] For Holstein's letter to Hohenlohe of 30 December 1887, see Rogge, *Holstein und Hohenlohe*, p. 306.

[3] Hohenlohe was blamed for being too indulgent towards the University of Strasbourg because he did not want to propose *Ministerialrat* Richter as permanent Curator of the University against the wishes of the professors. In a letter to Holstein of 25 December 1887, Hohenlohe emphasised that he objected to Richter not because the professors did not like him but because he was the tool of Friedrich Althoff, who was in charge of university affairs in the Prussian Ministry of Education. The draft of this letter, dated 24 December, is printed in Rogge, *Holstein und Hohenlohe*, pp. 305–6.

[4] Marginal comment by Holstein: 'I am afraid poor Hohenlohe will not last much longer. Too soft.'

fact that according to all the news reaching here from Paris, the French will not be ready for action for some time. I hear from different quarters that at the moment, quite apart from the pacific inclinations of the present French Government, things are still not in order there from a military standpoint.

Villaume[1] told me that he is sending a long report on the military situation here by tomorrow's courier. According to my impressions, with the possible exception of the Tsar, some Grand Dukes, and a few generals of Baltic descent, there is scarcely a Russian officer of any importance who does not think that war with the German Powers is virtually inevitable. Differences of opinion exist, inasmuch as a small group of specially ambitious and resolute generals (particularly Kuropatkin, Obrutchev, Dragomirov, Feldmann, Dokturov, and the War Minister,[2] who is influenced by them) want to go to war in the course of the present year because of the state of the armaments situation in Austria and Germany, while others want to wait until the completion of Russian military preparations. Those who hold this latter view entertain the hope that meanwhile they will succeed in loosening our relations with the other Powers. It is understandable that the Russians would prefer to take on Germany and Austria and England individually, as the Horatii took on the Curiatii. On the whole one can say that those circles here which have an interest in the maintenance of autocracy, at least of the House of Romanov, want to start with the otherthrow of Austria, while those who either desire, or are indifferent to, the fall of the dynasty want to begin with Germany.

It is remarkable that during the last fortnight there appears to be greater self-confidence than formerly. The military believe they have at present a great numerical superiority, that they are a match for Germany, and they do not doubt that war with both Powers would finally end in a Russian victory, under no circumstances in a lasting defeat. I also recently encountered similar opinions in society here. In confronting the great tendency of the Russians to be overbearing, a cool, even a disdainful manner and attitude is indicated on our part, and it should stay that way until it is obvious that there is an actual and genuine improvement here. The Russians like all Asiatics are only impressed by the crude treatment to which the Tartars and the Tsars have accustomed them for centuries and which a diplomat must display in a more polished way but can actually never wholly abandon here.

Klepsch believes that despite their overweening self-conceit, the Russians are not wrong in assuming that their army is at present in good shape; 'tremendous strides' have been made during the past ten years; the army has first-rate armaments with which it is thoroughly

---

[1] Karl von Villaume. Prussian Lieutenant Colonel; Military Plenipotentiary in St Petersburg, 1887–93; Deputy-Head of the Naval Cabinet, 1896. In his dispatch of 30 December 1887 Villaume came to the conclusion that no trust could be placed in the Russian protestations of peaceful intentions and that Russia's military measures should be watched suspiciously as long as 'the malevolent influence of the Pan-Slav party on the soldiers continues'. (From the Foreign Ministry files.)

[2] Peter Vannovski.

familiar; the fortifications in Poland are sufficiently complete to confront us with serious difficulties; also the fleet, railway network, and stores are in a better state than formerly; the morale of the army is good. Klepsch believes that the Russians have a great advantage in the fact that their Generals have more initiative than the Austrians. The latter are too afraid of responsibility, since they expect in the case of failure to meet with the fate of Gyulai[1] and Benedek;[2] the Russians know that even if something does go wrong this will not cost an otherwise useful man his career—'it didn't come off' is all that is said—and therefore they go in with more dash.

The public at large bases its hopes for a successful issue of the war chiefly on its memories of 1812. It is known here that our General Staff considers that the state of things has completely altered in seventy-five years and that the difficulties attendant upon an invasion of Russia are less than in Napoleon's day. The Russians nevertheless believe that in this we are deluding ourselves. They maintain that climate, distances, roads in Russia are the same as at the beginning of the century, the peasant just as poor and in consequence just as willing to sacrifice himself, and that the same resistance would be encountered now as then. Moreover foreigners who live here—Germans, Poles, English—are of the opinion that in event of war the Russians would prove to be very tough. Although I stressed the fact that the general feeling here had recently become more confident, I must add that the Russians never have feared war in the same way as the English did during the Afghanistan crisis or the Austrians in recent days. The Russians are too conceited and too impassive. Although practically every Russian complains and argues about the present state of Russia, not a single one—in contrast to so many Austrians and many Germans—has any doubts about the future of the Russian people, who are so solidly unified by nature of their soil, nationality, and religion. The majority of the Russians consequently think that at worst they would not lose too much; they are often in the mood of a man who stakes five marks against fifty marks in the belief that he stands to win more than he can lose. Loss of human life is a matter of indifference to them and a state of poverty does not specially worry them because the people would always have bread. Their 'Nichevo' is in this connection not a sham. The Russian is, all in all, morally more prepared for war now than any of our other neighbours. If it breaks out tomorrow most of my acquaintances will not be unduly depressed but will regard the matter more as a splendid adventure, and in case of necessity sit smoking their cigarettes on the ruins of their houses and *dachas*.

It is infinitely difficulty to say what is going on in the mind of Alexander III. 'This mind sees the world differently from other minds.'

[1] Franz, Count Gyulai von Maros-Németh und Nádaska. Commander-in-Chief of the Austrian Army in the Italian campaign, 1859. He was compelled to relinquish his command after the Austrian defeat at Magenta on 4 June.

[2] Ludwig August, Ritter von Benedek. Commander-in-Chief of the Austrian Northern Army in 1866. After the defeat by Prussia at Königgrätz on 3 July, he was relieved of his command and brought before a court-martial by order of the Kaiser.

What is certain is that the Francophilism and the enmity towards us would never have taken on such proportions here were it not that everyone was and still is convinced that this change of attitude was really approved by the Tsar. The latest events seem to confirm at least in part what the *Société de St Petersbourg*, pages 11 to 13, has to say about Alexander III's personal feelings towards Germany. After all that has happened, especially since the spring, the practical trustworthiness of the Tsar is still very much *sujet à caution* until he shows that he is willing and able seriously to restrain at least some of the Pan-Slav agitators. Undoubtedly the Tsar is frequently deceived, but as you so pertinently say, he as often grumblingly swims with the current with his eyes open. An affair that is now raising much dust here throws a revealing light on conditions here. Two brothers named Darvis, about thirty years old, inoffensive, sensible, quiet, and loyal fellows, who for their undoing jointly possess 36 million roubles, were suddenly and without any reason placed under official guardianship by an imperial *ukase*, and the trusteeship was awarded to the Imperial Counsellor Korobiin and to a brother of Polovtsov's,[1] each of whom receives a salary of 50,000 roubles. Behind this step lies an intrigue in which Vishnegradsky,[2] various grands seigneurs and some *jobbers*, as well as the trustees, had a hand, all of whom would like to get the Darvis millions for themselves. The Tsar allowed himself to be deceived by these people, just as today he allows Pobedonoszev[3] or Katokatsy[4], tomorrow Vannovsky or Kuropatkin, to lie to him. On the other hand the Tsar is sometimes less naive than is supposed abroad; instead he is more apathetic and timid. For example, he thoroughly understands the imminent danger to him and his rule arising from the importance and attitude of the Russian Press, yet he does not dare to do anything about it in a really effective and lasting way. Hence there arose a *circulus vitiosus*: the Tsar does not dare to deal firmly with the Press; as a result the Press continually resorts to its familiar agitation, and the Tsar then takes all this as the expression of the 'national will' which must be yielded to.

It is frequently assumed that another assassination attempt may be made soon. 'Some 15,000 students,' so the talk ran in a fashionable salon, 'are in the streets.' Let us assume that each has only three people interested in his fate, which already makes 45,000 embittered malcontents in the middle classes. *Il est à craindre qu'il s'y trouvera bien un ou deux qui essaieront un mauvais coup.*' The majority are for the students and against the inspectors about whose *'bêtise'* and *'canaillerie'* innumerable anecdotes are in circulation. The Rector of the University here, Vladislaev, published his lectures on 'The Psychology of the Soul' a short time ago and the book has already become a rarity at booksellers, fetching a high price. Pobedonoszev's favourite develops in his lectures, not in fun but in all seriousness, the notion that the feelings to which the soul of a good Russian is sensitive can be gauged mathematically just as

[1] Director of the Russian Imperial Chancellery.
[2] Ivan Vishnegradsky. Russian Finance Minister, 1887–90.
[3] Constantin Pobedonoszev. Procurator General of the Holy Synod, 1880–1905.
[4] Russian financial and Press agent in Paris.

temperature is gauged by the degrees on a thermometer. When he encounters wealth and rank equal to his own, he feels indifference; confronted with greater wealth and higher rank, respect; very great wealth and very high rank, astonishment and admiration; and before him who unites in his person and can apportion all wealth and all rank, namely the Tsar, boundless fear. On the other hand, those who are poorer and of lower rank must, each according to his situation, inspire contempt, disdain, disgust—feelings that can only be alleviated by the birth or family connections of the person concerned. '*La Grèce a eu*,' said one of His Majesty's aunts, '*le système de Platon, basé sur la beauté et la bonté; l'Allemagne celui de Kant basé sur le devoir; nous avons le noble système Vladislaev.*' A Rector like this confronts a youthful generation nurtured on Büchner, Proudhon, Rousseau, Marx, whose teachings moreover they have not digested and, if it be possible, exaggerate.

It is not likely that the regime that has existed here for the past six years can maintain itself much longer. It is only a poor imitation of the Nicholas regime which ultimately collapsed, although it was carried by quite different personalities from those who are now in power. The slow—everything in Russia goes very slowly!—undermining of the governmental system inaugurated in 1881 can have both warlike and pacific results. It is possible that internal unrest could distract attention from foreign affairs and it is also certainly possible that the increasing discontent might induce the Tsar to act forcibly abroad.

Churchill[1] is being greatly feted here. I was told in complete confidence that Giers sent his nephew Cantacuzène around the influential salons with the request that they should be as friendly as possible to Churchill. One of my Russian acquaintances spoke enthusiastically to Giers about Churchill '*qui parle avec l'éloquence d'un tribun*'. Despite some protests he was made a temporary member of the Yacht Club at the insistence of the Tsar's secretary Polovzov. It is definitely asserted that Lady Randolph brought with her a letter of introduction from the Princess of Wales to the Tsarina. On the 31st of last month the Churchills were commanded to a soirée at Gachina to which no ambassador was asked.

Besides Churchill, Polovzov is now piloting a distinguished Frenchman, Marquis Breteuil,[2] who was also at Gachina. After dinner Breteuil told the Tsarina very confidentially before two ladies, who immediately repeated it to me: '*Ah Madame, je suis si heureux, l'Empereur a semblé me donner raison quand je lui ai dit, qu'il ne devait pas s'allier avec la république pour que l'alliance de la Russie soit la récompense du rétablissement de la monarchie en France.*' The horror of some Francophils who were present at this statement of Breteuil's is said to have been very great. The Tsar, however, is almost alone in his antipathy against the Republic. Nearly all other Russians would at once ally themselves even

---

[1] On 5 January Bülow reported that Lord Randolph Churchill had assured Giers 'that his journey [to Russia] had no political character or purpose whatever.' (From the Foreign Ministry files.)

[2] Henri Charles Joseph le Tonelier, Marquis de Breteuil. French Deputy.

with the Radicals. Apart from the bond of their common hatred for us, the structure of Russian society is democratic; Communism is their ideal for the future, and hence they feel themselves attracted to Clemenceau and Floquet.[1] [...]

I hope you began the New Year in good health and spirits, may it be *felix faustumque* for us all. With best greetings and wishes from your sincerely devoted

Bernh. Bülow

248. Philipp zu Eulenburg to Holstein

Munich, 6 January 1888

My dear Baron,

I could not write to you sooner owing to the pressure of Court and social engagements and to the effects of a frightful cold.

I would have liked to have told you earlier that my efforts in regard to Prince Wilhelm and Herbert were not unsuccessful and that a talk between them produced the welcome result of an understanding about the matter in question.[2] Prince W. told me this news on my departure with such expressions of pleasure that I could not help realising how very upset he had been by the ill-feeling that had arisen. He came to Berlin from Potsdam with a basket full of chocolates for the children, had dinner served for me on a table in the royal apartment, and returned to Potsdam when I left at eight o'clock. I had written to ask him *not* to come—as indeed I always ask him not to advertise his friendship too much for fear it may hurt us both—but it was no use. It is not so easy to dissuade him from doing what he pleases—we will have our hands full because of that! His artlessness and disinterested friendliness give him a quite peculiarly fascinating charm, and he is one of those people who by their very nature arouse spontaneous sympathy. When he wears a crown he will awaken passions that will call into being a violent opposition by the sheer vigour of their expression. [...]

249. Heinrich VII Reuss to Holstein

Vienna, 9 January 1888

My dear Herr von Holstein,

Thanks for your letter of yesterday.

The Austrian General Staff officers are now saying that it was they who were clever. We advised them to get ready for war at an early date, to take measures to defend the frontier, etc. If they had fully

---

[1] Charles Floquet. French Radical Deputy; President of the Chamber, 1886–8; Prime Minister, April 1888–February 1889. As Prime Minister he combatted Boulangism and on 13 July 1888 he seriously wounded General Boulanger in a duel.

[2] On 28 November 1887 Prince Wilhelm was present at a meeting at which the founder of the anti-Semitic Christian Socialist Party and bitter opponent of the Social Democrats and Progressives, Court Chaplain Adolf von Stöcker, made a political speech. The Bismarck Press criticised Prince Wilhelm very sharply for allowing his name to be linked with Stöcker's. (See *Memoirs*, pp. 138–9; *Diaries*, pp. 362–3; *Aus 50 Jahren: Erinnerungen, Tagebücher und Briefe aus dem Nachlass des Fürsten Philipp zu Eulenburg-Hertefeld* (Berlin, 1923), p. 154.)

carried out what we expected of them, they would have provoked the Russians to war. And that would have been quite disastrous, because now we are telling them: you must first allow yourselves to be attacked on your own territory and only then will we come to your assistance.

This has all made for bad blood here—unjustifiably, you will tell me. That is true, but nevertheless these people had some small justification for believing that we would come to their support more quickly in a war with Russia. Kálnoky and Széchényi are behaving splendidly at this stage. They are trying to pour oil on troubled waters and are taking pains to restore confidence.

Old Albrecht is said to be very abusive. He is no longer here.

You are quite right *que nous avons été dans le vrai* in rousing these people to preparedness; they will still need it. Kaiser Franz J[oseph] thinks so too, by the way, as does Kálnoky.

The fact that the Italian troop-transports were not at once agreed to is due partly to our concealing the Silesian railways behind our neutrality. Nevertheless I regard the matter as settled because it will not be refused in the event of war.[1]

To our meeting on the 17th.

Your very devoted
H. VII Reuss
In haste!

250. Eberhard zu Solms to Holstein

Rome, 11 January 1888

My dear Herr von Holstein,

I cannot answer your extremely interesting letter of the 3rd of this month by one of equal value, but do not want to let the courier leave without for my part wishing you a Happy New Year. You will find anything that is worth knowing from Rome in my dispatches.

The paragraph in your letter, according to which Berlin seems to assume that Crispi is opposed to the participation of Austrian officers at the military talks in Berlin, induced me to follow up a report on this subject by an immediate telegram containing the information that Crispi considers that an understanding with Austria is also necessary on this point.[2] It appears from Baron Bruck's remarks that Austria entertains, or entertained, doubts about initiating military agreements with Italy. His efforts in this direction in Vienna have only produced the result that for the present he is to confine the subject of military collaboration merely to academic discussion. Major Engelbrecht says he has noticed (not from any remarks let fall by the Austrian Military Attaché) that

---

[1] The Italians offered to send a considerable number of their troops to the Rhine if France attacked Germany, provided that Austria would permit the use of the Brenner railway. When Reuss sought this permission on 7 January, Kálnoky postponed giving a definite answer. (*Grosse Politik*, vol. VI, nos. 1304, 1306, pp. 241–2, 244–6.)

[2] On 5 January Solms reported that Crispi had discussed 'academically' the question of Austro-Italian military co-operation with Bruck. Crispi wanted Austrian officers to participate in the Italo-German discussions. The dispatch did not reach Berlin until 9 January, two days after the telegram mentioned by Solms. (From the Foreign Ministry files.)

there is surprise in Vienna at Italo-German military negotiations without Austrian participation. I am nevertheless convinced that Berlin has kept Count Kálnoky informed about these negotiations, but that the Embassy in Rome has not been informed. Baron Bruck has not given me the slightest hint on this subject. Explaining the political situation, Baron Bruck drew the attention of his Military Attaché to the necessity of avoiding in his reports any derogatory remarks about Italian military conditions, so that Vienna would finally cease underrating too greatly the usefulness of Italian support. Colonel Forstner, who naturally does not know that Baron Bruck spoke to me of the matter, has ever since seized every opportunity of depicting the Italian Army to me in the most brilliant colours.

After the latest news of Russian military preparations—the Austrians say they know that another three Russian Army corps are to be sent into advance positions—His Highness [Bismarck] must have a desperately tough job of it with his peace endeavours. I know that Count Kálnoky learnt from Berlin that His Highness stands almost alone in this colossal task of maintaining peace, and that Count Moltke himself, like Waldersee, etc., is of the opinion that we should go to war. You will see from one of my dispatches today that Crispi secretly shares this desire.[1] There is no sign whatever in his case of distrust or even any passing fear. He hates Count Mouy.[2] May God preserve him at his post for a long time! His soirées make him a positive laughing-stock in society. One could not imagine anything more miserable. Üxküll, a diplomat of the old school, the long time friend of the German and Austrian Ambassadors, is the first to make fun of the Pan-Slavism of some of his subordinates and does not trouble himself much with politics. Although Baron Bruck and I are none the less fully aware of the necessity of keeping our eyes open, there has up to now been no reason for mistrust. [...]

Your sincerely devoted
Solms.

251. Heinrich VII Reuss to Holstein

Vienna, 21 January 1888

My dear Herr von Holstein,
Many thanks for your letter of 19 January.
Kálnoky spoke to me today in a resigned manner about Széchényi's reply; he could not expect anything else but had to write to Széchényi.[3]

[1] According to Solms' dispatch of 10 January Crispi had told him: 'I want peace and would like to preserve it, but I cannot deny that I am unable to see how Italy will unravel her problems with France in a peaceful manner. Our relations with France are growing worse and more insupportable every day, and they will not improve until we have had a good fight with France.' (From the Foreign Ministry files.)

[2] French Ambassador in Rome, 1886–8.

[3] Herbert von Bismarck wrote in a memorandum of 17 January: 'Count Széchényi today read to me the attached copy of Kálnoky's dispatch of 12 January. [*Grosse Politik*, vol. VI, no. 1192, pp. 79–81.] When I [...] expressed myself satisfied with the first part of the dispatch, Count Széchényi said: "Yes, but the heart of the matter comes at the end, where it speaks of finding a formula by which later on, if war seemed imminent, military agreements

I am convinced that he was forced to do so by the Kaiser, who is dreadfully afraid that he might possibly have to fight alone. Moreover Kálnoky continues to deplore the fact that we are not yet discussing any military measures for *the* eventuality. For [he] is firmly convinced that they will not fight without us. Since nowadays everything in a war depends on the first few days, we would lose the head start that would be so valuable for us both by discussions. He will not refer to the matter in future.

The soldiers now do not have the least idea of what they should do. Your surmise that militarily a period of marking-time will now begin will certainly prove correct. But in what way? Nobody seems clear about that.

Politically no change will be made despite the fact that there are many people who are inimical to us and who say that we would always leave Austria in the lurch. At all events the Kaiser and the soldiers show some annoyance; whether justified or not—*enfin*, it exists. If we were to try again to advise them to strengthen themselves militarily, they will think and say: you will not catch us a second time!

I have now instructed Deines (and do it myself) always to tell people in all possible detail about what *we* are doing to strengthen our position, which is anyway already much stronger than the position here, in the interests of peace. [...]

Your very devoted
H. VII Reuss

252. Heinrich VII Reuss to Holstein

Vienna, 28 January 1888

My dear Herr von Holstein,

The dispatch bag of the 24th was good; Dispatches Nos. 82[1] and 84[2] have had a stimulating effect here, especially on the Kaiser. Kálnoky, who during the whole of this ticklish business did not give up hope that in our own interests we would reach this conclusion,[3] has shown himself

could be concluded without derogating from the defensive character of our alliance." I told Széchényi I could not discuss this formula because at present there was no danger of a war of *aggression*.' (*Grosse Politik*, vol. VI, no. 1193, p. 82.)

Reuss concluded his official report of 21 January on his conversation with Kálnoky with the paragraph: 'I would like in this connection to remark with all deference that I do not think I deceive myself if I assume that Count Kálnoky was compelled by his very nervous Imperial master to pose a question which he was convinced in advance that we could not answer. He will drop any discussion of the matter and will continue to calm down soldiers here about the failure.' At the word 'failure', Bismarck commented: 'their blunder.' (From the Foreign Ministry files.)

[1] Published in part in *Grosse Politik*, vol. VI, no. 1197, pp. 86–7. The portion of the instruction that is not printed deals with Austrian operational plans in the event of war with Russia. The Austrian army was to take up a position not on the Carpathians but near Cracow, to maintain contact with the German Silesian Corps, and further was to have troops ready for an offensive against Odessa in conjunction with the Rumanian Army. (From the Foreign Ministry files.)

[2] *Grosse Politik*, vol. V, no. 1112, pp. 284–5. See also no. 1113, pp. 286–7.

[3] A paragraph in Dispatch No. 82 stated: 'If Russian preparations for war are pushed to such an extent that their offensive intentions become unquestionably obvious, we will in such a case mobilise so as to be ready to ward off the Russian attack on Austria; that will suffice to divert Russia *pro rata* from Austria.'

throughout the crisis as a sensible man. He told me that he now understands that the Chancellor had restrained our bellicose General Staff, but he wishes that this could have happened a little earlier so that the bewilderment that began to show itself here, especially among the soldiers, had never arisen. If I have done anything to promote this clarification it would be a great satisfaction for me. Here they have again begun to take courage. For a time they were under a wet blanket! I think they will now resume defense preparations here with greater enthusiasm.

I had already discussed the military part of 82 with Kálnoky when the warning-off telegram came.[1] He said that he could not believe that this exposé had been drawn up in agreement with Count Moltke. He readily agreed to my subsequent wish that he should regard our conversation as wholly academic. He will almost certainly not say anything about it to the General Staff in order to avoid confusing them anew.

Sturdza[2] has returned from Berlin delighted, only unfortunately he tells me that the Prince is complaining of sleeplessness and stomach trouble. That is not good news.

Széchényi wails about the endless rumours about his recall, particularly in our Press. Here too the impression created is unfortunate; denials have been issued, but Szögény says he cannot answer every article appearing in Berlin. He consoles him by saying that nobody thinks of replacing him. [...]

With sincere respect
H. VII Reuss

253. Bernhard von Bülow to Holstein

St Petersburg, 5 February 1888

Dear Holstein,

[...] Have you noticed that the *Warschawski Dnewnik* about a fortnight ago called upon the Poles finally to abandon once and for all the 'insensate hope' of a restoration of Poland with German help and instead to reach a reconciliation with Russia under the banner of Pan-Slavism? The moment was drawing near—Gurko's[3] paper continued—for the Poles to decide their 'life and death question definitely and for all time'. Russian overtures to the Poles are one of the most reliable symptoms of malice aforethought towards us. It may perhaps be difficult for the Austrians to induce the Poles to rise against the Russians, but an effective Russo-Polish reconciliation on the other hand belongs for a hundred reasons to the realm of utopias. One of these reasons is that a

---

[1] In a telegram of 26 January Reuss was instructed not to discuss the military portion of the dispatch with Kálnoky. If he had already done so he was to ask Kálnoky for the present not to inform the Austrian General Staff of it. (From the Foreign Ministry files.)

[2] On 21–2 January Sturdza visited Bismarck in Friedrichsruh and afterwards had talks in Berlin with Field Marshal Moltke, and others. Bismarck told Sturdza that a threat to the peace of Europe could only come from Russia. A strengthening of Rumania's defensive preparations would therefore contribute to the maintenance of peace. (From the Foreign Ministry files.)

[3] Joseph Gurko. Russian General. Governor-General of Warsaw, 1883–94.

Russia ruled in the spirit of Pobedonoszev and Delianov[1] cannot really be to the liking even of the Bulgarians and Serbs, let alone the Catholic West Slavs. As Ignatiev, Abaza,[2] etc., undoubtedly know, there exists an *'incompatibilité d'humeur absolue'* between the aspirations of the non-Russian Slavs and the extreme Caesaro-papism now ruling here. The latter can subjugate the *Bratuchkas*[3] by armed force—and that is what it is aiming at sooner or later—but its propaganda in peacetime will yield small returns. The articles in which Lemanski,[4] an intellectual leader of Pan-Slavism and the *Russkaia Myssl*,[5] frankly and penetratingly demonstrates this are among the most noteworthy pieces of journalism of the winter.

There exists, by the way, an antagonism between the economic and the political necessities of Russia similar to that between the system of domestic government and Russia's pretended international mission. A woman friend of mine recently told me : 'Nowadays not only agriculture throughout the whole of Russia, but also industry in the west and commerce in the south of the Empire, are sacrificed in the interests of the Moscow ultraprotectionists, and that solely because the latter have the ear of the autocrat. We must, in order to be able to breathe again economically, have a parliament in which every interest is represented, but that would result politically in anarchy and ruin. Hence we will never prosper.' If things continue to be managed here as they have been until now, I think it probable—as does more than one serious observer of Russian conditions—that despite Vishnegradski's jugglery with the budgets, Russia will proclaim national bankruptcy within three to four years. [...]

If at present much is being said here, and to some extent also in certain journals of the foreign Press, about the alleged great love of peace and quiet not only of the Tsar but also of the Russian people, it is to be taken very much *cum grano salis*. The Russian peasants, like peasants all over the world, with the possible exception of the Montenegrins, are certainly peace-loving. It is also true that they comprise nine-tenths of Russia's population. But although the influence of the *moujiks* upon the internal development of Russia is for many reasons great, and growing greater, they have nothing whatsoever to say in foreign policy, and like dumb sheep follow the impulses which emanate from 'society' (*Russkoie Obchtchestvo*). This society, which is more restless, conscienceless, and spoiling for a fight than any known to me in Europe, for the most part neither specially dreads war nor loves peace. Its ideal is not the age of Alexander II with its domestic reforms, but those epochs which were characterised by outward splendour, such as the reigns of Tsar Nicholas, Peter the Great, and, above all, the Tsarina Catherine II. Any improvement in the character and inclina-

[1] Rudolf Delianov. Russian Minister for Education, 1884–9.
[2] Alexander Abaza. Chief of the Economic Division of the Russian Imperial Council.
[3] 'Little brothers', an ironic term for the southern Slavs.
[4] Vladimir Ivanovich Lemanski. Russian writer and philologist. Professor of Slavic languages at the University of St Petersburg, 1865–90.
[5] A political and literary monthly review of outspokenly Pan-Slavist views.

tions of Russian society within the foreseeable future is in my opinion inconceivable. If we nevertheless leave the Russians in peace they will almost certainly, after the turn that things have taken in recent weeks, finally decide for the time being to wait and see. Whereas a powerful party was at work here in the late autumn in favour of commencing hostilities in the spring, the opinion at present is almost universal that peace is assured for several years. The Russians always jump from one extreme to the other. The present feeling amongst the majority of her fellow-countrymen was summed up by Countess Kreutz, when in the course of a confidential conversation she said: Russia at present does not want war but also does not really want friendly relations with Germany. She would rather suffer all sorts of evils—isolation, financial stringency, war, defeats—than return to the traditions of the last three Tsars. In this respect Alexander III will have to follow the voice of the people. Many diplomats here base their judgments of Russian conditions on the saying that the Russians always talk and never act. In the finest available portrayal of the Russian character, Goncharov's *Oblomov*, the hero of the novel is so involved in endless discussions that he does not contrive to get out of bed throughout the whole course of the first volume. But Russian history during the past two hundred years nevertheless proves that notwithstanding their Oblomov temperaments, the Russians have achieved much. I would take it as very probable that the Russians will make good use of the long respite that they now think they will have before the great decision, in order on the one hand to improve their military offensive power, and on the other to undermine our relations with other countries. Their activity on this latter count can be better observed in the seven or eight places that come into question than it can here. [...]

With best regards and wishes,
Your
Bernh. Bülow

254. Hugo von Radolinski to Holstein

[San Remo, 12 February 1888][1]

My dear friend,

The journey was terribly depressing, because Bergmann told me all the painful possibilities the future held in store for the unfortunate Prince. The Grand Duke and Grand Duchess of Baden met us at the station in Karlsruhe and were very sympathetic. When we arrived here everyone was deeply upset by the terrible events of the last few days and the operation.[2] I was very tired after the long journey and excused myself from dinner. The Crown Princess, however, summoned me at once today and greeted me *smiling as if nothing had happened.* I approached her in a very serious manner and let her see very clearly that I was not pleased by her cheerful behaviour. She told me that the opera-

---

[1] The letter was probably begun on this day. (See Ponsonby, *Letters of Empress Frederick*, p. 276.)

[2] On 9 February Dr Bramann had performed a tracheotomy.

tion was *not serious*, anyone could perform it, and any child undergo it. Shortness of breath had become somewhat pronounced and therefore the Crown Prince had undergone the operation. He would be completely cured in a short time, since it was now quite certain that it was not *cancer* but a simple perichondritis, which was not in any way malignant, and though it certainly called for much care, it was not fatal. A member of the family even said in front of Countess B[rühl] that the operation was not much worse than the removal of a corn. I am amazed by this optimistic attitude and can only explain it to myself by the fact that on the *preceding* evening, when their father *gasped* for breath like someone who was suffocating so that all who heard it were terrified, when their father could at any moment have suffocated, the young ladies, the son, and the future father-in-law[1] visited a tobacco manufacturer from Switzerland and danced until half past three in the morning. It makes a curious impression when one reads in the newspaper: the operation is arranged for tomorrow, and then immediately below: the Princesses were present at a ball at Herr Ormond's and danced until four o'clock. One is frankly revolted by such happenings. Dr Bramann was in a frightfully difficult situation. On Wednesday evening, without having been allowed to see the Crown Prince previously, he received the order to operate on Thursday. He was only allowed to examine the throat hastily just *before* the operation. He was told immediately afterwards to operate, as the doctors would not hold themselves responsible for the Crown Prince's life if Bramann did not immediately operate. Poor Bramann behaved magnificently. Under such conditions and battling with endless difficulties he summoned up his courage and performed the operation superbly, but all the time he had a revolver in his pocket, and had sworn to himself that if the operation miscarried he would at once put a bullet through his head. Bergmann told me afterwards that he was quite determined to do so. He really behaved superlatively well. He continually suffered insults for weeks on end—bad treatment *not only* from the other doctors, particularly Krause, but also from other people—because of his unselfishness and for the sake of the Crown Prince and the cause, for he knew that the moment must come when *he* would after all be called upon by the others to save the Crown Prince from suffocating. For weeks past he begged that the operation should be performed while it was still easy in order to avoid exposing the Crown Prince to the danger of suffocation and to spare him the agony of breathlessness, but he was openly jeered at and he was merely told that there was no danger. But when it could not go on any longer he was called upon and had to help. When, after it had been done, the poor invalid breathed freely and felt himself relatively at ease, Bramann got hardly a word of thanks. Everything that he does and advises is criticised and his achievement is represented as hardly worth mentioning. This disgusted those of us who stick together, and for that reason I regarded it as my duty to telegraph Count H. B[ismarck] to ask for a special mark of distinction for him. I am on tenter-hooks to see the sour looks when the

---

[1] The Grand Duke of Hesse. Prince Heinrich was engaged to his daughter.

promised decoration arrives. Yesterday I saw the Crown Prince for the first time. I got a bad shock. He looked twenty years older, his hair quite grey, his complexion pale, thin, noticeably thin, the temples and cheeks fallen in. He greeted me in a most friendly way with a smile that was so sad, wrote down for me that he had had dreadful nights. He looked so sad and at the same time so patient. I cannot tell you how terribly upset I was. The Crown Princess was there too, she beckoned me to leave after five minutes, and when I told her how thin I thought he looked, she said it was nothing, it was only because he did not have his false teeth in his mouth, it was only imagination, etc. What I felt you can imagine. Will she or can she not see how ill the poor man is? Two days ago he got up and on the first day spent some hours in an easy chair, yesterday he walked about in his room. Today as well. At the same time he suffers from tooth-ache and neuralgia, which also pulls him down. The cannula hurts him, he coughs frequently, and suffers from mucous secretion. All of which are inevitable accompaniments. Now for the doctors' opinions:

(1) Mackenzie maintains quite definitely: whereas earlier (in Nov.) cancer was a probability it is now only a remote possibility. All symptoms pointing to it have disappeared; he does not believe that cancer will still appear. Virchow[1] definitely stated that in the specimen he examined there was nothing suspicious. It is now only a perichondritis as a result of which the patient will in all probability die in three years, but he might also be completely cured. (The odds are seventy for the former and thirty for the latter supposition.) The odds in favour of a complete cure thus were still quite good, and he is very pleased with the Crown Prince's condition. The operation had been necessary, and now that it had been performed he finds the patient much better than during the past months. There is nothing to worry about in his appearance. By order and with the approval of the Crown Prince and Crown Princess, he had me send the *Staatsanzeiger* an account of the illness. This bulletin will reach Berlin one or two days before this letter; please read the *Staatsanzeiger*. It is such silly nonsense that it is almost incomprehensible. Nevertheless it gives a picture of Mackenzie's point of view. Bramann believes that what he says is full of medical contradictions.

(2) Bergmann and Bramann are convinced that it is cancer, and believe that everything Mack. says is nonsense, that he is deceiving himself and others for some dishonest reason. (Mackenzie now believes that Bergmann is not accustomed to treating throat diseases and sees cancer everywhere because he is only called in in cases of cancer to perform the operation.)

(3) Krause talks involved nonsense, swears it is cancer one day and the contrary the next.

(4) Schrader[2] does not know what to say, but when he is not overheard

[1] Dr Rudolf Virchow. Professor and Director of the Institute of Pathology in Berlin; Member of the Reichstag (Progressive Party), 1880–93. Virchow had been called upon to perform a microscopic examination of a specimen of the growth in the Crown Prince's throat.
[2] Surgeon to the Crown Prince.

by the Crown Princess he inclines to Bergmann's view. It is very easy to understand why the Crown Princess clutches at every straw, and continues to hope, but what I *cannot* understand is how she could suffer so unconcernedly the gasping and groaning of the unfortunate man, look on the operation—during which the Crown Prince could at any moment have collapsed and died—as child's play, and be capable of laughing and of sending the children, who are after all grown up, out dancing. It is a mystery to me.

Loë[1] and S[eckendorff] always have their heads together. The former invariably says something clever, and recently said: it was after all a matter of *absolute indifference whether the Crown Prince died in his own country or not*; he believes the Crown Princess would hold out to the last with colours flying. He always shares the Crown Princess' opinion, and you will see his benevolent influence in the matter of the return home. The doctor from Bolzano (Gries) is here now and has had long discussions with L. and Seck., probably everything is already arranged a for stay later on in Gries, which is a centre for splendid mountain tours and where S. can paint. Well, my dear friend. You now have a picture of our unhappy life and of all that is happening. The poor man is so dominated by her that he has no longer any will of his own. He suffers much and feels the iron hand within the velvet glove, but does not dare say anything. Our esteemed friend Minist[er] Friedberg will be interested to read this letter. Please give it to him *confidentially*, and also ask him, if he tells his friends about some things in it, not to mention the source. It would only make for bad blood, even more than has already been created, and ultimately would serve no purpose. Some things in it will perhaps interest Count H.B.

Yours affectionately
R.

Excuse this horrible scrawl. I am afraid you will hardly be able to read all of it. Moreover I ask forgiveness for the frightful style. But I am in a great hurry.

You can certainly communicate what is written above to some friends, including Mrs T.[2] and perhaps Lindau, naturally confidentially. I have one fear; if the decoration for Bramann, already promised by telegram, arrives the day after tomorrow, she will certainly seize this opportunity for inducing her husband to ask at once for a decoration for Mackenzie or Krause as counterpart to the decoration accorded to Br. It would be unjust, and I leave it to you to tell this to H.B., so that His Majesty may be approached in good time to stop it. The youngest son[3] is strongly influenced by the cousin[4] of our cry-baby[5] here. He (the honest sailor) was recently in Friedrichsruh, where the Chancellor put it to him that it was time his young master gave up a naval career in order first to serve in the army and then to be initiated into more serious state affairs. Now this did not suit the noble cousin of the noble S. at all.

---

[1] Walther, Baron von Loë. General commanding the 8th Army Corps; later Field Marshal.
[2] Mrs Julia Tyrrell.   [3] Prince Heinrich.   [4] Captain Albert von Seckendorff.
[5] Götz von Seckendorff.

He wants to keep the young man completely under his thumb in Kiel because he has made a comfortable nest for himself there and wants to lord it over him without any interference. An accident brought into my hands some sentences from a letter which he (S) wrote to the young man. I enclose these jottings, which have been copied down verbatim, for you in *absolute confidence*[1] and you will see from them how he criticises and sneaks on Caprivi, and how he acts contrary to the Chancellor's intentions (while seeming to agree with the Chancellor's views) in making the ingenuous suggestion that the Prince should stick firmly by the navy, and not go into the army, and that in Kiel, where a local administration is to be set up, he could after all also be employed in that. The notion of leaving Kiel does not please him at all. I suggest that you should communicate the enclosed document in *strict confidence* and in a suitable way to H.B. so that he can convince himself of the injurious influence S's cousin exercises over the young man. Prince H. told his father about this letter, and afterwards said to our friend that he was so pleased that his father would comply with his wishes, and he, after all, had the final decision in the matter. The Prince told me that he would never give up the navy. You can see from this how he does what S. says. Unfortunately the young man is very immature and has absolutely no judgment. He is still a child, who on the one hand realises the seriousness of the situation and of his father's illness, and on the other fools around with his sisters at balls. He can be influenced very easily. The enclosed letter from S. to P.H. is certainly complete nonsense. It reminds me of Loë's lengthy *exposés*, which he makes at every opportunity. Do you remember how you told me that Prince Heinrich was being stirred up against Cap[rivi]? Here we have the source.

The father's weak character allowed itself to be influenced by this silly letter of S's, and that sufficed to rouse him (the father) against Caprivi and also once more against the Chancellor. This last I do not know for certain of course, but I take it for granted. In all events the young man will be turned against His Highness because the latter will not consent to his, or better said, to S's plans. I still regard it as advisable that H.B. should be informed of this event, and possibly that he speaks to H.H. about it. Only I beseech H.B. most urgently *not* to name *me* as the source for the communication of the letter. [...]

Your faithful
Hugo. [...]

Postscript 15 February.
I have just received the telegram from the Chancellor and, acting as if I knew nothing of the matter, informed the Crown Princess, and sent it up in writing to His Imperial Highness. Her Imperial Highness was very sour about this act of grace,[2] and believes that the little operation did not merit a decoration. It was unfair to the others. Later the Crown Prince at her instigation wrote to me as follows: 'How hard for Krause, who has been with me at my request continuously since

---
[1] See Enclosure.   [2] The decoration for Bramann.

November. And Schrader? How painful too for Sir Mor. Mackenzie, particularly for Dr Hovell.[1] Once again an action of this kind has been taken without my being asked beforehand.' I at once replied that after all Bramann had saved his life and saved him from suffocation, whilst the others had up to now done nothing tangible.

If you consider it proper, please pass this on to Count H.B. in order to show how difficult the position of Bergmann and Bramann is here. The Crown Princess is completely enchanted with Krause and thinks him the best doctor and the most honourable man. Poor Crown Prince! Even at such moments he cannot judge for himself.

ENCLOSURE

Albert von Seckendorff to Prince Heinrich of Prussia

Copy

Secret 25 December 1887

After my visit to Friedrichsruh on 19 December, I have the impression that it could and should have served to throw a particular light upon the questions that so preoccupy Your Royal Highness.

(1) How the future of Your Royal Highness could be usefully mapped out in regard both to private and official life and

(2) What changes could be indicated as desirable in the present [...][2] of the national navy.

The Chancellor definitely expressed the opinion that with all due respect for the navy, the life of Your Royal Highness was too valuable to be exposed to the varying vicissitudes of that profession. The further exercise of naval duties was precluded not only on account of the personal danger involved, but because of the part to be filled by Your Royal Highness in the nation's life. It was the task of Your Royal Highness to establish a bridge between 'the present and the future' and at some future time to assist His Royal Highness Prince Wilhelm in the task of government. Your Royal Highness lacks legal and political knowledge, and a clear insight into military affairs, which are necessary requirements for Your Royal Highness. The Chancellor believes Your Royal Highness should read more of the great newspapers and follow political events. Your Royal Highness would be the most suitable person for important diplomatic missions. If possible you should be given command of a battalion on 1 January 1888. When I protested that at any rate a definite system must be followed, the Chancellor replied that a quick decision was the best. Later on, Your Royal Highness should work in a provincial administration or a Ministry. During the course of this exposition, I ventured to ask why the solution of the Brunswick problem had not at the time been allowed to serve as a step in the realisation of these statesmanlike hopes.

Although I am at heart in agreement with all this, I also believe that the political conception should not alone shape the future of Your Royal

[1] Dr Mark Hovell. English laryngologist; Assistant to Dr Mackenzie.
[2] One word illegible.

Highness, for there remains the necessity for military service and for military training. And further, the whole matter is bound up with the attainment of those intellectual heights of which Your Royal Highness is capable and intends to aspire. Political, military, and personal demands and restrictions must be weighed against each other in order that Your Royal Highness' personality may be developed so as to make of you the best servant of the State and the most prosperous head of an illustrious family. (!!!)

Just as Prince Bismarck sees the problem in the light of reasons of state, so must the military superiors of Your Royal Highness [...][1] the decisive opinion as to the ideal way to develop the general or the admiral in the person of Your Royal Highness.

The enclosed decision of the Head of the Admiralty,[2] however, from the outset subordinates the military to the political task, and therein lies the proof that the controversies that have occurred were not the result of professional considerations but were based on questions of principle. From the time of his first interview with Your Royal Highness, the Head of the Admiralty has taken the viewpoint which Prince Bismarck on 19 December very definitely indicated was his own, namely, that the navy was not a suitable profession for Your Royal Highness. General von Caprivi's remarks can be regarded as identical with the Chancellor's. As against that I was obliged, in accordance with the supreme commands of His Majesty the Kaiser and Your Royal Highness's instructions, to recognise as basis for the advice demanded of me the fact that Your Royal Highness would continue to serve in the navy. I have asked again and again that this principle should be brought up anew and decided upon unequivocally, because professional details are without consequence and cannot be discussed until the principle has been fixed and agreed upon.

At one time I advocated the regency in Brunswick. It was then said that Your Royal Highness was too good for Brunswick and that you could *not* be dispensed with for the navy and the state. Your Royal Highness felt a heavy load lifted from you when H.M's decision was taken, etc.

General von Caprivi summed up his decision by saying that a great personality could command an army without understanding anything at all about commanding a battalion. Hence service at the front could not be regarded as advantageous for Your Royal Highness.

The principal 'new ideas' can be easily carried out in Your Royal Highness' case because Your Royal Highness will be able to gain detailed information about the Civil Service and its operations from the administration that is to be established in Kiel. Up till now the navy alone has afforded Your Royal Highness satisfaction. To throw it overboard means the renunciation of skills which have not yet been tested in other ways. A combination of naval service and political duties can however fit one 'to help in the task of government in whatever capacity is demanded'.

Finally may I touch upon the second question discussed by the

[1] One word illegible.   [2] General von Caprivi.

Chancellor. It is the dearest wish of Prince Bismarck to regain General von Caprivi's superb abilities for the army. The fulfilment of this wish seems to be encountering difficulties on the part of Count Moltke, who has arranged for the assignment of more pliable material than General Caprivi personifies.

I could gain no support for the idea, which I mentioned casually, of entrusting the shortly to be created portfolio of the Navy Ministry to a civilian, for example to one of the shipowners belonging to the National Liberal Party. Sailors all over the world are well-known for holding steadfastly to traditional methods and to the ways of their profession. The creation of the German navy meant the fulfilment of a national wish. For that reason a mist of democracy settled round it which became appreciably denser under the command of a Prussian general with a liking for Parliament,[1] and under a second general,[2] who is engaged in the forcible extirpation of professional individuality, with the result that a vigorous flow of life blood through the main organs of the navy has for years past been prevented.

255. Philipp zu Eulenburg to Holstein

Munich, 20 February 1888

My dear Baron,

How grateful I am for your sympathetic interest in my fate![3] I really do not know how I have gained your friendship. I only know one thing —that I will *never* forget your interest in me, and that you can always definitely depend upon me whenever our paths may cross!

I wrote to Prince W[ilhelm] and am confident that he will put in a word in favour of my continuing in charge of affairs here. Whether that will do any good is another matter! He is so convinced of the importance of the rules of the service that the slightest remark on the part of my superior about inappropriateness would be enough to make him give up his efforts.

They have the strongest desire here to have me as Minister. Crailsheim[4] has expressed the greatest possible interest in it and is prepared to set *all* wheels in motion for that purpose.

I have asked him to exercise discretion. Such promotion is out of the question; efforts of this kind would only cause bad blood.

I will let my ship drift—if people wish me well, they will take care of me. I hate all *pro domo* activity.

---

[1] General Albrecht von Stosch.   [2] General von Caprivi.

[3] Count Werthern had been forced to give up his post as Minister in Munich to make room for Bismarck's son-in-law, Count Rantzau. Eulenburg believed this appointment would be a serious political mistake, for he did not think Rantzau would support the appointment of a Liberal government in Bavaria, which alone would check the growth of Roman Catholic influence in that country. It was Holstein's idea to secure the postponement of Rantzau's appointment until the autumn and to leave Eulenburg in charge of the Legation. By that time Prince Wilhelm would probably be Kaiser and things could then be arranged differently. (See Haller, *Eulenburg*, p. 38; *Diaries*, entry for 11 April 1888.)

[4] Christoph Krafft, Baron von Crailsheim. Bavarian Minister of the Royal Household and for Foreign Affairs from 1880.

The result of Werthern's brusque recall will be that the Regent will be annoyed. I sense a feeling of irritation in that quarter because he personally intervened in favour of W's staying on—now *he* is the cause of W's departure since he demanded the fateful dispatch.[1] He may also sense a 'want of confidence' in that W was recalled on account of the fulfilment of one of his wishes! Now that Lutz[2] has begun to make excuses, the whole business bears this interpretation. [...]

Your very devoted

P Eulenburg.

256. Hugo von Radolinski to Holstein

S[an] Remo, 28 February 1888

My dear Holstein,

Prof. Bergmann is leaving today for Karlsruhe to see Prince Wilhelm and will take these lines with him. I attach great importance to his seeing the Chancellor, and have already written to Count Herbert to ask him to secure an interview for Prof. Bergmann. Since, however, HB is away I address this request to you. Perhaps you will kindly arrange this and in doing so say that Their Imperial Highnesses would be pleased if the Prince would permit Bergmann to report to him on the Crown Prince's condition. It will certainly interest the Prince to learn from him what the prospects are for the future. Prof. Bergmann will call on you, and I would be grateful to you if you would receive him. He will tell you much that is of interest, especially about the strange illusions entertained by the lady and the way in which M[ackenzie] humbugs her.

I do not have any intention of leaving the Crown Prince *now* as you seem to think in your telegram of yesterday. If, however, I attach importance to his being transported to Germany while he is still capable of being transported, the reason is that some time ago he made me responsible for seeing that he would die in his own country. He also told Winterf[eld]. I had to promise him that if he were about to die, I would make arrangements that he died at home. Moreover I consider it undignified that the Crown Prince of the German Reich should die like a homeless wanderer in some hotel abroad. On account of the love shown for him in his own country, it would never be forgiven either him or *her* if he did not return home. Moreover climate has no influence on this disease. Furthermore it has already been definitely arranged that he should be in Potsdam in May. The only question is whether he must not return there sooner. S[eckendorff] and Mack[enzie] are alone in not wishing him to return; the former because he has a pleasanter time when travelling, in that he can meet more international adventurers; while in the case of Mack., because he knows very well that it will be all over with him when they are in Berlin. It will certainly not shorten the old

[1] The Prince Regent of Bavaria had asked Werthern to send a dispatch to Berlin saying that it was the hope of the Bavarian Government that he remain as Minister to Munich. The dispatch only hastened Werthern's recall, because Bismarck suspected he had inspired it himself. (*Diaries*, entry for 10 July 1886.)

[2] Johann, Baron von Lutz. Bavarian Minister-President, 1880–90.

man's life; for we know for a certainty that he longs for his son and wanted to come here himself. Incidentally, *I* can do nothing either for or against. Of course I shall stay here as long as I can be of any use. By the way I am of no use now. I have only been allowed to see the Crown Prince on two occasions for five minutes. I am staying on, however, because I will not leave the Crown Prince at this critical time. There is nothing to fear for the immediate future. Hence Bergmann is leaving and will return again in a fortnight.

Nobody here can get anything done, not even Bergmann and Bramann. *She* controls and decides everything, even changes what the doctors have ordered, and only trusts M[ackenzie] and Hovell, who keep on talking her into believing that the Germans do not understand anything about laryngology. It is scarcely credible, but she is still firmly convinced that he will yet get well, and that it is only the Germans who have inflicted such injury upon him during the last fortnight. If M. had operated, and if no other doctor had meanwhile made a mess of things, the patient would have been cured!!!! It makes one's blood boil when one hears these really criminal statements. I wish to God she were right, but unhappily, unhappily, it suffices to see the poor invalid to convince oneself that he has one foot in the grave, yet at the same time they say it is nothing, it is only a slight indisposition, just because he cannot go out into the open air. To be shut up for a fortnight was enough to make him look ill. S. chatters to everyone about how the Crown Prince is only temporarily indisposed and will soon be well again. It was childish to indulge in so many professions of sympathy when the illness was not in any way serious! Fool! [...]

Your faithful
Rad.

Can't you send me some political news? I am to see the Crown Prince soon and amuse him. It would interest him if I could tell him something that was of real interest.

257. Hugo von Radolinski to Holstein

S[an] Remo, 2 March 1888

My dear friend,

I can only now send you the two letters I wrote to you because Bergmann stayed on here and there has been no reliable opportunity of sending them till now.

Prince W[ilhelm] has just arrived, was welcomed affectionately by his father and coldly by his mother. He told me that he would stay here in order to compose the doctors' differences and to straighten out the cannula question. I am afraid that he will not achieve anything; father and mother are for Mack[enzie] and will not allow him to be attacked. The patient feels better today. He did not have a bad night, and Prince Wilh. thought his father was looking better than he had expected! They have all just left on a yachting trip. While they were away I visited the Crown Prince. Yesterday I too found him looking better than recently. But it was very distressing when he got a fit of coughing, because he choked a great deal and expectorated masses of bloody phlegm. Otherwise he ate well in my company—two cutlets, some rice, bread and butter and wine! with a good appetite. Thus I was easy in my mind for the moment. The final phase that Bergmann has been awaiting has now set in, and it must be used to get him home if they still want to. The doctors absolutely want him to be brought back because they cannot treat him from a distance for any length of time in the same way as if he were at home, and nothing can be obtained here that may be needed in a hurry. The doctors *absolutely* want him brought back. I *do not now interfere in this at all*, since you have advised me not to, and retain my freedom of action on all sides. I will accept no responsibility. Let the doctors alone decide and use their influence *with His Majesty* in due course.

How could you think that, in spite of all the unpleasantnesses, I should think of going away just now so long as any crisis is imminent or is to be expected? I do not think of any such thing, although I really *have nothing to do here* nor can I get anything done. There are many people here who are not to my liking, but both he and she are charming to me, and I certainly notice that she has the feeling that she needs me. For that reason she is very sweet to me. My chief endeavour is to dispel the acerbity between the doctors, and between the Crown Princess and the German doctors and her sons. But I am only successful to a small degree. I still believe, however, that I can say more to her and advise her more freely than anyone else. And that is quite a good thing. But I could not endure this perpetual shamming for long. I cannot approve of her attitude in the matter and cannot *rompre en visière* lest harm is done. I must therefore try to trim my sails. I hear to my deepest regret that Prince Wilh. is not particularly well-disposed towards Caprivi and does not like him. I attribute this to Capt. Seckendorff, who first roused Prince Heinrich against him, and then Prince Heinrich in his turn roused his brother against this first-rate man. You can thus see for yourself how injurious is Seckendorff's influence. The letter you received[1] will make this clear to you. A fool like Seck. in this way gains sufficient power to bring about events of vast purport. It is very very much to be regretted that such a capable man as Cap[rivi] should be ruined in the eyes of the future ruler by idle gossip. It would certainly be a good thing to bring this to the Chancellor's knowledge, or else you should tell H.B. so that he can tell his father. If only Caprivi could secure an important post while the Kaiser is still alive; later on it will be difficult.

What part is Alb[edyll] playing in the question of Prince Heinrich's employment? He is pressing for an answer from the Crown Prince to his letter about the employment of Prince Heinrich this year, and added in his telegram: the navy is becoming insistent. I therefore think that Alb. is also playing an anti-Chancellor role in the question of the transfer of Prince Heinrich to the army and his leaving the navy, and that he is

[1] See the enclosure to Radolinski's letter of 12 February 1888.

flattering Prince H while working to keep him with the navy. This must certainly be brought to the Chancellor's notice. There are a good many dangerous agitators and climbers about who are bad influences on the two Princes. The 'pious' general[1] should also be rendered harmless. At times the energy fails me for that sort of thing, and I would like to go away and never see them again. But calm yourself, dear friend. I will remain in the breach and will not give in as long as I can stand it. As I have already said, I have no intention for the present of leaving Their Imperial Highnesses, but my position is made difficult for me by some of the entourage. I repeat that both of *my* Highnesses are very nice and kind to me. Nevertheless there is nothing to be done. The doctors alone must come to an agreement among themselves. *I do not interfere in the matter of the homeward journey of the Crown Prince and will not exert any pressure in any direction.* My only pleasure here is to hear from you, so be so kind and compensate me for staying here by letting me hear from you often. Give me some political news that I can pass on so as to keep the poor man in touch with what is going on. Two words from you afford a clearer picture than a whole portfolio of dispatches.

The Crown Princess has herself told Bergmann that she would agree to the Crown Prince being taken back to Wiesbaden in three to four weeks, if by that time his condition had not improved. Now we will have to wait and see if she will do so. I think it would be a very good thing to give a hint to the Chancellor about the bad feeling against Caprivi on the part of the two Princes which Capt. Seck. has aroused. His influence over Prince H. is very harmful. *Adio*. Take some care of poor Julie[2] and Doudouce,[3] as you promised me. It is such a consolation to me to know that you are looking after my family.

Adio, my dear Holstein. God guard you. Write soon and forgive this scrawl.

Your H.

258. Holstein to Hugo von Radolinski[4]

5 March [1888]

Dear Rado,

Today I read extracts from your letter[5] to His Highness. For when Herbert went away H.H. ordered that political matters should be submitted to him by the officials dealing with them, and he particularly desired me to do so. As to the return home,[6] H.H. is of my opinion. His chief concern is that the Anglophils and the Democrats will raise a cry that it is murder. One must wait and see whether the Crown Princess *ex propriis* will bring up the question in regard to Wiesbaden.

I read him the section about Caprivi, and especially the conclusion where you say that much could be done more easily now than later. H.H. agrees in principle. As to Seck[endorff], though he does not question his maliciousness, he thinks he is a muddle-headed stupid fellow.

You want to have some political news. You know from the news-

---

[1] Waldersee. [2] Mrs Julia Tyrrell, Radolinski's sister-in-law.
[3] A nickname for Countess Lucy, Radolinski's daughter.
[4] From the Radolin Papers. [5] Of 2 March. See above. [6] Of the Crown Prince.

papers that the Russian *démarche*¹ has miscarried, in that Vienna, London and Rome have *unanimously* replied that they would only approach the Sublime Porte if they were told beforehand what proposals Russia would make in the event that Coburg² were removed or refused to do what he was told.

Up to now Russia has not made any reply but instead has gone ahead with her proposals in Constantinople in conjunction with Germany and France. Accordingly, the Porte will probably state in Sofia that it regards Coburg as illegal. But it is known already that the Bulgarians will only take notice of this communication in the event of its being made at the instance of *all* the Great Powers—which is not the case. The Russians will certainly now return to their system of bribery and insurrections—perhaps with greater success than hitherto, since the position of Coburg *s'en ressentira* because Uncle Aumale will no longer pay him the monthly allowance of 50,000 frs.³ [...]

Best wishes—which you will please pass on to Lyncker and Kessel.

Ever yours
Holstein.

259. Hugo von Radolinski to Holstein

S[an] Remo, 6 March 1888

My dear Holstein,

Things are very sad. Bergmann and Bramann are beside themselves over Mackenzie's treatment and his untrustworthiness. Since he would not believe in cancer and the consequences of the disease, Waldeyer⁴ was summoned to make an investigation. Mack. convinced himself of the presence of cancer. Nevertheless he allows the Crown Princess to entertain illusions and false hopes whilst he admits to the doctors and myself that the end is inevitable.

Bergmann presses *à tout prix* for a speedy return and has told Mackenzie that if it does not take place within four weeks, a return will be absolutely impossible. All this has been told to the Crown Princess by Bergmann. She has agreed to travel to Wiesbaden in the middle of April and reach Potsdam in May. Bergmann believes that it will not be possible to bring him further than Wiesbaden. He thinks that the patient will not live for more than six months. Mackenzie continually deceives and angers him. The cannula question still plays a part in it. Mack. believed that the bleeding would stop if his cannula were used, Bergmann gave way and the English cannula was used, but the bleeding did not lessen much. Berg. believes that the bleeding with the sputum will never stop because it comes from the decomposition of the tumour in the larynx. For some days past the patient is outwardly livelier and

---

¹ On 15 February, after previous consultation with Germany, Russia proposed to the Powers that a joint declaration should be handed to the Porte stating that the rule of Prince Ferdinand in Bulgaria conflicted with the terms of the Treaty of Berlin. (From the Foreign Ministry files.)

² Ferdinand of Saxe-Coburg-Gotha was elected Prince of Bulgaria by the Sobranje on 4 July 1887. His election was not recognised by any of the Powers.

³ The Duc d'Aumale was the fourth son of King Louis Philippe of France and the brother of Prince Ferdinand's mother.

⁴ Dr Wilhelm Waldeyer. Pathologist.

stronger and better—ever since he has been in the *open air*. He spends hours on the balcony and today he walked for the first time in the garden. The seeming improvement that Bergmann expected has now set in, but it will not last long, and then his condition will rapidly worsen. Although the Crown Princess has heard from all sides that cancer has been diagnosed, and that Waldeyer, whom Mackenzie recognises as an authority, also pronounces it to be cancer, she nevertheless obstinately maintains that it is all nonsense, that he will recover, and that he, Mackenzie, will prolong his life by all sorts of devices, etc. She is very optimistic and gay. God grant that she may be right.

I now see the Crown Prince daily for long periods and read to him. He is in good spirits and pleased to be going home. Bergmann asserts that cancer lasts longer in the North than in the South, and therefore wishes, in order to prolong the Crown Prince's life, that he should soon be taken northwards. The Crown Princess told me recently that she had received hints that the Government intended to introduce a Regency Law and that it was being drafted. I calmed her about this, but at the same time said that if a change of rules came about it would be impossible in these difficult times to rule from abroad without giving full powers to somebody (Prince Wilh.) in the country. The German Kaiser was certainly not like the Grand Duke of Hesse, who could live here and govern his country from here. She appeared to understand this. She thought that he should not abdicate under any conditions, and that if a Regency Law were passed without the Crown Prince's consent, then she and he would appeal to the nation in order to preserve their rights. She wanted me to write this to the Chancellor. Obviously I am not going to. But I would be glad if you would send me an official letter from the Foreign Ministry, if possible signed by the Chancellor or Herbert, which says what will actually happen about the Regency question if the Crown Prince succeeded to the Crown when he is abroad. She expects a definite statement about this from an authoritative source. She will submit it to the Crown Prince. Prince Wilhelm was very nice to his father, but the Crown Princess fumes over his behaviour and says that he acts as if he were already Kaiser. I must say that while here he was very nice in every respect.

Now that the doctors have *outwardly* composed their differences, and Bergmann has put upon Mackenzie the full responsibility for further treatment (which he did not really want to assume), the long bulletin that will appear today in the *Staatsanzeiger* was sent off, and Bergmann will leave tomorrow. Please arrange that *Bergmann is received by the Chancellor*. He will give him some *highly interesting* information that I cannot set down in writing. He is quite shocked about everything and leaves full of disgust. I like him very much and I think that his behaviour here was dignified and upright. His position was not easy. [...]

The Crown Princess has arranged to leave on 15 April for Wiesbaden, to stay there until 15 May, and then to celebrate Prince Heinrich's wedding in Potsdam.[1]

---

[1] The wedding of Prince Heinrich and Princess Irene of Hesse took place on 24 May 1888.

But if his condition gets worse, Bergmann will return here, and in that case the journey to Wiesbaden will take place *earlier*, possibly at the *beginning of April*.

God preserve you.

Your faithful
Hugo [...]

260. Philipp zu Eulenburg to Holstein

Munich, 17 March 1888

My dear Baron,

I have refrained from writing during the recent eventful days in order not to tire you.[1] W[erthern] received his *dimissoriale* on the 11th, with the instruction to present it whenever he saw fit. He cannot therefore possibly delay longer than after Easter. I do not believe that a new Minister will be appointed immediately because W. draws his salary until 1 July, and we are hardly generous enough to pay twice over. The feeling here about R[antzau] is *wholly* adverse. Princess Ludwig told a woman friend that this appointment would be painful not only for her and the Prince but for the entire House. 'We do not want this bit of Bismarck.' If the noble lady only suspected that possibly this 'bit of Bismarck', through partisanship against the present Ministry, could fulfil black[2] desires, she would not indulge in such harsh expressions. The Princess followed up this outburst with the remark that *I* alone would be welcome here.

Despite all this I look on my candidature as a mirage—unless Crown Prince Wilhelm acts forcibly as Kaiser. He is fully convinced of my usefulness in Bavaria. Nevertheless he will always listen at the decisive moment to the Prince and Herbert—which is only what we must fervently wish for! I think that it is indicated that for the present the matter should be postponed. I do not really know how far I can interest my cousin Kessel in this idea? And my cousin August E[ulenburg]? I too think it not impossible that R[antzau] is now exerting considerable pressure in the matter. [...]

With best wishes and thanks
In most sincere attachment
Ever yours
P Eulenburg

261. Heinrich VII Reuss to Holstein

Vienna, 5 April 1888

My dear Herr von Holstein,

I have always been afraid that this bomb would explode.[3]

---

[1] Kaiser Wilhelm I had died on 9 March and was succeeded by his son, Kaiser Friedrich III, who died on 15 June.

[2] A punning reference to the clerical influence in Bavarian politics.

[3] On 4 April Bismarck telegraphed: 'H.M. the Kaiser told me on the 31st of last month that Prince Alexander of Battenberg was expected at Charlottenburg on the 2nd of this month. At my request the visit has been forbidden by telegram; whether it has been definitely prevented I do not know. I have offered my resignation in case it takes place. Please report

Yesterday evening I talked for a long time with Kálnoky about the Chancellor's telegram.

He was at first very taken aback and could not understand the affair because he remembered previous statements by the Prince which indicated that as soon as Battenberg as a *private individual* wanted to marry the Princess he would regard it as a poor match but could have nothing politically against it; it then became a family affair.

The possibility that the Prince could resign *now* seemed to him too improbable and so dangerous for the whole European situation that he did not seem to believe in the seriousness of the threat. He thought that it was certainly consistent if the Prince, in accord with his earlier *opposition to* this project, threatened to resign. On the other hand he could not convince himself that the Battenbergiad was worth the taking of such a fateful decision. Prince Alexander's position in Bulgaria was overestimated; his return there was *only* possible if it came to war with Russia. He would then perhaps have a chance of being called back by the Bulgarians to lead them against Russia. At present and for so long as there was no war, Battenberg signified nothing and could not even be regarded as a pretender.

For these reasons, Kálnoky said, he could not suppose that the visit to Charl[ottenburg] and its possible results could cause the Russians to arrive at the conviction that our policy had altered.

Nevertheless he was unable to contradict when I pointed out that from my knowledge of the character and obstinacy of the Tsar this affair might easily become a source of suspicion in that quarter; and despite everything he was obliged to acknowledge the political consequences drawn by His Highness in the opinion the Prince requested of him.

Kálnoky seemed to be searching for the reason why his opinion had been requested: did the Prince wish to have his support for the views which he had expressed to me, or on the contrary was he looking for reasons that would make it easier for him to climb down? He is not clear about this. Hence there is no other course open to him except to say what he genuinely thinks. He told me that he greatly desires to fall in with what would be right in the Chancellor's eyes.

I have endeavoured to point out that one should not so much try to interpret the Prince's words, but that one should deal with the matter *just* as it was presented to us.

He deeply deplores this friction and hopes that, since time will have been gained by the postponement of the visit, the Prince will still find a way to solve this complicated affair. Our Kaiser could not exist without the strong arm of his Chancellor, who would be our sole salvation in the difficult situation in which we find ourselves.

by telegram whether you and Herr von Kálnoky share my view that this visit, which I suspect has been inspired by the Queen of England, would be regarded in Russia as an anti-Russian demonstration and an alteration in the policy we have hitherto pursued. This would be the effect here upon public opinion.' (From the Foreign Ministry files. A similar telegram was sent to St Petersburg. *Grosse Politik*, vol. VI, no. 1330, pp. 281–2.)

I have just talked the matter over again with Kálnoky. He repeated to me that it is still not clear to him whither the Prince was steering with such vigour. He has the feeling that the Chancellor is trying to bring about a crisis that would result in the disappearance of Battenberg from the Bulgarian scene once and for all. If this were successful, then there would be no need to fear Russia's ill-feeling with its undesirable consequences.

The reasons advanced to Salisbury seemed plausible to him and he himself had reached a similar conclusion.[1] Moreover he could understand that the Prince would prefer to see the whole affair dropped, if only on account of the Crown Prince.

A private letter from Berlin, which was not addressed to Kálnoky but was communicated to him and whose writer is unknown to me, discusses the whole affair and says: if Battenberg realises his wishes, it would only be a brief ray of hope in his life and he would soon vanish again.

With sincere respect
H. VII Reuss

262. Chlodwig zu Hohenlohe to Holstein

Strasbourg, 14 April 1888

My dear Baron,

I see in the *Berliner Tageblatt* and in other newspapers that Hatzfeldt and I have allegedly been sounded in connection with the possible succession to Prince Bismarck.[2] I cannot refrain from telling you that no such enquiry has been addressed to me. Obviously I would have replied to it in the negative.

With friendly greetings,
your most devoted
CHohenlohe.

263. Heinrich VII Reuss to Holstein

Vienna, 15 April 1888

My dear Herr von Holstein,

Many thanks for writing to me despite your indisposition. I hope that you are now quite well again. Your lines were of much value to me at a time when one is virtually reduced to wretched newspaper gossip. I now again have hopes that the Prince will stay on. I completely understand his attitude; either everything or nothing. I am only afraid that this unpleasant wrangling will use up his strength, which we so greatly need.

I have not noticed in any quarter that people here think that the Crown Prince[3] has again become completely Russophil. Certainly this is not the case in influential circles. He has made many friends here

---

[1] Bismarck feared that Queen Victoria was promoting the Battenberg marriage. He therefore instructed Hatzfeldt on 5 April to let Salisbury know that this marriage would compel Germany to adopt a more friendly attitude towards Russia. (See *Grosse Politik*, vol. VI, no. 1333, p. 289.) A similarly worded telegram was dispatched on the same day to Reuss with the instruction to discuss the matter with Kálnoky. (From the Foreign Ministry files.)

[2] See Rogge, *Holstein und Hohenlohe*, pp. 311–12.

[3] The future Wilhelm II.

during his frequent hunting-trips and the Kaiser likes him very much.
With best regards
Your most devoted
H. VII Reuss

264. Paul von Hatzfeldt to Holstein

London, 15 April 1888

Dear Holstein,

To my not inconsiderable astonishment, I find even in the political survey of the *Post* of the 15th the absurd report that, among other people, I too have been 'sounded' regarding the successorship to the Chancellor.

The thing is so absurd that I would be afraid of making myself ridiculous if I were to deny it in some official or semi-official way. For the same reason I abandoned my first idea of writing about it to Count H. Bismarck.

Since, however, there are perhaps people who have an interest in disseminating such lies, I ask you as an old friend to counter this rumour wherever you meet it with the most definite denial. I have not been sounded by *anyone*, and from *no* quarter, and, moreover, have *not* heard or received a *single word* about the alleged crisis except from the Foreign Ministry through official channels.

Nobody desires more than I that the Chancellor should remain permanently at the head of affairs, and this I have always said at every opportunity. I think I can pride myself that the Prince himself is in no doubt about this, and that he has not forgotten how I worked to the best of my abilities through three long years in Berlin towards this end. The Prince expressly recognised this when I took leave of him at that time and expressed his regret at losing my services, especially in this connection, because of my transfer.

The calumny in question could however find credence in other circles, and it cannot be a matter of indifference to me to be rendered suspect in this manner. You would therefore do me a service for which I shall be very grateful if you would most definitely state everywhere that you think suitable that the whole matter is a complete invention.

With best regards,
Your sincerely devoted
P Hatzfeldt.

265. Philipp zu Eulenburg to Holstein

Munich, 16 April 1888

My dear Baron,

You will be wondering why I did not answer your letter before today.[1]

---

[1] Holstein had written to Eulenburg on 12 April that Crown Prince Wilhelm had informed Herbert von Bismarck that he wanted Eulenburg to be left in Munich as Minister *ad interim*, and that later on he was to be given the post on a permanent basis. (Haller, *Eulenburg*, p. 38.)

I had influenza accompanied by headaches that completely prevented me from working. You can perhaps imagine with what feelings I read your letter—feelings that were heightened when the next post brought me a letter from the Crown Prince. The Prince has for some time past poured out his heart to me even more than formerly, in long letters that are all the more valuable because it is his habit to write very briefly. He feels *how* devoted I am to him, and I am not astonished that he wants to give me exceptional proofs of his friendship. You can also imagine how much this curious turn of events affected me, coming as it did after I had already received a letter from Rantzau in which he informed me of his appointment.[1]

I was in the painful position of having to observe the displeasure with regard to R's contemplated appointment as Minister which was far greater than I had expected and about which I could not report because it would only have been looked upon as a piece of work *pro domo*. I take it for granted that the general desire to retain *me* here will also have come to the ears of the Foreign Ministry and that I will have been regarded as the instigator of this agitation.

When under the pressure of the Chancellor crisis I received the telegraphic instruction to raise the question here of R's appointment, I thought the battle was lost and in the interests of the Service did all I could to lessen the ill-feeling about R. After he had spoken with the Regent, Crailsheim wrote me a letter of consent—but he enclosed a private postscript on a separate sheet. This ran: H.R.H. the Prince Regent expressed to me his *liveliest* regret that he was not receiving *you* as Minister.

It was not un-interesting for me to have the royal opinion in writing.

I cannot tell how things will now develop. Much depends on how long the Kaiser will live. I doubt if the Crown Prince will give up his ideas. It is not in his nature. But I am in a painfully difficult position and ask *you*, who have hitherto guided me in such a friendly fashion that I cannot think of it without feeling the *deepest* and *most sincere* gratitude, to continue to give me hints and tips!

I am in the *greatest* anxiety lest I should forfeit Herbert's friendship and the Chancellor's goodwill. Even though the Crown Prince alone is the driving force, I would still be irretrievably branded as a thoroughly infamous, intriguing and ruthless scoundrel. What will happen about R. once he is appointed *here*? I am completely in the dark about the matter because he will not *allow* himself to be influenced. Do you believe that the Bismarcks will be completely implacable?

They would in that case attack me officially in order if possible to gain a hold over the Crown Prince—and that too will not be exactly pleasant!

The political outlook here is beyond description! If the situation in Berlin continues this way much longer we shall have to start building the German Reich all over again.

In the next few days I shall be writing a political letter to Herbert.

[1] As Prussian Minister in Munich.

If he does not show it to you, please let me know. I will then send you a copy.

The Ultramontanes are working feverishly, and the Lutz Ministry has become an *absolute* necessity for us.

Every spark of sympathy for the Kaiser is extinguished!

With best regards and the most heartfelt thanks

Ever your faithful

P Eulenburg.

I could refer to the Crown Prince's letter when writing to Herbert asking him not to look for *me* behind the scenes. At the funeral[1] the Bavarian Princes exerted themselves in my favour.

266. Eberhard zu Solms to Holstein

Rome, 29 May 1888

My dear Herr von Holstein,

Your interesting letter of the 17th of this month leads me to indulge in personal considerations of politics, not normally a habit of mine.

It surprised me that you, who were of the opinion that time was running against us and in favour of our enemies, should have been opposed to the gas-tap experiment[2] (excellent simile). If reasons of higher policy were to require it, I would look upon the matter thus:

As a result of Russia's push towards the East and the uncertainty of France, it is improbable that peace can be maintained in the long run.

The mere passage of time will gradually endanger the bonds of our alliances.

An outbreak of war during the reign of the peace-loving Kaiser Friedrich would make it easier for us to fix the guilt upon the enemy and exonerate the successor, who would otherwise be held responsible for everything if the war broke out during his reign.

Up to this point the matter seems clear to me. I would, however, prefer either to have the boiler explode or to have temporary quiet; I don't like the gas-tap experiment; it is too *mesquin* to provoke a France that is preparing for the Exhibition and very anxious for peace, to war. We would only be doing Boulanger's work for him by taking a decisive step at the present moment that would provoke a war. If things went against us, he would carry along with him the parties that are at present still opposing him, whereas with a little patience there is the possibility that he might be forced to a *coup de tête* and that through this a revolution, perhaps a *pronunciamento*, might be set in motion. We would only bring odium on ourselves by pin-pricks that do not really achieve anything; furthermore, in order to have everybody on our side in a major war, we must above all be unquestionably in the right.

[1] Of Kaiser Wilhelm I.

[2] Holstein used this same metaphor in his *Memoirs,* p. 40, in discussing the outbreak of war in 1870: 'Bismarck handled the Hohenzollern candidature rather as one waves a lighted match over a gas tap to see whether it is turned on.'

In my humble opinion, I would favour sitting still until the moment came for being completely 'brutal'.

Here they are on the whole in complete agreement with the measures taken in Alsace-Lorraine.[1] It is the general opinion that it is quite a good thing once in a while to show one's teeth to the French, and some future action against Russia would also be found understandable. I thank God in such moments that I am only a tool in the hands of a master who from experience knows best what is to be done and when. [...]

Farewell. With best regards and thanks

Yours very sincerely
Solms

267. Eduard von Liebenau to Holstein

Potsdam, 1 June 1888

My dear benefactor!

[...] The pre-arranged interview between mother and son[2] took place today on the waters of the Havel. The high-born lady does not appear to have been very skilful. What she said was virtually the literal repetition of a letter that she had sent to her son many years ago and which at that time had already met with a cold reception. Both were in agreement that discord was being sown between them; only each sought the villain in the other's camp. The extremely detailed report of the discussion was of special interest to me in so far as it strengthened my conviction that the son will never allow himself to be carried away into extreme actions, and because I have found out what notions about the present domestic policy and its consequences are being instilled in the young man from a well-known quarter. More by word of mouth about this! Although this first approach has therefore produced few results, I still see one good result from it in the fact that at least for the time being there will be more frequent personal intercourse. Thus, for example, the son will today show his mother the new officers' mess which he has had built for the Guard-Hussars. Mutual attentions like this will at any rate cause the trouble-makers to become more cautious. I would have liked to have reported to Rado[lin][3] personally and asked him to pass on my impressions to you. But unfortunately our meeting was prevented because our telegrams crossed. Nothing is lost, however, because the Crown Prince is leaving this evening for Prussia and will have time to think over all that we were able to tell him. I am returning at the same time as he, and will call on you immediately after my return.

Your truly devoted
L.

---

[1] A Ministerial Order of 22 May 1888 directed that all foreigners crossing the French frontier into Alsace-Lorraine must have a passport bearing a visa from the German Embassy in Paris.

[2] Kaiserin Friedrich and Crown Prince Wilhelm.

[3] During the reign of Kaiser Friedrich III, Count Hugo von Radolinski was created Prince von Radolin-Radolinski.

268. Friedrich von Pourtalès[1] to Holstein

St Petersburg, 23 June 1888

My dear *Herr Geheimrat*,

Although I have only a few minutes until the courier leaves, I would like to use them to express my heartfelt thanks for your friendly lines (meanwhile burnt in accordance with your instructions) which reached me by the latest dispatch-bag.

The inimical attitude towards Austria is becoming increasingly accentuated here. In my humble opinion, the people here are at the moment basing their calculations increasingly on the hope that they will be able to settle with Austria *alone*. Hence the constant efforts to ascribe to Austria the role of disturber of the peace and, if possible, of aggressor, something that was again particularly noticeable in discussions of the Delegations' Sessions.

If at present the notion of a conflict with us is receding further into the background, the reason is that on the one hand they do not immediately want to drive the young Kaiser[2] too far into the arms of Austria, while on the other they do not have the same sanguine hopes about co-operation with France that they had about a year ago. France's suitability as an ally is now being seriously questioned because the latest developments in her internal situation give little cause for confidence.

In the accession of Wilhelm II they see 'the Bismarck sun rising again', and for this reason alone this event is hailed with mixed feelings. Since strict instructions have been given from above, the Press is exceedingly cautious in commenting on the accession. Unbelievable though it may sound, society up to the last moment seriously thought we were deliberately exaggerating Kaiser Friedrich's illness because we *wished* his early death.

Forgive me if I break off here. You will undoubtedly see the detailed letter I have written to the State Secretary.[3] With the request for indulgence for these hasty lines, I remain in sincere grateful devotion

Your obedient

F. Pourtalès

269. Friedrich von Pourtalès to Holstein

St Petersburg, 9 July 1888

My dear *Herr Geheimer Rat*,

[...] Our Kaiser's proposed journey has steadily become *le secret de la comédie* here, even though it is still being treated with some discretion in official quarters. I do not think that the journey will fail to produce the intended effect, for the Russians cannot but recognise in this visit a

---

[1] Friedrich, Count von Pourtalès. Temporary Assistant in the Foreign Ministry, 1886–8; First Secretary at the Embassy in St Petersburg, 1888–90; *Vortragender Rat* in the Foreign Ministry, 1890–9; Minister at The Hague, 1899–1902; Prussian Minister in Munich, 1903–7; Ambassador in St Petersburg, 1907–14.

[2] Wilhelm II. Kaiser Friedrich III had died on 15 June.

[3] Not found in the Foreign Ministry files.

clear proof of our sovereign's love of peace, as well as of the Kaiser's desire for his own part to do everything to cultivate friendly relations with Russia.

I share the opinion that the impression made by the visit will endure for some months; but it does not seem likely to me that it will exercise a more lasting influence over our relationship with the Empire of the Tsars. Moreover the opinion is even now too clearly visible that we need the Russians too much to spoil our relations with them permanently, and that for this reason we are 'running after' them. This notion may for the moment do no harm, but there certainly cannot be any doubt that the agitation will start again all the more furiously the moment they convince themselves of the incorrectness of this assumption. [...]

Your most obedient and gratefully devoted
F. Pourtalès

270. Alfred von Waldersee to Holstein

Berlin, 11 July 1888

My dear Baron,

Since No. 76[1] does not always know what No. 77[2] is up to, I am reporting to you confidentially that yesterday I polished off two bottles of Grünhäuser with His Highness the Chancellor, and that we drank a toast that the Devil take all our enemies.[3]

Although we took nearly one and three quarters hours over this performance, you must kindly remember in making any criticisms that at our age most achievements take longer than in the years of our stormy youth.

What would you say if Lindau were to publish somewhere or other an account of my visit to 77? I think it would put an end to certain newspaper gossip that has been going on now for months.[4]

I am convinced that you will be relieved to note that there is no longer any real foundation for such gossip, and I will sincerely try to avoid supplying any fresh material for it.

If at all possible, I will still come along in the next few days to bid you farewell.

As ever your sincerely devoted

A. Waldersee.

271. Alfred von Kiderlen-Wächter to Holstein

Yacht *Hohenzollern*,[5] 16 July 1888

My dear Herr von Holstein,

Don't think that you on your mountains are alone in enjoying yourself

[1] Wilhelmstrasse 76. The Foreign Ministry.
[2] Wilhelmstrasse 77. The Imperial Chancellery.
[3] See Waldersee, *Denkwürdigkeiten*, vol. I, pp. 412–13.
[4] Waldersee refers to rumours about his own pretensions to the Chancellorship.
[5] In March 1888 Kiderlen was recalled from Constantinople to take charge of Balkan and Near Eastern Affairs in the Foreign Ministry; during the summer of 1888 he accompanied the Kaiser on his political journeys as Foreign Ministry representative. It was in this capacity that he was now accompanying the Kaiser to St Petersburg.

and in filling your lungs with fresh air. Since yesterday afternoon we too have had the most magnificent weather with sunshine and, *ce qui es plus*, no wind. On Saturday evening, throughout the night of Saturday-Sunday, and yesterday (Sunday) morning it blew a bit. So far as I know, it was General Wittich[1] who opened the fish-feeding session. His Majesty's salon was fitted out in the daytime as a writing-room for himself and for His Excellency.[2] The first pangs of sickness unfortunately overcame the General precisely in this room and he quickly opened the window. Happily his cargo went out, but simultaneously a huge wave came in and flooded the newly furnished apartment. When the window was again found open in the evening, and water was pouring in, Prince H[einrich], who is very much the ship's captain, was not very pleasant to Gen. W., and when the General said that he was not responsible the Prince said curtly that in that case he would be grateful to him if he would also ask the gentlemen in his suite to be careful how they handled royal property!

The second person who paid tribute to the sea and could not appear at breakfast on Sunday morning was H.M. himself. His suite seemed to regard this with a satisfaction that could not be wholly concealed; 'If he were never sea-sick,' one of them said to me, 'we would always be on the water.' But it did no good, because when the vomiting (can this word be used with regard to such a lofty personage?) was over, someone tested the ground with the remark that this voyage was all the more interesting because one wouldn't soon again take part in such a thing.

'I shall travel this way each autumn,' replied H.M. 'and I shall take many more ships along.' The bit of rolling did not bother H.E. and myself.

If the visit itself can be linked with the Speech from the Throne in the Reichstag, in which mention was made of cultivating the friendship of the Russian Tsar, Seckendorff[3] harks back to the remark in the Prussian Speech from the Throne in which reference was made to the Prussian tradition of thrift. The congregation is already grumbling because they only get thin white wine instead of sherry, tea instead of beer in the evening, and pigeons instead of capons. However, I must confess that after dinner I reject the imperial 'Holländer' and set a light to my own tobacco.

Nobody here has any luck with 'reports', which H.M. avoids as far as possible; he only wants to amuse himself.

The entry into Kiel was very fine and a great success, the weather too had become 'serene'. The trip by boat through the harbour with its countless beflagged ships, sailors manning the yards (which is a very pretty sight), and the tremendous cannonade (ten guns fired by each of thirty-three ships) made a fine spectacle. Afterwards there was the naval review—first the ten ships escorting us sailed past us in line, astern, with bands playing and the crews giving three cheers; then came fourteen torpedo-boats at high speed in close formation in two wedge-

---

[1] Hans Heinrich von Wittich. Adjutant-General to Kaiser Wilhelm II.
[2] Herbert von Bismarck.   [3] Captain Albert von Seckendorff.

shaped flotillas. Finally we sailed out into the bay, let the torpedo-boats go by us again one by one, placed ourselves at the *tête*, and then sailed on in the formation that we have maintained up till now:

Hohenzollern

(*Kaiser*) capital ship	(*Baden*) Flagship
(*Friedrich d. Gr.*) capital ship	(*Bayern*) capital ship
(*Moltke*) Training ship	(*Blitz*) Sloop
(*Adalbert*) Training ship	(*Stein*) Training ship
	(*Zieten*) Sloop
	(*Gneisenau*) Training ship

Yesterday we let the ships pass in review, their bands playing after Prince H. had previously held a religious service aboard! Fleet manoeuvres are to be held today; arrival St Petersburg on the 19th, in Cop[enhagen] between the 27th and 29th; when we arrive in Sto[ckholm] I do not know.

Communication by sloop was impossible the first day; so she leaves today for the first time with dispatches, after having yesterday brought ashore the body of a sailor, who fell to his death on board one of the other ships.

We always take our meals at H.M.'s table; up to now the chief subjects of conversation have been shitting, vomiting, pissing, fucking; pardon me for hurting your ear with these harsh words, but I cannot choose any others if I am to give you a true picture.

Everything is very free and easy on board, one can go everywhere, smoke anywhere. But only in the morning is the dress really comfortable; we are in uniform throughout the day; fortunately I brought a greatcoat with me and with that it is really a quite comfortable attire.

Excuse the confused nature of this letter; but I wanted to give you at least a small idea of the situation; nothing interesting has happened.

Ever with sincere respect
Your most obediently devoted
Kiderlen.

If there is something you specially want to know, please write it on a card and send it to me.

272. Alfred von Kiderlen-Wächter to Holstein

Peterhof, 19 July 1888

My dear Herr von Holstein,

You can see from the address and stamp that we have arrived safely at the end of our journey. Since my letter left by way of Memel, we have had beautiful weather and everything has gone on merrily on board; especially so in the case of His Majesty. A bland cheerfulness pervades the whole company. H.M. has 'hoisted' (as we sailors now say!) a tremendous interest in naval matters. I am astounded the whole time at the skill with which Seck[endorff] understands how to insinuate himself and to bring his influence to bear in a partly confidential, partly obsequious, manner. While more seriously minded men (H.E.,[1] Dr Leuthold,[2] Bissing,[3] and myself) play their rubber of whist, there is continuous peering through telescopes, reading of signals, etc. Yesterday naval battles were played at—pardon, should have written 'practised'—to the accompaniment of much thunder from the guns, and afterwards we one and all shot with a revolver-cannon at a barrel thrown overboard as a target, which H.M. to his great joy also hit. H.E. also fired away very gallantly! Today there were lots of ships' manoeuvres in which with the best will in the world I could find little pleasure. In the evenings anecdotes, jokes, etc. But nothing to drink—which does not please H.E. nor me either exactly. On one occasion H.M. talked to us for a long time about the illness of K.F. III. I will tell you about this sometime. The quintessence was more or less that H.M. believed (he said time and again: 'That is my conviction') that Mackenzie came to Berlin with *English* instructions. The Queen, who at the time had heard that Kais. W. I's customary spring-time illness had just set in, had sent for M. and gave him instructions before his departure for Berlin. *At that time* Queen V. was quite blameless in the matter, afterwards unfortunately it was different, and no-one dared attack M. too sharply since otherwise he might throw all respect overboard and 'then she would be exposed' if he printed everything.

It was amusing to see how H.E. vainly sought to get hold of H.M. to report to him. Yesterday he eventually got hold of him for half an hour before lunch in order to read H.H.'s [Bismarck's] instructions to him.[4] Whether with much success I do not know. They were also presented to him in a French translation; but he seems to regard all this as very insignificant compared with the question of how he will bring in his fleet.

At four o'clock this morning Plessen[5] arrived on board with the pilot who had been sent to meet us. He brought the programme for the ceremonies that I here set down for your edification, although by the time you receive it newspaper reports will have rendered it long out of date:

1st Day. Thursday the 19th. Family dinner party—Marshal of the Court's dinner.

2nd Day. Friday the 20th. Visit to the fortress of Peter and Paul on board Russian yacht. Laying of wreath, etc. Visits. Lunch on board. Evening: travel by special train to Krasnoe-Selo. Ride through the Camp, Tattoo, Supper in Camp. Sleep in Krasnoe-Selo.

3rd Day. Saturday the 21st. Grand Parade (allegedly 60,000 men). Lunch. Travel by special train to Pavlovsk. Visit to Grand

---

[1] Herbert von Bismarck.
[2] Rudolf von Leuthold. Kaiser Wilhelm II's doctor.
[3] Moritz Ferdinand, Baron von Bissing. Aide-de-Camp to Wilhelm II.
[4] See *Grosse Politik*, vol. VI, no. 1343, pp. 311–14.
[5] Hans von Plessen. Prussian General; Aide-de-Camp to Wilhelm II; Commander of the Imperial Headquarters, 1892–1918.

Duchess Constantine, Queen of Greece, etc. Visits in St Petersburg. Excursion to the Point. *Dinner with Schweinitz* (I do not begrudge him that).

On this 3rd day, by Schweinitz's desire, German deputations from St Petersburg, Moscow, Riga, etc., are to be received. H.M. isn't at all enthusiastic about this. H.E. proposed that the heads [of the delegations] should be invited to dinner. Schw. did not want this (probably because these fellows with their German throats would make too big a hole in his champagne; he has in any event procured the cheapest, but no matter!).

4th Day. Sunday the 22nd. Church, and Protestant at that. The Kaiser wanted to omit this, but Schw. said that could not be done because of the impression it would make on the devout Germans, so here too a minor conflict. Next, Cossack riding exhibition, family lunch, and in the evening gala dinner. Later embarkation on board the *Hohenzollern* in order to sail in the early morning and to be in Stockholm in fifty-five hours, and of course the whole squadron must come along!!! Our Sovereign wants very much to lunch on board the *Hohenzollern* on Sunday and then show the Tsar one of his armoured ships—but this is still undecided. On Monday Vladimir is to parade the cavalry before him; whether he will stay long enough to be present nobody yet knows.

I can imagine how you will take pleasure in picturing to yourself all these little opportunities for friction.

I hope to be able to get out of Schweinitz's dinner! He has grown terribly old, and as he stood before H.E. with his little list of decorations he looked damned fragile. In reply to my very polite greeting he could think of nothing better than, after reflecting for a few moments, to give me his hand with a sour smile—*but he did not utter a single sound.* But enough of that!

But now as to our arrival. This morning at four o'clock the pilot arrived with Plessen—pardon, I see that I have already written this, but I was interrupted by a long visit from H.E. and afterwards Vitzthum.[1] I ask you to excuse the incoherence of this letter for that reason and because of other distractions.

Well, besides the programme Plessen also brought the news that 'the Tsar would leave Peterhof at 1:30 p.m.'. This was taken to mean that he would come to meet us on the steamer *Alexandria.* At the same time we were informed in what order the ships were to anchor in front of Kronstadt. As a consequence of this order, the squadron had to change round so that some training-ships were in the lead and only then came the battleships. H.M., very angry, had wanted to show off his battleships first. Seck[endorff] at last pacified him by plausibly convincing him that by coming along behind the battleships would make a far

---

[1] Friedrich, Count Vitzthum von Eckstedt. Secretary of Embassy in St Petersburg.

greater impression!!! Next he wanted absolutely to sail past the Tsar as Admiral at the head of his squadron, could also not be induced to put on Russian uniform, but continued to wear his newly designed naval uniform! Despite all the peeping through the telescope, no Tsar came into sight and we hove to and anchored. The Russians thought that the *Zollern* with their pilot on board would sail ahead and they were waiting from 1:30 p.m., the Tsar on his yacht, the Tsarina[1] on the landing-stage. Since they thought we would leave the squadron behind, the pilots for these ships did not arrive until after three o'clock. Once the ten pilots had been allotted to their ships, we steamed very proudly past fourteen Russian warships whose crews were shouting hurrahs, and then had to part from the squadron, because the Tsar's vessel lay behind Kronstadt. Finally, after we had decided to shed our tail (that is to say the squadron) a pinnace arrived with Alexei,[2] who from a distance was thought to be the Tsar. It was only with difficulty that our master was able to change his clothes *a la russki* and be ready at the right moment. He and all of us were now brought on board the *Alexandria* by Alexei's pinnace. Here there seemed to be some slight ill-feeling about our delay, for we were by now two and a half hours late. The small vessel was crowded with Grand Dukes of every age and every kind, Ministers, and some of the highest officers of the Court. The welcome accorded to the Kaiser was affectionate and A. III still has his old good-natured friendly smile. But the remaining public had become definitely nervous on account of the wait! We were asked by everyone about our delay.

The two Emperors sat by themselves for a long time. Ours spoke every now and then; one could see how the other was searching for a subject.

I naturally met masses of acquaintances, all pretty well unchanged; only three people were markedly older. General Richter,[3] Jean Galitzin,[4] and Cochonitz.[5] Vladimir spoke to H.E. of Serbia, but without any sign of annoyance. I hear from Pourtalès that among the Grand Dukes strong language is used on that subject.

A very ancient general, whose name I cannot at the moment recall, has been attached to the Kaiser. They must have brought him out of a fossil museum especially for this purpose; but the reason given is that he is the only one who has the ribbon of the Red Eagle!!! Thus he can only be given the Black, but will certainly be given a present instead, because the Black will not be given to an unknown corpse. The blessing and curse of the conferring of decorations has already begun, but the intention is to be *very parsimonious*.

We will now see how things go! The little that I have already seen I have now exhausted. Perhaps the next time I will be able to write you

---

[1] Maria Feodorovna, daughter of King Christian IX of Denmark.
[2] Alexei Alexandrovich, brother of Tsar Alexander III.
[3] Adjutant-General of Tsar Alexander III.
[4] Steward of the Russian Court.
[5] Schweinitz.

something more interesting. H.E. was complaining today that you were on leave and therefore he had nobody who wrote to him.

Ever with the most sincere and grateful respect
your most obediently devoted
Kiderlen

[...]

273. Alfred von Kiderlen-Wächter to Holstein

Between St Petersburg and Stockholm
25 July 1888

My dear Herr von Holstein,

While at Peterhof, it was not really possible to give you a detailed account of events and the general atmosphere there; there was too great a rush. But I will try to make up for the lapse as far as possible.

I am sure that I do not need to say much about the formal events, about which you will have read in the newspapers.

On the day after our arrival—that is on Friday—the Kaiser visited the Peter and Paul fortress. I was excused from this journey so that I could occupy myself with writing our names in the visitors' books of important and less important Grand Dukes and with leaving cards. I want to mention in this connection that on the day of our arrival there was a whole crowd of young Grand Dukes with the Tsar on board the *Alexandria* waiting for us—mostly quite good-looking, tall, but frightfully slovenly and bad-mannered fellows. After his return from the Peter and Paul Fortress, His Excellency [Herbert Bismarck] had his first talk with Giers.[1]

I can tell you the following about that:

His Excellency did not say a word about politics until finally Giers, after much gulping, said that now that they finally had an opportunity to meet, they might surely talk a little about politics. He repeated the old story about Bul[garia]; that Russia now did not want to make any move, but on the contrary wanted to wait and see. But she could never recognise the Coburger. He was always preaching to Persiani[2] to abstain completely from interference in Belgrade; did not want to interfere in any way in Serbian affairs, but hoped the Austrians would also follow a policy of non-intervention in Bulg. and allow things to take their natural course. Later on, in conversation, His Excellency summed up Giers' views as follows: Giers hopes that the Austrians will not take advantage of Russia's temporary lack of trump cards in the Balkans to take all the tricks. He (Giers) said later that Buri.[3] was after all the adviser to the Bulgarian Government and that without his approval nothing important was done. Giers finally voiced the fear that trouble might occur in Serbia which would induce the Austrians to intervene, and that would put him in an awkward situation. His Excellency replied that since the trouble between the King and Queen[4]

[1] See *Grosse Politik*, vol. VI, no. 1345, pp. 320–5.
[2] Russian Minister in Belgrade since 1878.
[3] Stefan Burián von Rajecz. Austro-Hungarian Minister in Sofia, 1887–95.
[4] In August 1888 King Milan of Serbia was divorced from his Russian wife.

had passed away without any upheaval, this fear seemed to him unwarranted—he therefore saw no black cloud on the horizon.

Neither Giers nor the Tsar spoke to His Excellency about Queen Natalie. (See end of the letter.) Aehrenthal[1] however told me that Giers had once said to him that our action had been *dur envers une reine*.[2] Giers also spoke to His Excellency about economic questions on which agreement might perhaps be reached; they (the Russians) were ready to withdraw many measures that in truth were causing hardship for Russia herself. His Excellency replied coolly that we could not be hurt further and had already fortunately discovered other markets. If he had any proposals to make, he could make them in writing through his Embassy.

I will at once add here some remarks about His Excellency's discussion with the White Tsar that lasted for an hour and a quarter.[3] I had got as far as this when

>'a storm arose upon the sea
>and rolling thunder crashed'

I was not seasick but writing was impossible (there were also various sufferers on board). Writing was also impossible in Stockholm, so that it is only now, during the voyage from Stockholm to Copenhagen, that I can carry on with the story.

Please excuse the blots on the letter. They materialised while my things were being brought on board the *Hohenzollern*.

Well then, the White Tsar received H[erbert] B[ismarck] in a very friendly manner, kept him for an hour and a quarter, and at the close of the audience conferred on him the Alex. Nevski with diamonds, as you already know. The Tsar did not say a word about Austria and Bulgaria, just as if they did not even exist. On the contrary he wanted to be told about the reign of Friedrich III, showed himself very badly informed about it, was very thankful for every detail. Among other things he very naively asked whether it was not the case, as had often been said in St Petersburg, that at Versailles[4] the words used were 'Kaiser and his successor', and that therefore the Imperial Crown did not as a matter of course come to Prince Wilhelm. This certainly did not now appear to be true. When HB informed him that this was all settled in the Imperial Constitution, he thanked him most heartily!!!

The Tsar then spoke of the Chancellor, to whom he sent kind regards, of the Kaiser, whom he knew and esteemed from earlier days, of friendship, etc.

It meant a great deal coming from him when in conclusion he said that the dynasties must stick together for the good of their peoples and

---

[1] Alois, Baron von Aehrenthal. Counsellor at the Austro-Hungarian Embassy in St Petersburg, 1888–94; Minister in Bucharest, 1895–9; Ambassador in St Petersburg, 1899–1906; Foreign Minister, 1906–12.

[2] On 12 July Queen Natalie of Serbia, who for a long time had been living in Wiesbaden, was requested by the local police authorities to surrender her son, the Crown Prince of Serbia. The police authorities were ordered to make this demand by request of her husband, the King.

[3] See *Grosse Politik*, vol. VI, no. 1346, pp. 326–33.

[4] At the time of the proclamation of the creation of the German Empire.

in order to check the increasing *radicalism*. (So he has at last understood that this is also becoming dangerous to him.)

The Tsar had previously also said that in Denmark the Queen[1] would talk about Cumberland[2] and ask that he be allowed to travel freely across Germany. It was a matter of indifference to him (the Tsar), his brother-in-law[3] was in any case an irresolute imbecile; he had often been told to make it up with Prussia, the Queen especially wished it. But C[umberland] had done nothing owing to lack of understanding and want of energy. But C. himself did want to safeguard Brunswick for his son, and for that reason wanted to renounce all other claims in some written form. Our Kaiser subsequently said he was in favour of granting him permission to cross Germany, but he would have nothing to do with anything else. This has been approved in Friedrichsruh in reply to an enquiry.

On the following day the Tsar again talked with H.B. for about ten minutes, expressed his satisfaction about the Kaiser's visit, and to the accompaniment of a contemptuous remark about Cumb[erland], said that he well understood that he (Cumberland) had only himself to blame if nobody wanted to negotiate with him now.

On the afternoon of the second day we visited the camp at Krasnoe-Selo where there was a cavalry parade and tattoo. The troops were drawn up along the whole length of the road (they looked fit and seemed to me smarter than they were four or five years ago) and shouted hurrahs not only three times as we do but for as long as any one of the long suite was still in sight. We rode round for an hour to the accompaniment of this din (the Tsarina and Grand Duchesses were in carriages, we were all mounted). One became quite dizzy from this Asiatic howling. Everyone subsequently gathered near a marquee for a great tattoo, prayers, firing of cannon, etc. This part of the programme vividly recalled to mind the third or fourth Act of *Fatinitza*. Later we all went to our quarters—we all stayed overnight in Krasnoe-Selo—and then there followed a family dinner-party and another given by the Marshal of the Court.

The latter was delayed for half an hour while we waited for His Excellency General of Infantry and Imperial Ambassador Herr Lothar von Schweinitz, who did not subsequently take the trouble to apologise. When at last someone was sent to look for him he was sitting quietly in his room and—had simply forgotten.

Next day there was a parade led by the Russian Tsar mounted on a small, horribly fat, horse. Our Kaiser mounted on his big elegant

[1] Luise, wife of King Christian IX of Denmark and daughter of Landgrave Wilhelm of Hesse.

[2] Ernst August, Duke of Cumberland and Brunswick had become Crown Prince of Hanover on his father's accession in 1851. In 1866, after the annexation of the country by Prussia, he had to go abroad, but on his father's death (1878) he clung to his rights as heir to the throne. In 1884, after the death of Duke Wilhelm of Brunswick, he was unable to assume his hereditary title and rule over the Duchy because he refused to obey the Prussian demand that he renounce his claim to Hanover; he received only Duke Wilhelm's private fortune.

[3] A sister of the Tsarina, Princess Thyra of Denmark, was married to the Duke of Cumberland.

chestnut subsequently led his regiment in parade, to the universal admiration of the Russians.

Here I want to insert *in the strictest confidence* something that Prince Heinrich told me yesterday evening. The Tsar had given him a regiment. Our Lord and Master then reproached his brother, saying that it was quite out of the ordinary and could not be done, one could only be a Colonel-in-Chief when one was a Colonel, but he, Prince H., was only a Lieutenant-Commander, that is to say Major. Prince H. has now established that there were no Majors or Lieut.-Colonels in the Russian Guards, and therefore the next highest rank after Captain was Colonel. He had this next highest rank and therefore was a Russian Colonel; *quod erat demonstrandum!!!*

The parade passed off brilliantly and in the Russian fashion there were all sorts of extra turns. In general what was done was done very well. It occurred to me at the parade, and still more next day at the cavalry manoeuvres, that the cavalry only make attacks in extended order, and that could be fatal to them some time if they came up against cavalry in closed order. The White Tsar was obviously in a good humour that reached its height when our Sovereign at lunch in the marquee replied in Russian to the toast given by the Tsar in French. This made a really tremendous impression on all the Russians, all the more so because it was quite unexpected. Our Sovereign said his little piece quite smartly and without stumbling.

After luncheon the Kaiser went to Pavlovsk to visit the Queen of Greece[1] and later drove to the Point through the city along decorated streets packed with cheering people. At nine o'clock Schweinitz finally had his blow-out with his dinner-party. For three days he did nothing but talk about this great historical event until finally the Kaiser became quite angry. In the evening the Kaiser travelled back by train. His Excellency went on to Madame Durnov's,[2] whence he eventually arrived at Peterhof by troika at six o'clock in the morning. Your Lordship's most obedient servant only got back at seven o'clock, after he had spent the night drinking with Pourtalès, Aehrenthal, etc. At nine o'clock the next morning there was the Church Service which Schweinitz had insisted should be held and at which nevertheless he himself was not present. There was no sermon but only a lengthy prayer for the White Tsar and 'his noble guest'.

Voce Madame Durnov I will tell you something with the request that it remain strictly between us. Also please do not say that I wrote to you on the subject if H.E. subsequently speaks to you about it.

For she spoke to him contra Schweinitz (which is nothing new), but she asked him, and expressed her request as the urgent desire of St Petersburg society, to send Bülow as Ambassador to St P. *Qui vivra verra!*

At noon there was a Russian Orthodox Service and afterwards a huge

---

[1] Olga, wife of King George of Greece and daughter of Grand Duke Constantine of Russia.
[2] Marie Durnov was the daughter of the Mistress of the Robes to the Tsarina, Princess Helene Kotshubey, and was married to General Durnov, President of the Pan-Slav Philanthropic Committee.

luncheon party on the terrace that included everybody. The programme for the following extra day, which our sovereign had agreed to, was for the first time definitely arranged during luncheon. On this as follows:

According to the original arrangements we were to have gone on board after the State dinner-party on Sunday evening and stayed there, either in order to sail during the night, or else entertaining the Russians to lunch on board the next day.

However, as I think I have already written to you, the Grand Duke Vladimir and Nicholas[1] had on the very first day of our visit made the Kaiser's mouth water (*sit venia verbo*) with the prospect of a large-scale cavalry review and in his first flush of excitement he had half-promised to attend. But, then he repented of it. He had to ask himself the question whether or not he would risk spoiling the good impression made by his visit if he stayed too long. The invitation, moreover, did not come from the Tsar, who is no lover of hard riding, while in addition Monday was 'St Olga's Day' and therefore a family feast. It was finally arranged, after our Sovereign had laid down to Vladimir as a condition for his coming that he would only stay on if the Tsar himself asked him to stay, that our Sovereign should accompany Vladimir to the camp while the Tsar remained in Peterhof. This was necessary because of the above-mentioned programme. On Sunday the Tsar, whose mood was improving all the time, suddenly said that he would go too.

Since, however, the Tsar does not like to get up as early as would have been necessary if they were to leave for the camp in the early morning, everybody left that evening for Krasnoe, where they stayed the night. I stayed behind in Peterhof and worked on coding with Vitzthum until 3:30 a.m.

A small point characteristic of our new Sovereign: up till then he could hardly be persuaded to attend to business. Suddenly that night at 12:30 a.m. (an hour after arriving in Krasnoe) he had Villaume dragged out of bed and questioned him for a whole hour about all sorts of things!!!

I think our Sovereign was not too pleased that the Tsar accompanied them. He had particularly hoped to have a really good gallop round on his horse and to take the jumps, etc., as he did in Potsdam when he last inspected the Hussars. He was therefore not at all pleased (pardon, my writing is terrible, but we are rolling again pretty badly) that he was given an eighty-year-old General Glinka as honorary aide-de-camp, and he now looked forward to chasing the old man *à la* Albedyll over the jumps. It was certainly a good thing that that had to be omitted because most of the time our Sovereign had to watch the manoeuvres in a neat and proper way from a marquee in the Tsar's company. It would hardly have made a good impression if an old Russian general had broken his neck.

Everything thus went off well with the exception of the manoeuvres by the Cossacks that were to have taken place on Sunday after Church,

---

[1] Nicholas Alexandrovich, son of Tsar Alexander III, Heir Apparent to the Russian Throne.

were then postponed to the evening, then to Monday, only to be finally abandoned because they don't know how to do their tricks any more. I cannot therefore judge whether they have acquired the characteristics of European cavalry instead.

On Monday evening there was another family dinner party, while we dined at the Marshal of the Court's table (one of the most foolish inventions on earth). During the voyage the Kaiser has told us something of the dinner party from which I have gained the impression that it was arranged specially for the Tsar, who delights in family life, and that at all events it considerably heightened his good humour and his pleasure at our Sovereign's visit. In the Alexandria Palace, for example, the Tsar and his son upstairs and our princes downstairs pelted each other with wet towels, etc. They certainly struck the typical domestic tone of the Peterhof Court of the Autocrat of all the Russians (excuse the writing, the rolling is getting worse!) I have not written to you about the State banquet. There is little to say about it; it passed off like all such ceremonies. The Tsar proposed the Kaiser's health in French and he replied in French with a toast to the Tsar *'et sa brave armée'*. There is a story behind this: In Krasnoe-Selo the Tsar drank to the Kaiser *'et son (sic!) brave armée'*. In the little speech which our Sovereign had learnt by heart nothing was said of the army and obviously he could not immediately add something about it in Russian. He therefore did so the following day. When Schneider, our special correspondent, had his attention drawn to the fact that our Kaiser had not mentioned the army in his toast at the camp, I advised him to telegraph only that our Kaiser had 'replied' in Russian to the Tsar's toast, in order to avoid newspaper gossip about it. You will have seen it in this form in the telegrams. On Tuesday morning the two Emperors with their suites visited our flagship *Baden*. Nothing was spared us: upstairs and downstairs—everything had to be seen, engine-room, galley, men's quarters, etc. Finally lunch on board the *Zollern* and a touching farewell. Whether it was the feeling as we steamed away of being free from ceremonial obligations, whether it was a good lunch combined with pleasure that the visit had gone off so well that induced a peculiarly festive mood—in short, H.M. was in the most boisterous spirits and, as you are accustomed to say, gave one one in the tummy, only this time quite literally. I, however, have always kept in mind the rule of conduct that you gave me.

I can sum up the general impression of the visit to St Petersburg thus: the Russians were never so conciliatory, so humble, so compliant, and in everything their efforts and desires to get peace and quiet, and to be freed from the nightmare caused by a worsening in their relations with us; hence also the fearful avoidance of all 'ticklish' questions.

Naturally we were received with open arms in Stockholm, and their sole endeavour was to amuse us to the utmost from morning till night. They were completely successful in this despite the indifferent weather.

At the State banquet to which all the heads of missions had been invited, the King[1] proposed a long and cordial toast to the 'brother

[1] Oskar II, King of Sweden, 1872–1907.

peoples of German origin, both to those who live in Germany and to those who are settled in the North'.

The Kaiser received the telegram announcing the birth of the fifth Prince[1] late in the evening of the day of our arrival (Thursday). When Seckendorff asked: 'Has Your Majesty in consequence any other orders about the journey?' H.M. replied with a laconic 'No'.

When on Friday morning we climbed an observation tower, a salute was fired in honour of the Prince by our own and the Swedish ships. This made an infernal noise in the harbour, which is shut in by low cliffs, to the great joy of H.M. The whole programme on board the ironclad *Baden* naturally had to be gone through again in Stockholm! The two heaviest armoured ships had, however, to H.M.'s deep regret, to be left behind at Oskar-Friederiksborg because their draught was too great to allow them to enter the harbour. And—oh, alas!—at Copenhagen we will have to leave *three* behind!

We do not arrive there till Monday morning, and only stay until the evening, so that we will not stay ashore overnight, which will certainly be a very great relief to the Danes in view of the shortage of accommodation.

The visit to the exhibition has been declined to my joy 'on account of mourning'.[2] (The reason is good!)

Then we go directly to Kiel and from there to Friedrichsruh where we arrive on Tuesday evening and stay the night. I do not know whether we are all going there.

Harmony has up to now—touch wood!—been preserved splendidly. General Wittich is a very understanding and quiet man and His Excellency always says: 'I work with him as with butter.' Only Major von Werthern, who has recently joined the Military Cabinet, and who followed us overland to St Petersburg, received a few raps over the knuckles when he wanted to play the part of a minor Albedyll in the question of decorations. There was also a small difference of opinion with Villaume, who had drawn up a list of decorations for some 400 people. When, however, he saw how the wind was blowing he quickly beat a retreat.

Above all, H.E. was annoyed when just by chance he learnt in advance that the Kaiser was to be asked to confer a number of Orders of the Crown, First Class, on people who had received the Red Eagle, First Class, years previously. That was, to be sure, a pretty *bévue*!

To conduct business with W.II is, however, in many respects not easy. It is so difficult to get hold of him for that purpose. Wittich has carried around with him during the entire voyage the new drill regulations, which are to be submitted in draft form to a Commission if approved by H.M. But H.M. could not be got hold of to approve them. Moreover Wittich reckons that there will be much more travelling, for apart from Vienna and Rome (probably in October), H.M. will probably

[1] Prince Oskar.
[2] The Kaiser did in fact finally visit the Exhibition of Industry and Agriculture in Copenhagen.

accept a number of hunting invitations. Wi. says he still lacks the ability to discriminate as to which should be accepted.

People are already asking what will happen when he gets home, where a whole pile of things await him. Everything is being staked on the energy of Herr von Lucanus.[1]

À propos, I forgot to tell you above that the 'Watch on the Rhine' was played at the end of the Swedish State banquet. Barrère, who was present, must have been pleased!

In conclusion I wish you a very happy holiday! If you have any questions please send me a line care of the Foreign Ministry. I will gladly answer everything in so far as it lies within my humble capacity.

Excuse this muddled screed, but I was frequently interrupted and wrote below the water-line by the light of a poor lamp.

In Copenhagen all Cumberland's suggestions, 'as well as all those emanating from the Prince and Princess of Wales'[2] are to be rejected outright, and as to the journey across Germany, they will be told that permission will be granted *if* Cumberland himself asks for it, which he has not done so far.

Ever in sincere respect and gratitude
Yours
Kiderlen.

Grand Duke Vladimir spoke to H.E. about the Queen of Serbia and called the King *'un chien en vérole, fils d'une putain'*. H.E. pointed to a father's right to his son and to the Francophil-Germanophobe sentiments of the Queen, with which Vl. expressed himself satisfied.

274. Friedrich von Pourtalès to Holstein

St Petersburg, 25 July 1888

My dear *Herr Geheimer Rat*,

The Kaiser-days are over; yesterday our young Kaiser with his squadron steamed away again from Kronstadt, and I am availing myself of the courier who leaves today for Berlin to tell you something about the way the visit went.

I must say first of all that it was not very easy for me to keep *au courant* of what was happening in Peterhof because Schweinitz, who had settled himself with Vitzthum in Peterhof, had left me in charge of affairs here. Therefore I only got to the Court for a few hours at a time, either for ceremonial occasions or through curiosity. I hardly need tell you how difficult it was on such occasions to speak to anybody even for a few minutes.

Without wishing to be too optimistic, I must say that I have gained the impression that the visit went off better than I had anticipated. The sole ground on which I had promised myself any good results at all

---

[1] Hermann von Lucanus. Head of Wilhelm II's Civil Cabinet, 1888–1908.

[2] Edward, Prince of Wales (later King Edward VII) and his wife Alexandra, daughter of King Christian of Denmark and sister of Tsarina Maria Feodorovna, wife of Tsar Alexander III.

from the meeting was that of the *personal* impression made on each other by these influential and highly placed personages, and I believe that it is in this field that it can be reckoned a success, which could under certain circumstances for a time bear good fruit.

I believe that our young Kaiser with his frank guileless character found favour in Tsar Alexander's eyes and by his mere presence dispelled much of the artificially created mistrust of him. But what does seem to me to have gone extremely well was a long audience which Count Herbert had with the Tsar. The State Secretary expressed himself as very satisfied with it, and said he had hardly ever before had an opportunity of speaking to a Sovereign as he had at this audience, which lasted for one hour and a quarter and at which the Tsar again and again started the conversation afresh with new questions.

As far as I can judge from the hasty and cursory accounts given to me of this conversation, Tsar Alexander expressed himself as greatly satisfied with the visit and voiced the conviction that it would bear excellent fruit. He would always welcome a renewal of such meetings. No mention was made throughout the entire conversation of Austria, Serbia or Bulgaria. Rather the conversation turned chiefly on English influence at our Court during the past four months and on the Cumberland question.

Count Herbert kept the conversation on this matter alive by speaking in great detail, and by touching upon many confidential aspects of the Battenberg marriage affair and the intrigues that went on at our Court during the ninety-nine days. The State Secretary told me he spoke so freely[1] that on several occasions he himself had the feeling that he had perhaps gone too far, and that he had hesitated to go further on this or that point. The Tsar, however, always encouraged him to speak openly about everything, and had shown by listening attentively and by frequently throwing in questions, that he was in the highest degree interested in everything the State Secretary had to tell him and that much of it was entirely new to him. Count Herbert again and again emphasised to me that he was completely surprised to find how responsive the Tsar seemed to be in a frank and sincere conversation and that during this talk he became more and more convinced that if the right person and one who would dare to speak openly to the Tsar, were to be found among statesmen here, much could be achieved through the loyal and upright character of the Tsar. Since, unhappily, there is no such person, much *mistrust* is sown precisely on soil that would be very receptive to *trust*.

I therefore believe that one must be on one's guard against indulging in over-sanguine hopes regarding the after-effects of the exchange of ideas that has taken place during the last few days. The disruptive endeavours that have perhaps been upset for a time will certainly be resumed, and it is impossible to arrange for meetings between the Emperors every two months.

I think that what can be considered a success is that we have shown

[1] Marginal comment by Holstein: 'probably too much so'.

that we did not *want* anything from this visit, but at the same time that we are not disposed to comply with certain demands that they would like to make of us. Giers did not really dare to come forward with any demands, but confined himself merely to expressing the hope in general terms that Austria would not receive our support if she tried to extract too much advantage from Russia's present wait-and-see attitude in order to gain further ground in the Balkan Peninsula, especially in Bulgaria. I believe that Count Herbert did not afford the Minister much opportunity to express himself more thoroughly on this question; he himself carefully avoided touching upon it, and when Giers managed at length to bring the conversation round to Bulgaria, he referred him to our well-known policy regarding Near Eastern Questions. If the people here want something done about the Bulgarian Question, then they should draw up some plan; we would then see whether and to what extent we could support it. They could hardly expect us to take the initiative in a question in which we had no interest; that was after all up to the Russian statesmen.

So far as I know the economic question was only touched upon in the State Secretary's conversation with the Tsar. The Tsar emphasised his wish for the establishment of good relations in this sphere without entering into details. He could not understand why it had never been possible in his father's time to conclude a commercial treaty. In view of the fact that the economic interests of both countries did not run counter to each other such a treaty should certainly be possible, and he would see to it that the question of the establishment of good relations in the economic sphere was more closely investigated here.

On his own initiative the Tsar also emphasised the necessity for collaboration between the two Empires against revolutionary tendencies.

I forgot to mention above that according to instructions from Friedrichsruh the answer to be given in the Cumberland affair is that there will be no objection to the request for permission for the Duke to travel through Germany.

But with regard to everything that concerns the assurance of the Brunswick succession for the Duke's son, we for our part have turned *la sourde oreille*. The Tsar has made arrangements for this question to be raised in Copenhagen. If this happens, then according to instructions from Friedrichsruh all discussion of this point is to be avoided.

One odd point: it appears from a question put by the Tsar to the State Secretary that His Majesty himself was in doubt whether Wilhelm II would be German Kaiser.

The Tsar was completely uninformed on this question of European constitutional law and listened with interest to Herbert's explanation without showing the least sign of embarrassment, or even looking as if he felt that he had lost face by his ignorance of things that are not unimportant!

Please excuse these hasty lines which unfortunately I have had to write much faster than I wished because yesterday afternoon an imperial command suddenly ordered the sending of the dispatch bag by today's express.

>With sincere esteem
>Your most obedient
>F. Pourtalès.

275. Alfred von Waldersee to Holstein

Lauterbach, 26 July 1888

My dear Baron,

It was a kind thought to enliven my quiet country life with a letter, for which I thank you heartily, as also for the enclosure.

That young people should have a passion for sea voyages is neither new nor particularly unnatural; but when old people make an effort to arouse this passion it is both in bad taste and also, as in the present instance, a mistake. In the general order of things, however, feet do not grow too big for their boots, and the time will come when the navy will clearly understand that it is only one part of our armed forces, and by no means the most important, though certainly the most costly.

It is to be hoped that by that time too much money will not have gone up the funnels.

The future will show whether the navy will have the men for its new organisation.

I am sorry to hear about the sort of table-talk that is going on because I had hoped that a change had taken place in this regard since 15 June.

That the presence of His Excellency [Herbert von Bismarck] does not improve the moral tone is bad, but unfortunately undeniable.

Like you, I do not indulge in any illusions about the probable success of the journey. I think everything will remain as before; if anything should have been achieved it will be a postponement of the clash with Austria; but who can prove whether this is advantageous to us; I would not attempt it. I am convinced that Kaiser Wilhelm made a very good impression, but that does not alter the situation as a whole.

I am sorry that I knew nothing about the journey to Copenhagen for I am of the opinion that an understanding can be achieved with the Danes that could be of great value to us.

My own observations and many talks with Stumm would have enabled me to offer some advice. [...]

Now that the weather has become fine, may my thoughts accompany you to the highest mountain tops.

>Your sincerely devoted
>A. Waldersee

276. Herbert von Bismarck to Holstein

Mainau, 30 September 1888

Dear Holstein,

[...] Krauel's unpleasantness to Peters[1] was at my orders. Peters is

[1] Karl Peters. Explorer and founder of the German Colonisation Society, 1884; Reich Commissioner in German East Africa, 1891-3. In 1893 he was accused of cruelty to the natives and recalled. He was dismissed from the Civil Service in 1897.

a thoroughly bad lot who has by this time inflicted irreparable injury upon the whole East African undertaking, and his complete removal must be insisted upon. I have frequently informed the East Africans about this; they face ruin so long as they have to do with such a fantastic dolt. I have also always said that the East Africans will come to a miserable end if Peters continues to be connected with them in any way. [...]

Farewell.
Ever your
HB.

His Majesty wanted to order a gunboat to go to Heligoland to keep watch so that, if Geffcken[1] attempted to reach the German coast in a sailing-vessel, he could be arrested at once. I have already telegraphed to His Highness [...] that the passenger steamers running between Cuxhaven and Heligoland are to be searched by the police to see if Geffcken is on board. Now you could perhaps first speak to Kayser[2] about the Imperial gunboat (about the practicability of such an arrest) and afterwards please inform H.H. of H.M.'s idea.

277. Otto von Bismarck to Holstein

Friedrichsruh, 3 October 1888

I cannot approve the procedure which you, Sir, according to dispatch No. A12364 of the 2nd of this month, have adopted regarding Gasnier's assassination attempt,[3] and I would have wished that the memorandum by the State Secretary of the 30th of last month—No. A12358[4]—had been brought to my notice before any decision had been taken in the matter. Correspondence with His Majesty the Kaiser in so far as it is not a matter of simple transmission, and in so far as it calls in particular for any form of political decision, is among the matters which I reserve to myself and which must necessarily pass through my hands. The memorandum by the State Secretary of 30th of last month was in accordance with its final paragraph to be brought to my notice in the

---

[1] Dr Heinrich Geffcken. Lawyer. Since 1872 Professor of Jurisprudence and Civil Law in Strasbourg; member of the Alsace-Lorraine Council of State, 1880–2. For many years he was an adviser and confidant of Crown Prince Friedrich Wilhelm. His anonymous publication of extracts from the 1870–71 war diary of Kaiser Friedrich in the October 1888 number of the *Deutsche Rundschau* (published at the end of September) resulted in his being charged with high treason.

[2] Paul Kayser. *Vortragender Legationsrat* in the Foreign Ministry, 1886–90; Head of the Colonial Division of the Foreign Ministry, 1890–6.

[3] On 28 August a Frenchman named Gasnier fired two shots at a French employee of the German Embassy in Paris without however wounding him. Holstein, who was acting as deputy for the State Secretary, had reported that a dispatch from Paris had depicted France's attitude to the Gasnier incident as unsatisfactory, and that in consequence he had inspired a sharp article in the *Post*. Bismarck commented on the margin: 'Premature!' (From the Foreign Ministry files.)

[4] Herbert von Bismarck had reported that the Kaiser had ordered that the Embassy in Paris should be requested to report on the French attitude to the Gasnier incident and that 'depending on the result of the report' the semi-official Press should adopt a sharp tone. Herbert von Bismarck had asked that the Chancellor be informed of the matter. (From the Foreign Ministry files.)

first instance and before anything was arranged. Similarly, inspired articles, which could influence our relations with France, should not be initiated by the Foreign Ministry unless I have previously seen the text. I can only judge after perusing the text whether I would have approved the publication of the article in the Press.

I would be obliged, Sir, if you would observe precisely the preceding instructions and communicate to me the correspondence emanating from the Imperial Court before action is taken upon it.

v. Bismarck[1]

278. Holstein to Hugo von Radolin[2]

5 October [1888]

Dear Rado,

I can imagine that you too have read the Diary[3] with interest. I find to my regret that the poor gentleman does not come out of it very well. With the exception of the extreme Progressives, the other parties come in for much unfriendly criticism. The present Kaiser is said to be very angry. It seems certain that Kaiserin Friedrich knew nothing about the publication beforehand.

Geffcken has said that he was given the Diary to read by Kaiser Friedrich and that he then made extracts from it. There are all sorts of indications that Geffcken—although neither a friend of the Reich nor a Liberal—had exchanged ideas on the most intimate footing with both Highnesses, His and Her, and exerted great influence, at least *before* the accession to the Throne. Afterwards—you may well have destroyed it. [...]

Best regards
H.

279. Ludwig von Raschdau[4] to Holstein

Rome,[5] 13 October 1888

My dear *Herr Geheimrat*,

Many thanks for your friendly lines which reached me in Pistoia. Since then we have been caught up in the Italian rush and it is only now —thanks to the refusal of an invitation to the parade—that I find an opportunity of answering you. You can imagine that on a day like yesterday I could not call a *single* minute my own, although I got up at six o'clock and went to bed at one. Meantime *in medias res* on the subject of your suggestions.

[1] See *Diaries*, entries for 22 October 1888.
[2] From the Radolin Papers.
[3] Kaiser Friedrich's Diary. See p. 296, note 1.
[4] Temporary Assistant in the Foreign Ministry, 1885–8; *Vortragender Rat*, 1888–94; Minister in Weimar, 1894–7. After 1890 Raschdau became one of Holstein's bitterest enemies. (See Ludwig Raschdau, *Unter Bismarck und Caprivi* (Berlin, 1939).)
[5] Raschdau was in the suite of Wilhelm II during the Imperial visits to Stuttgart (27 September), Munich (1 October), Vienna (3–4 October), and Italy (11–19 October). On 12 October the Kaiser paid official visits both to the Quirinal and the Vatican.

I will try to find your Professor[1] today or tomorrow. What I can then do for him shall be done.

I did not until now know anything definite of what you tell me concerning certain tensions. I do not see everything that comes in here, partly because at times His Excellency [Herbert von Bismarck] and my humble self live in different places (even in Munich we were not in the same place), partly because perhaps H.E. keeps the matters in question completely secret. Perhaps also, what you call high-pressure correspondence refers only to the general political dispatches on the conversations that have been held here and in Vienna. The long twenty-eight page Vienna dispatch[2]

[1] Pietro Blaserna.
[2] See *Grosse Politik*, vol. VI, no. 1352, pp. 346–9. The following passages from Herbert von Bismarck's memorandum about his conversations in Vienna were among those not printed in *Die Grosse Politik*. 'When I spoke to Kaiser Franz Joseph about the pan-Orthodox movement, I also mentioned the advances made by this movement in the Baltic provinces and emphasised the mistake made by the Baltic Barons in having Germanised their Latvian and Estonian tenants over the centuries. In the course of time this would probably result in the Baltic peasantry becoming radicalised, in part converted to Greek Orthodoxy, and finally to the expulsion of the German landowners, to the joy of all Slavs. At this point I switched rather quickly to the federalist movement of the Celtic tenantry against their Anglo-Saxon landlords in the hope that the Kaiser would perceive the analogy between these people and the German landowners in Bohemia and their radical Hussite Czech tenantry. [...]

'Count Kálnoky expressed some anxiety, in confidence, about the failure to decorate Taaffe, in view of the high decoration conferred on Tisza. I told the Count that this was merely the result of our Sovereign's conviction that, as the representative of Hungary, Tisza was our most reliable friend in the Empire, whereas Taaffe had done us the disservice of weakening the power of the cis-Leithanian half of our ally. At this stage Count Kálnoky wanted to talk about the language question, which is a legacy from the bad middle-class Liberal Ministry; but I cut this short by stating that the language question was a purely Austrian domestic issue, a matter of complete indifference to us. He could best judge that from the fact that we did not care at all whether or not the Magyars wholly absorbed the German-speaking Transylvanian Saxons; if instead of the Czechs any other foreign race inhabited Bohemia, a race as friendly to us as were the Magyars, it would not matter to me whether the Germans there retained or lost their language. When Count Kálnoky said that 25–30 years ago the Magyars had constituted the most dangerous opposition and were now outstandingly loyal, and that the same transformation could take place with the Czechs, I replied: "That is impossible; there are only six million Magyars in the whole of Europe; but the Czechs look upon themselves as the vanguard of the Pan-Slav Federal Republicans, and once they get hold of the Crown of Wenceslas, they will no longer be governable by the Austrian Kaiser." Count Kálnoky thereupon argued that the notion of the Crown of Wenceslas would never be a practical proposition, and when I asked him what he had really meant by the analogy with Hungary he kept silent, and only made the evasive remark that the propagation of the notion of the Crown of Wenceslas did not belong to Count Taaffe's system. When I requested him to define this system for me, he hesitatingly conceded that in his opinion indeed Taaffe had no system and he added: "But what do you want us to do? The Germans have made themselves impossible with the Kaiser, indeed shown themselves actually incapable of governing. [Marginal Comment by Bismarck: 'Unhappily yes!'] In addition, the Germans are divided into Ultra-Liberals and Clericals, for there are no Conservatives among us. Those who might be are absorbed by Clericalism. If the Germans had a man like Tisza and would follow him as unitedly as the Hungarians follow their leader, then a solution would indeed be easy; but as it is, Cis-Leithania with its mosaic of nationalities is frightfully difficult to govern, and if one wanted to draw the consequences, nothing remains except to do away with constitutionalism."

'*"Voilà le mot de l'énigme"*, I interrupted, "I am glad that you should mention this possibility."

'Count Kálnoky was somewhat put out by my concurrence and said that this radical method could not well be used on account of the Hungarians, who insisted that there should be a constitution in this part of the Empire too. After that I could not pursue this subject further, and only repeated to the Count my conviction that if Taaffe were to continue to govern for another ten years as he had done hitherto, the Crown of Wenceslas would be the inexorable

you should certainly see soon. The one for here[1] has not yet been written.

I cannot therefore tell you anything about the reason for this ill-feeling, which, as I have already said, I have not noticed. For I cannot believe that the acceptance of the visit to Leipzig (laying of the cornerstone of the Supreme Court of Justice), which His Highness [Bismarck] advised against for political reasons, caused this ill-humour. H.M. had accepted at the invitation of the King of Saxony[2] before he learnt of H.H.'s point of view. Nevertheless you could be right. After you drew my attention to it, H.H.'s request that he should be consulted before the appointment of Count Goltz (Oldenburg) struck me as remarkable. But again I have no definite indications.

The reception in Vienna appeared to me as a *succès d'estime*, to put it mildly—especially after Stuttgart and Munich. It is true that we *dii minorum gentium* in the last carriages could not see much of the first reception. But it was at any rate obvious to me that there was more curiosity than jubilation. Nor were there many decorations. The people in the Hofburg, on the other hand were very friendly, and relations with the Imperial Family seemed to me affectionate, despite Kaiser Franz Joseph's displeasure at T[aaffe] not receiving a decoration.[3] On this subject you will find some details in the above-mentioned Vienna report. Here in Rome—and from the outset in Italy—the welcome has been quite different. For instance, yesterday's scene beneath the balcony of the palace was *le comble de l'enthousiasme*. Upon our arrival here behaviour was unexpectedly sedate, although very friendly. Someone remarked—not without penetration, it seemed to me, though I cannot vouch for its absolute validity—that this young Kaiser had so impressed these people here (who think so very highly of themselves) that they felt they were experiencing a great event. On such ceremonial occasions the Kaiser looks very serious, almost hard, and in my opinion this suits the occasion. The soldiers are especially impressed by this Imperial attitude. But in general this manner is effective in those countries where the monarchy adopts a frivolous attitude. In society, however, the Kaiser displays his winning charm of manner.

Yesterday Rampolla[4] nearly tripped up.[5] You know that in accordance with H.M.'s wish, Prince Heinrich was not to wait in an ante-room but was to arrive half-an-hour later. Everything was arranged accordingly.

logical consequence. Since we therefore believed Taaffe to be weakening Austria, to our great regret, it could only be regarded as an expression of good-will towards the allied Empire if our Sovereign, when conferring decorations, omitted Taaffe, who was the ruination of his country.' (From the Foreign Ministry files.)

[1] There is no comprehensive report by Herbert von Bismarck of his conversations in Rome in the Foreign Ministry files. There are only two extracts from the letter written by Herbert von Bismarck to Holstein on 15 October (see below) and a report of a conversation with Crispi on Balkan problems.
[2] Albert, King of Saxony, 1873–1902.
[3] Eduard, Count von Taaffe. Austrian Minister-President and Minister of the Interior 1879–93. The Kaiser had hoped to weaken Taaffe's position by conferring the Order of the Black Eagle on Tisza, the Hungarian Minister-President, but not on Taaffe.
[4] Cardinal Secretary of State, 1887–1903.
[5] When Wilhelm II visited the Pope.

But when the Prince arrived, R. persuaded him to wait; His Holiness would summon him shortly. Count B[ismarck] intervened very firmly and, despite the persistence of the Cardinal, he said: *non, pas attendre!* A Papal Chamberlain at my side remarked that this language left nothing to be desired in the way of decisiveness. The Prince was then taken at once to the Pope. The whole presentation question was not altogether easy, as you will subsequently see from the exchange of telegrams. Incidentally H.M.'s private conversation with the Pope did not make any significant impression on the former. His Holiness appears to have made quite incredible political proposals regarding special alliances, etc.[1]

I must stop in order to catch the courier. Excuse the bad handwriting. I hope to be able to give you details later.

Your most obedient
Raschdau.

280. Herbert von Bismarck to Holstein

Rome, 15 October 1888

Dear Holstein,

Pourtalès' letter[2] is returned enclosed, with thanks. Crispi has just left me after a visit lasting an hour and a half; he is suspicious about the French intention to fortify Bizerta. Italy could not allow this because Sicily would then be caught in the pincers Toulon-Bizerta. Crispi thinks Bizerta very important and calls it militarily the most important position in the Mediterranean. He wants us to let our experts examine it from the standpoint of its importance for the Mediterranean and for a war with France. I promised him this and also to communicate the results of the examination to him. Please write accordingly to the General Staff and the Admiralty. [...]

The Pope very greatly bored us; a hypocritical Lenten preacher; the Kaiser is very disappointed with him. [...]

Ph. Eulenburg and Rantzau get on well; the latter indeed wants the former to stay on. But His Majesty wants to give Eulenburg a minor Legation as soon as possible, and I have advised His Highness to do H.M. this favour. But this *secretissimum, only* for you.

Our Kaiser does his job extremely well. He pleases and impresses everywhere he goes.

As ever
Your HB.

281. Herbert von Bismarck to Holstein

Naples, 17 October 1888

Dear Holstein,

Many thanks for your letter of the 14th with its enclosure which I return herewith. I am glad that I shall soon be home, for it is really

---

[1] See *Diaries*, entry for 22 October 1888.
[2] Pourtalès' letter to Holstein of 9 October. Not printed.

nerve-racking to attend to affairs in this state of hustle and hurried journeys, while thanks to the confusion and awkwardness of the Italian arrangements one is never easy in mind and can only partially enjoy the beautiful things here.

Nevertheless it was a real pleasure to me to see Naples again, especially since we are having magnificent weather and moonlight. Today's outing in the Bay was delightful and the wild enthusiasm of many hundreds of thousands is *beyond description*.[1]

I agree with you, and for the same reasons, that it is not very wise of my father to want to move to Berlin so soon. I first heard about this in a letter from my mother, who complained very much about this unexpected decision. I sought to oppose it in my reply, but do not believe I will succeed, because my father appears to be very set on it. I also believe that he is afraid that H.M. is escaping from his grasp. But that is quite unfounded. It is very easy to get along with H.M., at all events easier than with any other Sovereign with whom I have hitherto been acquainted. H.M. has been quite exceptionally nice to me throughout this journey and has often come into my room in the evening with his brother to recover from the day's exertions with the help of beer, cigars, and jokes. Everything goes splendidly, H.M. makes a first-rate impression everywhere, and for his part is thoroughly content, only disappointed with the Pope. His notes will amuse you.[2]

It is very possible that Rottenburg is quietly urging a return to Berlin.[3] I have no evidence for this because I do not get private letters from him.

Farewell—and to our meeting in four days.

Ever your
HB.

282. Eberhard zu Solms to Holstein

Rome, 2 November 1888

My dear friend,

[...] Yesterday I visited Countess Pecci, wife of the Lieutenant-Colonel of the Papal Guards and nephew of the Pope; she is a Spaniard with whom I became acquainted in Madrid and who has even dined with me accompanied by her husband; thus, a sensible woman. She asked me what the Kaiser thought of the Pope. I replied that the Kaiser had found him a venerable old man with whom conversation was somewhat difficult because the Pope never gave him time to utter a word. 'How true,'[4] said the Countess, 'he talks without interruption!' She then continued: 'Everything would have been all right if Count Bismarck had not forced Prince Henry into the apartment where the Kaiser and the Pope were engaged in a *tête-à-tête*.[5] He came in like a bomb and the

---

[1] In English in the original.

[2] See Diaries, entry for 22 October 1888. In the letter enclosing these notes, Herbert von Bismarck told Holstein that the portion of the notes dealing with the conversation between Wilhelm II and the Pope were dictated to him by the Kaiser verbatim. (From the Foreign Ministry files.)

[3] The reference is to Bismarck's return to Berlin from his estate in the country.

[4] The conversation with Countess Pecci is in French in the original.

[5] See above, Raschdau's letter of 13 October 1888.

Pope was extremely annoyed about it. My husband saw the whole business and everyone was dumbfounded. It is true,' the Countess added laughingly, 'you Protestants do not realise how important the Pope is.' I replied: 'But one cannot keep the brother of the Kaiser waiting in an antechamber, and the conversation had already lasted half an hour.' On the subject of the conversation I asked the Countess: 'But tell me, how is it possible that a man as clever and of such great wisdom as the Pope could possibly nourish the illusion that the Kaiser, who had come to Rome to pay a visit to his friend King Umberto, would inaugurate the alliance with Italy by helping to rob him of Rome and several provinces? The Pope could not believe this himself, and if he could not believe it, why this comedy? Everyone is agreed that from the moment Italy cedes the city of Rome to the Pope, the Holy Father would not be able to maintain himself there for a single hour unless he had an entire foreign army at his disposal.

'As long as the Papacy needed a principality, Providence provided one; today she has taken it away because it has become unnecessary, for one would have to be blind not to realise that ever since the Pope has been relieved of his sovereignty, his prestige is one hundred times greater than when he was at the head of a state which did not shine in its manner of government.'

'I assure you,' the Countess excitedly replied, 'that the Holy Father realises all that, but what is he to do? He is under pressure from the Cardinals; he cannot act otherwise!'

What the charming woman told me was in truth not new to me. But it is nevertheless interesting that a niece of the Pope who sees him frequently because her husband is his heir should be so outspoken.

In any case she is not too pleased with her uncle because he did not give her a single thing out of all the many beautiful gifts he received for his jubilee.

I think this little conversation will be of interest to you. I write to you about it because I did not want to make it the subject of a report.

Herr Crispi returned today.

Farewell and many thanks for your letter of the 24th.

With best regards
In friendship and devotion
Your
Solms. [...]

283. Anton von Monts to Holstein[1]

Vienna, 26 November 1888

My dear Herr von Holstein,

[...][2] The dangers to the Government arising out of differences of opinion within its own ranks are less imminent. Count Taaffe will undoubtedly always smooth over the differences between Schönborn[3] and

---

[1] From the Foreign Ministry files.
[2] The beginning of the letter deals with the position of Taaffe's Cabinet in Austria.
[3] Friedrich, Count von Schönborn-Buchheim. Austrian Minister of Justice, 1888–95.

Bacquehem;[1] if need be he will drop one of them. It is another matter with the increasingly domineering Finance Minister[2] (who is at the same time actually the mouthpiece of the Government) with whom Count Taaffe identifies himself more and more as time goes on. Herr von Dunajewski, however, aims at anything but a real reorganisation of the Austrian finances. Far too greatly influenced by the great financial powers, always placing his own and his native Galicia's interest in the forefront, the Minister has no time to spare for the critical economic situation. The population of Cis-Leithania, or rather certain classes, cities and provinces, are now making sacrifices that could hardly be demanded of a less well-disposed and hardworking people than are the German Austrians and Czechs. Yet notwithstanding all the new taxes, the balancing of the Budget is well-known to be still a *pium desiderium*. Meanwhile they continue to borrow merrily from Rothschild; it is obvious what the repercussions will be on property mortgages, and therefore on the entire economy, of the many millions in bonds bearing interest at over 5 per cent in specie that are annually thrown upon the market. And Dunajewski will hardly abandon paper currency and break off the close relations with high finance or introduce a just system of taxation. Economic necessity on the other hand may still perhaps reconcile races[3] which are now tearing each other to pieces in blind hatred but which nevertheless have been made dependent upon each other by close association and common interests through centuries. In recent times voices have often been heard criticising the monopoly system, the spoliation and overburdening of the lower classes, despite the fact that a thoroughly corrupt Press does its utmost to maintain a deathly silence about such things. The general discontent at the same time reveals itself in vague desires and the formation of political parties. Demagogues and anti-Semitic agitators of the lowest kind gain an otherwise wholly inexplicable number of fanitical supporters among the peaceful population. But were the movement to become an organised one, the Kaiser who unfortunately has neither interest in nor understanding of economic questions, would ultimately find himself forced to break with Dunajewski, who would probably involve Count Taaffe in his fall. I have allowed myself in the foregoing to touch upon a question that to my knowledge has up to now received little attention in Berlin—the undeniable economic decline, especially of the little man, in both halves of the Empire. The Austro-Hungarian peoples can only continue to bear the present military and financial burdens if their material conditions of existence are helped more than has hitherto been the case.[4] Yet everything has to give place to the political and national quarrels in Cis-Leithania, and to the feverish endeavour to consolidate the Magyar State in Trans-Leithania. Tisza as well as Taaffe have in this respect made many mistakes, and although both are personally thoroughly

[1] Marquis Olivier de Bacquehem. Austrian Minister of Commerce, 1886–93; Minister of the Interior, 1893–5.
[2] Dr J. von Dunajewski. Austrian Finance Minister, 1880–91.
[3] Marginal Comment by Bismarck: 'Hardly.'
[4] Bismarck: 'And not even then.'

honourable men, both have more than once stretched a point in favour of their partisans. Herr von Tisza now recognises his sins of omission but does not dare to act except with palliatives. The exceptional irresponsibility of the Cis-Leithanian statesman on the other hand makes him blind to any understanding. An Austrian Government which would courageously attack the severe economic decline and corruption and bring the great but still undeveloped wealth of this magnificent Empire into production could overcome many antagonisms. It would then be possible on the basis of the present Constitution to govern well;[1] and it would also be possible to reconstruct a purely Austrian middle-of-the-road party out of the moderate elements in what are now specifically nationalist parties, and—by a judicious control of new elections—a party which would not consist of the so-called Centre of the great landlords; the destruction of this party by Count Taaffe was one of his chief mistakes. [...] Allow me to take this opportunity to express to you my deepest respect and esteem.

Monts.

284. Heinrich VII Reuss to Holstein

4 December 1888

My dear Herr von Holstein,

[...] Széchényi insists on resigning. I have written to the State Secretary about it. Here they do not want to let him go because there is no one better to put in his place, and they do not want to experiment with an untried man. For this reason they desire above all that we treat the offended man in a friendly way and that we give him the Black Eagle on the occasion of the Kaiser's visit.[2]

Our Sovereign's letter[3] has made a good impression here and I have not heard any criticism. The reply[4] will be cordial and the Kaiser intends to revise it personally. It will be drafted in the Foreign Ministry and will be written out in the Chancellery. The telegram[5] has caused great joy!

Ad votam Széchényi, Kálnoky tells me he has talked the matter over with the Prince, and told him he wanted to withdraw him, but that he had no one better. Upon which the Prince replied that under those circumstances he had better leave Széchényi there, he was indeed an honest man, did no harm, etc. Under the circumstances it seemed

---

[1] Bismarck: '??'

[2] Kaiser Franz Joseph intended to visit Berlin in the Spring of 1889. In a letter to Holstein of 14 December Reuss wrote: 'Herbert will have told you how angry his father was when he received the suggestion that Széchényi should receive the Black Eagle on the occasion of the forthcoming visit of the Kaiser. If that is the way things really stand, then it would be better if Széchényi were to leave beforehand.'

[3] In a letter of 30 November Wilhelm II congratulated Kaiser Franz Joseph on the 40th anniversary of his accession to the throne and emphasised the community of interests of the allied monarchies. (From the Foreign Ministry files.)

[4] In a letter of 10 December Kaiser Franz Joseph expressed his gratitude. (From the Foreign Ministry files.)

[5] An official telegram of congratulation from Wilhelm II to Kaiser Franz Joseph on 2 December. It was published together with Franz Joseph's reply on 10 December in the *Reichsanzeiger*.

reasonable to him (K) that his Ambassador should also be treated decently. At the same time he quite understood that it would be better to recall Sz. At present that could not be done because he had no one else, but he was working on the question. He was now trying to console him. Because in general and also from a political standpoint he could not wish to see the Austrian Ambassador slighted by us.

Again best thanks for your friendly reception

Your devoted

H. VII Reuss. [...]

285. Heinrich VII Reuss to Holstein

Vienna, 10 December 1888

The idea of publishing the congratulatory telegram is a good one.[1] The more I see of people here, the more clearly I have been able to notice how uncertain the public at large has become about whether feeling in Germany is still as favourable to the alliance as formerly.

Here they know perfectly well what worries us about Austria; but people, especially our friends, see no help for the immediate future because Taaffe is again firmly in the saddle. They have to wait till that statesman has gone, and that may take quite a while. Therefore there is acute anxiety lest we become impatient and turn towards other friends.

The Hungarians take care not to mix in domestic affairs here. They will only do so if the Crown of Wenceslas, that is to say the autonomy of Bohemia, which is what the Czechs want, is established. The Hungarians could not tolerate that; they have too many Slavs on their side of the Leitha. They would, in that case, take a firm line and insist on the Compromise[2] and their Constitution, which guarantee one dualism *only*. Although the concept arouses enthusiasm in *every* Czech, the Kaiser will have nothing to do with the Crown of Wenceslas. As a proof of this resolve I can cite among other things the fact that Count Franz Thun,[3] who, in an election speech in the autumn, imprudently spoke of the coronation as a necessity to placate the Czechs, was privately reprimanded, and in consequence will not take his seat this winter in the Upper House but will instead travel in Italy.

Now as formerly I can only advise that we apply no further pressure here. All pressure will only produce the opposite result.

That does not mean that from time to time I will not draw attention to the fruits of the Taaffe system.

I have nothing new to write today about Crown Prince R[udolf], but will probably soon receive further information.

With best regards

H. VII Reuss

[1] See above p. 304, note 5.

[2] The Compromise of 1867, setting up the dual Austro-Hungarian Empire.

[3] From 1879 a member of the Austrian *Reichsrat*; from 1883 a member of the Bohemian *Landtag*; leader of the Czech Feudal Party; Governor of Bohemia, 1880–96, 1911–15; Austrian Minister-President and Minister of the Interior, March 1898–September 1899. He promoted the negotiations between Germans and Czechs over the so-called Bohemian Compromise of 1890.

286. Friedrich von Pourtalès to Holstein

St Petersburg, 28 December 1888

My dear Herr *Geheimer Rat*,

Permit me to send you my sincere good wishes for the approaching New Year. May the coming year bring you only days of health and happiness.

In accordance with your advice I have kept up my correspondence with Count Herbert and in that way have informed him of many personal observations, as well as of various things which could serve to illuminate the official dispatches.

Little has changed in recent weeks in the situation here. Excitement over the railway crash at Borki for a time displaced Persian affairs[1] as the centre of interest. Meanwhile tempers have calmed down very quickly on the latter question; in my opinion this speedy pacification is perhaps the most significant and interesting symptom of this whole episode. *À tout prix* they do not want to commit themselves in Asia, and undoubtedly listened very readily to the advice given them to that effect by English and French sources.

Sympathy for France is steadily increasing and is propagated by the Grand Dukes who have returned from Paris filled with enthusiasm for the attentions shown them there in the autumn. Parisian *élégance* and frivolity have an irresistible attraction for the Russians. I was very glad to see in a memorandum by the State Secretary,[2] a copy of which was sent here, that he had gained the impression from a conversation with Grand Duke Vladimir that this Grand Duke, who has the reputation of being our best friend, was not able to resist the fascination of the Parisian atmosphere. Our friends from the former reign are steadily dying off or losing influence, and however polite we are to the Russian Court, in my humble opinion sympathy for us—quite apart from what happens in the domain of special political questions—is steadily decreasing. [...]

With gratitude and sincere respect, I remain, my dear *Herr Geheimer Rat*,

Always your most obedient
F. Pourtalès.

[1] Pourtalès refers to the Anglo-Russian rivalry over concessions for trade and communications in Persia.
[2] See *Grosse Politik*, vol. VI, no. 1355, p. 353.

1889

287. Philipp zu Eulenburg to Holstein

Oldenburg, 4 February 1889

My dear Herr Baron,

[...] What do you think about Crown Prince Rudolf?[1] I think that the disappearance of this figure is not unwelcome to the friends of the Austrian alliance—in the event that the present Heir to the Throne does not arouse the particular displeasure of His Majesty. I do not know him, know nothing about him. I have found that in great affairs antipathy centres on one person who according to his behaviour at the time heightens or calms this antipathy in regard to the affair itself. H.M. does not love Austria. Crown Prince Rudolf's behaviour (no matter how unimportant this might have been in itself) was the barometer for the Kaiser's rising or falling aversion to Austria. It is to be hoped that a new figure of this type does not soon take his place! It is from this standpoint that I regard the situation.

I would be grateful to you if you would send me a short note about the real reason for his suicide.[2] The example given by that wholly demoralised creature to a Europe pulling down all that is sacred is downright dangerous! I feel more and more what our Kaiser signifies as a protector in a moral and political sense.

H.M. spoils me terribly. I keep this to myself and take pains to be friendly with everyone. Only thus am I able to keep lurking envy within bounds! [...]

In the most loyal attachment and gratitude.

Your most obedient

PEulenburg

288. Heinrich VII Reuss to Holstein

Vienna, 10 February 1889

My dear Herr von Holstein,

I was afraid from the very outset that the catastrophe here would produce a serious reaction in Berlin. Formerly it was the Crown Prince who afforded no guarantee for the future; and *he* was Germanophil. The present Heir to the Throne, that is to say the old one,[3] is a bigoted, sly man who poses as a *bonhomme*. The young one[4] may still develop

---

[1] Crown Prince Rudolf of Austria committed suicide on 30 January 1889. His successor as Heir to the Throne was the Kaiser's brother Archduke Karl Ludwig, who transferred his rights to his son Franz Ferdinand.
[2] No such note has been found.
[3] Archduke Karl Ludwig.   [4] Archduke Franz Ferdinand.

into something, but one does not know for certain. It is therefore not surprising that there should be a rash of new anxieties and that the Hungarian Parliament business should also play an important part.[1]

I had the same idea as you and spoke to Andrássy about it. He was astounded, but he had already blundered into the affair and had not thought of it from this aspect. Now Tisza's concessions are a settled matter.[2]

Kálnoky has learnt of the attitude in Berlin and is disturbed by it. He said: there seems to be uneasiness in Berlin about the succession to the throne. It is impossible to go on emphasising the solidity of our alliance; it has already been done formally so often. *Et qui s'excuse, s'accuse*. People will in the long run think that it is not as firm as it once was.

Kálnoky hopes that something can be made of the young man. The 30 January destroyed a great deal. Nevertheless Crown Prince Rudolf's certainly very morbid disposition allows one to think that it may not be a misfortune that he never ascended the Throne. [...]

With best regards
Your very devoted
H. VII Reuss

289. Friedrich von Pourtalès to Holstein

St Petersburg, 14 June 1889

My dear *Herr Geheimer Rat*,

I have not written in recent weeks because there was nothing special to report from here that was not included in the Ambassador's official dispatches.

Lamezan's[3] supposition that the situation here and the intoxication of the Russians as a result of their favourable financial position would cool off of its own accord has proved to be correct in that the value of the rouble has recently fallen to a not inconsiderable degree. This fall in the rate of exchange can probably be ascribed partly to the unfavourable situation in regard to exports even after the resumption of sailings, and also to the bad prospects for the harvest. It is, however, remarkable what effect the Tsar's toast at Peterhof[4] also had in this connection; the rouble fell by about two marks on each of the two succeeding days. This is a proof of how sensitive Russian credit still is to every puff of the political wind. Lamezan thinks that this sensitiveness has only increased

---

[1] The negotiations over a new Army Law in the Hungarian Parliament. The new law provided for the extension of the period of service of the one-year volunteers and for the setting of all examinations for officers in German, to the exclusion of the Hungarian language. No time-limit was set for this new law, whereas the Army Law of 1879 had been limited to ten years.

[2] The opposition of public opinion in Hungary to the new Army Law obliged Tisza to introduce amendments. Approval for the recruiting quotas was limited to ten years, and the Hungarian language was to be used more widely in the examination of officers.

[3] Ferdinand, Baron von Lamezan. Consul in St Petersburg, 1887–92.

[4] During the celebrations for the marriage of Grand Duke Peter Nikolaievich with Princess Militza, daughter of Prince Nicholas of Montenegro, the Tsar on 30 May proposed a toast in which he called Prince Nicholas the sole sincere and true friend of Russia.

after the conclusion of the conversion operation; he will go into this in more detail in a forthcoming report. If that is the case, then the effectual fulfilment of the Vishnegradsky Plan for a consolidation of the Russian finances will only be possible with a Russian foreign policy that is firmly and steadily directed towards peace. Recently, however, we have again had various occasions to see the nature of the influences to which this policy is exposed.

Although the flirtation with France has momentarily somewhat abated as a result of the Ashinov affair[1] on the one hand and the celebration of the centenary of the Revolution[2] on the other, the plans of a certain party here are still unchanged; nor do I believe that a common front between Russia and ourselves in the interests of the monarchical principle will really bring about a new rapprochement between Russia and ourselves.

The report which Yorck wrote a short time ago about the funds at the disposal of the War Minister for the purpose of making preparations for war during the coming five years is certainly not calculated to arouse any great degree of confidence in Russia's pacific intentions.

In my humble opinion too much importance should not be attached to the toast at Peterhof in itself. I believe that the words which have aroused so much justified attention are for the most part to be looked upon as the expression of a certain embitterment directed in the first place against 'the ungrateful Bulgarians, Serbians and Rumanians'. Moreover these words express the notion, so popular here just now, of an independent policy on the part of Russia, who does not need and therefore will not enter into any alliances. Far more important in my opinion than the toast itself are the commentaries on it which have been allowed to be published by the higher authorities. The fact alone that 'the powerful words of the Tsar' which have everywhere 'made such a tremendous impression' are praised to the sky suffices to permit the Pan-Slav newspapers, despite the censorship, to write as they like, and they more or less write nothing else than that the Tsar's words were directed against perfidious Germany. This is yet another step in strengthening the Pan-Slav doctrine that Germany is the source of all Russia's evils. At the same time, the fact that this interpretation of the toast has met with no check is a fresh proof of Tsar Alexander's overweening self-conceit and self-satisfied belief in his quasi-divinity! Just as on this occasion the strewers of incense met with a very friendly reception by the Tsar, so the time may come when they will convince him that his dignity has been insulted or that he has been impeded in the fulfilment of 'his mission'. The party in favour of action will undoubtedly adopt this method as soon as they think the right time has come.

[1] In February 1889 the French Admiral Orly ordered his men to fire on a group of Russians led by Ashinov who were on a pilgrimage to Abyssinia. They had landed in Sagallo in the sphere of interest of the French colony of Obock and had not obeyed the French order to leave the territory. The incident aroused much bad feeling in Russia, despite the fact that Ashinov was disavowed by the Russian Government.

[2] On 4 May the French commemorated the hundredth anniversary of the meeting of the Estates-General at Versailles.

It remains to be seen just how much opposition they will meet from a monarch whose indolent temperament is certainly opposed to military entanglements. I believe that one cannot count on very much opposition because Tsar Alexander, notwithstanding his apparent stubborness, is a weak character who can be influenced by individuals as well as by public opinion. This has been revealed in recent times in several cases—among others in the Hohenlohe affair.[1] It is surely significant that the mighty Ruler of the Russian Empire should on the same day allow a petition to be rejected which he himself had earlier given reason to hope would be granted. It was the same recently with the filling of the post of Minister of the Interior,[2] when the Tsar as a result of some kind of influence withdrew a decision which he had already as good as made. I fear that the anxiety is only too justified that the Tsar will let himself be driven so far by the Pan-Slav current that he will have neither the strength nor the energy to stand up against it.

As I have already indicated above, I also expect that our joint démarche in Bern[3] will have little effect in increasing recognition of the community of interests which unites the monarchical states. The impression made by the bomb incident in Zürich[4] is already partly obliterated, and the suspicion is steadily gaining the upper hand that in the Wohlgemuth affair we merely want to make use of the Russians. *'Nous ne pouvons après tout pas souffrir'*, it is now said in society, *'que Monsieur de Bismarck mange aussi la Suisse'*. [...]

With sincere esteem
Your most obedient
F. Pourtalès.

[1] After the death of Prince Peter von Sayn-Wittgenstein on 20 August 1887, the Wittgenstein estates in Russia passed to Princess Hohenlohe, the wife of Prince Chlodwig. According to Russian law the Princess was forced to sell these estates, because foreigners were not permitted to possess land in the western administrative areas of Russia. The law was enforced in this instance despite German protests.

[2] The appointment of Ivan Nicholaievich Durnovo as Minister of the Interior (1889–95) was made in the second half of May. In 1895 he became President of the Council of Ministers.

[3] On 21 April 1889 a German police inspector named Wohlgemuth was arrested in Switzerland on the charge that he had been engaged in procuring *agents provocateurs*. The German Government demanded his immediate release, and stated that Wohlgemuth had only been engaged in obtaining information about Social-Democratic and Anarchist activities in Switzerland. According to a telegram from Otto von Bülow on 30 April, the Swiss Federal Council resolved 'to abstain from legal proceedings out of regard for the Imperial Government, but to expel Wohlgemuth from the country'. The expulsion was immediately carried out.

In an instruction of 29 April Schweinitz was ordered to ask Giers whether Russia would be prepared in the monarchical interest to take common action with the German Government 'in order to remind Switzerland of her international obligations towards other States and to obtain her assistance in ending the criminal activities of conspirators on Swiss territory, or at least in restricting them'. On 2 May Schweinitz telegraphed that Giers had accepted the suggestion with 'lively satisfaction'. A Russo-German *démarche* followed on 12 June. The German Minister in Bern informed the Swiss Government that if Switzerland did not take steps to prevent a threat to the German Reich from revolutionary activities on Swiss territory, Germany would feel herself compelled to examine, in association with the Powers friendly to her, the question of 'how far Swiss neutrality is compatible with the maintenance of order and peace'. (From the Foreign Ministry files.)

[4] In March 1889 a bomb was exploded in Zürich. The political opinions of two of the men arrested in connection with the affair gave rise to the belief that the bombing incident was instigated by anarchists.

290. Anton von Monts to Holstein

Vienna, 23 June 1889

My dear Herr von Holstein,

May I request your kind indulgence in order to bring to your attention, privately and confidentially, the following remarks on the present situation in the Balkan Peninsula.

Count Kálnoky is perhaps regarding the situation in Serbia in too favourable a light; for instance he thinks, or pretends to think, that the Russians are only engaged in agitation there on a small scale, or not at all. The General Staff holds the contrary opinion. English sources, too, confirm that the rouble is circulating very freely in Serbia. I have received similar reports from private sources whose accuracy however I cannot check. Members of Garashanin's Party[1] even express the belief that the little King[2] will soon quietly be deposed—perhaps as early as the occasion of the anniversary of Kossovo.

Confronted with this situation, the Austrian General Staff is insisting that at least precautionary measures be taken so that if the occasion arose (if, for example, as General Beck says, Minister von Hengelmüller,[3] who is very unpopular anyway, were to be violently insulted) Belgrade could immediately be occupied. A *fait accompli* and ruthlessness never fails of effect with Slavs both great and small. Count Kálnoky has refused his consent to such preparations; they would cost money, they could not be taken without the fact becoming known, and could possibly turn out to be the spark in the powder-cask. Herr von Kallay, who was consulted about conditions in the zone of occupation, has said he will answer for the 500,000 Mohammedans and 250,000 Catholics who live there. As to the 600,000 Orthodox, they are only partly unreliable. On this matter, too, the Imperial and Royal General Staff judges the situation less favourably and reasons thus: encroachments by citizens of Serbia on the neighbouring Austrian districts populated by Serbians, or some form of provocation of Austria by Serbia at Russian instigation, is probable. Everything could be nipped in the bud by immediate intervention and the occupation of Belgrade by some 5,000 men. If the Serbian Army were to mobilise, an uprising in Bosnia would be the inevitable consequence, and thus they would succeed in pinning down three to four army corps.

I need hardly say that without instructions I have not discussed these possibilities even academically with either Count Kálnoky or Herr von Szögyény. Nevertheless it seems to me that these military calculations are not without sense. The already enraged feelings of the Hungarians towards the Serbians must also be taken into account, because if the occasion arose they would exert pressure upon the weak Central Government in Vienna to act. Major Deines says that, because of the lack of

[1] Milutin Garashanin. Serbian Minister-President and Minister for Foreign Affairs, 1884–7; Ambassador in Paris, 1894–8.

[2] King Milan had abdicated on 6 March. His successor was his thirteen-year-old son Alexander (1889–1903).

[3] Hengelmüller had already been replaced as Austrian Minister in Belgrade in February 1889 by Baron von Thommel.

mobility of the garrisons closest to the Serbian frontier, of which there are in any case only a few, it would take at least five days after the receipt of an order before even a small body of troops could be assembled at Semlin. And by that time the defence would have been so organised in Belgrade as to render a surprise attack out of the question.

In view of the speed with which events in Serbia have developed up to now, Berlin might perhaps consider the possibility of bringing pressure to bear here to ensure that Austria put herself in a position, as unobtrusively as possible, to throw at least some 5,000 men into Belgrade within twenty-four hours. An agreement to this effect at the time of the meeting between the Emperors in August could easily be made *post festum*.

There are so many powerful voices in the Crown Council here in favour of a prophylactic measure of this kind—Archduke Albrecht, General Beck, probably also the Hungarians—that Count Kálnoky and the Cis-Leithanian Cabinet would finally have to give way. Incidentally, the sympathy which today's issue of *Vaterland* displays for Serbia in discussing the prohibition of the Kossovo commemoration ceremonies in Hungary is symptomatic. [...]

Please accept the renewed assurance of my sincere esteem, with which I have the honour to sign myself,

Your most obedient
A. Monts.

291. Karl von Wedel to Holstein

Stuttgart, 25 June 1889

Dear Herr von Holstein,

I only received the enclosed letter[1] at the railway station last evening and therefore could not return it. Many thanks for sending it to me! Monts is certainly far too pessimistic. His proposal to prepare Austrian troops for an emergency would probably be regarded by the Russians as a form of provocation and perhaps be answered by similar measures on the Rumanian frontier, so that the odium for taking the first step would rest upon Austria. The Chancellor would in that case certainly advise against co-operation on our part. The predominant influential role that has recently been ascribed to the 'Austrian General Staff' is a myth, for Beck is far from being the man of action that he is represented to be. I think that in Monts' letter the wish is to some extent father to the thought. Two or three months ago Reuss wrote to me—or one of his reports mentions it—that Beck himself had said with great confidence that the situation in Bosnia was so well under control that even in the event of a European conflagration they would be able to hold the provinces with the forces stationed there. If there are 750,000 reliable inhabitants in Bosnia and 600,000 who are only in part unreliable, it is obviously nonsense from a military standpoint to say that three or four Army Corps could thereby be 'tied down'. Moreover the people in

---

[1] Count Monts' letter to Holstein of 23 June 1889. See above.

Vienna formerly had the thoroughly sensible idea of evacuating Bosnia if need be and withdrawing behind the Sava, instead of trying to hold these provinces with troops that could not be spared from areas where the outcome of the war, and therewith also the probable future fate of Bosnia, would be decided.

Kindest regards
Your sincerely devoted
Ct. Wedel

292. Holstein to Karl von Eisendecher[1]

Strictly Secret 5 July 1889

Dear Eisendecher,

Correspondence is not my long suit, but today I think I can be of use to you by giving you a few hints.

There are at present two points at issue between the Chancellor and the Kaiser. First—the question of the Russian conversion operation. Bleichröder and associates have already converted about 1,500 million of Russian securities, and more than that remains to be converted. Somebody has drawn the Kaiser's attention to the fact that *if* fate were to involve us in war with Russia, the vast quantity of Russian securities in German hands would be a source of danger, because they would afford the Russians ways and means of attacking our finances. Other objections, too, are raised against the conversion operation. In short H.M. has demanded that the latest conversion of 250 million railway preference bonds should be prevented and that the public be advised not to take up the newly converted stock, but instead to demand payment in cash. His Highness [Bismarck] resisted for a long time, but yesterday finally gave the order by telegram that the *Norddeutsche* should advise its readers to this effect. You will already have seen the article before this reaches you by the slow postal route. You will see from this submission of H.H. to H.M.'s wishes that he recognises after all the necessity of sticking to his post, even though it is no pleasure for him. For this reason I do not take too seriously the hint in today's dispatch to you that he is tired of it all.[2]

The Swiss affair is going badly.[3] Owing to the agitation of Rottenburg, who wrote the first articles in the *Norddeutsche* right at the beginning, and of Dr Kayser, who handed down the somewhat exaggerated legal interpretation, H.H. is handling this question in a manner

---

[1] From the Eisendecher Papers.

[2] In his dispatch of 4 July in reply to Eisendecher's report of 30 June (see p. 315, note 1) Bismarck concluded: 'I can only conduct policy as I understand it, and in any case I am heartily tired of it all. I have already noticed that contrary influences are at work on His Majesty the Kaiser along the lines of the policies advocated by His Royal Highness the Grand Duke [of Baden] and my strength is not sufficient to cope with contrary influences in counselling His Majesty.' (From the Foreign Ministry files.)

[3] See above, p. 310, note 3. The Swiss Government, in reply to the *démarche* of 12 June, had informed the German Government on 17 June that they could not abandon the rights of asylum and police, for these were expressions of Swiss sovereignty. On the following day Bismarck instructed the Foreign Ministry to secure the Kaiser's assent to the abrogation of the German-Swiss Immigration Treaty. (From the Foreign Ministry files.)

that threatens—we can say this between ourselves—to alienate German public opinion more and more. Even *before* the visit to Stuttgart,[1] the Kaiser (not Dr Kayser) had Berchem write to him that he hoped we would not get too heated about it and would succeed in avoiding a conflict. After his return from Stuttgart, H.M. expressed this same idea in more detail and more definitely through Berchem to H.H., and positively *refused* to sign the Cabinet Order for the control of passports. (This is *absolutely* secret!)[2]

Since it is thus difficult to get action through the Imperial Government, H.H. would like to have the individual states—Bavaria, Württemberg, Baden—take the initiative. As you know, there has been little response.[3]

The reason for this was expressed today by a National Liberal Bavarian deputy: people in Munich are convinced that in this way they would play into the hands of the Ultramontanes and would ensure them certain victory in the next elections, both for the Landtag and the Reichstag. A way out of this dilemma would therefore be, he thought, if the south German Governments declared that any initiative *qua state Governments* would be incompatible with state, or rather with local, interests, and would only serve to bring in anti-Reich elements at the next elections. On the other hand, the south German Governments would be willing to agree to a *motion by the Reich* in the *Bundesrat*, because thereby the Reich Government would openly declare that a matter of *high policy* was at stake. Even then, to be quite frank, the effect on public opinion would be bad, but not so bad as it would be if the State Governments were to take a hand in the matter *before* instead of *after* the Reich Government. The former—that is, to take the initiative —would certainly cause the fall of the Lutz Government, for instance.

This sounds sensible, although I am too out of touch with public opinion to form any personal judgment. At any rate I wanted to tell you this, because you will undoubtedly hear the idea expressed. I was not clear on one point, however: whether this Reichstag deputy had already been inspired by Lutz, or whether he intended to report to Lutz in this sense. And the three Governments will surely consult with each other, for it is out of the question that, for example, Baden should say yes and Bavaria, no. It would greatly ease your responsibility, however,—that is, your Grand Duke's—if he were to ask for Bavaria's opinion and leave the initiative to Bavaria.

I wanted to tell you this in your own interest, dear friend, because the Minister who in a moment of crisis gives useful advice *on his own*

---

[1] Kaiser Wilhelm II visited Stuttgart on 25–6 June.

[2] The Kaiser approved the abrogation of the Immigration Treaty. According to a memorandum by Berchem on 29 June, the Kaiser had nevertheless expressed the wish that things should not be pushed too far. He desired in particular that 'more rigorous passport control should be dropped because he knew it would severely injure the interests of Baden' (From the Foreign Ministry files.)

[3] On 20 June the Prussian Ministers in Munich, Stuttgart and Karlsruhe were instructed to find out confidentially how the respective Governments would react to the abrogation of the Immigration Treaty. The three governments expressed the view that the abrogation of the treaty would be detrimental to their countries. (From the Foreign Ministry files.)

initiative is subsequently a great man in the eyes of the Court to which he is accredited. The advice would therefore be that contact be sought with Munich and Stuttgart. Naturally you can only do this if you are certain that the Grand Duke will correctly interpret what you say.

If you would prefer to let things slide, you can comfort yourself with the thought that no immediate danger to the Reich can arise out of this question—at the most indirectly, through unsatisfactory election results, as this Bavarian said. For *me* the only sad thing is the reflection that as a result our old Chief should forfeit a bit of his hard-won popularity. Finally, the fear cannot be excluded that the Kaiser will again intervene personally in case the affair is not speedily settled, and then there might still be a serious row between them. This letter is obviously only for you personally. I know nothing and you know nothing.

Finally, as an old friend I would like to compliment you on the manly way in which you tell the truth.[1] Not everyone does it. I could have wished for your sake that your dispatch had been forwarded to H.M., but frankly it could have been dangerous further to arouse H.M. who is already well aware of the conflict of opinion between himself and H.H. in this matter.

Write me how the matter *really* stands and how things are going. As long as the tension lasts I will keep you informed of everything that can be of use to you that will not otherwise be dangerous. The complete fulfilment of this plan of action will *meo voto* not be possible because of the Kaiser's attitude, which is already known in Southern Germany. I would then be afraid that as a last resort H.M. would be directly played off against H.H. A conciliatory proposal will therefore be necessary which, without rejecting the proposed action, would postpone it, and thereby give the Swiss time to carry further the policy of effective redress which they have already begun. All this is merely my personal observation and opinion. You yourself will have to judge whether there is anything in this long scrawl that will be useful to you. I wrote only in the hope of calming you a little, for I have no doubt that today's letter from H.H. will affect you painfully in more than one respect.

In old friendship
Ever yours
Holstein

293. Holstein to Karl von Eisendecher[2]

11 July [1889]

Dear Eisendecher,

I awaited your letter with impatience to find out how H.H. would try

---

[1] Holstein refers to two dispatches from Eisendecher of 30 June and 3 July. In the first, Eisendecher reported a conversation with the Grand Duke of Baden who had expressed himself very sceptically about the action of the Reich Government in the Wohlgemuth affair, and indicated that 'for the first time he could not comprehend the motives and reasons underlying the policy of the Reich Government'. Eisendecher ended his dispatch of 3 July with the statement that the greater part of the Press and of the well-disposed population of Southern Germany would not understand punitive measures against Switzerland. (From the Foreign Ministry files.)

[2] From the Eisendecher Papers.

to bring you to order. That he thinks that he can win you over by gentle rather than by rough methods is a compliment.[1]

You are right in saying that they cannot in future expect you to give truthful reports of the state of opinion. But do not say the opposite of what is in fact true.

There is no question that we are helping the German Ultramontanes by the way in which we are behaving towards Swiss Social Democracy. For that reason I still continue to hope that the South German Governments will put a brake on the affair.

That H.H. should expect you to declare that there were no such things as semi-official newspaper articles is unfortunately a sign of the times.[2] He does not always restrict himself to what is plausible and people like ourselves who look upon him as on a principle that must be upheld as much as possible have the task of preventing these and similar exaggerations, which are a sign of the nervousness of old age, from becoming obvious. You know as well as I do that all the articles now published by the *Norddeutsche Allgemeine Zeitung* are published by the direct order of H.H. H.H. has simply run aground on the Swiss affair, and his position will get worse if he holds to his present course. He is very annoyed that the conciliatory remarks that H.M. is said to have made to the Neapolitan Swiss General Schumacher were published in the Press and were greeted with applause throughout the whole of Germany.

As a matter of fact the Swiss are trying to remedy the situation as quickly as possible by legislation. If a courteous Note were to arrive now, I do not see why the nonsense on the frontier should continue any longer.[3] But H.H. wants it to go on until winter. Obviously this will cause boundless discontent in Baden because foreigners will by-pass Baden. The lake district will lose, in particular. But what can we do about it? You at all events have done everything possible.

On the 20th I will be going to Schuls via Lindau.

Ever yours
Holstein. [...]

294. Holstein to Hugo von Radolin[4]

Berlin, 15 October 1889

Dear Rado,

[...] So the Russian visit is over.[5] The crowds' reception was icy. Kaiser and Chancellor did their best to offset the temperature on the

[1] In several dispatches Eisendecher was supplied with material with which to answer the objections raised in Baden against Bismarck's policy. In none of them was there any expression of dissatisfaction with Eisendecher personally. (From the Foreign Ministry files.)

[2] In reply to a dispatch from Eisendecher on a conversation with the Baden Minister Turban, Eisendecher was instructed to inform Turban that there was no such thing as a semi-official Press and that complaints about its behaviour were therefore uncalled for. (From the Foreign Ministry files.)

[3] A more rigorous customs inspection had been introduced by the Germans on the Swiss frontier. On 20 July Germany announced the abrogation within one year of the Immigration Treaty and its supplementary protocols.

[4] From the Radolin Papers.

[5] Tsar Alexander III visited Berlin from 11–13 October 1889. (See *Grosse Politik*, vol. VI, nos. 1358–9, pp. 359–62.)

streets by a great display of charm. Hence our Kaiser's speech at the luncheon for Alexander[1] and the Chancellor's appearance at the gala performance of the Opera.

The Tsar spoke to the Chancellor with some uneasiness about our Kaiser's visit to Constantinople. You will have read that the cancellation of this visit was represented in the Russian Press as the natural result of the Berlin visit. This result will nevertheless not now materialise.[2]

The Tsar is also said to have spoken anxiously to the Chancellor about Waldersee and his bellicose tendencies.

Cherevin[3] said to someone who told it to me: *'Le Chancelier se fait vieux, je le trouve beaucoup vieilli depuis deux ans.'* In response to the remark that the Chancellor was healthy and could last for a long time, Cherevin replied: *'Et bien, tant mieux, parce qu'il semble être à peu près le seul ici qui ne veut pas la guerre.'*

It is now said that the Tsar departed 'satisfied'. The calming down will doubtless last until our Sovereign gets to Istanbul.

The report about the bad reception of Kaiserin Friedrich in Copenhagen is said to have been deliberately spread by herself and Seck[endorff] and to have been quite untrue.

The Prince of Wales literally fawned on the Tsar,[4] and the Princess of Wales spoke in the bitterest way about Germany. Those two are supporters of the Russian-French-English alliance.

I forgot to say that the Tsar also asked the Chancellor whether we had no 'arrangement' with England.

Please keep the political part of this letter secret, except from Hatzfeldt. [...]

Always yours
H.

295. Herbert von Bismarck to Holstein

Monza,[5] 21 October 1889

Dear Holstein,

Crispi is annoyed with Taaffe's Austria, which is unfortunately also Imperial Austria, and though it is only over domestic *irredenta* difficulties these nevertheless touch him *to the quick*.[6] He is trying to get into closer touch with Russia, not only in the—utopian—hope of promoting the isolation of France, but also on account of his annoyance with narrow-minded Vienna with its Slav-Catholic colouring: *Ces messieurs d'Autriche sont toujours en retard d'une armée, d'une idée et d'une année,*

---

[1] At the gala luncheon on 11 October, Kaiser Wilhelm II drank a toast to the hundred years of friendship between the ruling Houses of Russia and Prussia and said he wanted to remain faithful to this tradition.
[2] Kaiser Wilhelm II visited Constantinople from 2–6 November.
[3] Adjutant-General to Alexander III.
[4] The Prince of Wales saw the Tsar in Denmark shortly before the Tsar's visit to Berlin.
[5] The German Kaiser and Kaiserin stopped in Italy on their way to Greece in order to visit the Italian King and Queen. (See below p. 319, note 3.) They arrived in Monza on 19 October and left from Genoa on the 23rd.
[6] In English in the original.

Napoleon I rightly said. The *sancta simplicitas austriaca* makes the juggling feat of the Triple Alliance increasingly difficult for us.

H.M. is in the best of humours and my reports to him pass off *comme sur des roulettes grassées*. Let us hope it will continue this way until we return. H.M. had invited himself to Monza again on 12 November to shoot pheasants, which thanks to the rain had to be left alive for the present. I disapprove of this renewed get-together from Venice, because Imperial visits lose their value when they are repeated too often, and also because *Re Umberto* will not be pleased at having to give up shooting pheasants for three whole weeks in expectation of another visit. [...]

Wishing you all that is good
Ever yours[1]
HB.

296. Eberhard zu Solms to Holstein

Rome, 26 October 1889

My dear friend,

Accept once more my most heartfelt thanks for all the favours and kindnesses which you showered upon me in Berlin. My feelings of friendship could not have been increased by the superb luncheons, but then the latter were far from exercising a prejudicial influence on those feelings, upon which they actually set the seal. Our conversations—especially at dinner on the last day with Waldersee—have subsequently occupied my thoughts a good deal, as you can readily imagine. They were extremely interesting, particularly because they cast quite a different light on the situation than does the usual dispatch-bag that is sent to me.

I found that it was no longer necessary, as I had previously assumed it would be, to make the latest peace moves palatable to Herr Crispi. He is delighted about the peaceful constellation that has taken shape as a result of the Tsar's visit to Berlin. He wants to see Russia satisfied so as to isolate France; he wants to see all movements in the Balkan countries suppressed; he has abolished the differential tariff with regard to France and is pleased with France's speedy recognition (which was carried out in the most polite manner) of the treaty with Menelik.[2] Damiani, Pisani,[3] Mayer[4]—all expressed themselves in a similar manner in favour of peace. Baron Bruck has been made thoughtful by the situa-

---

[1] In English in the original.

[2] Menelik II, Negus of Abyssinia, 1889–1914. Solms refers to the Treaty of Uccialli of 2 May 1889 between Menelik and Italy. According to the Italian version, Menelik accepted an Italian protectorate over Abyssinia. A supplementary agreement guaranteed a loan to Menelik for which the customs dues at Harrar were to serve as security. In case the interest could not be paid, Harrar was to be handed over to Italy.

[3] Alberto Pisani-Dossi (actually Carlos Dossi). Italian journalist and diplomatic agent; for a time he served as Crispi's private secretary; Chief of the Secretariat of the Consulta since 1889.

[4] Edmundo Mayer. Member of the Italian Foreign Ministry since 1875; for a time secretary to Depretis and Crispi; Minister in Belgrade, 1898; Ambassador in Washington, 1901.

tion, especially as Crispi is annoyed with Austria over the Trieste trials.[1] Count Kálnoky on the other hand is also annoyed because Crispi gave an instruction to Baron Blanc in the Bulgarian affair that did not conform with the Austrian one, after he must have learnt in time from Nigra of Kálnoky's intentions.[2] I am convinced that Crispi knew nothing of the matter and that neither he nor Damiani could have read Nigra's dispatch.

I am becoming convinced that Crispi has found out that the army is not so well prepared for war as he had previously supposed, that the rifles and the new powder are still not ready, that they would be happy to gain time to complete some ships, and that therefore he wants peace *but only for one or two years*. He replied to Baron Bruck's question: 'How do things stand as regards war and peace?' with an expressive and contented twinkle in his eye: 'The Kaiser believes peace is assured for two years, the Chancellor for one year; *voilà tout!*'

I feel confident from this that Crispi intends to sit still for the present and give us fewer surprises in the form of dangerous escapades.

Grand Duchess Katharina of Russia (actually Grand Duchess Georg of Mecklenburg), who has hitherto invariably ignored the Embassy, has sent her gentleman to me. I wrote my name in her book and have been invited by her to-day for two o'clock. I dine with her to-day at the Russian Ambassador's. Another result of the Tsar's visit!

The rain in Monza and Genoa was indescribable. Their Majesties must have had an appalling journey! You have surely heard about the arrangement to return to Monza from Venice in order to bang away at the 10,000 pheasants. The Kaiser wanted to leave his noble wife in Venice to let her recover from the sea voyage. He intended to go to Monza for two days. Her Majesty however was not pleased with the idea, and the Queen told her that she would feel that the Kaiserin had not enjoyed herself with her if she did not again accompany the Kaiser. I am curious to see what becomes of it all.

Farewell, dear friend. With the very best wishes

Your sincerely devoted
Solms.

297. Herbert von Bismarck to Holstein

Athens,[3] 28 October 1889

Dear Holstein,

[...] Russia does not want to be appeased with *Armenia*, where it does not want any extension of territory for religious reasons. It could only

[1] These were the trials of people who had been arrested in Trieste in connection with pro-Italian demonstrations.

[2] At the beginning of September Kálnoky had proposed to the Porte that Turkey approach the Powers on the question of legalising the position of Prince Ferdinand of Bulgaria. Turkey did not act on this suggestion when it became obvious that Russia would oppose this solution. The Italian Ambassador to Turkey was instructed to inform the Porte that in Crispi's opinion it would be inopportune to make any change in the *status quo* in Bulgaria. (From the Foreign Ministry files.)

[3] Kaiser Wilhelm II and Kaiserin Augusta had gone to Athens to attend the marriage of Princess Sophie of Prussia with Crown Prince Constantine of Greece on 27 October 1889.

be 'appeased' in Crispi's sense if Bulgaria were again to be made a satrapy under an *Orthodox* head as it was ten years ago—and that would only be the first bite.[1] Crispi's idea is tantamount to the squaring of the circle and is only worthy of notice as an expression of ill humour against Austria. The Greeks, elated by the wedding celebrations, seem to have gone mad again. Up to now I have avoided any kind of political conversation, but learn from the English Minister, Monson,[2] that Tricoupis[3] intends to deliver an aggressive speech next week at the opening of the Chamber, and to occupy Turkish islands in the Aegean Sea if the Sultan does not offer concessions to Crete. With a shrug I pointed to the isolation of Greece, which would make enemies of *everybody* by the use of violence, because *all* the Great Powers want peace in the Near East.

The celebrations are tiring; up to yesterday it was terribly hot, to-day cooler with a north wind. Wherever it borders on the wonderful transparent blue sea, the country is beautiful in the contours of its mountains, its southern colouration, and its reminders everywhere of Classical times. Otherwise, apart from the raising of currants, it is desperately barren, arid, stony, dusty and forsaken, the veritable island of the damned, *a most beastly, damnable country*.[4] There is great enthusiasm everywhere on the streets of Athens, probably counting in advance on future German support for Greek aspirations, towards which, fortunately, H.M. is completely cold. Le Maistre[5] did several silly things, embroiled himself with the navy which has criticised him in higher quarters, so that unfortunately H.M. is annoyed with him. I have calmed things down.

I am feeling quite well on the whole, only I sprained my ankle badly by slipping in Genoa harbour on a wet day, and this causes me considerable pain, especially when standing. The nicest experiences I have had here were two swims in the Aegean Sea. The huge suite returns home overland from Istanbul. I therefore hope to be in Berlin on 10 November.

Ever your
HB.

298. Bernhard von Bülow to Holstein

Sinaia, 28 October 1889

Dear Holstein,
[...] King Carol maintains that there are only a few Russian troops

[1] According to a memorandum by Herbert von Bismarck of 20 October, Crispi told him on the previous day that he did not approve of Austria's attitude with regard to Bulgaria (see p. 319, note 2) because it could bring Russia into an embarrassing situation which would endanger the peace. The Italian representatives in Constantinople and Sofia had therefore been instructed to advise against any step that might change the existing situation. Russia must be 'appeased', possibly with Armenia. (From the Foreign Ministry files.)

[2] Sir Edmund Monson. English Minister in Athens, 1888–92, in Brussels, 1893–6; Ambassador in Paris, 1896–1904.

[3] Charilaos Tricoupis. Greek Minister-President, 1886–90, 1892–5.

[4] In English in the original.

[5] Rudolf Le Maistre. German Minister in Athens, 1887–90.

stationed in Bessarabia and on the Rumanian frontier in general. This would indicate that the Russians are holding all their forces together against Austria and ourselves. Hence it is the more important for Austria not to divide up her forces. The Pan-Slav programme in the Balkan Peninsula is apparently aimed, during the period of peace still granted to Europe, at persuading the Balkan peoples in the event of war to attack Austria in the rear and so to prevent a full-scale campaign against Russia. Thus two Pan-Slav newspapers published in Belgrade— *Odjek* and *Correspondence Balcanique*—have recently proposed a Serbian-Bulgarian-Rumanian alliance. These papers say more or less that Bulgaria should depose its Ferdinand, form a Zankov[1]-Karavelov Government, and then join with Rumania and Serbia under the aegis of Russia to form a Balkan Confederation for the purpose of realising in common their national aspirations. If the Russian plan of setting her small neighbours at Austria's throat in a time of general conflagration succeeded, then we would have to bear the whole brunt of the Russian attack. I am certain you will agree that I should regard as my chief task the prevention of such an eventuality. To prevent the Rumanians from falling into the Russian trap, it is essential to pay a certain amount of attention to their expansionist aspirations—obviously in a suitable manner and with all due caution. When the Pan-Slavs continually remind the Rumanians of the three million Rumanians living in Austria-Hungary, the Rumanian claim to Bessarabia should at least not be rejected too sharply by the other side. For all Rumanians suffer from megalomania and the thought 'my fatherland must be greater' runs through all their heads. The King recently unburdened himself to me— in the course of a quiet walk, without witnesses—of the most extraordinary notions. He mentioned the fact that in Serbia there was a party that desired union with Rumania, touched again on the project of a Bulgarian-Rumanian personal union, described the idea of the union of all nine million Rumanians as a dream that would not of course be realised in our lifetime but might be in the distant future; and finally he expounded on Bessarabia as though it were an acute and urgently vital question for Rumania. The Rumanian expansionist aspirations cannot be completely ignored, otherwise these people will take the side of those who are always willing to promise everything at the cost of others.

The greatest obstacle in the way of collaboration between Rumania and Russia fortunately continues to be their fear and dislike of the despotic Russian governmental system, which pays no regard to foreign susceptibilities. The more skilful the Austrian representation is in the Near East, the more will Austria's policy of respect for the autonomy of the Balkan peoples arouse sympathy among them. This policy is unfortunately too often carried out by clumsy agents, whereas the Russian wolf looks after his affairs through the agency of his foxes.

Since Bratianu's fall we have in general made some progress here. Bratianu's followers and the members of the Junimea Society have

[1] Dragan Zankov. Russophil Bulgarian politician. Minister-President, 1883–4.

remained anti-Pan-Slav, whereas the former Slavophil Conservatives and dissident Liberals are becoming more and more anti-Russian and pro-Austrian, so that a sudden return to their former attitude is becoming increasingly difficult. The dark spot in the situation continues to be the apathy displayed by the present Government towards the unceasing underground agitation of the Pan-Slavs. The Government has taken no steps against either the picture peddlers, who have again made their appearance, or against the Russian trade centre planned by Hitrovo, whose commercial travellers (i.e. Pan-Slav emissaries) are to travel all over the country. I have confidentially suggested to the Austrian *Chargé d'Affaires*[1] that he use his influence to persuade the Rumanian Opposition Press and the Austrian Press to throw somewhat more light on these proceedings in order to force Katargi's[2] Government to take a stand against these intrigues. [...]

With kindest regards
Yours
Bernh. Bülow

299. Heinrich VII Reuss to Holstein

Vienna, 5 November 1889

My dear Herr von Holstein,

Many thanks for your letter of the 3rd, which I have dealt with according to your wish.

I can understand why we do not hit the Russians over the head with a club; but to treat them kindly is love's labour lost, I have long been convinced of that. I also believe that Alexander III is for the moment under the spell of Wilhelm II's well-known charm and that H.H. [Bismarck] has temporarily persuaded him not to believe all the lies he hears. But how long will that last! I am sorry that they will not be going through Hungary on this trip. It is a bit far to go from Gödöllö to Innsbruck, although the ruler here is not afraid of fatigue.

The hints about Rome were very helpful to me. I am ceaselessly harping on the necessity of this alliance for Austria, as you know. I would like to know what was said about it in Friedrichsruh.[3] [...]

With best wishes
Your very devoted
H. VII Reuss

[1] Probably Count Nicholas Szécsen von Temerin, at that time First Secretary of the Austro-Hungarian Legation in Bucharest. Ambassador to the Holy See, 1901–11, in Paris, 1911–14.

[2] Laskar Katargi. Rumanian Minister-President and Minister of the Interior, 1889; December 1891–5.

[3] Kálnoky had just spent two days in Friedrichsruh as the guest of the Chancellor. On 7 November Bismarck telegraphed to Wilhelm II: 'Count Kálnoky left me on the 4th after a satisfactory exchange of views about current problems, including the difficult Austrian relations with Italy and Bulgaria.' On 8 November Reuss reported that Kálnoky, who had just returned, had informed him that Bismarck appreciated Austria's difficulties in her relations with Italy. Count Kálnoky had assured him, however, 'that Austria would cultivate her relations with Italy in every possible way'. (From the Foreign Ministry files.)

300. Holstein to Hugo von Radolin[1]

28 November 1889

Dear Rado,

[...] Complaints from everyone that H.M. dodges political reports. At the same time he reads thirty to forty newspaper clippings one after the other and makes marginal comments on them. A curious personality. Yet I confess a certain liking for him. The Kaiserin has made great progress in public opinion. [...]

Best regards
from your
H.

301. Holstein to Hugo von Radolin[2]

5 December 1889

Dear Rado,

[...] With regard to Waldersee's position your informant may be right. W., driven by his wife, is still a partisan of Stöcker—but the Kaiser spoke to Helldorff[3] last Sunday in a determined way against this extreme tendency and empowered Helldorff to spread his remarks confidentially. At Verdy's dinner the Kaiser drank Wald.'s health saying: 'Well, here's luck, poisoner' which was certainly a two-edged compliment. [...]

Goodnight
Ever your
H.

[1] From the Radolin Papers. [2] From the Radolin Papers.
[3] Otto Heinrich von Helldorff-Bedra. Leader of the Conservatives in the Reichstag.

1890

302. Holstein to Herbert von Bismarck[1]

24 January 1890

Dear Herbert,

I did not sleep much after our talk. What disturbs me particularly is the thought that the timidity you inspire in people prevents them from being entirely frank with you either about their own views or about public opinion.

A position like your father's can be undermined only gradually, but there is at the moment no doubt that disruptive forces are at work. There is a great deal of bitterness in Parliament, and from there it is spreading rapidly to the Kaiser above and to the electorate below. The idea persists that Prince Bismarck does nothing himself and prevents others from doing anything, and unless this idea is killed at the source it will before long materially alter the Prince's position, *inside* Germany at least.

As regards the Anti-Socialist Law, the Conservatives are saying openly that *nothing* but the attitude of the Government (i.e. His Highness) prevents them from passing it without the expulsion clause, while reserving the right to make it more stringent if necessary.[2]

As for the question of the protection of labour which has suddenly become the vogue, opposition is made difficult because it can be shown that the system is in fact working well in Saxony, to which H.H. often used to refer as a model of administration.

Much more is being said about his attitude to labour questions, but I do not care to repeat it because the subject is outside my province. I will just confine myself to a few main points and can only say that at present H.H. stands very much alone. The Government supporters, even those of the Centre—e.g. Hüne[3]—think he is, in one way or another, making their position vis-a-vis their constituents unnecessarily difficult.

Even H.H.'s *positive* proposals are being eyed with suspicion and examined for ulterior motives. Considerable harm was done in this

---

[1] Note by Holstein: 'Copy made in bed.' (See *Memoirs*, p. 157.)

[2] In October 1889 Bismarck brought before the Reichstag a bill which would have made the Anti-Socialist Law a permanent and integral part of German public law. The existing law contained a clause which entitled the police to expel Social Democrats from their homes. This power of expulsion was rejected by the Reichstag commission. The Conservatives finally voted against the Anti-Socialist Law on the grounds that the entire Law was worthless without this clause.

[3] Karl, Baron von Hoiningen-Hüne. From 1877 Member of the Prussian Chamber of Deputies; of the Reichstag 1884–93. He was one of the leaders of the Conservative-aristocratic wing of the Centre Party.

respect by the plan to reinforce the garrison here, which of course became known.[1] It was regarded as an unnecessary measure and the conclusion was drawn that H.H. intended to cause alarm. It is with the same feelings that people are now awaiting his speech in which, it is said, he intends to introduce the Red Spectre. Conversely the Kaiser is gaining ground in many quarters because people say he does make some effort in his desire to arrive at the facts. One would hail this phenomenon with unmixed satisfaction if the Chancellor were not thereby the loser.

Under these circumstances it is inadvisable to push things to extremes, as H.H. may have made up his mind to do during his solitary walks.

You know how H.H. would often say, when things were not going as he wished: 'Really, people behave as though I were the only person with an interest in the Reich.' This idea might be put to good use *now*.

To turn from problems to people. Acting on my belief that a concession in the Maybach[2] affair would have a good effect on the Kaiser and throughout the Reich, I made rapid enquiries about Thielen[3] and discovered that he and Fleck[4] are the only two competent officials in Maybach's department. A further outstanding personality in the division of mines is a Herr von Heyden-Rynsch;[5] although a lawyer, not a miner, he is regarded as the most suitable successor to Hüssen,[6] whose appointment is said to cast a shadow on Maybach's administration because of some suspicious marriage connection. There is only *one* opinion on Hüssen's inefficiency.

I have heard nothing about Thielen being related to Bötticher.[7] That would not be a crime in itself. But we still have Fleck. As things stand today, almost *anyone* would be better than Maybach.

Rottenburg's recommendation of Golz[8] shows that he is bent on preventing Maybach's departure; Trippelmann[9] knows H.H. better than almost anyone, and is aware of H.H.'s feelings about military encroachments on civilian affairs.

Rottenburg is still the nihilist he always was, and is pushing things towards a crisis so that at least he will not go down alone.

Your very weary
H.

303. Friedrich von Pourtalès to Holstein

St Petersburg, 9 February 1890

Dear *Herr Geheimer Rat*,

I want to take advantage of to-day's favourable opportunity to thank

---

[1] See *Memoirs*, p. 146; Bismarck, *Die Gesammelten Werke*, vol. VIc, no. 129, pp. 119–20.

[2] Maybach's Ministry, which at this period administered the state coal mines, was accused of serious mismanagement in this field. (See Eulenburg, *Aus 50 Jahren*, p. 287.)

[3] Karl von Thielen. From 1887 Head of the Hanover railways; Prussian Minister of Public Works and Head of the Reich railways, 1891–1902.

[4] Director of Communications in the Ministry of Public Works.

[5] Superintendent of mines; Chief administrator of mines in Halle.

[6] Chief Superintendent of mines; Head of Division I in the Ministry of Public Works.

[7] Karl Heinrich von Bötticher. Prussian Minister of State; State Secretary of the Ministry of the Interior, 1880–97.

[8] Gustav Golz. Lieutenant-General and Chief of the Corps of Engineers.

[9] A nickname for Rottenburg.

you for your kind letter which I found extremely interesting. I had in fact intended to write to you by the last courier, but he was called away so suddenly that I could not carry out my intention because I happened to be hunting that day.

I wrote to His Excellency about a fortnight ago[1] and emphasised that our wish to settle the date of His Imperial Majesty's proposed visit here[2] had been fulfilled more swiftly and more easily than I had expected. I then tried to point out that in my humble opinion, now that it was certain that the Russians were more or less intent on this visit, it seemed to me highly desirable that from now on they should be made to take the initiative in the matter. Fortunately it appears from the dispatch[3] recently sent to Villaume that this is now our intention.

Our relations with Russia are now tolerable, as good as we can hope for under the present circumstances. We can no longer count on love, so that tolerable relations can be based only on mutual respect. Courteous treatment and a constant renewal of the proof that we were not the ones who wrecked our former good relations are certainly indicated, but I regard all exaggerated expressions of friendship, and particularly the constant seizing of the initiative, as extremely dangerous. Such behaviour makes the Russians either suspicious or still more demanding. The only person on whom we can work with any assurance of success is the fat Tsar, but he prefers to be left in peace as much as possible.

It is interesting to see how the Chancellor really succeeded this time in dispelling all the Tsar's mistrust of *him*.[4] People are still talking about it, and in this connection General Cherevin told me recently that this meeting and the preceding one[5] were as different as black is from white.

I have referred purposely to *the Chancellor*, for the Tsar does not trust the Kaiser an inch; it is precisely on this point that you can see the cloven hoof in the whole business. In other words, for the next few years, so long as the Chancellor is alive, it suits the Russians very well to jog along with us on our present footing, but the trouble-makers here will certainly see to it that no lasting cordial relationship develops between the two countries, and particularly between the two dynasties. And so I remain of the opinion that if His Imperial Majesty pays the Tsar too many civilities on his own initiative, he is greatly compromising his dignity without any tangible result. The way these civilities are returned here is plain from the fact that at his birthday luncheon Tsar Alexander was wearing neither the famous monogram nor any Prussian decoration.

In general people here are not talking politics much this year. The

[1] Pourtalès' letter to Herbert von Bismarck has not been found in the Foreign Ministry files.

[2] The reference is to an invitation to Wilhelm II to take part in the Russian manoeuvres.

[3] In a dispatch of 31 January Villaume was instructed to reply to a possible invitation to Wilhelm II that the end of August would be suitable. (From the Foreign Ministry files.)

[4] During the Tsar's visit to Berlin, 11–13 October 1889. (See *Grosse Politik*, vol. VI, nos. 1358–9, pp. 359–62.)

[5] On 18 November 1887. (See *Grosse Politik*, vol. V, nos. 1057, 1129, pp. 203–5, 324.)

interest of society is focused almost exclusively on performances of Russian plays which are given in various salons twice or three times weekly. It is a fairly harmless way of satisfying national vanity. It is a remarkable symptom of conditions here that they had no hesitation in performing in a salon Tolstoy's *The Power of Darkness* which was, I am sorry to say, put on recently in Berlin. This is actually a piece of Zola filth, but it excites immense admiration here simply because it is Russian.

But now I must conclude, with the assurance of my continued respect and gratitude.

Your obedient servant,

F. Pourtalès.

304. Friedrich von Pourtalès to Holstein

St Petersburg, 22 February 1890

Dear *Herr Geheimer Rat*,

Many thanks for your last letter and the friendly advice it contained.

People here are, in my opinion, inclining more and more to side with Prince Bismarck, who is regarded as the exponent of a pro-Russian policy, and to criticise the Kaiser, who is thought to be exposed to, and receptive to, anti-Russian influences.

The reception accorded here to the Kaiser's manifestos[1] showed this very clearly. Most people think them a youthful prank of which the Chancellor disapproves. I do not think the *Grashdanin* would have carried that outrageous article the other day, which the Embassy forwarded to Berlin, unless it was known that such language would not be unwelcome in the Anitchkov Palace.

None of this would matter much here if it were not, as I believe, a new factor impeding the re-establishment of really intimate relations between Russia and ourselves. In this connection, the one thing which makes any impact here (I mean on the Tsar) is a reference to our common monarchical interests. Now that people have become convinced that the Chancellor desires friendship with Russia (I nearly said 'at any price'), he is represented as the sole champion of the true monarchical principle in Germany, the young Kaiser on the other hand as one who in the thoughtless arrogance of youth is undermining his own throne.

This much is certain: whereas formerly, e.g. during the Ninety-Nine Days, the Russians automatically sided against the Chancellor whenever they got wind of a disagreement between him and the sovereign, now the opposite is the case. I can on this occasion simply repeat: the successful result of this recent meeting still persists in that the Tsar trusts Prince Bismarck, but as regards relations between the two monarchs, any impression which Tsar Alexander may have momentarily

---

[1] Two pro-labour manifestos which were published on 4 February in the *Reichs und Staatsanzeiger*. One of them was not countersigned by the Chancellor. (See *Memoirs*, p. 148.)

retained of their personal contact in Berlin can now in my opinion be regarded as effaced. This emerges very clearly from the way every single act of our Most Gracious Majesty is criticised in Russian society, even by the Grand-Dukes. The breach is in fact too great to be easily healed. They only trust the Chancellor because they are certain he wants to spend the last years of his life in peace, and that peace for the next few years also fits in with Russian intentions. And so I return to the opinion already stated, namely that a *modus vivendi* between ourselves and Russia is possible, but that a striving for Russian friendship is futile and dangerous.

It is indeed extraordinary that whenever Tsar Alexander has met Schweinitz recently, he has not once enquired after our royal family, and has in fact hardly mentioned our Most Gracious Majesty's name. The Tsarina is the same: the most she does is to ask some question containing barely concealed criticism about events at the German court.

The Tsar has never touched on the question of the invitation to the manoeuvres, but it is quite certain that it is being discussed in military circles and is regarded as a *fait accompli*. But one could definitely not assert that people here are looking forward to this event with particular pleasure.

And so I beg leave to conclude for the present, with the assurance of my deepest respect.

I remain always
Your most obedient servant,
F. Pourtalès.

305. Heinrich VII Reuss to Holstein

Vienna, 25 February 1890

My dear Herr von Holstein,

I had been uneasy for some time at hearing nothing from you; it seemed an evil omen. Now that I have at last learned the facts from another quarter, I understand the reason for your silence. It seems that the breach can no longer be healed. You always saw this coming and rightly foretold who would prove to be the stronger. If it comes to a complete break, a deep impression will be made abroad. 'Our oppressor has been laid low', some will exult, while others will complain 'the greatest guarantee of peace has been destroyed'. People here will swell the latter chorus. Kálnoky is badly upset by the increasingly insistent rumours. The Austrians, with their fervour for peace, looked upon Prince Bismarck as the moderator of [the Kaiser's] youthful exuberance, despite the latter's well-known Nordic sympathies. I had not expected the moment to come so soon when he would wish to be his own Chancellor. But there will have to be someone to take over the office in name at least, and who will that be? I do not expect you will answer this question but I cannot resist putting it.

With best regards
H. VII Reuss.

306. Paul Kayser to Holstein

28 February 1890

Dear *Herr Geheimrat*,

His Highness has issued a memorandum[1] stating that the draft bill for the protection of labour is not to be introduced before the end of the *Conference*.[2]

His Majesty is furious about this and has added marginal notes that he does *not want this*, but that the bill should be proceeded with independently.

H.M. *sent for me* and I tried to explain that this was no misfortune; but he would have none of it and declared a spoke had been put in his wheel and he would not allow that sort of thing.

When I heard this I pointed out to H.M. that H.H.'s memorandum had not been drafted in the Foreign Ministry and doubtless they would find common ground again provided the international Conference concluded its labours *very soon*. In the meantime, I said, we would need four weeks after the document came from the Ministry of State; that would take at least another week, so we had five weeks to play with. By that time the Conference might well be over. The Kaiser seemed to *approve* of this solution; he told me and, previously, Herr von Bötticher, in specific terms, *that to his mind all difficulties between himself and H.H. had been smoothed out.*

I leave it to you to decide what use to make of this, *if any*—at any rate I was anxious to give you further evidence of how much I deserved to be excluded from the Conference, and what a useful influence I might have exerted there in the interests of reconciliation.[3]

In great haste,
Your devoted servant,
Kayser.

307. Wilhelm von Bismarck to Holstein

2 March 1890

Dear Holstein,

[...] I am not satisfied with the 'reconciliation' between H.M. and H.H. In my view the position is as confused as before, and the tension continues. I am more and more afraid I shall be proved right in my belief that they will not stick together beyond the summer, unless a violent struggle with the Reichstag over the military question draws them together again for a time. Their mutual suspicion seems to me as

---

[1] Memorandum by Bismarck of 26 February 1890. See Bismarck, *Die Gesammelten Werke*, vol. VIc, no. 436, pp. 432-3.

[2] The International Conference for the Protection of Labour, which met in Berlin from 15 to 29 March.

[3] Kayser wrote to Holstein on 27 February. 'I am writing this after a sleepless night. Never in my life has anything made me so angry as the plan to exclude me entirely from the international Conference. That is my reward for offering my services to the State Secretary unreservedly and without recompense, for disregarding my health and well-being, and for experiencing so much worry and agitation over the last few weeks in my efforts to end the quarrel between H.M. and H.H.'

lively as ever; I gather this from Press observations on the crisis, which after all are put out by someone, and from the circumstance that the *Norddeutsche Allgemeine Zeitung* prints them. And I do not think the present Ministers will continue to work in peace and harmony with H.H. Bötticher has been playing a double game and will undoubtedly continue to do so. H.H. knows this and will *never* trust B. again.[1]

Goodnight,
Yours,
B.B.

308. Friedrich von Pourtalès to Holstein

St Petersburg, [19] March 1890

Dear *Herr Geheimer Rat.*

I began a letter to you on two separate occasions, but both times I decided not to send it because I was afraid of giving you incorrect or incomplete information on the questions raised in your last letter.

But of course we have now been overtaken by events.[2] It would, I think, be premature to express an opinion at once on the impression Prince Bismarck's resignation will make here, and the reaction it may have on Russia's relations with us.

It was only yesterday that people here began to believe seriously in the Imperial Chancellor's resignation and to think about the consequences of this event. Most people who have discussed the affair with me have expressed the utmost astonishment that the Kaiser can have brought himself to accept his resignation. The Russians cannot really grasp the idea yet that the great man who has directed our policy for a quarter of a century is to make way for a successor; the impact of the *fact* itself is for the moment so powerful that its *consequences* are not yet being considered.

I do not really know what Shuvalov was doing here apart from visiting his newly-engaged son.[3] But I think his sudden appearance in St Petersburg was connected less with Near Eastern affairs than with the situation in Germany. I am inclined to think either that he judged it necessary to come, or that he was summoned here to give a personal report on the situation in Berlin.

He seems to have convinced Tsar Alexander that Prince Bismarck's resignation will not cause any shift in our foreign policy; such at least was the purport of one or two hints Giers dropped in strictest confidence to Schweinitz. Giers emphasised that the Tsar now felt absolute confidence in our Kaiser, particularly as the representative of the monarchical principle.

I candidly confess that I was struck by this statement in that I had formerly assumed, from various rumours coming from the Anichkov

---

[1] See *Memoirs*, pp. 143–4.

[2] On 18 March 1890, in response to the Kaiser's second demand, Bismarck handed in his resignation, which was accepted by two Orders in Council of 20 March. (Bismarck, *Die Gesammelten Werke*, vol. VIc, pp. 435–8.)

[3] Paul, Count Shuvalov. Russian Ambassador in Berlin, 1885–94. Shuvalov had gone to St Petersburg on 27 February. (See *Grosse Politik*, vol. VII, p. 3, note **.)

Palace, that the Kaiser's recent activities in the field of social welfare seemed highly suspect to the Tsar and had estranged him still further from our sovereign. How far Shuvalov may have influenced the Tsar's opinions on this point I do not venture to say.

The Tsar sent for Schweinitz today before his departure for Berlin. The audience is taking place at this very moment, and I am intensely anxious to know the outcome.[1] It is interesting, at a time like this, to observe how the Russians judge our young ruler.

Only a few months ago all that was known of him was that he liked travelling about and spreading alarm, and would occasionally deliver a fiery speech. People watched this with a certain rather malicious pleasure. It was as if they said: 'We need only sit back and let things take their course. The Chancellor, who in any case wants peace at any price now, has only a few years to go, and Germany will certainly not grow more powerful under this young Kaiser.'

Things are now substantially changed. Various events have taught the Russians that Kaiser Wilhelm II represents a force to be reckoned with. But his most recent conduct has at the same time provoked a change in anti-German circles here.

It is of course common knowledge that democratic ideas are widely disseminated throughout the Russian middle classes. Such people cannot but welcome sympathetically the Kaiser's initiative in the labour question. Thus there have recently been signs of a changed atmosphere in precisely those circles where a hatred of Germany and the desire to settle accounts with us were particularly strong. One may quote as an instance the attitude of certain papers like the *Novosti*. Without overrating this change in the atmosphere, I do not think one can ignore it in any appraisal of the situation.

On the other hand recent events in Germany have caused some shaking of heads in conservative circles (if this term can be used at all in the situation here) where monarchical considerations still caused many people to desire co-operation with Germany; these events, together with the already existing antipathy to Germany and things German, have destroyed any remaining spark, perhaps not of pro-German feeling, but of desire to be on good terms with us. These circles see our young Kaiser's behaviour as the action of a frivolous young man who is thereby undermining his own throne and the monarchical principle in general. In these circles I heard it said repeatedly yesterday that Prince Bismarck's resignation makes war seem more likely.

But that must be all for to-day. You can imagine the anxiety with which I await further developments at home, and how grateful I should be if you would drop me a line occasionally.

I remain with sincere respect
Your obedient servant,
F. Pourtalès.

---

[1] See Schweinitz, *Denkwürdigkeiten*, vol. II, pp. 396–7. Schweinitz spoke with the Tsar on 19 March and left for Berlin the same evening.

309. Holstein to Karl von Eisendecher[1]

[26 March 1890]

Dear friend,

Just as I sat down to write I heard cheering in the street. His Highness is driving past to wait upon the Kaiser as Colonel-General.[2]

Since, while you were here, we discussed everything frankly together, I have little new to tell you. The immediate cause for the break arose from His Highness' refusal to allow the Ministers access to His Majesty without his own approval. His Majesty first made a personal request that such access be granted, and then sent General Hahnke[3] to His Highness asking him if he would cancel the order restricting access.[4] His Highness replied he was not in a position to do so. It is alleged that His Majesty thereupon sent someone else to point out the necessity, under the circumstances, of their parting company.

All this has no doubt given you enough to think about, so I will not burden you with my own reflections.

I deplore the fact that Herbert is also going. As a mediator between his father and His Majesty, he would have enjoyed considerable status with the latter and would have kept open the possibility of His Highness' subsequent return.[5] I tried all conceivable means, even going to Bleichröder and asking him to try to influence Prince Bismarck—not out of friendship for Herbert, but to prepare for a possible return of his father. Bleichröder did it, too. His Highness, however, rejoined that he could not possibly urge his son to remain. Herbert expressed himself in very moderate terms to me, and as reasons for resigning his office adduced health and the attitude of the Reichstag. To which he added His Majesty's methods of work.

I have no idea who will now replace Herbert. Alvensleben[6] has apparently no wish to do so. His Highness recommended Bernhard Bülow and Stirum to Caprivi. What is your opinion? As for me I should then leave. It would not greatly surprise me. In any case, one will now have to forego that calm sense of security which one had hitherto enjoyed in one's position.

Best regards
Holstein.

310. Karl von Eisendecher to Holstein

Karlsr[uhe], 4 April 1890

My dear Holstein,

The most astonishing things are happening; judging by your letter

[1] From the Eisendecher Papers.

[2] On 20 March Bismarck was appointed Colonel-General of Cavalry with the rank of Field-Marshal. On the 26th he had a farewell audience with the Kaiser. (Bismarck, *Die Gesammelten Werke*, vol. XV, pp. 528, 530.)

[3] Wilhelm von Hahnke. Aide-de-Camp of Kaiser Wilhelm II; Head of the Imperial Military Cabinet, 1888–1901.

[4] The Cabinet order of 8 September 1852. Printed in Heinrich von Poschinger, *Denkwürdigkeiten O. von Manteuffels* (1901), vol. II, p. 247.

[5] See *Memoirs*, p. 149.

[6] Friedrich Johann, Count von Alvensleben. Minister at The Hague, 1882–4, in Washington, 1884–6, in Brussels, 1886–1901; Ambassador in St Petersburg, 1901–5.

you did not expect M[arschall][1] to succeed Herbert any more than I did. I hear, not from local sources but from my sister in Berlin, that the Grand-Duke of Baden is said to have played an important part in this appointment. What is your own attitude? And don't you think that Berchem, Lindau and one or two other greybeards in the Foreign Ministry have serious doubts about whether they should remain at their posts? We feel flattered here,[2] but we are experiencing some difficulty in finding a successor for the Behrenstrasse.[3] [...]

I just spoke briefly to the Grand-Duke on his arrival; I shall make no attempt to see him, but shall wait until His Royal Highness feels the need to talk to me. I have the definite impression that he played a considerable role in Prince Bismarck's overthrow. On the other hand, if I am correctly informed, Kaiserin Fr[iedrich] seems to have sided whole-heartedly with our old chief. His departure from Berlin must have been an overwhelming experience. According to Prince Max's[4] account, Berlin has scarcely ever seen anything to equal it.

Hitherto I have tried in vain to adapt myself to the new conditions; in particular the future of our overall European policy seems to me rather uncertain. The Chancellor[5] and M[arschall] are rather out of their depth, and you are really the only man in the Foreign Ministry who is completely *au courant*.

I should be extremely grateful to you for any news. What are Herbert's plans? Sooner or later he is bound to come back, and it is understandable that for the time being he declined to remain.

M[arschall] and I were boyhood playmates in Frankfurt; I like him very much, personally. He is younger than I am, incidentally; younger than the newly created 'Excellency', B[erchem], and of course, than yourself.

      Best regards from your old faithful
               Eisendecher.

311. Holstein to Herbert von Bismarck
   Copy
               5 April [1890]
Dear Herbert,

Your present reserve makes it plain to me, after talking with Bill, that we still hold divergent conceptions about professional obligations.[6] Perhaps time will bring a change. Considering our past association, I think it desirable that we should not take personal leave of one another at a moment of discord.

[1] Adolf Hermann Marschall, Baron von Bieberstein. Minister representing Baden in Berlin, 1883–90; State Secretary in the German Foreign Ministry, 1890–7; Ambassador in Constantinople, 1897–1912.

[2] About the appointment of Marschall, the Minister of Baden to Prussia, as German State Secretary.

[3] The Baden Legation in Berlin.

[4] Prince Max von Baden. German Chancellor in 1918.   [5] Caprivi.

[6] Herbert von Bismarck had quarrelled with Holstein because he had shown Caprivi a copy of Germany's Reinsurance Treaty with Russia. (See *Memoirs*, pp. 129–32, and Holstein's letter to Eisendecher of 16 April 1890.)

I am therefore bidding you farewell in this letter and I send you my sincere wishes for good health and your future.

Ever yours,
Holstein.

312. Herbert von Bismarck to Holstein

5 April 1890

Dear Holstein,

I see with regret from your letter just received that, for no reason, you have withdrawn your acceptance of the invitation for this evening which I gave you yesterday; for you give no reason in your letter. Since you speak of our past association you will understand my particular regret that *you* should be the only one of all the Foreign Ministry officials who seems to begrudge me this final honour in the house I am now about to leave.

As for the conversation with Bill of which you write,[1] I know nothing about it so I can make no comment—and professional obligations only existed between us as long as I was Head of the Foreign Ministry. However, only the Head is entitled to define the nature of such obligations; thus there can be no such thing as a different conception between him and the other officials. You are most unjust to reproach me with reserve.

Last Friday, when I was late and hurrying to dinner and you stopped me on the stairs, I told you I should be glad to see you on my return from Friedrichsruh. I have been back for three days, doing nothing but clearing out and packing up and not stirring from the house, but the first news I have of you is to receive at this very moment your refusal of my invitation. Time will bring changes enough; I hope they will be happy ones for you and that the future fulfils all your hopes. Since you avoid me it will be some time before we meet again, for I am unlikely to return to Berlin.

Farewell.
Yours ever,
H. Bismarck.

313. Philipp zu Eulenburg to Holstein

O[ldenburg], 8 April 1890

Dear Baron,

Your letter reached me in Amsterdam a couple of evenings ago, together with one from Fischer,[2] which I sent off at once to His Majesty with a letter of my own, a copy of which I enclose.[3] You will gather from it that I spoke to Trost in Stuttgart. The mood in Bavaria is *ugly*, and I shall ask His Majesty in Bremen on the 21st whether I may give

---

[1] See below, Holstein's letter to Eisendecher of 16 April 1890.

[2] Dr Franz Fischer. *Justizrat*; the Berlin correspondent of the *Kölnische Zeitung*. Fischer's letter has not been printed.

[3] See enclosure.

the Regent some information myself at the beginning of May. Under prevailing conditions I think that Rantzau, if only as B.'s son-in-law, is positively dangerous. But in view of public opinion I should think it still more dangerous to remove him *forthwith*. It is a disaster we have to reckon with.

A report on opinion here, intended for the Kaiser, will reach you tomorrow. It is better for me to write to you and for His Majesty to receive this letter from *Caprivi*. We must see to it that H.M. grows to like Caprivi as much as possible—and it will considerably strengthen H.M.'s confidence in C. if he sees that my letters go through this channel.

Don't you think so too?

Sincerely, your very faithful,
P.E.

I can also say more about Rantz[au] in a letter to you than if I wrote direct to the Kaiser. Under the present circumstances that is important.

ENCLOSURE
Philipp zu Eulenburg to Kaiser Wilhelm II[1]
Copy

O[ldenburg], 8 April 1890

Your Majesty,

I have the honour to enclose with my most humble respects, the copy of a letter by Dr Fischer (*Kölnische Zeitung*), the contents of which, I have no doubt, will prove to be of great interest to your Majesty.

The fact that Fischer, who has not written to me for a very long time, feels compelled to send me this report on public opinion, is evidence of its importance. Yet I would respectfully and earnestly *entreat* Your Majesty not to plan a wider programme so soon after the successes in the Council of State and the Conference, which were beyond all expectation.[2] Germany is nervous as a result of Prince Bismarck's retirement and the period that preceded it. Like a fever patient, her first need is a peaceful sleep to help her recover. Your Majesty informed me in Berlin of your intention to be satisfied for the present with the reforms of the Council of State and the Conference. I am therefore at a loss to account for the source of the official articles in the *Reichsanzeiger*.[3] I regret to have to confirm Fischer's observation on the general mood in the Reich, so far as Bavaria and Württemberg are concerned. During my short stay in Stuttgart I had an interview with a close friend of Crailsheim, Dr Trost, a counsellor on religious affairs. I was able on this occasion to do a good deal to further Your Majesty's interests, but it was a drop

[1] Printed in part in Haller, *Eulenburg*, p. 78.

[2] Both the *Staatsrat* and the international conference for the protection of labour had drafted programmes to improve the conditions of the workers.

[3] An officially inspired pro-labour article, which appeared in the *Reichsanzeiger* at the beginning of April, was widely interpreted as encouragement for the Social Democrats and was the reason for the above-mentioned letters by Fischer and Holstein. (See Haller, *Eulenburg*, p. 78.)

in the vast ocean of feeling created in Munich by Lerchenfeld's[1] biassed dispatches and Rantzau's inactivity (which may be forgiven under the present circumstances)!

Your obedient servant
E.[2]

314. Eberhard zu Solms to Holstein

Rome, 11 April 1890[3]

P.S.[4]

We had a court banquet yesterday. Only the Heads of Mission and their wives, and Count Goltz[5] (who is leaving), apart from the Cabinet Ministers.

When the royal party arrived Their Majesties addressed only a few words of greeting to particular persons including myself. The King spoke of nothing but the Model 88 gun. Then we went in to dinner. I was seated next to the Duchess of Genoa, the Queen's mother, and sister of the King of Saxony, whom I had already met on her honeymoon and later saw much of in Dresden. When she discussed our recent personnel changes, though cautious in what she said, she kept raising her eyes to heaven. The innovations were decidedly not to her taste. The old lady summed up her opinions in the words: 'Rather young, rather young!' I took advantage of the occasion to show her the situation in a somewhat rosier light. After dinner we stood about talking interminably. We were not drawn up according to rank but were standing about informally. When the King reached me he spoke first of the services we had again rendered to the Italian finances in Berlin and thanked me for our successful support.[6] Then he touched on Prince Bismarck's resignation, so I seized the opportunity of giving him some idea of the situation and of the excellent choice H.M. the Kaiser has made; I emphasised particularly that our foreign policy would continue to follow the same course as hitherto, and that things would run as smoothly under General Caprivi as under Prince Bismarck. The King replied: *'Oui, je crois bien que tout ça marchera parfaitement et qu'il n'y a pas de danger.'* He said this as he was shaking hands with me and turning to my neighbour, but I had the feeling that there was no inner conviction behind the words. And he did not converse with me so long as usual (though I may be mistaken); it seemed to me that he was glad not to have to pursue the subject further.

Ah well, we must give the rest of the world time to adapt itself to the new situation. It's a slow business!

Ever yours
Solms.

[1] Hugo, Count von Lerchenfeld. Bavarian Minister in Berlin, 1880–1919.

[2] Wilhelm II's answer, a copy of which was in the Holstein Papers, is printed in Haller, *Eulenburg*, p. 78.

[3] The date was written by Holstein.

[4] The first two pages of this letter are missing.   [5] Karl August von der Goltz.

[6] At the beginning of April 1890 an agreement had been reached between a number of Berlin banks and several Italian banks concerning the settlement of some Italian financial obligations. The Foreign Ministry had used its influence to obtain a solution satisfactory to the Italians. (From the Foreign Ministry files.)

315. Holstein to Karl von Eisendecher[1]

B[erlin], 16 April 1890

Dear Eisendecher,

I had already begun two letters to you, but they had to be abandoned under the pressure of work.

I was much interested by your remarks on the causes of the crisis. In my opinion, however, the main cause was the obstinacy of the B[ismarck]s, father and son. We discussed this, to be sure, while you were here. The two fallacies—'The Kaiser must be handled firmly' and 'The Kaiser will not conceivably get rid of Prince Bismarck'—did a great deal of harm. I also think it highly probable that the Kaiser vented his indignation to his uncle.[2]

Furthermore, as I remarked in my letter to H.B. of 24 January[3] about which I told you, His Highness had gradually become isolated because he himself avoided contact with political circles. This fact was confirmed in a way which even I found surprising when yesterday in the Landtag not a single party could find a good word for Prince Bismarck, not even the Conservatives. I find that quite incredible, but significant.

I fell out with Herbert right at the very end.

On the day of the investiture[4] Caprivi asked to see a secret document[5] which the Kaiser wished to discuss with him immediately afterwards. I let him have the document, to Herbert's unbounded fury. Bill, to whom I mentioned the matter, said (and I tell you this in complete confidence); 'You ought to have told Caprivi that you knew nothing of the matter.'

A commentary is hardly necessary.

As I was not prepared to admit that I was wrong, I took leave of Herbert by letter,[6] and received an irritable reply.[7] And that was that. I will show you the correspondence when you visit me here.

Apparently the Bismarck family are highly incensed; they are abusing me as they have already abused countless others; I am also being reproached for remaining in the service.

What sort of personality Marschall is I still do not know. He can hardly be faultless, or he would not be human.

He is very sound on the files; it remains to be seen how he will succeed in dealing with the *Reichstag*. I think a great deal both of Caprivi's character and of his abilities. His speech yesterday[8] has met with general approval. I have very little business with him.

I must stop now.

Best regards
Yours,
Holstein.

[1] From the Eisendecher Papers.
[2] Grand Duke Friedrich of Baden.   [3] See above.
[4] For the Chapter of the Order of the Black Eagle on 22 March.
[5] The Reinsurance Treaty with Russia. (See *Memoirs*, pp. 129–32.)
[6] See above, Holstein's letter of 5 April 1890.
[7] See above, Herbert von Bismarck's letter of 5 April 1890.
[8] In the Prussian Chamber of Deputies on 15 April 1890.

316. Heinrich VII Reuss to Holstein

Vienna, 18 April 1890

Dear Herr von Holstein,

I really think Kálnoky knows nothing definite about the matter in question;[1] otherwise he could not have spoken to me to-day as he did. There is nothing unusual in his speaking of Prince Bismarck's friendship for Russia which had often caused him embarrassment; he has always spoken in those terms. Hence I felt no obligation to enlighten him, but I just used the agreed formula, that we had never adhered more closely to the [Austrian] Alliance than at present.

On the whole he gave me the impression of already slipping quite comfortably into the new relationship and of no longer regretting the old so much as at first. He was well pleased with the first speech made by our Chief.[2] He felt that the subject of the semi-official Press was a bit too delicate to be treated in the way that it was. [...]

I am still not in a position to report on Italy. Kálnoky was gratified that we had procured money for the Italians, since this showed the Italian opposition that the Triple Alliance had material advantages.

Many thanks once more for the friendly reception you gave me in Berlin.

With best regards
Your devoted,
H. VII Reuss.

317. Philipp zu Eulenburg to Holstein

Oldenburg, 25 April 1890.

Dear Baron,

When you spend two full days attending a Kaiser who is being officially honoured on land and sea, you simply must have sleep to keep up your strength, but my sleep was *snored* away by Waldersee (we were sharing a cabin) in a way that beats anything I have ever known.[3] You will understand that on my return I was in no state to write to you but, limp as a rag, had to clear up the routine business that had accumulated just before I left. Today I am back to normal—largely due to my anger over Prince [Bismarck's] unrestrained behaviour.[4] What a pitiful spectacle! I agree with H.M. that there should be no counter-attacks at the moment. The government's dignified reticence is making a good impression. Fundamentally it will be strengthened rather than harmed by Prince Bismarck's behaviour, which I find inexplicably foolish.

I have so much to tell you about my trip with the Kaiser that I prefer to give you a *verbal* report and shall mention only essentials here.

[1] The German Reinsurance Treaty with Russia.
[2] See above, p. 337, note 8.
[3] The Kaiser had travelled to Bremen on 20 April to pay an official visit to the city. Eulenburg shared improvised sleeping quarters with Waldersee on board the *Hohenzollern*. (See Eulenburg, *Aus 50 Jahren*, p. 245, note 1.)
[4] After his resignation Bismarck made highly unfavourable comments on government policies in interviews with the Press and sharply criticised the Kaiser's labour programme.

H.M. showed by his silence that he approved of the Italy-England-France relationship, and as a result of [my] report he has probably come round to the views I share with yourself and Kiderlen.[1] H.M. thinks that political opinion in Italy and England will very soon right itself. They cannot, he thinks, fail to notice eventually that the sole purpose of our polite attitude is to emphasise the idea of international peace. I remarked that a further display of politeness on our part might lead England to reach an agreement with France which would at once be evident in great difficulties in Africa; this the Kaiser appeared to appreciate fully. H.M. is unlikely to initiate any fresh attempts towards a rapprochement with France, but I think it desirable to discuss the question soon at a conference with him.

H.M. was kind enough to bring with him the copy of his letter to Kaiser Franz Joseph, together with the latter's reply, for me to see.[2] The copy of H.M.'s letter fills FIVE *closely-written pages of* FOLIO. The mere bulk of this letter, written in his own hand and composed ABSOLUTELY WITHOUT ASSISTANCE, is evidence of how much trust now exists between them! And the contents present a *really excellent* picture of the development of this regrettable crisis, and touches chords which deeply moved Kaiser Franz Joseph. His reply *could not* be more friendly. He completely understands the Kaiser's conduct, and concludes with the accurate observation that the best proof of H.M.'s objectivity is the choice of a Chancellor like Caprivi, from whom he had parted on thoroughly 'bad terms'. H.M. thought that Kaiser Franz Joseph's recent visit to Munich will have contributed towards calming down the Prince Regent, but agrees to my doing what I can to pacify His Royal Highness on my way to Stuttgart.

Bill Bismarck, with whom I talked a good deal in Bremen, has a fairly sensible grasp of the overall situation. But he became 'Bismarckian' when he said: 'From the moment the Kaiser came to the throne he intended to get rid of my father in about a year's time. Since then Bötticher and Marschall have kept things hot and finally brought him down.'

I replied: 'My dear Bill, you can't believe what you say—it's just nonsense.' But he insisted that Marschall had made use of the Grand-Duke of Baden to worm himself into the Kaiser's favour. He would like to become *Chancellor*!

General Count Wedel sat next to Bill during the banquet on board the *Fulda*, but after the meal he came to tell me what Bill had said. Apparently they treated him [Wedel] badly and coldly at Friedrichsruh. The key to the pot of gold is now in the Castle of Berlin! I could see a *complete* transformation. He even made nasty remarks about his friend Herbert.

[1] See Kiderlen's letter to Eulenburg of 16 April 1890. (*Grosse Politik*, vol. VII, no. 1543, pp. 267–70.)
[2] Kaiser Wilhelm's letter to Kaiser Franz Joseph of 3 April 1890 and Kaiser Franz Joseph's reply of 12 April are printed in Dr Hanns Schlitter, 'Briefe Kaiser Franz Josephs I und Kaiser Wilhelms II über Bismarcks Rücktritt,' *Österreichische Rundschau* (1919), vol. LVIII, pp. 100–8.

Waldersee is not going along to the fiords;[1] Versen,[2] Count Görz, Hahnke, Güssfeldt,[3] Kiderlen, Hülsen[4] and myself. Waldersee has more or less taken a back seat but is treated *very well* by H.M.

You cannot ride all the good horses in your stable every day. But you still appreciate them.

The Kaiser was *most appreciative* of Caprivi and Marschall. He told me this in all sincerity. [...]

With best regards
Your faithful
P.E. [...]

318. Heinrich VII Reuss to Holstein

Vienna, 5 June 1890

My dear Holstein,

Bravo! I should like you to know that it is a long time since I read anything which gave me such pleasure as a certain two documents![5] They reveal a clear-cut policy and give an excellent directive. Mind you, they will pull a long face in St Petersburg; even so there is a certain charm in being sent about one's business in so disarming a manner. I have already written to the Chancellor to say that the more we can utterly convince people here of the honesty of our policy, of the fact that we have no ulterior motive, the more caution will they display, and avoid everything which might cause us embarrassment. [...]

With best regards
Your very devoted,
H. VII Reuss.

319. Georg zu Münster to Holstein

Paris, 11 June 1890

Strictly confidential

My dear Herr von Holstein,

As you know, I have been to England to attend my son's wedding, and I have chosen to describe my impressions to you in the form of a highly confidential private letter.

Sensible Englishmen considered H.B[ismarck]'s visit to London as extremely tactless; I was very glad to be there so soon afterwards in order to correct many entirely false opinions that had taken root. He spoke of nothing but 'the dismissal of my father' and constantly repeated the old story that the Kaiser thrice sent to the Prince to ask whether he was still unwilling to hand in his resignation.

Lord Salisbury seemed to be pretty well informed via Malet. He told me that H.B. had adopted a very cautious and correct attitude towards

---

[1] After Kaiser Wilhelm II's visits to the King of Denmark in Helsingör (30 June) and the King of Sweden and Norway in Christiana (1 July), he began a cruise along the Norwegian coast on 5 July, and returned to Wilhelmshaven on 28 July.

[2] Max von Versen. Prussian general. [3] Dr Paul Güssfeldt. African explorer.

[4] Dietrich, Count von Hülsen-Haeseler. Aide-de-Camp; Head of the Military Cabinet 1901–8.

[5] See *Grosse Politik*, vol. VII, nos. 1378–80, pp. 29–36; these documents laid down the new policy towards Russia after the non-renewal of the Reinsurance Treaty.

him, but he had heard that in other places and with other people he had let himself go and displayed the greatest bitterness towards the new regime. As regards our colonial policy, and this has been repeatedly confirmed by very important people, he is said to have boldly affirmed that his father and he had in fact never seriously desired this policy, and that *they* would easily have reached an agreement with England!!! That really is rather hard to take!! All in all H.B.'s behaviour made a bad impression, and as for his father, all reasonable people hope he will abandon his journey to England and will at least keep clear of London.

Turning now to the general attitude towards Germany, my impressions are not at all encouraging; a swing of opinion has taken place which gives me pause, and you know that I do not readily see things in too dark colours. Whereas Lord Salisbury and his adherents and, I believe, still a majority in Parliament, desire good relations with Germany and wish to avoid all conflict in the colonial sphere and to reach an agreement, there is on the other hand a party gaining ground which will have nothing to do with an agreement with Germany but wishes to abandon England's old traditional policy in order to seek other alliances and to draw closer to Russia. Lord Randolph Churchill is the principal spokesman of this idea, and he has won more support than I thought possible the last time I was in London.

There is already one member of the Cabinet who supports this idea: Lord Knutsford, the Colonial Secretary.[1] Rosebery, who is certain to be reappointed Foreign Secretary, and Sir Charles Dilke, who will still be an influential figure, may be friends of H[erbert] B[ismarck], but they are no friends of Germany; the Prince of Wales' son-in-law[2] is an ardent member of the East African Company and no friend of Germany: he seems to want to become the English Wissmann.[3]

While still Ambassador in London, I foresaw very clearly the inevitable outcome of the violent, reckless way in which Prince B[ismarck] launched his colonial policy and unleashed his savage Press campaign against England. I gave repeated but fruitless warnings—unfortunately no one would listen.

Even those Englishmen who regard Russia as their natural foe and Germany as their natural friend are indeed deeply shocked at the way we conducted our colonial affairs. Envy and rivalry play their part too; in Central Africa the two Companies[4] are at each other's throats and are setting their two countries against each other. Their violence and virulence is the greater because they are both in grave financial difficulties. And the English Company is doing very badly, is losing credit and is unable to raise more money. The wily director, Mackinnon,[5] accordingly enlisted Stanley,[6] whose stand against Salisbury is intended to pull

[1] Sir Henry Holland, Lord Knutsford. Colonial Secretary in the Salisbury Cabinet, 1887–1892.

[2] Alexander William George Duff, Duke of Fife.

[3] Hermann von Wissmann. African explorer; Governor of German East Africa, 1895–96.

[4] The British East Africa Company and the German East Africa Company.

[5] Sir William Mackinnon. President of the board of directors of the British East Africa Company, 1888–95.

[6] Sir Henry Stanley. Explorer and journalist.

the chestnuts out of the fire for the English Company and the British government, just as we have unfortunately tried to do for our own. He will not succeed, but he is putting the British government in a very difficult position, which is to be particularly regretted at the moment because Hatzfeldt's negotiations are also being made more difficult. I told Hatzfeldt of my misgivings and my reflections; he thinks them ell-founded, though perhaps he expresses his uneasiness less openly than I do. He hopes to reach an agreement with Salisbury over East Africa through direct negotiations; but this will be very difficult because Salisbury can make no concessions to us that might endanger his position. But the less *Geheimrat* Fiasco di Carolinas y Samoa[1] has to do with the affair, the better. The Carolines fiasco[2] set us at odds with Spain, which is of less consequence; but the Samoa fiasco[3] cost us our well-earned influence there and the Americans have as a result acquired for their own use the only good harbour in the island. The third fiasco that could be brought about by this *Geheimrat*, unless he is firmly held in check, would be the most dangerous of all, for it would drive England into the arms of Russia and France, and I need hardly underline to you the dangers of that. As an old diplomat and a true German patriot, my advice, given with the deepest conviction, is that we should at this moment deal most cautiously with England and France, especially as the time when we could in some measure rely on Russia *has gone*. The French people and their present rulers still definitely wish for peace, but both, rulers and people, are feeling their power which they are beginning to overrate just as they often underrated it after the war. Since last year the army's confidence in itself and the people's confidence in the army have grown apace, and thus, despite this love of peace, the fear of war has much diminished.

Please convey my best regards to the Chancellor and the State Secretary. You will probably be informing them of the contents of this letter; but otherwise it is intended for you alone.

With deepest and most friendly respects,
Your devoted,
Münster

320. Eberhard zu Solms to Holstein

Rome, 13 June 1890

My dear friend,

In your last letter of 5 June you asked me: 'What is Crispi's feeling about Caprivi? Does he take him seriously?'

---

[1] The reference is to Krauel.

[2] See *Diaries*, entry of 23 August 1885 *et seq.*

[3] At the end of 1888 the indigenous Samoans revolted against German influence in Samoa and the ruler supported by the Germans, King Tamasese. A Conference on the Samoan question met in Berlin from 29 April to 14 June 1889, attended by representatives of Britain, the United States and Germany. By the Samoa Treaty of 14 June the islands were declared neutral territory in which nationals of the signatory states would enjoy equal rights; the independence of Samoa was recognised and the signatory states agreed to take no unilateral action and to put forward no separate claims. Malietoa, who had been exiled by the Germans in 1887, was recognised as King, and a special authority composed of representatives of the signatory powers was set up to supervise Samoan affairs.

Once he had overcome his first alarm at Bismarck's retirement, Crispi very soon developed complete confidence in the new Chancellor. He has told me so repeatedly, and since he is no phrase-monger and there is also no reason to withhold one's confidence in the Chancellor, I have no doubt of the sincerity of his assurance.

I regard as still more important Crispi's remarks in this connexion to other ambassadors.

I therefore asked Baron Bruck: 'What does Crispi think of Herr von Caprivi?' Bruck replied: 'He's formed no opinion so far. Since Bismarck went, the Kaiser is everything to Crispi. He swears by the Kaiser alone. He does not know Herr von Caprivi yet. As soon as they have spent half an hour together the new Chancellor will soon take that place in his esteem which the former one used to occupy. He has all sorts of questions to discuss with him, and that is why I consider it so extraordinarily important that there should soon be a meeting between the two statesmen. It would have enormous influence on Crispi's position if Herr von Caprivi could arrange a rendez-vous in Milan, for the Radicals always reproach Crispi with going to Friedrichsruh every year to get his instructions without ever receiving a visit in return.'

Some time ago when I called on Damiani he remarked to me: 'You know, your Chancellor, Caprivi, is growing in stature every day as a statesman! How lucky you are to have a man of such calibre again!'

I have noticed that in other circles people speak of Herr von Caprivi with great regard and respect; we are envied particularly by Crispi's opponents, who repeat incessantly, as I have already told you: *'Nous cherchons notre Caprivi.'* [...]

Farewell until we meet
Your faithful and devoted
Solms.

321. Alfred von Kiderlen-Wächter to Holstein

Christiansand,[1] 7 July 1890

My dear Herr von Holstein,

A slight storm came up during the crossing from Christiana to Bergen, so, like true mariners, we have put in at Christiansand.

We are making excursions to the mountains; 'we' are the retinue on board the *Hohenzollern*, while H.M. is on board the *Kaiser* and is completely the sailor.

Very many thanks for your kind and interesting letter; I do appreciate your kindness in having found time to write to me despite your present burden of work.

Herr von Marschall will have told you about Christiana. Everything went smoothly, more or less without disagreements, apart from one or two tiffs with Senden.[2] But Güssfeldt is annoyed at having been awarded only a 'cross', as a captain (cavalry), whereas he thinks of himself, as a

---

[1] During Kaiser Wilhelm II's Scandinavian journey.

[2] Gustav, Baron von Senden und Bibran. Admiral; Head of the Imperial Naval Cabinet 1889–1906.

'scholar', entitled to a star. He sat chewing it over for three days!!! That's how people behave who are constantly proclaiming, 'these baubles mean nothing to me'. What a joke. Hahnke's rage is amusing too. H.M., as a special favour, included him in the party aboard the *Kaiser*; now he has to sit there the whole time watching regattas etc. and occupies a lieutenant's berth. In addition, being of course a mere general, he is treated badly by the naval officers!

I have not yet managed to speak much to H.M. because he is entirely monopolised by the navy, but I should just like to state two facts here:

Each time we met he expressed his satisfaction that the 'new regime' was going so well and, secondly, he said of his own accord how glad he was we had reached agreement with England about Africa.[1]

Concerning Münster's dispatch on opinion in Paris[2] he said: what a master-stroke to give the English the protectorate over Zanzibar and thus to set them at odds with the French. It would therefore be a good idea if you sent everything here that came in along those lines, to keep him in the same favourable frame of mind about the treaty. As long as H.M. remains on board the *Kaiser* he is of course exposed to navy influence.

I hope we get away from here tomorrow; we shall then leave the squadron in Bergen.

Prince Heinrich went off to-day in the *Irene* to celebrate his dear wife's birthday in Kiel on the 11th; he will then rejoin us in Molde!

I hardly think we need follow the French example and devise a Press-law now in case of general mobilisation (see military dispatch from Paris).[3] If this should be the view of our Military Attaché, H.M. can easily be talked out of it.

I have, of course, so far been unable to bring up the question of a Governor for East Africa. For that I need a period of quiet, and I shall never find it so long as the fleet is with us. Word has just gone round that we are to weigh anchor early tomorrow morning. After long consultation with the Admirals a decision seems to have been reached that the fleet will not in fact be leaving us. I hope to goodness it turns out differently. (1) It is not good for H.M. to be stuck on a ship for days on end. (2) The fleet is doing absolutely *nothing* at present, yet this is its main training period. Everything is regarded more or less as a game. This entirely between ourselves.

So far I have managed to have a brief audience with H.M. at least once a day, often under a flimsy pretext by way of the Civil Cabinet, and then with bad grace on His Majesty's part. The idea is that when I really do

[1] The Anglo-German Colonial Treaty of 1 July 1890, whereby Germany renounced far-reaching claims in East Africa and received the island of Heligoland in exchange.

[2] In his dispatch of 29 June on the political situation in France, Münster had stated that the French Foreign Minister was being generally attacked on account of the Anglo-German Treaty on Heligoland and Zanzibar. (From the Foreign Ministry files.)

[3] The Military Attaché in Paris, Huene, had reported on 28 June that the question of the organisation of France's internal affairs in the event of war was being widely discussed. The War Minister apparently intended to eliminate all possible danger from the Press in such an eventuality. Wilhelm II commented in a marginal note: 'Right for us too. What are our plans?' (From the Foreign Ministry files.)

want something, he will by then have got used to my face. I must confess that up to now, after exerting a little pressure, I have always been given audience and have always been well received.

Ever your obedient servant
Kiderlen.

322. Alfred von Kiderlen-Wächter to Holstein

Olden, 15 July 1890

My dear Herr von Holstein,

We have been held prisoners here by the rain for three days now, but we are in the best of tempers; it is a strain, though, to keep the conversation going all day long. [...]

Towards H[erbert] B[ismarck] there is boundless fury; I discussed this at length with H.M. the other day.

H.M. has also spontaneously assured me on several occasions recently that [he] will undertake *no* obligations in St Petersburg;[1] he is—now at any rate—quite definite about that.

He is quite delighted with the 'new regime' as he calls it. Moreover he expressed today—*avis au lecteur*—his particular satisfaction with the choice of documents which are being sent to him. This again gave rise to comparisons between then and now.

No news. His Most Serene Majesty caught a salmon yesterday, a fact I record here for the edification of his faithful vassal. [...]

Your most obedient and devoted
Kiderlen.

323. Karl von Eisendecher to Holstein

Karlsruhe, 18 July 1890.

Dear Holstein,

Now that you are more or less the absolute ruler one ought really not to plague you with letters. [...]

The Gr[and Duke][2] has recently shown unusually great interest in military matters, of which, according to those competent to judge, he understands very little; he will take part in the autumn manoeuvres, on which he is very keen. His intimates maintain that the martial exploits of the late Gr[and Duke] of Mecklenburg[3] even at that time awakened in H.R.H. a certain military ambition, which is now emerging more and more; he regards it as his destiny to command an army in the event of war, and his military entourage is said to be partly in favour of these ideas.

Politically the Gr. is in some respects deeply pessimistic. He sees in Russia a constantly lowering cloud. Like the Gr[and Duchess], he

---

[1] Kaiser Wilhelm II intended to visit the Tsar in mid-August. The visit took place from 17–23 August.
[2] The Grand Duke of Baden.
[3] Friedrich Franz II, Grand Duke of Mecklenburg-Schwerin 1842–83, who had distinguished himself in the wars of 1866 and 1870–1.

appears to detest His Highness [Bismarck] more and more. Their attitude is characterised in her words, which are, I think, authentic: 'And they want to put up a monument to a man like that!'

Even I am probably still suspected a little of leanings towards Fr[iedrichs]r[uh] and of antagonism towards the present regime—*most* unjustly, since my admiration for Bismarck the man is in no way connected with the political change. No one could deplore more than I do the statements to the reporters emanating from Fr[iedrichs]r[uh];[1] and moreover I know from you how things stood before the break, and that the situation was rapidly becoming impossible.

The Baden heir-apparent[2] will, if I am not very much mistaken, one day turn out to be a rather embarrassing Federal Prince; he is generally regarded as holding strictly separatist views; although completely under the thumb of the Grand Duchess, as a military superior he is said to be remarkably hard and brusque. Both in temperament and character he is strikingly reserved, highly suspicious and easily offended—these two latter qualities are also found to a certain extent in his father, the Grand-Duke. [...]

My very best wishes for a good summer.

In friendship, as ever your devoted

Eisendecher.

contents strictly confidential please[3]

324. Alfred von Kiderlen-Wächter to Holstein

Storfjord, 19 July 1890

Confidential

My dear Herr von Holstein,

In spite of rain etc. this trip, too, is proving satisfactory in every way.

In very intimate conversation with me, H.M. occasionally spoke of Caprivi and particularly of yourself in *the most cordial terms*, which gives me sincere pleasure. Less cordial towards Herbert, Verdy (whose departure in October seems certain) and *Lerchenfeld*. H.M. sees right through the latter; I must tell you more of what H.M. said about him and also about you when we meet. Please remind me. H.M. does not regret Berchem's departure in the least. But he holds the mistaken opinion that a B[erchem] Ministry in Bavaria would be of advantage to us. I shall try to get Eulenburg to talk him out of that. His friendship with the latter is firmer than ever. *Completely secret:* please discuss this with no one (except of course the Chancellor if you should think it necessary): Leuthold told me that when H.M. was still Prince Wilhelm, Eulenburg and he dabbled in spiritualism; Leuth. took him to task about it recently and asked him to give it up. E. promised to, and indeed there will probably be no more séances with mediums, but they will have

---

[1] See p. 338, note 7. Bismarck continued to criticise publicly the Kaiser's domestic and foreign policy. In an interview with the editor of the *Frankfurter Journal* published on 11 July he criticised adversely the Anglo-German agreement of 1 July and discussed in detail his differences of opinion with the Kaiser on social policy.

[2] Friedrich II, Grand Duke of Baden 1907–18.   [3] In English in the original.

conversations on the subject. More when we meet. In all other respects Eulenb. is a good influence. And so I would ask for the strictest discretion. [...]

If the Chancellor were still in Berlin at the end of this month, it might perhaps be a good idea—for what my opinion is worth—if he came to Wilhelmshaven, where H.M. is staying four full days if not five. It would be a good thing if the Chancellor took him under his wing to prevent him from falling entirely into the navy's clutches. H.M. has told me a good many stories. Here, as a sample, is a good one about Liebenau: When the Prince of Wales was in Berlin and a state banquet was to be given in his honour, the new Chancellor had just arrived from Hanover. H.M. happened to ask Lieb: 'I suppose you have informed the Chancellor?' Lieb: 'He is not in Berlin.' H.M.: 'Oh, yes, he arrived today.' Lieb: 'Maybe, but he has not yet called on me officially, and so I am obliged to ignore him.'!!!!!! H.M. told me this himself!

By the way, Waldersee seems to have had a considerable hand in Prince [Bismarck's] overthrow: more than I thought. No doubt you know the details better than I do. He has not yet dared to attack Caprivi, whom he hates from the bottom of his heart, probably as much as Prince Bismarck. H.M. made a clear-cut pronouncement on this matter: 'If the Chancellor *demands* anyone's dismissal, he must go, even if I myself like him.' That referred in the first place to Berchem, but it goes for others too. I fear for W., his star is on the wane, and, so far as I have been able to discover, the cause must lie in a *tête-à-tête* he had with H.M. immediately after the crisis.[1] I have been unable to find out *what* took place. I need hardly urge you to treat all the foregoing with discretion.

I hope you find your work congenial, for you must have a great deal now.

Ever your most obedient and devoted
Kiderlen.

325. Holstein to Karl von Eisendecher[2]

20 July [1890]

My dear Eisendecher,

Your letter[3] just reached me this morning (Sunday) and I have read it with great interest. But I, in my loneliness, was even more affected by the fact that it came from you than by its contents. What experiences we have been through together. Without going into cause and effect— we understand each other—I must state that, deep down, one can still sense the *fact* of the change-over.

Fortunately I have such an enormous amount to do that I have not much time for reflections of that kind. One of the things I brood over is the question, where shall I go when I leave the service? I do not

[1] On March 17, during military manoeuvres, there had been a difference of opinion between the Kaiser and his Chief of Staff over the criticism of the way the tactical exercises had been carried out. (See Waldersee, *Denkwürdigkeiten*, vol. II, pp. 119–21.)
[2] From the Eisendecher Papers.   [3] Of 18 July. See above.

wish to go just yet, because it might at the moment be difficult to replace an elderly and experienced official like myself. But the idea has certainly occurred to me. Your remarks on 'ruling' do not fit the facts. Both our new Chiefs have a strong instinct to rule for themselves. But I and my only assistant Raschdau are so overburdened with work that I am seriously considering whether to propose Marschall's recall, though he really ought not to be back before the 8th. What you say about the heir apparent does not make pleasant reading. I take less seriously the Gr[and Duke]'s military aspirations because I am beginning to think the danger of war is far more remote than people think.

Warmest regards,
Your
H.

326. Paul von Hatzfeldt to Leo von Caprivi[1]
Copy.

London, 21 July 1890

Your Excellency,

I beg to express my most sincere thanks for the renewed proof of your confidence as shown by your sending me the memorandum enclosed in Dispatch No. 548,[2] and beg at the same time to be allowed to develop, confidentially and with the utmost frankness, my own personal views on the questions treated therein.

First of all I think one is justified in assuming that Signor Crispi, by engineering the Tunis incident on the basis of hitherto unauthenticated reports, completely misjudged the political situation in Europe, as he has often done; unless of course, he is convinced that domestic difficulties make it necessary for him to gain a tangible advantage for Italy at any cost in order to reconsolidate his position. In the present case I incline to the latter assumption, for it must be perfectly obvious to Crispi that he has chosen the most unfavourable moment imaginable to confront his best friends with the alternative either of falling in with his whim and running the risk of complications which might lead to war and which on such an occasion would be roundly condemned by public opinion in every country, or else of deserting him in such a situation, thereby dangerously strengthening that party in Italy which aims at an alliance with France and Russia.

With this in mind we must, I think, examine the question of the extent to which we should support Italy, if at all, from the double standpoint of our treaty obligations and, independent of them, our political

---

[1] From the Foreign Ministry files.

[2] Dispatch No. 548 of 18 July forwarded Caprivi's memorandum of 17 July (*Grosse Politik*, vol. VIII, no. 1872, pp. 245–8) with a request for Hatzfeldt's comment. Crispi had informed the German government of an alleged treaty between France and the Bey of Tunis, whereby after the death of the Bey the French protectorate was to be transformed into French sovereignty over Tunis. Caprivi wrote in his memorandum: 'The Italians appear to be preoccupied with the idea: it might lead to war, and they want us to recognise that this would constitute a *casus foederis*.' (See *Memoirs*, pp. 151–5.)

interests. On the first point it is my opinion that the text of Article III[1] of our secret treaty which has been sent me cannot be interpreted as an unconditional obligation on our part to support the Italian demands. The hypothetical fact (*ce fait*) does not exist so long as the change in Tunis that Italy refuses to accept has not actually occurred; and, even supposing Tunis is covered by our treaty, one could in my opinion successfully refute the idea that the subsequent coming into force of the treaty with the Bey would in fact introduce any change in the actual state of possession which would prejudice Italy. France already exercises complete governmental control in Tunis which she would under no circumstances renounce, and the renunciation of the Bey and his rightful heirs would therefore not materially alter the situation there either to France's advantage or to Italy's detriment.

Since, therefore, it is possible for us not to recognise unconditionally the treaty obligations imputed to us by Italy and to offer Crispi our friendly advice to refrain from too strident an insistence on them, it is my personal opinion that the affair presents itself to us in quite a different light when we consult our political interests quite apart from any treaty. Italy's inclusion in the Triple Alliance, despite her indifferently reliable government and her indifferently well prepared army, arose from the realisation that such a reinforcement of the counterweight against the inevitable alliance between France and Russia in the next European war was absolutely imperative. But our aim was, I believe, not merely to add weight to the peace-loving powers, but even more to prevent Italy—which is notoriously always in quest of acquisitions which she picks up where she can—from aligning herself with the Franco-Russian group and thus upsetting the balance of power to our immense disadvantage. So far as I am aware, Prince Bismarck also took constant care in recent years to keep Crispi in the proper channel by official and by repeatedly exercised personal influence, without, so far as was possible, appearing to lecture him, in order to forestall any rash behaviour on his part.

As far as I may allow myself to express an opinion, this situation has since remained unchanged. Even though Europe may have become convinced of the pacific intentions of Tsar Alexander himself, which may have some connection with Russia's lack of military preparedness, there has nevertheless been a sharpening of tension in the Near East since [his accession], as events in Crete, Serbia, Bulgaria etc. in recent years have shown, and the possibility of an outbreak of war in the Near East which could involve Europe, has been constantly present, if indeed it has

[1] Article III of the separate treaty between Germany and Italy of 20 February 1887 ran as follows: 'S'il arrivait que la France fît acte d'étendre son occupation ou bien son protectorat ou sa souveraineté, sous une forme quelconque sur les territoires Nord-Africains, et qu'en conséquence de ce fait l'Italie crût devoir, pour sauvegarder sa position dans la Méditerranée, entreprendre elle-même une action sur les dits territoires Nord-Africains, ou bien recourir, sur le territoire français en Europe, aux mesures extrêmes, l'état de guerre qui s'ensuivrait entre l'Italie et la France constituerait *ipso facto*, sur la demande de l'Italie et à la charge commune des deux alliés, le *casus foederis* avec tous les effets prévus par les articles II et V du susdit Traité du 20 mai 1882, comme si pareille éventualité y était expressément visée.' (*Grosse Politik*, vol. IV, no. 859, pp. 258–9.)

not actually increased. Unconditional refusal to give Italy the support she is at present demanding would probably further increase the Near East danger which is threatening the peace of Europe, even if Italy did not turn right about and join the opposite camp; France and Russia would certainly interpret Italy's secession from the peace-loving Alliance as a considerable weakening of it, and might feel tempted to precipitate a conflict over the Near East question and, concomitantly, a decision on the question of political mastery in Europe.[1]

If these assumptions are correct, one is in my opinion justified in concluding that our own interests dictate, even now, the maintenance of friendship with Italy by every means which can be employed *without endangering peace*.[2] A further encouragement to do so lies, I think, in the circumstance that a rejection on principle of Italy's demands would also cause the other Powers to suspect that we were abandoning our entire former policy and might even be contemplating a complete change of front. If I may make this last point quite explicit, I really cannot see how, in view of our absolute need of support from friendly Great Powers, we could in that event escape a renewed rapprochement with Russia; we should then, of course, be obliged to further her designs in the Near East at Austria's expense.[2] At such a turn of events a certain person at Friedrichsruh would hardly deny himself the satisfaction of reminding public opinion through his usual channels that we are throwing away the Italian Alliance so carefully won by Prince Bismarck's statesmanship and that we have now felt obliged to seek Russia's friendship, just as he had vainly counselled before his resignation.[2]

If, therefore, in view of the considerations adduced above, we decide to maintain the Italian Alliance, there is I think the further point in favour of this policy, namely that it can probably be pursued under present conditions without exposing us to the danger of complications which we cannot possibly desire at the moment. From all we know of Crispi's pronouncements and from all similar experiences of him in the past, we can almost categorically assert that he does not believe in the possibility of regaining Tunis from the French, nor does he seriously intend, on account of this dispute, to involve his country in a war in which he might well stand alone against France. He is equally well aware that by a political rapprochement with France he will not induce her to renounce the realisation of her aims in Tunis. Thus all France could offer him as a reward for a political agreement would be the prospect of *future* advantages *after* a victorious war in Europe. But we, together with our allies, can do this equally well, indeed with greater prospect of success,[3] and Crispi will hardly fail to realise this. And finally, the Italian communication[4] which accompanied Dispatch No. 548 already stated that Italy was at present requesting purely diplomatic action and would be satisfied with guarantees of her interests for the future. If I may venture to add my opinion on the attitude towards Italy

---

[1] Marginal note by Kaiser Wilhelm II: 'Very likely.'
[2] Kaiser Wilhelm II: 'Yes.'   [3] Kaiser Wilhelm II: 'Correct.'
[4] Printed in Crispi, *Memoirs*, vol. II, pp. 440–1.

in the present situation most consonant with our overall interests, I think I must briefly outline in the following sentences the tone I think we should adopt:

Even though we regret that the Italian Government, without first reaching a confidential agreement with us, has chosen the present unfavourable moment to broach a problem which could, if handled overhastily, result in serious complications, we are of course prepared to examine it in that friendly spirit which corresponds to our close relations with Italy, in particular to consider means of affording a just satisfaction of Italy's claims without prejudicing the peace of Europe. The extent to which our treaty obligations are involved cannot be perceived at a glance, for the fact upon which the Italian complaint is based has not yet been established beyond all doubt. According to the information on the subject, which is available to the Italian government itself, an agreement exists which may not come into force for years and which would not essentially alter the actual state of affairs. Signor Crispi would therefore do well to realise that even if friendly governments were prepared without more ado to create serious trouble with France in circumstances offering no prospect of immediate danger to Italian interests, they would find no sympathy and obtain no co-operation from parliament or public opinion in their countries. It would therefore be in Italy's own interest to await the agreement between the friendly Powers already being negotiated,[1] and meanwhile to see that the fact of the treaty concluded with the Bey is proven beyond a doubt. With this proviso, the three nations in question will in all probability reach agreement on the steps they could take to help Italy without endangering the peace. Precisely because of our treaty with Italy we think we can claim of Signor Crispi the favour of allowing us, in the interests of peace, the necessary time to do this. Naturally we have no intention of trying to elude any obligations which would result from the treaty, and we should therefore not avoid closer examination of this question if the above-mentioned confidential discussions between the Powers produced no result. But it is in Italy's own interest, as Signor Crispi will not fail to realise on closer examination of the problem, to prefer without question the possibility of an agreement between the friendly Powers on a *démarche* in Paris or perhaps subsequent compensation for Italy.

I have attempted in the foregoing pages to give my personal opinion of our overall political interests and to outline our treaty position, thus complying to the best of my ability with Your Excellency's kind request in Dispatch No. 548. May I therefore beg your indulgence for this candid and confidential exposition?

I hope I shall be fulfilling Your Excellency's intentions if, on this basis and in accordance with my former reports, I do my utmost to prevail on Lord Salisbury to adopt a co-operative attitude on this question.[2] I should like in this connection to emphasise particularly that according to all my experience it would be quite futile to strive for separate action by the English government in Italy's favour, since Lord

[1] Kaiser Wilheim II: 'Yes.'   [2] See *Grosse Politik*, vol. VIII, Chapter LIII B.

Salisbury always attaches the utmost importance to his ability to justify in Parliament his attitude in such questions by joint action with other Powers; in this case he is particularly apprehensive lest public opinion in England should, on being informed of this incident, pronounce a definitely unfavourable verdict on Signor Crispi.

With sincere respect

I have the honour Sir, to remain,

Your devoted

P. Hatzfeldt.

327. Philipp zu Eulenburg to Holstein

Drottningholm near Stockholm, 1 August 1890

Dear Baron,

Forgive me for taking so long to reply to your letter of 4 July.[1] During H.M.'s holiday trip I wished to spare him as far as possible any news and conversation which might remind him too vividly of the Berlin atmosphere. And so I waited for an opportunity to occur naturally—and I candidly confess that I found it most unpleasant to discuss with H.M. the subject you touched on. But the Kaiser's objectivity and perspicacity quickly helped me over my disagreeable opening. H.M. said: 'You're not telling me anything new. I have already noticed signs that Waldersee was scheming against the Chancellor. He is an intriguer pure and simple and wishes to become Chancellor, although I have told him *I* shall *never* appoint him. As for his notions of a future alliance with Russia, well, politics are none of his business! That is *my* concern. He will kindly refrain from meddling in such matters. He also asked me whether he could accompany me to Russia. Of course I refused. W. is too closely connected with the Press. No doubt Zahn[2] is behind this: I shall replace him.' This topic, as you can see, was easily dealt with. H.M. has ceased to let Verdy worry him. 'He's already done for,' he said recently. The second point you raised, which we have so often discussed together—H.M.'s winning in the manoeuvres—was *quite new* to the Kaiser. I had to brace myself before embarking on it, because one dislikes saying unpleasant things to people one is fond of! But after careful consideration I forced myself to do so! H.M. became *very heated* and proved to me by an exposition of the military situation that he had won 'according to the rules' and that the whole story was an invention of Albedyll's aimed at harming Waldersee and getting himself out of a tight corner. I said: 'But I beg Your Majesty to consider that when the monarch is involved everyone strives to concede him the victory. It's human nature.' H.M. replied: 'Such a conception implies a grave affront to all my commanding generals, who likewise regard me simply as a commanding general. Moreover, I have never assumed command except when the corps was in retreat. Thus I did *not* always win. Moreover if any commanding general opposing me in battle were to act

[1] The letter was primarily concerned with Waldersee and Holstein's suspicions about his efforts to undermine the position of Caprivi. (From the Eulenburg Papers.)

[2] Major in the General Staff in charge of Press affairs. Both Holstein and Eulenburg suspected him of influencing the Press on Waldersee's behalf.

dishonestly towards me, I should *dismiss him from the service at once.*' I told him I was glad to hear this opinion and that I should make use of it when the occasion arose. When the Kaiser remarked during the course of the conversation that he hoped the army was satisfied he was *capable* of victory, I said twice that I should be very glad to learn some day that he had been defeated and that I thought it desirable in the common interest that this should happen once in some of the forthcoming manoeuvres.

Finally the Kaiser told me he would make use of the contents of our conversation in the after-manoeuvre discussions or on other occasions. H.M. rejected absolutely the suggestion that he should withdraw *completely* from active participation in the manoeuvres. He regards himself as perfectly entitled to undergo military training—and, after all, we can hardly find fault with him for that. We must just wait and see what will be the practical results of my observations. I was very surprised to notice that this topic was *completely new* to H.M. During our discussion H.M. was so heated that my secretary, who was working in my cabin two doors away from us, asked me whether H.M. had been reading me some document—the Kaiser's voice had sounded so consistently loud.

I find it remarkable that no soldier has yet had the courage to discuss this question with H.M. The fact is they all go in holy terror of H.M. I see this more and more clearly, and a very good thing it is! H.M. also drew attention to Waldersee's talents as a commander during this conversation. What H.M. resents is the way he has exploited his close relationship with H.M. for his own purposes. H.M. holds the very correct view that people should work for *him* and not for themselves. That was of course Prince B[ismarck]'s opinion too!

The latter's behaviour is a very great, if not the greatest, object of H.M.'s interest. H.M. seems to me to have become rather more touchy on the point, for he told me: 'I shall intervene if I am asked to by public opinion.'

This trip abroad is unfortunately not conferring any tangible benefit on H.M. His restlessness has increased rather than diminished and he takes too little sleep. Leuthold, who incidentally is seriously ill, told me plainly things could not go on like that. I too feel that H.M. is doing himself harm and simply must have eight hours' sleep if he wants to keep going any longer. These Scandinavian voyages are a sort of fiord carnival. It is in fact H.M.'s 'season'—minus feminine conversation, which is as he likes it.

I am leaving Stockholm for Liebenberg on the 10th and shall be in Stuttgart on the 15th. In Gastein from the 20th onwards. Could we meet? Will you be passing through the Tyrol? *This year I am able to talk* and feel quite fit! I have so much to tell you.

My wife sends her best wishes. I got back here to-day after a mad trip straight across Norway.

In true friendship
Your very devoted
Philipp Eulenburg.

P.S.

Berchem also came up in conversation with H.M. He referred to him in friendly terms and said, when I spoke of his possible political role in Munich, that it would not be a bad thing if he became Minister there. I said we could not use him because of his Ultramontane associates, and developed this idea. H.M. listened to me in silence. But H.M. became angry when I mentioned how Berchem had told me *you* were the cause of his retirement. I am happy to be able to pass on to you the Kaiser's following remarks: 'I should not have believed B. capable of it! Anyone who attacks Holstein attacks me. I rely on H. and look on him as a tower of strength even though I do not know him personally. I am glad Caprivi relies on him so firmly. I am sorry not to know H. personally, but I have no wish to disturb his habits and to force myself upon him. He has arranged his life after his own fashion. No doubt he has his own good reasons for it.' [...]

Finally, I can tell you that your ideas about M[arschall] are, fortunately, quite unfounded. Bearing in mind that M., who is aware of our friendly relations, could say nothing but good of you in a simple conversation, I brought him round to the subject via Berchem, and I can only say that the simple, unaffected way in which M. spoke of you excludes all possibility of a rift between you. A propos of the conflict with Berchem, the expression occurred: he could not imagine the Foreign Ministry without you. And he spoke of you with the utmost *gratitude*. As a result of this conversation I can look ahead quite calmly and can foresee from now on only superficial differences over certain vexatious subjects. I am not mistaken. Do me the favour of believing in my intuition in this matter.

Will you write and send me your address?

I hope this letter reaches you before you leave Berlin.

Best regards
E.

328. Alfred von Kiderlen-Wächter to Holstein

Berlin, 21 September 1890

Dear Baron Holstein,

I returned safely from the manoeuvres yesterday evening, and I am now hastening to send to Dresden the letter I promised you.

First of all many thanks for your kind letter which reached me in Liegnitz.

The only 'news' is the following:

The entire manoeuvres marked the final stage in the decline of Waldersee's status in H.M.'s eyes.[1]

His influence was at an end ever since that occasion at G.H.Q. which you doubtless recall, when the Kaiser so severely criticised the tactical exercises problem set by W. in front of all his subordinates.[2] Since H.M. called on W. in the morning for a walk in the Tiergarten (this was at the height of the Bismarck crisis) we assumed at once, you remember, that something must have occurred as they walked and talked

---

[1] See Waldersee, *Denkwürdigkeiten*, vol. II, pp. 144–7.   [2] See p. 347, note 1.

together. I have since had this confirmed by two of H.M.'s remarks which have been passed on to me. Immediately after that stroll, on his way home, H.M. said to his adjutant: 'I don't understand W.; he's my Chief of General Staff, and ought not to worry his head about things which don't concern him.'

Later, after the criticism, when Hahnke spoke to H.M. at W.'s request and observed that the criticism had been rather severe, H.M. merely replied: 'I only wanted to show him that I could live without him.'

And then, as I was returning from the provincial dinner in Glücksburg with H.M., and we were alone in the cabin, he suddenly began talking about Württemberg conditions, the army corps stationed there, etc., and said: 'What do you say to my sending W. there?' As you can imagine I was completely dumbfounded, but of course I showed [no] surprise but warmly applauded this decision. But H.M. disliked breaking the news to W. 'Then he'd resign,' he said and appeared *for the moment* to find the prospect painful. H.M. actually wanted me to sound W.! As you can imagine, I refused to do anything of the sort! H.M. having said once or twice, 'I imagine the Chancellor has no objection to the idea', I sent a personal report on the matter to Berlin. The Chancellor replied by a personal letter written in his own hand. The address, too, was in his own handwriting and the envelope was marked: 'private and personal'. This letter suffered a curious fate. It arrived in Holstein the day we left; as a result of incorrect information from the Court Marshal's office the courier made for the *Mars*, where H.M. was breakfasting with the navy, instead of to Gravenstein where I still was. On board the *Mars* the courier was now informed, incorrectly, that I had already left. The courier now began to lament that the letter had been entrusted to him most particularly, in short, this was reported to the Kaiser. H.M. said: 'There is sure to be something urgent for me inside' and then—opened the letter with the words: 'Let's commit a breach of confidence for once!'—!!!! The letter merely instructed me to tell H.M. that the Chancellor agreed entirely with the idea of W. for Stuttg., and that he withdrew the candidate he himself had put forward, Haeseler;[1] H.M.'s suggestion was much better. Thus the 'breach of confidence' did no harm, and may have done good. I wonder if one of his motives may not have been the secret urge to have a peep behind the scenes for a change?

The very day after the arrival in Breslau H.M. summoned me and told me he had had a word with W. (By the way, I forgot to say above that along with his command in Stuttg., W. was to be given, to soften the blow, the inspectorship of the Bavarian forces, held hitherto by Blumenthal.[2]) Now, the crafty W. at once pretended he was very glad

[1] Gottlieb, Count von Haeseler. Prussian General; Quartermaster in the Great General Staff; Commanding General of the XVI Army Corps in Lorraine (Metz), 1890–1903.

[2] Leonhard, Count von Blumenthal. Chief of the General Staff of the Schleswig-Holstein Army 1849–50; of the combined mobile corps deployed against Denmark in 1864; of the Army of the Crown Prince of Prussia, 1866, 1870–1, Commanding General of the IV Army Corps, 1871; Inspector of the 4th Army, 1888–92; of the 3rd Army, 1892–8; from 1888 General Field-Marshal.

to go, but pointed out to H.M. that Prince Leopold of Bavaria was senior to him in the service, and could therefore not be subordinated to him. Resultant embarrassment of H.M., whom Hahnke advised to let the inspectorship wait a little. H.M. then told me he did not intend to take a decision but would await the Chancellor's arrival, and has requested me in the meantime to describe the state of affairs to him. So when the Chancellor arrived H.M. told him he was handing the matter over to him and asked him to have a talk with W. but that he was reluctant to 'force' W. The Chancellor then talked for an hour with W., who seemed prepared to acquiesce in the matter; the Chancellor, I think, told him pretty bluntly that 'there was simply no room for him here'. W. asked for a few days in which to think it over (probably to send a telegram to his wife, who had of course no wish to leave Stöcker, the Berlin court, the newly founded Young Men's Christian Home, and so on). Two days later he *wrote a letter* to the Chancellor, who lived ten minutes away, who had called on him, and whom he saw daily. He dropped all his previous arguments and said—it was quite cunningly thought out—that he would be unable to enter upon his duties in Stuttg. with the necessary creative zest.

Hahnke says he thinks it was a mistake not to go to Stuttg.; W. would certainly not last much longer here, and H.M. would not make him such an offer a second time. I am afraid H. is right.

Loë (VIII Corps) now heads the list of candidates. When H.M. returns from Mürzsteeg on the 7 or 8 October the Chancellor is to lay a definite proposal before him. For this purpose the Chancellor will leave shortly for Stuttgart 'to pay a return visit to Mittnacht'.[1]

The King of Saxony was also asked for his opinion in Rohnstock, but he does not seem *au fait* with the situation here; his first suggestion was Prince Wilhelm von Württemb., with a military assistant; his second suggestion was—*horribile dictu*—Verdy!!! Fortunately they are both definitely out of the question. Verdy goes on 1 October. To be succeeded most probably by Kaltenborn.[2] So that is how things stand at the moment.

During the manoeuvre H.M. tried to trip up W. whenever he could. On the last day but one of the manoeuvre, the 19th, H.M. was commanding the Sixth Corps against the Fifth. According to the exercise set up by W. he was to attack the Fifth Corps when his division was separated by the Weistritz, and suffered a resounding defeat. There was admittedly a slight flaw in W.'s planning of the exercise, but, as the Chancellor said to me, H.M. did not correct it but made it still worse through one or two gross errors.

During the final critical discussion on the 20th, H.M., after defending his troop dispositions and thanking W. in rather general and grudging terms for directing the manoeuvres, said to him: 'If our exercise had been set up differently, yesterday might well have proved more instruc-

---

[1] Hermann, Baron von Mittnacht. Minister-President of Württemberg, 1876–1900.
[2] Hans von Kaltenborn-Stachau. Prussian general, who in fact succeeded Verdy as Minister of War.

tive and more interesting.' It was noticed, too, that he did not shake hands with W. as he usually did.

In the evening Versen had the cheek to say to H.M., 'I must say, all question of monarchical principle apart. I have never seen such a dashing attack (the one which was repulsed).' H.M. turned away. A high-ranking person summed up the scene in the words: 'Versen was trying to lick H.M.'s boots but he wasn't having any!'

A very serious matter has been going on these last few days. The Cabinet had proposed to His Maj. that Forckenbeck[1] should be confirmed in office as Lord Mayor of Berlin. When Lucanus put the matter to H.M. in Rohnstock, he said no. Then the Chancellor spoke to H.M., pointed to the reasons behind the Ministry of State's opinion, said it would be impossible to push through the new local government organisation if a conflict now arose in the realm of urban organisation; the people of Berlin would re-elect Forckenbeck or someone worse, and in the end it would be necessary to resort to government by special commission; in that case the honorary town counsellors (two-thirds of the whole) would relinquish their posts, in short an impossible situation would be created. H.M. stuck to his opinion. The worst of it was that he had already rather committed himself by telling some Conservatives in Breslau: 'I'll never confirm that fellow in office,' etc.

The Chancellor was most depressed and was already talking of the resignation of the Cabinet which no longer enjoyed H.M.'s confidence. Lucanus stepped in and said Forckenbeck was not worth that. A compromise was finally reached whereby the question will once more be submitted to the decision of the Cabinet.

On the way back from Liegnitz the Chancellor was quite cheerful again and told me confidently: 'The Kaiser will give in this time.' Lucanus thinks so too. [...]

Our relations with the Austrian visitors were most cordial.[2] The Chancellor seems to have made a great friend of Kálnoky. H.M. went for a walk in the grounds with Kálnoky for over an hour and told him about everything, in particular about one thing which no longer exists.[3] Kálnoky may well have felt as if he were skating on thin ice.

The Chancellor's comment to me was: 'I have no objection to *H.M.'s* discussing that. I refrained from doing so myself; I thought that Kálnoky might say to himself: this time it was admittedly Prince Bismarck's doing, but such behaviour is part of their Prussian character and may recur.'

But the whole encounter passed off most satisfactorily.

Meanwhile Muraviev has presented the memorandum promised by

[1] Max von Forckenbeck. Member of the Prussian Chamber of Deputies from 1858; of the Reichstag from 1867; co-founder of the Progressive Party, 1861, of the National Liberal Party, 1866; Lord Mayor of Breslau 1873; of Berlin 1878–92.

[2] Kaiser Franz Joseph, accompanied by Kálnoky, visited Wilhelm II in Rohnstock from 17 to 19 September and attended the Silesian manoeuvres. (See Enclosure.) The only document in the Foreign Ministry files relating to this meeting is a dispatch from Reuss dated 21 September, stating that Kálnoky had expressed his satisfaction and that of his Kaiser with the result of the visit.

[3] The Reinsurance Treaty with Russia.

Giers covering his talks with the Chancellor in St Petersburg. The Chancellor told me—I've not yet seen the text—that it was quite harmless, not even complete, and contained more of Giers' opinions than his own. 'In any case,' the Chancellor added, 'I let Giers do most of the talking and played a listener's role.' After Muraviev had read out this *opus* he said that though he had no instructions to that effect he thought it would be a good idea if the Chancellor would confirm *dans un petit billet* that this had in fact been the content of the St Petersburg conversations. When the Chancellor refused, Muraviev wanted at least some confirmation in writing that he had read the document to the Chancellor.

The Chancellor replied with a smile that this was surely unnecessary between gentlemen; he would never repudiate his interview with Giers and with him, Muraviev. 'Then he went off with his tail between his legs' said the Chancellor in concluding his description of the scene.[1]

And he said, quite rightly, 'with a document like that which says nothing they could do far greater mischief than with one stating something definite.' But how people do fuss about 'something in writing' and how sensible to give nothing away![2] [...]

Of course praise was again lavished on the navy, although the landing exercise was a complete travesty. It was so overdone that even Hollmann[3] felt quite embarrassed at such praise and told me so in Holstein. Then he repeated it to the Chancellor here.

Verdy has been dismissed once and for all and is going on 1 October. He did not cut a good figure in the manoeuvres.

The Chancellor also told me that there had been a new development in the bronze versus cast steel dispute, in which H.M. had sided with Krupp[4] and advocated cast steel while Verdy had advocated bronze. The devotees of bronze were constantly making great play of the fact that bronze does not crack. Now, three bronze cannons have recently cracked. The Chancellor said to me: 'That's a great triumph for H.M.; I said nothing to him about it in Rohnstock. He might have made his pleasure sound a trifle too emphatic in front of all the Austrians.' And the Chancellor would like to be rid of the affair again because, as he rightly says, it is really none of his business. But I find it encouraging, in view of H.M.'s nature, that he now passes on everything to the Chancellor. It would in itself be better if H.M. would observe departmental proprieties more. [...]

Crispi has enquired about the date of the Chancellor's visit to Italy, which he had tentatively arranged for the end of September or the beginning of October.[5] The Chancellor wrote in the margin: 'Reply

---

[1] Kaiser Wilhelm II paid a visit to Tsar Alexander III in Narva and Peterhof from 17 to 23 August 1890. That was the occasion of the talk between Giers and Caprivi. (See the latter's memorandum of 8 September, *Grosse Politik*, vol. VII, no. 1612, pp. 352–3.)

[2] Disappointed by the German refusal to renew the Reinsurance Treaty with Russia, Giers had repeatedly expressed the desire to get something in writing, no matter how general, to take the place of the lapsed Treaty. This was the main purpose of his talk with Caprivi, described above.

[3] Friedrich von Hollmann. Admiral; State Secretary to the Imperial Naval Office 1890–7.

[4] Friedrich Alfred von Krupp. Head of the big German armament firm.

[5] Count Solms had reported this on 15 September. (From the Foreign Ministry files.)

that I cannot yet fix a date.' Our view here—and I assume you agree—is that if Crispi is actually expecting the Chancellor now, whether justifiably or unjustifiably, then the Chancellor must go for the good of the cause. I would suggest that the Chancellor, who is going to Stuttgart anyhow in the next few days, should go on to Italy via Munich and on his return journey should pay Kálnoky a brief return visit.

I will let you know later what decision is reached.

While I was busy writing this letter I received your kind letter together with the interesting photos from Pontresina. Very many thanks. I am filled with admiration at your climbing expeditions, though I do not envy you. I would not climb up there for a kingdom—not even for my own Württemberg!

You will have news of Lindenau from Prince Radolin whom I saw in Liegnitz and to whom I send my kindest regards.

When Marschall was away for a few days (a week, I think) Raschdau 'directed' the Ministry, as he put it!

Also enclosed is a letter from Reuss.[1]

I look forward to seeing you again on the 10th. Perhaps you will give me your address after you arrive in Dresden, in case I have anything to add to this letter.

With sincere regard, as ever your most obedient and devoted

Kiderlen.

ENCLOSURE

Heinrich VII Reuss to Alfred von Kiderlen-Wächter.

Vienna, 21 September 1890

Dear Kiderlen,

I have not yet thanked you for your kind letter from Gravenstein.

Our Austrian guests arrived home from Silesia this evening extremely well satisfied. According to Kálnoky everything went off splendidly, no discords. The Chancellor has made a very good impression on Kaiser Franz Joseph and Kálnoky is amazed at his knowledge of affairs and the general situation, which revealed exceptional gifts and enormous industry.

K[álnoky] says they got on very well together and their political opinions completely coincided.

I am very glad the affair was such a great success. My one regret is that K[álnoky] had no opportunity to have a talk with you.

Nothing to report here. With best regards.

Your devoted

H. VII Reuss.

329. Alfred von Kiderlen-Wächter to Holstein

Berlin, 30 September 1890

My dear Baron,

As a postscript to my last letter I must tell you that a dispatch has

[1] See enclosure.

come in from Pourtalès,[1] according to which Giers has indulged in expressions of apology and regret for Muraviev's request for something in writing from the Chancellor; this had certainly not figured in his instructions and he, Giers, attached not the least importance to a *bout de papier*; his communication had been a matter between one gentleman and another, for which one does not request a receipt as though from one's banker; Muraviev had acted with the best intentions but with excessive zeal, etc. etc.—*Risum teneatis*.

We have talked round the Chancellor who had already sent Crispi a letter declining his invitation. He sent for me yesterday morning to ask me one or two things about Friedrichshafen where he is to go at the Kaiser's request. Since he said he then intended to go on to the Mainau and to Munich, I took the liberty of making another enquiry about Crispi. The Chancellor said that urgent business (Forckenbeck, the Stuttgart command), made it imperative for him to be back here on 10 October, the day of the Kaiser's return, which left too little time, otherwise he would 'be very glad to go to Rome'. Now I saw what was up and said, quite calmly: 'Then Your Excellency would like to look round Rome too for a few days?' When he assented at once, I asked him at least to empower the Foreign Ministry to inform Crispi through Solms that the Chancellor would be happy to visit him now but that pressure of work would leave him time for only a flying visit, and that he would very much like to see that great statesman, Crispi, for a longer period, etc.

The Chancellor consented. Then Marschall started on him and got him to agree that a telegram should be sent to Crispi stating that the Chancellor was prepared to travel to *Milan* if Crispi wished to see him now, otherwise they would meet in Rome later and for a longer time. The Chancellor imagines Crispi will drop the idea now but I think he will seize on the offer at once. Unfortunately the telegram cannot be sent off until replies have come in from Stuttgart and Friedrichshafen. I shall not feel satisfied until the telegram is on its way to Rome.[2] [...]

With sincere regard, as ever your most obedient and devoted

Kiderlen.

330. Holstein to Hugo von Radolin[3]

Berlin, 5 November 1890

My dear Rado,

[...] Pourtalès arrived yesterday, but he is still on leave until the 20th to shoot chamois. He says that the ideal Ambassador for St Petersburg is yourself. I think so too of course, but I'm very doubtful whether we could push through your appointment for St Petersburg.

---

[1] Pourtalès to Caprivi, 24 September 1890. (*Grosse Politik*, vol. VII, no. 1614, pp. 355–6.)

[2] Caprivi visited Munich on 5 and 6 November; on 7 November he met Crispi in Milan. (See Crispi, *Memoirs*, vol. III, pp. 5–11.)

[3] From the Radolin Papers.

At the moment opinion would not favour this idea, so we must see that the decision is put off, i.e. that Schweinitz is left there a while longer.

With best regards
Your,
H. [...]

331. Philipp zu Eulenburg to Holstein[1]

St[uttgart], 1 December 1890

My dear friend,

You can imagine the effect produced by your communication relating to Munich and my future![2] Our letters crossed in the post, so that I see myself behaving—*sans comparaison*—like a pregnant woman who complains that her husband does not get her with child![3] How has this sudden change come about? I suppose it may be precisely as a result of that business about which I was lamenting.[4] The thought of moving out of our scarcely completed house in Stuttgart almost alarms this unfortunate family man! When is the catastrophe to occur? After all the fuss, I can hardly believe that the time has come—and I would beg you to consider that I may not come up to your expectations in Munich. Life weaves myths around people and situations, but woe to the man whom fate leads out of the myth!—were he never so wise, he would be condemned, whereas the most foolish figure within the myth can even become a hero.

Please write and tell me the further development of this affair. [...] Another letter has come in from Crailsheim with any number of requests. But for your 'Munich news' I should have gone on strike! As it is I will play the intermediary yet again. I wonder what the Chancellor thinks of H.M.'s request? It seemed to me that Prince B[ismarck]'s successor had wanted to keep on the son-in-law[5] out of courtesy to a colleague. I should *feel very keenly* the departure of any colleague *on my account*! I have the misfortune to approach life with too great a sensibility. Whether, like yesterday evening in Tübingen, I am making comic speeches with Prince Wilhelm at the 'Swabians' bottle party, whether I am doing my job, looking after children, composing ballads, or drinking Goldlacher with you at Borchard's—I always enter into it *completely*. And that will finally be my undoing. The wisdom of this world—but not its *riches*—lies in objectivity. And I shall console myself with that, even though my coffin will be made a few years earlier.

Your ever faithful
P.E. [...]

[1] Printed in part in Haller, *Eulenburg*, p. 61.
[2] Holstein had informed Eulenburg on 27 November that it was proposed to transfer him to Munich at the Kaiser's request. (See Haller, *Eulenburg*, p. 61.)
[3] In a letter of 28 November Eulenburg had complained to Holstein of the unpleasantness caused him by the Bavarian government's habit of using him as confidant.
[4] The reference is to a misunderstanding between Crailsheim and Caprivi.
[5] Rantzau.

332. Holstein to Maximilian von Brandt[1]

26 December 1890

Your Excellency,

There is nothing in particular going on in the field of foreign politics, though things are not so quiet as the newspapers would lead one to assume. The fact is that nothing reaches the Press now—not from us at least.

The Mediterranean goes on seething gently. Those half decayed Barbary Coast countries favour the development of political bacilli. It is always *possible* for trouble to flare up there suddenly, though in the main I rather think the quiet note in politics will persist until the Russians have their new rifle—in about two and a half year's time. [...]

Domestic affairs are going quite well on the whole. Caprivi has the Kaiser's confidence. The Kaiser, after having just had a heated conversation with Waldersee,[2] said recently in Königswusterhausen: 'I've just repulsed an attack on Caprivi. There is no hope whatever of driving a wedge between C. and myself. I know perfectly well why Waldersee always tries to do so; he'd very much like to become Chancellor himself.'

I deplore the increasing acrimony between ourselves and the General Staff, on objective grounds. I have enjoyed good relations with Wald. for very many years, but I have felt annoyed with him recently for failing to recall our Military Attaché in Rome,[3] who is playing a private political game which happens to be anti-Crispi.[4] He actually uses him for *political* reports. It was precisely for this *political* reporting, which Caprivi has now expressly forbidden, that Waldersee put in a plea to H.M. in Wusterhausen, but H.M. took the Chancellor's side.

For my part I passionately hope there will not be another violent change for the time being. The Reich would suffer from it.

I wish you a Happy New Year, although this letter will arrive rather belatedly.

I remain, Your Excellency,

Yours most sincerely,

Holstein.

[1] From the Brandt Papers.
[2] See Waldersee, *Denkwürdigkeiten*, vol. II, pp. 165–70.
[3] Colonel von Engelbrecht.
[4] See Waldersee, *Denkwürdigkeiten*, vol, II, pp. 170–1.

1891

333. Heinrich VII Reuss to Holstein

Vienna, 11 February 1891

Dear Baron,

I have been most interested to observe from recent dispatches that the Russians are up to something again. Shuvalov's effusive utterances to the State Secretary[1] do not seem entirely due to deep drinking, as happens so often with him, in which case what he says is meaningless. I am strengthened in this belief by Count Schweinitz' dispatch.[2]

I can hardly believe it was *only* alarm at the spread of republicanism that made the Tsar let his luncheon get cold. He also wanted to throw us a bait, and to remind us of the advantage of an alliance which did not include Austria. If he also aimed at spoiling our taste for Austria by prophesying chaos in the Danube Empire after Franz Joseph's death, then I think he was rather wide of the mark. For this, surely, is more likely to happen in Russia; if the worthy Alexander III were to meet a violent end, the resultant chaos in nationally unified Russia would be more dangerous to us than such chaos in Austria, despite her many nationalities.

For this reason, and for others known to you, I do not think this graciously dangled bait is tempting enough to swallow; on the contrary I think it imperative to continue the sensible policy pursued hitherto and to cultivate personal relationships between the sovereigns without entering into conspiracies against Austria. But it still is a good idea to make the Tsar's flesh creep with the threat of republicanism. While on this subject Schweinitz might have pointed out to him that, thanks to France's really ridiculous flirtations, republican ideas will reach Russia (World's Fair[3]) and that this constitutes a far greater danger to monarchical Russia than a republican victory in, let us say, Portugal. If the republican bogey served to link the Tsar again more closely with the older monarchies, that would indeed be best, and he might in the end even become convinced that the House of Habsburg is one of the monarchies in question.

[1] See Marschall to Reuss, 30 January 1891. (*Grosse Politik*, vol. VII, no. 1616, p. 362.)

[2] On 28 January Schweinitz had reported a long conversation with Alexander III, in which the Tsar expressed his fear of the spread of republicanism in Europe and emphasised the necessity of collaboration between the monarchies. In particular the Tsar regarded the situation in Spain, Portugal and Italy as menacing, and thought the existence of the French Republic a serious threat to monarchical interests. This conversation, which also touched on the subject of Austria-Hungary, interested the Tsar to such an extent that he did not break it off in spite of the Tsarina's hint that luncheon was waiting. (From the Foreign Ministry files; see Schweinitz, *Denkwürdigkeiten*, vol. II, p. 419.)

[3] The World's Fair which was being planned for Moscow.

Kálnoky, in planning the Archduke's journey,[1] was probably acting upon this idea. In fact he is simply imitating what our Kaiser is doing, without indulging the slightest hope that such visits will contribute towards an agreement between Austria and Russia in those spheres in which their common interests have conflicted hitherto.

In view of the Tsar's continued mistrust of Kálnoky, it is not to be expected that Austrian proposals (for combating republicanism) will create a good impression or produce any effect in St Petersburg. I think I may conclude, from a statement made towards the end of secret dispatch no. 60,[2] that we still wish to bring the Tsar back into closer relations with the other monarchies (even though little hope is entertained that this would succeed) and thus that an attempt could be made to do *something* in that direction, but with no hint of what this is. This 'something' can refer only to Portugal.[3] It is common knowledge that Kálnoky has been at work here before us and has also made various attempts in England to combat the dangers to the Portuguese dynasty which may result from British policy. He has, it is true, a very low opinion of the King and his Ministers, but he never tires of urging them to take a strong line. And so I think that if we are planning any step of this kind we should be well advised not to keep it secret from Vienna. Otherwise if the facts become known, Kálnoky might see in our silence a lack of trust, a decline in our usual intimacy, and might take offence. You will agree with me that this would prejudice our relations. I should particularly like to avoid this at a time when people here are imagining that the close military relations so important to the Austrians may suffer because of Waldersee's retirement.[4]

Kálnoky is satisfied with the progress of the Archduke's visit to St Petersburg. He told me yesterday that, as usual, the Russian Press was now saying the exact opposite of what it said during our most gracious Majesty's visit. *Then* it was: come along with us and let those damned Austrians go; but *now* the Russians are whispering in the Austrian's ear: if only you'd drop the Germans, Russia would very easily reach an agreement with Austria. Kálnoky regards neither of these insinuations

---

[1] Archduke Franz Ferdinand had arrived in St Petersburg on 6 February on a visit to the Russian court. (See Kálnoky's dispatch to Wolkenstein of 12 February 1891. Wolfgang Hermann, *Dreibund, Zweibund, England, 1890–95* (Stuttgart, 1929), pp. 153–4.)

[2] Schweinitz' report of 28 January had been communicated to Reuss in dispatch no. 60 of 7 February. This dispatch had concluded by stating that the Tsar's anxiety at the possible spread of the republican system might perhaps result in Russia's drawing closer to the other monarchies. (From the Foreign Ministry files.)

[3] Disputes between Britain and Portugal over rival territorial claims in East and South Africa led to a serious crisis between the two countries in January 1890. On 11 January 1890 Britain presented Portugal with an ultimatum to withdraw all fighting forces drawn up along the Shiré and stationed in Makoli territory or in Mashonaland. Indignation in Portugal over the Government's acceptance of the ultimatum forced the Ministry to resign and gave rise to widespread republican agitation. The various attempts to reach an understanding with Britain throughout 1890 were met with fierce popular opposition, and were accompanied by increasing republican activity so that the Portuguese monarchy was seriously endangered.

[4] As Chief of the Army General Staff on 2 February 1891. Waldersee was appointed General in Command of the IX Army Corps in Altona. His successor as Chief of the General Staff was Count Alfred von Schlieffen.

as sincere; he is amused by them and has given orders that the Austrian Press shall not react to them.

With best wishes
Your very devoted
H. VII Reuss.

334. Paul von Hatzfeldt to Holstein

London, 11 February 1891

My dear Holstein,

I observed a certain caution in to-day's dispatch because I have the impression that it may be better if certain considerations do not yet reach the files.[1]

But if you wish to know my opinion I will outline it now as briefly as possible.

The more I reflect on it, the more firmly convinced I become that a Portuguese Republic, which would soon be followed by a Spanish Republic, would constitute well nigh the *greatest* political danger to the Triple Alliance, and to each separate member of it, most especially to us. I have not a shadow of doubt that the setting up of an Iberian Republic which would not only deliver France from any anxiety about Spain, but would also inevitably cause the entire peninsula to depend on her, would give the French fresh courage to attack us and might touch off another war. You saw how they gave themselves airs in Paris immediately after Crispi's downfall.[2] Just add to that a Republic in Spain and Portugal with the hope of a similar revolution in Italy and the results would be incalculable.

That is the standpoint upon which I work, and it forces me to the opinion that we must try every possible means of effectively combating that danger. Our common interest in preserving the monarchy is also involved, and—but only secondarily—the repeatedly discussed colonial question.

If my view of the danger to be averted is correct, we must consider by what means our end may be attained, which friends we can count on and which enemies we must reckon with. The one thing we must certainly not do is to sit with our hands in our lap.

It appears certain that Spain will take no independent action without the encouragement and moral support of powerful friends, particularly when the sacrifices and effort demanded of her appear to promise no tangible advantage. The advantage could consist only in an annexation which would correspond to a national wish and would thus, if successful, strengthen the monarchy in Spain. The encouragement and moral

[1] In a personal letter to State Secretary Marschall of 5 February 1891, Hatzfeldt had reported a conversation with Salisbury which considered in detail the problem of a possible republican revolution in Portugal and its consequences. In particular the question of Spanish intervention and the future of the Portuguese colonies was discussed. In the dispatch of 11 February Hatzfeldt reported that he had, as instructed, informed Salisbury of the conversation between Schweinitz and the Tsar (see above, p. 363, note 2) and also of Spain's rapprochement with Italy. (From the Foreign Ministry files.)

[2] The Crispi Ministry had fallen on 31 January 1891.

support, if not more, can come only from the Triple Alliance and England. Only by these Powers will Spain—quite justifiably—be convinced that she can act without danger from outside and that neither France nor Russia will intervene.

Stumm's arguments are superficial, as they must be since they are based on a different premise—the intervention without personal advantage.[1] Nor am I convinced that even present-day Spain could not deal with a revolutionary Portugal. Salisbury, as you know, thinks that she could, and I share his opinion on this point. But I go still further. If the Spaniards are content to set up an observation corps along the frontier when the Republic is proclaimed in Lisbon, then I am convinced the days of the Spanish monarchy are numbered. The situation cannot therefore get any worse, even if the success of Spanish intervention remained militarily doubtful. In view, therefore, of the political danger, which I consider of primary importance, our interest, i.e. that of the Triple Alliance and England, requires that the attempt be made.

Now if we first consider possible friends and enemies, it is clear that all the Powers with the exception of Russia and France would approve of Spain's action. I think that Tsar Alexander, in view of his horror of republicanism in Southern Europe, would not support the French. But in that case the French would, at the most, grouse in private. The worst we have to fear from Russia, as you say yourself, is an invoking of the unselfishness clause;[2] which would perhaps make it impossible to settle the colonial question at present. But even at the worst I do not think that too dear a price to pay for the strengthening of the Spanish monarchy, which is anti-French and allied with Italy.

When we examine the means by which this aim may be pursued, we must not deceive ourselves; *no one* will wish to act *first* and *in isolation*, England least of all, because an English Minister risks his neck if he is found guilty of such secret agreements. But I am convinced that we can do nothing without England—quite apart from the colonial question. S[alisbury] is brooding over the affair; he is still wavering and would prefer the Spaniards to come forward with proposals, which they will not do without encouragement. There are thus only two courses, if we recognise the necessity of this action and realise that England must participate:

either we drop a hint to the Spaniards (directly or via Austria) to instruct their envoys in London to discuss the situation in strictest confidence with S. and to put forward their *wishes*

or—and this still seems to me the right step—we first try to reach *complete* agreement with S. direct, as soon as we can assume with tolerable certainty that he is in favour of doing so. I feel convinced that,

---

[1] In a dispatch from Madrid of 31 January which was communicated to the Embassy in London, Stumm reached the conclusion that Spain would intervene to re-establish the Portuguese monarchy only if she were certain of the support of the other monarchical states in Europe, but that this support would presumably only be forthcoming if Spain sought no national advantages for herself. (From the Foreign Ministry files.)

[2] That is to say, that the Powers should not seek to benefit from Portugal's domestic disturbances by seizing Portugese territory.

if he does indeed decide upon action, *only* our collaboration will give him the courage to expose himself to the unpleasantness he may suffer here as a result of this affair. If this secret agreement is achieved—and its provisions would have to be precisely determined—we can then jointly request the Austrians to drop a hint to the Regent.[1]

I can see no other course, unless we are prepared to wait until the catastrophe is upon us. Whether or not it will then be too late from every point of view is another question. In that event the Spaniards would not be prepared and would lose valuable time. Negotiations between the Powers and the Spaniards would take weeks. The Republic in Portugal would gain time to organise itself and to get in touch with its sympathisers in France and Spain, who would then set in motion every possible means, even attempted revolt, to prevent any intervention in Portugal.

But if our plan is to meet with success it is obvious that on the day a Republic is proclaimed in Lisbon, Spain must go into action on land and by sea.

So now you know my views and I have only a few words to add on the colonial question.

Make no mistake about it, we can achieve a satisfactory result in this matter only by coming to a previous understanding with England. I feel convinced that S. will not shun such an arrangement if it takes place simultaneously with the political agreement. In that case it would obviously be an advantage for S. to be certain in advance of our support in this question too. But I very much doubt whether he would still be a party to it *after* the catastrophe had occurred. My own feeling—which, as you say, is often right—is that he imagines that the object in question, at any rate in the East, would then fall like ripe fruit into England's lap. Every agreement with Portugal would then lapse, British companies and adventurers, whose name is legion, would close in from all sides and take possession. And afterwards the British government would merely say, as it has done so often in reply to Portugal's claims, that it was not in a position to expel its fellow countrymen. *Et le tour serait joué.* Will anyone make war on England for that, or even pick a serious quarrel? I think *not*.

And so this consideration also points to our reaching *prior* agreement. Goodbye for now. If you think that my modest personal opinion may interest Herr von Marschall, then I leave it entirely to your discretion whether you show him this letter. The only reason I refrained from burdening him with a personal letter to-day is that I have nothing new to say on the matter and could only set out my personal view, and this, considering I had not been invited to do so, might have seemed to him rather impertinent.

With best wishes,
Your
P. Hatzfeldt.

---

[1] Maria Cristina, widow of King Alfonso XII of Spain.

335. Georg zu Münster to Holstein

Paris, 5 March 1891

Private and Confidential
My dear Holstein,

[...] Kaiserin Friedrich's visit here would have done good if it had lasted four days at the most, as my daughter and I expected, and if the royal lady had brought a more tactful escort than Seckendorff.[1] In fact these ten days have merely cost a good deal of money, created widespread annoyance and in many respects done actual harm.

The reaction of public opinion, I am glad to say, is so strong that the political harm will not be so great as I originally feared. The tightening-up of passport regulations has some good aspects but also much that is dangerous.[2] It is a good thing for the Alsatians to realise the harm being done to them here by Déroulède, the Boulangists and the chauvenists. And it is a good thing for them to see that we have taken the matter seriously. I think, too, that it is a good thing that these stringent passport regulations provide us with the means of depriving Déroulède and the Alsatian malcontents of their most effective method of agitation. But it is my firm hope that the Kaiser, provided he acts correctly and acts fairly soon, will abolish the detested compulsory passport regulations, thereby winning over and making happy the greater part (i.e. the *better* part) of the population of Alsace. At the same time we should have to demand certain guarantees from the French government against the League of Patriots and Déroulède, and threaten even harsher measures if they were not forthcoming!

I should not express this idea if I were not firmly convinced that the passport regulations are antagonising the Alsatians still further and have provided Alsatian agitators in France, on whom we cannot keep an eye here, with a powerful means of stirring things up, done us no good [*sic*]. Everything I [have] heard from soldiers or from *German* chauvenists, of whom we have many in Alsace, has failed to convince me. If the Alsatian administration, despite the extensive police powers it can command, is incapable of holding in check pro-French agitation or of winning over the Alsatians by a policy of rigorous justice without enforcing compulsory passports, then it is worthless.

The danger of tightening up regulations at this moment is that nothing which seems prompted by anger is good politically.

Moreover, the present decrees are so harsh that many of them violate the Treaty of Frankfurt. And we must not entirely forget that on the material level not only Alsace-Lorraine but also some of the South German states are badly hit by them—nor can we be completely indifferent to public opinion in Europe.

[1] The Kaiser's mother had visited Paris, 18–27 February. Her visits to St Cloud and Versailles, which vividly recalled the recent war with Prussia, enraged French public opinion. (See *Grosse Politik*, vol. VII, nos. 1545–54, pp. 271–85; Rogge, *Holstein und Hohenlohe*, pp. 349–56, 360.)

[2] In reply to Parisian demonstrations against Kaiserin Friedrich, Wilhelm II issued an order rigorously enforcing passport regulations in Alsace. (See *Grosse Politik*, vol. VII, p. 285, note ***.)

Please take what I have said as information kindly intended; I should be glad if you shared my opinion. Please convey my best wishes to Herr von Marschall.

> Ever your good friend and devoted servant,
> Münster.

336. Georg zu Münster to Holstein

Paris, 9 March 1891

My dear Holstein,

Thank you very much for your kind letter. I am not surprised to learn from you that you all abused me on the 26th,[1] first because abuse is a special characteristic of the Berliner, and secondly because to those unable to observe events on the spot there seemed ample grounds for doing so. But I do take some credit for the way things turned out—it was not easy. No one has ever spoken so plainly to the French statesmen as I did without harming Germany or endangering his own position, and I was very well aware of the *dangerous* possibilities. Let me just briefly recall the last two days of the visit.

Lord Lytton[2] called on me at noon Monday to tell me Queen Victoria was getting worried and had asked him to enquire whether it would not be more prudent to let the Kaiserin leave secretly that evening, during the night, or on Tuesday morning. I replied that her visit had quite definitely lasted far too *long*, that I had said so to Count Seckendorff, with no result, and had also hinted as much to the Kaiserin, *but* now that we had arranged for the French and British Press to announce her departure for Friday, a secret departure *before* then would look like ignoble flight, and I therefore categorically refused to comply with such a proposal. I then went straight to Ribot,[3] the Foreign Minister, said as much to him, made the situation perfectly clear to him, and made him *responsible* for anything that might happen. The Minister was obviously dumbfounded, admitted I was right, actually thanked me for speaking so frankly and firmly, and said: 'You are quite right. Her Majesty must *not* leave before Friday. I grant you that now; we should show ourselves incapable of appreciating and honouring so noble a guest.' M. Ribot then asked me to take all necessary decisions and make arrangements with the officials he would be sending me.

The departure had been fixed for 11:30, by the Calais train, but on the suggestion of the Northern Railway Company, which seemed very anxious to please, this time was reserved for baggage and servants, the Kaiserin's departure being fixed for 10:10, by the Boulogne train, and a special train was put on from there to Calais, which the police required in any case for her arrival and embarcation in Calais. There was some

---

[1] Because of the incidents that had taken place in connection with Kaiserin Friedrich's visit to Paris.

[2] Edward Robert, Earl of Lytton. British Ambassador in Paris, 1887–91.

[3] Alexandre Ribot. French Foreign Minister in the Freycinet Cabinet, 1890-2; in the Loubet Cabinet, 1892; Minister-President and Foreign Minister, December 1892-March 1893; Minister-President and Finance Minister, January–October 1895.

talk of the Kaiserin driving to the station in an ordinary hired cab, but I would not hear of it and drove Her Majesty in *my carriage* bearing the German cockaid, a procedure entirely approved of and actually desired by the Prefect of Police, H. Lozet, who consistently displayed great energy and ability. Between the Embassy and the station there were four policemen posted every hundred yards, two on either side of the street. There were not many people, but they were all quiet and many of them cheered. I felt a trifle worried as we approached the station because quite a considerable crowd converged on the station entrance.

But the people took up their positions calmly and raised their hats as if at a word of command. When I remarked on this later to the *Chef de la sûreté publique*, who was also going to Calais, he replied: 'I was sure nothing would go wrong, for half of that crowd consisted of my plain-clothes police, who were explicitly ordered to knock down (*d'assommer*) anyone who so much as opened his mouth, and they'd have done so too.'

The people of Paris refused to get excited—only the stupid artists did that.[1]

I lost four pounds in those ten days, as well as my money, and yet you Berliners still curse me!! That does beat the devil!!! [...] Now, do confess you abused me unjustly, and do keep alive your friendship for me.

Yours ever in warmest friendship,

Münster.

337. Paul von Hatzfeldt to Holstein

[London], 15 March 1891

My dear friend,

Just a few hurried lines to tell you my only reason for not writing about the Iberian question is that there is nothing new to report. Salisbury has obviously mastered the facts, and I should not think it right to take the initiative repeatedly, *unless* something occurred to alter the situation, or else a move were made in Madrid or, still better, in Vienna, which I could then support.

Even though I think I must await one of these two contingencies (and I hope I can count on agreement in Berlin) that does not prevent me from sounding the terrain from time to time. Only yesterday I asked Salisbury whether he was still of the opinion that Spain was in no danger. He assented, introducing yet again the expression that there was *'une bonne tête'* (the Regent) in Madrid, and so there was nothing to worry about. Referring to the London negotiations with Portugal I jokingly observed: 'You are in an excellent position from which you can profit. Either Portugal gives in to your demands, and in that case you will get what you want; or the government in Lisbon falls and you will pick up her colonies like ripe fruit.'[2] He said nothing to contradict me, and smiled with gratification to think I had grasped the subtleties of the situation.

[1] Kaiserin Friedrich's interest in art and her visit to a few ateliers provoked particular anti-German demonstrations and declarations by French artists. (*Grosse Politik*, vol. VII, no. 1549, pp. 275–9.)

[2] In French in the original.

Assuming we desire to prevent this from happening, there are only two methods: either the Powers state that in the monarchical interest they are opposed to the plundering of the Portuguese and must insist on a fairer treatment of Portugal in this matter, in which case there is just a chance that S. may reach a rapid agreement to avoid running into difficulties—or else Kálnoky is prevailed on to raise here in London or via Spain the question of possible intervention and I am instructed to support this.

If nothing is done, things will take their course. One fine day the Portuguese monarchy will disappear, the Spanish and possibly the Italian monarchies will be threatened, and France will rub her hands for joy.

I leave it to you whether you show this letter to the State Secretary; I should not like to burden him myself with these observations, or my bad writing.

Every good wish,
Yours ever,
P. Hatzfeldt.

P.S. You might also consider whether we could drop S. a friendly hint that we cannot countenance too great a colonial expansion by England through the possible annexation of the Portuguese colonies, and that we might therefore—if this occurred—raise a protest, if there had been no prior agreement with us over the *political* question.

In a telegram from Marschall drafted by Holstein, dated 18 March (no. 53) Hatzfeldt was instructed to inform Lord Salisbury that the British attitude towards Portugal was arousing the suspicion on all sides that England wished to acquire the greatest possible amount of Portuguese colonial territory. In view of public opinion in Germany, the German government would find it difficult to avoid participating in joint counter-measures by the Powers. The German government, in view of its good relations with England, would regret this, and hoped therefore that Lord Salisbury would do his utmost to spare Germany this necessity. The telegram concluded: 'Your Excellency will perhaps find an opportunity of mentioning that the annexation of Portuguese colonial possessions, particularly on the *East* coast of Africa, vitally concerns German interests.'

Hatzfeldt replied by return that he had drawn on this telegram during his interview with Salisbury, and had the impression that the latter 'given *absolute* secrecy, would be inclined to reach agreement with us, for certain contingencies, on the possessions clearly indicated at the conclusion of telegram no. 53; he recognises our interest in them as a Power with mutual frontiers'.

On 19 March Hatzfeldt telegraphed for instructions as to whether he should influence the British government towards a more lenient attitude to Portugal or should be a party to negotiations concerning the partition of the Portuguese colonies. He added that the previous day when he mentioned to Salisbury Germany's interest 'in an annexation of Portuguese possessions on the *East coast* [of Africa], [Salisbury] had replied : *"alors, divisons."* '

Marschall instructed Hatzfeldt by telegram on 20 March that Germany's position in Europe made acquiescence in the partition of the Portuguese colonies impossible, but that it was more difficult to refuse Zanzibar and Pemba, British-controlled islands off the coast of German East Africa, as compensations. Germany's main interest, however, was the preservation of the Portuguese monarchy. Any action by England failing to take into account German interests, which were shared by other Powers, would compel the German government 'to bow to outraged public opinion in Germany and to reach agreement with France on a common approach to the Egyptian question, in exchange for her most binding promise, perhaps made publicly, not to attack Germany for a number of years'. Considerations of this nature might prove useful to Salisbury if he were urged either by England or by South Africa to adopt harsher measures against Portugal. A possible solution would be to submit the Anglo-Portuguese dispute to arbitration, or to lay it before a Congress.

Hatzfeldt replied on 21 March that he too regarded the preservation of the monarchy on the Iberian Peninsula as the main issue, and that a republic there would strengthen France 'and would probably hasten the outbreak of war. If the Portuguese monarchy should fall, the only remaining possibility was a Spanish entry into Portugal and its subsequent annexation by Spain, together with an Anglo-German agreement on the future of the Portuguese colonies. If Spain could not fulfill her allotted role and if it came to compensation negotiations, England would probably not cede Zanzibar but might cede other parts of Africa not at present forming part of Portuguese possessions. A further consideration was that too much pressure on England to show a more conciliatory attitude towards Portugal might overthrow the Salisbury Cabinet, which was certainly not in Germany's interests and might result in a swing by England towards France and Russia.'

In his reply of 22 March Marschall stressed yet again Germany's desire to preserve the monarchy on the Iberian Peninsula, if necessary even by a Spanish annexation of Portugal with the support of England, and emphasised in the event of compensation negotiations Germany's interest in Zanzibar and Pemba, in which case German South-West Africa might be considered as equivalent to Germany's new acquisitions. (From the Foreign Ministry files.)

338. Holstein to Paul von Hatzfeldt[1]

TELEGRAM

Berlin, 23 March 1891

Private, not to be referred back

England is now playing up the Triple Alliance and playing down France for Egypt's benefit, whereas in the Portuguese question, the consequences of which imply the disintegration of our system of monarchical alliances, she is doing the opposite, i.e. playing up France and playing down the Triple Alliance. The feeling that England had duped them, which everyone, governments as well as people, would inevitably experience, is a danger to England to which it would be as well to draw Ld. Salisbury's attention while there is still time. England is endangering her future in India (including Egypt and Morocco) just for the sake of forging ahead in Africa *somewhat faster*; for the next great European conflict would in any case leave her a fairly free hand in Africa, and at *that* juncture the question: republic or monarchy? would turn on other factors than the Portuguese constitution.

We have learned from recent dispatches from Tangier that England is aiming at acquiring Tangier and Cape Spartel at the earliest favourable opportunity—this and Egypt make *lasting* co-operation with France impossible for England. On the other hand an *ad hoc* agreement between the Triple Alliance and Russia and even with France is *logically not unthinkable*, on the basis of a *postponement* of the Balkan question and the question of *revanche*. There have been similar conditional adjournments in the past. As regards Russia, Prince Bismarck's statement that England would find it easier than Austria to reach agreement with Russia dates from a time when Egypt was not yet a British possession.

Résumé: *For the moment* Ld. Salisbury should be satisfied with a moderate success and should not put pressure on the friendly Powers which wish England every advantage compatible with their own security.

A moderate success, together with the preservation of the Portuguese monarchy, is easier to obtain than the absorption of the Portuguese republic by the Spanish monarchy, together with simultaneous colonial indemnity for us. If England does *not* commit herself to supporting Spain, the suspicion cannot be excluded that she would like to cause a European conflict over this question but *without* participating herself. In that case there would be no annexation, and republicanism would spread. If England gave the Spaniards assurances that she would take their side in the event of Franco-Russian intervention, such an intervention would become highly improbable because of the dynamic superiority of England and her allies—but in any case this situation is not so easy to obtain as the preservation of the Portuguese monarchy.

The foregoing is not a set of instructions but merely my personal view for you to consider.

Holstein.

[1] From the Foreign Ministry files.

Hatzfeldt telegraphed on 24 March that he had discussed the contents of Marschall's telegram of 22 March during a three hour interview with Salisbury. The British Prime Minister had not fallen in with the suggestion that Germany should receive colonial compensation from Britain in the event of a partition of the Portuguese colonies. When Hatzfeldt hinted at the possibility of a monarchical coalition against Britain, Salisbury replied that if such a coalition threatened to materialise Britain would reach an agreement with France even if it meant sacrificing Egypt. Salisbury did say, however, that in view of the interest of the Triple Alliance Powers in preserving the Portuguese monarchy, he was prepared to consider communicating to the governments of Germany, Austria-Hungary and Italy the terms Britain intended to offer to Portugal.

On receipt of Hatzfeldt's telegram Holstein drew up the following memorandum, which, with the exception of the passages in parenthesis, was sent on the evening of 24 March as a telegraphic instruction to Hatzfeldt over Marschall's signature. (From the Foreign Ministry files.)

339. Memorandum by Holstein[1]

Berlin, 24 March 1891

The course of the Anglo-Portuguese negotiations so far has clearly shown that England is guided exclusively by colonial considerations and occasionally disregards her European interests.

But it is precisely these European interests which unite us with England; the colonial interests divide us from England, particularly Germany and Italy.

Our task now is to recall England to the consideration of her *European* interests. This can come about only if England suffers a check in the Cape Colony. She will suffer this as soon as it becomes obvious that there is some obstacle besides Portugal to the pursuit of British colonial interests beyond a given point. Such an obstacle will exist the moment the three allied Powers declare that they object to sacrificing the present peaceful balance of power in Europe to their friendship with England.

(Germany in particular has to consider the incidental circumstances that the Cape Colony, as the possessor of Mozambique, would be an unruly and undesirable neighbour for us. But we showed last summer in the East Africa Agreement[2] that we rate our European relations higher than our colonial interests. If it were now merely a question of the latter it would probably not be difficult to obtain some compensation or indemnity from England. But the significance of the colonial question entirely disappears in this case when compared with the progressive jeopardising of the system of monarchical alliances which would be the

[1] From the Foreign Ministry files.   [2] See above, p. 344, note 1.

direct result of the fall of the Portuguese monarchy. For the powers of resistance of the Spanish monarchy, which would in that event be *principally* threatened, seem to be still further reduced at this very moment and for the immediate future by the uncertain prospects of the defence of Cuba.)

Portugal's isolation hitherto is proving a temptation to which the British government's political *sang froid* threatens to succumb. Hence the first task of the three Powers is to lessen that temptation in their own interest as well as in England's obvious interest. This task could be discharged by a step which would show England that the interests of the Portuguese monarchy are bound up with those of the [three] Powers and consequently with England's interests. (In doing this we would have to show the British government the greatest possible consideration, first by keeping this absolutely secret from foreign Powers, secondly by keeping Russia out of the affair at first, since she might favour joint action *for* the monarchical principle and *against* England.)

Lord Salisbury's remark that England might possibly be obliged to reach agreement with France, even if it cost her Egypt, can be taken as an empty threat because even if England pursued very ambitious aims in Central and South Africa, their attainment would certainly weigh too lightly when compared with giving up the connection with India. There is on the contrary a further hint, besides what we have heard from Morocco, that England is bent on making this connection still more secure by the appointment there of the new British Minister Euan-Smith[1] who won his spurs in preparing the ground for the British protectorate over Zanzibar.

(Assuming for the moment that England rates her interests in Central and South Africa so far above all others that she really is considering a rapprochement with France even though the three friendly Powers would like to bring their main interests in Europe more in line with English interests in Africa, then the policy pursued hitherto by the Triple Alliance towards England would thereby be characterised as fundamentally mistaken. In that case the three Powers and Italy whose monarchical interests and, consequently, whose national unity would be most threatened, would be faced with the necessity of thinking of a practical remedy in time. But for the moment we still refuse to believe there is any such necessity.)

We shall for our part ensure that the three Powers act in such a way as to make it as easy as possible for the English to comply. And for that reason we wish England to initiate the confidential discussions *à quatre*, as was Your Excellency's own intention. The raising of the Portuguese claims beyond the minimal requirements of existence, which Lord Salisbury fears, would conflict with the interests of the three Powers, who request nothing but an acceptable outcome whatever it may be.

[1] Sir Charles Euan-Smith. British Consul-General and diplomatic representative in Zanzibar, 1887–91; Minister in Tangier, 1891–3.

I shall now await to hear from Your Excellency whether the English approach to the three Powers will soon be forthcoming. Otherwise the pressure of events will force the initiative upon the three Powers.

Holstein.

340. Paul von Hatzfeldt to Holstein

25 March 1891

My dear friend,

I am very glad to see from the latest news from Berlin that the solution I suggested (whereby S[alisbury] would communicate his latest conditions to the three Powers in strictest confidence) is approved. I shall of course do my utmost to persuade him to do so, but I must have *a little time*, because S. is travelling and will not reach his destination for two or three days.

His misgivings over the proposal will probably be twofold: 1. anxiety lest the Portuguese hear of it and then become more intractable; 2. fear lest people *in London* hear of it and reproach him not simply with submitting to the interference of a third party but with actually provoking it, in fact with submitting England's well-founded claims to the decision of a third party!

In your assessment of the situation please never forget that *foreign* considerations always take second place—first place is taken *always* by *domestic* considerations. Because of this our appraisal of English policy is sometimes wide of the mark if we assume that foreign considerations (India, Morocco and even Egypt) *must* be the deciding factor in certain cases. It is therefore *by no means impossible*, believe me, for S. to be obliged to swing right round, against his will and judgment, should public opinion become heated over foreign interference, which could be presented as a coalition against England—and this is quite possible.

You know better than I what the effect would be on Italy, already wavering, if the prospect of the possible protection of the British navy were withdrawn.

I urge you to grant me two things to render my present task easier: 1. an assurance that the three Powers will observe the *utmost* discretion in Portugal if S. does inform them of his intentions; 2. an assurance that if they find his conditions acceptable they will throw their weight into urging their acceptance in Lisbon. (I should have to be empowered to promise S. this.)

As regards Egypt do not forget that there is a group in this country, and in Parliament too, which favours giving up Egypt and coming to terms with France. And so the idea would not be impossible by any means.

But I think we must consider above all the fact that S.'s fall would be a great misfortune for us. His fall could very easily come about if this affair were not handled very skilfully. If it appeared to the public that the British government saw arrayed against it a *monarchical coalition* in support of *P.*, then I think there would be the very imminent danger that S., wishing to submit to pressure for reasons of foreign policy which the public found completely incomprehensible, would thereby compass his fall.

Dixi et salvavi animam meam, while bowing to superior wisdom in other things. But I must never be reproached later with failing to draw attention to the danger.

With warmest regards,
P.H.

P.S. With reference to the conduct of business I should like to point out that *from tomorrow until the following Tuesday* not even Sir Ph[ilip] Currie will be at the F.O. There is therefore at a time like *this not a soul* about for me to speak to, even if the world went up in flames.

341. Paul von Hatzfeldt to Holstein

14 April 1891

My dear friend,

[...] Don't expect any particular activity or communications from me before S[alisbury] returns (on the 17th). Then presumably the Port[uguese] affair will be our main topic of conversation, assuming I know by then what is thought of the plan in L[ondon] and in what respect *we* think moderation desirable.[1] But at the same time do not forget that my prospects of success in these negotiations depend *entirely* on my being able to guarantee to S. certain concessions from the other side. If I am not able to do so, he will probably hesitate to confide to me his most recent ideas.

As you know, I do not at the moment think we can pursue anything seriously or systematically in Morocco.[2] And in any case I must avoid creating the impression of wishing to force the pace or of forcing unsolicited favours on him. Believe me, I should do no good by that, merely harm. I can only *tâter le terrain*, and indeed most cautiously and when a favourable opportunity arises, when S. happens to have time and inclination for the exchange of general political ideas, which is not always the case. If I can then find a suitable opening without revealing the existence of any plan back at home, you may rest assured I shall not let it slip. S. is used to hearing me express independent and sometimes rather bold ideas and assumes I am allowed some degree of independence and that I sometimes put forward my own schemes in Berlin only after discussing them with him. This is an advantage in that when, in the excitement of conversation, I let fall my unexpected

[1] Since Lord Salisbury was reluctant to communicate the draft of the treaty between Britain and Portugal to the Triple Alliance Powers officially, the German and British governments had agreed that Germany should request Portugal to inform Germany of the treaty. The Portuguese government had declared itself in agreement with this. The draft was handed over in Lisbon on 15 April and communicated to the German government officially by Portugal and unofficially by the British government. (From the Foreign Ministry files.)

[2] Hatzfeldt had reported on 27 March that Count Tornielli was highly suspicious of British aims in Morocco. Hatzfeldt was informed on 31 March that Germany had every reason to promote British aims in Morocco and that Italian and Spanish opposition to such British expansion could probably be bought off with compensations. Hatzfeldt was instructed to try to talk the subject over with Salisbury. (*Grosse Politik*, vol. VIII, no. 1916, pp. 294–6; see also nos. 1918–19, pp. 296–8.)

and unusual ideas as though they were inspirations of the moment, he does not immediately see your shadow behind me and assume you know about them or agree with them. When incidents occurred in the past (e.g. Samoa) I told him more than once: if I were taking the decisions in Germany I should have acted quite differently, *and done this or that.* Then sometimes he talks freely too and discusses the idea I have thrown out, without being afraid of committing himself by anything he says. *Ce sont les petites ficelles du metier.* But they can only be used successfully when you can command both time and opportunity.

As regards the proposed meetings with R.[1] I must assume for the moment that S. replied to Rome direct. You can imagine how glad I should have been to see it come to pass and that I did my utmost from this end. The misgivings which prompted S. not to go—apart from the wish to be left in peace—seemed to me to be these: 1. the fear that R. might make all kinds of requests which S. would be unprepared for, and 2. that people at home would conclude he was reaching secret agreements and would on that account create difficulties for him in the House and in the Press. [...]

15 April

[...]. I should be very glad to know your opinion of the overall situation. I don't like the look of it, though I do not believe there is any immediate or impending danger. Italy is my main anxiety, however correctly the present cabinet may behave, and I am afraid we shall not be able to restrain her much longer because her need for funds and the rapprochement with France connected with it will constantly increase. There are in addition the Russian preparations on the frontier which cannot be denied, and the English elections due in the autumn of '92, the outcome of which no one can foresee. The Conservatives are by no means certain of victory, even though their position has materially improved because of the dissensions in Ireland. If there is a Gladstone Ministry, during which Italy could hardly count on the support of the British Navy, then it would scarcely be possible to retain her any longer in the Alliance, and there would then be imminent danger that Russia, ready for battle, certain of French support and not needing to fear England, would judge the time ripe to lay down the law to Austria and—should we wish to help her—to attack us too.

Thus our position could by next year—if not before—become really serious.

It is not for me to decide whether in these circumstances we should look more closely at Tornielli's[2] idea, doubtless conceived for other reasons, of an attempt at reaching a binding agreement with England.[3]

[1] Antonio, Marchese di Rudini. Italian Minister-President and Foreign Minister, 1891–2; Minister-President, March 1896–May 1898. Rudini wished for a meeting with Lord Salisbury who was staying at Cannes. The meeting did not take place. On 23 April Solms reported from Rome that Lord Dufferin, the British Ambassador, had expressed his regret that no meeting had taken place and added that generally speaking Lord Salisbury disliked such meetings. (From the Foreign Ministry files.)

[2] Giuseppe, Count Tornielli Brusati di Vergano. Italian Ambassador in London, 1889–95; in Paris, 1895–1908.

[3] See *Grosse Politik*, vol. VIII, no. 1706, p. 43.

But, I hasten to add, it is very doubtful whether the attempt would succeed. We might have to content ourselves with proposing slight alterations in the text of the existing agreement, and seeing how far we could get that way.

Another equally important point would, I think, be the re-establishment of close relations between the Porte and England, which would increase the Sultan's confidence and would lay him under an *obligation* to seek England's help under given circumstances, which he has been merely *entitled* to do hitherto. Do you think this aim an impossible one? The idea would have to be first mooted in Constantinople and the Sultan clearly shown that it was in his interests to be sure of England's possible intentions. If he has a talk with White and tells him he will undertake, given certain conditions, to seek help from England under the terms of a treaty, provided there was no doubt that England would also feel bound to give a treaty guarantee, I think it possible that Salisbury would be prevailed on to provide a written statement to that effect. What reason could he indeed adduce for not responding in the same spirit to such an overture from the Sultan? Perhaps you will think the matter over. If it is not done now it will become necessary later on when the Russians are on the move, and then it may be too late.

If the great crisis in Europe comes upon us overnight and finds us alone but for Austria, without Italy and with a Gladstone Ministry in England, perhaps even with a Republic in Lisbon and Madrid, we may be obliged to turn to Bismarck's formula and make our peace with Russia *à tout prix*, i.e. by sacrificing Austria. Thus all the fruits of our policy hitherto would be forfeit and we should moreover be obliged humbly to acknowledge that His Highness [Bismarck] was in fact the great master who alone is capable of guiding our destinies.

Good-bye for today my dear friend, and once more very many thanks for your letters.

With warm regards,
Ever yours,
P.H.

342. Heinrich VII Reuss to Holstein

Vienna, 2 May 1891

My dear Baron,

Since the dispatch concerning Italy reached me yesterday evening the affair has been satisfactorily settled.[1] I cannot see Kálnoky before the evening but I am certain he will give his consent.

You were dissatisfied with my reporting of this affair. The situation was this: You wrote and told us that Caprivi *must* be able to reply to possible enquiries by Bismarck that we had *not committed ourselves further* in the Middle East than in his day.

But Articles VI and IX (in No. 1) envisaged 'Further Commitments

[1] The renewal of the Triple Alliance. (Dispatch no. 278 of 30 April 1891. *Grosse Politik*, vol. VII, nos. 1421–2, pp. 95–7.)

by Germany'.[1] I thought therefore that I was carrying out your intentions when I in my turn emphasised my misgivings, which you shared, and I thought this would make the Chancellor more wary of these brazen Italian attempts.[2]

Kálnoky himself had already stated his willingness to accept VI and IX (from No. 1) though criticising them in the same way we did. So no objections were raised in this quarter to the version we desired.

I have observed with pleasure how very skilfully you have steered round the reefs. It is a *very* good thing that it is settled. [...].

With every good wish,
Yours very truly,
H. VII Reuss.

343. Paul von Hatzfeldt to Holstein

London, 6 May [1891]

My dear friend,

[...] Incidentally, the Portuguese are hagglers, always coming along with more trivialities and so making things very difficult for me.[3] And they look on me and treat me as *their* representative receiving instructions from them. If this goes on I shall tell them where they stand. My general plan of campaign, as you must long have realised, is this: 1. to settle all outstanding problems except Manica.[4] When that is achieved, both sides will think twice before ruining the whole thing simply for the sake of Manica. 2. in this way to confront both parties ultimately with the pleasant fact that I, as an unbiased mediator, declare that I shall decide against whichever side wrecks the affair because of trivialities, that I shall communicate this officially to Berlin and shall cease all further mediation.

For the moment will you just make sure that Soveral[5] is empowered to sign the document as soon as I can report agreement here. [...]

Farewell, I am dog-tired.

Yours sincerely,
P.H.

White has not yet breathed a word!

344. Anton von Monts to Holstein

Zillerthal, Riesengebirge, 23 July 1891

My dear Baron,

I hope Your Excellency will graciously permit me to submit to you

---

[1] The extension of Italian demands are explained in a dispatch from Marschall to Reuss of 25 April 1891. (*Grosse Politik*, vol. VII, no. 1416, pp. 88–9.)

[2] Reuss to Caprivi, 27 April 1891. (*Grosse Politik*, vol. VII, no. 1417, pp. 90–1.)

[3] Germany had taken over mediation in the Anglo-Portuguese negotiations. The Anglo-Portuguese treaty was signed on 11 June 1891.

[4] The question involved freedom of navigation on the Pungwe River, which was the direct waterway through Portuguese territory to Manica and Eastern Mashonaland.

[5] Luis Marie Pinto de Soveral. Portuguese Secretary, then Minister in London, 1897–1910.

personally and confidentially a problem which does not in fact come within my province.

As you know, the commander of our field artillery gunnery school has just been sent to Austria to find out about their artillery potential. I had the opportunity of becoming acquainted with Lieutenant-Colonel von Reichenau before he left for the firing range. One sensed immediately during detailed discussions of Austrian military matters and the role of the artillery in modern war that this highly intelligent officer had come with extremely low expectations. I was interested to hear more details of the result of his observations, and Herr von Reichenau also thought a further discussion desirable; and so a second meeting was arranged shortly before I went on leave.

Herr von Reichenau began our conversation with the rather gloomy assurance that his fears had been far surpassed. The Austrian artillery had made no essential progress since Königgrätz and lagged some twenty years or so behind our own or the French artillery. The Lieutenant-Colonel explained this in a way that even the layman could follow, with a wealth of detail. Though he had never observed it personally, according to the information he had received the Russian artillery, in addition to its numerical superiority resulting from a partial wartime footing, must be at least the equal of the Austrian artillery in marksmanship. But, given the same proficiency, the great numerical superiority of the Russian artillery would turn the scales.

Although I hold a far from optimistic view of Austria and her army and have on the contrary always been at pains to describe truthfully the many serious shortcomings of our one dependable ally, I was positively alarmed by Reichenau's statements and assertions. In my humble opinion the Russian infantry's long-established excellence in passive resistance compared with the very moderate reliability of the Austrian infantry (a result of its dual nationality), calls for outstanding performance precisely from the Austrian artillery. And the victory of the army fighting in Poland is a matter of life and death to the Habsburg Monarchy in view of the hostile Balkan States which are simply waiting to pounce and the inevitable revolts in certain Hungarian provinces in the event of defeat. The consequences for ourselves and for the greater part of our army deployed along the Rhine are obvious.

Putting these ideas into words I asked Reichenau whether he thought there was any possible remedy. The Lieutenant-Colonel, after stating that it was hardly possible that the Imperial Austrian artillery alone should have lagged behind in its development, replied that he had only the slenderest hope. The renaissance of an army or of one of its branches could only come from within. The officer class of the Austrian artillery, as he had noticed when he met the younger men, contained some outstanding elements, but the highest positions were held exclusively by second-rate figures. Even so, once a disease is recognised it is always possible to treat it. The Austrian artillery could undoubtedly learn a great deal from us, but the devising of a method whereby our experience could be made available to the Austrians was a matter for the highest military direction and for the Chancellor. In view of the importance of this affair he would try to enlist the personal interest of the Chief of the General Staff and if possible of His Imperial Majesty. But the overriding need was no doubt to put the influential people at the Foreign Ministry in possession of the facts. And so in his country's interest he was actually requesting me to try to draw attention to this question which so vitally concerns us.

This affair falls really within the Ambassador's province, but he is on leave and there has not been any close contact so far between Ratibor[1] and Reichenau. And so I decided to comply with Herr von Reichenau's request and, since you, my dear Baron, have so often given me proof of your goodwill in the past, I decided to make these gloomy observations of one of our officers the subject of a personal letter to you.

On his return to Berlin Herr von Reichenau will prepare the briefest possible memorandum, intelligible to layman and soldier alike, setting forth, in as military a style as is practicable (to avoid too great a divergence from former military reports) the defects of the Imperial Austrian artillery. Technical appendices will furnish the evidence for his statements. The Lieutenant-Colonel will make no proposals in this memorandum because this lies outside the scope of his assignment. But in his opinion a really intelligent senior military figure invested with full powers and assisted by a junior field artilleryman could contribute enormously towards the regeneration of the Austrian artillery. The transfer of Austrian staff officers to German commands would also do good. But the prime and imperative need is for money.

It would of course be the diplomats' business to win over the people in Vienna and Pest. I believe that the monarchy could at this moment raise ten to twenty millions more for armaments. In Hungary the taxes are even less heavy than in Austria, the projected tax reform here and the currency regulation will also help, and in addition the Vienna Stock Exchange is the only one to remain unaffected by the great financial calamities; finally both halves of the Empire have wiped off their deficit. Thus a quicker rearmament tempo would be perfectly possible and is in view of the world situation imperative. But the artillery has at present no smokeless gunpowder, there are not enough horses in the stables, it will take three years before the infantry is fully equipped for war—and so on.

In conclusion I should like to add that the three officers sent here in the spring also went back not greatly edified by what they had seen of the three branches of the army in Vienna. The Ambassador urged them to express their great satisfaction to their fellow officers. Similarly Herr von Reichenau will only sing hymns of praise in public, but he is afraid that the Russians and the French, who have their representatives amongst the artillery in Vienna, are fully informed of the inadequacy of the Austrians' artillery, the Galician fortifications, their stock of arms and so forth.

[1] Max, Prince of Ratibor and Corvey. First Secretary at the Embassy in Vienna, 1890–4; Minister in Athens, 1902–6; in Belgrade, 1906–8; in Lisbon, 1908–10; Ambassador in Madrid, 1910–18.

While assuring you once more of my respect and my unchanging gratitude and loyalty I beg to remain, my dear Baron,

Your obedient servant,

A. Monts.

345. Alfred von Kiderlen-Wächter to Holstein

Bergen, 3 August 1891

My dear Baron,

Since I must assume I shall not now meet you in Berlin, I would like to make one more brief resume, *for your ear alone*, of my impressions of our trip.[1] They are, unfortunately, not exactly favorable in one respect: since last year H.M.'s autocratic tendencies have markedly increased. This *sic volo sic jubeo* obtains in matters both great and small. And—quite between ourselves—it is not accompanied by any serious scrutiny or weighing of the facts; he just talks himself into an opinion. Anyone in favour of it is then quoted as an authority, anyone who differs from it 'is being fooled'. For example, H.M. has decided that a state of acute distress exists in Russia; anyone who says things are not so bad as H.M. supposes is falling into Vishnegradsky's trap; and the suggestion that it would be better to underestimate the position than to overestimate it and imagine that Russia is ruined for years to come only meets with a pitying smile. At the same time he illogically rejects the idea that countermeasures against Russian war preparations would thereby become less urgent. You can see from various marginal comments on newspaper clippings I have sent that his own opinion always is that in view of the increase in our neighbour's armies we should also ask for greater appropriations. But I do not want to spoil your leave, and will offset these pessimistic statements with the brighter side of the picture; namely the feeling which prevails (at present at any rate) that we cannot manage without Caprivi and that we do not wish to impose fresh military demands immediately but rather in three years' time.

It would perhaps be better to say nothing to the Chancellor of my observations, to avoid causing him unnecessary annoyance. But I should just like to add *for your benefit* an anecdote that throws a sidelight on H.M.'s thought processes. H.M. is growing a beard, a fact that provides one of the more interesting topics of conversation on board: 'This will fix the portrait painters.' 'They'll have to alter the imprint on the ten-mark and twenty-mark pieces.' 'People will collect the coins showing me without a beard.' 'Yes,' and he banged hard on the table, 'with a beard like this you could thump on the table so hard that your Ministers would fall down with fright and lie flat on their faces!!!!!!!!' Comment unnecessary. But I trust the beard will be shaved off again in Berlin (he started growing a full beard two years ago) and then the ideas connected with the beard will tend to disappear too.

I am sorry I cannot report anything more cheerful, but I really did feel like getting it off my chest.

[1] Kiderlen had accompanied the Kaiser on his annual Scandinavian cruise.

See that you don't let such ideas spoil your holiday, for which I send my very best wishes.

Ever your most obedient servant,
Kiderlen.

346. Alfred von Kiderlen-Wächter to Holstein

Kiel, 10 August 1891

My dear Baron,

[...] The Chancellor left at 2:13; he will tell you himself all about his talk with H.M. I feel much easier in my mind since seeing him after this interview. The situation seemed to us really serious because of H.M.'s incessant talking himself into the need for an army bill, which he discussed constantly with his 'restricted retinue' for no other reason than to win authoritative approval.[1] H.M. does not seem very enthusiastic about me either, because I took the liberty of occasionally toning down the everlasting sighs he heaves both in words and in marginal notes. Eulenburg will no doubt give you more details. If not, I will tell you some day in Berlin. (And I'll try to endure doing so!!!) [...]

During this trip three telegrams have come in from people not of royal blood, condoling with the Kaiser on his accident. They were signed, 1. 'Caprivi' 2. 'Bernhard von Bülow' 3. 'Marie von Bülow née Princess Camporeale.' Dear me! There's an example for us to follow!!! If they had a lot of children like Schweinitz, would each one telegraph specially?! [...].

Ever your devoted and obedient servant,
Kiderlen. [...].

347. Hugo von Radolin to Holstein

Jarotschin, 13 August 1891

My dear friend,

Now the celebrations in Posen are over I must send you my report. Everything passed off very pleasantly at Trachenberg and the Kaiserin was as usual extremely cordial and agreeable. I shared the Kaiserin's

---

[1] In the years 1889–90, Verdy, the Minister of War, had unsuccessfully tried to carry out a large-scale reorganisation of the army by means of a complete change in the system of universal military service. In consideration of the hostile attitude of the Reichstag, Caprivi restricted himself to introducing the so-called Little Army Bill as a counter-measure to the military preparations of France and Russia. This was passed by the Reichstag on 28 June 1890. At that time the Radical Party (*Freisinnigen*) had introduced a proposal to cut down compulsory military service from three to two years. This proposal was rejected. On 15 June 1891 the Kaiser surprised the Chancellor with the demand that a large-scale reorganisation of the army be vigorously pushed through the Reichstag. The Kaiser, supported only by an Aide-de-Camp and without consulting any of his responsible officials, had personally prepared a plan for this purpose. He announced his 'holy' resolve never to agree to the two year military service. On 16 June Caprivi, who believed that the Kaiser's plan could only be put through by a *coup d'état* which would not be supported by the other governments of Germany, tendered his resignation. (The Kaiser's proposal and Caprivi's resignation are printed by Heinrich Otto Meisner, 'Der Reichskanzler Caprivi,' *Zeitschrift für die gesamte Staatswissenschaft*, 1955, vol. III, pp. 741–5.) The Kaiser grudgingly gave way, but the struggle over the reorganisation of the army and the two year military service continued.

compartment on the journey from Trachenberg to Posen, and she told me all about the Paris affair[1] and complained very much of Münster's lack of tact; she told me she would have preferred to leave earlier but M. had persuaded her to stay; she would never have visited the Embassy but for M.'s constant urging. She thought it most tactless to hold big receptions in embassies etc. without approaching Carnot,[2] and she thought it foolish to go to Versailles. But M. had been so imperiously insistent that she gave way, though making him accept the responsibility. She asserted that M. had, in the hearing of *foreigners*, referred to Baroness Mohrenh[eim][3] as *'canaille'*, which explained the Russian-inspired article in the *Matin*. She had not complained of M. to his superiors because she likes him, but she confessed to me that she was furious with him and his boundless vanity and tactlessness. And the Kaiserin severely censured the way the journalists had been insulted. If she had stayed at the hotel quietly and incognito, as she had often done before, then she could have visited the artists' studios etc. unmolested. The artists, too, had been offended by M.'s arrogant bearing. [...]

Yours as ever,
Rado [...]

348. Paul von Hatzfeldt to Holstein

London, 16 September 1891

My dear friend,

[...] Today's article in the *Standard* will not displease you.[4] Nor is it without significance even though it may not be directly inspired. In addition to having the courage to state openly where England would stand in certain contingencies (and this, in view of conditions here, is remarkable enough!) it is in my opinion particularly important in that the Sultan can deduce from it that the present British government *would* intervene in certain circumstances provided he himself *acted* accordingly.

The question now is—and I should welcome a fresh directive on this —what should be *our* attitude *here*?[5] My general view is that until England takes the initiative we should keep in the background over this

---

[1] See above, Münster's letters of 5 and 9 March 1891.
[2] Sadi Carnot. President of the French Republic, 1887–94.
[3] Wife of the Russian Ambassador in Paris.
[4] On 16 September 1891 the Powers were informed by the Porte that Russo-Turkish negotiations had led to an agreement allowing free passage through the Dardanelles for the so-called Russian 'Volunteer Fleet'. At the same time a false report was circulated that British troops had landed on Mytilene. As a result of these events the *Standard* published an article stating: 'The Russian government would lull itself into a most dangerous illusion if it imagined that Great Britain would, in any circumstances, suffer Russia to obtain command of the Dardanelles.'
[5] In a dispatch of 19 September Rotenhan wrote to Hatzfeldt: 'Your Excellency has been familiar with our policy for many years and is therefore aware that it has always been regarded as one of our tasks to rid the English of the idea that we and our allies are called upon to defend British interests at the exit of the Black sea. We can confidently leave to British statesmen the decision on the nature of the interests Britain must defend in the Straits. We have no advice to them and will most certainly not force any upon them. But if Britain intervenes herself to protect her interests at that point and desires our friendly support, any British requests in this matter can count on a kindly reception by us.' (*Grosse Politik*, vol. IX, no. 2113, pp. 68–71.)

Dardanelles question and avoid any action that might be regarded as provocative in St Petersburg. And I think such reserve justified by the mere fact that England, so well known for her tendency to let someone else pull her chestnuts out of the fire, will then—as is already obvious from to-day's article in the *Standard*—more readily grasp the necessity for acting independently and coming out into the open.

But this caution, to which in general I subscribe, does not, I think, preclude our working secretly at *both* ends—Constantinople and London—for a political rapprochement.[1] Only a few days ago, immediately after the change of Ministers in Constantinople,[2] I should have judged this inadvisable and impracticable. But since then there have been signs indicating that the Sultan does in fact shrink from throwing himself unreservedly into the arms of the Russians and the French. There is further proof of this in a telegram from Joseph [Radowitz] communicated to me to-day concerning the Sultan's statements to Wh[ite].[3] If, according to this, it were in fact possible to bring about an agreement on Egypt, the possibility ought not, I think, to be neglected. I humbly submit that the question whether England can in the event count on the Sultan and his army when the great crisis arises is also of incalculable importance *for us*, may indeed be the *most important* question of *all*. Austria would at once find herself in a totally different position vis-à-vis action by Russia if Russia had to reckon with the Turkish army at the same time. But the supremely important circumstance for us is that England, where public opinion is notoriously erratic and is making it difficult even for the present government to pursue an energetic policy, will stand by the Triple Alliance at the critical moment far more easily if it can be explained to public opinion that England can count on the Turkish army.

Thus the question so vital *for us*, namely whether the weight of England and her navy will one day tip the scales in our favour, will probably depend to a very great extent on England's ability or failure to reach agreement with Turkey. But the *first* step towards it and the *preliminary condition* for it still remain an agreement over Egypt.

Unless I receive contrary instructions I shall, when I have an opportunity, have a highly confidential talk both with S[alisbury] and Rust[em] along these lines—i.e. in favour of such an agreement. Rust., I should add, is at Eastbourne at the seaside but comes to town occasionally and I shall probably see him during the next few days.

[1] In order to ascertain whether the Sultan's mistrust of Radowitz expressed in June 1891 (see *Memoirs*, pp. 99–100) was a symptom of an anti-German shift in Turkish policy, a new channel for confidential communications to the Sultan was opened up, with Wilhelm II's consent, by-passing Radowitz and using Hatzfeldt and Rustem Pasha, the Turkish Ambassador in London.

[2] The Grand Vizier Kiamil-Pasha was relieved of his duties on 3 September. He was replaced by the Governor of Crete, Djevad-Pasha.

[3] Radowitz telegraphed on 14 September: 'The Sultan has now had a personal and highly confidential talk with Sir W. White about Egypt and has himself laid great emphasis on the idea of a Convention with the primary task of preserving her sovereign rights; he thought all the rest was "details over which agreement could be reached". Sir William replied cautiously but cordially and sent in a report of the conversation.' (*Grosse Politik*, vol. VIII, no. 1803, pp. 176–7.)

The overall situation seems to me very serious, not because of a Russo-French alliance, which can scarcely yet have been concluded.[1]

In my opinion the danger lies in the increased self-assurance of the French. Any repetition of the Schnäbele Case[2] might lead to most serious consequences to-day. But I am convinced nothing could be more dangerous for us than for war to break out on German soil and particularly between ourselves and France. I have, as you know, frankly stated this view to Cap[rivi] and I firmly persist in it. Thus I regard it as our primary task to avoid *all* disputes with France and—should war eventually prove unavoidable—to employ all our strength and skill in ensuring that the bombshell bursts in the Middle East or the Mediterranean. *We* must *on no account* appear, or be represented as, Europe's disturber of the peace!

If I have stated above that to me the danger does not lie in the alliance still to be concluded, and therefore *not* in St Petersburg, I would ask you not to misunderstand me. I have not the slightest doubt—and never have had—that Russia will join forces with France one day, unless we do what Prince Bismarck would have done and come to terms with her at Austria's expense. On the contrary, my anxieties on this score have been further deepened by much that I have since heard. A Russian lady who has been a friend of mine for many years, and whom I met recently in Wiesbaden, told me a great deal which impressed me the more in that she is a really intelligent woman, maintains one of the best-known salons in St Petersburg and is by no means enamoured of the French or of an anti-German policy. Amongst other things she told me the following: 'I was present at the time of the coronation and I saw the reception of the Tsar in Caucasia. I had thought I would never see anything comparable in the way of popular enthusiasm. Well, I was wrong and I can assure you that this was far surpassed by the enthusiasm of the Russian public during the visit of the French fleet.[3] I am absolutely convinced that if the Tsar had tried to oppose the public demonstrations, they would have taken place anyway, in spite of and if necessary even against him.'[4] When I said that if her remarks were well-founded they might provoke the fear that the Tsar, despite his well-known peaceful intentions, might one day be pushed still further by this same public opinion, my friend replied that such an event was unfortunately by no means impossible. [...]

I should also like to mention that I met Morier recently at Ems while he was there for a couple of days to call for his family. It was clear from what he said that he read no significance whatever into the Kronstadt incident and thought the Tsar's consistently peaceful intentions when in Russia were the only reliable guide. There is no doubt that he has sent home a dispatch stating as much, but S., who knows him, will hardly

---

[1] The first step towards a Franco-Russian alliance was taken in August 1891 in the form of an agreement to consult in case of a threat to peace, or if one of the parties were menaced by aggression.   [2] See p. 226, note 2.

[3] The visit of a French squadron under Admiral Gervais to Kronstadt, July 23–August 8 1891.

[4] The entire quotation is in French in the original.

have been much impressed by it. It would be more dangerous if he told the Russians that the English think everything is perfect and will certainly take no action. When I can I will talk to S. about him, but on the purely personal level. Thanks to H[erbert] B[ismarck]'s former activities, S. cannot now get rid of him. [...]¹

Yours sincerely [...]

349. Philipp zu Eulenburg to Holstein

Jagdhaus Rominten, 3 October 1891

Very many thanks, my dear friend, for your interesting photographs which I am returning herewith, and thank you for your letters. For an amateur the photographs are most remarkable.

With my head still full of all my Liebenberg affairs I am not in a fit state to enjoy my stay here in this most attractive spot, which H.M.'s kindness makes still pleasanter. I thought H.M. would return by 3 October at the latest, but the good weather and a return of good hunting only yesterday have made our return journey uncertain, thus causing me great embarrassment. Yesterday we found an enormous eighteen-tined stag which H.M. had wounded a few days ago. To-day we bagged a huge twelve-tined stag. The size of the game here is fantastic.

Politics have been hardly discussed. I have had to sing and tell stories. The Chancellor's Osnabrück speech² appears to have annoyed him somewhat. H.M. said to me: 'Now, what is this speech aiming at? First, the Chancellor could have mentioned it to me beforehand, secondly in such grave circumstances he exposes himself to the danger that next time he will be driven *ad absurdum* by public opinion, and thirdly we *need* a mood of unrest in Germany so as to push through the unavoidably necessary military increases. Such a mood suits me perfectly, for if the German lights his pipe and puts on his dressing gown he simply cannot be governed.' I replied that a mood of permanent unrest in Germany would benefit the opposition and Prince Bismarck *alone*, and in addition our credit would sustain losses we could ill afford in view of the next war. I said Miquel was already upsetting the financial situation by his frankly outspoken pessimism. If this pessimism were erected into a *system*, the consequences would be incalculable. H.M. said: 'The key to the whole situation is the urgent necessity for strengthening the army. That is the goal which *must* be reached. I have sought the opinions of the King of Saxony, the Regent of Bavaria, etc., and have received, particularly from the former, wholehearted agreement. The Prince Regent also agreed with me—but he is like an old peasant who finds everything too dear. The situation in Russia is incalculable. No one

¹ In December 1888 the *Kölnische Zeitung* published an article attacking Sir Robert Morier and asserting that in 1870 Morier, as Chargé d'Affaires in Darmstadt, had betrayed details of German troop movements to the French General Bazaine. In a letter to Herbert von Bismarck Morier protested against this statement and, dissatisfied with Herbert von Bismarck's reply, turned over the correspondence to the Press. In the resultant Anglo-German Press war, the British Press unanimously supported Sir Robert Morier's position.

² Caprivi's speech of 27 September in the Friedenssaal (where the treaty ending the 30 Years' War was negotiated) in which he expressed the opinion that the peace of Europe was not in danger for no government desired war.

can tell the outcome of this famine. According to a secret report the Warsaw hotels are already being used as winter quarters for the troops! That is not merely military activity, it is mobilisation!' These utterances will give you a clue to his political mood—and how his energies are directed towards expanding the army.[1]

4 October

I was too much in demand yesterday to be able to finish my letter. I have just read Hatzfeldt's letter aloud to H.M.,[2] and we appended more far-reaching observations to some of his exposés. H.M. found himself in complete agreement with H.'s views, and *wishes you to be told this*. H.M. fully understood the idea that conflict must not break out between ourselves and our neighbours. Deines' dispatch[3] came in today from Vienna, reporting the refusal of the military estimates, with an accompanying dispatch from Reuss.[4] H.M. was extremely angry with the Austro-Hungarian attitude. Praised Deines' communication and blamed Reuss' attempt to gloss things over. H.M. said something like this: 'Austria's inaction throws everything on to *our shoulders*. They do not stand by us, they simply leave us in the lurch in military matters! *We* are now more than ever obliged to go ahead—and as his contribution the Chancellor makes a peace speech in Osnabrück.'

H.M. was very pleased with the way the Russian loan was dealt with. Our conversation touched on this several times and each time H.M. was delighted with Marschall's handling of the situation.[5]

However pessimistic H.M. may be on foreign policy, his views on home affairs are growing more and more optimistic. The rise of Socialism does not disturb him in the least—indeed, he disputes the possibility of its spreading in the army and also regards the outbreak of a major revolutionary movement as impossible. This would give Herrfurth[6] and Berlepsch[7] something to think about! [...]

Every good wish

P.E. [...]

[1] The Kaiser's desire to increase the size of the army and his opposition to the two-year military service was supported by almost all his generals and by the Bismarck Press. On 3 August 1893 Caprivi finally succeeded in securing the passage of an Army Bill providing for a large increase in the size of the army, but as a concession to the opponents of army reorganisation in the Reichstag he at the same time reduced the period of compulsory military service from three to two years. Holstein had recommended this compromise—the adoption of the two-year service plan—in a letter to Eulenburg of 5 September 1892. (From the Eulenburg Papers.)

[2] Hatzfeldt's letter to Holstein of 16 September. See above.

[3] Deines had reported on 28 September that the increased demands of the Austro-Hungarian Minister for War had met with a refusal from the Austro-Hungarian Finance Ministry. (From the Foreign Ministry files.)

[4] In a dispatch of 29 September Reuss explained that the refusal of the increases was attributable to the clumsiness of the Minister for War and insufficient contact with the Finance Minister. (From the Foreign Ministry files.)

[5] On 28 September Marschall had telegraphed the Kaiser to say that in reply to an enquiry by the banker Mendelssohn concerning taking up the new Russian loan, he had stated that the German government would not adopt any attitude to the question officially. The semi-official German Press campaign against the Russian loan, however, had persuaded Mendelssohn to inform the Russian Finance Minister that he did not wish to take up the loan. (From the Foreign Ministry files.)

[6] Ernst Ludwig Herrfurth. Prussian Minister of the Interior, 1888–92.

[7] Hans Hermann, Baron von Berlepsch. Prussian Minister for Trade and Industry, 1890–6.

350. Paul von Hatzfeldt to Holstein

London, 4 November 1891

My dear friend,

[...] When you consider the quite extraordinary conditions I am up against here you will perhaps not think my impression exaggerated that over the last few days great headway has been made in the problems confronting us—more even than I had hoped.

This applies particularly to Tuat[1] and the setting up of closer relations between Rudini and Salisbury.[2] As regards the first of these two points, Salisbury's remark to Tornielli[3] implies more than I had hoped for, and, provided Tornielli has accurately reproduced it in Rome, it may serve as a sufficient basis for concerted action in Morocco and possibly even in Paris. I am sure you passed on at once to Solms the text I told you of; he will thus be in a position to exercise appropriate influence and at the same time to discover whether Tornielli's reporting was accurate. As a further precaution in this matter I have just written to Salisbury advising him to telegraph to Dufferin the text he communicated to me so as to avoid misunderstandings.

And so this affair has probably reached the stage we both desired, provided Rudini plays his part in Madrid, where powerful support seems very necessary. Meanwhile rest assured, and please assure Launay too, that the situation here is exactly as you had supposed, i.e. Salisbury attaches the greatest importance to there being no perceptible *initiative* on his part, but he is prepared for his participation to be subsequently disclosed within diplomatic limits laid down by himself. All we need for the moment is to *hold him to that*. Should it come to a direct discussion of the question between Paris on the one hand and Italy and England on the other, that would not lead to war, but relations between France and England would certainly not improve and an agreement between Italy and England on Mediterranean questions would thereby find further confirmation and justification in the eyes of the world.

I can therefore only advise you in the strongest terms to recommend to Rudini a most ready acceptance of Lord Salisbury's recent utterance.

I should like to add a point I forgot to include in my dispatch,[4]

---

[1] On 20 October the Italian government asked what attitude Germany would adopt if France carried out its threat against Morocco to occupy Tuat. The German reply, drafted by Holstein, pointed out that this was a good opportunity for Italy to show England that she was not willing to do England's work without England's help. (*Grosse Politik*, vol. VIII, no. 1924, pp. 301–3.)

[2] Solms had reported from Rome that Rudini had told him how worried he felt about Salisbury's reserve towards the Italian Cabinet, and had asked Solms to discover from Hatzfeldt whether the fault lay with the person of the Italian Ambassador in London, Tornielli. In a telegram of 4 November Hatzfeldt reported that he had brought the matter up with Salisbury. He said Salisbury's reserve was based on fear of Italian indiscretions and imprudent disclosures in Blue Books, but he had no objection to Tornielli. Hatzfeldt's proposal to keep in touch with Rudini by means of personal letters met with Salisbury's approval. (From the Foreign Ministry files.)

[3] On 3 November Salisbury made the following statement to Tornielli: 'In the event of Spain's wishing to support Morocco's rights over Tuat, the British government, which shares this view of the Sultan's rights, would support any diplomatic action by the Spanish government.' (*Grosse Politik*, vol. VIII, no. 1933, pp. 309–10.)

[4] Of the same day. The main points of Hatzfeldt's conversation with Salisbury are given in the letter. (From the Foreign Ministry files.)

namely that Salisbury in conversation with me has repeatedly and emphatically stated that the French assertion that England, in a colonial agreement with France,[1] recognised Tuat as a French possession, is unfounded.

On the question of a closer exchange of ideas between Salisbury and Rudini, the outcome of my strenuous efforts is also better than I had hoped. Salisbury, who has so far refused to commit himself to anything out of sheer anxiety, gave way yesterday, and I feel sure he will follow my advice provided I can find him a way that will protect him from indiscretions and disclosures in Parliament. Launay can and must help here by secretly obtaining for me Rudini's authority to assure Lord Salisbury that he will if need be regard secret information as private property and treat it as such. [...].

Best wishes
P. Hatzfeldt. [...]

351. Paul von Hatzfeldt to Holstein

London, 9 November 1891

My dear friend,

[...] In order to make Salisbury's mood quite clear to you I am seizing the opportunity I expected to have to-day of sending you a belated copy of his personal letter on Tuat[2] about which you already know. You can see in it his caution and timidity, but you will at the same time notice that he insists that *both Tangier and Paris* should be prepared to make a declaration supporting Spain. And so for that reason alone it would be a mistake for the Italian envoy in Madrid and the Spanish envoy here merely to talk of giving *advice* in *Tangier*; the affair would then be shelved indefinitely and its force seriously weakened.

While again emphasising this for reasons you are aware of, I venture to point out that the report reaching Rome via Launay and communicated to me to-day, stating that a point in its favour was the intention here of proposing a *simultaneous* approval both in Paris and Tangier, is not entirely accurate.[3] I have considered very carefully the plan of campaign for Spain, which is the reason for my reproducing it word for word in my telegram. As must be obvious from the telegram in question, this plan comes under the following three heads:

1. The Spanish Ambassador must first express a request for support,
2. After Salisbury has expressed his *willingness* to do so, he should communicate the programme drawn up by me, or a similar one, and,
3. Finally, *when* agreement has been reached, he should suggest that a similar statement should be made to the Sultan. Hence, *successive*, not *simultaneous* action.[4]

[1] On 5 August 1890 a treaty was signed between France and England regulating their respective zones of influence in West Africa.

[2] Of 5 November. See Enclosure.

[3] See *Grosse Politik*, vol. VIII, no. 1935, pp. 311–12.

[4] Hatzfeldt had submitted this plan in a telegram of 7 November. He had proposed that the Spanish Ambassador in London, now that Salisbury had agreed to take action on the Tuat question, should make the following statement: 'The Spanish Ambassador in Paris, in a

I think this necessary to prevent Salisbury, whom after all I know, from shying away before the start.

Whether my friend [...]¹ is the man to carry this out skilfully is another question. It would be a good thing if I could get my oar in first.

We have made greater headway with Salisbury than I hoped. We might therefore hope something will come of it, but I mistrust this calm in Madrid and *even in Rome too*. They are very glib with their promises so long as they can complain of inactivity and caution here, but they appear to hesitate when this obstacle is removed and they have to take action themselves. Does this spring from a secret wish not to spoil relations with France completely? I do not know. I suspect Spain of being reluctant to deprive herself completely of the possibility of a subsequent acquiescence in French *proposals for a friendly partition* of Morocco which will be made sooner or later. Thus I have grave doubts whether Italy, even if she makes a serious effort in Madrid, will bring about honest and appropriate action here! [...].

In any case I hope to leave here soon and to come first of all to Berlin. There is so much I should like to discuss with you—particularly one matter that worries me greatly; I mean Kálnoky and our relations with him, which seem thoroughly unsatisfactory. There exists, I think, a misunderstanding which could, given mutual goodwill, be cleared up and removed.² Why not bring him and Caprivi together to talk things over personally? I can—simply for lack of time—only hint here at what I mean, but even so you will certainly understand me: there is in my view *no* question of our acting *pari passu* with Austria in all Middle East problems that arise, as is assumed in the memorandum communicated to me to-day.³ Even Salisbury realises we cannot, and indeed ought not do so in the interests of peace, and *Kálnoky* would doubtless realise it too if it were put to him clearly. The thing he may *not* understand—and if I am not deceived he is quite right—lies in a totally different sphere. Do you remember the theory propounded so often by Prince Bismarck, namely that Austria may count on us only when she is *attacked*, not when she *attacks*, even though circumstances may *oblige* her to attack in self-

---

conversation held at his own request with the French Minister for Foreign Affairs, will state on behalf of his government that Spain 1. recognises the Sultan's claim to Tuat as justified, 2. must declare herself opposed to any unilateral alteration of the *status quo* in Morocco. As soon as this is done, the English and Italian Ambassadors will in their turn officially inform the Minister that their respective governments associate themselves with the Spanish view on both counts.' (From the Foreign Ministry files.)

¹ Name illegible. Presumably the Spanish Ambassador in London.

² In reality the tension between Germany and Austria-Hungary was far more than a misunderstanding. Vienna was dismayed by the vacillation in the direction of German policy, and Berlin feared that Austria-Hungary might go over to the side of Russia. (See Aehrenthal's report to Kálnoky of 31 January 1892 about his talk with Kiderlen, in Hermann, *Dreibund, Zweibund, England*, pp. 154–6.)

³ On 3 November the Austrian Chargé d'Affaires in Berlin had read Kiderlen a letter from Kálnoky concerning Austria's attitude towards Turkey. Kiderlen's memorandum on the subject was sent to London on 7 November with an accompanying dispatch from Marschall. Kálnoky had tried to make it clear that Austria would proceed only *pari passu* with Germany in Middle Eastern questions. Kálnoky had apparently still not realised, Marschall said in his dispatch, that Germany could take no initiative in Middle East questions, but that this still must come from Austria in conjunction with England. (From the Foreign Ministry files.)

preservation? I need hardly tell *you* the aims of this theory. I have always expected and feared the harm it was bound to do eventually by destroying confidence. And *there*, if I am not greatly deceived, is the root of our present trouble.

I shall discuss this further if my hope is realised of actually talking over all our current problems with you soon.

Goodbye then, with my warmest wishes
P.H.

I hope there will be another letter from you by the next courier.

ENCLOSURE

Salisbury to Paul von Hatzfeldt[1]

Copy

5 November 1891

Private

My dear Count Hatzfeldt,

The memorandum of our conversation which you inclose to me is, with respect to China,[2] as far as I remember, correct: with respect to that concerning my language to Count Tornielli there is one omission of importance. I said that I did not look upon the question of Tuat as in itself closely touching any British interest. I should not therefore volunteer any diplomatic action to Spain: but if that power should express a wish for our concurrence we should at their request be willing to express it both in Tangier and Paris.

In neither case does the subject matter appear to me to be urgent enough or important enough to justify my taking any step which would remove my communications upon it out of the category of *verbal* expressions of opinion.[3]

Believe me
Yours very truly
Salisbury.

352. Paul von Hatzfeldt to Holstein

11 November 1891

My dear friend,

Now we have a nice mess in Madrid![4] Unless we follow the sugges-

[1] In English in the original.

[2] In view of the anti-foreign disturbances in China in the summer of 1891, the diplomatic representatives in Peking had recommended in a protocol of 9 September that the Powers employ stern measures against China. On 4 November Hatzfeldt had sent Salisbury a written account of their conversation of the previous day. Regarding China they had agreed to counter any possible French request for action against China by pointing to the calm which at present prevailed there. In the event of further disturbances all the great Powers were to confer afresh. (From the Foreign Ministry files.)

[3] On 7 November Hatzfeldt sent this personal telegram to Holstein: 'During yesterday's conversation it became clear, as I had expected, that Salisbury's personal letter sprang from a fear that if the wording of his statement [see above p. 390, note 3] (which he and I had agreed on) were simply passed on without explanations, he would be too far committed and might possibly encounter difficulties here.' (From the Foreign Ministry files.)

[4] The Spanish Foreign Minister had informed Stumm that he was unable to make formal proposals to Lord Salisbury and to Paris, for Spain must not abandon her attitude of caution

tion I made to-day by telegram[1] and make at least a final effort here to persuade the Spaniards to make a proposal in the more *modest* form of supporting *advice* to *Morocco*, then we must regard the whole affair as having come to nothing.

Salisbury, with whose entire outlook I am most familiar, will note with satisfaction that he was right about the Spaniards and will gladly resume his *liberté d'action*, i.e. *liberté* to do nothing at present. You will understand that at once when you recall that in the first place he had a holy terror of involving himself in difficulties here, and secondly he does not think British interests in Morocco are really threatened by Tuat. That group of oases deep in the southern desert is in itself immaterial to him since he does not wish to have it. What interests him is the possible partition of Morocco later, and he is not greatly troubled by this future problem because, rightly or wrongly, he is convinced that England will *then* still be in the position to make sure of what seems to her a necessary *share of the booty* (particularly as regards Gibraltar) by means of friendly negotiations with the interested parties, supported if necessary by the presence of the British Navy.

In these circumstances he had, while succumbing to my persistent urging that he should support Spain, no other aims but the following, which he never concealed from me:

1. to keep on good terms with Italy, because I had been drumming it into him for weeks that this was absolutely indispensable;

2. to represent Spain as the party mainly concerned and to oblige her to state her position. If Spain agreed to this, he, Salisbury, could justify in London his support of Spain if the need arose, whereas any initiative of his own would have been roundly condemned. In addition Spain was so far committed that the subsequent temptation for her to acquiesce in French partition proposals was, if not entirely removed, certainly considerably diminished.

3. finally, without provoking a conflict, to give the French a little *avertissement* and thereby to warn them against any further effective action in Morocco.

Now, in my opinion the Spaniards are complete dolts to let slip such an opportunity, which may never recur. The reasons they adduce will not hold water. If Tetuan[2] really meant what he is alleged to have told Cambon some time ago, the Spanish Ambassador in Paris could perfectly well repeat *exactly the same thing*—for there is *no* question of *more*— without thereby prejudicing Spain's precious friendship with France to any *great* extent; provocation of a conflict was ruled out beforehand by Salisbury in agreement with Italy. And so, if Tetuan *now* refuses to say in Paris, where he has the support of the two Great Powers, the *same thing* he is alleged to have told the French *alone* in Madrid, there are

which circumstances had hitherto imposed: 'Spain had already made perfectly clear to France that her attitude towards the Tuat question was unchanged; to repeat this in Paris would appear there as a challenge, and Spain would at once appear as the Power which had prompted the other two Powers to action.' (*Grosse Politik*, vol. VIII, no. 1936, pp. 312–3.)

[1] *Grosse Politik*, vol. VIII, no. 1937, pp. 313–14.

[2] Carlos O'Donnell y Abrey, Duke of Tetuan. Spanish Foreign Minister, 1890–2.

only two conceivable possibilities : either he did not speak so definitely to Cambon as he claims, —*or* circumstances have since arisen which *now* make him feel it undesirable to make exactly the same pronouncement in Paris[1] [...][2]

[1] See *Grosse Politik*, vol. VIII, nos. 1938–43, pp. 314–17.
[2] The end of the letter is missing.

1892

353. Paul von Hatzfeldt to Holstein

London, Wednesday 6 January 1892

My dear friend,

I have just come up to town again for a couple of days, mainly to see how the land lies, because there is nothing in particular to do at the moment until something comes through from the Sultan.[1]

Yesterday Salisbury and I chatted for half an hour at random about all kinds of things, and on the whole I had the impression that his timidity and his desire to hold as far aloof as possible from everything are on the increase in view of the elections.

I began by attacking him about the article on Tuat in the *Standard*, for which he disclaimed all responsibility. But this time I insisted, and pointed out that the *Standard*, though not his organ personally, was nevertheless the organ of the Conservative Party now at the helm. I asked him what must be the effect of such statements in Madrid and Rome, just when agreement has been painfully reached on an approach to the Sultan of Morocco?[2] This went home and he finally said: 'What shall I do; do you want me to issue a *circular* about it?' I replied: 'At the moment I want nothing at all, nor have I any instructions, but I must point out to you that it must arouse suspicion in Rome and Madrid when the *Standard* says that Tuat lies in the French sphere of interest. There is surely also the further question of the effect the announcement will have on the Sultan that you are going to seize Tangier.'[3]

I hope you agree with me that I could not go further. But see if you think you can discuss this with Launay. Rudini could instruct Tornielli to obtain in conversation an assurance that the British government does *not* share the questionable attitude of the *Standard*.

The French Press, so far as I can see, seems infuriated with the *Standard*'s designs on Tangier, and this has its good side. Incidentally, Lord Salisbury did not deny this *arrière-pensée* yesterday, but simply said

[1] In November 1891 the Sultan had requested German mediation in the Anglo-Turkish negotiations concerning Egypt. The Germans expressed their conviction that England's agreement should be obtained. After lengthy discussions about whether the negotiations should take place in London or Constantinople, Radowitz reported on 12 December that the Sultan would now present his negotiation proposals in London. These proposals had not yet reached London by 6 January. (From the Foreign Ministry files.)

[2] On 18 December 1891 the representatives of England, Italy and Spain handed a Note to the government of Morocco proposing that the Sultan should request France to substantiate her claims to Tuat. A Note on this subject was handed to the French Chargé d'Affaires on 11 January 1892 by the Moroccan government. (From the Foreign Ministry files. See *Grosse Politik*, vol. VIII, no. 1943, pp. 316–17.)

[3] Here Hatzfeldt is reproducing the gist of the *Standard*'s leading article of 4 January.

nothing about it. When I jokingly remarked: 'You know, you don't need to tell me anything about it, for I can imagine just what you would do and what you would take,' he just laughed heartily.

I should of course not regard it as a misfortune if France and England fell out over Tangier. But I am not quite clear at the moment whether France might not willingly comply over this if she could at the same time pocket a good slice of Morocco. What is your own impression? One of the French papers—the *Débats* if I am not mistaken—says that the formidable position England would command given Gibraltar *and* the points on the opposite coast, could under *no* circumstances be granted her. If this is the authoritative French view it might be desirable for England to act to-day rather than tomorrow!

I am very glad Solms has calmed down Rudini about Salisbury's letters.[1] His dissatisfaction would be unfounded in so far as his own letter also contained mere generalities and there was thus no reason to require or expect the reply to say more or to deal more fully with specific questions. I leave it to you whether to quote this to Launay as my personal opinion. But for your ears I must add that there is *now absolutely nothing more to be done* here and that we must therefore *bide our time*. During our conversation yesterday I referred to Rudini and Salisbury's letter to him, and let fall the remark that he, Salisbury, seemed not to have touched on the well-known agreement with Italy. He replied: 'Why should I have mentioned that? The agreement isn't worth very much.' I replied with a laugh: 'You are quite right there, but that's not my fault; I suggested to you an alternative wording more than once and my modest drafting abilities are always at your disposal.' He laughed too, but did not pursue the subject further and I am, as I said, convinced that there is nothing to be done at present in that direction.

I still consider the Egyptian question as the most vital issue, and so I sent you a telegram yesterday.[2] I am, if I may say so, convinced that it is *most* important for me to be on the spot when the memorandum does arrive, for me to see the Sultan's envoy *before* his first conversation with Salisbury and if possible to have a talk with the latter beforehand too. We *must* expect one or two unreasonable demands from the Sultan and if the envoy confronts Salisbury with them without any preparation we run the risk that Salisbury, who can be very abrupt and who treats the Sultan abruptly partly out of calculation, will reply with a curt refusal.

---

[1] According to Solms' dispatch of 26 December 1891, Rudini had informed him that in a letter to Lord Salisbury he had emphasised the fact that Italy adhered to the agreements made in February 1887. In his reply, couched in the most friendly terms, Lord Salisbury had not mentioned this point. Solms explained to Rudini that this caution was conditioned by the forthcoming English parliamentary elections. (From the Foreign Ministry files.) At approximately the same time, Rudini expressed himself unfavourably to Baron Bruck, the Austro-Hungarian Ambassador in Rome, about 'Germany's nervous English policy'. The mere appearance of Count Hatzfeldt in the Foreign Office aroused disagreeable feelings. The Italian Minister thought that Germany was not the Power to arouse England from her innate condition of lethargy. (Bruck to Kálnoky, 5 January 1892. Hermann, *Dreibund, Zweibund, England*, pp. 152–3.)

[2] On 5 January Hatzfeldt had requested Holstein by private telegram to inform him at once of the arrival of a Turkish envoy with the Sultan's proposals. (From the London Embassy files.)

I have, it is true, forestalled this a little and he has promised me not to reject the documents on the spot and without consulting me, but one cannot count much on that if it contains really unreasonable proposals, so that it is still of the utmost importance that I should be able to prepare the ground in both quarters, once things reach that stage. If you still want to leave Joseph [Radowitz] out of things I should think Goltz[1] could manage since the Sultan has already expressed his intention of sending his envoy to me.

Thank you very much for Kiderlen's letter to Goltz, with which I naturally agree.[2] Goltz will probably express himself rather less forcibly to the Sultan but there is no harm in that.

If in the end he fails to reach a decision, we shall simply have to treat him harshly the next time he wants anything and make it clear to him that we are dropping him. That would probably do the trick. But we must at the same time realise that the people who depend on him, like Rustem, the Turk in Berlin,[3] and perhaps even Goltz, will not deliver any really unpleasant message to him because he regards *them* as responsible. The only man left to do *that* is Joseph, and we should have to school him exactly in what he must say. [...]

My best wishes for the New Year,
Ever yours
P.H. [...]

354. Paul von Hatzfeldt to Holstein

Tuesday, 19 January 1892

My dear friend,

[...] I have just come up to town to welcome Prince Leopold[4] and possibly to see Salisb., who is not due here until Friday.

Before that I saw Rustem, who knows nothing but does *not* think Shakir[5] likely[6]; he believes it far more probable that the Sultan will send his private secretary (name escapes me!). In that case it would be a

---

[1] Kolmar, Baron von der Goltz. Prussian officer serving with the Turkish army, 1882–95; from 1896 with the Prussian army as Chief of the Corps of Engineers and Pioneers and General Inspector of fortifications; Commanding General of the 1st Army Corp, 1898–1902; from 1907 General Inspector of the 6th, later of the 2nd Army Inspectorate.

[2] General von der Goltz, in several letters to Kiderlen and Holstein towards the end of December, had informed them of the Sultan's wish to conduct the negotiations on Egypt in Constantinople. The Sultan requested that Radowitz be instructed to undertake a role of intermediary similar to Hatzfeldt's in London. Kiderlen, in a letter of 1 January 1892, requested Goltz to inform the Sultan that Germany would act in the capacity of mediator only if negotiations were entered into in London immediately. Otherwise Germany would withdraw completely, for if Germany's part became known, both her position and Salisbury's would be compromised. Goltz informed Holstein in a letter of 11 January that he had communicated this to the Sultan and that the Sultan had stated that he would send an emissary to London on 14 or 18 January who would make contact with Rustem Pasha and Hatzfeldt. (From the Foreign Ministry files.)

[3] Tewfik Pasha. Turkish Ambassador in Berlin, 1886–95; Foreign Minister, 1895–1909.

[4] Prince Leopold von Hohenzollern had come to the funeral of Albert Victor, Duke of Clarence, eldest son of the Prince of Wales, who had died on 14 January.

[5] Shakir Pasha. Turkish Marshal; Adjutant-General to Sultan Abdul Hamid II.

[6] Holstein had telegraphed to Hatzfeldt on 14 January that Shakir Pasha would probably be entrusted with the mission to London. (From the London Embassy files.)

good thing for me to see him. If Shakir does come I am still in some doubt what to do and Rustem shares my doubts. He himself will probably plead illness so as to render Shakir fully responsible for the *échec*, and also because he would feel insulted if someone were sent inferior to him in rank. In my case things are different. It might be a good thing for me to excuse myself on the grounds of indisposition and not to appear. But I should thus leave him a clear field and should make it easier for him to carry out his intended intrigue. There is another way which I would ask you to reflect on: without showing the least *empressement* I should allow the envoy to seek me out and I should say curtly and decisively:

1. As a *private individual* and out of *personal* friendship for the Sultan, I gave him some advice at his request;[1]
2. whether he follows it is quite immaterial to my government, since it has no interest whatever in Egypt;
3. I promised my personal help here *on the assumption* that the Sultan recognises the correctness of my view and *acts accordingly*. If not, I do nothing. I shall not be a party to bringing about an undoubted *échec* in the negotiations. Finally
4. If negotiations were being carried on here on a different footing—a thing I can easily check—I should discharge my personal responsibility to the Sultan by writing him a personal and private letter by a reliable route recounting progress here, thus certainly forestalling any inaccurate accounts.

However pro-French or pro-Russian the fellow may be, he is above all afraid of his master and will take good care not to run any risk himself. This is Rustem's opinion too. Provided the envoy could lie to the Sultan without danger, he would probably try. But he would realise that *my* letters cannot be suppressed, that I can keep a very accurate check on him here and that, if he lied, the Sultan would hear of it from me.

I am, as I said, still in doubt, but I beg you to think the matter over. I think the best course at present is to wait and see what happens and who is sent and then to act accordingly. [...].

Best wishes,
P.H.

355. Leo von Caprivi to Holstein

Berlin, 27 January 1892

My dear sir,

I have the honour, in obedience to His Majesty's command, to present to you with this letter The Cross of the Commander of the Order of the Royal Household of Hohenzollern, which His Majesty has conferred on

---

[1] In a memorandum of 13 October 1891, Hatzfeldt advised the Sultan to conclude a treaty with England as soon as possible and at all events before the next elections. By ceasing to insist that a term be fixed for the evacuation of Egypt, in exchange for an English guarantee of his sovereignty, the Sultan might secure a closer political relationship with England. (*Grosse Politik*, vol. VIII, p. 179, note **.)

you. I may add that this mark of favour is made on his Majesty's own initiative and that His Majesty chose to-day[1] so as to render still more precious this distinction which will by His Majesty's wish henceforth rank above the other Orders. With the expression of my sincere congratulations and unfailing respect,

I remain

Your obedient servant,

Caprivi

356. Philipp zu Eulenburg to Holstein

Munich, 28 January 1892

My dear Holstein,

The note I sent yesterday[2] was almost a reply to the questions you ask me to-day.

Since I, like you, am Conservative at heart, but since, again like you, I peep over the top of the Conservative battlements and look round to spy out what should and should not be done, my attitude towards the present skirmish[3] is very simple: I still think that co-operation between the Centre and the Conservatives is a dangerous experiment—not only in Prussia but particularly throughout the Reich.[4] Any forcing back of our present state into a government by the Centre in alliance with the ultra-Conservatives is a measure which will lead to a crisis in which the government will come off *worst*. The Prussian government just as much as the Imperial government. The struggle of the united Liberals will be the more violent in that their banner will read *suprema lex salus republicae* as against *suprema lex regis voluntas*.[5] His Majesty's vigorous emphasis on the personality of the monarch will stamp the imprint of absolutism on the brow of any Conservative-Centre government, and no one will believe the constitutional safeguards—in the end not even the moderate parties, which in my view form the *natural* basis nowadays for monarchical government. All attempts at a too powerful forcing back of the body politic have in every state throughout the centuries resulted in the powerful recoil of the compressed spring. Only a gentle, steady pressure, now forcing now yielding, has maintained strong governments. Having travelled about the Reich a good deal I am a tolerably good judge of the danger to Germany, rocked to her foundation since

---

[1] The Kaiser's birthday. (See Rogge, *Holstein und Hohenlohe*, pp. 377–8.)

[2] Not found.

[3] On 27 January 1892 Holstein had written to Eulenburg about the difficult situation in Parliament that had arisen because of the Prussian School Bill introduced by Count Zedlitz, the Prussian Minister for Ecclesiastical Affairs. Holstein's letters to Eulenburg during this period are filled with concern about this problem. (From the Eulenburg Papers.) The 'skirmish' mentioned by Eulenburg above developed into one of the most serious crises of the Caprivi era.

[4] The School Bill, by giving great power to the churches in the Prussian educational system, was intended to secure the support of the Conservative and Centre Parties for the government.

[5] In a letter to Eulenburg of 16 November 1891 Holstein had characterised the Kaiser's inscription in the Golden Book of the City of Munich: '*Regis voluntas suprema lex*' as 'ludicrous' and a 'national misfortune'; in response to this, the slogan was being heard: '*Salus publica suprema lex.*' (From the Eulenburg Papers.)

the death of the old Kaiser. I told you yesterday that a Liberal alliance at this moment would spell danger to the government. In Bavaria and Württemberg the concept of the Reich is enshrined only in Liberal hearts. Very slowly, and finally in greater numbers after the commercial treaties, those elements who felt dissatisfied after Bismarck's retirement have in part begun to support the present government. The Liberal alliance in the re-emerging Kulturfrage would lose the Imperial government the whole of Württemberg, the greater part of Bavaria and probably the greater part of the other Federal States too, and, with drums beating, they would all desert to Friedrichsruh—to their former love. The Imperial government would retain the Ultramontane Federal States—i.e. those ultramontanes who support the Kaiser, not the particularists. Thus the gain bears no relation to the loss. Something similar would take place in Prussia, as you know better than I do.

These parliamentary power relationships certainly explain the government's deliberation as to whether perhaps most may be achieved by relying on a majority. And of course the certainty of a parliamentary majority is of the utmost importance in connection with our vital military requirements and other matters. But reliance on a majority, a reliance which entails such great and grave risks, only appears justified if the government is *firmly* resolved, *directly* they have attained their ends, to start a campaign and to undertake a reform of the electoral system, etc. etc. If there is *no* such intention, then of elementary necessity the spring recoils, bringing in its train constitutional discussions at least, which imply other embarrassments for the monarch apart from parliamentary government.

Those are more or less my ideas, which I could develop much further if my wearisome, tedious convalescence did not imperiously bid me stop. You can see that I substantiate my anxiety with arguments. I cannot but express the wish that, by a reconciliation of the moderate parties—if that is indeed possible—we may *avoid* complications bringing in their train untold difficulties for the government.

The introduction of the primary school law was not a mistake, provided the government was *consciously* making a move towards the Centre so as to provoke these crises I hinted at.

Let me have news of you soon; in the sick-room one is consumed with impatience.

Your faithful
P.E.

357. Philipp zu Eulenburg to Holstein

Munich, 29 January 1892

My dear friend,

I can still vividly recall the time when we saw in Prince Bismarck's leaning towards the Centre, in those secret matters transacted not through representatives abroad but through Berchem, a great danger to the Reich which was removed by his retirement!—and now!?

Judging by the Chancellor's attitude I see no possible way out, for if he is *bent* on giving the Centre a trial he will not be prevailed on to amend the School Bill—which in any case presents the greatest difficulties. The only possibility I can see is for His Majesty to influence members of the *Chamber of Deputies*—there is little chance of success with the Upper House.

I think the affair is hopeless. The Bill was a political error.

The Liberals' struggle will become unpleasant. The fear that measures taken by the Centre and the Conservatives may drive the Social Democrats to acts of violence and thus result in a changed electoral procedure drives them frantic. There are all kinds of surprises in store for Caprivi! An immediate swing away from the Centre at the first demand they make would be the only possibility of success later on. But the government would emerge from the incident weakened. Throughout the Reich confidence would be shaken. Miquel's resignation now would *also* mean shattered confidence throughout the Reich. The National Liberal hero in the Prussian Ministry was a kind of guarantee to the South German Liberals.

If Miquel resigned at this juncture he would enjoy *enormous prestige* throughout the Reich. Relations between him and Friedrichsruh would then become interesting; if Prince Bismarck wished to turn to his own advantage the powerful stream of popular feelings for Miquel, he would be obliged to reckon with M. If he does not, but abides by the viewpoint of the pamphlet *Bismarck und der Hof*,[1] then we must expect a breach in the united Liberal Party.

30 January 1892

Your telegram agreeing with my views reached me yesterday evening.[2] Caprivi's speech which I read this morning excludes any activity on my part. But I am gratified that as a result of my last letter[3] His Majesty talked things over with Zedlitz.[4] His wishes regarding an agreement between the parties must be *allowed to leak out only so far* that they do Caprivi *no harm*. A certain awareness of the royal wishes will turn public animosity away from his *person*—and will on the other hand throw into relief the fact that he *has subordinated voluntatem regis voluntati Cancellarii*.

There is enormous interest here in events in Berlin. I shall talk to Crailsheim about it one day soon. His Majesty's ideal is, as you know, the formation of two major parties in the *Landtag* and the *Reichstag*. I imagine therefore that these events will not be greeted unsympathetic-

[1] Early in 1892 a pamphlet called *Bismarck und der Hof*, written by a certain Max Bewer, had been published in Dresden. In German Government circles the authorship of the pamphlet was ascribed to Bismarck himself. The Kaiser labelled it as 'scandalous'.

[2] Holstein telegraphed on 29 January. 'I advise you do nothing now, for it might easily harm Caprivi. Writing tomorrow.'

[3] Letter of 28 January. (Printed in Haller, *Eulenburg*, p. 68.)

[4] Robert, Count von Zedlitz und Trützschler. Head of the administration in Posen and President of the newly founded Colonial Commission, 1886–91; Prussian Minister for Ecclesiastical Affairs, March 1891–March 1892. He fell as a result of his failure to secure the passage of his Primary School Bill. (See above, p. 400, note 4.) Head of the administration of Hessen-Nassau, 1898–1903; of Silesia, 1903–9.

ally by him—even though in Germany more than in any other country such desires are quite illusory!

We shall have some appalling experiences in the elections. Ah well, who knows what it may be good for! Prussia's star has not yet faded and each man must stand firmly in the breach! This post in South Germany is not easy. I hope you have 'primed' Saurma[1] well.

Your faithful
P.E.

358. Holstein to Kaiser Wilhelm II[2]
Copy

Berlin, 30 January 1892

Most illustrious and all-powerful Kaiser:
Most gracious Kaiser, Lord and King:

Your Imperial Majesty has been graciously pleased to remember me. For the first time in thirty-four years' service I have received a Prussian decoration independently of precedence or chronological sequence. It is precisely now when, partly for reasons of health, I am living as a recluse, that this high distinction, as also Your Majesty's gracious recognition in the *Tiergarten* recently, came as a surprise indeed. Everything I can do belongs in any case to Your Majesty by right. I owe Your Majesty a debt of gratitude for all Your Majesty's particular favours towards me.

It is with deepest respect that I remain
Your Imperial and Royal Majesty's most humble and truly devoted

Holstein.

359. Philipp zu Eulenburg to Holstein

Munich, 4 February 1892

My dear friend,

[...] I must congratulate you on the Star of the Hohenzollern Commanders as being a *quite exceptional* mark of His Majesty's confidence. If you but knew *what value* he attaches to his Order of the Household! It almost borders on eccentricity—and how the class of the decoration enhances the value! I would say that no more profound, sincere and genuine thanks could be bestowed on you—knowing His Majesty as I do. And because of this quality in this demonstration of favour, I rejoice in my Kaiser, who, impervious to the envious strivings of inferior natures, says: I give according to *merit*, to whom I have found to be loyal. [...].

With warmest wishes
Your faithful
P.E.

360. Paul von Hatzfeldt to Holstein

Hastings, 9 February 1892, evening

My dear friend,

[...] I have instructed Metternich[3] to send a detailed dispatch by

[1] Saurma was about to become Prussian Minister in Stuttgart. [2] From the Radolin Papers.
[3] Paul, Count von Wolff-Metternich zur Bracht. First Secretary at the London Embassy, 1890–5; Consul-General in Cairo, 1895–7; Prussian Minister in Hamburg, 1897–1900;

tomorrow's courier about the highly undesirable incidents at Akaba and Aden,[1] and I have provided him with the necessary material. If things are really as they were reported to Rustem from Constant[inople], then the Sultan's annoyance is indeed understandable. They have played into the hands of those elements desirous of preventing any agreement on Eg[ypt]. For the moment we can only wait and see what action will be taken here. S[alisbury] knew nothing so far about the Akaba incident and said he wished to recall Rustem at once for information. Let us hope this will be of a nature that will enable him to reassure the S[ultan], also concerning the Aden incident, which in itself is less important. In this case one may still hope that the S. may think better of it and may finally send Tewfik.[2] If he hesitates much longer it may easily happen that my colleague here will simply not risk embarking on anything more before the elections. At any rate I am expecting you to agree with my having refrained also in this case from sending any further message to the S. via Rustem's good offices.

I must also mention (leaving it to you what use you make of it) that Deym,[3] who is shortly going on leave to Vienna, came to see me yesterday after expressly requesting an interview. He told me the following: The last time he was at home, K[álnoky] instructed him to obtain a more precise wording of a certain document in the files[4] but left to him the choice of timing and any other details. But he, D., had refrained from making any move because he was quite convinced that before the elections it would be useless and unlikely to succeed. He attached the greatest importance to knowing whether I shared this view, for his Chief was certain no one knew the situation here better than I do. I replied that I must admit that he, D., was right. At this moment and before the elections there was undoubtedly nothing to be done about it, a fact I nevertheless deeply deplored because the document in question was unfortunately cast in rather vague terms. D. then replied that it did at least contain definite assurances on one or two points; namely in the event of a threat to Constantinople, and also in the event of its ruler entering upon hostile alliances. But there was the fact that S. had repeatedly assured him that his probable successor (Ro[sebery]) completely shared his views on these questions and would insist that the assurances in question were fulfilled should the need arise. D. followed

acting Ambassador in London 1900–1; Ambassador in London, 1901–12; repeatedly Foreign Ministry representative in the Kaiser's retinue.

[1] There had been violations of Turkish territory along the Egyptian frontier and near Aden.

[2] Lieutenant-Colonel Tewfik Bey, the Sultan's Aide-de-Camp. The Sultan hesitated between sending Tewfik to London or once again proposing Constantinople as the seat of negotiations. (From the Foreign Ministry files.)

[3] Franz, Count Deym. Austro-Hungarian Ambassador in London, 1888–1903.

[4] The exchange of notes between Italy, England and Austria of December 1887 for preserving the status quo in the Near East. Salisbury had always regretted this connection between England and the Triple Alliance, but had felt it was necessary to prevent the formation of another Three Emperors' League. (See Theodor Bayer, *England und der Neue Kurs, 1890–95* (*Tübingen*, 1955), chapter 3.) In the next two and a half years, when the possibility of a Russian seizure of the Straits had to be reckoned with, Kálnoky tried to bind England more firmly to the Triple Alliance on the question of the Straits and the Balkans, and to persuade England to make a common front against the Franco-Russian alliance in the Mediterranean area.

this with the question whether I believed this or whether, if the elections gave us a change of government, I expected different treatment of those questions. I said that in general I did not doubt Ro's agreement with S. in these matters, but that I did think for many reasons you must be prepared *at least* for vital and not always welcome *nuances* when your successor carried out your policies.

It might be a good idea if Reuss were in a position to check in what way D. reports on these questions in Vienna, in particular on my own statements. [...].

With warmest wishes
Your
P.H.

361. Philipp zu Eulenburg to Holstein

Munich, 14 February 1892

My dear Holstein,

[...] The opinion you expressed to me in your letter of the 10th that it was better in the end to swing towards the Radical Party, [Freisinnigen] which is composed of *Germans*, than to surrender to the Centre, which is *Roman*, is *quite correct* in its judgment of *South German* interests, but I fear this does not fit Prussia's case, and I am afraid such a swing would strengthen tendencies there which would *endanger* the monarchical principle. In view of Prussia's ascendancy it needs careful thought. From the point of view of German politics, the logical step still seems to be reliance on the *moderate parties*. Particularly as South German Radicals (except Frankfurt, part of Baden and part of Württemberg) are closer to National Liberalism than to Democracy. But how can we strengthen these parties and weld them together? Exhortation will not do it. I am afraid the moderate parties gain adherents and achieve unity only through *fear*, i.e. as a result of dangerous outbreaks of Social Democracy, and I question whether the Chancellor's programme may not lead precisely to that. If you can think of any other method I shall be only too glad, for I entirely agree with you that the experiment with the Centre, if it overthrows the Ministry here, may introduce ultramontanes into the *Bundesrat* indefinitely. I make no secret of the fact that the difficulty in joining forces with the moderate parties lies mainly in '*summa lex regis voluntas*'—quite apart from Friedrichsruh. You probably think so too.

I am watching the development of the School Bill with the utmost anxiety for I cannot yet think the Bill is dead. [...].

Your faithful
P.E.

362. Philipp zu Eulenburg to Holstein

Munich, 22 February 1892

My dear friend,

[...] Your last letters put me into an *appalling position*![1] I have not

---

[1] In letters to Eulenburg of 16, 17, and 18 February, Holstein once again discussed the question of the Prussian School Bill. He had heard from Köller, the President of the Prussian

yet written to the Kaiser because I had to talk to various people first so as to obtain an *absolutely* clear picture of the situation likely to arise here if the School Bill were passed by courtesy of the Centre. The results of my investigations are most *depressing* and I am prepared to write, but I should first like to submit the following to your consideration, and I should be grateful for a reply.

The more H.M.'s attention is drawn to the dangerous consequences of the School Bill, the more easily may annoyance with Caprivi gain a hold. But that simply must be avoided. You know H.M. is inclined to criticise Caprivi—and I assume he is already silently reproaching him over this school question. Since Prince B[ismarck]'s intention of exploiting the school agitation for his own purposes in the Upper House represents a national danger, it is my conviction that the School Bill must not get as far as the Upper House. Burying the Bill beneath a committee may be one way out, but this continued unrest is most harmful. I favour a definitive solution. A withdrawal would weaken the government, because most unfortunately Caprivi committed himself too far—quite unnecessarily. Why not remove Herrfurth, replace him by Zedlitz, and then withdraw the Bill under the pretext of a newly appointed Minister for Ecclesiastical Affairs? That would at least appear a sufficient motive in South Germany. In Prussia the motive would seem rather more flimsy—but in the end it would also be accepted. I cannot imagine the Chancellor would stand by Herrfurth if H.M. urged this solution on him. As I said, I think it is *dangerous* to force the Kaiser into adopting measures aimed against Caprivi. I have observed here that even the Bavarians, worried as they are by events in Berlin, *shudder* at the thought that Caprivi might go. 'The thermometer measuring confidence in Prussia's leadership, standing at 25° *before* the School Bill, has now already fallen to about 5°', I was told yesterday by a loyal citizen of the Reich who is very familiar with conditions here.

Write and tell me your opinion soon—but believe me: any prolongation of the unrest by obstruction in committee is almost as harmful as a definitive decision meaning victory for the Centre; any strengthening of H.M.'s mistrust of Caprivi is actually dangerous.[1]

Your faithful
P.E.

Chamber of Deputies, that the Bill could easily be killed in commission, and advised that the Kaiser instruct Köller to do so if a Bill could not be passed that would be approved by the National Liberals as well as by the Centre and Conservative Parties. Otherwise Bismarck could exploit the situation by attacking the School Bill in the Upper House and in this way win over all political groups opposed to the School Bill. Such tactics on Bismarck's part would leave the Kaiser helplessly dependent on the Centre and the extreme Conservatives. Holstein strongly advised Eulenburg to warn the Kaiser of this danger, and to persuade him to instruct Köller to bury the School Bill in committee. (From the Eulenburg Papers.)

[1] On 1 March Holstein wrote to Eulenburg that Göring, the Head of the Reich Chancellery and an old school friend of Caprivi, was of the opinion that a 'bogging down' of the School Bill was the best thing that could happen under the circumstances, for if the Bill failed to pass Caprivi would almost certainly fall. (From the Eulenberg Papers.)

363. Paul von Metternich to Holstein

London, 24 February 1892

Dear Baron Holstein,

You will see from my to-day's report about Anglo-Turkish negotiations over Egypt[1]

1. that Lord Salisbury definitely *wants* to negotiate and that this desire causes him to forget even the question of expediency involved in the *where*;
2. that he probably sets too great hopes on the alleged liking of the Sultan for Ford[2]
3. that it will depend upon this Ambassador's greater or lesser degree of ambition whether the negotiations take place in Constantinople or London—provided that the Sultan comes out into the open with his proposals and that these can be discussed at all from the English standpoint.

The reasons why Salisbury no longer thinks that London is a good place for negotiating are old and out of date and humbug. He simply believes in Ford's star. If Ford becomes *afraid*, or if he is made afraid, and in consequence does not let his star be seen, then I am convinced that Salisbury will again be willing to let the negotiations take place here. He is on the wrong track *only* in regard to the place for the negotiations; he has more courage than formerly so far as the affair itself is concerned, otherwise he would now gladly give the Sultan the cold shoulder. I explain the greater courage by the attitude of the Opposition, who had promised a particularly violent attack on Salisbury's Egyptian policy in the debate on the Reply to the Speech from the Throne, which in the end did not take place. Salisbury's Egyptian policy is popular here, and therefore the Opposition does not dare openly and plainly to press him to evacuate the country. Their official line is to say they approve Salisbury's policy on the Nile, but they never forget to add the hope that conditions will very soon permit the English to fulfil their word and to withdraw. With the first line they calm the Liberal voters and try to calm the fears of English capitalists on the Nile, and with the perfidious addition they keep French hopes alive and French friendship warm; what people in Constantinople and Egypt think about all this is a matter of indifference to them.

Salisbury was visibly surprised yesterday when I made use of the argument supplied me by His Excellency [State Secretary Marschall] that we knew for certain that if he should negotiate in Constantinople the Sultan would regard it as 'weakness'. He was not exactly pleased by the word, but it made an impression. If we keep a close watch in Constantinople, and find out at once if the Sultan does confide in Ford,

---

[1] Metternich's report stated that Salisbury had informed him he would instruct the new English Ambassador, Sir Clare Ford, to find out what the Sultan's intentions were with regard to Egypt. Salisbury was afraid that the Sultan might not consent to an agreement arrived at in London. (From the Foreign Ministry files.)

[2] Sir Francis Clare Ford. English Ambassador in Madrid, 1887–92, in Constantinople, 1892–3, in Rome, 1893–8.

then perhaps the favourable moment will have arrived to try again to persuade Salisbury to hold the negotiations *here*. [...]

With kindest regards,
Ever your most devoted
Paul Metternich.[1]

364. Philipp zu Eulenburg to Holstein

M[unich], 5 March 1892

Dear friend,

As matters stand I am of your opinion, though with a *heavy* heart: postponing the School Law is the only possibility.[2] Whether Göring is right in his opinion that Caprivi will resign if the Law does not come into force or rather if the Kaiser refuses his consent, is something I cannot judge. In such cases a great deal depends on the way the thing is done. Nevertheless, the *danger* of Caprivi's resignation is alone sufficient to justify preventive measures. There can be no doubt that postponement, with the accompanying agitation, will have serious consequences in Southern Germany, and it is only with the greatest reluctance that I will work toward this end. [...]

With affectionate greetings
Yours faithfully
P.E.[3]

365. Philipp zu Eulenburg to Holstein

M[unich], 22 March 1892

Dearest friend,

I have just received a telegram in code, but cannot decipher it before the post goes.

A reply in haste that I think cousin B. Eulenburg quite *extraordinarily* good as Minister-President. But see to it that he does not accept *any* administrative department for the present.[4]

He is a *gentleman through and through* and an *indescribably* good-natured man.

That is what we need in order *to make Caprivi's position bearable.*

[1] On 26 February Holstein sent Metternich the following private telegram: 'Letter received. The Sultan's desire to negotiate in Constantinople could be exploited by having Lord Salisbury let him know that the English Ambassador was instructed to enter into negotiations if definite proposals were made to him from the Turkish side.' On the same day Hatzfeldt telegraphed to Holstein that he had spoken in this sense with Salisbury. (From the London Embassy files.)

[2] See above, p. 406, note 1.

[3] The crisis over the Prussian School Bill came to a head at the meeting of the Crown Council of 17 March, when the Kaiser declared he would not accept a Bill that was not acceptable to the moderate Parties. Caprivi stood by Zedlitz on the School Bill question, and both men handed in their resignations. The resignation of Zedlitz was accepted, as was Caprivi's in his capacity as Minister-President of Prussia. Caprivi stayed on as German Chancellor and Prussian Foreign Minister, however. His successor as Minister-President of Prussia was Count Botho zu Eulenburg, a cousin of Count Philipp.

[4] In August 1892 Count Botho Eulenburg, the new Minister-President of Prussia, became Prussian Minister of the Interior as well.

As a departmental Minister my very conscientious cousin would possibly get involved in all sorts of unnecessary details and be incapable of carrying out his *particular task*.

I am quite impartial and *never* pursue family but only *Kaiser*-policy.

I had never thought of cousin B. but I am absolutely convinced that he alone is the right person.

Hohenzollern[1] as Chancellor would be a puppet. Perhaps you would like that—forgive this expression that just slipped out.

Your old faithful
P.E.

366. Philipp zu Eulenburg to Holstein

M[unich], 26 March 1892

Dear friend,

I have just written the enclosed letter.[2]

You will see from it that I am in favour of a line of action that is not too different, and that I regard this as *absolutely* necessary—otherwise I would not have written.

If it will not work with B. Eulenburg and Caprivi—it will not work with Caprivi at all.

I am afraid that Caprivi's prestige has suffered greatly in the Kaiser's eyes. For that reason C.'s depression makes his dismissal a constant danger. It is necessary that he should be morally roused in every way. I am writing to him tomorrow—with the emphasis on wishes here.[3]

I cannot say that my position in regard to Caprivi is *pleasant* but I will try to surmount it. The attacks on Caprivi in the Conservative and Centre Press are also most disagreeable to me. I hope that this affair can at last be brought to an end if a conciliatory line is followed in both directions.

I am busy on every hand trying to calm excited feelings, and for that reason there will be no official dispatches for the present. I have no time to spare for them. You will see how matters stand at the moment from the enclosed *s.p.r.* letter.

Your sincere friend
P.E.

Please be kind enough to forward the letter enclosed in the diplomatic bag to H.M. at once.

367. Georg zu Münster to Holstein

Paris, 15 May 1892

My dear Herr von Holstein,

Many thanks for your friendly letter. I have read the article in the *Fortnightly Review*[4] with interest, although the political part of it is the

---

[1] Prince Leopold. Head of the non-regnant branch of the House of Hohenzollern.
[2] Not found.   [3] See Haller, *Eulenburg*, p. 71.
[4] Reverend Richard Haweis, 'The Coming Crisis in Morocco', in the April number of the *Fortnightly Review*. (See *Grosse Politik*, vol. VIII, nos. 1944–5, pp. 317–19.)

phantasmagoria of an impractical clergyman. I endorse every word of the first part, which describes the advantages that a European Power could gain from this country so richly blessed by nature and so ravaged by barbarism. I know a good part of the Moroccan coast, Mogador, [...],[1] Tangier and also the district around Tetuan *de visu*, and have always thought that that is the only remaining *spot on earth* that in *our hands* could become the *most lovely colony*. Unfortunately I must admit that this could only happen after great changes and wars, and will probably never happen. To achieve it no sacrifice would seem to me too great, whereas everything we undertake in the negro part of Africa only kills white men and swallows up money, of which we still have none to spare, besides *definitely weakening* our position in the world. Who knows whether our grandchildren will not try to exploit our rights and our influence in Morocco where it would pay and where both men and horses [...][1] are first rate.

The present situation in Morocco will continue for the same reasons as will the Turkish Empire. So long as there is no war in Europe, France, Spain, and England will keep one another in check, and none of the Powers will start a war on that account. [...].

As always, your most friendly and devoted

Münster.

368. Paul von Metternich to Holstein

London, 18 May 1892

Dear Baron Holstein,

[...] Yesterday I sounded Salisbury about Egypt. I began with the well-known Berlin telegram about the Sultan's health which had so greatly enraged him.[2] Salisbury thought it was not impossible that Armenians here had inspired the telegram. From the Sultan to Egypt was then only a step, and Salisbury told me approximately the following:

The Sultan still would not speak openly. Now and then he made a start but that was all. He—Lord Salisbury—would still be happy to lend a hand to raise the Sultan's position with regard to Egypt in the eyes of the *Mohammedan* world *if he only knew how*. In the last analysis that was probably all the Sultan really cared about, and it was not a question of establishing a position of actual power in Egypt. I replied that so far as I could remember, the Sultan wanted, among other things, to be represented in Egypt by Turkish troops. From everything that Salisbury told me in this connection, he does not have the slightest intention of going beyond the 'symbolic action'. But it seems to me very doubtful whether he will even go *so* far. He says that the answer to the question whether a small Turkish garrison could be allowed to come to Egypt depends above all on the attitude of the Egyptian Government. In the difficult situation of 1884, he himself had proposed joint action by Turkish and English troops in Egypt, but had immediately met with

---

[1] One word illegible.

[2] Count Metternich refers to a Reuter telegram sent from Berlin on 10 May according to which reports were circulating in Berlin that the Sultan was suffering from insanity.

stiff opposition on the part of the Egyptian and French Governments. When I said I was doubtful whether France would adopt the same attitude nowadays, Salisbury remarked that the traditional policy of France was directed towards making Egypt independent of Turkey, and *red tape traditions*[1] always exercised great influence upon the course of French foreign policy. I jokingly replied that the new tradition in France appeared to me to be less concerned with the independence of Egypt than with obstructing English policy there as much as possible. At which he exclaimed: 'That is not the new but the old French tradition, which from time immemorial has been one of frustrating England's plans all over the world!' You will gather from all this that he will not even use Egypt as an object of barter. Nor does he have any illusions that he can promote a reconciliation with the Sultan if he does him a favour in Egypt. He still considers the Sultan to be incalculable and an uncertain customer who should gradually accustom himself to the fact of the English occupation of Egypt. Otherwise he is trying to strengthen the Sultan as a possible ally against Russia by using the saying 'and if you aren't willing, then I'll use force'. Recently Salisbury, in speaking of the favourable financial situation of Turkey, expressed the idea that the Eastern Question would perhaps find an unexpected solution in that Turkey, by its progressive development, would be in a position to help itself, and especially if the rich land of Asia Minor were opened up by railways. I replied that that would very probably enrich English and other commercial people, but that it was very questionable whether commercial exploitation by Europe would restore internal strength to Turkey.

I am certainly not a courtier. I have just returned from the *Drawing Room*,[1] which interrupted me in the middle of this letter. The air at Court has a deadening effect upon body and mind. Nevertheless I will try to add a few words about Morocco. In my last letter[2] I was somewhat disturbed about whether you wanted my personal opinion after all. But you now write that you found my letter not uninteresting, and that encourages me to send you some of my ideas on the, as you call it, 'distant but great' Moroccan danger.[3] You will see from my report to-day that Salisbury also regards it as 'distant but great'.[4] In general it can be said that it is impossible to foretell whether a flabby English Government will not at some time, for the sake of a momentary peace, surrender vital English interests and try to come to an understanding

---

[1] In English in the original.   [2] Not found.

[3] In the files of the German Embassy in London there is a telegram of 6 May from Holstein to Metternich that states: 'Letter received. [...] I wish to inform you personally and confidentially that a concession by England in response to Turkish-Russian-French pressure in Egypt would at this moment be dangerous for us, in as much as it might perhaps amount to a partial compensation for an eventual English action against Tangier and bring the possibility of Anglo-French agreement over Morocco somewhat nearer. This is something we cannot desire.'

[4] Metternich had reported that Salisbury had described the Moroccan affair 'as for the moment completely quiescent'. On the other hand it could very suddenly—for example, in the event of the Sultan's death—acquire the importance of a second Eastern Question. (From the Foreign Ministry files.)

with France about Morocco, that is to say over a real partition. But I cannot see what England can offer France in order to make the Straits of Gibraltar English on both sides. Egypt is surely too high a price. England would in that case surely prefer to make the Straits of Gibraltar into a sort of Suez Canal under international protection. She would not need to give anything to obtain that. I do not believe that Syria can become an object of barter. In the first place England has no rights there and therefore nothing to give away. She can therefore only promise to look on quietly in the event of France's establishing herself there. But it is also questionable to me whether France would desire this under the present circumstances, since she would easily come into conflict with Russia over the Orthodox and Roman Catholic religious communities. Furthermore, Turkey still exists and will perhaps exist longer than Morocco. But chiefly and above all, England cannot permit France to secure a firm foothold in the eastern regions of the Mediterranean. England would then come between two fires and France, with the possible support of the Russian Black Sea fleet, would gain a near and convenient base for operations against Egypt. Moreover England now has sufficient reason to be afraid of French sea power in the Mediterranean. But quite apart from the question of barter, the most important thing in my opinion is the fact that *every* Anglo-French partition of Morocco would mean bad business for England. England owes her position in the world largely to the lucky circumstance that nowhere, except in Canada for which she will therefore not fight, has she a powerful neighbour across the frontier. If the Sebu, or any other line, were to become the frontier between France and England in Morocco, then French military power would be permanently at her throat. From Toulon France can strengthen her already considerable military forces in Algeria at will. England cannot maintain a standing army in Morocco to defend her eventual share of Morocco, and would therefore be at the mercy of the favour and disfavour of French arrogance. The incongruity between prestige (based on clever diplomacy and fortunate frontiers) and real power would then be quite obvious for the first time, to the disadvantage of England. The struggle would no longer be fought out on the sea but on land, and there, as everyone knows, England is *nowhere*.[1] [...]

Always yours
Paul Metternich.

369. Holstein to Hugo von Radolin[2]

1 July [1892]

Dear Rado,
You are acceptable to the Sultan.[3] The matter is thus arranged. What do you intend to do about your estates? Is Haak to have complete control?

[1] In English in the original. [2] From the Radolin Papers
[3] As Ambassador in Constantinople.

Re your appointment, an attempt was of course made to keep Radowitz there. But everything is now settled.

I am writing in great haste.

Lay me at the feet of the Princess,[1] if there is still room.

Your
H.

370. Paul von Hatzfeldt to Holstein

Ems, Villa Dreix, 1 July 1892

Dear friend,

Since you have not yet written to me, I assume that the storms of war have died away for the present and that His Highness has not started another offensive.[2] This will still come, about that we must not deceive ourselves. In my humble opinion it will then be advisable *for the time being* to observe *great composure in the manner* of our replies and also to preserve the appearance that we are only acting in self defense, and that only *with bleeding hearts* did we criticise the demigod of the past. Everything I see in the Press about public opinion strengthens me in this opinion. The situation obviously is that the great majority condemn H.H.'s action, and even his friends have little to say in his defence, but that everyone, including the vast number of impartial and honourable people, is painfully disturbed by the thought that a conflict could arise which would result in hurling from his pedestal the sole remaining representative of the great past. Therefore it seems to me that moderation is called for; this will be all the easier to exercise because it will hardly be preserved by the other side. For should H.H. take up the cudgels he will hardly show moderation (which he has never known) and he himself will then probably supply the means for a severe counter-attack, which would then have the approval of the great majority of the nation.

If in the foregoing I have said things that you know just as well as I do, my excuse is that this very important question intensely preoccupies me here, perhaps even more than in Berlin where I was close to the developments.

The second excuse for writing to-day is a letter that has just reached me from Salisbury by way of Malet which I enclose (with a request for its return).[3] In the first place you will notice that he himself sets no great hopes on the outcome of the elections. The information about

---

[1] On 4 June 1892 Radolin had married Countess Johanna von Oppersdorff. His first wife, Miss Lucy Wakefield, had died in 1880.

[2] In June 1892 Bismarck went to Vienna to attend the wedding of his son Herbert with Countess Marguerite Hoyos. An audience with the Austrian Kaiser was refused him after the personal intervention of Wilhelm II (see his letter to Kaiser Franz Joseph of 12 June 1892, *Österreichische Rundschau*, 1919, vol. LVIII, pp. 109–10) and of Caprivi, who feared that Bismarck might use the opportunity to discredit the present regime in Germany. (Holstein's part in this affair can be seen in his letters to Eulenburg in the Eulenburg Papers.) No member of the Austrian Court or of the German Embassy staff attended the wedding. Afterwards Bismarck bitterly attacked the German Government in Press interviews and in public speeches. (See also Rogge, *Holstein und Hohenlohe*, pp. 386–9, 391–4.)

[3] See Enclosure.

Tricoupis' intentions was obviously given to me in the hope that we for our part would also warn the Sultan; perhaps you will see what can be done about it. If there are no reasons against doing so (I know of none), I think it would be advisable to fulfil his wish, and to inform Salisbury of this as quickly as possible through Metternich. I am not surprised because I know Tricoupis. For that very reason the affair is not without its dangers, because most probably he is speculating on the result of the elections in England and Gladstone's warmer sympathy with Greece. Even Rosebery feels this sympathy, although at the time, under the pressure of circumstances and the other Powers (I will not take into account my own energetic endeavours towards that end), he took part in the demonstration at Piraeus.[1]

You know as well as I do what kind of crisis *can* arise in the Near East *if* Tricoupis this time acts decisively in regard to Crete, especially after the possible *avènement* of Gladstone. What would be the attitude of France and Russia *now*? That is not quite clear to me and it would be of great importance to know the answer. Nevertheless we should not lose sight of the fact that in this danger for the Sultan there is an opportunity for us to regain *completely* or in part the influence over him which was unfortunately lost. If Rad[olin] were only there in time to exploit this opportunity if it presents itself, for that is something Joseph [Radowitz] will certainly *not* do!

If you think it advisable for me to reply by letter to Salisbury from here and to draw special attention to any particular point, then please let me know as soon as possible. Perhaps this reply would best be sent by cipher-telegram through Metternich as a *private* communication for Salisbury. This would also be a special act of courtesy to him, and is all the more to be recommended since it is to be hoped that he will return to power again soon in the event that the Grand Old Man now hoists him out of the saddle. [...]

With kindest regards
Yours
PH

ENCLOSURE

Salisbury to Paul von Hatzfeldt[2]

Dear Count Hatzfeldt,

I see by the papers that you are at Berlin. I venture, therefore, to send you a letter through the British Embassy in order to thank you very much for your kind telegram from Italy about my carriage accident. As you possibly may have seen I came by no harm: but I could not write to you to tell you this, or to thank you, as you did not give me your address. I also write to tell you—as I may be out of office before

---

[1] In April 1886 Turkey had appealed to the Powers to stop Greek military preparations for forcing a frontier revision upon Turkey. Notes by the Powers to Greece of 26 April and 6 May were backed up by a naval demonstration outside the harbour of the Piraeus. On 10 May an international naval force blockaded the Greek coast.

[2] In English in the original.

I see you again—that Tricoupis has plainly informed Monson that he intends to take the first opportunity of seizing Crete; and Monson thinks that Tricoupis is in earnest. I think a hint of the danger should be given to Yildiz.[1] I would instruct Ford to tell the Sultan; but His Majesty does not believe a word we say. Believe me

Yours very truly

Salisbury [...]

371. Paul von Hatzfeldt to Holstein

Ems, 10 July 1892

Dear friend,

[...] Why no word from you? I would have been glad to hear how things were going, in general and in particular; whether you sent the warning about Tric[oupis] by some means to C[onstantinople] and the message I suggested to Sal[isbury].[2] Meanwhile the prospects for the latter apparently are turning out more and more as I told you I thought probable, namely, that Gl[adstone] will certainly return to power with a *small* majority. *Politically* that would be better for us than if S. were to win with a small majority because he would then be very weak. So far as one can tell, however, Gl. in the same situation will very quickly be at the end of his resources, and I am told that he himself knows this very well.

In my opinion the new elections are of the *greatest* importance for the future development of the foreign policy of the whole of Europe, and hence for us. I regard as the second most important point—I hope you agree—the restoration of our influence in Const., and for that reason urgently hope that with the appearance of Rado[lin] there—I wish he could be there by tomorrow—an entirely new era will begin. Almost the entire advantage which we can expect from having a Conservative Government in England, in the event of the development of a European crisis, will be determined in large part if not exclusively by how the situation develops in Const., and for that reason this is something we cannot watch too closely. I have no voice in the matter and can only express my opinion, which you might regard as my political testament.

I am afraid that in regard to His Highness things are developing as I expected and that he will not give up the struggle. Caprivi's position is now a good one, however, because even [Caprivi's] opponents will not follow the Prince through thick and thin. The only thing that gives me cause for anxiety is Caprivi's worry, which was clearly discernible in his remarks to me, that he was not in sufficiently 'good company' if he did not above all have all Conservatives behind him. As you know, I am personally no Liberal, but I cannot close my eyes to the fact that 'good

---

[1] The country residence of the Sultan.

[2] On 9 July the German Minister in Athens, Wesdehlen, was instructed by telegram to warn his Turkish colleague. In a dispatch on 11 July Wesdehlen reported that he had carried out the instruction, but that the Turkish Minister did not think that Tricoupis would shortly find an opportunity for an attack on Crete. The report was forwarded to London on 17 July. (From the Foreign Ministry files.)

company', that is the support of the Conservatives and the more or less fashionable people, nowadays promises little *political* advantage if one is restricted to them, in fact they can in that case almost be a danger. Quite apart from the fact that to-day no government can have much success in the long run without respecting so-called public opinion in certain questions (nobody could have less regard for it in general than I), we need a parliamentary majority for questions of the greatest importance upon which our external safety depends, and this we can never get from the Conservatives alone—or rather from *part* of them, because you cannot count on any more. But a parliamentary majority alone is not enough. The continued self-sacrifice of the country and its assent to ever greater burdens can only be assured by a government in two ways: either through tremendous successes like 1866 and 1870, or if this seems excluded as it does now by present circumstances, then by assuring that they are borne by the force of 'public opinion'. The government can and must in this connection represent the most moderate and conservative standpoint, and nobody will blame it for that. It must not, however, be in any doubt about the fact that *our* Conservatives do not represent this 'public opinion', which may be essentially wrong but which is indispensable. [...]

Kind regards

372. Alfred von Kiderlen-Wächter to Holstein

Skanör,[1] 13 July 1892

Dear Herr von Holstein

This international exposition is a bad business.[2] You have seen H.M.'s attitude to it in his marginal comments.[3] In addition to that H.M. said: 'Six months ago when there was first talk of an international exposition I urgently requested the Chancellor to put a stop to it. He then wanted to wait and see. I have however repeatedly told him that I was opposed to it; but he has always shut up like an oyster and now we have a pretty kettle of fish; if it is now stated that I do not want it, then people will again say I do not know what I want and had changed my mind; and yet from the outset I left no doubt that I was against it, and have asked Caprivi to oppose it. At the time of my visit to Stumm,[4] I told an industrialist (H.M. mentioned the name which I have forgotten), who spoke against the exposition, that that was also

[1] Kiderlen was with the Kaiser on his annual cruise to the Norwegian fjords.
[2] On 15 January 1892 the German Commercial Congress passed a resolution in favour of an international exposition in Berlin.
[3] In a report of 4 July, Caprivi had drawn the Kaiser's attention to 'the mounting feeling in favour of an exposition in Berlin' and had sent him a memorandum on the subject addressed to the Federal Governments. These Governments were asked to investigate the question whether Germany should hold an international exposition in Berlin before 1900, that is before the international exposition in Paris which was to be held in that year. Wilhelm II in his marginal comments expressed himself sharply against the proposed international exposition. (From the Foreign Ministry files.)
[4] Karl Ferdinand, Freiherr von Stumm. Industrialist and politician; Member of the Reichstag, 1867–81, 1887–1901; Co-founder and leading member of the German Reich Party. He was a personal friend of Kaiser Wilhelm II.

my opinion and that he could tell everyone, and that the people who were opposed to it should express their views in the Press.'

This was roughly how H.M. expressed himself and in doing so he was more depressed than angry. I admit he has a right to be annoyed that Caprivi, after he knew H.M.'s definite attitude on the matter, had allowed himself to be sucked into the affair without having discussed it with H.M., and that, without further reference to H.M., he should have approached the Federal and French Governments. Nor could I say anything in Caprivi's defence because I knew absolutely nothing about the matter. Since the Chancellor knew H.M.'s views it would have been better if he had not brought up a matter that H.M. had heretofore opposed by so abrupt a means as a personal dispatch. I sent H.M.'s marginal comments by telegram to give the Chancellor a chance to veer around before it's too late. I do not know what the Chancellor's own views are in the matter. After he published the Karlsbad letter,[1] I always thought he was at most an unwilling supporter. Moreover I must also admit that H.M. is right in thinking that, assuming the Government wanted to have the exposition, they should have taken the lead and the initiative instead of letting themselves be slowly dragged along by 'public opinion'. From a material standpoint I cannot presume to answer the question of whether or not to hold an exhibition. In my telegram I have acted solely on the supposition, based on the repeated and at times very sharp remarks of the Kaiser, that H.M. will *not* give way in this matter, that therefore the Chancellor must give way in order to avoid a conflict if that is still possible, and that if it is decided not to hold an exposition this must be made known as quickly as possible. On this there are a few more marginal comments by H.M.

What do you think of the Chancellor's action in proposing Ph. Eulenburg for Vienna to H.M. without saying anything to anybody? (Doubtless to get rid of him in Munich!) The Chancellor told me on the day before my departure, and thus *after* he had seen H.M. for the last time and had already made his proposal, that we should try to keep Reuss and that he had as yet not made *any sort* of decision.

I had written this letter up to this point when I got your telegram about the exposition.[2] Despite my own reservations, I spoke to the Kaiser today in *your* sense about the matter. He said: 'I cannot decide in favour of the exposition, the economic disadvantages for us would be too great. (H.M. always speaks to me in this connection of an article that appeared months ago in the *Schlesische Zeitung*, which I dimly remember; it emphasises, I think, workmen crowding to Berlin?

---

[1] A letter of 20 May addressed to the executive committee of the Association for the Promotion of Industrial Activity in Berlin, in which Caprivi agreed that everything possible should be done to increase German exports. 'An international exposition in Berlin would serve this purpose only if it were successful, whereas failure would mean not only pecuniary sacrifice but might also affect the prestige of German industry and commerce abroad in a manner injurious to our export trade.' Caprivi therefore advised the postponement of an international exposition until success could virtually be assured.

[2] Not found.

Gabriel¹ will certainly find it.) Bötticher knows my views. I must take the decision here and go ahead.'

I now regret all the more that the Chancellor sent his report directly to the Kaiser without putting me in a position of knowing the Chancellor's views and of discussing them with H.M. In the report all sorts of things were mentioned which the Chancellor had already done, but *without* the Chancellor's taking up a definite stand *for* the exposition. The result is that H.M. has now firmly put himself in the opposition camp by his marginal comments. I can now do little more in the matter; the Chancellor must fight it out in Wilhelmshaven.

The enclosed marginal comment on the Army Bill² will please you. You can show it to the Chancellor and therewith perhaps make him understand that H.M. is completely convinced that he has therein clearly indicated that it is his pleasure that he should not now introduce the Bill. [...]

Always your most obedient
Kiderlen. [...]

373. Alfred von Kiderlen-Wächter to Holstein

Trondheim, 20 July 1892

Urgent

Enclosed a copy of His Majesty's handwritten letter to the Chancellor, prepared in secret.³ When H.M. (with Eulenburg) gave me the first page to read and asked my opinion, I said I was glad the letter was couched in a friendly spirit for the Chancellor. Whereupon H.M. replied: 'I would certainly not have a row with him over the Crystal Palace; I would be running the risk of his offering me his resignation.' You see therefore that the letter is at all events *intended* to be friendly, despite its sometimes crude, sometimes arrogant inquiries *in fine*. Please emphasise that there.

Afterwards H.M. said further: 'I have put this in writing because in that way I can more emphatically emphasise my position as King and Father of his Country; it might easily seem provocative if I as a young man were to say anything like this orally to someone much older. I hope that will be avoided by the letter.'

Personal feelings in regard to the Chancellor are *good* because H.M. recognises the *necessity* for retaining him; but I cannot believe that H.M. will give way in the matter (exposition) itself.

In great haste
K.

Just now H.M. has ordered that you are to receive a copy. You have it therefore *de plein droit*.
K.

Once again I expressly emphasise that the passage in which H.M. thanks the Chancellor for his care for H.M.'s popularity *could* sound ironical but *is not meant in that sense*. You can definitely assure the Chancellor

[1] Adviser for Press affairs at the Foreign Ministry.   [2] Not found.   [3] See Enclosure.

that that is the case. It would not be advisable, however, to tell the Chancellor that Eul. and I have seen the letter *any more* than that you have received a copy.

ENCLOSURE
Kaiser Wilhelm II to Leo von Caprivi
Copy

Trondheim, 20 July 1892

My dear Caprivi,

I have read with interest Your Excellency's letter on the subject of the commotion over the Berlin Exposition.[1] I thank you very much for your frank expression of opinion regarding the handling of this affair. Although I do not underestimate the reasons which seemingly argue in favour of the encouragement of the project, yet I am nevertheless unable to accept them fully. The idea of an exposition for Germany (with Berlin as the place where it is to be held) is indeed nothing new. And it has every now and then made the rounds of the newspapers. A real enthusiasm for it has nevertheless never and nowhere shown itself. For that reason also discussion of it has always remained purely academic. Such was the state of things this spring when the idea again made its appearance. I then told you that I was absolutely opposed to it and did not desire that it should be put into effect or allowed to gain strength. The reasons are known, I do not need to repeat them. Moreover I informed you of the *factum* that the same question was brought before Prince Bismarck two and a half years ago. The former Chancellor settled the affair at that time, since his views completely coincided with mine, by roundly refusing the proposal of the group favouring the scheme after he had had an audience of me, and he indicated that an exposition was not feasible and also that it was not approved by me. All outcry in favour of an exposition thereupon ceased. Since then my views have not altered in any way, the Paris Exposition has on the contrary strengthened them.

When you say in your letter that you did not want to give an outright refusal in your answer from Karlsbad because you had previously recognised the possibility that the idea of an exhibition might become the subject of a national movement, then it would seem in my opinion to have been doubly important to have countered the possibility with a decisive No. In this connection a reference to the decision taken by Prince [Bismarck] after an audience of the Kaiser would not have failed of effect, and would probably have nipped every movement in the bud. This procedure would at the same time have precluded the possibility to which Your Excellency alluded that P[rince] v[on] B[ismarck] might *now* come forward in support of the idea of an exposition.

The fame of the Parisians gives the Berliners no peace. Berlin is a great city, cosmopolitan (perhaps?), therefore it must also have an exposition! It is easy to understand that this line of thought is very

[1] See p. 416, note 2.

understandable and acceptable for *Berlin* hotels, theatres, music-halls, etc. They will be the only ones to profit from it! Hence the propaganda. But the *proton pseudos* is to be found in the conclusion that it was the tourist traffic alone that brought Paris such good returns. This is completely false. The hundreds of real millionaires who settled there to *live*, and to amuse themselves for months, and who attract new acquaintances from all countries—it is all this that has fattened the calf. Paris is after all—what I hope Berlin will never be—the greatest whore house in the world, hence another attraction quite apart from the exposition. There is nothing in Berlin to hold the foreigner with the exception of a few museums, palaces, and the soldiers. He has seen everything with the red book in his hand in six days, and then goes on with an easy mind and with the feeling that he has done his *duty*. The Berliner does not understand this and would be thoroughly offended if one told him so. But that is exactly what stands in the way of an exposition. I am deeply moved to see from your proposal—to place me at the head—how you are trying, in these times that are so difficult for us both, to find a good opportunity to increase my subjects' affection for me, and I warmly thank you. But my will is firm as a rock, and I will hold fast to what I hold right, and no devil—not even Prince Bismarck—can dissuade me. I will not have an exposition because it can injure my fatherland and my capital! Moreover we Hohenzollerns are accustomed only to advance slowly and painfully amidst trouble, conflicts, party divisions, and lack of appreciation. How often have my ancestors, most recently my grandfather who rests with God, had to battle for measures in direct opposition to the will of the uncomprehending populace which first opposed, then criticised, but finally blessed them. *What do I care about popularity!* For as the guiding principles of my actions, I have only the dictates of my duty and the responsibility of my clear conscience towards God. Dear Caprivi, think of it, I was prepared for bullets and dynamite when I ascended the Throne and I am still alive! Yes—even the Socialists say that one can talk to me; well! more cannot be expected in two years after Prince [Bismarck] and the disappearance of the Socialist law. Our time will come as for everyone. Let us be patient and persevering, let us do our duty whether people are annoyed or not, it is all the same. Respect will come, it is already 'on the march' owing to your distinction and my trust in God. Only *trust in my leadership* and fight bravely where I point the way, and we will have no trouble in managing the *canaille* either in this affair or later on in *rebus militariis*! Moreover I am glad to have learnt from the Press that the 'national movement' is weak. The *Freisinnige, National* and *Münchener* are already issuing warnings against it. Hence don't worry! As my Berliners say, the exposition is done for. [Ausstellung is nich]. Farewell, best greetings to your colleagues and counsellors, as well as to Holstein.

Your very affectionate King
Wilhelm I.R.

374. Philipp zu Eulenburg to Holstein

Trondheim, 20 July 1892

Dear friend,

I have just written by H.M.'s command to my cousin Botho E[ulenburg]. He is to talk to Stolberg[1] or any other of the participants about the attitude of the *Post*. Further H.M. advised my cousin to maintain the closest contact with Caprivi and to assist him in an advisory capacity in all Press matters, etc. I have as far as possible endeavoured to act as a conciliator between H.M. and the Chancellor. The tone of the letter of which you are to receive a copy shows that H.M. does not want any serious conflict.

Your position is tremendously powerful and the firm confidence which H.M. has in you bears a truly fine and assured character. You can imagine how glad I am!

The conversation turned once more on the Vienna Embassy.

Wedel has (so far as I can *sense*) a sort of promise from H.M. of an embassy. *But not for Vienna in particular*.[2] H.M. emphasised that— though God alone knows what course the affair will suddenly take. But I don't think I am wrong in assuming that a piece of advice reaching H.M. FROM YOU would straighten the matter out in the desired way.[3] [...]

With kindest regards
Yours faithfully
PE

Best thanks for your letter. It pains me that you are grinding away when you need a holiday more than all of us together.

375. Valentine Chirol[4] to Holstein[5]

London, 20 July 1892

My dear Baron Holstein,

[...] The moral of the last elections is the decay of Gladstone's personal influence, and the increase of Chamberlain's.[6] I am very hopeful as to the future from a patriotic point of view. The existence of a Radical party is a fact which one may deplore, but which has to be faced, now that our institutions have been placed on a democratic basis. But I believe the knell of the old narrow-minded, insular Radicalism has been sounded, and that possibly after a series of internal

---

[1] Otto, Prince zu Stolberg-Wernigerode. Vice-President of the Prussian Ministry of State, 1878–81; Lord High Chamberlain, 1884–94; Member of the Reichstag (Independent Conservative), 1871–8; President of the Prussian House of Lords, 1872–6, 1893–6.

[2] At the desire of the Kaiser, Prince Reuss was to be replaced as Ambassador to Vienna because of the critical attitude both he and his wife had taken towards the German government's activity during Bismarck's visit to the Austrian capital. (See above, p. 413, note 2.)

[3] Eulenburg means that Holstein should work to get him the ambassadorial post in Vienna.

[4] Correspondent of *The Times* in Berlin, 1892–6; Deputy-Director of the Foreign Department of *The Times*, 1896–9; Director of the Foreign Department, 1899–1912.

[5] From Baroness von der Heydt's collection of typewritten copies of Holstein letters. The original has not been found. The letter was written in English.

[6] In the General Election of July 1892 Gladstone was returned to office with a narrow majority that depended upon the support of the Irish Home Rulers.

crises and electoral struggles, there will emerge a young Radical party under Chamberlain's leadership, as thoroughly Imperialist, etc, as thoroughly conscious of the world wide range of our interests and duties, as the Conservative party has always shown itself to be. Under Chamberlain and Rosebery the Radical party might possibly embark upon risky experiments in domestic legislation, (but it is not from those that I apprehend any serious danger as I believe the practical common sense of the nation will counteract any pernicious tendencies), but on questions of Imperial policy it will be guided by broad and statesmanlike principles, and it is just with regard to those questions that it is most important for an ignorant electorate to be in the hands of able and sensible leaders.

Nor must it be forgotten that in the event of Chamberlain ultimately regaining his proper position as leader of the Radical party, the experience he has gained during his alliance with the Conservative party will prove of the greatest value in placing on a footing of mutual respect and forebearance the relations of the two parties in the state when once the irritating and sterilising question of Home Rule has been eliminated.

I confess that if the outcome of the process of disintegration and reorganisation which evidently awaits the Radical party, were to bring Chamberlain into office in 1894 and 1895 with Rosebery at the F.O., as a *fin de siècle* Palmerston, I for one should be ready to welcome such a consummation with the utmost composure. [...]

Believe me with all grateful regard,
my dear Baron,
Yours sincerely
Valentine Chirol.

376. Philipp zu Eulenburg to Holstein

Rominten,[1] 30 September 1892

Dear Holstein,

On my return yesterday evening, H.M. himself read to me my memorandum of the 24th, which I enclose, 'in order to talk to me about it'.[2] After each sentence he said to me: quite right!—found only 'compromise with Caprivi' wrong and wanted to substitute for it 'concession to C'.

The places that are underlined aroused his special approval. H.M. *demanded* after this discussion that we must act *very energetically* in this sense. I therefore ask you for your part to initiate some kind of campaign which will make it perfectly clear that H.M. is not afraid of dissolving the Reichstag in the event that the Bill is thrown out. This pressure must be brought to bear on the Centre and Progressives.

[1] Eulenburg had accompanied the Kaiser on a hunting trip to Rominten in East Prussia.
[2] The problem concerned the proposed new Military Service Bill to reduce compulsory military service in the infantry from three to two years, but with the provision for a substantial numerical increase in the standing army. Caprivi favoured reducing the period of compulsory service as a concession to liberal opinion in the Reichstag, but encountered stubborn opposition from the Kaiser and most of the military leaders on this point.

After the election at Löwenberg[1] the latter will be worried. All doubt that H.M. is in earnest will then disappear from the minds of the other Parties. My argument about 'Bismarck as saviour' had an absolutely convincing effect. H.M. has again taken the memorandum from me to make use of it in writing to Botho Eulenburg. (This in strictest confidence!) H.M. is of the opinion that we should start an official campaign. People should also understand that if he made full use of the added clause about the three year period of military service he meant the *full utilisation* of the three years (which would have imposed a *great* burden on the people). [...]

In great haste
Your
PE.

I will write to the Chancellor—about the bill.

H.M. has not yet brought back my memorandum and these lines must go. I will send it to you by the next post.[2]

377. Philipp zu Eulenburg to Holstein

Rominten, 2 October 1892

Dear friend,

Even before I had read your letter,[3] which just arrived, I had spoken with H.M. about St Petersburg. I said that unfortunately Schweinitz could not be kept there very much longer and that I thought it would be useful to set up a *salon* Radolin in competition with the *salon* Montebello.[4] We had no one who could be more competent to represent us.

'Why did you not say so sooner,' said H.M., 'now it is out of the question. I cannot immediately make another change in Constantinople.

---

[1] At a bye-election for the Reichstag in Löwenberg the Conservative candidate received 4,932 votes, the German Liberal 3,596. The National Liberal candidate received only 433 votes.

[2] In his covering note to Holstein of 30 September Eulenburg wrote: 'Memorandum enclosed. Please *regard it as the expression of H.M.'s* [wishes] and *make energetic use of it!* H.M. has just spoken to Mirbach-Sorquitten [Member of the Prussian House of Lords and of the Reichstag] in *exactly* the sense of the memorandum. Thus the fabricated myth will surely collapse.'

Eulenburg's memorandum of 24 September 1892 is published in Haller, *Eulenburg*, pp. 92–5, with the exception of the following paragraph: 'The disaster [e.g. the failure to carry the Army Bill through the Reichstag] will make itself felt *at home* in the following manner: Prince Bismarck has the inclination to get an embassy for Herbert B. But he will *not* write the letter demanded by His Majesty asking for an audience to make an apology because he thinks he will lose the respect of his party by making such an apology. If however public opinion believed that His Majesty's Government had given an irrevocable proof of its weakness, that is to say had ruined itself by bad management, he would *no longer* have to fear having to make his apologies to His Majesty *since he would then come as the saviour of the fatherland* and *as the saviour of His Majesty*. At such a moment the Prince's supporters would not only not deplore such an apology but would applaud it. In such circumstances however not only would Count Caprivi's position be impossible but, what would be far more serious, His Majesty would be delivered with tied hands to the Prince. It would mean the bankruptcy of the Kaiser.'

[3] Of 1 October 1892, in which Holstein strongly advised against Berchem as Ambassador to Russia and suggested Bernhard Bülow. (From the Eulenburg Papers.)

[4] Adrien, Count Montebello. French Ambassador in Constantinople, 1886–91, in St Petersburg, 1891–1903.

Besides Radolin is so superb that I would not like to be deprived of him at the *most important post.*'¹ I said: 'For that Your Majesty has B. Bülow.' 'He must go to Paris,' H.M. replied. 'I am sticking to that. Münster will get a stroke or something else will happen to him—hence Bülow must be free. I cannot play at juggling with the ambassadors.' He then continued: 'Since my relations with St Petersburg really no longer exist, it no longer matters much *who* is there. I also regard Constantinople as *more important.*' I thereupon allowed myself to raise some more particular objections. Then we were interrupted. I will return again to the subject. I think Berchem is less in question than Wedel. So far as I know, H.M. still has *no* general fixed plan with regard to personnel. I can talk about Berchem—there are a good many interesting things that can be said about him. We must reckon with Wedel somehow and somewhere. The best would be to wait for another year and then to play *praevenire.* Rome or Madrid. It will be difficult to do it in any other way.

I want to say something about the journey to Vienna.² I would rather Kiderlen went than I. You cannot think how repugnant it is to me 'to be gossiped about' as a favourite, intriguer, etc. There is probably enough of this as it is—but I have certainly not provoked it.

I doubt whether H.M. will agree. I can only do it if I suggest K. as a welcome addition to the gay travel group, many of whom are friends of his; and even then it is uncertain. But the visit should be *entirely* of an intimate nature. For the rest I thoroughly agree with your arguments. [...]

Yours faithfully
PE

378. Paul von Hatzfeldt to Holstein

28 November 1892

Dear friend,

I can subscribe *word for word* to the *English sentence* in your letter and you can therefore see that as usual we agree in principle. If you had any doubts about it, I cannot have expressed myself clearly in my last—very hastily written—letter.³

What caught my attention in the dispatch⁴ and what is still not clear to me, is *whether* and *if so why* you now consider the moment has come to raise the question here and to provoke a more or less binding statement about it.

---

[1] See also the brilliant testimonial given to Radolin by the Kaiser in his letter to the Tsar of 26 April 1895 when Radolin was made Ambassador to St Petersburg. (*Briefe Wilhelms II. an den Zaren, 1894–1914*, edited by Walter Goetz (Berlin, 1920).)
[2] Kaiser Wilhelm II visited Vienna from 11–13 October. In his letter to Eulenburg of 1 October, cited above, Holstein had advised that Eulenburg or Kiderlen accompany him.
[3] Not found.
[4] In a dispatch sent on 17 November, Marschall asked Hatzfeldt to find out the attitude of leading English statesmen towards a possible Russian advance on Constantinople and whether England would counter a Russian move against India by an action in the Black Sea. (*Grosse Politik*, vol. IX, no. 2127, pp. 88–9.)

I would ask you to note carefully in this connection that I—as I have already emphasised in my report[1]—do not in any way deny the existence of the opportunity if it is determined by reasons other than those already known to me, and that I only believe I should recommend the *postponement* of the question because of how matters stand *here*. It is my firm conviction that R[osebery] is at present wholly powerless to give me any kind of answer *as a Minister* without asking the others, and that the result would to-day undoubtedly not be satisfactory; it might on the contrary lead to R.'s resignation in case he wished to insist on giving us a satisfactory answer.

For *these* reasons, which you now know exactly from my very detailed report, I must—always presuming that there are no other compelling reasons—vote in favour of postponing the question until the spring when it will be possible to see whether the present company may be expected to remain in office for a long time. If this were the case, then in my opinion the moment would have arrived in which to put the question here clearly and definitely, and you need not worry yourself that I would fail to put it with the desired clarity. I think that—if as already said no other reasons exist—*up till then* it is in our interest to assist in *strengthening R.'s* position, for which purpose he is himself working very skilfully, and certainly not to render it more difficult. He is indeed not a *certain guarantee* that the right thing will meanwhile be done in *all* cases—I am far from wishing to assert that—but at least we know this much about him, that he *wants* to do the right thing, even if he cannot always admit it and perhaps cannot always get it put through, and especially that he will *prevent* damaging escapades. What we also know is that the Russians and French are not certain of peace so long as he is there, and that they will probably take care not to bring about any kind of crisis so long as they are not sure that the people here will put up with everything.

If however the Russians should really advance *on India*, which I do *not* believe, then I could only say: *tant mieux!* A real threat to India would achieve what we cannot achieve, namely it would drive public opinion over to the side of the Triple Alliance and make it impossible for Gl[adstone] to lean further towards France or Russia. If it came to war over it, we could wish for nothing better than that things should at first go badly for the English, for then they would be *compelled* to throw themselves into the arms of the Triple Alliance in order with its help to repair the damage in the Black Sea.

You see, dear friend, that at bottom we are as usual in agreement, with the sole difference that I want to gain three months' time for

[1] In his report no. 773 of 24 November Hatzfeldt replied that while he believed Lord Rosebery personally wished to maintain a firm policy towards Russia, Germany should not prejudice Rosebery's position within the Gladstone Cabinet by demanding definite statements on policy from him. Hatzfeldt recommended that Germany should wait until February or March 1893 to see whether the Gladstone Government could maintain itself in power before asking definite questions. (*Grosse Politik*, vol. VIII, no. 1744, pp. 93–6.) In his report no. 774 of 24 November Hatzfeldt said he thought every English government would counter a Russian move against India wherever it considered action practicable. (*Grosse Politik*, vol. IX, no. 2128, pp. 90–4.)

reasons of expediency, as I explained in my report in great detail. As to the question which will possibly have to be raised here eventually, I would like to ask whether, when it really comes to the point, we cannot and should not take action here in conjunction with our allies, *or at least with Austria*. The impression would surely be quite different if both Powers were simultaneously to say in a quite friendly manner here: 'We do not want anything from you and up to now have not demanded anything. But in continuing our present policy, which obliges us to bear increasingly heavy military burdens, we are also defending great English interests in the Near East, and therefore are indirectly defending India. We no longer want to bear these burdens alone or sacrifice our lives for English interests if England will not act with us, or does not recognise that English interests are involved. In that case, England should not be surprised if we for our part do not take these interests into account and prefer some sort of understanding with Russia and France (which, especially with the former, is certainly conceivable for Austria and ourselves) to the continuance of the present situation with its unforeseeable burdens and dangers.'

Now I ask you to believe, dear friend, that because I plead for a postponement for the above reasons, I am not therefore inactive in the matter in question. Here is an example. In the course of my latest conversation with R. we touched on former days and His Highness' [Bismarck's] policy. I made this an excuse to mention his theory about the division of the Near East into spheres of interest, and let fall a few remarks which *he* could interpret as though I did not consider it impossible *in the future* that Austria, if she could no longer carry the existing burdens, might recall this once rejected theory and withdraw her opposition. R. was *extremely impressed* by this notion and exclaimed: 'That is impossible if only because that would leave only Italy and England in the Mediterranean.' I laughingly replied that I was glad to hear from his own lips that Italy could rely on England's protection in the Mediterranean. And now you will see R.'s fear of my compromising remark: he was embarrassed and hastily said: 'No, no, I did not mean *that*—but she could count on the *possibility (la possibilité)* of our acting with her.' But my words gave him a shock and you can be certain that he will not forget it. On the following day I visited Ph. Currie[1] who asked me in the course of conversation whether I must not admit that R. was manoeuvering extremely skilfully, so that without saying a word or provoking a discussion with his colleagues he let everything continue as before in foreign policy, and meanwhile continually strengthened his position and independence. I answered that I certainly was astonished at R.'s skill, but that it was not easy to explain his position and the domestic reasons for his attitude to others on the Continent, or to convince them that R.'s stubborn reserve in regard to the great political questions could be combined with an intention to deal with those questions if they arose in the same manner as L[ord]

---

[1] Sir Philip Currie. Under Secretary of State in the Foreign Office, 1889–94; Ambassador in Constantinople, 1894–8, in Rome, 1898–1903.

S[alisbury] would have done. This remark will also find its way to R. and make him think.

Naturally such things are only intended to prepare the terrain for the eventuality that I should find myself in the position of being able to speak directly and frankly to R. about the situation, which I will naturally not fail to do if he gives me an opportunity. It may come sooner than I can foresee, since R. *likes to gossip with me*, and he has often asked me that if I wanted to talk to him I should not come on his regular day for receiving visitors so that we would have more time for gossip. I only want to avoid making him anxious and cautious by taking the direct initiative in such a question, and in this I hope you will agree that I am right.

I now pass to the second part of your letter which deals with our attitude to the general situation. *Certainly* it would not suit us if others withdrew from the game and left us 'in the lurch'. How much I share this opinion can best be seen by my reply to S[alisbury] at the time of his leaving office when, as you know, he foresaw a reconciliation between ourselves and the Russians. I told him then that in my private opinion this was not impossible if England under Gl[adstone] failed to appreciate her own interests;[1] but I would tell him even more in confidence, now that he was virtually a private individual: as a result of a mistaken and inactive policy here, a situation could arise in Europe which would even force me (whose political leanings he knew) to advise—if I were asked —that we, owing to the threat to our position from two fronts, should do everything in our power to seek a rapprochement with R[ussia].

This remark corresponds completely, I should add, to my honest opinion and I would not hesitate to act accordingly if the case cited really occurred. I would perhaps even go further than recommending that we 'sit still' if I have rightly understood this expression in your letter. We must in my opinion never let ourselves be *isolated* and must have a connection to the right *or* to the left. It also seems to me to be questionable whether merely sitting still would be enough to bring about the understanding with the R[ussians] which we would then need as a guarantee against other threatening dangers. We *must* of course be ready to make certain concessions—that seems clear to me at least— if we want to get out of the difficulty and into a situation in which we could concentrate our entire forces against the West. That was, as we know, H.H.'s very simple idea, about which he himself talked to me on many occasions. He said: 'The alliance between the Russians and France causes me no anxiety because I will always keep it within my power to purchase Russia's *neutrality* in the event of a Franco-German war, and we don't need anything more.' The calculation was absolutely correct and would probably even today still prove to be correct. It would only be a question of the *price* for such neutrality, and on closer inspection that would turn out to be pretty high. It can perhaps be summed up in the harmless sounding phrases: 'Germany has no direct interest in the Near East and can calmly look on if Constantinople falls

---

[1] See *Grosse Politik*, vol. VIII, no. 1744, pp. 93–6.

into Russian hands.' You know what I think about it and that in my eyes this is a fallacy. It is my firm conviction that, although we have only an indirect interest in the shaping of events in the Near East, this interest *is none the less great*, simply because the preservation of the Austrian Monarchy as a counter-balance to the hostile element of Pan-Slavism is of the utmost importance for us, and the advance of Russia to the Dardanelles, which would mean that all the Balkan countries would fall under Russian influence, would in all probability be the beginning of the end for Austria. Whether this happened with or without Austria's consent does not affect the final result either for us or for Austria, which already has trouble enough with its Slav populations. Therefore the statement would seem justified that for us a policy of sitting-still would not settle the matter and that we would have to pay an extraordinarily high price for Russia's friendship or her eventual neutrality—unless you believe she would be willing to settle for less, which is something of which I cannot as yet convince myself.

Notwithstanding all this I would, as I said, not hesitate under certain circumstances to follow this course either, if we were convinced that Austria and Italy were unreliable or really not sufficiently armed to the full extent of their capabilities, or that Gl.'s Government were firmly established here and that we could not count on its genuine co-operation under any circumstances, not even for England's own interests in the Near East and in the Mediterranean.

Do these hypothetical conditions already exist in whole or in part? If the train of thought I have developed is correct, this would be the question that would have to be answered before taking a decision to depart from the policy we have hitherto followed. My knowledge of the state of affairs in Vienna and Rome is naturally incomplete and I would be very grateful for any information. At the present I have only impressions on the subject which are perhaps wrong or unfounded. Of Italy I have the impression that up to now the influential people there are sincerely trying to fulfil their obligations towards us, and despite the pressure brought to bear on them are determined not to allow the army and navy to be weakened. In Vienna we have K[álnoky], with whom it is often difficult to deal because of his vanity. The Austrians may also make the mental reservation that for them it would be pleasanter and cheaper if Germany were to take upon her shoulders the greater burden for armaments. Does this unpleasant and perhaps not altogether loyal conduct justify the conclusion that Austria would possibly not come in with her whole strength even if the vital interests of the Austrian Monarchy were to be primarily at stake? I openly admit that I am unable to conceive of the possibility of such a suicidal delusion. As you will remember there was once under His Highness [Bismarck] a danger with regard to Vienna: this was that Austria might counter the well-known concept of the 'two irons in the fire' by deciding to come to a direct understanding with Russia—even at the cost of great sacrifices. I can see no other danger to-day, and that one is *meo voto* impossible as long as Austria is convinced of our loyalty to the alliance and of our loyal co-operation, and of this she can surely have had no doubt since the appointment of Caprivi.[1]

There remains England, and about the situation here I have expressed myself very fully. Allow me, while I am at it, to close with a commonplace which is nevertheless valuable for the light it throws on the whole problem. The very uncomfortable position in which we find ourselves to-day has been developing for a long time, and you and I, if I do not deceive myself, saw it coming long ago. Any child could have foreseen that the time *must come sometime*, as it did even earlier for Austria and Italy, when the burdens would be too expensive and too heavy to bear, *et tout cela* for the sake of a problematical peace in which, moreover, according to the predictions of competent military authorities, our military chances are steadily getting worse. Nothing could be done about that, and nobody could and would accept the responsibility for a breach of the peace. But I think we must make it clear to ourselves that this situation will inevitably become more and more uncomfortable the longer this armed and uncertain peace endures, and that the moment must inexorably come when everyone will have expended the last of his strength and can go no further. The crisis will then be inevitable unless one or another of the Powers, such as Russia through famine and nihilism, or France as the result of a socialist revolution, previously suffers an internal collapse and disappears from the game. I will say nothing about Austria and Italy who also do not stand on too firm a footing. It is dangerous however to look too far into the future, and I think we must restrict ourselves to the consideration of the possibility that is always with us that the crisis may suddenly burst upon us overnight at some point. In that case, the *great point* for us in my humble opinion is to know *beforehand* exactly *what* we want, not to be *surprised* by events, and *under no circumstances* to allow ourselves to be forced into an *isolated position*.

What I would like to repeat once more because I regard it as extremely important is: I do *not* believe in a serious advance by the Russians against India as things are to-day, and the English probably do not believe in it either—unfortunately! The Russians are not so stupid as to make such a mistake. What would be the consequences of it? 1. it would drive public opinion in England and even the weak Gl. into the other camp; 2. it would give the Triple Alliance, especially Austria, a better position, no matter how things went in India, since either (*a*) the attack on India is at first successful because of the weak English defences, in which case England *must*, in order to extricate herself from the affair, *seek* the friendship of the Triple Alliance for the purpose of continuing the struggle in a more favourable quarter; or (*b*) the Russians sustain defeats and are compelled to throw in all their forces, in which case the situation will be even better for us, and especially for

---

[1] See Kálnoky's dispatch to the Austro-Hungarian Ambassador in St Petersburg of 12 February 1893 in which the question of Germany's earlier rapprochement with Russia was raised and the prerequisites for a pacific policy on the part of Austria. (Hermann, *Dreibund, Zweibund, England*, pp. 157–8.)

Austria, which will perhaps get an opportunity of making good Andrássy's mistake of not dictating to the Russians sword in hand when they were helplessly bogged down in Turkey.

There is a great deal more that causes me deep concern. But you are doubtless already sufficiently appalled by the amount of reading that has been forced upon you, and I will therefore at last release you. I hope you will accept as an excuse for my long report and this equally long 'outpouring' the fact that I am dealing with the most important question that faces us, and that I feel the full weight of my responsibility for every opinion I have expressed.

Finally, I just want to say that I also agree with you that for the present we must drop the idea of an agreement with the S[ultan] over Eg[ypt], unless R[osebery] sooner or later feels strong enough to express a desire for it himself. This will hardly escape our notice, and in that case we will have to think it over again.

Meanwhile I would *very* much like to know how Rad[olin] found things in C[onstantinople]. If he manoeuvres correctly, as I expect he will, he must shortly be in a position to enjoy the confidence of the Sultan (who likes him personally) without having to put himself *en avant*.

Kindest regards.

If you think it can be of any service, it goes without saying that you can make use of this letter in whole or in part as you please.

1893

379. Holstein to Karl von Eisendecher[1]

1 January 1893

Dear Eisendecher,

Many thanks for your good wishes. I need them, for in the course of this month my left eye is to be operated on for cataract and it seems to me that under the circumstances I cannot remain very much longer in the Service.[2] Kiderlen already does most of the work. I predict a great career for him if he remains in good health.

I wish you, dear friend, good health above all. As you see, once again nothing has come of the *revirement*.

Your old friend
Holstein.

380. Holstein to Kaiser Wilhelm II

Draft

Berlin, 26 January 1893

Most [gracious and all-powerful Kaiser!]
Most [gracious Kaiser, King and Lord!]

A half blind but very loyal subject lays his best wishes at the feet of Your Majesty[3] and at the same time offers his thanks for to-day's gracious recognition. May Your Majesty be granted to use the exceptional gifts that Providence has conferred upon you for the good of the Reich. May the nation recognise what it possesses in Your Majesty.

In this latter regard I venture a respectful word of advice: Let Your Majesty cause the sunshine of your favour to shine more widely than hitherto. A bullet penetrates more deeply, but grapeshot is useful for a closely packed crowd. Nobody knew that better than Your Majesty's deceased Grandfather. If Your Majesty were to talk to fifty people for two minutes, instead of to ten people for ten minutes, you would have forty more enthusiastic supporters who would proclaim far and wide: 'He spoke to me!' An extract of loyalty gained in such a way should not be missing from any monarchical household in these times of republican epidemics.

In the event that Your Majesty should deem it necessary to bring to

---

[1] From the Eisendecher Papers.
[2] Holstein's eye was operated on successfully in March 1893. See Rogge, *Friedrich von Holstein*, pp. 162–3.
[3] For the Kaiser's birthday on 27 January.

the cognisance of the undersigned, who must helplessly submit to it, the All-Highest displeasure owing to any possible breach of regulations, nobody would be more suited to be the executor of this penal order—both for his natural gifts and for abilities learnt at Court—than Count Phil. Eulenburg (I ask that you graciously take note of the Christian name).

Now a final request; namely that Your Majesty most graciously tear this letter, which has no claim to historical preservation, into quite tiny pieces *immediately*. For I distrust the Imperial writing-table in regard to discretion, just as I distrust everything that I do not know well.

In most profound veneration I remain
Your Imperial and Royal Majesty's
Most humble and most faithful
H[1]

381. Bernhard von Bülow to Holstein

Bucharest, 3 February 1893

Dear Holstein,

I have seen with sincere regret from your friendly letter of the 21st of last month that your eye trouble has become more serious than I had thought. I heartily hope that the coming operation will prove successful.

My wife and I know of many cases in which cataract has been operated on successfully and the operation resulted in the restoration of normal vision. Our very experienced German family doctor here tells me that the relatively easy operation for cataract almost invariably proves successful.

At all events I would like to tell you that our best wishes accompany you. That you could leave the Service is a thought that you—permit me in this instance to violate the '*Ne sutor supra crepidam*'—should never entertain and that all those who have the interests of the Service and the country at heart must at all events protest against. Apart from objective considerations, I want you to stay on above all because of my personal attachment to and admiration for you, which stem from memories of my apprentice years in Paris; ever since that time I have owed you a debt of gratitude, which the passage of time has not lessened, for the unforgettable stimulus and help of every sort that you gave me. I can hardly

---

[1] Marginal Comment by Holstein: 'Since then he has actually seen more people.' As a convinced monarchist, Holstein was much concerned about the weakening of the monarchy under Wilhelm II, a concern that is evident in his letters to Eulenburg during this period. Holstein sharply censured the Kaiser's passion for travel, his dislike of serious work, his frivolous attitude towards affairs of state, his delight in smut, and his utter lack of reliability. He complained about the Kaiser's irresponsible interference in foreign policy, and he repeatedly warned Eulenburg against any attempt on the part of the Kaiser to increase his personal authority by a *coup d'état*. His efforts to rule Germany as an absolute despot had already gone too far. 'Nowadays no European nation is ruled in the way he is ruling,' Holstein said. 'He is not the man and this is not the time to play with a nation as though it were a big toy.' Holstein had grave doubts as to whether Wilhelm II would die on the throne, but he thought it more likely that a republic would succeed the monarchy than that the German Reich would collapse altogether. Wilhelm II was making the whole world nervous. 'He is walking on the edge of a precipice [...] while under attack from the great statesman whom he dismissed.' (From the Eulenburg Papers.)

visualise the Foreign Ministry without you and I hold firmly to the hope that the operation will bring about a complete cure. [...]

                          Always your faithfully devoted

                                          Bernh. Bülow

382. Paul von Hatzfeldt to Holstein

22 March 1893

Dear friend,

[...] You will remember that a few months ago I sent you a long letter[1] in which I expressed the opinion, which you shared at the time, that *if* Gladstone remained in office it would be advisable to let the people here see in a tactful way that if they expect *favours* from us, we would expect reciprocity from them.[2] For my part, I still hold to this opinion, and it seems to me that since the great decision on the Home Rule question is still impending, on which the existence of the present Cabinet depends, it would be advisable to begin to consider the position we intend to take here.

To begin with, I can surely assume that there can be no question for us of changing the course of our major policy, since this is rendered virtually impossible by our position within the Triple Alliance. There are however, a good many nonpolitical questions, or questions which have very little to do with politics, in which we might or might not do England a good turn without its conflicting with the political principles of the Triple Alliance, while England can help us on many similar points if she has the honest desire to do so. It is to *this* sphere that my proposal refers.

Furthermore, from my knowledge of conditions and personalities here, I am of the opinion that it would be highly impractical, if not the greatest mistake, to try to secure the support of the Gladstone Cabinet in questions like those I have just indicated by confronting it either openly or in a disguised form with the prospect of a change of policy in the event of a refusal. First of all they would not believe that we were serious, and besides I cannot avoid a feeling of concern that Ro[sebery], who is *extremely sensitive and resentful personally*, might *ultimately* be pushed into an undesirable course by *repeated* threats of this kind.

But I go even further and believe that we will achieve more in the above-mentioned sphere, where we are dealing with a question of mutual *favours*, if we abandon the method of *announcing in advance* that unpleasant things will happen if the principle of reciprocity is not observed.

My proposal would be that in every area where England has been accustomed to small favours from us, we instruct our representatives always to wait until their English colleagues have expressed a wish, and then to reply with the greatest friendliness that they have no instructions, but do not doubt that the wish would be fulfilled if the

---

[1] Of 28 November 1892. See above.
[2] See Rosebery's dispatch to Malet of 11 January 1893 dealing with Anglo-German relations. (Bayer, *England und der Neue Kurs*, pp. 113–14.)

English Government were to drop a hint about it, either through Malet or through me, *in Berlin*.

This would be understood here immediately, and then they would have the choice either of dispensing with the favour or of coming to us —most probably the latter. Our position would thus be *far more favourable* than if *we* are always obliged to formulate our wishes here which can conveniently be shelved if they cannot say Yes and do not want to say No. Suppose, for example, that a case were to arise similar to the recent one in Cairo, and that Leyden[1] expressed himself as I have suggested and Ro. then came to see me about it.[2] I would reply in the most friendly way : so you want us to do you a favour? Certainly, with the greatest pleasure, for that goes without saying between friendly governments. And that reminds me of something I had just wanted to speak to you about : we too have a small request with which you might help us. If I take it upon myself to see that your request is fulfilled, perhaps you would allow me to report that you will fulfil our request with the same readiness.

Believe me, our position would thereby be incomparably better than by continuing the system of general and vague threats which was already used by His Highness [Bismarck].

As I already mentioned, there would in my opinion be time enough to operate in this way if the development of events here forces upon us the conviction that a change of Cabinets cannot be expected in the near future, which is something I do not at present believe will happen. Since we may soon know one way or another, and since new questions may come up on the matter of 'favours', it would be very useful to me to find out soon whether my proposal is approved in general, and whether I should act in accordance with it here.

Best wishes

H.

383. Paul von Hatzfeldt to Holstein

Cowes,[3] 2 August 1893

Dear friend,

[...] As I had expected the latest crisis[4] has come to nothing and it

[1] Casimir, Count von Leyden. First Secretary at the German Embassy in London, 1888–1890; Consul General in Cairo, 1890–3; Minister in Bucharest, 1893–7, in Tokio, 1898–1901, in Stockholm, 1901–5.

[2] Leyden reported in December 1892 that the Egyptian Government had asked the Powers for permission to devote the sum of 60,000 Egyptian pounds annually from the savings derived from the conversion of the privileged debt for the purpose of increasing the strength of the army. Marschall instructed Hatzfeldt to inform Rosebery that Germany was ready to give her consent if England desired it. (*Grosse Politik*, vol. VIII, no. 1814, p. 184.) On 6 January 1893 Leyden was instructed to tell Lord Cromer that the unfriendly English attitude towards German railroad construction interests in Asia Minor compelled Germany to withhold her permission for an increase in the strength of the Egyptian army. (*Grosse Politik*, vol. VIII, no. 1816, pp. 185–6.) When Rosebery expressed his concern over Germany's changed attitude, Hatzfeldt asked him to co-operate 'in overcoming the existing difficulties'. (*Grosse Politik*, vol. VIII, no. 1818, p. 187.)

[3] Kaiser Wilhelm II was at Cowes on the Isle of Wight from 27 July to 8 August for the Cowes Regatta.

[4] Frontier incidents between Siam and France in May 1893 led to the dispatch of two French gunboats to Siam. The gunboats reached Bangkok in July and were fired upon by Siamese

almost seems as if the French demand that the English gunboats should withdraw from Bangkok[1] was either never made at all or else only by the French Admiral, and could therefore be disavowed in Paris. At all events my other assumption has also proved to be correct, namely that the slightest firmness in London would be enough in such cases to bring the French to a standstill and to a policy of greater moderation. This experience will not have been lost upon Rosebery and will encourage him to show greater firmness in any similar incidents.

Although the whole situation today seems to indicate that no further serious development is to be expected, I still do not regret that the day before yesterday I sent you such a detailed telegram and presented my opinion on questions about which I think we have to make up our minds once and for all.[2] I would therefore even to-day think it highly desirable that the Chancellor should express an opinion on these questions, and that I should receive as full and comprehensive an elucidation as possible, since my entire behaviour towards Rosebery must be determined by it. Do not let us make any mistake about the fact that as things are, the hints that I eventually give to Rosebery about the course to be adopted have an almost decisive effect upon him. If, however, on some possible future occasion, I were through my advice to put him on the wrong track or one that did not correspond to our wishes because I was not sufficiently well-informed about our possible decisions, the ensuing damage would be wellnigh irreparable.

Up to now I have only received from you a telegraphic reply to the first part of my long telegram of the 31st, but not to the second and more important part of it.[3] But I have the impression from your letter of the 29th that *the moment England was really at war with France* you would favour the unconditional support of England by Italy, whom we would then have to support. I do not know whether I altogether understand your ideas and their implications, but would like even now to draw attention to the fact that we would thereby in no way escape the risk, which you have hitherto rightly borne in mind, that we would be left in the lurch by Mr Gladstone after we had pulled *his* chestnuts out of the fire, and that we would then find ourselves in the situation of having to

batteries. On 20 July the French Government presented an ultimatum to the Siamese Government demanding the cession of all Siamese territory east of the Mekong river. The Siamese Government rejected the ultimatum and the French Government ordered a blockade of the Siamese coast. The situation caused a crisis in Anglo-French relations because England wished to preserve Siam as a buffer between Burma and French Indo-China. On 1 August the Siamese Government yielded to renewed French demands and the crisis came to an end. A Franco-Siamese Treaty was signed on 2 October 1893.

[1] On the night of 31 July Queen Victoria sent a dispatch from Lord Rosebery to Kaiser Wilhelm II which ran: 'French Government demands that we withdraw our gunboats from Bangkok. I have refused this request. Desire to see Count Hatzfeldt immediately in London.' Kaiser Wilhelm II interpreted this dispatch as indicating a serious danger of war between England and France, in which England would find herself obliged to appeal to German assistance. (*Grosse Politik*, vol. VIII, no. 1752, pp. 107–8; Haller, *Eulenburg*, pp. 88–90.)

[2] On 31 July Hatzfeldt telegraphed to the Foreign Ministry that illness had prevented him from seeing Lord Rosebery, but that the delay was welcome because he wanted to know what official reply he was to make to Rosebery about Germany's attitude. (*Grosse Politik*, vol. VIII, no. 1753, pp. 108–10.)

[3] The reply was drafted by Holstein. (*Grosse Politik*, vol. VIII, nos. 1756–7, pp. 113–16.)

face the consequences without England. If you want me to, I will gladly develop these ideas more fully. But you must surely agree with me that if war broke out between France and England, and Italy then took England's side with Germany behind her, Mr Gladstone would have no scruples about using this as a means of bringing pressure to bear on France to make a separate peace with England and leaving us to bear the brunt. It seems to me that there cannot be any question but that the French would enter with pleasure into an arrangement which would result in the withdrawal of England and her fleet, which is still greatly feared, and would permit them to attack Italy and ourselves with their whole strength—perhaps increased by the addition of the Russian army.

There is on the other hand no doubt in my mind that if a war with France really appeared to be imminent, Rosebery would see the necessity and have the desire to establish firmly the fact of England's close association with the Triple Alliance. I therefore believe—provided that a case of unavoidable war should really arise here—that we would not even encounter serious difficulties if I were to answer his question about our attitude by saying that we would be glad to advise Italy to come to the active support of England—in which case, as he knew, we would then have to support Italy—if we were given the guarantee that England, for whose sake we had entered the fight, would remain at our side to the end. It seems to me that in such a case the principal and indispensable condition would be an unconditional guarantee by the British Cabinet that it would not conclude any separate peace with France and her allies without the agreement of Britain's allies.

I might perhaps speak otherwise if Salisbury were in control of English policy, but I think that even in that case I would support a serious attempt to reach an agreement which, even though it served no other purpose, would afford *him* the means by which to remain firm in the face of possible fluctuations in public opinion and in Parliament.

From what I have seen, I do not believe, as I said, that war will break out, not so much because the people here would not make such a decision under any circumstances, but because in Paris they will, as I predicted, give in the moment they see the slightest signs of firmness here; it is because they do not feel certain of Russian support after all and are therefore trying to avoid having the affair develop into a European war. The chances that a conflict may yet break out therefore lie only in the possibility that the French Cabinet will fall, or that some unforeseen incident may occur to inflame anew the public opinion on both sides. [...]

Best wishes
PH.

384. Paul von Hatzfeldt to Holstein

London, 7 August 1893

Dear friend,

Since the official courier who should have left this evening was sent off earlier while I was away, I could not avail myself of that opportunity of writing to you. Kiderlen will send you these lines from Heligoland.

I. H.M. spent nearly one and a half hours with me this morning and was in full and ready agreement with my opinion on *all* questions that are dealt with in my long telegram of the 5th[1] and in the replies to it sent to me from Berlin.[2] Since the Foreign Ministry is also in agreement with me, I now know what I shall possibly have to do. *Until then*—and this H.M. most expressly approved—I will as far as possible have to avoid making it appear as if we wanted to *exert pressure*, namely because (1) it would make the people here gun-shy; and (2) because the latest events have shown that at the slightest feeling of being threatened the people here will take a stand *of their own accord*, and in that case our situation in regard to the guarantees we intend to demand would be incomparably better.

II. H.M.'s conversation with Ro[sebery] after the recent dinner in Osb[orne].

H.M. assures me that in the course of the conversation, which in any case only lasted about ten minutes, nothing much was said about the situation, and H.M. refrained from expressing any views of his own from which any conclusion could have been drawn as to his intentions.

H.M. was particularly struck by the fact that R. repeatedly let fall the remark that the crisis was only *temporarily* over.

III. The grandmother,[3] whom I had not seen at all up till now on account of my illness, summoned me to-day to a brief private audience, and as we were alone she talked to me *quite confidentially*, also about the situation.

At first she very warmly praised Ro., whose position was difficult. He had some, though not all, of his colleagues against him. But he possessed the necessary strength if a serious question arose to hold fast to what he held to be right. When I observed that Gladstone seemed not to bother much about foreign policy and also to have little understanding for it, she strongly agreed and—with an expression showing the very reverse of esteem—said that she had recently tried to speak with him about the serious current problems, but that he had behaved as though he were completely at a loss. She therefore assumed that he would not interfere and would let Ro. alone.

What specially struck me was that Grandmama—just as in the case of Ro. to H.M.—repeatedly remarked that the crisis was *only temporarily* over. With regard to her neighbours she seemed to be as annoyed as she was mistrustful, and on one occasion the un-parliamentary expression 'impudent' escaped her in speaking of their actions.

We then spoke about the Mediterranean and the demonstration by the Russian Fleet.[4] At first she did not seem to take this too seriously, described it rather as something incomprehensible. But when I let fall

---

[1] Apparently an error on the part of Hatzfeldt, because no telegram from Hatzfeldt of 5 August was found either in the files of the Foreign Ministry or in those of the German Embassy in London. (See *Grosse Politik*, vol. VIII, no. 1753, pp. 108–10.)

[2] *Grosse Politik*, vol. VIII, nos. 1756–7, pp. 113–16.   [3] Queen Victoria.

[4] Hatzfeldt refers to the forthcoming visit of the Russian Fleet to Toulon.

the harmless remark that its significance, if any, surely depended upon whether the affair took on a permanent character, she became excited and exclaimed twice in succession : 'But that cannot be allowed.'

She mentioned with pleasure that the young Pharoah,[1] who had achieved nothing in C[onstantinople], had now given satisfactory assurances here.[2] I remarked that I had heard—and H.M., who knew him, had confirmed this—that the young man was quite uncommonly sly and adroit. He had obviously quickly understood that nothing could be gained in C. and that he must seek support elsewhere. The temptation to seek such support not here but in Fr[ance] will almost certainly soon be offered him, and then it will be a question of what he will do. She replied : 'But he will get little enough from France!'

The remainder of the conversation turned on personal and unimportant matters. The preceding remarks of Grandmama, which she would certainly not have made to any other foreigner, I naturally ask to be kept *strictly secret*, which does not mean that if you think it useful you should not read them to the Chancellor or Herr von M[arschall]. Otherwise please keep them absolutely secret. [...]

Good-bye for today, dear friend, let me hear from you soon again.

Best wishes.

385. Paul von Hatzfeldt to Holstein

17 September 1893

Dear friend,

Since I found out from the telegraph office that my telegram to you[3] actually reached you, I conclude from your silence that you are unable to give me the proposed rendezvous. I am sorry for many reasons. I would have *very* much liked to see you, and it would certainly have been good to have been able to talk over much about which one cannot easily write.

In regard to Ems nobody knows better than I how useful it would be for me, and nobody can more greatly regret that it cannot be done. There are private reasons of which I was not previously aware that have absolutely compelled me to abandon it. In every other respect I am looking after my health as much as I can. After I got over the afterpains of Cowes I have not been at all unwell, and I feel myself physically and morally able to do as much work here as anybody else for a long time to come. Obviously I have the greatest confidence not only in your friendship but in your judgment and your knowledge of affairs, and

---

[1] Abbas Hilmi II, Khedive of Egypt, 1892–1914. On 15 January 1893 the Khedive had dismissed three Ministers whom he had considered too submissive to England. On 18 January he yielded to English pressure and appointed a Ministry approved by England.

[2] The Khedive had gone to Constantinople to visit the Sultan on 10 July. According to a telegram from Radolin on 20 July, the Khedive had suggested that the Sultan address a Circular Note to the Powers requesting their intervention in bringing about a settlement of the dispute over the respective rights of the Sultan and the Khedive in Egypt. On 21 July Radolin was instructed to inform the Sultan that raising the Egyptian Question at the present time would be extremely dangerous. (*Grosse Politik*, vol. VIII, no. 1843, p. 213 and note *.) On 24 July Rosebery thanked Count Hatzfeldt for Germany's aid in influencing the Sultan. (*Grosse Politik*, vol. VIII, no. 1845, p. 214.)   [3] Not found.

therefore have no doubt that starving heirs are doing their best to unseat me. Nevertheless I am doubtful whether for the present they will find in H.M. favourable terrain for such intrigues. As you know I had a long talk with H.M. before his departure. I laid before him my views on the situation in considerable detail, and also on our tasks here as I see them, and I met with the *most complete* agreement. Still more (please treat this information *strictly* confidential) H.M. repeatedly said to me at the close: 'Should you find that the reserve you feel is still indicated here, and with which I fully agree, meets with doubts in the Wilhelmstrasse, or if they try to force you out of your reserve, then write to me *direct* without hesitation and I will see to it that you have no difficulties.'

I do not need to tell you of all people, dear friend, that I have neither made use of this unsought for permission nor mentioned it in Berlin, where it would have caused unpleasantness. As you know it is not in my nature to tread secret paths, and least of all would I do this in regard to Capr[ivi], whose confidence I believe I have earned. If that should change, which I hope will not be the case, I would then have to consider whether I should make use of this permission, but then I would also openly say so.

At all events I cannot suppose after the frank exchange of views in Cowes that H.M. feels any ill-feeling towards me. I can believe this all the less because—I add this in the strictest confidence—I have just rendered him a not inconsiderable service in a very delicate family affair and he recently sent me his warmest thanks for my endeavours in that regard.

It is completely clear to me—and I believe to you too—that there are people in the Foreign Ministry who are inferior in every respect, who are my enemies as well as yours, and the enemies of our friends. Their subterranean intrigues may become dangerous if one allows them to go on for too long. On this question I can only say: *avisez*, so that this subterranean danger does not become greater. In this connection, believe me, I am far more concerned about the *political* than the personal danger, for political danger would appear soon enough if these people ever gained power and authority. I could defend myself readily enough, but the political damage would be immeasurable.

As a proof of how gladly I listen to your advice, look at my last long report in which I presented to the best of my ability my views as to my present task.[1] In this connection, I would like to note that my view in Cowes as to the reserve to be observed here for the time being has been corroborated to an extent far greater than I had expected. At present R[osebery] is obviously afraid of being too friendly to us and of being pushed too far, though he reserves the possibility of throwing himself into our arms again in case of need. I would regard it as infinitely wrong and injurious to show anything but reserve towards him, or to take any kind of initiative. The people here must learn to see that if they recognise their own interest and meet *us* honourably, we will fulfil our

---

[1] See *Grosse Politik*, vol. VIII, no. 1759, pp. 117–19.

part as before, but that until then we will not run after them and *possibly* —that is to say if they are determined to follow an equivocal policy— will even be able to get along without England. R. especially must be given the feeling that we have confidence in him *personally* but that we conclude from his behaviour that he has to contend with great difficulties, and that until he has overcome them and gained the upperhand we will not press him in any way; until that time, however, we have no intention of setting foot on the oscillating plank of English friendship.

If we act according to this precept, which in my firm opinion is the only right one for the time being, then *if* the case arises that they need our friendship they must make the *first* step, and then our situation would be *incomparably* better. If the case does not arise we lose absolutely nothing by our present restraint, for you may rely on it that as long as the present anxiety and irresolution persist here no pressure on our part will produce any result.

I need hardly assure you that I do not consider my political wisdom to be infallible. But you may believe me when I say that I have a pretty exact knowledge of the situation here, especially of my friend R. with his good qualities *and his singularities*.

Although I would like to spare you from having to read a too lengthy letter, allow me to illustrate my ideas by a few examples. Some newspapers have announced that a visit by the English fleet to Italian ports is being considered[1]—an idea that *I* gave to R. before Cowes and that I had trouble in making plausible to him. Since his return from Hamburg, despite the fact that I have seen him repeatedly and we have talked freely about all sorts of things, he has *not let a word* escape him about this matter.[2] Furthermore he has not said anything whatever about the negotiations over Siam that are still in progress in Paris, the extent of the English demands, etc, and the *sole* remark which I have been able to extract from him on this subject since his return was the statement that Develle[3] was doing his utmost to evade Dufferin's communications by staying away. Nor has R. since then returned to his former favourite topics—the state of affairs in the Black Sea, Turkey, or Egypt.

I am as you know at present far from thinking that R. has changed his whole political outlook, and believe only that he has temporarily applied the brakes for opportunistic reasons and for the sake of his own position. But even if this assumption is correct, it is in my humble opinion sufficient to draw the correct conclusion about the present attitude of Gladstone and some of his colleagues in order to impose upon ourselves the greatest reserve and abstention from any initiative with regard to European politics.

I flatter myself that *you* will agree with me. The attempts of the above-mentioned inferior Great Men in the Foreign Ministry to explain my reserve—the result of careful reflection—by charging me with

[1] An English naval squadron under the command of Admiral Seymour visited Taranto from 16 to 20 October 1893.

[2] See Hatzfeldt's dispatch to Caprivi of 19 September. (*Grosse Politik*, vol. VIII, no. 1760, pp. 119–22.)

[3] Jules-Paul Develle. French Minister for Foreign Affairs in Dupuy's Cabinet, 1893.

incompetence and lack of zeal is something that accords so little with my whole past history that I refuse to be irritated. If these people are not taught their place and succeed in making their influence felt without my being able to find protection from them, then indeed I must think over a resolute and energetic defence against such slanders.

In the event that I do not receive any other definite instructions, I will abstain from any initiative in regard to international affairs. Up to now Ro. has not taken any initiative either. In addition, we are now approaching the slack season. There is not a human being of any importance in town. R. goes shortly to Balmoral and will then stay on his estates in Scotland *provided* that no new difficulties in Paris demand his return here. In that case I cannot with the best will in the world for the present write interesting political reports unless I am to invent them to please Raschdau.

Finally, dear friend, I must say a few words about colonial policy since it is related to international policy, and ask you to read the lengthy dispatch sent to me some days ago on that subject,[1] if you have not already done so.

Nobody disputes less than I the unfriendliness—which I had always expected—of the Colonial Office under Gladstone's administration; I agree with the presentation of the case in the dispatch and with the conclusion that we should not conceal our displeasure. Although I can obey an order that is given to me in regard to policy and its execution, I cannot give up all claim to a dissenting opinion or to tell you about it confidentially.[2]

As you will remember from our correspondence about this same question at the beginning of the year,[3] we were then completely in agreement that we should not *threaten* the people here with reprisals in Egypt or elsewhere, but must show by our *actions* that we intend to repay their unfriendliness in the same coin. The statement which Leyden was ordered to make in Cairo at the time[4] did not fail its effect, as we know, even though the language used towards Malet in Berlin (about which I only know from hearsay) may have been a little too severe, and as I sensed here, R. felt almost personally insulted by it.[5]

The latest dispatch now reverts to the earlier standpoint, which you and I at the time recognised as erroneous, namely, to give the people here an *avertissement* which, even though clothed in friendly language, is to indicate a change in our *political* attitude. After reading the dispatch you will agree with me that in executing *this* instruction, no matter how much I may twist or turn, and no matter how much I may emphasise our personal regard for R., it will in effect amount solely to a

[1] Rotenhan to Hatzfeldt, 10 September 1893. (*Grosse Politik*, vol. VIII, no. 2018, pp. 402–5.)

[2] In the dispatch of 10 September, cited above, Rotenhan wrote: 'If the unfriendliness of English officials in colonial matters continues, we will not be able to avoid exercising greater reserve in our general political relations with England than we would otherwise do or than we ourselves (apart from colonial affairs) would wish. I request Your Excellency to talk over these matters with Lord Rosebery in a friendly way at a suitable opportunity.'

[3] See above, Hatzfeldt's letter of 22 March 1893.

[4] See above, p. 434, note 2.   [5] See *Grosse Politik*, vol. XIVii, no. 3966, pp. 453–4.

threat against the *Government*, and will undoubtedly be understood by R. in that sense. But instead of being flattered or pacified by the friendly remarks addressed to himself, he will, as I know from experience, on the contrary object that *he* always, and nearly always successfully, took the greatest trouble to secure the fulfilment of our wishes by the Colonial Office and that therefore a change of attitude on our part in foreign policy, which shatter precisely *his* position, would be a *personal* and *insulting injustice* to *him*. I have not the slightest doubt that he would interpret it in this way.

Under these circumstances I can only urgently recommend the abandonment of an *avertissement* in this sense, and in case no improvement takes place here in regard to the treatment of colonial questions, to show by our actions that we must insist upon reciprocity. *First* of all I would, if possible, restrict myself to the colonial sphere, and I should think that in Africa, where our interests frequently clash, we could find an opportunity of doing the English a service and therefore also of doing them a disservice and being disagreeable. Only *secondarily* would I think it desirable again to choose Egypt for a demonstration of displeasure, because the matter would therewith immediately come into the sphere of major policy and on a question about which England is particularly sensitive. For that reason it would assume here the character of an unfriendly political act, and would deeply hurt Lord Rosebery in particular who is looked on here as our friend.

In *each* instance, even if it be Egypt because we really found no suitable opportunity in Africa, we must in my opinion neither *threaten beforehand* nor, if we make a demonstration at some point, allow ourselves to be drawn into expositions and declarations about our behaviour. My friend R. will, as on the last occasion in Cairo, immediately discern our motive and either himself draw the moral or ask for an explanation. In the latter case it would be easy, even if it were a matter of some colonial discourtesy, to answer that the Colonial Division is now just as independent of the Foreign Ministry as the Colonial Office is of the Foreign Office; like R. with his Minister for the Colonies, we could *ask* our Colonial Division to reconsider a matter if we considered it important, but that just like Rosebery, we could never do so with any guarantee of success. If only for this reason, it would be advisable that we for our part should also restrict ourselves to the colonial sphere.

What I will do in the meantime if I have the opportunity is to express to Ph. Currie, who understands *à demi mot* and immediately repeats everything to R., my *personal* anxiety lest we should again have trouble with the Reichstag because of the unaccommodating attitude of the Colonial Office.[1]

Now good-bye for today, dear friend, do not be angry with me for this long expectoration and please let me have news soon. I hope your holiday in the mountains did you a lot of good.

Kindest regards
PH.

[1] See *Grosse Politik*, vol. VIII, no. 2019, pp. 405–9.

386. Paul von Hatzfeldt to Holstein

London, 19 October 1893

Dear friend,

I do not for a moment believe *at the present time* in any attempt by the Russians to force the Straits. Their faith in the *misère* here does *not yet* go so far. Later *je ne dis pas*, provided that by that time further proofs of weakness here make them *certain* that they can permit themselves to do so without being punished. But then the Russian Fleet will sail in from the Black Sea, and that is what one calls *jouer le tout pour le tout*—for then it will not be a matter of England alone, but of Austria and in the second place of her friends. For England it will then be a question not of Constantinople alone but of the whole Mediterranean, and nobody can give the Russians a guarantee that even present-day England will sit quiet, especially since *then* she will not need to fight alone, and even if we were able to sit still, she would be standing *dos à dos* with Austria and with Italy.

Nothing will happen about Morocco at present as far as one can see, and consequently I have only a slight interest in it. Here too they want only peace and the *status quo* for the time being, and the new English representative has been repeatedly instructed to maintain a very calm and cautious attitude and thereby gradually to build up good relations with the Sultan. [...]

I fully agree with your opinion that the miserable weakness shown here in regard to Siam, etc, will encourage others, above all the French, to become more and more insolent, and you will see from my to-day's reports that Rosebery *himself expects this*.[1] What makes him gloomy makes me pleased as Punch. I would give much if I were quite certain that the French would become downright impertinent as a result of Russia's embraces and tread heavily on the corns of the English everywhere—Egypt, Madagascar, Tuat, etc, etc. That is the most likely chance—and by no means beyond the bounds of possibility—that they will really get angry here one of these days and that Rosebery will compel the Grand Old Man and his followers to keep quiet. The English as you know are peculiar people, and a government here can possibly give away a great deal without the public, which by and large is stupid, understanding what it is doing. But if I understand the people here, they will not swallow an impertinence even in form. Let us hope that the French in their frenzy push matters to that point—be it over Egypt or anything else. I for my part would do all I can to help things along, for I think we are agreed that nothing would be better than that the *first* shot on the peace of Europe should be fired from English or French guns.

Do not think that because he has horses at Newmarket Rosebery is simply simulating depression. When business is over, he is an English-

---

[1] In two reports on conversations with Lord Rosebery and Sir Philip Currie, Hatzfeldt stated that Rosebery had expressed great concern about the future, since after the visit of the Russian Fleet to Toulon he expected that France would be less conciliatory towards England. (From the Foreign Ministry files.)

man and does not allow himself as we do to be prevented by political worries from enjoying life. Especially, and above all, he is *un ambitieux*, and if he can find an opportunity of tripping up his political enemies and of playing a great part over their dead bodies he will quite certainly do so.

Ceterum censeo let me for the present act here as I see fit: gentle encouragement but no initiative. If it does no good—and that does not depend on us but on the French—it can at any rate do no harm. In case Roseb. resigns, or is forced to resign, we can always throw the whole crowd overboard. [...]

Kindest regards and always yours
PH.

387. Paul von Hatzfeldt to Holstein

London, 8 November 1893

Dear friend,

Ph. Currie is back and I paid him a visit yesterday. [...]

In the course of our entirely confidential conversation (during which Currie continually showed a lively desire to establish confidential relations between ourselves and Ro[sebery]), I found an opportunity to recall former days and to remind him of Salisbury's words when leaving office: *quand je reviendrai je suppose que je vous trouverai dans les bras de la Russie.* Without stressing the point, I let him see a certain anxiety on my part that this prophecy might be fulfilled some day after all, *if* they continued to behave as they were doing now. Times were serious, as Ro. had recently emphasised, our position was imperilled from several sides, and everyone must sometime finally make up his mind where his safety lay, etc. All this was of course expressed as my personal opinion, and not at all as a threat but rather as a painful concern lest the result of my long years of work here—the drawing together of our two countries —should in time be seriously endangered by the wretched policy of the present Cabinet (not Rosebery's).

This trend of thought was extremely distasteful to Currie, who sincerely desires political co-operation between us. He took the greatest trouble to prove to me (1) that Ro. had the best intentions and was unchanged; (2) but that it would be the *greatest misfortune* if he were forced to resign and were replaced by one of Gl[adstone]'s radical friends, Kimberley[1] or somebody else, who could perhaps direct foreign policy here into wrong paths from which it might subsequently be very difficult to turn back. He hinted that as long as one could not 'get rid of' Gl., one should be glad to have Ro., who was the only person who wanted to carry on Sal.'s policy and who, even though he could not always secure the acceptance of his wishes, at all events would prevent a real change in the course that has hitherto been followed.

[1] John Wodehouse, Earl of Kimberley. Secretary of State for India and Lord President of the Council, 1892–4; Secretary of State for Foreign Affairs in Lord Rosebery's Cabinet, 1894–5.

Since I had to avoid that Currie, in reporting our conversation to Ro., should make it appear that *I* was *opposed* to him (Ro.) *personally*, I agreed that we could never have a better or even as good a successor, spoke in a very friendly way about him, and expressed the best intentions of obliging and helping him personally to the best of my ability—always with the small reservation that if he clung to his reserve with regard to the discussion of problems I could not and would not press them, and must leave it to him whether he wished to maintain contact with us or not.

I hope that my behaviour on this occasion, which I believe was the only possible attitude in the circumstances, will be approved. Its object was *de laisser une porte ouverte à l'entente* but at the same time to show that we have become more cautious and have become conscious of the fact that possibly we can also manage without England.

It is quite clear to me from Ro.'s and Currie's remarks that they are beginning to be *seriously* worried here about our wavering and that (apart from reports they say they have received from Berlin) my reserve has really contributed to this feeling and was thus the right policy to adopt.

The best proof of the anxiety now prevailing here seems to me to be Currie's assurance in the course of the above-mentioned conversation that they are *not* thinking here of *any understanding with France*, an assurance that he would scarcely have given to me without Ro.'s knowledge.

You know better than I the practical worth of such assurances. I would never advise that we should clutch at this straw if ever any service were demanded from us in return which would involve us in the slightest trouble elsewhere. Remember how I expressed myself in Cowes against any positive action without definite reciprocity, and at that time things were seemingly much better than they are to-day. I hold to this opinion all the more firmly now and will therefore maintain my present attitude of reserve for the time being until they show us unequivocally that they intend to resume the discussion of political questions with us on the former confidential basis. If that happens, we can maintain friendly relations and talk over everything among ourselves. But should actions of any kind be called for, then the question of reciprocity will immediately arise.

I naturally leave it to your discretion to use the foregoing in any way you see fit. I have not reported all this but have written privately, so as not to prejudice the question as to what and how much is suitable for the archives and for communication to H.M. Besides I can speak more freely in this manner than in an official dispatch.[1] [...]

Kindest regards,
PH

---

[1] There is no evidence in the Foreign Ministry files that any official use was made of this letter.

388. Paul von Hatzfeldt to Holstein

London, 18 November 1893

Dear friend,

After all that I scribbled together yesterday with my writer's cramp, I am so done up that with the best will in the world I can only write you another few words.

In my long report I mentioned practically everything that was said in the course of the conversation with Ro[sebery],[1] and I await instruction regarding further dealings with him.[2]

If you want my humble opinion I would say the following: I have no doubt that Ro., who is very pessimistic, expects a crisis soon, and that *that* is the reason why he is again flirting with us. I also think that if the French furnish him with a suitable motive he will gladly attack them: first of all because since the last humiliation[3] he has felt an even greater hatred for them, and secondly, because in that event he would play a great role. Nor have I any doubt that he will then try to make certain of Italy and ourselves.

For us the affair *meo voto* turns on this: that we could take this chance without compromising ourselves by making a move anywhere. If action is demanded of us, we will refuse with thanks if simultaneous guarantees are not offered us.

Moreover you can rest assured that it is a matter of complete indifference to me personally whether we treat R. well or badly. If we want to or must make a change, I have not the least objection to bad treatment. I would in that case, as I recently wrote to you, only like to have the guarantees from the other side that we still lack here.

It is a great pity that we cannot talk over the situation fully!

If I am well enough at Christmas time I would like to go to Sommerberg for about a fortnight. Perhaps we can then arrange a meeting. Writing is a poor substitute for it.

Best wishes.

---

[1] In his report of 18 November Hatzfeldt gave a full account of his conversation with Lord Rosebery. After a long discussion of England's attitude in the Siam Question and of the reserve which he had afterwards maintained in regard to Germany, Lord Rosebery declared that serious complications could not fail to appear before long. England would in that case look for the support of Germany and her allies. Rosebery was pressing in the Cabinet for an increase in the English fleet in order to be armed against all eventualities. At the end of the report Kaiser Wilhelm II made the marginal comment: 'Rosebery's recent sudden change-over, that surprises Hatzfeldt and has led to a return to such a frank and confidential discussion, is due to my initiative. For I let Rosebery know through a confidential channel quite bluntly that I would not stand this game of hide-and-seek with me any longer, and that if he set any store at all by my friendship and affection, and if he counted on favours, he must return to the old relationship of complete honesty. Otherwise I will not talk to him again. It seems to have worked.' (From the Foreign Ministry files.)

[2] In an instruction of 24 November Hatzfeldt was instructed to recommend to Lord Rosebery that he continue to cultivate Anglo-Italian relations, and above all that he strengthen the fleet and its harbours in the Mediterranean. (From the Foreign Ministry files.)

[3] Over Siam.

389. Paul von Hatzfeldt to Holstein

London, 29 November 1893

Dear friend,

[...] Incidentally, dear friend, you over-estimate Ro[sebery] when you take him for a cunning knave. *Entre nous soit dit*, I am more and more convinced that he is not equal to his difficult post either in vision and understanding or in energy. Besides he is no diplomat and does not understand the importance and significance of his own actions and words, nor of his omissions. In addition there is his vanity, but especially an excessive personal touchiness. If you keep this picture before you, many things will become more comprehensible to you.

It is a pity that I cannot have an hour's talk with you. We may soon be standing at a cross-road! [...]

Always your
PH

390. Holstein to Paul von Hatzfeldt[1]

9 December 1893

Dear friend,

We have now heard from two sides that the Austrians are negotiating with St Petersburg over the Straits or the Balkans.

Since Reuss's connections are not clear to me, I have sent the enclosed Promemoria[2] to Philipp Eulenburg who is going to Austria to hunt and who will see Kálnoky.

After reading the P.M. you will hardly be able to accuse me of having taken the initiative for a change [of policy]. But naturally I too have no intention of waiting until we are left alone with England.

The successive discouragements came in this order: first the Italians were discouraged by England's attitude—even in Salisbury's time. As you will see from to-day's reports from Reuss, Italy's discouragement has now affected Kálnoky;[3] although I admit that Kálnoky's discouragement has a tendentious quality, rather as if he were looking for an excuse for a change.

England has simply exhausted the patience of her friends; she now stands, as you very rightly told Ro[sebery], very close to the cross-roads.

England must do two things: build up her naval armaments quickly, also make arrangements for crews and docks, etc, in the Mediterranean; and, diplomatically, maintain closer contact with Rome and Vienna, particularly with Rome—but then Ro. must express himself more clearly than hitherto. He must consider which is the lesser evil—danger of

---

[1] From the London Embassy files. See also Kálnoky's dispatch to Deym of 7 December 1893. (Partially printed in Hermann, *Dreibund, Zweibund, England*, p. 161.)

[2] See Enclosure.

[3] In two reports from Vienna of 5 December Reuss reported that after his return from Italy Kálnoky had expressed himself very pessimistically about the political situation there. Kálnoky had expressed the fear 'that the state in which Italy finds herself might make the English very cautious about engaging themselves more closely with this kingdom'. (From the Foreign Ministry files.)

some indiscretion, or a change of policy on the part of Austria and Italy. He must also treat Crispi decently because he is very susceptible to it.

In no eventuality, however, will *we* step to the fore in Balkan or Mediterranean problems. If we see that the interested parties do nothing, then we change our policy, that is we let the Russians flow peacefully into the Mediterranean and wait to see what happens.

Solms has been given a hint to resign. He was no longer up to the job in view of the increasingly difficult situation in Rome. Bernh. Bülow is to replace him and Leyden is going to Bucharest. Both appointments are still secret.

Kindest regards
Yours
Holstein

ENCLOSURE

Memorandum by Holstein
Copy   8 December 1893

Prince Reuss recently said here—he had not reported it—that in Vienna Count Wolkenstein was vigorously advocating a Russo-Austrian understanding over the Straits and that Count Kálnoky was considering it.

From another source we heard that Italian diplomats believe they know that Austria has sounded St Petersburg about an understanding over the Balkans.

If the latter were reached, it would be welcomed *by us*. We can presume that our standpoint is known. Even if, as a result of obtaining control over the Dardanelles, Russia's influence were to extend itself over the rest of the Balkan Peninsula, *we* could look on calmly—and we have said so often enough. Our role in this connection is made easier by the fact that Austria's freedom of action in Balkan questions is not restricted by the Triple Alliance Treaty. Austria acts there in her own right and on her own responsibility. That means therefore: if, after Austria has opened the way to the Straits, Russia advances further than the Vienna Cabinet would like, the result of this Austrian action remains purely an Austrian affair which does not impose on us any further care or responsibility.

For Austria the question will certainly be less easy to decide. The Vienna Cabinet will of course have to reckon with the possibility that Italy for her part will also conclude an agreement with Russia—first over Albania—and that England would retire in discouragement from the Mediterranean. *If* these two possibilities were to become actualities, then the result for Austria of an agreement over the Straits could be summed up in the word 'reprieve'.

Undoubtedly such an agreement would contain a very serious danger for Austria, and it is a question whether conditions are so pressing that the conclusion of that convention is called for *just now*.

It will be many years before Russia's new arms are ready. The administrative branch of the army has shown itself unequal to the demands made upon it during the past years of scarcity.

Austria could therefore reasonably wait and see whether the dawning conviction in England of the necessity for defending England's interests by England, or by England in association with others, will lead to any practical result.

As to Italy, conditions there are not nearly so desperate as Count Kálnoky pictures them after his talk with the pessimistic King Humbert. This does not mean that Count Kálnoky *needs* a pessimistic opinion of Italy's abilities as friend or foe to motivate a rapprochement with Russia. His present attitude may be simply the concrete expression of an instinctive feeling which Count Kálnoky—whom Count Launay described as *anti-Italian jusqu' au bout des ongles*—has held all his life.

Prince Bismarck was opposed to *our* helping to defend the Dardanelles. He advised division into spheres of interest because he no longer entertained any hope that they would be defended by *England*, Austria, and Italy.

If Prince Bismarck were still Minister today he would perhaps advise that Austria should wait for the time being to see whether England were seriously preparing the defence of her Mediterranean interests.

Under the present circumstances, however, when Prince Bismarck does not know the true situation and continues to live in the past, it is not impossible that the Austrian flirtations in St Petersburg may be directly traced back to *his* advice. A short time ago the Bismarck Press actually gave a hint to the Italians about coming to an understanding with Russia—perhaps in order thereby to bring pressure to bear on Austria's decisions. Immediately after this report of an alleged approach by Italy to Russia appeared in the Press, Count Kálnoky undertook the journey to Monza.

It would be of importance for the policy of the German Government to learn that Austria did not fear any prejudicial results from an agreement with Russia over the Straits and in particular none for the relations between the Austro-Hungarian Monarchy and England and Italy.

391. Bernhard von Bülow to Holstein

Vienna, 10 December 1893

Dear Holstein,

Philipp Eulenburg assures me that I owe my appointment as Ambassador[1] in the first place to your good offices. I would like once more to say how grateful I am to you. It will be my constant endeavour to keep your trust. I would be happy if in full agreement with your views and aims I were to be successful in becoming a useful diplomatic instrument in Rome. Please make use of me in every way. On the other hand I hope you will allow me to call on you for advice in the numerous instances in which I will need it. The more you honour me with your guidance, the happier I will feel. In this hope I enter on my new post without fears.

Eulenburg arrived yesterday evening but left again this morning for

---

[1] In Rome.

Silesia. Hence he could not see Kálnoky this time. However he is coming back here Friday evening for two days. I will call on Kálnoky early tomorrow in order to arrange a talk between him and Eulenburg for Saturday morning.[1] Your promemoria,[2] letters, and the secret London dispatch,[3] have been carefully read and discussed by Eulenburg and myself. Eulenburg will speak to Kálnoky in the sense you indicated —which should be at about the right moment.[4]

Wolkenstein has also told me that in his opinion Austria must give way in the Dardanelles Question as well as over Bulgaria. No reliance could be placed on England, she will never fight. And Italy, apart from her political untrustworthiness, was in a state of economic disintegration. There can be no doubt that Wolkenstein expressed the same ideas to Kaiser Franz Joseph as also to Kálnoky.[5] He has spoken to Reuss in similar terms on many occasions. I heard from his brother—the Lord High Steward—that Wolkenstein was pleased with his audience of His Imperial and Royal Apostolic Majesty.

I feel that Kálnoky would prefer to make concessions to the Russians in the Dardanelles Question rather than in regard to Bulgaria, because on the one hand the Catholic dynasty there is very dear to the pious Arch-House and on the other out of regard for the Magyars. The greatest impression would be made if Eulenburg were to present Kálnoky with the arguments furnished by you (Italy–England) in order to make it clear to him that Austria could isolate herself by making precipitate and excessive concessions to Russia. Obviously I will not say anything to Reuss on this subject. Incidentally, while Wolkenstein is orating in this way and Aehrenthal-Lexa[6] is intriguing in St Petersburg, the Vienna correspondent of the *Kölnischen Zeitung* told Lichnowsky[7] that he is always being exhorted by the Imperial and Royal

---

[1] On this subject see Haller, *Eulenburg*, pp. 137–8.

[2] Of 8 December. See above.

[3] Of 6 December. Hatzfeldt reported that he had spoken to Rosebery on the subject of the distrust aroused in several European capitals by English apathy and weakness. Italy felt herself exposed to a French naval attack unless she could count on the timely aid of the English fleet; while Austria feared that England might show herself to be indifferent to the fate of Egypt and Constantinople. Rosebery agreed that such mistrust of England must be removed, and thought that this could best be achieved by a strengthening of the English fleet which would leave no doubt of England's intention to uphold her role in Europe. (*Grosse Politik*, vol. IX, no. 2137, pp. 102–5.)

[4] Eulenburg reported to Caprivi that he had spoken to Kálnoky on 16 December 'and had sought to turn his thoughts into the direction in which, so far as I know, the views of Your Excellency lie, that is to say in regard to demanding political activity on the part of England and strengthening Italy'. (*Grosse Politik*, vol. IX, no. 2138, pp. 105–9.) See Kálnoky's highly unfavourable reaction in his dispatch to Szögyény of 29 December 1893, in which he spoke of the 'obvious confusion and lack of leadership in the [German] Foreign Ministry', the nervous unrest and suspicion of Austria on the part of the 'little lords' in Berlin, and their jealousy of Austria's 'position of leadership' in the Triple Alliance. (Hermann, *Dreibund, Zweibund, England*, pp. 159–60.)

[5] See *Grosse Politik*, vol. IX, no. 2140, pp. 110–11.

[6] Alois Lexa, Baron (from 1909 Count) von Aehrenthal. First Secretary at the Austro-Hungarian Embassy in St Petersburg, 1888–95; Minister in Bucharest, 1895–9; Ambassador in St Petersburg, 1899–1906; Foreign Minister, October 1906–12.

[7] Karl Max, Prince von Lichnowsky. First Secretary at the Embassy in Vienna, 1894–9; *Vortragender Rat* in the Foreign Ministry, 1899–1904; Ambassador in London, 1912–14.

Foreign Ministry to be as anti-Russian as possible in his writing and to stir up feeling in Germany against Russia. [...]

My wife sends you her kindest regards together with her most heartfelt gratitude and I remain in constant admiration and loyalty.

Your

Bernh. Bülow.

392. Paul von Hatzfeldt to Holstein[1]

London, 13 December 1893

Dear friend,

Ro[sebery] was away for several days and will not be returning until to-day, so that I could not see him sooner. [...]

En attendant permit me to make a few remarks.

Le noeud de la situation is obviously in Italy, and the further course of events will depend upon what happens there.

It is therefore clear that my task here, as you also admit, must be directed towards securing for the Italians the greatest possible peace of mind. From this standpoint I have tirelessly preached to Ro. on the subject of the strengthening of the fleet. That this will be done even if Ro. does not stake his head upon it now seems to me to be no longer a matter of doubt. Public opinion is steadily growing stronger in support of it and the Government will *have to* do it whether they like it or not.

Now you indicate in your last letter that to calm Italy, and presumably Crispi, *more* than that—assurances—will be necessary.

In regard to this matter I would first like to draw your attention to one or two points:

(1) Ro. can reply: 'In August last year, at your request, I gave a written statement drafted by myself by which, so you yourself assured me, the people in Rome were *completely* satisfied and set at ease.[2] What is your reason for concluding that now, when in addition the fleet is to be strengthened, this is no longer the case and that they again require assurances? Neither in Rome nor here through Torn[ielli] has any such desire been hinted at by a single word.'

(2) If I speak to Ro. about this I must bear in mind the possibility that he will ask Torn. whether in Rome they no longer consider the statement of August last year to be sufficient, and why. If the latter replies that in Rome they do not want or demand anything, then Ro. will be mistrustful of us, and of myself in particular, and will think that we want to harry him without any reason.

I do not need to tell you that despite everything I will do my part. But it would be very useful with regard to the considerations set out under 1 and 2 if Crispi could be induced to let the people here know of his keen desire for further reassurance. Torn. must at least be given instructions so that he does not contradict me!

[1] Holstein sent a copy of the letter to Eulenburg. (From the Eulenburg Papers.)
[2] A statement of September 1892. (See *Grosse Politik*, vol. VIII, no. 1740, Enclosure, p. 89, and no. 1737, pp. 82–4.)

I am still too exhausted to-day to write more fully, but I think I will shortly be able to send a courier to Berlin again, and will then give the reasons for my *credo* in regard to the whole situation. For to-day only this much more: It is my conviction that Austria will never *gladly* consent to allow the Russians complete liberty of action in the Near East. The most mediocre statesman in Vienna can see for himself that in that case—once things had gone so far—it would no longer be possible to call a halt. In other words—that then sooner or later all the Slavs left in the Austrian sphere of interest after such an agreement would irresistibly gravitate towards Russia. What would then remain of Austria, since expansion towards Germany is out of the question? All they would get by such an agreement with St Petersburg would be a reprieve for their own existence.

If Austria does that—which she can never do *gladly*—then she will only be driven to it for three reasons, either individually or collectively, and these are:
1. Collapse of the Triple Alliance because Italy can no longer be held;
2. England's complete abandonment of the policy followed by Lord Salisb[ury] in the Near East;
3. the conviction that she cannot count on us either, and therefore would face a Russian advance *alone*.[1]

Finally, dear friend, you know that I honestly do not want to get the Vienna post. But I do find it shocking that in such serious times our representative there, who, although on terms of intimate friendship with the leading Minister, nevertheless is apparently incapable of knowing his intentions and of influencing him.

Kindest regards from your
PH [...]

393. Paul von Hatzfeldt to Holstein

London, 20 December 1893

Dear friend,

[...] The choice of Currie[2] is a good one. But I deeply deplore losing him here. He had influence over Ro[sebery] as representing tradition and greater knowledge of affairs, and I could say things through him that I did not want to say directly to Ro. To-day when I visited him to congratulate him, he mentioned Radolin, whom he does not yet know, and seemed to want an introduction to him. I said: 'My friend Radolin will be very pleased to make your acquaintance and certainly will do all he can for you personally. Unfortunately it will not be in his power to do more because we no longer mix in affairs there.' He: 'But why not?' I: 'Why should we mix in things that do not directly concern us if those who are directly interested do not do so?' He: 'But how have we shown then that we would not do anything?'

[1] In this connection, see Kálnoky's dispatch to Calice of 15 December 1893 (Hermann, *Dreibund, Zweibund, England*, p. 162) and the Minute by Currie of 22 November 1893 (Bayer, *England und der Neue Kurs*, pp. 115–16).

[2] As British Ambassador to Constantinople.

I : 'To discuss that would take us too far, but the *fact* is that nobody will any longer believe that you will.'

He then spoke of Austria, which also seemed to be withdrawing from the Near East, and said that in Vienna they had probably become anxious because they saw that *we* did not want to help them in that quarter. I replied that one could hardly be astonished that we had no desire to face the possibility of standing there *with Austria alone* against Russia and France. There could be no question of that. But this eventuality would occur if Italy deserted *because she was left in the lurch by England*.

All this gets back to Ro., and *meo voto* I must now *quite calmly* wait and see whether he gets the shivers and what he then does. If he again tries to talk things over, then *meo voto* it is up to me *to listen* but *at the same time* to let him feel that empty words are to-day *no longer* enough.

Currie's successor here will be Sir Thomas Sanderson,[1] well-meaning but fairly insignificant.

Good-bye for today, dear friend. Best wishes for Christmas and the New Year.

I am not yet well enough to travel to the Rhine, and must wait some days, but hope to be there for the New Year.

Kindest regards from your

PH.

394. Heinrich VII Reuss to Holstein

Vienna, 23 December 1893

My dear Baron Holstein,

Permit me to accompany a dispatch about Kálnoky's remarks on the relations between Austria and Russia with a few observations.[2]

I would submit that these remarks should be regarded as private and that *for the present* there should be no reaction to them. The matter up to now does not seem to me to have been sufficiently fermented.

But I would be most extremely grateful if I could learn your opinion on his ideas about the spheres of influence, in order to be able to follow your line in further conversations with the Minister.

I have the impression that Kálnoky agrees with Nigra that England will not close the Straits to the Russians by force. If one were to abandon the Straits to the Russians, he would regard this as a lesser evil for Austria and peace than if Austria were to be drawn into a fateful war with Russia over them. At all events he has no desire to be pushed to the front by the English in this matter if it should come up.

If his idea should be right that Russia, having secured free passage,

---

[1] Sir Thomas Henry Sanderson. Permanent Under Secretary of State in the Foreign Office, 1894–1906.

[2] Dispatch of 22 December 1893. Kálnoky told Reuss that in his opinion Russia had abandoned her ambitions with regard to Bulgaria and that Russian policy was concentrated on obtaining free passage through the Straits. The Straits, he added, lay outside the present Austrian sphere of interest. (*Grosse Politik*, vol. IX, no. 2141, pp. 111–14.)

will come into conflict with France over the balance of power in the Mediterranean, then we could not ask for anything better.

With my best wishes for the New Year that is about to begin,
I am as always,
Your very devoted
H. VII Reuss.

395. Chlodwig zu Hohenlohe to Holstein

Strasbourg, 31 December 1893

My dear Baron,

I cannot allow the year to close without sending you my most heartfelt good wishes for the New Year and without thanking you for much friendly advice which you have given to me during the present year. The few men who seriously mean well by the Kaiser are being viciously persecuted by the Press and also by certain bureaucratic circles. It is necessary to hold together. You know that you can count on me. [...]

With friendly greetings
Your most devoted
C Hohenlohe.

since then often thought about it, and am therefore in a position accurately to reproduce the content and in fact practically every word of the passage in question.

Geheimrat Wilke asked whether I knew any details about the relations between Count Arnim and Count Henckel. At the Embassy these relations were the subject of much comment; but since nobody had enquired into them more closely, I knew nothing definite and consequently had to answer Wilke's question in the negative.

Before the court I gave my evidence for the most part without cross-examination and in context, and had no reason to mention Henckel's letter, about which I had not known in Paris and which I had only recently been shown in Berlin, since the judge did not ask any particular questions about the matter. The details can be seen in the official reports of the trial.

Henckel's letter was not read in court.

Some years later while Prince Bismarck was still living in the old house, and thus before June 1878, the following took place:

During a luncheon at the Prince's at which Count Guido von Henckel was present, the question of Count Arnim's speculations was brought up for discussion. Count Henckel defended Count Arnim, and also himself at the same time, and expressed himself more or less in these words: 'If I had allowed myself to get mixed up in any thing like that, I would indeed have been a fool.' To this Prince Bismarck (in substance) replied: 'I know what I know *from the documents*.' And when Count Henckel repeated his first statement in almost the same words, Prince Bismarck again replied that he derived his knowledge from our documents. After which there was silence for a time.

Two of the luncheon guests—both still living—came down to my office immediately after the luncheon and, independently of each other, related what had happened in exactly the same way.

The Prince's allusion to the documents on that occasion accords with the same train of thought that inspired the allusion in yesterday's *Zukunft*: 'Herr von Holstein knows the documents.'[1] I doubt that I will be forced to make known the contents of that letter of Henckel's.

ENCLOSURE

Guido von Henckel to Harry von Arnim
Certified Copy

Neudeck, 30 August [1874]

Dear Count,

I received your friendly letter of 13 July in Moscow during a journey through Russia from which we returned a fortnight ago. Since it is risky in view of your high office to entrust a letter addressed to you to the post, I am sending you these lines by my wife, who leaves today for

[1] Maximilian Harden's journal, *Die Zukunft*, raised the question as to whether Holstein had 'played a part, and if so what part, in the conflict between Bismarck and Arnim' and whether it was not Holstein who in the first instance had planted suspicions about Arnim in Bismarck's mind. 'Herr von Holstein is alive, he has the documents at his disposal, he can reply.' ('Bismarck und Arnim', *Die Zukunft*, 13 January 1894, Vol. VI, p. 61.)

Pontchartrain while I am making my final preparations to go to my hunting lodge in order to devote myself undisturbed to looking after the deer in the rutting season.

It is very kind of you to remember my humble part in the final settlement of the milliard [loan] in such an appreciative manner. I take credit only for having succeeded in acting as an *eminence grise*, and not to have pushed in with those heavy flat feet of which the French so accuse us. However, my name would never have been mentioned if there were not such well-cultivated relations between the lowest officials in the Ministries and the Berlin Press. I am keeping a few *curiosa* to tell you about in person; the funniest thing of all was the astonishment of the *Jesuitenbanner* that the affair had been arranged so smoothly.

I predicted the uncanny success of the loan, but once again nobody here would believe me. I showed my own confidence in the transaction very profitably in my country-bumpkin way by participating in the loan to the extent of six millions and within eight days selling at a profit of five francs. One should not allow French securities to cool off in one's safe.

Bleichröder as usual behaved foolishly, which did not astonish me.

My best wishes for the purchase of Nassenheide.[1] I was certain that Leo Henckel[2] would behave as a gentleman and not withdraw. But it has been a bitter affair for him.

The mysterious undertaking with a great future has not yet been born. If anything should come of it you will be informed in good time.

I am sincerely glad that my financial advice has agreed with you. I will add to-day that unless you need ready cash, do not sell Laura, Plessner and Zinkhütten preference shares (to-day at 115). I would put a limit on Laura of 210 and on Zinkhütten of 120. I firmly believe in this course. If anything, I would get rid of Plessner.

In Russia we got as far as Kazan, the capital of Tatary.

To our meeting in the middle of October.

With the most profound consideration
Your very devoted
Henckel-Donnersmarck.

In attestation of the accuracy of this copy
Berlin, 20 July 1894.
G. Willink
Geheimer Hofrat
Director of the Cipher Office

(Seal of the Cipher Office)

399. Bernhard von Bülow to Holstein

Vienna, 14 January 1894

Dear friend,

After arriving here in the evening of the day before yesterday, and

[1] In 1874 Count Harry von Arnim bought the former estates of the Counts Henckel at Nassenheide and Bueck in the district of Randow.

[2] Leo, Count Henckel, Baron von Donnersmarck. Chamberlain and Governor of the Palace to the Grand Duke of Saxony.

despite the fact that my time was somewhat occupied with domestic affairs, I called to-day on Kálnoky in order (in view of the coming change of representatives here) not to leave him under the influence of the views of Prince, and especially of Princess, Reuss.

Kálnoky said that he regretted Prince R.'s resignation, but nevertheless spoke calmly about this affair. Since the Bismarck wedding[1] the Prince's position had been barely tenable, and his health was in reality very poor. It was nonsense to talk of intrigues against R., as certain scandalmongering papers were doing. Incidentally, and in complete confidence, Kálnoky said that the 'grave-digger' of Prince R. was his noble wife, who had been guilty of many indiscretions and much tactlessness.

Going over to political affairs, Kálnoky at first turned the conversation to the subject of Italy. He was no longer quite so pessimistic about conditions there as he was four weeks ago, but he is nevertheless still very pessimistic. A financial stabilisation was impossible without fundamental reforms in taxation and administration, and without the former Italy, even if she did not meet with a catastrophe, would at all events be impotent in foreign affairs. In Sicily the newly-restored peace was only a sham,[2] and a thorough-going agrarian reform was indispensable. Since his last Ministry Crispi had become both physically and mentally more feeble, Blanc was unsteady and unreliable, King Humbert lacked initiative and energy. Italy's allies could not proffer advice in the question of a reduction in the strength of the army; the Italians must settle that for themselves. I emphasised in reply that from private information I had received from Italy, I judged the situation there to be indeed difficult, but by no means desperate. *Alios jam vidimus ventos.*

On his own initiative—I refrained from touching upon the matter even by implication—Kálnoky started to talk about the Dardanelles Question.[3] He emphasised in this connection—not without vigour—that if England left him in the lurch in this question he could not oppose Russia alone. The Dardanelles in themselves lay outside the Austrian sphere of interest. The Straits at present were the sole object of Russian policy. The Russians did not want Constantinople but only freedom of passage through the Dardanelles for their Black Sea Fleet. He thought that Russia, 'as formerly in the Reichsstadt Agreements',[4] would now once again be prepared to declare Constantinople a neutral and independent city.

I replied that in principle we always wanted as few differences as possible between Austria-Hungary and Russia. As the expression of my purely personal opinion based on my six years' experience *in*

---

[1] See above, p. 413, note 2.

[2] Serious peasant revolts in Sicily during the autumn and winter had been ruthlessly suppressed by the Italian army.

[3] Without informing the Germans further, Kálnoky empowered Deym to raise this question in London on 25 January 1894. (Hermann, *Dreibund, Zweibund, England*, pp. 169–71; Bayer, *England und der Neue Kurs*, pp. 62–3.)

[4] The informal agreements of 8 July 1876 between Russia and Austria.

orientalibus, I added that, if Austria-Hungary brought the Russians the keys of the Dardanelles, Russian influence would irrevocably triumph not only in Sofia, but also in Bucharest. Moreover, the moment any such intention became manifest, Italy might endeavour to outdo the Viennese Cabinet in St Petersburg, and England, in a mood of discouragement, would withdraw from the Mediterranean.

Kálnoky was obviously made thoughtful by these remarks that I threw out as carelessly and casually as possible. He said that he would indeed only give way to the Russians in the Straits Question with great reluctance and very much *à contre coeur*. But without England he could not oppose an empire of a hundred million inhabitants which was striving with the whole pressure of its enormous power to achieve this aim. He must know in advance where he stood with England. He did not at present want to press Lord Rosebery, but to leave him time to digest the pills administered by Hatzfeldt and Deym.[1] Sooner or later, however, he must have a clear-cut statement as to how far he could rely on the material and effective support of England in any future opposition to Russia on the Dardanelles Question. He owed that to the Kaiser as well as to the Parliaments of both halves of the Empire to whom he was responsible. Public opinion in both Cis and Trans-Leithania must be made to understand that the Habsburg Monarchy could not fight singlehandedly for the Dardanelles.

I drew Kálnoky's attention to the fact that there were recent indications of a gradual awakening of the British lion. Kálnoky did not contest the importance of Dilke's speeches, in particular those advocating a strengthening of the fleet; he also conceded that any future English government would be more capable of action than the present Cabinet presided over by Gladstone, but he also emphasised that a good many politicians in England greatly underestimated the importance not only of the Straits but also of the Mediterranean for the British Empire.

I would sum up my general impression by saying that Kálnoky has already considered the question of an understanding with Russia over the Dardanelles Question not only *dans son for intérieur* but also with others. Certainly with Wolkenstein and Aehrenthal, probably also with Kaiser Franz Joseph, perhaps also with Wekerle[2] and Ludwig Tisza. Whether also with Lobanov I cannot decide. Kálnoky would in my opinion—particularly with regard to the Austrian position on the Lower Danube—greatly prefer if Russia did not succeed in getting her way in the matter of the Straits. He nevertheless will not stand up singlehanded against Russia without England's effective support. It is therefore possible that Kálnoky paints the possibility of an Austro-Russian understanding over the Dardanelles in somewhat harsh colours because he hopes in that way to arouse England from her egoistical apathy. His ideal at the moment, it seems to me, would be that Rosebery should expressly and unreservedly accept the points formerly stipulated with Salisbury.[3] If Kálnoky were at some time to set foot on the slippery

---

[1] See *Grosse Politik*, vol. IX, nos. 2142-4, pp. 114-24.
[2] Alexander Wekerle. Hungarian Minister-President, 1892-5; Minister-President and Foreign Minister, 1906-10.   [3] The Mediterranean Agreement of December 1887.

slope of concessions to the northern Great Power by means of an Austro-Russian bilateral understanding over the Straits, it would, according to what I know of the situation here, be virtually impossible to foretell how far he would slide. [...]

Munich, 16.1.94.

I took this letter with me to Munich in order to read it to Philipp Eu[lenburg] for his information. I go on to Rome this evening. With kindest regards and best wishes

Always yours
Bernh. Bülow.

400. Statement by Herbert von Bismarck[1]

Berlin, 10 January 1894

'Count Herbert Bismarck has had nothing whatever to do with the attacks made on Herr von Holstein in connection with the recent discussion of the Arnim affair in certain newspapers such as the *Zukunft*, *New York Herald*, *Kladderadatsch*,[2] and was himself surprised to see them.'

Count Herbert Bismarck accepted the above declaration word for word on 18 January 1894 in the residence of His Excellency General of Cavalry and General-Adjutant Count Heinrich Lehndorff in the presence of the two signatories.

Count Dönhoff Friedrichstein
Count Friedrich von Pourtalès

401. Letter of 2 February 1894 from *Kladderadatsch* to Herr...... in reply to a question as to the identity of 'Oyster-lover, von Spätzle, and Count Troubadour' who have recently been so often mentioned in the *Kladderadatsch*.[3]

I reply to your most justifiable question with pleasure. *Oyster-lover* is *Wirklicher Geheimer Legationsrat* von Holstein, the senior *Rat* in the Foreign Ministry, who behaved perfidiously in the Arnim trial and then four years ago at once turned his back on Bismarck. He is regularly consulted by Caprivi and Marschall, who are not professional diplomats, and decides most things. An intriguer through love of intrigue. A passionate consumer of oysters.

Von Spätzle is *Geheimer Legationsrat* von Kiderlen-Wächter,[4] Director of the official Press Bureau, whose influence is unbelievably far-reaching, and who by means of cleverly chosen intermediaries influences even decent people in such a way that their Editors-in-Chief often know

---

[1] See Rogge, *Friedrich von Holstein*, pp. 168–70.
[2] See the following document.
[3] This letter was intended for private circulation but was published in the *Frankfurter Zeitung* on 7 March. Kiderlen thereupon challenged the writer, Polstorff, to a duel and wounded him. (See Ernst Jäckh, *Kiderlen-Wächter der Staatsmann und Mensch* (Berlin und Leipzig, 1924), vol. I, pp. 96–9; Otto Hammann, *Der neue Kurs* (Berlin, 1918), pp. 94–7.)
[4] The word *Spätzle* (little sparrow) is the name of a famous dish from Kiderlen's native province of Swabia, but it was clearly also intended as a reference to Kiderlen's notorious enjoyment of scandalous gossip.

nothing about it. Extraordinarily clever, adroit, and frivolous man of the world.

Count Troubadour is Count Philipp Eulenburg, Prussian Minister in Munich, clever careerist, writes verses, composes and sings his songs to his own accompaniment in High and All-Highest circles.

In recent years Holstein and Kiderlen have consistently tried to widen the gulf between the Kaiser and Bismarck, especially by nasty stories that are cleverly disseminated in various newspapers and subsequently brought to H.M.'s attention as products of the pro-Bismarck Press. In addition they have forced out or thrust aside able and independent Ministers, in order to give posts to insignificant but compliant people. Thus it is that the excellent Schlözer has been replaced by the incapable Otto von Bülow, and at the important post of Constantinople, the clever Radowitz has been replaced by the commonplace Radolin. Moser[1] had to leave here *solely* because Count Eulenburg wanted to place his friend Varnbuler[2] here who would otherwise have been without a roof over his head as a result of the withdrawal of the Württemberg Legation in Vienna. And because Eulenburg himself wants to go to gay Vienna, Prince Reuss must leave there. Holstein and Kiderlen are the worst, but Eulenburg is peculiarily dangerous because he is *persona gratissima* with the Kaiser, whom he accompanies every summer on his voyage to Norway.

In the autumn, when the Kaiser visited Babenhausen, Eulenburg was already there (from Munich), whereas the Prussian Minister in *Stuttgart* (von Holleben)[3] was only summoned shortly before H.M.'s departure.

All these things have long been talked about in that part of society here which moves in diplomatic circles. But it was only two months ago that we first obtained such authentic information that we could act with decision. After the publication of Issue no. 53 [*sic*][4] last year, Caprivi sent *Kammergerichtsrat* Wichert, the dramatist and author of *Aus eigenem Recht*,[5] to us and asked us to stop the attacks; he had to defend his officials and Holstein was an honourable man and a Civil Servant. We replied that we unfortunately were better informed than he himself was. Since that time, every issue has been eagerly awaited in official and even higher circles and has been carefully examined, but no steps have been taken either against us or in defence of the honourable officials.

Caprivi has been urged from many quarters, especially by high-ranking officers employed in diplomatic posts, to throw out the two fellows. But he would reply: 'Yes, that is all very easy to say!' Obviously he is afraid to take vigorous action on account of the influence which Kiderlen and Eulenburg have with the Kaiser.

[1] Württemberg Minister to Berlin, 1890–4.
[2] Axel, Freiherr von Varnbüler. Minister from Württemberg to Berlin since April 1894.
[3] Theodor von Holleben. Minister in Tokyo, 1885–91, in Washington, 1891–3, in Stuttgart, 1891–7; Ambassador in Washington, 1897–1903.
[4] This should read no. 52, which was the issue of the *Kladderadatsch* in which the article 'Der Vierte Mann im Skat' appeared.
[5] Ernst Wichert's play was enjoying great success in Berlin during the winter season of 1893–4.

In Issue No. 4 of last week we again tried to lure the foxes from their filthy lair with the coarsest attacks. It seems that they intend to swallow even this in silence, no matter how disgraceful such an ostrich-like policy may be for the Government of the German Reich.

We will let the matter rest for the present because in the first place it is repugnant to have anything further to do with such spineless people, but also out of regard for our readers.

We realised from the beginning that outsiders would and could not understand the allusions, but we did not hesitate to pose such a riddle to our readers because it was in the interest of an important and a just cause.

I not only empower you to communicate all these details to everyone who has an interest in them, but I even ask you to do so. It is a matter solely of facts which we shall be glad to prove.

Yours very faithfully
W. Polstorff,
Editor of *Kladderadatsch*.

402. Paul von Hatzfeldt to Holstein[1]

London, 15 February 1894

Dear friend,

My impression is that *both parties*[2] would *like* to come to an understanding—whereby each would obtain as much as possible and give as little as possible.

Therefore the question seems to me to be: do we *still* want the two to come to an understanding over the point in question,[3] and if so, will it be possible—as D[eym] hopes—to find an acceptable basis for it?

I have in general behaved towards R[osebery] as a friendly listener and only made some factual remarks. R. had decided that he would talk to me purely personally and as a friend, and I demanded the same right for myself so that I could express an opinion on any matter on which I had not been officially informed. With this reservation I have touched chiefly on two points: 1. I have expressed the purely personal opinion that his supposition that K[álnoky] now preferred the other way[4] was unfounded. So far as I knew, things were still as I had always pictured them to him, R., namely, that K. will not consider the other way until he is *finally* convinced that this one[5] is *hopeless*, and for that nobody could blame him. 2. When he began to talk about *us* and our present enquiry,[6] I replied that I had always told him frankly and definitely that we could not tread upon a certain bridge,[7] and that the people here

---

[1] See Hatzfeldt's telegram to the Foreign Ministry of 14 February. (*Grosse Politik*, vol. IX, no. 2147, pp. 127–9.)   [2] Austria and England.
[3] The co-operation of Austria and England in preventing Russia from gaining free access to the Mediterranean through the Straits.
[4] An understanding with Russia. (See Hermann, *Dreibund, Zweibund, England*, p. 164.)
[5] Co-operation with England against Russia.
[6] The Italians had asked that Hatzfeldt should sound the British as to a possible Anglo-Italian agreement. (*Grosse Politik*, vol. VIII, no. 1987, pp. 358–60.)
[7] That is, that Germany could not become directly involved in the affairs of the Near East. (See Hermann, *Dreibund, Zweibund, England*, p. 163.)

must think that over and be in no doubt about it. Unfortunately I had tried to do so in vain for seven years. 3. In order not to frighten him off completely, I seized the opportunity when he spoke about himself of slipping in the remark that to my knowledge everyone thought highly of him personally, but not of his playmates. I therefore could not be astonished if K. demanded guarantees for their good behaviour.

Deym definitely wants to find a basis for negotiation and is advising his Government to this effect. He probably assumes that R., even though he does not at present think it possible to give any guarantees other than his own word, would become more amenable if he were to receive a *practical* proposal, the acceptance of which would not compromise him *too greatly* here.

What seems to me to be of particular interest for us in this affair is the attempt that is being made here to get K. to accept undertakings against *le troisième larron*.[1] If this were to succeed I would not be sorry. But if I were K. and wanted to go into the matter at all, I would reply only with: If I take up a hostile attitude towards *le troisième* in your interest, you must then naturally undertake *to do so yourself* and to bear the consequences *with* me. You know what I mean without further elaboration of the idea.

As for ourselves in this connection, it seems to me that the matter is fairly simple provided that this latter course is at all to our liking. If we were asked we would [say]: If K. thinks it important to come to an understanding on the basis proposed by R., we have no objection. If as a result he were to get into trouble with the *troisième larron* and were molested by this party, then he knows—and can also tell this to R.—what we have promised him for such an eventuality.[2] That is sufficient, and we will go no further so long as R. and his friends for their part regard caution as the mother of wisdom.

R. is quite clear in his own mind that here they will have to sound the retreat from the Mediterranean if *both* enemies[3] act together, and about all that they would have to abandon there. He will therefore think twice before he definitely rejects a proposal from K. that is at all acceptable, provided that he will not be irretrievably compromised by it. His fear of that can be judged from his remark to D[eym]: *il s'agit de ma tête dans cette affaire*. [...]

Kindest regards
PH.

403. Paul von Hatzfeldt to Holstein

London, 28 February 1894

Dear Holstein,

You will see from my to-day's report[4] how matters stand. *Mais c'est le ton qui fait la chanson* and in this connection I can only say that not

---

[1] *La troisième République*. Rosebery has asked the Austrians whether Austria and her allies would protect England's flank against France if England were to oppose a Russian attack on the Straits. (See above, p. 463, note 1.)
[2] The terms of the Triple Alliance.   [3] France and Russia.
[4] *Grosse Politik*, vol. IX, no. 2150, pp. 131-4.

only Rosebery but also Deym—and so presumably his master too—are eager for an understanding.

Is this really so desirable for Austria? It is not my task to look into that nor into what advantages it offers England; the question is what *we* would gain from it. I await your instructions in the matter and will act accordingly. Meanwhile I have listened in a friendly way and, with all due reserve, have not only discreetly offered encouragement but also, as you see from my report, drawn attention to the disadvantages. Deym has been (up to now) very receptive to hints (for example, that it would after all be of little value without a *note* from Ro. and that the latter must commit himself *positively* so that, if the case in question should occur, he would reach an agreement with Austria over how to deal with the matter and possibly go to war if the agreement called for it. Once they get down to details and to drawing up a draft, there will be a good many other things to consider that would take me too far afield at the present time.)

I must not forget to add here that Ro., in explaining the situation in the Mediterranean and the chances for England there, referred to the fact that England was on the best possible terms with Spain and Portugal and in event of war could unquestionably count upon a friendly attitude in those countries. He assumed that Greece alone would take the side of Russia.

If the occasion arises, he will act in the Mediterranean with overwhelming naval strength. You will at once have realised, as I did, that that would be very easy if he were able to use the Channel Fleet and did not need to fear France.

What would be our interest in the matter *if* we are not engaged elsewhere? I have recently written you my opinion about this[1] but since then the situation has been substantially altered by the renunciation of material assistance. With this reservation I can see no disadvantage for us in allowing Austria and England to reach an understanding here, and even to promote it if, as I told Deym, we remain in the background. The advantage would be—it seems to me—that Austria, even if she only promised diplomatic pressure, would therewith be still further engaged against France, and that England would be deprived of the temptation of one day coming to an understanding with Russia or France—a temptation that in my humble opinion we must not underestimate.

At all events I believe that if we do not take advantage of this opportunity for an understanding with Austria over the Near East, a second will hardly offer itself.

I hope the courier will bring me a letter from you with a hint as to what object I—openly or clandestinely—should aim at. My friend Deym has the best intentions, but needs a little guidance in order to steer around the reefs and to avoid missing favourable opportunities. [...]

                                           Kindest regards
                                                 from your
                                                      PH.

---

[1] In the letter of 15 February. See above.

404. Holstein to Hugo von Radolin[1]

3 March, [1894]

Dear Rado,

Since Kiderlen has chosen this very moment to go on leave, we here are up to our ears not only with business but also with personal matters.

Now I would like to ask you to do something. I cannot know how soon I shall have to fight a duel.[2] At the moment I know nobody whom I can challenge, at least not in such a way that the other person could not settle the affair by an explanation. One such incident is already settled.[3] But things may be different next time.

Do you think it would be very disagreeable for General Bissing to act as my second in case of need? He would be particularly welcome to me because of his resolute character.

Will you write to him about it? Since I know him so little I have no claim on him whatever, and must therefore be prepared for a refusal on some excuse or other.

You will do me a great service by doing this. If meanwhile you have reason to think that it *would* be disagreeable to the General for personal reasons, then do not write to him at all.

Your old
Holstein.

405. Chlodwig zu Hohenlohe to Holstein

Strasbourg, 6 March 1894

My dear Baron,

Yesterday I forgot to say that in my opinion a legal prosecution of the *Kladderadatsch* is not only unnecessary but even dangerous because no actual slander in the sense of Berlin law exists and the *Kl.* would therefore be acquitted. I am for my part starting cautious enquiries into the identity of the men behind the *Kl.* If I should learn anything I will immediately send word.

With friendly greetings
Your most devoted
Hohenlohe.

406. Holstein to Hugo von Radolin[4]

Berlin, 12 March 1894

Dear Rado,

Heartiest thanks for your letter of the 8th.[5] Things are different to-day to what they were on Saturday when I wrote to you.[6] Negotiations were then in progress over my demand that Herb. Bismarck should *publicly* make it known that he had nothing whatever to do with the

---

[1] From the Radolin Papers.

[2] On account of the articles in the Press attacking Holstein. Holstein was trying to discover who was behind the attack.

[3] See above, Herbert von Bismarck's declaration of 18 January, and also Rogge, *Friedrich von Holstein*, pp. 168–70.

[4] From the Radolin Papers.   [5] Not found.   [6] See above, Holstein's letter of 3 March.

attacks on me. The declaration appeared in the *Hamburger Nachrichten* on Tuesday morning, and as an honourable man I must believe it.[1]

For the moment I therefore have nobody against whom I can proceed. Pourtalès conducted the affair splendidly.

It was very kind of you to have taken up my cause immediately.

Remember me to the Princess and the Countess, and give Lindau my kindest regards.

Your H.

407. Holstein to Guido von Henckel-Donnersmarck
Copy

Berlin, 31 March 1894

Count Guido von Henckel-Donnersmarck.

The attitude taken by the *Berliner Neuesten Nachrichten*, which takes its orders from you, in regard to the campaign of the *Kladderadatsch* against the Foreign Ministry and myself, has convinced me that you are primarily responsible for this campaign.

I herewith charge you with the responsibility, and will send my second in the course of the day.

In the event that you do not accept my challenge, I would no longer be able to regard you as a man of honour.[2]

Holstein.
Wirklicher Geheimer Legationsrat.

408. Paul von Hatzfeldt to Holstein

London, 4 April 1894

Dear friend,

I was very glad again to hear from you at long last.

Since the decision has been taken I will naturally refrain from any intervention here.[3] I agree with *you* that the suggestion in question,

---

[1] This was a second declaration by Herbert von Bismarck that Holstein demanded in order to put an end to all misunderstandings about the incident. (Rogge, *Friedrich von Holstein*, pp. 168–70.)

[2] On 4 April 1894 Count Henckel's second, General Alfred von Waldersee, sent the following letter to Holstein's second, General Moritz von Bissing: 'Sir, I have the honour to inform you that Count Henckel cannot see that he is called upon to take part in a duel for which he has not given even the slightest cause. He reserves the right to take steps with regard to the provocation emanating from Herr von Holstein.' On the same day Holstein wrote to General von Bissing: 'My dear General, You inform me that Count Waldersee has written to you on behalf of Count Guido Henckel to the effect that Count Henckel rejects my challenge. In view of this declaration I draw particular attention to the final sentence of my letter of 31 March addressed to Count Henckel.'

[3] On the question of opposing a Russian demand for the free passage of the Straits. Rosebery, who had become British Prime Minister after Gladstone's resignation on 3 March, informed the Austro-Hungarian Ambassador that the British navy would fight Russia unassisted in the Mediterranean, provided that the Triple Alliance would see to it that France remained neutral. (*Grosse Politik*, vol. IX, nos. 2148–50, pp. 129–34.) Germany rejected Rosebery's plan because it would mean that the Triple Alliance would be obliged to define its attitude in the event of an Anglo-Russian conflict over the Straits in advance, whereas Britain herself assumed no obligations whatever and retained the freedom of decision as to whether and when she would oppose a Russian attack on the Straits. Britain could thus

in so far as it had taken shape *at all up to now*, is to be looked upon as froth. On the other hand I believe that it was not impossible that if negotiations between here and Vienna had been continued, they would finally have resulted in finding a better formula which would also have been more desirable for us. Moreover the fact of the *continuation* of the conversations would in itself have been desirable, as Cap[rivi] expressly recognised, and this result, it seems to me, could have been achieved without our having had to commit or to compromise ourselves if we had avoided an absolute refusal and only said: in *this* form we would have to commit ourselves *only* and to carry all the burdens. If you, by further conversations in Vienna, can find a formula involving *equal* obligations and *equal* burdens for all, we would be prepared to examine it more closely.

As the matter stands to-day there is a reason to fear that both parties are discouraged and will drop the business. Indeed, I regard this as highly probable because I can hardly doubt that in Vienna they will use our refusal to explain their lack of success here.

I will be glad if this fear is proved groundless. [...]

Kindest regards
PH

409. Holstein to Philipp zu Eulenburg[1]

TELEGRAM

B[erlin], 4 April 1894

Private

Last Saturday I wrote a letter of challenge to Count Henckel in which, referring particularly to the significant attitude of the *Berliner Neuesten Nachrichten*, I declared him to be a leader in the campaign against me and held him responsible.[2] Immediately afterwards General Bissing challenged him on my behalf. Henckel named General Count Waldersee as his second.[3] After three days of negotiation, in which my second displayed the greatest determination, Count Waldersee to-day wrote him a letter in which he rejected a duel in Count Henckel's name because the latter had given no cause for it. The declaration which my second demanded to be used if occasion arose—was also refused.[4]

I thereupon wrote a letter to my second which he has forwarded to Count Waldersee. In this I made particular reference to the final

force Germany to carry out a plan to which Germany had previously committed herself. Furthermore it would fall largely to Germany to keep France neutral—by force, if necessary. Should Germany be forced to declare war on France, Germany would be the aggressor and would almost certainly be drawn into war with Russia. The result would be the dreaded war on two fronts. (*Grosse Politik*, vol. IX, no. 2153, pp. 138–42; see the extracts from the Austrian documents published by Hermann, *Dreibund, Zweibund, England*, p. 165 *et seq.*, and Rosebery's dispatch to Malet of 3 January 1894. Bayer, *England und der Neue Kurs*, pp. 115–16.)

[1] Eulenburg was at this time in Abbazia where he had been staying with Kaiser Wilhelm II since 20 March.
[2] See above. Holstein's letter of 31 March.
[3] See Waldersee, *Denkwürdigkeiten*, vol. II, p. 312 *et seq.*
[4] See Enclosure.

sentence of the letter of the 31st of last month to Count Henckel, which ran: 'In the event that you do not accept my challenge I would no longer be able to regard you as a man of honour.'

Copies of the letters are being sent to you this evening.[1]

I leave it to you as to whether to inform His Majesty.[2]

Holstein.

ENCLOSURE

Declaration[3]

Because of attacks which have recently been made in the Press against officials of the Foreign Service and especially against himself, and because of the attitude taken in this matter by certain newspapers, for example the *Berliner Neuesten Nachrichten*, Herr von Holstein has found reason to make me in part responsible for these attacks and even to demand personal satisfaction from me.

In consequence, I herewith declare on my word of honour that I have no connection whatever with these attacks, that to my knowledge no discussions have ever taken place in my house with the object of inspiring or promoting such attacks, and that in general I disapprove of all these attacks most strongly.

I empower Herr von Holstein to publish the foregoing declaration.

410. Philipp zu Eulenburg to Holstein

5 April 1894

Note for Holstein

H.M. said after I had read him the telegram:[4] 'Bravo! That is my old Holstein! Plucky and won't stand any nonsense! He is now well out of it: a declaration from Herbert, one demanded of Henckel—who will now hang anything on him? Telegraph him immediately that I am *very* glad—also particularly with his choice of a second.'

H.M. ordered me to inform Plessen, and in the afternoon elicited words of such unmistakable praise from Plessen, Moltke,[5] Leuthold, etc, that the impression made was striking. The conversation always culminated in the expression: 'My old Holstein is a splendidly plucky fellow. If everyone was like him affairs of State would be in better shape.'

---

[1] In a letter to Eulenburg of the same day, Holstein explained in greater detail the reasons for his challenge to Henckel and for proceeding 'against enemies which I certainly did not make in my *private* life'. He urgently appealed to Eulenburg to secure him the support of the Kaiser. 'If His Majesty *takes no steps* against Henckel,' Holstein said, 'he will be taking the side of my enemies.' Eulenburg's marginal comments, perhaps written at a later date, reveal that he was gravely embarrassed by the position in which Holstein had placed him. (From the Eulenburg Papers.)

[2] Eulenburg telegraphed Holstein from Abbazia on 5 April: 'His Majesty very pleased about your behaviour, instructs me to telegraph this. Letter follows.'

[3] This was the declaration which Holstein demanded from Count Henckel, a copy of which he sent to Eulenburg.

[4] Holstein's telegram to Eulenburg of 4 April. See above.

[5] Kuno, Count von Moltke. Aide-de-Camp to Kaiser Wilhelm II. Later Military Governor of Berlin.

I heartily congratulate you on this *decisive* and lasting success—but you strongly furthered the tendency which you attacked in the *exposé*[1] that you gave me to bring along. Well, that has nothing to do with the matter! I am *glad*.

Your old
PE.

411. Moritz von Bissing to Holstein

Potsdam, 6 April 1894

My dear Herr von Holstein,

[...] I did actually speak to Herr von Wedel[2] yesterday evening, but only to ask him to give me time for a talk with him this afternoon.

In the course of this conversation I informed him of the mission with which you had entrusted me, and after I had told him all that was worth knowing, I mentioned to Herr von Wedel my intention to call a meeting of the Mess Committee for next Monday in order to obtain a decision as to the attitude to be adopted towards Count Henckel. [...]

I am of the opinion that there is nothing more that you need to do, indeed I am of the opinion that [...][3] for the reasons communicated to you verbally it would not even be advisable. I am especially opposed to the use of the Press, so long as it is possible to avoid it, and most particularly so long as the letter from Abbazia[4] has not arrived here. According to what Herr von Wedel tells me it is certain that the Mess Committee will demand from me a written or oral report on the whole affair, based on the documents. For that purpose I want a copy of the letter which you sent to Count Henckel and I ask you to send me this here as quickly as possible. [...]

Your most devoted
Freiherr von Bissing.

412. Moritz von Bissing to Holstein

Potsdam, 8 April 1894

My dear Herr von Holstein,

[...] Yesterday I put the protocol that I recently drafted with you[5] into proper shape and added it to the documents. It is an ingenious and I think a clear account that leaves no room for doubts about the negotiations between Waldersee and myself, between you and me, and between Waldersee and Henckel. I will be able to give the Mess Committee the desired explanation, armed as I am with this report and the accompanying evidence—letters, declaration, and counter-declaration. I will also make suitable use of the permission given to me to

---

[1] Not found. Eulenburg undoubtedly refers to Holstein's efforts to calm the Kaiser's impulsive behaviour.

[2] Wilhelm von Wedel-Piesdorf. Minister of the Royal Household, 1888–1907.

[3] One word illegible.

[4] Bissing probably refers to Eulenburg's note of 5 April 1894 (see above), which Eulenburg had promised in his telegram to Holstein of the same day. (See p. 469, note 2.)

[5] Not found.

declare that you are prepared to fight a duel with a proxy of equal rank.[1]

A telegram will best reach me here, and if necessary I will be at your disposal in the shortest possible time.

With deep regard
Your most devoted
Freiherr von Bissing.

413. Moritz von Bissing to Holstein

Potsdam, 17 April 1894

My dear Herr von Holstein,

I acknowledge the receipt of your friendly letter of yesterday with most sincere thanks. I rejoice with you that everything was approved at the All-Highest level there and that they are satisfied with what has been done. If I have really contributed to bring about a more temperate appreciation of the situation by my letter to Plessen, it would be a great satisfaction for me. It is a mystery to me from what quarter the conduct of your opponent has met with justification. [...]

Your very devoted
Freiherr von Bissing.

414. Heinrich VII Reuss to Holstein

Vienna, 19 April 1894

Dear Herr von Holstein,

I will not lay down the baton without taking leave of you. We have worked together for many long years and, thanks to your support, not badly. We have always on the whole understood each other well because we had the same aims in mind, and I am anxious to express to you my thanks for the kind help that you have often given me. I do not need to tell you first of all that it will not be easy for me to leave the diplomatic service in which I have worked throughout a long life. But I do not regret for a moment having taken the decisive step. *Un homme d'esprit doit savoir se retirer à temps!* The honours that are heaped upon me, and the flattering *Ordre* which has been made public and makes me feel ashamed, confers on the whole affair *the* character which I wished it to have. Many people to be sure ask themselves: if he was such a first-rate fellow, how could they let him go? That is a matter of indifference to me; I leave without resentment, and if others understand that they must be thankful to me for having spared them the need of committing an injustice.

Allow me to express the wish that you may yet remain for a long time in the diplomatic service. The tradition of a great age lives on in you *alone*, and you make up for what in other places is unhappily wholly wanting: knowledge of diplomacy and understanding in handling foreign governments.

---

[1] Bissing tried to explain Henckel's need for a deputy in a letter to Holstein of 9 April: 'I have lately had the idea that Count Henckel might let a nephew fight the duel of honour in his place because I got the impression that the Count must be physically unwell; otherwise I have no reason for such an idea.' (See Rogge, *Friedrich von Holstein*, p. 170.)

I will come to Berlin in June and then hope to pay you a visit.

With my best wishes for your welfare, I ask you to retain your friendship for me in the future and am

Your very devoted

H. VII Reuss.

415. Moritz von Bissing to Holstein

Potsdam, 26 April 1894

My dear Herr von Holstein,

I received yesterday from Minister Wedel the information that the Mess Committee had resolved to declare:

'that at the present time it was not in a position to be able to adopt an attitude in regard to the affair between Herr von Holstein and Count Guido Henckel von Donnersmarck.'

I have not spoken to any of the Committee members and therefore cannot give you an explanation of this decision. Since on your behalf I demand nothing, and the Committee took up a completely neutral standpoint, I regard the matter as closed for the present, although the manner of its settlement is not satisfactory. [...]

With the highest regard I have the honour to remain

Your very devoted

Freiherr von Bissing

416. Holstein to Moritz von Bissing

Copy

Berlin, 26 April 1894

My dear General,

Since no demand was made from our side, and our only intention was to prevent the possible growth of a legend by communicating the authentic facts, I too am of the definite opinion that by the declaration by which the Mess Committee takes cognisance of the communication the whole affair is settled not temporarily but *finally*. I leave it to you as to whether it is advisable to bring this point of view to the attention of Minister Wedel in a short note.[1]

(The rest is thanks).

417. Holstein to Hugo von Radolin[2]

30 April [1894]

My dear Rado,

I am glad to hear that you and your family are well again. This time of year should indeed be quite superb in Constantinople.

I send you my heartiest thanks for your good offices with General

---

[1] In a letter to Holstein of 27 April, Bissing showed that he wanted to pursue the matter further. No reply from Holstein has been found. For the final outcome of the affair, see the Holstein-Bissing correspondence of August and September 1898.

[2] From the Radolin Papers.

Bissing. He handled my interests in the Henckel affair in splendid fashion. It was not our fault that Henckel did not respond. This affair is now at an end. Meanwhile I doubt that there will be peace until one or another of the cowardly blackguards who are behind the Press agitation is rooted out. [...]

Your old
H.

418. Bernhard von Bülow to Holstein

Rome, Wednesday, 2 May 1894

Dear friend,

My sincere thanks for your friendly letters of the 18th, 21st, and 30th of last month. As I immediately telegraphed, I have written to Philipp Eu[lenburg] and—*Secretissimum!*—to my brother Adolf in the indicated sense, making use of your arguments. Essentially I am in agreement with your point of view, and I will do what I can elsewhere in support of it.[1]

Personally, I have really—three times underlined—no other desire than to remain in Rome.[2] I would be a fool if I were to prefer any other Embassy to my uniquely pleasant and comfortable existence here—let alone the worrying and thankless Berlin. My wife thinks as I do. Donna Laura loves you more than she can say; but if you take us away from here she will tell you: *C'est fini nous deux.* Moreover I can be more useful here than anywhere else in the present state of affairs. Finally I ask you not to forget that after I have been so well received here, the Court, the political world, and even public opinion would be deeply wounded if I did not remain here for a number of years. Do not let us give Engelbrecht the pleasure of seeing me make way for him here [...].

With affectionate greetings from my wife and Donna Laura—Blaserna also always asks about you—

Always your truly devoted
B. [...]

419. Hugo von Radolin to Holstein

Pera, 10 May 1894

My dear friend,

Your long friendly letter gave me great pleasure and I conclude from it that—thank God—things are going well for you. You can be proud of your success. You have acted every inch the man and shown enormous courage. The attitude of the other side is quite unbelievable. You can now await what comes with peace of mind. Delbrück told me the details and I am glad that B[issing], despite his friendship with Wal[dersee], behaved so splendidly. The good cause must triumph.

---

[1] Bülow refers to the question of the possible fall of both Caprivi and Marschall.
[2] Bernhard von Bülow was commonly regarded as the next State Secretary of the Foreign Ministry.

The only thing I am sorry about is that I was not in Berlin to help you with my feeble powers. You did not need me, but nevertheless I would gladly have been with you. An additional friend never does any harm. Words cannot say how I have suffered *for you* and felt for you. [...]

In haste

Your Hugo

420. Georg zu Münster to Holstein

Paris, 31 May 1894

My dear Herr von Holstein,

Many thanks for your letter. You will see from my report about the situation how I regard the crisis and its consequences.[1]

I greatly regret the departure of Casimir Périer[2] because I am on the friendliest terms with him and could speak to him quite frankly and openly, as I could with no other Minister. The new one, Hanotaux,[3] is a real French bureaucrat who thinks himself far bigger than he is. One could deal with him alone, but there are two quite young Ministers who have all the bad characteristics of our assistant judges and the dashing lieutenants, Delcassé[4] and Poincaré,[5] who continually want to interfere in foreign affairs, and this triumvirate, to whom the good Dupuy[6] will leave foreign affairs, can do many stupid things. They will be cautious in regard to us and I strongly advise caution in regard to them. The hatred of these men is concentrated on England and they will try to get us to pull the chestnuts out of the fire for them—especially in Africa.

The Government that has resigned had begun to adopt a friendlier attitude towards Italy. That is something the present Government will not do, and hence Ressmann[7] regards this change of government as very unfortunate. The immediate future will be quite interesting. Congo and Siam will be two hard nuts for Hanotaux.

As always most sincerely yours

Münster.

P.S. As to Africa, the French will play us off against the English in order to take our place later on. Take care that Kayser does not make this game easier for them.

M.

[1] In a report of the same day Münster analysed the situation resulting from the formation of the new French Cabinet. He warned especially against possible attempts on the part of Delcassé and Hanotaux, who were both anti-English, to play off Germany against England in Africa. (From the Foreign Ministry files.)

[2] Jean Paul Casimir Périer. French Prime Minister and Foreign Minister, December 1893–May 1894; President of the Republic, July 1894–January 1895.

[3] Gabriel Hanotaux. French Foreign Minister in the Cabinets of Dupuy, 1894–5; Ribot, 1895, and Méline, 1896–8.

[4] Théophile Delcassé. French Colonial Minister, 1894–5; Foreign Minister in the Cabinets of Brisson, Dupuy, Waldeck-Rousseau, Combes, and Rouvier, 1898–1905.

[5] Raymond Poincaré. French Minister for Education, April–November, 1893, January–October 1895; Finance Minister, May 1894–January 1895, March–October 1906; Deputy-President of the Chamber, 1895–8.

[6] Jean Dupuy. Director of the *Petit Parisien*; Prime Minister and Minister of the Interior, April–November 1893, May 1894–January 1895, November 1898–June 1899.

[7] Italian Ambassador to Paris, 1892–5.

421. Philipp zu Eulenburg to Holstein

R[ominten], 26 September 1894

Dear friend,

Only a few words by the courier. I think you will gradually come to believe in my objectivity *even in this situation*.[1] One can do no more than take up the cause of Fischer's rash *exposé*.[2]

Yesterday I had another talk with H.M. which proved *nothing can be done to alter* the decision to bring a workable law before the Reichstag.

King Albert is playing the decisive part in this affair.[3] He will also write to the Chancellor.

My attempts to urge caution were wrecked by the subject of the speech in Königsberg,[4] etc. H.M. *has pinned himself down*—or let himself be pinned down (?).

Marschall will personally have to bear the consequences for not having let Kid[erlen] go to Königsberg as adviser!

In my opinion we are faced with a Chancellorship of Botho [Eulenburg] and a State Secretaryship of Bernhard [Bülow] *unless* Caprivi takes it upon himself to act vigorously in the Reichstag.[5] If Caprivi refuses to act, then Botho will suddenly emerge as an energetic Phoebus from the clouds. For Miquel[6] will *never* be Chancellor.[7]

---

[1] Under the influence of the industrial magnate Karl Ferdinand von Stumm and as a result of a series of political strikes and anarchist outrages, the Kaiser not only abandoned his original pro-labour attitude but became greatly incensed against the Social Democrats, whom he equated with the anarchists. The assassination of the French President Sadi Carnot by an Italian anarchist on 24 June 1894 led to a demand by the Kaiser for sterner anti-revolutionary laws in Germany. (See the Kaiser's order to the Chancellor of 16 July 1894, printed in Egmont Stechlin, *Staatsstreichpläne Bismarcks und Wilhelms II, 1890–1894* (Stuttgart and Berlin, 1929), pp. 186–8.)

[2] Not found.

[3] Since the beginning of September the Kaiser had been in East Prussia attending the autumn manoeuvres. Here he was under the influence of the Kings of Saxony and Württemberg, the Prussian Minister-President Botho Eulenburg, and the East Prussian nobility. The Chancellor had not accompanied him. The Kaiser allowed himself to be persuaded of the necessity of changing the electoral laws in Germany by decree in case the present Reichstag failed to accept a more stringent anti-revolutionary law. (See Waldersee, *Denkwürdigkeiten*, vol. II, p. 325; Zechlin, *Staatsstreichpläne*, pp. 191–2.)

[4] On 6 September Wilhelm II made a speech at a banquet for representatives of the province of East Prussia in which he sounded the cry: 'To battle for law and order against the parties of revolution.' This speech, made without previously consulting the Chancellor, was interpreted as a statement of the Kaiser's intention to proceed with his anti-Socialist programme.

[5] The Prussian Minister-President Botho Eulenburg was in favour of a more stringent anti-revolutionary law, and expressed his willingness to face the consequences of a *coup d'état* that might be necessary to effect its passage. He believed, however, that such legislation should not be confined to Prussia but should be extended to the whole of Germany. (See Botho Eulenburg's letter to Caprivi of 8 September 1894 in Zechlin, *Staatsstreichpläne*, pp. 113, 189–91.) Caprivi, although willing to consider a moderate extension of certain legislative regulations, doubted whether stiffer anti-revolutionary laws would have much effect, and he doubted whether the Reichstag would pass them. (See the Minutes of the Cabinet meeting of 12 October in Zechlin, *Staatsstreichpläne*, pp. 193–204.)

[6] Dr Johannes Miquel. Co-founder of the *Nationalverein*; one of the leaders of the National Liberal Party in the Prussian Chamber of Deputies and in the Reichstag from 1867; Lord Mayor of Frankfurt-am-Main, 1879–90; Prussian Finance Minister, 1890–1901.

[7] Miquel, the Finance Minister, was a political opponent of the Chancellor, but he nevertheless supported the more moderate ideas of Caprivi concerning changes in existing legislation. (Zechlin, *Staatsstreichpläne*, pp. 112–13.)

Two things are absolutely necessary at this moment:
1. Caprivi must not become annoyed for any reason and demand his dismissal. He *would receive* it.
2. An understanding must be brought about between him and Botho by all means.

H.M. said to me: 'I have prepared the *terrain* for the Chancellor to take action in such a way that he must take the jump. I hope he does *not refuse!*'

H.M. will not hear of an exceptional law—only of a *serviceable* extension of the penal legislation.

Urge Caprivi to take action—I will advise Botho to *moderation* when I see him on 2 October at the marriage of his brother in Pressin. The two men *must* find a common ground, otherwise the existing system cannot be maintained.

I am working on an *exposé* for H.M. in which I am depicting the dangers *in the Reich* and in regard to Bismarck.[1]

Thank Kiderlen for his letter.

Yours faithfully
PE.

In the greatest haste.

422. Philipp zu Eulenburg to Holstein

R[ominten], 27 September 1894

Enclosed, dear friend, is a very hastily copied promemoria that I will read to H.M. on his return from hunting—or hand to him.

If you have any other arguments, please write to me. *It is very necessary.*[2]

Today the apothecary[3] is here—he leaves this afternoon. I doubt if he is up to any good. He probably brought poisoned pills along.

I will give H.M. the promemoria as an antidote.

Your faithful
PE

ENCLOSURE

Copied very hastily! R[ominten], 27 September 1894

The dangers attached to the introduction of a stern measure in the Reichstag are undoubtedly serious. It is only possible to count on the acceptance of a *very moderate* measure. The moment this limit is exceeded, the opposition of the majority will force the Reich Government to dissolve the Reichstag in order to maintain its prestige.

There is the *possibility, but not the certainty*, of getting the measure through the new Reichstag. It is far more likely that there will be a conflict between the Reichstag and the Reich Government which could only be ended by radical measures (alteration of the franchise, perhaps

---

[1] See below, the enclosure to Eulenburg's letter of 27 September.

[2] During this period of crisis, Eulenburg received a steady stream of letters of advice from Holstein. (From the Eulenburg Papers.)

[3] Nickname for Hermann von Lucanus.

force of arms). The difficulties that would arise in the Reich would be more or less of the following nature :
1. Since the constitution of the Reich has become a part of the constitutions of the Federal States, but since there are also responsible Ministries in some of the Federal States, these Governments would be impeached by their Landtags if they took the side of a Reich Government that had violated the constitution of the Reich. For this reason these Federal *Governments* cannot be counted on in a conflict of this nature, and the Kings of Bavaria and Württemberg would have to take up the fight within the confines of their own lands, whether or not they retained or dismissed their Governments. Nor would they be able to find any other Government willing to take up this conflict, and would therefore have to carry on the fight against the current *personally*. Neither the Prince Regent[1] nor King Wilhelm of W[ürttemberg] would be suited for this purpose. Neither has the nerve to battle through against possible revolts (a certainty in Stuttgart).
2. The only way in which they could come to an understanding with the Reich Government and take part in the conflict would be on the basis of a revision of the *Reich* constitution of '71 by which, for example, the Bavarian Government could demand as compensation for an alteration in the franchise advantages that must alter their existing position in the Reich to the *disadvantage of a governing Prussia*. That is the basis on which the Bavarian and Württemberg Landtags might consent to negotiate. But Prussia could not tolerate any such weakening of its position, and consequently a conflict could arise out of the—perhaps sincere—intention of the Federal *Princes* to stand by Prussia which would require the use of arms.
3. Thus there emerges out of this the picture of an internally disrupted and badly shaken German Reich. Tremendous damage would be done to its national and international reputation. It would be the moment for a French invasion.

A conflict in the Reich also gives cause for hesitations in another respect :
4. The agreement of Prince B[ismarck] with H.M.'s declaration may be sincere.[2] In the event of a conflict in the Reich with all its consequences—that is to say a state of chaos—H.M. would be compelled *par la force des choses* to ask for B.'s help. That would be Canossa—and the Kaiser would have lost the game. 'He would be squeezed against the wall until the pips squeaked'—which was the intention at the time of the Bismarck conflict in 1890.

It is incontestable that out of the present situation there can arise an opportunity for the Bismarcks to take their revenge, and therefore the behaviour of the Prince and his Press is to be watched with *extreme caution*.

---

[1] Prince Luitpold of Bavaria.
[2] The Bismarck Press had praised the Kaiser's Königsberg speech and supported his appeal for unity against the forces of revolution.

In an article in the *Hamb[urger] N[achtrichten]* Prince B. allowed his opposition to the franchise that he himself had introduced to be described as a figment of the imagination. Nevertheless the article concluded with: up to the present no necessity had arisen for a change. It would appear from this that the Prince would lend his help *under certain circumstances*; but also that he is in the position to *refuse* his help until one is ready to negotiate with him.

423. Philipp zu Eulenburg to Holstein

Secret R[ominten], 28 September [1894]

Only a word dear friend! The situation is improving. Botho E[ulenburg] has just written to me that he hears from Bötticher that the Chancellor has the intention of bringing in a bill which *corresponds with Botho's ideas*.[1]

I told this to H.M. *after reading* him my little promemoria. H.M. was obviously pleased and said: 'I have committed myself so far that the Chancellor can count on firm support from me if he introduces a sensible bill.'

I must go to dinner.

Your
PE

424. Maximilian von Ratibor to Holstein

Vienna, 22 October 1894

Confidential

My dear *Herr Geheimer Rat*,

I have been informed by a proved and benevolent source that in political circles here (Deputies, Members of the Upper House, officials) the fact that the Ambassador Count Eulenburg is so seldom in Vienna is a subject of lively discussion. They say that this cannot go on permanently, the intimacy between the two Empires must ultimately suffer from it, it almost looks like contempt on the part of Germany when for the greater part of the year she is only represented in Vienna by a *Chargé d'Affaires*, etc. I believe I am able to deduce from the manner and way in which the matter was told to me that similar thoughts are entertained in the Imperial and Royal Austro-Hungarian Ministry, and also in the Austrian Ministries. Almost every time I meet anyone I am again and again asked the question, 'when is your Chief coming back?' And this question does not always sound like a mere polite enquiry, even though no hint is ever so clearly made that I would be forced to understand it. Since Kálnoky returned from Pest he was extremely friendly to me personally whenever I met him, but in regard to official matters very reserved and inaccessible. I think it is not impossible that by this he wished to show me that he wanted once again to be able to speak with the 'Ambassador'. Perhaps the preceding

[1] For stringent anti-revolutionary legislation.

has some bearing on the Austro-Hungarian attitude in matters connected with trade relations with Spain, about which I reported on the 14th of this month and again today.[1] A remark by Kaiser Franz Joseph is also frequently quoted. He is supposed to have said repeatedly: 'I greatly regret the departure of Reuss, with whom I could talk as with a friend.' I look upon it as my duty to bring this matter to your attention in complete confidence, and to add to it the request that you will most kindly inform Count Eulenburg, to whom I would also have written today by the official courier if the time had not been so pressing.[2] With the expression of my most highest regard I have the honour to be

Sir,

Your most obedient
M. Ratibor

425. Holstein to Adolf Marschall von Bieberstein

B[erlin], 26 October 1894

With your Excellency's permission, I have sent private telegrams to deal with official matters in the interest of the Foreign Ministry.

In the spring of 1893, before my operation for cataract, the then existing papers of this nature as well as the replies were, as Your Excellency knows, destroyed.

I believe the moment has now come in which to destroy the drafts of private dispatches and replies exchanged since that time in order to forestall any possible indiscretion. I ask Your Excellency to approve this destruction.

Holstein
Wirklicher Geheimer Legationsrat.[3]

426. Holstein to Bernhard von Bülow[4]

TELEGRAM

Berlin, 26 October 1894

Private

Caprivi and the Minister-President have both tendered their resignations and both have been accepted.[5] The Kaiser intends to unite the

[1] These reports have not been found.
[2] In his reply to Ratibor of 30 October, Holstein sharply criticised the unfriendly attitude of political circles in the 'mosaic-monarchy'. (From the Eulenburg Papers.)
[3] Marginal Comment: 'Approved. Berlin, 26 October 1894. Marschall.'
[4] From the Bülow Papers. Published by Rogge, *Holstein und Hohenlohe*, p. 412.
[5] The Kaiser had for some time been prepared to accept the resignation of Caprivi owing to the Chancellor's reluctance to push some of the Kaiser's favourite legislation through the Reichstag. The Prussian Minister-President, Count Botho zu Eulenburg, was willing to carry through such legislation even at the risk of a *coup d'état*, but the refusal of the other governments of Germany to back up Prussia evidently persuaded the Kaiser himself to adopt a more moderate policy, and he therefore accepted Botho Eulenburg's resignation when it was offered. The Kaiser's decision to accept Caprivi's resignation was spurred on by an article that appeared in the *Kölnische Zeitung* on 25 October giving an accurate account of the imperial conversation with Caprivi of 23 October and stressing the irreconcilable breach between the political views of the German Chancellor and the Prussian Minister-President. (See Rogge, *Holstein und Hohenlohe*, pp. 409–13.)

offices of Chancellor and Minister-President,[1] has now summoned the Ministers of Bavaria, Saxony, Württemberg, and Baden for consultation. The State Secretary makes his going or staying dependent upon the choice of the successor.[2]

Holstein.[3]

427. Georg zu Münster to Holstein

Paris, 12 November 1894

My dear Herr von Holstein,

[...] As you will have seen from the newspapers, and to-day in a report[4] from Schwartzkoppen,[5] the arrest and the prosecution by military court martial of an artillery captain named Dreyfuss[6] [sic], a brother of the big industrialist Dreyfuss [sic] from Mühlhausen, is creating a great uproar. He is supposed to have handed over important documents to a foreign Power.

Naturally, the *Soleil* immediately carried the information that Dreyfuss [sic] was in touch with Schwartzkoppen. Here at the Embassy and also in Berlin at the Intelligence Bureau of the General Staff nothing is known about this officer. The Italians say the same thing, and so we do not know with whom and for whom, or even whether he has committed treason at all. In this connection it came out that forty-eight Dreyfusses, most of them Jews, were serving as officers in France. [...]

In the hope of soon having the pleasure of receiving a letter from you, I remain, as I have for years,

Yours in friendliest devotion
Münster

428. Paul von Hatzfeldt to Holstein

London, 12 November 1894

Dear friend,

[...] I need hardly tell you how sorry I was, both personally and

---

[1] The offices of German Chancellor and Prussian Minister-President had been separated after the School Law crisis in March 1892.

[2] Caprivi was succeeded by Prince Chlodwig zu Hohenlohe, who was recommended to the Kaiser by the Grand Duke of Baden and Count Philipp zu Eulenburg.

[3] For Holstein's role in the fall of Caprivi, see Meisner, 'Der Reichskanzler Caprivi', *Zeitschrift für die Gesamte Staatswissenschaft*, vol. III, p. 732 *et seq*. In a letter to Philipp Eulenburg of 30 October 1894, Holstein wrote: 'I hear there is already a good deal of agitation going on against me in the Hohenlohe family. Thus Hammerstein [the editor of the *Kreuzzeitung*] told Alexander Hohenlohe [Prince Chlodwig's son] that *I* had inspired the article in the *Kölnische Zeitung* [see p.479, note 5] that led to the break between Caprivi and Botho. In reality, I did not inspire *a single* article relating to the crisis or the anti-revolutionary law, with the exception of the article in *The Times*.' Many years later, after his own break with Holstein, Eulenburg commented on this letter: 'Perhaps Hammerstein is not altogether wrong.' (From the Eulenburg Papers.)

[4] Not found.

[5] Maximilian Schwartzkoppen. German Military Attaché in Paris, 1891–7; Aide-de-Camp of the Kaiser from 1896.

[6] Alfred Dreyfus. Temporarily attached as *stagiaire* to the French General Staff. He was arrested on 15 October and charged with treason. On 22 December he was condemned by a military court martial *in camera*, degraded, and sent to Devil's Island, a penal colony off the coast of French Guiana. The Dreyfus case became one of the greatest moral and political issues in recent French history. It was not until after a series of trials ending in 1906 that his innocence was finally established.

officially, about the resignation of Caprivi. I wrote to him at once to thank him for the kindness he had always shown me. Now, as regards his successor (from whom I only to-day, incidentally, received a very friendly note), I have a notion—if it is false, I hope you will tell me so—that you were not altogether uninstrumental in this selection. I also consider it the best choice that could be made under the circumstances, in so far as I can permit myself an opinion from here. With him there is surely no need to fear upheavals, and other, perhaps dangerous, candidates are kept at a distance.

I cannot deny, however, that I am disturbed by the rumours in the newspapers about a contemplated *coup d'état* over the laws against the anarchists and a change in the electoral system, and also about the stirrings of particularism in South Germany. I hope that there is no truth in all that and that you will very soon calm my fears about it. [...]

Now please tell me one thing: is it true that Hohenlohe is going to Friedrichsruh, and that in general he intends to consult His Highness [Bismarck] constantly, with the consent of His Majesty? In that case it seems to me that His Highness might just as well move back into the Wilhelmstrasse, and the rest of us could pack up.

With warmest greetings for the present, dear friend, and do not punish me too severely for my long silence.

Always your
PH

429. Holstein to Hugo von Radolin[1]

Berlin, 8 December 1894

Dear Radolin,

I can commend Mr Chirol to you very warmly; he was until now the correspondent of *The Times* here, and now unfortunately he is going to Egypt. If the English Government were even approximately as clever and as sensible as he, then England would have a different position in Europe from the one she has now. Ch. was formerly also a member of the diplomatic corps and has a very influential position in London.

If he brings up the subject or throws out feelers, you may tell him *confidentially* what it is that we have against the present English Government: unfriendliness towards ourselves, lack of energy in political questions in general (for instance, Tripoli).

The English are now trying to sow distrust of us in various Cabinets because of our relations with France, although every sensible man must see that between ourselves and France there can never be anything more than peaceful business [...],[2] never friendly relations.

As for Turkey and specifically the Straits, England refuses to commit herself; she can therefore not expect that other Cabinets—Rome, Vienna, or even Berlin—should commit themselves while England runs along loose. We, just like England, will deal with actual cases.

So there you have a topic for conversation. I consider this conversation

---

[1] From the Radolin Papers. [2] Part of a word illegible.

more important than one with Currie, because Chirol is better disposed towards us and at the same time is *at least* equally influential. If you give a dinner while Ch. is there—the more elegant the better—invite him. He fits in everywhere, and he is, as I said, a *reliable* Englishman; but of course always an Englishman.[1]

The office has just sounded the end of the work day.

Since the beginning of the new regime, nothing has happened here from which one can draw conclusions one way or another. Hohenlohe shows great experience in official routine. Let us hope that his health holds out.

Remember me warmly to the Princess.

Your old
H.

430. Paul von Hatzfeldt to Holstein

London, 19 December 1894

Dear friend,

There is nothing new to report, so I will therefore restrict myself to these lines.

The report from Eulenburg[2] which was enclosed with your dispatch[3] did not surprise me and, in so far as I can judge, it correctly pictures Kálnoky's attitude. One point deserves *particular* attention: that Kálnoky has intentionally and repeatedly avoided expressing himself on the *future* position of Austria with regard to certain eventualities. It seems to me that this permits the observation that Austria wants to preserve a free hand in case of a threatening shift among the Powers in order to make a separate peace with her former opponent, to whom everyone else is now paying court.

If it is true, as you too assume, that the existence of Austria would be hanging in air if Russia were to advance in the Near East with the agreement of the other interested Powers, and Austria were in that case not able to count on us—if this assumption, with which I completely agree, is correct, then it is understandable that Vienna should be thinking ahead of time of finding a way out of this blind alley.

On the other hand, Kálnoky has as yet no right to lay the responsibility for the aforementioned eventualities at *our* door. He can not expect us on that account to allow ourselves to be stepped on here in all questions involving our special interests. Nor could he expect us for Austria's sake to agree to Rosebery's proposals whereby we were to commit ourselves and run serious risks without being certain of reciprocal action by England. On the contrary, it was up to Kálnoky to lay the basis for an agreement here in which we could participate. If we had *then* refused to participate, he would have been able to complain with

---

[1] Holstein wrote on 18 January 1895: 'Your news about what Chirol said was very interesting. The Russian-French-English combination does not worry me. *Those* acorns will never grow into great oaks.' (From the Radolin Papers.)

[2] Of 4 December. (*Grosse Politik*, vol. IX, no. 2168, pp. 172–6.)

[3] Of 13 December. (*Grosse Politik*, vol. IX, no. 2169, pp. 176–9.) These two documents were sent to London on 13 December. (From the London Embassy files.)

justification that the vital interests of Austria were not given adequate consideration by ourselves.

From this standpoint, I consider your dispatch to Vienna—about which you wanted my modest opinion—sensible and moderate. If Eulenburg uses it *correctly*, it can in my opinion serve our interests in two ways:

(1) leave Kálnoky in no doubt that we do not intend to allow our feet to be stepped on here, nor to be lured into slippery territory,

(2) but that we are following these matters attentively and will perhaps be willing to reach an understanding about them with our allies, and especially that we would not tolerate a threat to Austria's territorial integrity *any more than we would tolerate a threat to her position as a Great Power*.

In *that*, it seems to me, lies the heart of the matter. For the *fact* remains, one may argue about it as one will, that England is now casting about elsewhere, a policy that England blames on our alienation of herself, and that this casting about *might* lead to the formation of a group that would be extraordinarily dangerous to Austrian interests.

Eulenburg can now do *much* in Vienna, if he is really as outstanding as His Majesty pictured him to me last summer in Cowes.

I must incidentally agree with one of Kálnoky's remarks about England. The danger here does not lie in offending some Minister or other, but in the possible shift of so-called public opinion, which is by the way already making itself felt as a result of the estrangement between us; and even Salisbury will not be able to contend with it if, by the time he returns to office, public opinion has turned decisively against the Triple Alliance.

This was the reason why I recommended at the time of the last Cabinet change that we regard Rosebery as the bridge that would, without too much difficulty, carry us over to the return of the Tories. I never expected great things or decisions of him, and for that reason I warned against being over-hasty almost two years ago in Cowes, when His Majesty wanted to jump in right away on the Siam business.[1] If it had been possible for us to remain on terms of mutual confidence with him until the return of Salisbury, then the danger that is feared in Vienna—that public opinion will turn completely before the next change of Governments and will then also bind the hands of the Tories—would be out of the question or at least be very much reduced.

Therefore my opinion is and remains that we should not allow our feet to be stepped on here and naturally not entertain any propositions that do not make for reciprocity, but at the same time we should leave a loophole for agreement and not totally destroy the hope that we might again become 'friends'.

As regards Vienna and Rome, I have no doubt that in both places they are deeply disturbed about the future. No matter how competent Bülow is or how well his reports are written, I cannot see in that any

[1] At the end of July 1893. See above Hatzfeldt's letters to Holstein of 2 and 7 August 1893.

guarantee that Blanc—whom I have never much trusted—will not in the long run jump out of the straight and narrow path. Incidentally, in that respect one cannot count on *any* Italian, and furthermore Blanc may be ousted again within a few weeks.

Finally, as regards the Dardanelles question (in which, in my humble opinion, we should sit very quietly and passively), it seems to me that the question would not by any means be solved if the Russians were really to turn down the right of passage because they were obliged to share it with others. Once Russia had completed her preparations in the Black Sea, the position of her fleet even in this case would be *incomparably* superior to that of the English, as Salisbury has always recognised. In addition, there is the added danger to-day that in case of a conflict, the English fleet would *simultaneously* have to face the French. I have hardly any doubt that this situation would immediately arise, little as the French might otherwise like to allow the Russians into the Mediterranean. The main object for France for the time being *must* be to avoid losing Russia's friendship and to drive the English from the Mediterranean. Everything else they can regard as *cura posterior*, especially since the French, if left alone with the Russians in the Mediterranean, would be by far the stronger maritime Power and could in addition purchase the aid of Italy, which, as soon as the fear of the English ships was removed, would fall into her lap like ripe fruit.

One may therefore twist and turn as one will: the solution of the Dardanelles question will in all probability decide the domination of the Mediterranean and for that reason would result in a regrouping of the Powers.

For *us* there is, so far as I can judge, only one correct policy in the matter in case England does not want to bind herself to the Triple Alliance, and that is: *wait*, without committing ourselves in *any* direction.

I am certainly no admirer of the Gerlach policy at the time of the Crimean War,[1] because quite apart from everything else, it had false illusions about the European significance of Prussia. To-day the situation is different and this world-shaking question can hardly be settled without us. The more the rival Powers commit themselves to each other, the more certainly they will have to come to us. But that depends above all, I repeat, on our sitting absolutely quiet until the right moment. [...]

Best wishes from your
PH

431. Paul von Hatzfeldt to Holstein

London, 22 December 1894

Dear friend,

[...] I would be in complete agreement with your telegram to

---

[1] Despite his desire for close political relations with Russia, Leopold von Gerlach, the Adjutant-General and trusted political adviser of King Friedrich Wilhelm IV of Prussia, had advocated an uncommitted, independent foreign policy during the Crimean War.

Bülow[1] *if* the information in question had not been communicated to St Petersburg.[2] I have not the slightest doubt, since it is obviously in the Russian interest to alienate us from our former friends, that this information has long since been made known here, and probably in Vienna and Rome as well. But in that case what authority will your otherwise absolutely correct advice carry in Rome? I assume that it will create the following impression: our friends have already covered themselves in St Petersburg without considering whether in doing so they were selling out our interests; but all the same they want *us* to hold fast to the English with whom *they* want nothing to do. They thus want to retain *two* blocs, but they want to retain freedom of choice for themselves if it should come to blows, depending on whether they consider the one side or the other stronger and more dependable. England *alone* with her wretched policy is, without the Triple Alliance, an unsteady reed on which we cannot lean. The *other* group, to which Germany, and perhaps for the same reasons Austria too, is inclined, would be the stronger. Let us therefore make our arrangements in good time with Russia which will be the predominant partner in that bloc, and then we will be covered for any eventuality.

This, it seems to me, will be the reasoning in Vienna and Rome. Nor can we be surprised about it, because *everyone* holds his own skin dearest.[3]

Incidentally, the case is not new and you may remember that several years ago there was a similar one under Prince Bismarck. At that time I had to bring to His Highness' attention the fact that our allies were growing mistrustful owing to our unsteady policy, and that something had to be done to reassure them.[4]

[1] Bülow had telegraphed the Foreign Ministry on 18 December that Baron Blanc saw in England's flirtation with Russia over the Armenian question only a symptom of British weakness, and that he was anxious to see to it that Italy's own relations with Russia should be at least as close as the relations England felt she could arrange with Russia. The Foreign Ministry replied on 19 December that Blanc should consider primarily what the Italian position in the Mediterranean would be in case England, discouraged by the Italian attitude, withdrew from the Mediterranean altogether. 'Italy, which would certainly carry more weight in questions concerning the Near East in collaboration with England, would therefore do well to avoid burning bridges for future co-operation with England on account of the Armenian question.' (*Grosse Politik*, vol. IX, nos. 2193–4, pp. 215–16.)

[2] In a marginal comment at the end of Hatzfeldt's report no. 697 of 11 November, the Kaiser wrote: 'A *highly confidential* conversation today with Colonel Swaine gave me the opportunity casually to throw out the question as to whether Rosebery's statements about an understanding with Russia included the Dardanelles as well as India. It was not difficult to see from his answer that this was essentially the case; and that they were already seriously considering the question of free passage. Hatzfeldt has smelled it out absolutely correctly, and should keep up a sharp lookout. At the end of the conversation I remarked *en passant* that if England were really seriously trying to assure herself of the good neighbourliness of Russia in Asia by giving up the Dardanelles, it was to be hoped England would inform the other Powers about it in good time and not offer them a *surprise à la Congo treaty*; this would hardly be conducive to John Bull's good health. The Colonel was entirely of the same opinion and promised, if he heard more about the question, to make use of this *hint*. W[ilhelm]. Inform Hatzfeldt of this immediately. Also St Petersburg, Rome, Istanbul, Vienna.' (*Grosse Politik*, vol. IX, no. 2161, pp. 153–60.) According to the Foreign Ministry files, this information was not communicated to St Petersburg, but Hatzfeldt was not notified of this fact.

[3] See *Grosse Politik*, vol. IX, no. 2172, pp. 182–3.

[4] See *Grosse Politik*, vol. IV, no. 926, pp. 368–73.

To-day the matter is more serious than it was at that time for two reasons:

(1) because of our attitude in St Petersburg,

(2) because Vienna and Rome see the estrangement between ourselves and England.

Whether that can still be changed is not so easy to say, and it is hardly worth considering because we can hardly retrace our steps on the path we have now taken to the East. I have no doubt whatever that *Blanc and Kálnoky* will only turn to St Petersburg with a heavy heart, because it is clear as daylight that this *can* only be a *pis aller* for them, whereas their true interests lie on the other side. This is as true of Austria as it is of Italy. The former can twist and turn as it will, it will be sorely weakened and its vital interests will be threatened if the present development of things continues. Italy for its part cannot, if events develop in a logical fashion, escape the fate of having the French instead of the English in the Mediterranean, and thus lie with its open coast in a more or less French sea. Italian expansion on the north coast of Africa will then in addition be as good as finished.

Here too they will not turn to Russia *gladly*, above all not the Conservatives. But in the end they will join in the general chorus against the wicked Germans, and Salisbury will be able to do nothing to counter that when he returns to office.

You pose the question as to what caused the changed attitude in Wallace,[1] who was usually so well disposed towards us. None other than what I believe I have already mentioned, that he senses the coming about-face of public opinion, and, as *The Times* always does, is changing his tune in time.

Finally, as regards *our* interests, as things stand now I can only say that to the best of my knowledge and understanding I feel that it all depends on two points:

(1) not to allow the mistrust in Vienna and Rome to grow further, and to prevent both from an ostensible shift to Russia while the situation is still so obscure;

(2) to remain passive here, take no initiative, but allow the hope to remain that we will stand firmly *by our allies*, and therefore, if England comes to an understanding with *them*, we will maintain a *friendly and benevolent* attitude towards her.

I consider this to be incredibly important, because the worm may turn and they may realise here that nothing can be done with the Russians (*Moscow Gazette*) or that their prices are too high. Besides, I share the opinion that within a few months Salisbury will probably be back at the helm, and he, if his majority is not altogether too small and public opinion had not been completely misled against us, can inaugurate a better policy.

I agree absolutely with your opinion, my dear friend, that a Dardanelles *defensive* bloc would be infinitely better. Only I cannot

---

[1] Sir Donald Mackenzie Wallace. Director of the Foreign Department of *The Times*, 1891–9.

quite follow you in the belief that this would have been impossible. In my opinion this was ruined *in Vienna*. If Kálnoky had had the courage at the time to say to Rosebery: 'Your proposal is unacceptable as you have formulated it. I herewith propose another solution, and if *you* accept it, I will promote it with *all my strength* in Berlin and Rome.' If he had done that, there would have been the possibility of an understanding. If Kálnoky could be induced to do this, it would not even now be *impossible*, and Salisbury would be happy, you may rest assured of that, to find at hand something stemming from his predecessor that he can grasp firmly.

A warm farewell for the present, and with the best wishes for Christmas. I *must* close, because there are only a few minutes before the courier leaves.

How happy I would be to talk to you for an hour!

Best wishes from your
PH

432. Philipp zu Eulenburg to Holstein

Vienna, 23 December 1894

My dear friend,

These lines are intended to reach you on Christmas Eve and bring you a warm and whole-hearted greeting from the entire family, which counts you among those friends to whom it is closely attached! You cannot believe how much you are talked about! Ever since you visited poor little Adina[1] at the hotel you have so to speak come alive in the nursery; before, you were surrounded by a mysterious veil.

As we think of you with loving thoughts, so your thoughts will be with us. But I also hope that you will not be too lonely. You have, heaven be praised, old and good friends and firm connections in Berlin. The people who do not hate you love you all the better. This must serve as a sort of compensation for you. Unusual characters are bound to have unusual destinies. The humdrum of daily life assumes a different aspect in you.

You will be receiving a fairy tale with music from Bote and Bock, who published it. Perhaps this little effort will please you since it is about 'freedom'—which is after all a fairy tale.

A. Hohenlohe[2] will have told you the reasons why I did not come to Berlin at this time but preferred to visit the Reich Chancellor in Podiebrad, and I hope you approved.[3]

Now farewell. I will write you something political in the next few days.

Your faithful old
PEulenburg.

[1] Countess Alexandrine zu Eulenburg. Oldest daughter of Count Philipp.

[2] Alexander, Prince zu Hohenlohe-Schillingsfürst. Son of Prince Chlodwig and personal aide to his father during the latter's Chancellorship; later Head of the Administration of Upper Alsace (Kolmar).

[3] Eulenburg was going to Podiebrad, where the Chancellor was spending the Christmas holidays, to discuss with him the rumours about a change of Chancellors and his intended visit to Friedrichsruh. (See *Fürst Chlodwig zu Hohenlohe-Schillingsfürst. Denkwürdigkeiten der Reichskanzlerzeit*, edited by Karl Alexander von Müller (Stuttgart and Berlin, 1931), pp. 24–6.)

433. Georg zu Münster to Holstein

Paris, 27 December 1894

My dear Herr von Holstein!

[...] The Dreyfus Affair has raised a great deal of dust here, and the filthy Press has stirred up still more dust in order to gather dirt to throw at the Embassy and at me. In order not to disturb our relations with France, I have dealt with the matter from a personal standpoint by telling the people here that I could easily grow tired of allowing myself to be maligned here; whereupon there was no lack of apologies and declarations of friendship.

The secret has been well kept and nobody knows what really happened. The Embassy had nothing to do with the matter, but the Intelligence Bureau of the General Staff is very careless and can easily compromise us here. I think that it was the plan of invasion of an army through neutral Belgium that was betrayed. Right at the beginning, just after the trial, there was a rumour mentioned by Clemenceau in his *Justice* to the effect that an invasion through Belgium was intended, that there existed a plan listing the military roads and billeting districts, and that it was this that Dreyfus had betrayed. The Belgian Minister[1] drew my attention to it and was very excited about it. Antisemitism has played a great part against Dreyfus; he cannot be completely innocent, for seven officers, even if they are Frenchmen, would not unanimously condemn a comrade if they were not convinced of his guilt.

I hope to come to Berlin for a few days on the 14th of January, and am very much looking forward to discussing domestic and foreign policy with you and to observing the situation in Berlin at closer range.

Please extend my best greetings to Prince Hohenlohe and Herr von Marschall.

With friendliest greetings
Yours sincerely
Münster

[1] Baron von Anethan.

1895

434. Philipp zu Eulenburg to Holstein[1]

Vienna, 11 January 1895

My dear friend,

A good many days have gone by since I received your last kind letter.[2] I was not very well; terribly tired and run down, like an old cart horse that finds every effort too great.

In your last letter you paid me too many compliments about my understanding and my heart. I am after all only trying to stand by you with my warm friendship as best I can—above all to give you my hand in spirit when I find you are suffering! So don't let us talk about understanding and heart, but of friendship, which is *a matter of course*. You see, dear friend, I worry and torture myself AS YOU DO. So let us not talk to each other in polemics, but let us fight side by side *without thinking about ourselves*. We have no time for that.

Neither of us will change. That we have worked together so long is proof of that, and upon this we can look with pride and the consciousness that we will always *remain* the same in our true friendship and in the way we see things. [...]

Politically there is nothing in particular to report now that Kálnoky has 'returned to the fold'.[3] It would, however, seem desirable to me if the Chancellor were at some time to tell Szögyényi that it would be a good thing if we kept Crispi energetic. My to-day's report about 'Kálnoky and Italy'[4] will give you the key to my request. So it would be good if this remark appeared to be spontaneous—not as though I had made a report. That might otherwise make Kálnoky suspicious of me—and now he eats out of my hand.

Our relations with the new Tsar do not please me a bit, and I am watching H.M.'s family politics with real anxiety. It is a blessing that he has now moved into the palace at Berlin.

Always faithfully
Your
PE

---

[1] Partly printed in Haller, *Eulenburg*, p. 185.

[2] Of 1 January. (See Haller, *Eulenburg*, pp. 184–5.)

[3] Eulenburg wrote in a report to Hohenlohe of 14 December 1894: 'I do not think I am deceiving myself in informing Your Highness to-day that Count Kálnoky—probably after a good deal of deliberation—has come to the conclusion that the existing position in the Triple Alliance together with a connection with England—be it ever so loose—is a sounder basis than the clay feet of the League of the anti-German great Powers of Europe.' (*Grosse Politik*, vol. IX, no. 2170, pp. 179–81.)

[4] In his report of 10 January, Eulenburg said that Kálnoky had spoken in most derogatory terms of Crispi, and would apparently have preferred Rudini as Minister-President. (From the Foreign Ministry files.)

435. Bernhard von Bülow to Holstein

Rome, 15 January 1895

Dear friend,

Excuse me for daring to write to you in pencil. I have only half recovered from an attack of influenza that kept me in bed for several days. But I would not want to let tomorrow's courier go off without thanking you warmly for your kind lines of the 8th of this month. I do not need to tell you that, although your interesting news explains many recent events, their contents also makes me worried and depressed. Rest assured that I will continue to do everything possible so far as my means permit to preach prudence and caution to the authorities to whom I have access. Philipp E[ulenburg] shares our views in theory, but he nevertheless occasionally lets me know that my advice tends to accord with my desires, whereas the facts he has to reckon with are irreconcilable. My *ceterum censeo* remains: no further changes in the key positions! If these are avoided, I am not without hope. I have stressed especially that, apart from the general need for stability and calm, a really serious domestic conflict would seriously curtail H.M.'s freedom of action, especially in the choice of his advisers, and I have repeatedly referred to the feelings in the South and have warned against any loosening of the ties that bind the Reich. I will be happy if I can be of further service to the good cause in the future. In this respect I am completely at your service—I see in that only the fulfilment of a patriotic duty—, but there is one service I do not wish to render under any circumstances, nor can I do so: I will not and can not follow a summons to Berlin. Apart from compelling personal reasons, I am, *vanité à part*, needed here in the foreseeable future for official reasons. You will see from the contents of my present report[1] how complicated and difficult both the domestic and international positions of Italy are, and they will remain so. [...]

Your sincerely devoted
B.

436. Philipp zu Eulenburg to Holstein

Vienna, 22 January 1895

Dear friend,

I wrote the enclosed letter, as you will see, on *14 November*.[2] I think you will see from it how objective I was and not blame me if H.M. should prefer to leave me in Vienna.[3]

I received *no* answer to this letter. In a letter to me written a short time later, H.M. did not mention the contents of my letter of 14

---

[1] See Bülow's report of 13 January. (*Grosse Politik*, vol. VIII, no. 2005, pp. 381–3.) Further reports by Bülow dealt with Italian domestic problems and the King's opinion of the situation. (From the Foreign Ministry files.)

[2] Not found. See Eulenburg's letter to Hohenlohe of that date. (Hohenlohe, *Denkwürdigkeiten der Reichskanzlerzeit*, pp. 13–14.)

[3] Hohenlohe had suggested that Eulenburg become Minister of the Royal Household because it seemed likely that Wilhelm von Wedel-Piesdorf would not be able to retain that position. (*Ibid.*, p. 30.)

November. So he regarded the matter merely as a piece of advice given by somebody else, which is what it was intended to be.

Would it really have been the right thing to do to move me from here??

I am writing to Hohenlohe by the same mail to put myself at his disposal.[1] But I will already say in this letter that I would not take the post without certain misgivings, partly material, but also partly connected with the position itself. I will write you the details when the matter has progressed further.

I was disturbed to hear that you were ill; especially since you did not say *what* was wrong with you. Please explain!

Your old faithful
PE

437. Holstein to Bernhard von Bülow[2]

Berlin, 23 January 1895

Dear Bülow,

The realisation that I am essentially in agreement with you on all important questions is a great comfort to me.

I heard several times from our friend in Vienna.[3] He squints occasionally, but when he opens his eyes he sees with uncanny accuracy. Now we must not lose our heads, but see what is to be done.

The short speech Hohenlohe gave yesterday,[4] all his own idea and the expression of his personality, is in my opinion a little masterpiece. Everyone can see that the speaker has definite objects in view, but nobody *has* to feel that he is meant if he doesn't want to. That Stirum ran up the steps after the speech and shook the Prince's hand effusively is delightful. The position of the Prince is improving, I am glad to say. It is obvious that he is not an orator, but an old experienced statesman. Marschall's big speech[5] was a surprising success; his position has improved greatly as a result. He could use it.

One thing troubles me. His Majesty constantly reverts in his marginal notes—he did so again this evening—to 'the need for the monarchies to consult' about the steady deterioration of conditions in France, about what should be done about such conditions and the soil from which they sprang.[6]

---

[1] Letter of 22 January. (*Ibid.*, p. 30.)

[2] From the Bülow Papers. Only a typewritten copy of this document was available to the editors.

[3] Philipp zu Eulenburg.

[4] In a speech before the Prussian Chamber of Deputies Prince Hohenlohe had defended the Ministry of State against charges of internal dissension and had denied rumours about prospective ministerial changes.

[5] On 14 January in the Reichstag, on the question of the protection of Germans living abroad.

[6] Eulenburg had reported on 17 January that in Kálnoky's opinion the resignation of Casimir Périer was a victory for the Socialists, and that this example would inspire revolutionary parties in other countries. The report was submitted to the Kaiser on 23 January. He commented at the end: 'It might perhaps be in order to get used to the idea—as Sonnemann [publisher of the *Frankfurter Zeitung*] told His Highness [Hohenlohe] last autumn—that something surprising may happen in Paris. I therefore think it would be useful to begin *highly confidential* enquiries among the monarchies for reaching an understanding about a common line we can take in case of need.' (From the Foreign Ministry files.)

We of all people are the last who should propose general measures that are directly or indirectly aimed at France. *On nous enverra promener*, because people would suspect us of chauvenistic intrigue.

For a stylist like yourself it will not be difficult at some time to make a reference to 1792 to an appropriate authority and to mention incidentally the usefulness *de laisser cuire dans son jus*, especially after some prominent Italian has said something to that effect.

Hohenlohe shares our opinion completely—I say our, because I would be insulting you if I had any doubt about yours. Nor do I doubt that His Majesty will very easily see the point at issue. [...]

Your sincerely devoted
Holstein

I assume that you have written recently in detail to Vienna???

438. Chlodwig zu Hohenlohe to Holstein

25 January [1895]

H.M. was just with me. I presented the case, and H.M. has given up the idea of conferring the rank of Minister of State on Eulenburg.[1] After consulting the Minister of War, I suggested that he be made a Lieutenant-General. Lucanus is to have a rank directly behind that of the Minister of War. That is all the same to me. The ministerial conference took place shortly before H.M.'s arrival. Everything went off perfectly. H.M. came to justify his marginal comment opposing my report.[2] He said he would hear nothing about an action by the Powers against France. Therein he agreed with me. What H.M. is considering is the following: he fears that in the event of the formation of a revolutionary socialistic government, one or another of the *monarchical* governments might betray the solidarity of the monarchical governments for reasons of self-interest or because of weakness and establish relations with the revolutionary government in France. H.M. would like to prevent this and make certain that the solidarity of the monarchical governments did not 'crumble'. 'How this is to be arranged,' so says H.M., 'is a problem for cleverer people than I.'

CH.

439. Hugo von Radolin to Holstein

Pera, 25 January 1895

My dear friend,

[...] I feel it is important to be on good terms with the Russian Ambassador[3]—of course without running after him, like Cambon or Currie—because it is a fact that the Russians, thanks to gold and their position as a neighbouring Power, are the ones who will in the end do

---

[1] August zu Eulenburg is meant. (See Hohenlohe, *Denkwürdigkeiten der Reichskanzlerzeit*, pp. 36–7.)

[2] See p. 491, note 5.

[3] Alexander Nelidov. Russian Ambassador in Constantinople, 1883–97, in Paris, 1903–10.

everything they please. Neither we nor our friends will be able to stop them when the hour strikes; and so in my opinion it is a good idea to make *bonne mine à mauvais jeu,* and to extract what advantages there are from the inevitable. This is of course music of the future, but to me it seems indicated to tune our violins ahead of time, of course being very careful not to offend anybody. It seems very possible to me that at the given moment the Turks will try to settle accounts with the Russians when they see no other way out, and their good friends of former times, the English, will leave them sitting in the mud as usual. The idea of many Englishmen about a possible understanding between Russia and England over the passage through the Straits is very foolish (about that I will report in greater detail some time). Nothing could be more desirable to the Russians than the present closure, and they will never help in opening the passage. The only people to whom this would be an advantage would be the English. The Russians, however, know very well that they can break out of the Black Sea whenever they like, whether the Straits are closed or not. But they feel much more strong and secure when they are closed. The few sorry forts on the Bosporus or the Dardanelles will not stop them. That the Sultan realises this can be seen from the fact that he will not make up his mind to fortify the Bosporus effectively. I repeat what I have now written frequently— that the Russians are the only ones who conduct their policy with an exact knowledge of their goals. They have time and do not hurry. At the same time they know how to be pleasant and smooth in dealing with the Turks, and they spend a fortune in the palace. [...]

Your faithful
Hugo.

440. Paul von Hatzfeldt to Holstein

London, 30 January 1895

Dear friend,

The speech of President Krüger[1] had a very disquieting effect here, and Kimb[erley] has just poured out his heart to me about it.[2] The Government is doing its best here for the Boers (Swaziland),[3] even put the damper on Rhodes,[4] and things like that speech worsen an already difficult situation. People here are extraordinarily sensitive about South Africa. The Government is especially anxious to prevent public opinion from turning against *us* on account of such speeches, *especially now*, when K[imberley] wants to reach a closer understanding with us about Moz[ambique] and in general wants to make extensive arrangements in colonial matters.[5]

[1] Paul Krüger. President of the South African Republic, 1883–1900.
[2] On 27 January Krüger made a speech to the Germans of Pretoria on the occasion of the Kaiser's birthday in which he indicated his desire for German support against England.
[3] Swaziland had been granted to the Transvaal in December 1894.
[4] Sir Cecil Rhodes. Prime Minister of the Cape Colony, 1890–6.
[5] On 30 January Hatzfeldt telegraphed to Berlin: 'Lord Kimberley just told me that he has agreed with the Prime Minister shortly to discuss with me in strictest confidence the bases for an eventual partition of Mozambique.' (From the London Embassy files.)

Moral: The moment is as favourable for colonial questions as is conceivable here. I must therefore *very shortly* be prepared for a confidential talk about Moz. and other questions, probably the hinterland of Togo, and in order not to lose the opportunity it is necessary for me to know *exactly* what we *want* and what we *don't* want. Therefore I beg you most urgently to grant my telegraphic request for *immediate* instructions. The main question is above all whether we want access to the Niger if we can get it here, even though we might thereby collide with the French and risk their displeasure.[1]

It is high time for the courier!

Best wishes
H.

441. Holstein to Chlodwig zu Hohenlohe
Draft

B[erlin], 1 February 1895

As there is now no longer any doubt that my remaining in the Foreign Ministry is among those obstacles that make the establishment of the close relations with Prince Bismarck desired by His Majesty more difficult, I regard it as my duty to remove the obstacle represented by my person. As a second consideration there is my cataract trouble that would in any case have caused me to resign in the not too distant future.

Under these circumstances, I request Your Highness to be kind enough to take steps to arrange for my resignation from the imperial service. At the same time I wish to remark that this request is the expression of a firm resolve.

As my eyes have been injured in the service, I have a right to the pension provided by law.

Finally, I wish to express to Your Highness my deep and heartfelt thanks for the kindness and trust with which Your Highness has honoured me for so many years.

H[olstein]
Wirklicher Geheimer Legationsrat

442. Paul von Hatzfeldt to Holstein[2]

London, 8 February 1895

Dear friend,

I saw with pleasure from your letter that you are well once again and back at your post. On the other hand, I am *beside myself* about what you tell me about your plans!

Our friendship is too old and too solid for you not to allow me to ask you *what* made you adopt such an extreme resolve. *What* has happened

---

[1] On 31 January Marschall telegraphed that Germany could not agree to the English occupation of Delagoa Bay or anything else prejudicing the interests of the Transvaal. 'In the hinterland of Togo we want access to a point on a navigable section of the Niger.' (From the London Embassy files.)

[2] The last part of this letter is printed in *Die Grosse Politik*, vol. IX, no. 2224, p. 252.

to make it intolerable for you to continue in an occupation which you love and in which you are useful to others? If I ask this question, you must not forget that I know *nothing* except what I read in the newspapers!

What I do know however, my dear friend, is that *without* you the cart will go *into the mire*. You know that I am no maker of compliments, so that this is my honest conviction.

I am of course certain, even before you answer my question, that you must have good reasons. But are they sufficient to outweigh the damage that your departure would have *on the whole*? Allow me to doubt *that* for the time being, just as I think that you are too modest to admit to yourself what consequences your departure would have for our foreign policy and thus for the country. There is *no one* at hand who can half-way replace you, who can keep things in the right channel and—not least important—who can prevent mistakes and jumping off course.

No one can do that better or anything like as well as you—because this I know for certain: that H.M. has a high regard for you, and that Hohenlohe too places the highest possible value on your assistance. The latter will therefore always be prepared to listen to your advice and through him you can always bring your opinion to bear on H.M., to suggest the right policy and in *many* cases to prevent the wrong policy. So do me the favour to think it over again carefully before you give up the game.

There are certain things, of course, that would make it impossible for you to stay on: for instance, if H[erbert] B[ismarck] moved back into the Wilhelmstrasse. But is that likely?

I need hardly tell you that my inability to come and talk all this over with you makes me more depressed than ever. When this will be possible depends on when this Siberian temperature ends. Then ten horses won't be able to restrain me.

Apart from colonial questions, about which I am writing to-day, I see only two important things here: the Italian negotiations, in which I have done everything possible and have so far at least prevented their break-down[1] (incidentally, take my word for it that Blanc is a thoroughly unreliable rascal, about whom Bülow seems to have illusions), and the situation in China.[2]

The latter stands in the forefront in that a crisis must now come soon which will either unite the three Powers (England, Russia, France) in joint decisions—perhaps even in joint actions—or it will provide the proof that they cannot reach an understanding and that each must look out for himself and take what he can. If we want something, as I am forced to assume from previous communications, then it is time to make

[1] The Italians asked for German support to persuade England to demonstrate her friendship to Italy by ceding the port of Zeila in British Somaliland which Italy needed as a base against Abyssinia. (See *Grosse Politik*, vol. VIII, nos. 1998–2015, pp. 375–93.)

[2] On 1 August 1894 war broke out between China and Japan over Korea. On 6 October, after a succession of Chinese defeats, the British Government invited Germany, France, Russia, and the United States to join in intervention in the Far East. The intervention failed because of German and American unwillingness to participate. (*Grosse Politik*, vol. IX, nos. 2215–17, pp. 243–4.)

up our minds about it. If we continue to wait, then we have *one* good chance that the three will *not* reach an understanding and that we can then throw our weight on the side of the one that suits us best, either Russia or England. But that is *one* chance, and things *may* turn out *differently*. But by what arguments we will then persuade the Chinese to reward us for our previous reserve which was even contrary to their interests, this I really don't know. Furthermore, it seems to me that it is impossible to wait much longer to begin negotiations with the Chinese, because as matters stand there now there soon won't be any more government in China.

Goodbye for to-day, my dear friend, and do not forget my request to hear from you very soon how things stand in Berlin and what has happened recently.

Best wishes from your
PH [...]

443. Holstein to Bernhard von Bülow[1]

15 February 1895

Dear Bülow,

[...] You probably heard that the Kaiser had a long talk with that ex-Jesuit Hoensbroech.[2] Lucanus arranged that. Various signs indicate that Hoensbroech as well as Lucanus spoke against Marschall because the latter has pro-Centrist tendencies. (And how else is he to secure the passage of the Government bills?)

They are now in a hurry about getting rid of Marschall because he is making a position for himself in the Ministry of State and is a decided support for Hohenlohe. So far they have succeeded in making H.M. unfavourably disposed towards Marschall.

A second attack is being directed against both Hollmann and Marschall. The commanding Admiral,[3] egged on by a few young place-seekers, has sent a memorandum with all sorts of cutting remarks about the Reich Navy and the Foreign Ministry to the Kaiser and the marine authorities with the demand that the colonial troops be subordinated to the commanding Admiral. Hollmann has threatened to resign, and Hohenlohe wrote the Kaiser yesterday that he shares the views of Hollmann.[4]

This morning H.M. did not go to see either the Chancellor or Marschall, something he usually does after taking his walk; they say too that he is in a rotten mood. Naturally! All the people to whom he talks are anti-Government, and the latest method of the Fronde—that of praising the Kaiser at the expense of the Government—can hardly fail in its effect. Since I, as I wrote you recently, have already straightened

---

[1] From the Bülow Papers. Only a typewritten copy of this document was available to the editors.

[2] Paul, Count von und zu Hoensbroech. In 1892 he left the Jesuit order and in 1895 became a Protestant. (See Hohenlohe, *Denkwürdigkeiten der Reichskanzlerzeit*, pp. 38–42.)

[3] Wilhelm von Knorr. Commander-in-Chief of the German Navy, 1895–9.

[4] See *Ibid.*, p. 43.

out my accounts with heaven, I can observe things calmly. But in all this I am sorry for the Kaiser who has no notion what kind of future he is preparing for himself. He does not suspect that the most popular man in Germany would be a Chancellor who was known to press his thumb in the Kaiser's eye and who obviously did so.

Incidentally! Poschinger,[1] who is parading around here as the messenger of Bismarck, said the day before yesterday that when relations between the Kaiser and Friedrichsruh had improved a little more, then Bismarck would advise making Radowitz State Secretary in the Foreign Ministry. I suspect that the latter would be sent to Paris after a few months and H[erbert] B[ismarck] would then move in here.

All the above is only for your information, my dear friend, because I can imagine with what excitement you are observing these events.

There is nothing to be done for the time being.

Yours in friendship
H. [...]

444. Holstein to Bernhard von Bülow[2]

TELEGRAM

Berlin, 17 February 1895

Private

Things got more serious recently. On Thursday the Minister of War had a scene with the Kaiser because the latter doubted the loyalty of the Catholic officers. The Minister of War was so angry about it that he told Herr von Lucanus yesterday that in his opinion the entire Ministry should resign, or pose conditions. The whole agitation, in which Hoensbroech is only *one* instrument, is directed against the 'Catholic' Prince Hohenlohe.

I suspect that a crisis is almost upon us in which the Kaiser and his previous advisers will play a sorry role, whether Prince Hohenlohe's cabinet stays on or is replaced by people who are energetic by nature or are made so as a result of recent experience. I will now write to Count zu Eulenburg who to-day asked what had suddenly happened. The whole crisis was unnecessary. Intrigue and irritated nerves.

Holstein

445. Bernhard von Bülow to Holstein

Rome, 18 February 1895

Dear friend,

[...] After receiving your letter of the 7th of this month, I wrote at once in detail to Philipp E[ulenburg]. In my (very full) letter I warned against rash decisions and a too sudden turn to the Right, against any action within the country without being certain of the unconditional support of all the Federal States, against a legitimist crusade against

---

[1] Heinrich, Ritter von Poschinger. Historian.
[2] From the Bülow Papers. Only a typewritten copy of this document was available to the editors.

France, as well as against another *Kulturkampf*, and above all against any changes in the top positions. I supported and proved my warnings by countless arguments drawn from the actual situation and from the lessons of history. After receiving your letter of the 15th of this month and your yesterday's telegram,[1] I once again sent an urgent telegram to Philipp E. My telegram concluded: 'In the interests of His Majesty I ask you most urgently to do everything in your power to prevent changes in Berlin.' Although I am far from failing to recognise the seriousness of the situation, still I do not by any means regard it as hopeless. My hopes in this respect are based on the fact that as His Majesty just parted with Caprivi in the previous autumn, he will undoubtedly not want to part with Hohenlohe now. I am supported in this opinion in that—please regard this information as absolutely secret!—ex-Ambassador Stumm recently wrote to his nephew Müller: 'Hohenlohe has not lived up to my expectations. The dawn is still a long way off!' What Ferd. Stumm means by the dawn you can imagine.[2] [...]

Your sincerely devoted

B. [...]

446. Philipp zu Eulenburg to Holstein

Vienna, 19 February 1895

Secretissime. Only for yourself!

Dear friend,

When I arrived here yesterday I found all the letters describing the situation. Reading them took about an hour and my head was spinning so much that I went to bed. After thinking it over for some time I feel that the basic purpose is not to overthrow Hohenlohe, but to get rid of *Marschall*. They don't dare touch Hohenlohe (1) because they have to bear in mind that H.M. will not now provide Europe with the spectacle of another change of Chancellors, (2) because his position has grown much more secure and people are convinced that his age imposes narrow limits on him anyway.

No, believe me, the *opponents of Caprivi* are so angry only because Hohenlohe took over *Marschall*. Marschall is making these people strain every effort, and they will stop at nothing to overthrow this man from Baden 'who harmed Prussian agricultural interests'.

The opponents of Marschall are successful because Marschall has just as little ability as Caprivi to win friends among the entourage of H.M.

The entourage of H.M. has *not* turned against Hohenlohe because he has the kindly manner of the grand seigneur and is polite by nature. Although the stupid Court ladies may talk against the *Catholic* Chancellor, this issue is only taken up by the military and civilian entourage of H.M. in order to bring up Marschall's 'undignified' flirtation with the Centre Party.

You know that H.M. has felt a pronounced antipathy to Marschall

[1] See above. [2] Bismarck.

for almost two years. I myself, I freely admit, only agreed to the inclusion of Marschall in the Hohenlohe Cabinet *out of consideration* for you. What good would it have done if I had presented my arguments to you *against* his inclusion in those critical days? You presented us with a *fait accompli* and made it a condition for your own continuation in the service!

The weakness of the Hohenlohe Cabinet lay and lies in Marschall, because he has no friends in Prussia and because the Kaiser hasn't liked him for two years—he feels an antipathy for him, as I just said.

Now that I have received a letter from H.M. and *two* written at his orders, all of which describe Marschall's behaviour in inviting Lieber[1] and his assumption that H.M. should speak with him as inexcusable, I no longer have the slightest doubt that H.M. *wants* to get rid of him but doesn't quite know how to go about it.

I could do no more than ask H.M. to avoid all surprises and to wait until the end of this session of the Reichstag. Then we would see.

Now the business is more or less up to Hohenlohe. Will Hohenlohe make this a Cabinet question or not?

I tell you frankly that in my opinion Hohenlohe would be stronger if Marschall went, because in the long run the antipathy of H.M. will become unbearable and because the King after all has the right to select his own Ministers.

But it is above all important that such a change should not occur now, but possibly *after* the session of the Reichstag, and that a Chancellor crisis be avoided.

At the same time H.M. should realise that a stronger line against the Centre would be *dangerous* at the present moment, and that the Anti-Revolutionary Bill must be passed in its present form.

I attach no importance to the highly superfluous remarks of Dönhoff.[2] It is certainly not intrigue but a bit of self-importance that will make no particular impression on H.M. if it is accompanied by an explanation from the Prince. We are a long way from a *coup d'état*.

Everything depends on convincing H.M. that the present Anti-Revolutionary Bill *must* pass. I will write to him about this to-day.

In great haste
Your faithful
PEulenburg

447. Holstein to Bernhard von Bülow[3]

B[erlin], 21 February 1895

Dear Bülow,

I don't know if you have any doubts, but I have none, that at the

[1] Dr Ernst Maria Lieber. Member of the Reichstag, 1871–1902, and leader of the Centre Party since the death of Windhorst in 1891. The Kaiser accused Marschall of having secured Lieber an invitation to a Court ball without informing him. The Kaiser had severed all relations with Lieber on account of Lieber's attitude to the Army Bill. (Hohenlohe, *Denkwürdigkeiten der Reichskanzlerzeit*, p. 40.)

[2] See Holstein's letter to Eulenburg of 24 December 1894. (Haller, *Eulenburg*, pp. 182–3.)

[3] From the Bülow Papers. Only a typewritten copy of this document was available to the editors.

psychological moment His Majesty will finally say: 'My dear Bülow, I am counting on you; do me the favour of taking over the Foreign Ministry.'

Whether you can then refuse without the danger of quarrelling or breaking with H.M. only you can judge. I can not.

With the present anti-Catholic agitation and the artificial awakening of the 'Evangelical' party consciousness, Radowitz would be impossible under the Catholic Prince Hohenlohe. The very suggestion of making Radowitz State Secretary would be certain proof to the present Chancellor that he was to be removed as soon as possible and replaced by a Protestant.

Alvensleben can't do the job; specifically he can't make speeches and he is too old to learn.

Varnbüler isn't a Prussian and is still very inexperienced, although very clever.

Monts would be suitable. But then he would have had to be—if only for six months—Minister to some post besides Oldenburg, for instance to the Holy See. If Phil. Eulenburg now proposed a change of Ministers in Rome to H.M. or to the Chancellor, then we would have an unobjectionable candidate for the post of State Secretary in the foreseeable future.

But those who are pressing H.M. to get rid of Marschall *right away* are really trying to foment a crisis. The Centre would probably reply to the dismissal of Marschall with the rejection of various bills. That would mean the 'Dissolution, with the Agrarian programme'. The new Reichstag would undoubtedly be agrarian, that is, with a Socialist-Agrarian rather than a Conservative majority. *The influence of the Kaiser would thus be paralysed*. For do you think that *this* group, probably with Herbert Bismarck at its head, would have any consideration for the wishes of the Kaiser once it was in the majority?

Yesterday a well-informed man told me: 'The Kaiser doesn't *suspect* who the real Chancellor candidate of the agrarians and bimetalists is: it is Herbert Bismarck. His recent speech on bimetalism, which was greeted with almost fanatical applause, was regarded as a Chancellor's speech.'

Of course people think quite rightly that the father would stand behind the son with his advice.

The dismissal of Marschall *now* would have to be considered as the beginning of a Chancellor crisis, and would, I think, be so considered by Prince Hohenlohe; it would certainly also be so considered by the agitators, among whom Count Moltke, the Aide-de-Camp, is *said* to be very conspicuous since his last trip to Friedrichsruh. I don't know what Varnbüler thinks. He hasn't visited me for a long time.

Briefly then, if Marschall is under all circumstances to be removed here and possibly placed in Bötticher's job, as the Bismarcks demand, even that might be arranged decently if enough time is allowed. In four months, that is *at the end of the sessions*, you could be brought in; in about seven months, Monts could be brought in.

But I fear that temperament is more powerful than reason. I have noticed this increasingly recently, and it is precisely that that gradually makes one discouraged.

The fight we waged for so many years *to preserve the independence of the Kaiser* is in the process of ending in defeat, that is, of placing the Kaiser in a position of constraint. This constraint will exist as soon as the Reichstag is no longer a patchwork, like the present one, but one in which a party can impose its will, especially when it is composed of such rebels as those 'economic reformers'.

And do you think that if the Kaiser then appeals over the head of Parliament to the German Princes, that *they* will run interference for him against the Reichstag and the Constitution?

About four weeks ago I spoke with a man—whom you also know—who sees the Kaiser frequently. I had not seen the person in question for a long time. He joined me and poured out his heart to me. 'If one hears what is being said, if one sees how His Majesty is steering *blindly* towards his doom—it makes one weep.'

As a characteristic item I would like to mention that among the reasons advanced for Marschall's speedy dismissal is his unpopularity with the Kaiser's *entourage*. That surely allows one to conclude that some of the main agitators are in that entourage.

The preceding arguments are based on the assumption that H.M. has not reached some agreement with Prince Bismarck whereby the latter is accorded influence of one sort or another on the *direction* of affairs of state. If this should nevertheless have occurred, one could only say that H.M. must know—is old enough to know—what he is thereby doing.

If such an agreement has not been made, then it cannot be denied that H.M. is by his present behaviour following a course whose immediate aims do *not* correspond with his intentions and whose dangers seem to be hidden from him.

Ever your devoted
Holstein

Just as I had finished this letter I had the opportunity to make *certain* from a remark of Hohenlohe's that he would regard an attack on Marschall *now* as one against himself. But on the other hand I also learned from a very secret communication that—as one might have assumed—the intention on the part of our enemies of involving Hohenlohe in the crisis actually exists.

The whole affair is a sneak attack, taking advantage of the nervous irritability of the Kaiser.

Postscript, 7:45 p.m.

The Kaiser has just informed Hohenlohe in a long and courteous letter (in his own hand) that, although with regret, he has given in to the latter's arguments and is prepared to agree to the dismissal of Schele,[1] the Governor of East Africa. A serious quarrel had flared up between him and Kayser, and it seemed very likely that Kayser would come out on the short end against the military.

---

[1] Friedrich Rabod, Baron von Schele. Governor of German East Africa, 1893–5; Aide-de-Camp of Kaiser Wilhelm II.

The letter of H.M. at least shows clearly that for the time being at any rate he intends to keep Hohenlohe.

So for that reason I also hope that Marschall, whom the Chancellor regards as indispensable in the Council of Ministers, will yet be available to him for a while longer. Perhaps the present mood of H.M. will yet emerge from its critical stage. But that should not prevent sending Monts to the Vatican shortly. I should imagine that the *fear* of Monts as prospective State Secretary might keep many quiet who are now intriguing against Marschall in the Foreign Ministry.

448. Philipp zu Eulenburg to Holstein

Vienna, 22 February 1895

Dear friend,

Your dispatch just arrived—five minutes before the last opportunity to send a dispatch bag.

I am sending you a poor copy of the letter to H.M.[1] Please give it to the Chancellor with my apologies for having forgotten to enclose it in my letter. I was in a great hurry—as I am to-day.

Your faithful
PE.

A letter from H.M. *just* arrived.

Everything consigned to the realm of rumour, with considerable heat—and everything agreed to:

Marschall stays, Hollmann stays,[2] Schele goes, Kayser stays, Golz goes. He concludes: 'If Hohenlohe goes, I go too!'

The letter expresses complete devotion to Hohenlohe.

I will write more about it tomorrow.[3]

ENCLOSURE

Philipp zu Eulenburg to Kaiser Wilhelm II

Vienna, 20 February 1895

Your Imperial and Royal Majesty,

Permit me, as a result of news from Berlin that indicate a certain political unrest, to bring the following observations most humbly to the attention of Your Majesty:

The foundation for Your Majesty's political position might well be termed your firm adherence to Prince Hohenlohe, because a Chancellor crisis such a short time after the resignation of Caprivi, which after all made Europe nervous, would *personally completely discredit* Your Majesty *before all Europe*. With remarkable speed Prince Hohenlohe has created an important position for himself both at home and abroad, and has succeeded in calming the atmosphere. Whoever might try to influence Your Majesty against the 'Catholic' Chancellor would be acting in bad faith—like Harden in the *Zukunft* and the people who back him.

[1] See Enclosure.
[2] See above. Holstein's letter to Bülow of 15 February.
[3] See below.

One way to remove the Prince would be the case Your Majesty and I discussed in such detail at Rominten—the possibility of a conflict between the Kaiser and Reich in the event of a conflict in the Reichstag about anti-revolutionary measures. The serious objections to such a conflict, indeed the conviction that such a conflict could not be fought out until *all* the Federal Governments were *united* against the conditions in the Reichstag, about which the majority of the German people is also profoundly indignant—all this has led Your Majesty to consider the necessity of going forward *gradually*, step by step, and of gaining a footing by legal means. Your Majesty cannot depart from this course without being accused of grave inconsistency. Whoever would advise such a thing is either *completely naive* politically or is also—*mala fides*. Because anyone agitating for this crisis in the Reich intends to 'fish in troubled waters'—and I have my own ideas when I hear the outcry from the Friedrichsruh crowd against the present Anti-Revolutionary Bill which Your Majesty ordered with wisdom and wise foresight.

The crisis agitation is promoted by the various efforts to spoil the present favourable attitude towards the Anti-Revolutionary Bill. Such an effort would be to antagonise the Centre Party, on whose support the passage of the Bill *to a large extent* depends. The Centre has indicated its support WITHOUT demanding payment in return. That after all is something that deserves recognition. Under such circumstances it is of course important for the Centre to preserve a belief in Your Majesty's *objectivity*. Your Majesty remains *above all* a Protestant Kaiser—*but* as German Kaiser two-fifths of the population under Your Majesty's sceptre are Catholic. The belief that Your Majesty might be hostile to this group would drive the Centre into opposition against the Anti-Revolutionary Bill, which would fail to pass, the Reichstag would be dissolved, there would be a Chancellor crisis—and: Your Majesty would have worked for the *tertius gaudens*! There was something of this in the frank conversation with Count Hoensbroech—I humbly beg to be forgiven for my audacity!—but for two-fifths of the German Reich he is a priest who has broken his oath. What would *we* say if Frommel[1] turned Catholic, were received in the castle in Vienna by Kaiser Franz Joseph, and told the Kaiser that he felt free for the first time in the company of the Apostolic King?

Everything has a certain relationship with everything else—and demands great caution, great reserve.

The eventual resignation of Marschall is a case in point. I do not doubt that Prince Hohenlohe will give in to Your Majesty's desire, but the time must be selected with great care. The disquiet that this resignation would cause must be avoided at all costs during the debates over the Anti-Revolutionary Bill. The time can best be chosen by Prince Hohenlohe, whose Ministry Your Majesty after all accepted as it stands.

With this I close my epistle—with a feeling of discomfort because I was unable to unfold a pleasant picture for my beloved Kaiser! But my

---

[1] Emil Frommel. Court chaplain.

conscience compelled me to warn Your Majesty. I may of course be mistaken in many respects—but still something would remain that would be good for Your Majesty to know.

And so I beg forgiveness!—and again, forgiveness!

449. Philipp zu Eulenburg to Holstein

Vienna, 23 February 1895

Dear friend,

Yesterday I wrote Marschall a reassuring letter, and with a clear conscience; H.M. ordered me to do so *specifically*, and even says in his letter to me: 'That business about the ball has been forgotten.'[1] So his dismissal, or transfer, has definitely been *postponed*.

Still, *we* should realise that after the Reichstag session a change will have to be inaugurated *very* quietly. I agree with you that Monts must be considered a candidate. He is a man in every respect. I had considerable opportunity to see him here. His attachment to you and admiration for your worth is boundless. We agreed on that score—and the fact that you have really treated me quite badly recently was immaterial.

The agitation against Hohenlohe *does not bear the stamp* you think. It is there, I don't doubt, but it didn't reach H.M. in the way you may imagine. H.M. replied to an exposé I had written on the basis of Alexander H[ohenlohe]'s letter:[2] 'I give you my Imperial word of honour that these are *phantasies—nothing* of that sort has reached my ears. I think that should satisfy you!'

So at any rate H.M. didn't notice the attack on Hoh., and it would be ruthlessly suppressed if it should occur. It would be impossible to express oneself in a friendlier, more attached, or more appreciative way than H.M. did in writing about the Prince. Even the energetic conclusion: 'If H. goes, I go too' expressed a great deal, even though meant in jest. No, my dear friend, things aren't *yet* so bad as you think. And what attitude did H.M. take to the Hollmann crisis, to Schele? In so different a way from what you, Alex. H., and Marschall feared that I am rather annoyed that you should have given me *such* a fright!

From my letter to H.M. you will see that I said everything there was to be said and that *nothing* was glossed over. Nor has H.M. rejected this point of view—but I would like to add that this demonstrates even *more* willingness to meet Hohenlohe's wishes. There lies the centre of gravity—and that has *not* shifted as yet. Quite frankly, I was not 'necessary'.

You are quite right, however, in writing about the objectivity that makes it possible for us to work together better than with anyone else. How can a small difference of opinion on some matter be important

[1] See p. 499, note 1.
[2] Letter of 17 February 1895. (Hohenlohe, *Denkwürdigkeiten der Reichskanzlerzeit*, pp. 42–4.)

enough for us to 'growl' at one another?[1] This was done only by *you* and I am heartily glad if you want to be 'nice' again.

Your old faithful
PE

450. Philipp zu Eulenburg to Holstein

Vienna, 28 February 1895

Dear friend,

To-day only a word. I am overtired and have a cold and will write tomorrow.

Everything in good order so far as H.M. is concerned—even in *superlatively* good order.

Please see to it that the *Kölnische Zeitung* and similar papers known to be in close contact with the Foreign Ministry do not take too sharp a tone against the Agrarians, despite the fact that the latter had the *colossal effrontery* to make fun of the Kaiser's fine speech at the Provincial dinner.[2] Otherwise there will be a reaction on the part of these people, and they would refuse *to vote funds for the cruisers*.[3] Then, however, H.M. might turn very sharply against them, and Hohenlohe would be left 'on the see-saw'.

H.M. is now behaving so *sensibly* about the Conservatives that we can't allow him to be pushed into another course. For the two to remain together (H.M. and Chancellor), it is important to remain *moderately conservative*.

Believe me!
In haste, your very [ ][4]
PE

451. Philipp zu Eulenburg to Holstein

1 March 1895

FOR YOUR INFORMATION ONLY

Dear friend,

Once again I got no chance to write. A long conversation with Lobanov, on which I will report,[5] forced me to miss the dispatch bag. So, more tomorrow.

I just wanted to tell you to-day that H.M. heard that Wald[ersee] wanted to stay with H[erbert Bismarck] when he received the Bl[ack] E[agle] O[rder]. H.M. then indicated to W., not directly but in a roundabout way, that that was *impossible*. W. then stayed in a hotel.

---

[1] See Holstein's letter of 21 February 1895. (Haller, *Eulenburg*, p. 186.)

[2] At a dinner of the Provincial Diet of Brandenburg on 23 February the Kaiser spoke of his desire to do something for the lasting benefit of the peasantry, but he warned against exaggerated expectations for no class should expect to be favoured at the expense of another.

[3] On 8 January and again on 8 February the Kaiser publicly expressed the need for an increase in the German fleet.

[4] Word missing.

[5] The report is dated 2 March. Lobanov told Eulenburg about the difficulties that awaited him when he took over the Foreign Ministry in St Petersburg: the disorganisation in the Ministry caused by Giers' illness, and especially the strong influence exercised on the Tsar by his mother. (From the Foreign Ministry files.)

H.M. is of the opinion that W. is *au fond* glad of this opportunity to have a reason to cut H[erbert].

Please *destroy* these lines, which contain an indiscretion. But I couldn't help telling you about this decision of H.M.'s on his own initiative while you are working *so hard*. It also helps to confirm my opinion that the gulf between H.M. and H. is *unbridgeable*.

Your old faithful
PE.

452. Holstein to Hugo von Radolin[1]

Berlin, 2 March [1895]

Dear Radolin,

During the past six weeks great efforts have been made here to get rid of Marschall. However, his position to-day is more secure than it was before. There are many factors that make him the most successful parliamentarian of the entire present Cabinet; Miquel is the only one who might be his equal. And in the Ministry itself M. is making a position for himself, despite latent opposition.

The two Eulenburg brothers[2] and Lucanus are regarded as the active opponents of M. And the Bismarcks probably won't strew roses in his path either.

It appears that there will soon be a parliamentary debating battle between M. and Herbert Bismarck, who is gradually assuming a leading role among the wildest Agrarians. I am looking forward to this speech tournament.

All the efforts on the part of M.'s opponents were frustrated by his success yesterday. The Kaiser is happy as a lark about his four cruisers.[3] [...]

Lay me at the feet of your ladies.
With a warm shake of the princely paw
Your
H.

453. Paul von Hatzfeldt to Holstein

London, 6 March 1895

Dear friend,

[...] Incidentally, since we also have other things to discuss (Mozambique, Togo), I will again be seeing Kimberley in the next few days and China will automatically come up.[4] I would like to leave him the initiative as much as possible, because the more they try to force us to drop our reserve here, the better the situation is for us.

---

[1] From the Radolin Papers.   [2] August and Botho Eulenburg.

[3] On 1 and 2 March the Reichstag passed a Government request for a large increase in the navy, including four cruisers.

[4] A Chinese peace mission was sent to Japan late in January, 1895, but the Japanese refused to negotiate because the Chinese delegates had not been invested with adequate authority. Peace negotiations finally began at Shimonoseki on the island of Honshu in March 1895.

Meanwhile, my dear friend, it might be in order for us to make up our minds as to *what* we actually want and should do *pour le cas*. It is of course possible that the situation will *not* arise, but then it may, and if things develop so that a very confidential discussion becomes opportune, it would not be good if I were forced to restrict myself to broad generalities.

How things will develop seems to me at the moment to be still incalculable and one can imagine all sort of possibilities. The only thing about which I don't think there is any doubt is that the Japanese will make very large demands. If this proves to be the case, then the situation Kimberley envisaged will arise that the demands will be rejected by Peking even if Li Hung-chang[1] believes they have to be accepted. In that case Kimberley expects the Japanese to press on and capture the capital, the flight of the emperor, *et tout ce qui s'ensuit*. But it seems to me that the possibility also exists that the Powers most immediately concerned will intervene at once if Li Hung-chang is presented with demands which they believe conflict with their own interests (like Russia, which demands the complete and *actual* independence of Korea). Whether the three Powers in question will agree on a common stand, or, if they fail to do so, each presents his own viewpoint, remains to be seen.

In both cases, providing the Japanese do not give in to foreign pressure, Kimberley will be right in that Peking will fall and the Chinese Empire will collapse into a state of chaos. The question that concerns us, it seems to me, will then be the following: what position will the three Powers take, and what should we do to safeguard our position and our interests?

It seems probable to me if it comes to that, that at least an effort will be made to adopt a common policy to prevent the continuation of the war, the break-up of the Chinese Empire, and to arrange a peace satisfactory to the participants. It is my impression that in consideration of our position and prestige in the world we cannot avoid taking part in the exchange of views, discussions, and possible action. As things stand it seems to me we could do so without running great danger of annoying Russia and at the same time being of service to England. The Russians want above all the actual, not only the formal, independence of Korea, and they quite agree to that here.

If it appeared—and it should soon be obvious—that England or one of the other two Powers were at the same time seeking *special* privileges (through special negotiations with China or in some other way), then we could not be denied equal privileges. The *precondition* for this in my opinion is that now, as soon as difficulties are apparent in the peace negotiations, we take part in the exchange of views of the Powers and show clearly that in a question as great as this we have a right to be heard and we intend to be heard.

I thought, my dear friend, that you would permit me to give you my

---

[1] Li Hung-chang. Chinese general and statesman; chief Chinese Plenipotentiary at the Sino-Japanese peace negotiations in 1895.

modest opinion as to the course we should follow, something I do not think should be done in an official report if one is not asked. *Vous en ferez ce que vous voudrez*, and I only hope that you will tell me some time whether and to what extent you agree with me.

Here, by the way, they still have so little idea of what they want that they aren't even certain whether they should agree to the cession of Formosa to Japan or not. Nor are they absolutely certain as to whether they should refuse to allow the Japanese *any* annexations on the mainland. If the Japanese should content themselves with occupying certain territories temporarily until the peace conditions have been fulfilled, they would hardly raise serious objections.

Many thanks for your last letter. I need hardly tell you how pleased I am that everything is temporarily going more smoothly. Let us hope it stays this way. (Do you know what H.M. said about Caprivi? 'He never did me a single favour.' Would it not be possible to do this in certain things from time to time and thereby make it possible to be less tractable in other things? This I cannot judge, but I am obliged to think of the past, when His Highness [Bismarck] saved up his influence and his stubbornness for particularly big issues in dealing with H.M., but gave way on matters that concerned him less deeply.) [...]

And now, dear friend,
With best wishes
Your
PH [...]

454. Bernhard von Bülow to Holstein

Rome, 10 March 1895

Dear Holstein,

As I telegraphed you, I lost no time after the receipt of your serious letter of the 21st of last month[1]—before the arrival of H.M. in Vienna[2]—to write most urgently to Philipp E[ulenburg]. Since I was and am convinced that H.M. does not want to part with Prince Hohenlohe, I stressed especially that the departure of Marschall would shatter the Chancellor's position almost beyond repair: indirectly, because the Chancellor could not get along without Marschall's parliamentary-bureaucratic-ministerial support; directly, because public opinion would see in M.'s departure an advance notice of the resignation of the Chancellor as well. I added how and why I also agreed with you that later and under changed circumstances Monts would be a splendid successor for Marschall. I assume that our efforts have not been in vain. Philipp E. has meanwhile telegraphed to me: 'Berlin storm has passed over, Marschall stays.' Rest assured that I will in future too be glad to do what lies in my humble power to preserve us from other changes which (quite apart from the need for some peace and a certain con-

---

[1] See above.
[2] On 26 February Kaiser Wilhelm II had gone to Vienna to attend the funeral of Archduke Albrecht.

tinuity) would mean a leap in the dark as things stand to-day. We need steadiness, thoughtfulness, and the avoidance of all extremes. [...]

With warmest greetings and wishes
Ever your sincerely devoted
B.

455. Hugo von Radolin to Holstein

Constantinople, 20 March [1895]

My dear old friend!

You, who always keep me in your kind thoughts and take care of my interests, have arranged this unexpected honour for me.[1] I am certain of it, although no one has told me so. For otherwise I do not think that they would have thought of me. So, many thanks dear old friend. I will write to you as soon as I receive the telegram from H.M.

Your
Hugo.

456. Philipp zu Eulenburg to Holstein

Vienna, 7 April 1895

Dear friend,

Osten-Sacken[2] came yesterday. He had the special permission of Tsar Nicholas to do so, and was *commissioned* to talk things over with me. This shows that the Russians are *well-disposed*, although they want to wait and see. I am just composing the report,[3] which will be of interest to you. It is to go off tomorrow afternoon. As you can imagine, I gave Osten-Sacken a thorough indoctrination.

Among other things, I advised him to confide in Hohenlohe, never to by-pass Marschall, and never to forget to seek *advice* from *you*. I therefore ask you, for *my* sake, to be sure to receive this *most distinguished* man, whom I have known for years and who has the *best conceivable* feeling towards us, and to give him your counsel.

I told O.S. that you were so anxious for good relations between Berlin and St Petersburg that from you he would under all circumstances receive advice which would be best for our *mutual* interests.

He asked me to write to you and to commend him to you.

During our endless conversation, I found Osten-Sacken to be very *reasonable*, *calm*, and *lucid*. He seems to have communicated his instructions accurately. To these he added a flood of personal opinions that were of great interest.

Deepest thanks for your letter. You are obstinately silent about your health. How are you? Thank goodness you seem to be in a fairly good mood. Apparently things are not going too badly.

Your old faithful
PE.

[1] Radolin's appointment as Ambassador to St Petersburg.
[2] Nicholas Dimitri, Count Osten-Sacken. Russian Ambassador in Berlin, 1895–1912. Osten-Sacken had been designated as the successor of Prince Lobanov, who had become Russian Foreign Minister in March.
[3] *Grosse Politik*, vol. IX, no. 2313, pp. 348–51.

Postscript

O.S. *thanks his lucky stars* not to know the Bismarcks. He never saw Herbert, and certainly will not invite him. He expressed himself in the strongest terms about his last unqualifiable speeches, which he considered barbarous. In St Petersburg they were terrified that he might come.

E.

457. Paul von Hatzfeldt to Holstein

17 April 1895

Dear friend,

Things are moving fast at present, and everything I might write to-day will be superceded by the telegraph.

The situation has now developed that I often enough predicted to Kimberley in the past, namely that events would find us all unprepared unless we agreed in time about the possible eventualities and the attitude we intended to take about them.[1]

To-day, a conference is the only thing we can still do, *if* it isn't even already too late for that. And if we do want one, there is in my opinion only *one* way to arrange it: by a previous understanding with Lobanov. I do *not* think that the French will take the initiative in this matter, but I do think they will go along if this is what Russia wants.

In general we have arrived at a point (something you and I have always tried to avoid) at which in fact everything depends on the Russians, who are fully conscious of their weight and demand that this be recognised as the precondition for every favour. Ph. Eul[enburg]'s report[2] could not have been more instructive in this respect, and we will see a good deal more of this sort of thing. In addition, as you yourself now believe, Lobanov is by no means a friend of ours. Perhaps you will remember that I predicted this years ago when his appointment[3] was first mentioned, in '80 or '81 if I am not mistaken. I do not consider this any particular insight on my part, because I have known him since my earliest youth and had plenty of opportunity to observe him in Constantinople.

Nevertheless I quite agree that we should try to get on good terms if we know *how* it will benefit us—something that I have always regarded as a precondition, as you know. Unfortunately, I do not see anything very satisfactory in what O[sten]-S[acken], evidently under instruction, had to say in this regard. [...]

Afternoon

I have just seen Sanderson, who showed me the telegram from Tokyo about the peace terms.[4] We will soon see whether Russia will

---

[1] On 17 April the Treaty of Shimonoseki was signed ending the war between China and Japan.
[2] See p. 509, note 3.   [3] As Ambassador to Berlin.
[4] China was to cede Formosa, the Pescadores Islands, the Liaotung Peninsula (including Port Arthur) to Japan, pay a large indemnity, and sign a treaty of commerce opening seven additional Chinese ports.

swallow them, possibly because they have already been bought off by the Japanese, or whether they will demand revision, in which case a conference would be called for.

If Russia contents herself with accepting compensations, a general process of grabbing will probably begin. What will *we* do then? I have not yet been informed what Brandt thinks about this!

And now belated thanks for your letters.

It is a crying shame that Radolin, who has known Lobanov for years, isn't in St Petersburg now, for everything depends on getting him to talk! No chargé d'affaires can do that, no matter how clever he is, least of all with that haughty Lobanov.

And now goodbye for to-day. If things turn out so that the Japanese can take over their plunder without interference and keep it, then I may hope to see you shortly in Berlin.

With best wishes
Your PH.

458. Philipp zu Eulenburg to Holstein

Carlsbad, 3 May 1895

My dear friend,

I had wanted to write to you earlier about my particular pleasure about your Far Eastern policy, but I was incapable of doing so.[1] I was much sicker than I myself thought, and during the first part of my stay here I was in a very serious condition. [...]

I can only follow the course of events through the newspapers, and am amused at the embarrassment of the French patriots as Münster promenades arm-in-arm with Faure.[2] They sent my old friend Lecomte[3] to the Embassy in Berlin. He was previously at the Vatican. He is one of the secret admirers of Germany and is an advocate of a Franco-German rapprochement. He was sent to Berlin in a tremendous hurry—so he wrote to me from Rome. Whether that has any significance I am in no position to judge. In all events he is a thoroughly honourable person, strikingly clever. You may perhaps think *too* clever. But he employs his talents in the cause of peace.

I cannot deny that this new turn against Albion warms my heart.[4]

---

[1] After the publication of the Treaty of Shimonoseki, Russia informed Germany that the Japanese peace terms obliged Russia to advise Japan to give up her demand for the Liaotung Peninsula. (*Grosse Politik*, vol. IX, no. 2244, p. 270.) A telegram drawn up by Holstein was sent to the German Minister in Tokyo on 17 April informing him that Germany intended to join in the protest. (*Ibid.*, vol. IX, no. 2245, p. 270.) By supporting Russia in the Far East, Germany not only diverted Russian pressure from the West, but forced Russia's ally, France, to co-operate. On 23 April Russia, France and Germany presented separate statements advising Japan to retrocede the Liaotung Peninsula in return for an increased indemnity. (*Ibid.*, vol. IX, no. 2252, pp. 275–8.) England took no part in the intervention on the grounds that the Japanese peace terms did not infringe on English interests. (*Ibid.*, vol. IX, no. 2239, pp. 266–7.)

[2] Felix Faure. President of France, January 1895–February 1899.

[3] Raymond Lecomte. French Secretary of Embassy in Berlin, 1895–1907; Minister in Teheran, 1908–18.

[4] The Japanese did not consent to retrocede the Liaotung Peninsula until 5 May. Meanwhile there was considerable speculation about what attitude England would take should constraint against Japan be necessary.

The centre of our future development lies in world trade, and our deadly enemy in this field is England. No matter whether Rosebery or Salisbury is in power. That Russia is shifting her centre of gravity towards the Far East—something to which I drew attention in my reports very shortly after my transfer to Vienna and as a result of my close relations with Lobanov—seems to me now to be quite obvious. It was therefore undoubtedly right to define our position *at once* wherever a conflict between Russian and English interests manifested itself. In the future development of the great commercial questions, our place can *only* be at the side of Russia. I think that Lobanov has grasped this very well. There is only the question as to how far he has won over the young Tsar to this idea.

Austria takes a bitter-sweet view of these developments.

Kálnoky undoubtedly feels himself left behind, despite his long relationship with Lobanov. He is undoubtedly peeved by our attitude which assures us the first *pas* in St Petersburg. But on the other hand he finds Russia's shift towards Japan and China and the Siberian railroads agreeable. The easing of tension in the Balkans makes the prospect of the renewal of the Three Emperors' League seem more probable and possible to him. Hand-in-hand with that, however, will go an increased antipathy towards Italy. Or does he dream in angry and jealous moments of an Austrian-Italian-Spanish-English connection, with the domination of the Mediterranean? I don't *yet* think so. *For the time being* the Three Emperors' League is his ideal, and though he might have preferred that *he* and *Lobanov* had politely invited us to join, he will also accept if *we* and Lobanov ask him. [...]

Your old faithful
PEulenburg

459. Paul von Hatzfeldt to Holstein

London, 11 May 1895

Dear friend,

It would be very nice indeed if we could arrange for *Russia* to reject the French wishes without reference to ourselves.[1] But Lobanov will have no desire whatever to do so, as I feared from the beginning, and the anger of the French if they fail to get what they want will probably be directed against us.

I completely agree with the desire not to estrange the English from Russia completely. But how can this be done if Lobanov himself, according to his own statements, wants nothing better than to keep the English out of any future negotiations in Tokyo? It is clear that the present English Government, if they are asked to take part in the

---

[1] Hatzfeldt had been informed in a telegram of 4 May that the French Ambassador had mentioned the Pescadores Islands for the first time and had tried to demonstrate 'that through the present arrangement Russia would get what she wanted, but that France and Germany would get too little if the Pescadores Islands were left entirely in the possession of Japan'. (*Grosse Politik*, vol. IX, no. 2260, p. 284.) The French move was supported by Spain. (See also vol. IX, no. 2269, pp. 292–3.)

negotiations, will not take sides against Japan, so France and Russia *cannot* want English participation.

At the same time, I should like to say now that I am most doubtful whether the English Government would accept an invitation to participate. Considering their lack of logic and consistency anything is possible, but for the time being it seems to me very unlikely. On the other hand I think it fairly probable that if they are invited by us, they will be conceited enough to say immediately: there is just another example of the fact that other people can't get along without us, they are running after us again, and we are after all the masters of the situation when we choose to be.

If we nevertheless wish to operate here in the manner in question, then I would suggest that we say the following: 'We have always regretted your non-participation. Now there is a new development in the situation that will make it possible for you to come in with honour. If you wish to do so and inform us of this confidentially, we are prepared to suggest your participation and if necessary to insist upon it. But if you do not wish to do so even now, that is naturally your affair entirely. We have again wanted to show you that *we* don't desire England's isolation. We cannot separate ourselves from the others or, alone, even prevent them from pursuing their own interests, which may also create a threatening situation for English interests.'

This is in my opinion the tone that would have the greatest prospect of being attended to here and that *might* bring about English participation.

If you people want me to take this line, please give me the signal.[1]

Best wishes from your

PH.

460. Holstein to Hugo von Radolin[2]

Berlin, 14 May [*1895*]

Dear Radolin,

You fell right into the middle of things, nor can you, I think, complain about inadequate instructions. From telegrams alone I cannot yet judge how you carried them out. But it would seem to me that you allowed Lobanov to have the last word more often than necessary. However, that is no final judgment. Let us wait and see what the reports have to show.

The German standpoint is a very clear one and has not changed *in any way* from the beginning. We have no intention of allowing the Pescadores, about which not a word was said before, to be inserted belatedly into the programme.[3]

---

[1] Germany and Russia agreed that they should support France no further than in seeking assurances from Japan that European shipping would as before be assured free passage through the Straits of Formosa. The participation of England was not considered necessary or desirable. (*Grosse Politik*, vol. IX, nos. 2270–1, pp. 293–5.)

[2] From the Radolin Papers.   [3] See p. 512, note 1.

The significance of the recent telegram from Formosa is indirect.[1] How does the Governor of Formosa know what the Chinese Ministry in Paris is negotiating with the French? He was informed about it from Peking in order to keep alive the spirit of resistance of the people against Japan. The rebellious velleities in Formosa are in part natural, in part artificial. The simplest thing would be to leave Japan with the problem of pacifying Formosa. That will give them something for their army to do. China *and France* on the other hand would probably like to use these disturbances as an excuse to prevent the annexation.

In haste and fatigue

Your H.

461. Holstein to Maximilian von Brandt[2]

Berlin, 19 May 1895

Your Excellency

[...] Telegrams came from two sources yesterday saying that the Chinese Minister in St Petersburg—the little fellow's name is Hsii,[3] is it not?—is working with success on arranging a loan[4] with Russian and French participation, to the exclusion of German capital.

If our bankers are so dull-witted, there is nothing to be done. The Government cannot and will not play the part of Chief Banker. The most we can do is to inform them of news that comes in. But even this has its difficulties, because when Marschall sent for Hansemann[5] and Schwabach,[6] he found that the former was out shooting roebucks, and the latter was rinsing himself out.

The water is still cloudy in politics, too. France would like to have something to show for it. We have nothing against this on principle, but we don't want the—temporary—agreement to be delayed or possibly endangered on that account. [...]

Your Excellency's very devoted

Holstein [...]

462. Maximilian von Brandt to Holstein

Wiesbaden, 23 May 1895

Dear Sir,

[...] You do poor Schwabach an injustice; he left only after Herr von Mühlberg[7] and I had told him that it was probably not necessary for

[1] The German Vice-Consul in Taipei telegraphed on 10 May: 'Governor of Formosa informs me that through the Chinese Ministry in Paris negotiations are being carried on with France about French objections to the annexation of Formosa. France seems willing, but no firm agreement as yet; French warships expected here.' (*Grosse Politik*, vol. IX, no. 2267, pp. 289–90.)

[2] From the Brandt Papers.

[3] Hsii Ching-cheng. Minister to St Petersburg and also to Berlin, 1891-8.

[4] A loan to China for the payment of the war debt to Japan.

[5] Adolf von Hansemann. Berlin banker. Head of the *Diskonto-Gesellschaft*.

[6] Julius Leopold Schwabach. Partner in the banking house of Bleichröder; head of the firm after the death of Gerson Bleichröder in 1893.

[7] Otto von Mühlberg. *Vortragender Rat* in the Foreign Ministry 1885–1900; Under State Secretary, 1900–7; Prussian Minister to the Holy See, 1907–18.

him to stay; we were quite content to have him go, because as long as he was in Berlin, Rothschild[1] knew everything that was going on there, and this seemed at the present stage of the affair to be superfluous, to say the least.

I don't know how the loan question stands, because the enthusiasm of the Chinese for me has naturally cooled off greatly since my departure from Berlin, but I would assume that the things going on in St Petersburg are chiefly intrigues of the *Crédit Lyonnais* which is working against the French banks that co-operate with Berlin. I readily believe that Hsii lends a ready ear to such things for compelling reasons, but I doubt that Tientsin or Peking would at this moment run the risk of offending us on the loan question. [...]

Your sincerely devoted
M. v. Brandt

463. Leo von Caprivi to Holstein

Torgau, 1 June 1895

Dear Herr von Holstein!

Many thanks for your friendly letter. On this occasion I denied myself the pleasure of looking you up in Berlin because I did not wish to go up to the 'bureaux' and because I made a resolution to avoid all political conversations, a resolution I would not be able to keep when together with you. For seven months I have not talked about politics and have even almost gotten out of the habit of reading the newspapers.

But the next time I come to Berlin I will be glad to let you know.

Meanwhile I wish you all that is good, namely health, and remain in grateful remembrance.

Your old Chancellor
Caprivi

464. Holstein to Hugo von Radolin[2]

Berlin, 4 June 1895

Dear Radolin,

Why didn't you write all those interesting things contained in to-day's letter[3] in your official reports? This way you hide your light under a bushel.

It was really very skilful of you to find out from Witte[4] what he wanted. France furnishes the fifteen million pounds,[5] Russia furnishes

---

[1] Alfred de Rothschild. Partner in the banking house of N. M. Rothschild and Sons, London. A good friend of the Schwabach family.

[2] From the Radolin Papers.

[3] Not found in the Holstein Papers. There is an excerpt from Radolin's letter of 1 June in the Foreign Ministry files. Radolin thought that Witte was trying to aid the French in the matter of the Chinese loan in order to float a large Russian loan in France. Lobanov had denied all knowledge of the matter to Radolin.

[4] Sergei Witte. Russian Finance Minister, 1892–1903; President of the Council of Ministers, 1903–5; Plenipotentiary at the peace negotiations with Japan in Portsmouth, 1905; Minister-President, 1905–6.

[5] Towards payment of the Chinese war debt.

the guarantee,[1] and in that way keeps her hand on China's throat. I quite agree with your view that it would be better not to bother Witte any further about business matters for the time being. Perhaps you might invite him to a formal banquet some time. [...]

The ticklish point in the Far East at the moment is Korea.[2] What do you hear on the subject? But the matter should come up of itself in conversation; you must not show any interest. What does Lascelles think about it? I suspect that despite the clamour in the Press, the Russians will do nothing *for the present*.

I must close. Marschall, Pourtalès, Mumm[3] are away, so you can believe that I am not eating my bread in idleness.

Your faithful
H.

If I might offer some advice, it would be this: take pains to write interesting reports on the Kaiser's account. But then be careful in your criticisms about things which, if repeated in St Petersburg, might cause trouble for you. One never knows. [...]

465. Holstein to Maximilian von Brandt[4]

Berlin, 9 June 1895

Confidential
Your Excellency

I have the honour to return the manuscript[5] herewith, with the commentary of *Legationsrat* Klehmet.[6] Although it was such a short time since you were working on this problem in the Foreign Ministry, the situation has changed as a result of the partial Russo-Chinese loan of sixteen million pounds. In the opinion of all financial experts, this partial loan makes the arrangement of a greater loan, which China would need to meet Japan's demands in full, impossible in the foreseeable future. Under these circumstances we cannot advise the Japanese to evacuate Liaotung, and have said so in St Petersburg. Gutschmid[7] has been instructed not to take part in the discussions on implementing the peace treaty until further notice, but without naming the real reason.[8] This will only be done when we receive *official* word that China has actually contracted the loan that will in effect make her a protectorate of Russia.[9]

[1] For the repayment of the French loan.
[2] At the beginning of the war with China, Japan had forced Korea into an alliance and Japanese troops continued to occupy many strategic points. The Japanese policy to reform Korea was meeting with considerable resistance within the country and from Russia.
[3] Alfons Mumm von Schwarzenstein, Baron from 1903. *Vortragender Rat* in the Foreign Ministry, 1894–8; Chargé d'Affaires in Washington, 1899; Minister to Peking, 1900–6; Ambassador to Tokyo, 1906–11.
[4] From the Brandt Papers.
[5] Not found.
[6] Reinhold Klehmet. Temporary assistant in the Foreign Ministry, 1894–5; *Vortragender Rat*, 1896–January 1908; Consul in Athens, 1909–11.
[7] German Minister in Tokyo, 1891–7.
[8] Telegram of 7 June 1895. (*Grosse Politik*, vol. IX, no. 2276, p. 301.)
[9] See *Grosse Politik*, vol. IX, no. 2280, pp. 303–4.

The Chinese are the dupes in this case: a Russian protectorate; the evacuation of Port Arthur postponed *ad infinitum*.

With deepest respect, but in haste and fatigue

Your Excellency's very devoted

Holstein

466. Holstein to Hugo von Radolin[1]

TELEGRAM

Berlin, 9 June 1895

Private

The Russian Ambassador here is beginning to realise that we are taking the matter seriously.[2] Detailed telegram follows.[3] Await Russian initiative, then present our point of view firmly but dispassionately. The experiment of the present German regime in collaborating with Russia for the first time in several years has not turned out well. The Press here is criticising the German Government for having fallen between two stools by separating itself from England.

Holstein

467. Georg zu Münster to Holstein

Paris, 11 June 1895

Confidential

My dear Herr von Holstein!

Your friendly letter gave me great pleasure and the dispatch about Japan greatly reassured me.[4] I cannot deny, and say so quite frankly, that I felt there were serious objections to and was much concerned about our sudden initiative and co-operation with Russia and France. These objections were two-fold. First I feared that we might be pushed further than would be desirable. This fear has been removed by the dispatch and your letter. Second I feared—and I still have this objection—that Russia especially, which now praises us to the skies, will curse us and turn against us if we do not go as far as Russia may have hoped. We may easily have the same experience as we had after the Berlin Congress. You think I am an enemy of Russia. In some respects I am, not for personal reasons, but because I know how great the hostility is against everything German, and because I know people and conditions in Russia as few persons in Germany do. Nevertheless we must do everything to avoid a break with Russia, we must keep relations on the best possible footing, but we should not *allow ourselves to be misused*. The quite unnatural love affair between the Republic and the absolute Tsar is, like the bastard of a lioness and a tiger, not the product of love but of evil (as the owner of a menagerie told us) and above all of evil towards ourselves and the newly created German Empire.

[1] From the Radolin Papers.   [2] The Franco-Russian loan to China.
[3] Radolin was informed by telegram no. 126 of the same day of a conversation between Marschall and Osten-Sacken. Marschall had informed the Russian Ambassador that Germany's confidence in Russian policy could only be restored by internationalising the Franco-Russian loan, and allowing Germany full participation. (From the Foreign Ministry files.)
[4] Of 8 June. (*Grosse Politik*, vol. IX, no. 2279, pp. 302–3.)

If we could begin to weaken or completely dissolve this affair it would be a very good thing, and in that case our action vis-à-vis Japan would have been the right thing to do. But it is still too early for that. The Government here is too weak, the so-called patriots here and the Panslavs too strong for us to drive a wedge between them yet. There are a few signs that this may be possible later, however. The young Tsar of Russia is still very much under the influence of his mother, who, although she didn't want Lobanov at first, is completely reconciled to him and is supposed to be completely under the influence of the Slavophiles herself. I knew Lobanov when he was assistant to Timachev, the Minister of the Interior, at the time of the emancipation of the serfs. At that time he was enthusiastic about a constitution and had a nihilist mistress. He has always been our enemy, why should he not still be so? He will certainly be our enemy as long as he can win his spurs thereby.

I have great hopes, incidentally, that the German sympathies of the Tsar will come to the surface and that his admiration for his mother will not last too long.

I completely agree with you that the more the Russians gravitate towards the Far East, the better it is for us, and the fact that a Power has arisen there with which they have to reckon is all to the good of the West—only the West should not make common cause with them. This is also the opinion of sensible Frenchmen like Hanotaux. If we now begin to withdraw out there, his position will be difficult. I will therefore have to be very careful in dealing with him.

The latest stroke of the Russians, the guaranteed Chinese loan of 400 million francs, is most disagreeable to him. And it was a real *coup de Jarnac* on the part of the Russians. [...]

With friendliest greetings, always your sincerely devoted

Münster [...]

468. Holstein to Hugo von Radolin[1]

Berlin, 11 June 1895

Dear friend,

As Marschall has gone to dinner, I will sign the cover letter for the telegram from Tokyo,[2] and will add nothing more *officially*.

Privately I would like to add that the Russians have behaved vilely. Whether a few German bankers got a part of the Chinese loan was immaterial. The catch is that the present partial loan of Russia has made the big war loan impossible. We can hardly urge the Japanese to evacuate if their war indemnity hasn't been secured. Gutschmid has now received a telegram instructing him to stay away from the negotiations for the time being.[3] Let's see how far the Russians and French get with the Japanese *without* us. Lobanov will still have the opportunity to regret his present conduct. But for the moment it is a defeat for the

[1] From the Radolin Papers.
[2] Gutschmid's telegram of 7 June. (*Grosse Politik*, vol. IX, no. 2277, pp. 301–2.)
[3] Telegram of 7 June. (*Grosse Politik*, vol. IX, no. 2276, p. 301.)

German Government, and I would not be averse to advising Marschall to take this opportunity to resign. I would of course resign too. I have been sick of official business for a long time, and would find it amusing to watch things from the outside—especially if H[erbert] B[ismarck] should then come to power, something an influential Agrarian group is trying to achieve. We may assume that Papa Bismarck would not allow tricks like that loan *coup* to go unpunished.

But don't talk to anyone there about my intentions.

I haven't seen the Princess[1] since last Wednesday. As you know, when I am in a very bad mood I keep strictly to myself.

Your instruction remains: take no initiative; if people talk to you, point out that in principle we still regard the definitive occupation of Liaotung as being contrary to German interests, but that we can't enter into negotiations about an evacuation *date* so long as the prospects of Chinese payment of their war debts to the Japanese are as uncertain and dim as they now are; that we will also find ourselves obliged to communicate our views to Tokyo and Peking.

All this calmly and coolly, without being brusque. You can also, depending upon the mood you encounter, show a few signs of regret that the joint action, which you felt had promised so much in the way of a friendly rapprochement, should have ended in this way.

You will see from Gutschmid's telegram that the Japanese are not by any means ready to give in.

Incidentally, I almost forgot to mention that the instruction to Gutschmid does not extend to the demilitarisation of the Pescadores. He should only negotiate for the free passage of the Straits of Formosa and for the non-transferral of these islands by Japan to a third Power. He has already received a telegraphic correction.[2]

Farewell, my dear friend. However the matter may turn out, you handled yourself well so far as I can judge from here.

Your very disgusted old
H.

So—don't be the *first* to give in. Leave that to them. But under all circumstances remain calm and polite to the last rung of the ladder. [...]

469. Chlodwig zu Hohenlohe to Holstein

16 June 1895

What you predicted has happened. Bill[3] says he cannot give his father friendly advice but only bring him an imperial command.[4] If he does this, however, he owes it to his father to regard this as his *last official act*. Furthermore, he thinks that any warning would anger the

---

[1] Princess Radolin.

[2] Of 8 June. (*Grosse Politik*, vol. IX, no. 2278, p. 302.)

[3] Wilhelm von Bismarck, who had been appointed Head of the Administration in East Prussia in March 1895.

[4] The Kaiser had suggested that Count Wilhelm von Bismarck be summoned to Berlin and requested to persuade his father to restrain his criticism of imperial officials. (Hohenlohe, *Denkwürdigkeiten der Reichskanzlerzeit*, pp. 76–9.)

Prince, who always maintains that he has the right to criticise. He thinks, by the way, that his father will keep quiet. Under these circumstances I am sending him back to Königsberg. The Kaiser had already given up the idea of receiving the Count.

CH.

470. Holstein to Hugo von Radolin[1]

Berlin, 18 June 1895

Dear Radolin,

My compliments. You did all that splendidly. Now Lobanov is evidently trying to frighten us, but in that he will hardly succeed.[2]

To me the most striking of all your interesting news was that *Mohrenheim* was working against the Witte project. Do you see any reason for it? I can only see that Mohrenheim, whom Lobanov would like to replace with Polovzov, wants to administer a set-back to Lobanov on his own account.

As Hatzfeldt has the advantage over me in knowing Lobanov personally, I sent him the night before last by courier your letter to Marschall, the most important reports, and a lengthy cover-letter,[3] with the request that he send me his opinion by telegram, in fact by *private telegram*, because only in that way can he express his opinion freely.

It is just being decoded by the Coding Office. Half past eight in the evening. The courier leaves at nine thirty. It is no longer possible to write up a dispatch. So I will send you the opinion of our old friend *in natura*.[4]

The first page shows what I knew already: that he didn't approve of the entire action on principle.[5] But there was nothing else to be done. One day at the beginning of March I asked Marschall: 'Do you think that we could sit by calmly in case Russia and France both tried to seize some Chinese territory? I for my part would have nothing against it.'

[1] From the Radolin Papers.
[2] On 7 June Radolin was instructed by telegram to inform Lobanov that in view of the news of the negotiations for a Russo-French loan to China, Germany was unable to advise Japan to evacuate the Chinese mainland. In a long report of 12 June (*Grosse Politik*, vol. IX, p. 303, note **), Radolin said that he had carried out these instructions on that day, but that Lobanov was unable to understand the German position. In a private letter to Marschall of 13 June, Radolin added the information that, upon informing Lobanov that Germany could not advise Japan to evacuate, the Russian Minister had said: 'Do you mean that as a threat?' A German effort to prevent the conclusion of the Russo-French loan to China by the offer of an Anglo-German loan arranged by German banks and the London branch of the House of Rothschild failed, and on 6 July the Russo-French loan was signed in St Petersburg. (From the Foreign Ministry files.)
[3] Holstein's letter of 16 June has not been printed.
[4] See *Grosse Politik*, vol. IX, no. 2315, pp. 353–5.
[5] In his telegram of 18 June (see note 4 above), Hatzfeldt stated: 'In the case in question, I am of the opinion that our participation [in the Far Eastern Triplice] was actually welcome to Russia; first, because the possibility of keeping the Japanese off the Chinese mainland in the interests of *Russia* would thereby be considerably increased; second, because England would be politically isolated; third and above all, because the weak French Government, which at first objected to being involved too far in the Chinese affair because of public opinion, was absolutely compelled by our adherence to go with Russia through thick and thin.'

'No', he replied, 'That would be impossible on account of the Kaiser and also German public opinion.'

I then said: 'In that case we must take the initiative *either* to curb the Japanese acquisitions so that no one has an excuse to take anything; or to take part in the action and to grab when the grabbing begins.'

The next day, the 6th of March, we sent the warning telegram to the Japanese (to which they paid no attention) in which we informed them that the annexations on the mainland would make for intervention.[1]

When the Japanese showed their intention of occupying part of the Chinese mainland, *we* were the first to propose intervention *to preserve the status quo on the Chinese mainland*. Russia and France accepted this programme without enthusiasm, and have since then made every kind of effort to extend it. But we are standing firm, because there is no way of knowing what might otherwise happen. We have labelled every such extension as a *novum*, and as such unacceptable. But if Russia insists on another programme, she will have to reach an agreement with us first about the 'conditions'. We will *not* be treated as a vassal who *must* co-operate under all circumstances. In that case we will see who begins to get cold feet first; we will also see whether the young Tsar likes this kind of policy. The silent opposition of Mohrenheim makes me suspect that a set-back on the loan question would affect the Tsar as set-backs usually affect people; to the detriment of the person who proposed it.

Lobanov for his part is trying to intimidate us: the St Andrew to Faure,[2] joint Franco-Russian entry into Kiel;[3] he expects to frighten us with nonsense like that.

As you can see from the foregoing, Marschall and I are in complete agreement with the second and third pages of Hatzfeldt's telegram. The State Secretary has empowered me to send you the telegram as a supplement to your instructions. *But I make it a point of honour with you that you burn the three pages on the same day you receive them.* You can make a few notes from them, or have Hacke[4] do so.

Now farewell. Be tough, officially. Socially, be yourself and a little Puckish.

Your old H.

471. Valentine Chirol to Holstein[5]

Peking, 21 June 1895

Confidential
My dear Baron Holstein,

I have delayed writing to you for some time as I wanted to get (as far as possible within the limits of such a short visit) a thorough grip of the situation before putting pen to paper.

---

[1] *Grosse Politik*, vol. IX, no. 2226, p. 253.

[2] On 15 June a special envoy dispatched from St Petersburg arrived in Paris bearing the insignia of the Order of St Andrew for President Faure.

[3] To celebrate the opening of the Kiel Canal in June 1895.

[4] Attaché at the Embassy in St Petersburg.

[5] From the Papers of Baroness von der Heydt. Only a typewritten copy of this document was available to the editors. The document is in English in the original.

One of the strongest impressions I have gathered here is that of the utter worthlessness of China as a positive factor in the political equation of the Far East. As a negative factor she may have her uses, like any stone which may drive an express train off the line if placed in the proper position. She is an immense agglomeration of human beings, but she is not a Nation, nor does her cumbersome and effete bureaucracy represent a State. As for the individuals who compose what by an excess of courtesy is styled the Chinese Government, I can only say that the average Turkish Pasha or Persian Khan is an enlightened upright and cultured statesman compared with these people. I cannot imagine anything more discouraging than to have to treat with them of important matters on any basis than that of physical force. It is useless to invoke principles of honour, of which they have no practical experience, or to appeal to the logic of history, for they are ignorant of its most elementary facts, or to urge considerations of national interest, for they are concerned only with their own personal interests. I had a long interview with the Yamen the other day, and I came away with the feeling that the whole world of ideas in which the Western mind moves is no less alien to them than are to me the discordant tones of their uncouth tongue. Face to face with a most difficult and complicated situation, their attitude is chiefly marked by a sort of fatuous imbecility made up in equal parts of helplessness and arrogance. What indeed is one to expect of a Board constituted as the Tsung-li-Yamen is to-day! Of its ten members only one has ever been out of China, and barely half have ever been outside the walls of Peking. The wisdom of their sages, which is the Alpha and Omega of their vaunted education, consists of unexceptionable platitudes which have about as much influence upon their actions as had on ours the beautiful aphorisms which we used to copy out of a model book for our boyish writing lessons. Outside of their official relations with the foreign representatives they neither have nor seek any knowledge of the outer world. History, geography, the achievements of modern science, the influences which mould the policy of western states, public opinion, parliaments, the Press, are words which convey no sorts of meaning to their ears. A remark I made with regard to the Austro-German alliance elicited the instructive fact that they had no precise idea of what Austria was, but had got her somehow mixed up with Holland, who, as a colonial power, counts in fact for much more in their estimation. Another remark bearing upon the relations between France and Tunis led in the same way to the discovery that they had never as much as heard of Tunis or of an African Empire of France, though they appeared to have some knowledge of Egypt, derived seemingly from French sources! Yet they talk glibly and write with a facile pen of the balance of power in Europe and profess to know all about the relations of the European States. And these men form the Board of Foreign Affairs, and their ignorance is an ocean of learning compared with that of the other departmental officials and palace eunuchs who pull the strings of Chinese statesmanship!

I have dwelt at some length on this point because this imperviousness to Western modes of thought and action constitutes a Chinese wall of intellectual petrifaction which European diplomacy can only break through with a battering ram. I confess I had never entirely realised it from anything I had read about China and yet it must be realised before one can grasp the difficulties of the Chinese problem. Looking at this problem from an Englishman's standpoint, it presents itself, I must say, just now in a very ugly shape. Not the least unpleasant result of the war is that it has exposed the weakness of China, and with it the hollowness of the political combinations which we have based for years past on her eventual co-operation with us in various Asiatic questions. That is not however the worst result, though it is serious enough. The fundamental mistake we made was to my mind that we did not interfere this time last year to prevent the war. We could and ought to have forbidden China to run the risks of a campaign for which we knew her to be unprepared. Our traditions and the preponderancy of our interests in China entitled us to take the matter into our own hands and had we done so on our own initiative and responsibility I don't believe a single Power would or could have objected as our action could only have made for peace. Nor do I think that there would have been much opposition if even at a later date, say after the Yalu River and Pingyang,[1] we had interfered on our own account and without trying to draw others after us, in order to stop further hostilities. We should even then have saved some shreds of China's reputation and might have secured sufficient authority over her to compel her to put her house into something like order against future emergencies.

How far it would have been wise for us to join with you and France and Russia merely to modify the terms of peace after its conclusion, seems to me a more open question. That we or any other Power, having no reason to promote the aims of Russian policy, can be really interested in driving Japan off the Asiatic mainland, I for my part fail to see. But for the very same reasons which explain Russia's objection to seeing Japan firmly entrenched in a continental position, it is rather a contingency which we ought to welcome. As for the arguments that the presence of the Japanese in the Liaotung peninsula would be a constant threat to the independence of China, I can hardly imagine that anybody ever took it *au sérieux*. At any rate subsequent events have shown that China's independence may be much more gravely threatened in other quarters and by other methods. I would even go further and say that the maintenance of China may be and is eminently desirable, if it means the maintenance of an independent China, but that it is quite another question if China is to be maintained only as a subservient instrument for Russia and France to play upon.

On the other hand I admit that our abstention has materially facilitated the establishment of Russia's present predominance at Peking. But I am inclined to look upon this as a merely temporary evil, and as a lesser one than the permanent estrangement of Japan by our participation in an

[1] Japanese victories in the war against China, 21 November and 16 September 1894, respectively.

unfriendly intervention. If the British Govt. is prepared to take one or other of the vigorous measures by which it is always within its power to bring a country like China to its bearings, our influence in Peking need not long remain eclipsed or at any rate our interests can be otherwise safeguarded. My only anxiety on this score arises not so much out of intrinsic difficulties of the situation here as out of the well known weakness of the Govt. at home. In this case however I doubt whether even the present Cabinet can close its eyes to the consequences of the prolonged effacement of our legitimate influence in China. The commercial as well as the political interests enjoyed are too vast. We might perhaps have been lulled into a sense of false security if France and Russia had been content to go to work more cautiously and slowly, but their impatience to show that their preponderancy means nothing short of our exclusion, has prematurely exposed their hand.

If I write to you freely it is not only or mainly in acknowledgment of the confidence with which you have always honoured me, but because I am convinced that in spite of keen commercial rivalry, nowhere keener than in the Far East, between England and Germany, the political and in the long run the commercial interests too of both countries are, if not identical, at least parallel here as elsewhere. From that point of view I was never disposed to cavil at Germany's decision to associate herself with French and Russian intervention rather than with our abstention, as it was evidently calculated to mitigate the dangers of joint action limited to F. and R. and I have been only strengthened in that view by the frantic efforts which France has been making ever since to shake off your company and monopolise Russia's. Never have I seen the French carry on their courtship with Russia in such an unblushing fashion as at Peking. It was the French Minister[1] who organised the whole *mise en scène* of the joint French and Russian audience[2] which was the first public advertisement of the Franco-Russian liaison to the exclusion of Germany. It is the French Minister who sings Russia's praise every day at the Yamen and extols her power and generosity at our expense and yours. In fact not the least curious feature here is that the French Minister seems to do all the work of the Russian Legation as well as of his own. Count Cassini[3] very rarely goes outside his garden walls, but M. Gérard goes round every morning to confer with him, then on to the Yamen of which he takes possession for hours at a stretch and away back to his Russian colleague to report progress. Even in the matter of the Russian loan, it is he who is the mouthpiece of Russia's threats and blandishments and lies. Still, grotesque as some of these outward manifestations of the F.R. alliance may be, it is undoubtedly

---

[1] August Gérard. French Minister in Peking, 1893–7. See *Ma Mission en Chine, 1894–1897* (Paris, 1918).

[2] The French and Russian Ministers presented jointly letters from their Governments to the Chinese Emperor officially notifying him of the election of M. Faure as President of the French Republic (17 January, 1895) and of the accession of Nicholas II as Tsar of Russia (1 November, 1894). (See Chirol, *The Far Eastern Question* (London, 1896), p. 68.)

[3] Russian Minister in Peking, 1894–8; Ambassador in Washington, 1898–1905; First Delegate to the Conference of Algeciras, 1906.

for the moment a formidable combination here. We have already had one very unpleasant experience of it, as you will doubtless have heard from Baron Schenck.[1] It remains to be seen whether it will be equally powerful in the matter of the Russian loan where your opposition is added to ours. But I have no great confidence, though the Chinese are beginning to feel alarmed, and it is dawning upon them that the offer of a loan from a friendly Power at the point as it were of the bayonet is rather a novel and disquieting proceeding.

If it is carried, it will, I imagine, be the starting point for the *mise en coupe réglée* of China to the greater glory and profit of the F.R. alliance. That neither of them wants to see China enter upon the path of real reform and progress is obvious, for a weak China best serves their ulterior purposes. France especially desired nothing better than continuance of the troubled water in which she can fish at Russia's elbow: how, *vide* the part she played as prompter in the Formosa farce.[2] The lukewarmness of the French Minister with regard to the recent outrages in Sechuan[3] and the revival of anti-foreign feeling throughout the country is equally significant, for French subjects happen to have been the chief sufferers. Whilst M. Gérard loses no opportunity of impressing upon the Yamen that China owes her continued existence only to France and Russia, he apparently has no objection to the Chinese officials exploiting the intervention of the three Powers as a proof of the subjection in which the Son of Heaven still holds the nations of the outer world, in order thus to rehabilitate in the eyes of the people the authority of the Central Government, on condition of course that its authority be henceforth at the disposal of F. and R. But if F. and R. cannot be counted upon to promote those solid reforms upon which the development of legitimate trade must in the future depend more than upon anything else, there are ample indications that they mean to reap for themselves the full harvest of such enterprises as are likely to yield more immediate returns, i.e. the construction of railways, the refurbishing of the Chinese army and navy. All that others may look for is the gleaning of their leavings. When one considers the vast material resources of such a country as China, if it were once opened up fairly and freely all round to European enterprise, one feels that it ought not to be abandoned without a struggle to the exclusiveness of Franco-Russian preponderancy. For us of course, still more powerful considerations preclude our acquiescence in a consummation equally fatal to our political prestige in Asia as to our commercial interests.

However I cannot claim any title to trouble you with my speculations as to the future. My purpose in writing is only to submit to you a rough

---

[1] Baron Schenck zu Schweinsberg. Minister in Peking, 1893–6.

[2] In May Formosa declared herself an independent Republic and resisted Japanese occupation. According to Chinese statesmen, France was encouraging Formosan resistance. (See *Grosse Politik*, vol. IX, no. 2267, pp. 289–90; *Documents Diplomatiques Français*, Première Série, vol. XII, nos. 1, 39, pp. 1, 49.)

[3] An outbreak of anti-foreign demonstrations in May, resulting in the destruction of property of several European missions.

sketch of the present situation as it strikes my mind whilst still fresh to these new surroundings.

I hope I have not wearied you. My stay here has been so full of interest to me that I may deceive myself as to the amount of interest which can be conveyed to others.

My further movements are still undecided. I am inclined to stay on for a while to watch further developments, but I am here practically on leave, though of course I do not omit to keep *The Times* confidentially *au courant*, and they may think that my absence has already been sufficiently protracted.

With best remembrances believe me,
dear Baron Holstein,
yours very sincerely,
Valentine Chirol

472. Hugo von Radolin to Holstein

St Petersburg, 25 June 1895

My dear friend,

A thousand thanks for your kind letter[1] and the encouragement. It is difficult to deal with people of bad faith, and unfortunately that is the case here. I am sending you a copy of the article from the *Börsen Zeitung* as it stands, as there is no time to prepare a report. It is characteristic, and you can see from that how angry they are with England and secondly with us because we are working against the stratagems of Witte in Peking. He has a bad conscience, and the general belief is that this attempted *coup* in the matter of the independent loan has either failed or will meet with great difficulties on the Russian side. Witte is furious and has let down his mask, for he is supposed to have said that cost what it may (no matter how much sacrifice or how many millions it may cost Russia, and though it may bring no profits whatever) he *will* push through his *coup* in Peking. He will certainly pay thousands in the way of bribes to the Chinese, and he knows that the latter, like the Russians, are susceptible to bribery. I fear that he will in fact accomplish everything in Peking by such means. Perhaps the English are also paying well out there, but I should think that Witte will pay more. He is a thoroughly dangerous man, and too dangerous an adventurer to be the Finance Minister of such a great state as Russia. I can imagine an adventurer like that in a young state like Bulgaria. But I fear—or hope—that he will be ruined *here* in time. For the moment he has the ear of the Tsar, whom he impresses by his raw ruthlessness. All the other Ministers are *nothing* in comparison to him. Lobanov at any rate is not equal to him and has neither the brains nor the energy—or so it is generally said—to take over the difficult problems that Witte has created. As I have heard from various sources, Lobanov is discouraged and very angry. The general opinion about Witte's big projects is that he will certainly not pull off the big loan to China because the French

---

[1] Of 18 June. See above.

have already begun to withdraw from the smaller loan and have taken over only five-eighths, leaving the Russians with three-eighths, whereas in the beginning they declared grandly that France would take over the guarantee. The Russian action is the most flagrant example of bad faith I have ever seen. I hope we will succeed in giving the Chinese some backbone so that they don't succumb to Russian blandishments. But it will be difficult to overcome the Russian bribes to the Chinese. Witte has an enormous number of enemies here, but his cheek and ruthlessness are so great that no one can get at him. As I know for certain, he is playing a game of *desperation*. He knows that he has enemies who are powerful and can damage him in the eyes of the Tsar. For that reason he has now made this bold move in China and hopes in this way and by a great success to consolidate his political position permanently. It is really quite clever of him to try to bring China under *Russian* influence through his cunning. It is a step towards *world* domination which Witte has made his goal, and with that he flatters the Tsar, who is impressed by Witte's grandiose ideas. [...]

God preserve you, my dear good friend

Your
Hugo [...]

473. Holstein to Hugo von Radolin[1]

Berlin, 27 June [1895]

Dear Radolin,

Your reports give a complete picture of the situation.

If the Russian loan project really does fail, then we will have taught the Russians a lesson such as they have not received for many a year.[2] Let them then by all means send the Order of St Andrew to Hanotaux, or perpetrate any other kind of perversion in Paris.

It will then be up to us, since we were proved right in the matter, to behave urbanely; by that I mean that you should pretend to take Lobanov seriously when he assures you that he knew nothing about the whole business and that it was all Witte's doing. *To make Witte the scapegoat: that is the most practical solution—also for us.*

But—we aren't quite so far yet. With the vast funds for bribery he has at his command, Witte may yet overturn everything. [...]

I had reached this point when an important telegram arrived from Tokyo.[3] I am sending it to you. You will receive the directive by telegram the day after tomorrow.[4] In my opinion our standpoint remains the same: we can go on negotiating about everything else in Tokyo: (1) Freedom of trade in the Straits of Formosa, (2) Inalien-

[1] From the Radolin Papers.
[2] According to reports from London and St Petersburg, it seemed probable that the Russo-French loan to China would not be concluded. (From the Foreign Ministry files.)
[3] Telegram no. 50 of 27 June. (*Grosse Politik*, vol. IX, p. 304, note **.) The Foreign Ministry's reply to Tokyo (*Grosse Politik*, vol. IX, no. 2281, pp. 304–5) was prepared by Holstein after consulting Hatzfeldt by telegram and securing his agreement. (From the Foreign Ministry files.)
[4] No such directive was ever sent to St Petersburg.

ability of the Pescadores, (3) Fixation of the additional war indemnity for the evacuation of Liaotung; but *not* the *date* of evacuation *so long as* China is not in a position to determine the date of *payment*.

But, as I said, other directives will follow. Until you receive them, these will apply.

I think you will receive a telegram in the course of Saturday.

Socially, be as free and active as possible. Gradually try to bring together people (important ones, of course) who still have some sympathy for Germany or who at least have none for France.

Do not for heaven's sake show the poor opinion you have of most of the people there. Everything is observed and becomes a subject for gossip.

Your half blind old
H.

Lobanov must be pleased about Salisbury.[1]

474. Holstein to Hugo von Radolin[2]

Berlin, 2 July 1895

Dear Radolin,

I will be as brief as possible for the sake of my eyes.

In my opinion our position is a good one; it has improved thanks to the fact that we can now count on an energetic policy on the part of the English. We will go along with the Triple Alliance and preserve a free hand with regard to the rest of the world. The Russians will need us before we will need them. So for the time being we will sit quietly and wait.

I have recently gained an increasingly firm impression that the Russians are trying to steer things so as to provoke a war between the *three* Powers and Japan. The Russian proposals all have an insulting quality. They would like to anger the Japanese; that is, with the condition that Russia doesn't fight the war alone.

The French seem gradually to be noticing something of this Russian plan, and they apparently have a terrible fear of a war in the Far East, especially since they doubt (with reason) whether we would collaborate in a war unnecessarily provoked by Russia.

It is most significant that last Thursday the French representative in Tokyo stated that 'he was expecting instructions hourly',[3] whereas Hanotaux to-day told Münster that the Minister in Tokyo had received his instructions a fortnight ago.[4] So the Frenchman obviously has received word not to come out with his instructions until he sees for sure that we will go along—that is, that we too are determined to throw the Japanese out of Liaotung under all circumstances, even if China does not pay a war indemnity. Well, in the latter case we will *not* play. But we will not say so specifically yet.

---

[1] On 25 June Lord Salisbury had become Prime Minister for the third time.
[2] From the Radolin Papers.
[3] From Gutschmid's telegram no. 50 of 27 June. (See above, p. 527, note 3.)
[4] Telegram from Münster of 2 July. (From the Foreign Ministry files.)

I was much amused that Lobanov received your communication last Wednesday about the demilitarisation of Port Arthur with considerable aplomb.[1] *Immediately* afterwards, however, he must have sent instructions to Hitrovo to go ahead again and reject all Japanese demands, naturally together with France and ourselves.[2] Whether my instruction to Gutschmid[3] will please the Russians is uncertain. It contains nothing about throwing people out at all costs. It was sent off three days ago, but there has been no report yet about the resumption of negotiations, not even whether the Frenchman came forward with *his* instruction.

I think it would be a good idea if at this very time you used some plausible excuse to go to Finland, leaving behind only the Second Secretary. Hohenlohe and Marschall are away too. Let's see what the Russians will be able to accomplish now. [...]

            Farewell
            Your faithful old H.

When you say goodbye to Lobanov, talk about everything but don't broach the Far East. He won't broach it either, he still isn't sufficiently thick-skinned. If he should bring up the subject, tell him verbally that you knew about the instruction to Tokyo in general terms, but that you didn't know whether negotiations were going on. Our Minister was instructed to report whether the French directive had arrived; no such report had as yet been received. Be calm, friendly, say no more than necessary.

475. Holstein to Hugo von Radolin[4]

6 July 1895

Dear Radolin,

Yesterday the Russian Ambassador was with me for one and a half hours trying to prove to me that Russia, and especially Lobanov, was blameless;[5] he didn't care so much what I thought of Witte and Rothstein.[6]

The loan in itself is of course not very important. But the incident was symptomatic; to be treated like *this* just after we had rendered Russia a significant service! But we will preserve a calm, friendly, and

[1] On 18 June the German Government informed the Japanese Ambassador in Berlin that if Japan demanded that the Powers assume responsibility for the demilitarisation of Port Arthur, the Powers might demand that Japan demilitarise the Pescadores Islands. To this Lobanov commented that he did not wish to become involved in a purely Sino-Japanese question. (From the Foreign Ministry files.)
[2] From Gutschmid's telegram no. 50 of 27 June. (See above, p. 527, note 3.)
[3] Telegram of 29 June. (*Grosse Politik*, vol. IX, no. 2281, pp. 304–5.)
[4] From the Radolin Papers.
[5] The Foreign Ministry had just received word that left no further doubt that the Russo-French loan to China had actually been concluded. (*Grosse Politik*, vol. IX, no. 2283, pp. 305–6.) According to a joint memorandum by Mühlberg and Holstein of 5 July, Osten-Sacken explained that Lobanov believed the international action had come to an end with the Japanese promise to evacuate the Chinese mainland. Lobanov had known nothing about plans for an international loan. Hence the Russian Government had tried to secure the entire sum needed to pay the war indemnity for China. This effort had failed due to the Anglo-German counter-measures. (From the Foreign Ministry files.)
[6] Russian financial agent.

somewhat indifferent manner. Don't betray your feelings, and don't take it too much to heart yourself.

To-day's dispatch about the loan was written by Mühlberg, who treated it as a financial question. The wording was somewhat incautious; for that reason I added the instruction to destroy the document at the end.[1]

The decisive matter in our relations with Russia will probably be whether the young Tsar will want to play a political role, or whether he will continue to be uninterested. The latter eventuality would be unfortunate for our relations with Russia.

That you should *now* try to make contact with the Tsar seems to me to be hopeless. Hence it would be better not to try.

Perhaps something can be done next winter when everyone is back in St Petersburg.

Monday, when I repay [Osten-]Sacken's call, I will express myself as follows; it would be absurd for a great country to alter its political course in any way on account of a loan. Nevertheless the action of the Russian Finance Minister, which very much offended public opinion in Germany, will oblige the German Government to be a shade more careful in everything concerning Russia to prevent a storm from breaking out in the Press.[2] (This is in preparation for our not co-operating as a matter of course in throwing the Japanese out of Liaotung, at any rate not before the war indemnity has been settled. If the Russians want to arrange that alone with the French, *habeant sibi*.)

Have you noticed a nuance of change in Lobanov's behaviour since Salisbury appeared on the horizon?

So don't broach the Far East on your own initiative.

With warm greetings

Your H. [...]

Please also destroy this letter.

476. Paul von Hatzfeldt to Holstein[3]

London, 10 July 1895

Brandt visited me for over an hour yesterday. He does not think that the Japanese in Tokyo will create serious difficulties about the money question, but that they will demand a guarantee that Liaotung not be handed over to *someone else*. So we will have to wait and see, just as we will have to wait to see whether Korea will be brought up for

---

[1] See p. 529, note 5. In the section of this dispatch not printed in *Die Grosse Politik*, Radolin was informed that the conclusion of the Russo-French loan to China would make it impossible to secure the funds necessary to pay the rest of the war indemnity. Germany must therefore reserve her decision as to whether she would join Russia in forcing Japan to evacuate Chinese territory. (From the Foreign Ministry files.)

[2] On 8 July Holstein wrote to Prince Hohenlohe: 'Sacken came to see me, probably as a result of a hint from Your Highness, and I repaid his call to-day. I put the entire blame on Witte and Rothstein and told him that by acting in this way the Russians had placed the German Government in an awkward position vis-à-vis German public opinion and had obliged the Government henceforth to be *très prudent* in everything that concerned the Far Eastern question.' (Hohenlohe, *Denkwürdigkeiten der Reichskanzlerzeit*, p. 84.)

[3] This extract from a private letter was found in the Foreign Ministry files.

discussion. Strangely enough, Brandt thinks the Russians would be quite content if the Japanese declared their intention to remain in Wei-hai-wei because of insufficient payments or guarantees.

For my part I can see no reason to modify Gutschmid's instructions in this way.[1] If that is what the Russians want, they should tell Berlin about it and we can then see whether and what they will offer.

Naturally I do not think that we should have a serious difference with them over the money question. But I will always be of the opinion, which I have frequently expressed, that we can only get on good terms with them, especially with Lobanov, if the latter sees that we will not put up with bad treatment and that we wish to be accorded absolutely equal rights.

The *worst thing* that can happen in Tokyo would be if the Russians and French arranged the affair alone and we withdrew. *Et après?* Meanwhile there will be the elections here, and we will see whether Salisbury, if he gets an actual majority, will allow things to take their course in Asia without putting in a word.

For the time being he is more disturbed about Armenia than anything else because he foresees the dissolution of the Turkish Empire, which he has always regarded as a misfortune.[2] If I were in Constantinople, I think I would secretly try to secure the appointment of Reouf Pasha[3] immediately,[4] with or without instructions.

Finally a most confidential and interesting remark of Salisbury who was yesterday *en veine de causeur*. When we spoke about Morocco, he let fall the remark: 'Partition there will probably occur at the same time as in Turkey.' I: 'In that case I know what *you* will take and *how* you will take it. You will innocently send down a few ships and occupy the exact point of the coast that you want.' Salisbury laughed heartily and said: 'Quite right, that is probably how it would happen.'

Hatzfeldt

477. Holstein to Hugo von Radolin[5]

Berlin, 15 July 1895

Dear Radolin,

Hacke tells me you have given up the idea of Finland. *Officially*, as things are now, the *villegiatura* would have been more desirable than not, in order to show people that Germany is neither in a hurry nor afraid.

At the moment the Russians are chiefly concerned with the evacuation of Liaotung, and would like to make use of *us* in the process. The instruction to Gutschmid—the long one, which you saw[1]—is of course *not* to their liking, and they would like to have it changed. They are very peeved that neither Hohenlohe nor Marschall are here, and that they can't get at H.M. either. Osten-Sacken, whom I received at the request of Phil. Eulenburg and who stayed for one and a half hours, told

---

[1] See above, p. 529, note 3.   [2] See *Grosse Politik*, vol. X, nos. 2394–6, pp. 39–41.
[3] Turkish General, former Minister of War.   [4] As Governor of Armenia.
[5] From the Radolin Papers.

Alexander Hohenlohe yesterday that the Foreign Ministry was now *un simple bureau de transmission*—because we now take everything *ad refer*.

For the time being our position as a matter of course is: to sit tight. People will need us soon enough. As the *Gaulois* said recently: 'The side to which Germany inclines will carry the most weight.'

At the moment the Russians are working hard to intimidate England and Italy.

Naturally you will not now go to see Witte. If you run into him, he should be treated with the 'haughty languor' that poor old Friedberg[1] used to admire so much in you.

The position of the German Ambassador in St Petersburg has of course been badly damaged by the Aide-de-Camp tradition of Schweinitz and Werder. In your place I would simply preserve the serene calm of the *grand seigneur* without any particular political interests when dealing with the *gros* of St Petersburg society. I would treat political conversations as exceptions, and select the people for them. Avoid Poles.

Farewell, dear friend. Unfortunately I still have much writing to do to-day.

Your old H. [...]

478. Paul von Hatzfeldt to Holstein

London, 17 July 1895

Dear friend!

I don't know whether I gave you the correct impression about Salisbury's remarks.[2] In so far as I can form a judgment based on an acquaintance of many years, I am of the definite opinion that his remarks were only the expression of serious concern that he might be driven further than he would like in the affair in question by the stubbornness of the Sultan and by public opinion here.[3] So far as I know, he still holds the opinion that the preservation of Turkey is a significant English interest, and therefore it cannot be assumed *de parti pris* that he has other ideas that do not accord with this view. But he is too practical a statesman not to reckon with the consequences, no matter how undesirable he might find them, that would result from renewed pressure of the three Powers in Constantinople.[4] As the last of these consequences he regards the possibility of the break-up of Turkey and its whole or partial division, and is preparing 'to make the best of it'. I do not think, however, that one can conclude from this that he would not greatly prefer to forestall these eventualities and persuade the Sultan to make it easier for him to do so by sensible concessions.

[1] Heinrich von Friedberg, the former Minister of Justice, who had died on 2 June 1895.
[2] See *Grosse Politik*, vol. X, no. 2396, pp. 40–1.
[3] British public opinion, aroused by the so-called Armenian massacres of August and September 1894, continued to demand that the British Government compel Turkey to adopt a programme of administrative reform.
[4] In April 1895, an investigating commission consisting of Russian, French, and British delegates had recommended an innocuous reform programme for Turkey, but the Sultan had not yet acted upon it.

Incidentally, Rustem was just here to see me. He has no news whatever from Constantinople and is very much afraid that his master will be stubborn and stand by the selection of Shakir Pasha.[1] To-day he tried in vain to speak with Salisbury, and I fear that this will also be difficult to do during the next few days. Salisbury is in Hatfield, and from the remarks of Sanderson I have the impression that he will come here as little as possible until after the elections, because as long as he doesn't know what kind of majority he will have, he does not wish to be forced to take a stand on present problems of foreign policy.[2]

As concerns our position, in my humble opinion we should temporarily sit back and *wait*. It seems to me that we are virtually compelled to do so, if only by Lobanov's activity on the loan question. We found in St Petersburg that we could not count on reciprocity whenever we supported them with *empressement*. Although we should avoid reprisals or even a show of ill-tempered anger, we should at the same time avoid forcing our friendship upon them. The more reserve we now show, the more we can expect that Lobanov will need and seek our help, and then the moment will have come to name our price. If this case does not arise because Lobanov thinks he can get along with the friendship of France, then we will have lost nothing because our last experience has already proved that he only regards us as a third wheel to his cart and treats us as such. Like you, I am therefore of the opinion that we should calmly allow him to proceed if he wants to straighten out the Japanese business with the French alone.

The same principle of waiting seems to me to be indicated by the state of affairs in England, too, where one cannot yet foresee what the position of the new Cabinet will be and which paths Salisbury will follow in consequence. As I mentioned earlier, we can only expect an active policy on his part if he has a strong majority—let's say a minimum of fifty. Even then it is not absolutely certain whether he will simply return to his former policies and seek closer relations with the Triple Alliance and with ourselves, or whether he may not possibly try to reach an agreement with France on colonial matters and at the same time get on good terms with Russia. I am inclined to assume the former, but cannot yet guarantee it. There is the problem that Lord Salisbury believes in the fact of an estrangement between Germany and England caused by the mistakes of the Rosebery Cabinet, and that he has not yet decided whether our former intimacy can be restored and whether we might not demand too high a price. Despite our confidential relationship, he has not yet tried to discuss this question with me and has confined himself to following my suggestions on particular problems, perhaps in the belief that a rapprochement and better relations will follow in due course.

With regard to this situation too, I think we should calmly await the

[1] The Sultan wanted to appoint Shakir Pasha to supervise the implementation of the reform programme in Armenia. It was he who was supposed to have suggested using the Kurdish irregular cavalry whose ferocity in suppressing the Armenian revolt of August 1894 had been the principal factor in arousing the indignation of European public opinion.
[2] The general elections of July 1895 resulted in a great victory for the Conservatives.

course of events here in that we receive warmly every friendly gesture, but do not commit ourselves further to this course as long as Lord Salisbury does not show a definite desire to resume his former policy of friendship towards the Triple Alliance.

There is no doubt in my mind, from what I know of Lobanov, that he is following the development of affairs in England with the greatest attention and that in particular he is watching all signs that might indicate a renewed intimacy between ourselves and England. The position he takes towards us will therefore depend to a large extent on whether he feels there is reason to believe that such a renewal is imminent. The question is the more important to him since he can be in no doubt that a real rapprochement between England and the Triple Alliance would result in a renaissance of the latter. Nor will he fail to realise what the consequences of this would be for Russian policy in the event of another crisis in the Near East.

In any case, in view of the preceding considerations, there is no doubt in my mind that our interest—which is our primary concern—definitely indicates that we should adopt a policy of biding our time on both sides. There is no need to fear that important European questions will be decided without us, and we can on the contrary count on the fact that the Powers or groups of Powers involved will hardly commit themselves to far-reaching plans without having assured themselves of our attitude. We can then calmly consider which side can offer us greater security and greater consideration for our interests.

I would very much like to learn whether and to what extent you agree with my views. For my part I am so convinced of their accuracy that I would see no objection to expressing them as my *personal* opinions to Lord Salisbury if he brought up this subject in a confidential conversation. [...]

With warm regards
Always your
PH.

479. Paul von Hatzfeldt to Holstein

London, 26 July 1895

Dear friend,

[...] I of course understood the remark at the end of telegram no. 234 that there is more elbow room in Asia than in the Mediterranean.[1] To that I would comment that I am *firmly* convinced that Salisbury *urgently* hopes the Russians will bog down in the Far East. He *hopes* that a great part of their strength will thereby be withdrawn from Europe and that they may yet be involved in a war with Japan. Believe me, that is his *inmost* thought. Precisely for that reason he will not want to *offer* them anything in Asia; perhaps too, because he does not

---

[1] In this telegram of 25 July Hatzfeldt was informed that the German Ambassador in Constantinople had been instructed to recommend that Turkey give in on the Armenian question. (*Grosse Politik*, vol. X, nos. 2401–3, pp. 44–5.) It was also indicated to Hatzfeldt that Lord Salisbury might more easily reach an understanding with Russia in the Far East than in the Mediterranean if he so desired. (From the Foreign Ministry files.)

want to preclude the *possibility* of himself taking sides in the matter later, if it should come to that.

This path towards an understanding between England and Russia (offers in the Far East) is therefore eliminated. Salisbury will be even less inclined to offer the Russians other territorial advantages. That will only come if things develop in such a way on account of Armenia that the break-up, or rather the partition, of Turkey seems inevitable. In *that* case Salisbury would, I think, not fail to acknowledge that Russia should receive a substantial portion. Whether or not it would come to a break over the question of *what* everyone should get is another question which would take me too far afield.

In this situation, which can in time or even overnight lead to serious complications, I am more and more convinced that we should not commit ourselves *until* one side or the other guarantees our security and grants us compensatory advantages. If the Russians do so, something I have seen no sign of yet, fine, *mais sans tergiversations* and in black and white. If a powerful English Government would be willing to establish relations with the Triple Alliance so as to safeguard the latter against all eventualities, that too would be fine. But *until then* we should in my opinion keep our hands free so as to be able to cast our sword into the scales in such a way as would best suit us and our interests.

From this standpoint I would be in favour of our taking part as little as possible in the further negotiations in Tokyo. *Si les choses se gâtent*, that is, if the Japanese are stubborn and the Russians should become disagreeable, I would be in favour of our gradually pulling out altogether by allowing the Russians *in a very friendly way* to arrange the whole business exactly as they wish, which they are quite powerful enough to do, especially with the French.

The more restraint we show now, when there are some dark spots on the horizon, the more people will take us into account and ask: what does Germany intend to do, and whom does she intend to attack if it should come to war?

I see only *one* objection to this attitude, and that is the danger that that mighty unknown Goluchowski,[1] either from fear or malice, might play the *praevenire* and reach a direct understanding with Lobanov about the Near East. This danger—whether it exists or should be feared I don't know; Ph. Eulenburg will have to be asked about it—is something we will have to risk. It consists, to put it briefly, in the possibility *that Russia would then no longer need us*. [...]

With kindest regards
Your PH.

480. Hugo von Radolin to Holstein

St Petersburg, 6 August 1895

My dear friend,

Tomorrow, on Prince Lobanov's reception day, I will probably take

[1] Agenor, Count Goluchowski. Austro-Hungarian Minister in Bucharest, 1887–94; Foreign Minister, 1895–1906.

the opportunity to express my opinion about the fifty million Taels which the Japanese are demanding for Liaotung.[1] As I suspect that Lobanov will *avoid* bringing up the Japanese-Chinese business, as he has before, I will probably have to twist the matter in such a way as to force him to talk about it. It is really amusing that ever since the day he spoke about the threat,[2] he has not mentioned the subject again. He must have a bad conscience; for otherwise it would have been natural for him to have mentioned at least the avowedly unclarified question which Witte brought up to justify his partial loan.[3] Highly characteristic of the thinking of Witte is his remark to the Chinese (in my to-day's report[4]) that they should on no account say anything about the prospective loan, especially not to the *Germans*. If one recalls that all this happened after he assured me in the most positive manner that Russia definitely would not take part in the loan. False as Lucifer. I suspect that if I mention the enormous Japanese price for Liaotung to Lobanov, he will use the same indignant language as he did towards the Japanese. Lob. in fact seems to be adopting a habit of flaring up whenever he has no arguments. Incidentally, he is now often in the country and it is almost impossible to see him except on his reception day. Nor have I in my whole life ever seen so much laziness as in the Ministries here. All the officials arrive at eleven or twelve o'clock and disappear at four never to be seen again. During office hours they do nothing but smoke and promenade in the corridors. For that reason things go even more slowly than in Turkey. [...]

Your faithful
Hugo [...]

481. Chlodwig zu Hohenlohe to Holstein

Alt-Aussee, 6 August 1895

My dear Baron,

Your suspicion that it was Eulenburg's idea that we should support the Russians and French on the Japanese money question[5] is correct to this extent: I discussed with Eulenburg H.M.'s wish not to allow the Russians and French to proceed alone in the Far East, and I did not preclude the consideration that in abandoning our action in the Far East, we would also abandon all possibility of territorial gain and of securing a coaling station, and that at the end of our action in the Far East we would have nothing more to show for it than the alleged defeat on the

---

[1] See *Grosse Politik*, vol. IX, no. 2284, pp. 306–7.   [2] See p. 520, note 2.

[3] On 27 June Radolin had reported that Witte, in order to justify the Russian action in the loan question, had spread the information that Germany had been the first to make unilateral loan proposals in Peking. (From the Foreign Ministry files.)

[4] The reference is to Radolin's report of 3 August in which he stated that he had heard that Witte had forced the Chinese to accept the loan by informing the Chinese Minister in St Petersburg that, if the loan did not go through, Russia would see to it that Japan did not evacuate the occupied territories. At the same time he had forced the Chinese Minister to promise to keep the matter secret from Germany. (From the Foreign Ministry files.)

[5] The Russians wanted the Japanese to lower their price for the evacuation of the Liaotung peninsula. (See *Grosse Politik*, vol. IX, no. 2285, p. 307.)

loan question. Like you I could wish that we could now 'go our own way' and that we were out of the business; but how would this be possible unless we withdrew with empty hands? I would be grateful to you if you could explain this to me. Eulenburg merely said the same thing that Rotenhan had reported on the occasion of his audience with H.M.[1] According to Rotenhan's report on his conversation with the Russian Ambassador,[2] I think I may hope that the money question will not present insurmountable difficulties for further co-operation with Russia. Should the Russian Government make us a mediation proposal which did not specify the amount of the monetary indemnity but which made evacuation dependent on the payment in cash only, instead of on the conclusion of a trade treaty as well—in that case, and here I agree with you, we could declare ourselves satisfied.

Now that I already have Rotenhan's report about his conversation with the Russian Ambassador, I am prepared to wait for Radolin's report on his talk with Lobanov.[3]

With friendly greetings
Your most devoted
CHohenlohe[4]

482. Alfred von Kiderlen-Wächter to Holstein

Cowes,[5] 7 August 1895

Dear Holstein,

Hatzfeldt will write to you about politics. The day before yesterday, after having had dinner with Queenie, H.M. had a lengthy talk with Salisbury.[6] Immediately beforehand H.M. talked with Hatzf., so that he didn't allow himself to be carried away into anything dangerous. The most important part seems to have been that H.M. defended the idea that Turkey wasn't going to collapse as quickly as Salisbury thought.

Yesterday H.M. returned around three after having had lunch on the *Meteor*. He said the Queen was anxious to have him talk with Salisbury again, and so he sent a message to Osborne that he wanted to see Sal. at four, whereupon the latter simply sent word that he was sorry not to be able to come, but that he had been ordered to see the Queen at four. Nothing was said about whether he would then come later. H.M. then sent another message that Sal. should come to see him after seeing the Queen, and that H.M. would wait for him until half past six. This

---

[1] On 30 July. (*Grosse Politik*, vol. IX, nos. 2286, 2318, pp. 308, 358–60.)
[2] On 2 August Rotenhan had given the Russian Ambassador the memorandum printed in *Die Grosse Politik* (vol. IX, no. 2287, pp. 308–9). According to Rotenhan's own record of his talk with the Ambassador, he had confined himself to giving the memorandum a conciliatory interpretation so far as Russia was concerned. (From the Foreign Ministry files.)
[3] Radolin reported on 9 August that Lobanov still maintained the Japanese price for Liaotung was too high. (*Grosse Politik*, vol. IX, nos. 2289–90, pp. 310–14.)
[4] On 10 August, before Radolin's report of 9 August had arrived in Berlin, Hohenlohe wrote to Holstein: 'If we now don't succeed in getting something out of the Far Eastern business, then it would really be better if we tried to withdraw.'
[5] Kaiser Wilhelm II was visiting England from 4 to 16 August.
[6] See Hatzfeldt's telegram of 7 August. (*Grosse Politik*, vol. X, no. 2385, pp. 25–7.)

message didn't reach Salisb. before he went to the Queen, and afterwards it was apparently not delivered to him, because after seeing the Queen he did not go to his rooms but to the park. Hatzfeldt then wrote in the evening (yesterday) asking Salisb. to come to see H.M. today.

To that Hatzf. received this reply, a copy of which is enclosed.[1]

Hatzf. is of the opinion that everything happened as the latter says, and that Sal. really *must* go to London tomorrow. It seems to me, however, that the Marquis certainly didn't show much enthusiasm. Well, all that really makes no difference—I am quite happy that the talk did not take place; I have more confidence in Hatzf.'s talks with Sal. than in those of H.M.!

The one reason I can think of why Sal. might have deliberately avoided a talk with H.M., as he actually avoided one with the fat Wales, would be on account of the following circumstances:

As you know, the Queen spoke with H.M. about Wolseley[2] as the successor of Malet.[3] The main purpose in sending Wolseley is to get rid of him here and to make Connaught[4] Commander-in-Chief. H.M. of course knows that too and that is why he is so much for Wolseley for he thinks it is 'most important' (!) that Connaught be made Commander-in-Chief. (*Meo voto* we can accept Wolseley if he is good enough for the English!)

Now it is possible that the Queen worked out this little plan with her nephew without first asking Salisb., in the certain belief that he would make no difficulties for her on this point as Rosebery would have done. Now perhaps Salisb. bucked after all—because it is certainly strange that he said nothing about it either to H.M. or to Hatzf. In that case it is quite possible that it was for this reason that he did not want to see H.M. again, to avoid having to talk with him about Wols. But these are only guesses on my part.

Well, at any rate the visit to Hatfield (isn't that the name of Salisb.'s estate?) has definitely been abandoned. Fat old Wales has again been inconceivably rude to H.M. On our arrival he let H.M. wait three-quarters of an hour before he came on board. When H.M. was talking with Salisb. the day before yesterday, Wales came up twice to interrupt the conversation. The first time he completely failed, but the second time he succeeded in separating them.

Otherwise nothing interesting from here. [...]

H.M. gave the English a special treat by bringing along a fleet of four battleships and a dispatch boat. They block the course of the

[1] See Enclosure.

[2] Garnet Joseph, Viscount Wolseley. Leader of the British Campaign in Egypt, 1882; Commander-in-Chief of the Army in Ireland, 1890–5; of the British Army, 1895–9.

[3] Malet had resigned as Ambassador to Berlin on the grounds of ill health. He presented his letters of recall to the Kaiser on 23 October 1895.

[4] Arthur, Duke of Connaught, third son of Queen Victoria. Commander of the troops in the Bombay province, 1886–90, in the southern district, England, 1890–3, at Aldershot, 1893–8; Commander-in-Chief in Ireland, 1900–4; Inspector-General of the forces, 1904–7; Commander-in-Chief in the Mediterranean, 1907–11; Governor-General and Commander-in-Chief in Canada, 1911–16.

racing vessels, every few moments they get an attack of *salutirium*, the sailors are flooding Cowes, the Queen has to invite the commanders, etc.! [...]

Now, *valete*.

Yours
Kiderlen.

ENCLOSURE

Lord Salisbury to Paul von Hatzfeldt[1]

Osborne, 6 August 1895

My dear Ambassador,

I very much regret the misunderstanding which upset the gracious plans of the Emperor. I was caught in the rain and did not return until 7:40.

Even more unfortunately, I have certain appointments in London that I cannot fail to meet, and I deeply regret that I will be obliged to leave very early in the morning. I am most terribly sorry.

Always yours, but in a great hurry because the Queen is coming.

Salisbury[2]

483. Hugo von Radolin to Holstein

St Petersburg, 10 August 1895

My dear friend,

I did not think I should report everything officially that Lobanov told me on my latest visit (Thursday) about which I am reporting in greater detail to-day.[3] I will tell you about it, and you can do with it what you like. Only L. told me all this *confidentially*. Please read my to-day's report. L. told me: 'Your Emperor, before leaving for Cowes, had us informed that he would support Russian policy in the Far East, and he gave us the most positive assurances. But I fear that there are some cross-currents in your Ministry that are opposing the intentions of the Emperor, whom I admire very much. I do not know the gentlemen in Berlin, but it seems to me that they are hostile to us. A pedantic bureaucracy reigns in your country that does nothing but counter what the Emperor desires.'[4] To this, the reply I recorded in my report, only in more precise and sharper terms than I used there. In saying this, he probably wanted to express his anger about our failure to accept with enthusiasm Witte's filthy operations and constant deviations from the programme. Now he is again trying to screw down the just and moderate Japanese demands, as is the custom in the Orient in all business affairs. As he told me at the time when the question of the

[1] In French in the original. The original copy of this letter is in the London Embassy files.
[2] See also Salisbury's letter to Hatzfeldt of 8 August. (*Grosse Politik*, vol. X, no. 2386, p. 27.)
[3] Radolin's report on his talk with Lobanov of Thursday, 8 August, is dated 9 August. (See above, p. 537, note 3.)
[4] In French in the original.

demilitarisation of the Pescadores came up :[1] 'It's not in the programme, but it makes no difference, one can always *try*.'[2] In the same way he now wants to *try* to screw down the Japanese demands. All that without any justification. If the Japs had demanded 25 million, he would have tried to screw it down to 12½. If they had demanded 100 mill., he would have proposed 50 mill. In the present case, however, he is taking the line of the 'incredible size' of the demand. I tried to force him to prove to me why he wanted to fix the price at *exactly* twenty-five mill. After all, Liaotung could not be priced at its real worth, but only according to the value it had for one party or another. He was unable to do so. I had trouble keeping my temper and preserving a calm and moderate manner towards him. His arguments were not those of a statesman but of a Jewish money-lender's pimp, something he probably learned from Witte. But I do think he will allow himself to be reasoned with during the negotiations; because he constantly said—after he expressed himself so positively about the excessive amount of 50 mill. and had after all put this question in the *fore*front: 'For me the financial question is secondary, we can discuss that during the negotiations. For me the essential thing is to fix the date of evacuation as soon as possible.'[2]

Continued, 13/8/95.

I interrupted my letter because the courier wasn't going until this morning. I have reported at length about everything that has happened since I saw Lob. again to-day and demonstrated our friendship by meeting his wishes concerning the Jap-Chinese trade treaty for the date of evacuation.[3] But he always comes back to the problem that it is impossible for China to pay 150 mill. Taels at one go. If the payments were divided, however, it would be possible for China to pay the 50 mill. Taels to regain Liaotung as well. He has urgently requested that this payment not be made now, but at the same time as the *second* 100 mill. Taels, and in the same six instalments as these last 100 mill. Taels, as arranged in detail by the provisions of the Peace of Shimonoseki. To-day I again haggled with him for over an hour. If the Imperial Government agrees to this *later* payment, that is the postponement of the 50 mill. to the second part of the war indemnity, then I think that he will not take a rigid position on reducing the 50 mill. to 25. He will of course *try, pro forma*, but he will not be adamant.

If it is at all possible, I would be very happy if you would agree to Lobanov's wishes about *postponement* in order to give the Chinese the leeway to pay this 50 mill. with the second half of the war indemnity. These negotiations with L. are not pleasant, he is terribly tough and stubborn. But I didn't give in either, and tenaciously replied to all his arguments. It was not easy to get him to concede the 50 mill. if they were to be shifted to the second half of the war indemnity. He insisted again and again on reducing the 50 mill. to 25 mill., in which Montebello of course honourably supported him. I must close, the courier is just off. I am so sorry not to hear anything about *how your eyes are*. I cannot tell

---

[1] See *Grosse Politik*, vol. IX, no. 2270, pp. 293–4.   [2] In French in the original.
[3] See *Grosse Politik*, vol. IX, nos. 2291–2, pp. 314–15.

you how much we speak and think of you. God be with you. Johanna and Doudouce send you warmest greetings.

Your faithful
Hugo [...]

If it is possible for us, I would personally be very happy if we could grant the *urgent* Russian wishes about the date of payment, especially if it is true that H.M. promised his support in the Far East so definitely. It would certainly help a great deal to calm the present anger against us and would remove France's excuse to play the part of the only trustworthy friend. I don't really see how one can reach agreement about the amount of compensation for Liaotung unless *we* too make at least some concession. A remarkable thing is that P[rince] L[obanov] always talks about the *disinterestedness* of Russian policy in the Far East. Is it possible that he does so to prevent us from having—and expressing—the idea that *we* want something (a coaling station) too? I don't know why, but L. frequently mentioned how splendidly he gets along with Ld. Salisbury. Prince L. seems to place special value on establishing the date of payment independently of the trade treaty. His pressure to get us to agree to his wishes on this matter gives me the impression that he really needs us very much. I also forgot to say that P[rince] L. maintains that the Japanese are not at all concerned about the full payment of their war indemnity and he could therefore not concede that the Japanese would delay their evacuation for this reason or that they had the intention of doing so. The Japanese were just as certain of receiving the second half of the war indemnity as the first, which had been assured them through the Russian loan. In other words he wanted to say that *we* were to blame for the delay and for dragging out the negotiations.

484. Philipp zu Eulenburg to Holstein

Vienna, 11 August 1895

Dear friend,

[...] I can't get over not having seen you in Berlin! I had *so much* to talk over with you and to tell you.

During the trip my time was so completely taken up by H.M., and I didn't even have Kistler[1] along to whom I could dictate if things had to be done in a hurry, so that I couldn't keep you *au courant* as I would have liked and *as you should be*. I cannot do without your advice, your friendship, your experience. I suffer if I cannot be in constant contact with you. H.M.'s confidence has only increased with the years—but with that, my responsibility and the burden has also become much greater. I cannot bear all that *alone*. I also feel tired and miserable. Sometimes, when I might have time to communicate [with you] (in writing), I am so exhausted, so talked out, that I have to lie down in bed instead of writing.

[1] Prince Eulenburg's private secretary.

Now you may have some idea what it meant to me to have missed you!!

If it would be possible for you to visit me in Vöslau, do so. You would thereby not only be doing me but perhaps the state a favour. So many questions of domestic and foreign policy come up that should be talked over. I have need of advice. And although I can get along better on my own than formerly, I DO NOT WISH TO DO SO. We belong together—I can never free myself from this conviction, which is a *good* and righteous one.

Your old faithful
PE

Many thanks for your dispatch about the new English Ambassador. It shows that Salisbury is bringing up heavy artillery to win over H.M.

A hero! A general! An Englishman![1]—who can withstand that! Poor Osten-Sacken! [...]

485. Anton von Monts to Holstein

Munich, 14 August 1895

My dear Baron,

[...] Ph[ilipp Eulenburg] was in Munich a few hours before going to Ischl, very run down, very full of complaints about the strains of sea travel. Bülow, whom I visited for a day in Hall, was not without anxiety that the Cause, Vienna, and his other work might be too much for Ph. In fact, Vienna alone can give a hard-working official more than enough to do, but Ph. can only devote a small part of his time to the Embassy. The Sorcerer's Apprentice is without any doubt very industrious, full of interest and love for his work, but the gaps in his education and training are after all becoming very noticeable. A good Second [Secretary] as a prop would be very much in order in Vienna. [...]

Once more I repeat the request that you take a trip and relax a little. You are too valuable a piece of capital, and the Fatherland will have need of your dividends for a good many years to come.

As ever, my dear Baron,
Your most obedient and faithful
AMonts

486. Paul von Hatzfeldt to Holstein

14 August 1895

Dear friend,

The stay in Cowes and everything connected with it was after all very strenuous for me, so you must not be angry with me for not having written during that week.

H.M. was, as I should like to state at once, quite particularly gracious

---

[1] Eulenburg refers to the possibility of Wolseley becoming British Ambassador in Berlin. The appointment actually went to Sir Frank Lascelles.

and confidential, and I didn't notice the slightest tendency on his part to avoid a tête-à-tête with me. He allowed me to give a most detailed report about Eastern affairs, showed great interest and understanding, and, as you already know, was in agreement with everything. Unfortunately, two things aroused a certain annoyance: (1) the abortive rendezvous with Salisbury, who had been summoned to the Queen and therefore could not come. The whole business arose from a misunderstanding in that the Kaiser had understood that the Queen desired an audience for Salisbury, whereas the Queen herself told me that the Kaiser had misunderstood her and that she had only expressed the hope that the two would once again meet in England [bei ihr]. (2) the question of the Ambassador for Berlin. Now H.M. had been looking forward to having a Field-Marshal[1] with a suitable wife, and is peeved that this is not going to happen. Here they are probably just as peeved about the desire to get the person in question out of the way.

As you already know, Salisbury was somewhat more reserved yesterday[2]—why, I don't know—and so I at once pulled in my horns as well. If I were to show greater eagerness, I would only risk making Salisbury mistrustful. If he himself comes back to the matter of his own accord, then I can enter into an exchange of ideas without having given the appearance of taking the initiative. A crisis in the Eastern Question is not yet imminent, and we will have time to consider what role will be the most advantageous for us in the business. Added to that is the fact that the French are definitely seeking a rapprochement with us, so that it is advisable first to see clearly what they have in mind. The purpose I originally had in mind with Salisbury—to persuade him to make concessions to the Italians, will of course have to be postponed for the time being. In this connection I must observe that I am now no longer certain what the Italians really want. In a conversation I just had with General Ferrero,[3] I found my idea confirmed that the Italians don't really care any more about the question of the right of their agents in Zeila to display their colours.[4] He then told me that he intended to see Salisbury to-day, and in order not to forget anything, he wanted to give him a sort of memorandum listing the Italian desires. At first he wanted to show me this memorandum, but he then thought better of it and in doing so was unable to conceal a certain embarrassment; he confined himself to saying that he thereby merely wanted to prove that it was actually in England's own interest to preserve Italy's influence in Abyssinia and to prevent the latter from becoming a French protectorate. It did not contain an actual request. In that case what do the Italians want?

The Italian Ambassador is going on leave next week by the way, and is going first to see Baron Blanc in Chambéry.

Lord Salisbury is incidentally convinced, as I should like to note here,

[1] Lord Wolseley.
[2] See *Grosse Politik*, vol. X, no. 2387, p. 28.
[3] Italian Ambassador in London, 1895–1901.
[4] Lord Salisbury had also mentioned this in his conversation with Hatzfeldt. (See above, note 2.)

that concrete concessions to Italy, either in Zeila or anywhere else, are not at all the correct means of binding the Italians to the Triple Alliance or rather to England, and that this purpose can only be achieved by offering the prospect of such concessions in the future. I think he is not altogether wrong in this belief.

With respect to Armenia, Salisbury told me yesterday that the three Ambassadors would first ask the Sultan whether he would not also concede two or three further points, and that the affair would thus drag on for a little while longer. So apparently he still doesn't know how far Russia and France will go along with him or whether they will allow him a free hand if the need should arise. His disinclination to permit serious disagreements with the Porte to come up is in my opinion quite sincere. Yesterday he again repeatedly termed it a serious error on the part of his predecessor to have stirred up the whole question, which was now causing him great embarrassment.

What do you say to the circumstance you already heard about that both Salisbury and Courcel yesterday talked to me about Morocco, even though in a different sense?[1] I cannot help feeling that the people here may, if other expedients don't work or seem too expensive, arrive at the idea of buying the French with Morocco and thereby driving a wedge between them and the Russians. I don't believe they have any definite intentions of doing so as yet; on the contrary, I think they are keeping the opposite game in reserve, that is of buying off Russia with Constantinople and the Dardanelles, thereby separating the Russians from the French and in that way getting a free hand in dealing with the latter.

As for Lobanov's wishes concerning Japan, I will telegraph you my opinion to-day[2] and will confine myself here to the one observation that the urgent requests of Lobanov confirm the accuracy of the view I have often expressed—that Lobanov will only become friendly and pliant if one deals with him firmly. [...]

Now one more thing *in strict confidence*. Kiderlen may perhaps already have told you that in leaving, H.M. quite unexpectedly positively ordered me to write to him directly and personally in the event that anything important happened here with regard to the Near East and a possible partition.[3] I need hardly tell you that if this should become unavoidable, I will do so in the way we have already agreed upon. Kiderlen even thought it might have its good side.

---

[1] See above, p. 543, note 2.

[2] Holstein had informed Hatzfeldt of Lobanov's proposal (*Grosse Politik*, vol. IX, no. 2292, p. 315) and asked for his opinion on the subject. Hatzfeldt replied that Germany should avoid exerting any pressure on Japan, and before making any decision should consult Paris about the Russian proposals. (From the Foreign Ministry files.) For the German reply to Lobanov, see *Grosse Politik*, vol. IX, no. 2293, pp. 315–16.)

[3] At the interview between Wilhelm II and Salisbury at Cowes on 5 August, Salisbury hinted at the advisability of partitioning the Ottoman Empire as the best solution of the Near Eastern problem. (*Grosse Politik*, vol. X, no. 2385, pp. 25–7.) Salisbury had already discussed this possibility with Hatzfeldt. (See *Grosse Politik*, vol. X, no. 2396, pp. 40–1 and chapter LX.) There is no further information about the Cowes interview in the Foreign Ministry files or the files of the London Embassy.

And now farewell, my dear friend. In the hope of seeing you soon again.

With best wishes
Your
PH

487. Hugo von Radolin to Holstein

St Petersburg, 28 September 1895

My dear good friend,

[...] I have just received H.M.'s telegram saying that Colonel von Moltke[1] is coming with a letter.[2] I am glad he is coming while L[obanov] is away; because there is then a greater chance that Tsar N. will agree with what H.M. says. I have no idea what the letter may contain. The main thing, that is the second Chinese-Russian loan affair, will surely not be mentioned. I am sending you a newspaper clipping[3] about the new Russian-Chinese bank that is about to be established. You will see from that how far from innocent the matter is. It simply means that they are trying to keep the second loan in their pocket as well, while at the same time bringing China under Russian influence. Shirshkin[4] is of course denying that Russia has any intention of even joining in the second loan. But that is just as untrue as the earlier assurances of Witte. It would seem to me that we shouldn't again allow ourselves to be squeezed out, and that if they play a *dishonest game* with us, we should, so long as they still need *our* assistance, withdraw our participation from the *whole* affair and declare that we will support the two allies *no further against* Japan. There is no doubt that they need us *at the moment*. In a short time, however, when things are more settled there, they can *both* perhaps get along *without us* and then we will have to face the consequences. I think that it would be most unpleasant for the Russians if we withdrew *now*; for they are said to be very weak in the Far East. But as they are convinced from previous experiences that we will always support them in the end, in spite of every disloyalty on their part, they do not hesitate to affront us again and again. This would be the case if they actually arranged the second loan as they did the first. If the Russians and the French divide up the influence in China between them, can't we then step forward with our conditions? Can't we present our demands for a coaling station or for a large colony in China? Tsar N. seems to agree to this in principle. Has not the moment come for us to prepare the way seriously and in specific terms? The Press in Russia has feared for a long time that *we too* might want something and has expressed itself vigorously against this presumption. Please write me a line about what you think about this in

[1] Helmuth Johannes Ludwig von Moltke. Aide-de-Camp of the Kaiser; later Chief of the General Staff. Nephew of the Helmuth von Moltke who was Chief of the General Staff to 1888.

[2] Letter of 26 September 1895. *Briefe Wilhelms II. an den Zaren, 1894–1914*, edited by Walter Goetz (Berlin, 1920), pp. 294–6. See also *Grosse Politik*, vol. IX, p. 365, note **.

[3] Not found.

[4] Assistant to the Russian Foreign Minister, 1891–6; Director of the Foreign Ministry, 1896–7.

principle and whether *I* should be doing something about it.¹ My one great fear is that Witte, with the aid of the French, will once again freeze us out of the loan. I would like to do everything to avoid receiving a second affront of this nature. Witte is playing a *gros jeu*, and he seems to be winning at it. I am curious as to whether he is negotiating with our bankers in Berlin and what is being arranged there, or whether in fact, as he maintains, he is only there for his health. Could there be any truth in the rumour that he has cancer and has hardly two more years to live? We have been more loyal and open in supporting the Russians in this whole business than any other state is likely to be again. We have supported them through thick and thin and have swallowed the pill of the first loan by making *bonne mine à mauvais jeu*. It was and is surely very wise of us not to let those two operate *alone* out there but to have joined them—no matter how disagreeable this may have been to the French. But now the reckoning—and our reward—must come in the form of a settlement in China. This won't be altogether easy, to be sure, because the Russians still have in their favour the *appearance* of not wanting anything tangible for themselves. Apparently they don't want *territories* at the moment, but if they secure a powerful influence in China and the right *to use* railroads, etc., this would be even more dangerous and important than territorial aggrandisement in those desolate lands. The second loan in particular, if made by the Russians without our participation, would give them an enormous preponderance in China, and in my opinion no one could blame us for opposing it and taking care of our interests as we see fit. Personally I would be terribly sorry if it should prove necessary to end our collaboration with the Russians in the Far East; because this would mean that our relations which have happily improved would once again become quite poor and strained. But if it should come to that, it would be better that it came at a time when it would still be useful to us. I still have hopes that the Russians will resume their old friendship with us and that we will collaborate as good neighbours and bearers of the monarchic tradition. I consider it my first duty to do everything I can to be on the best possible terms with the Russians, and am trying as hard as I can to meet them half-way, and I am trying not to show my feelings when dealing with people of whom I think less than little. And I think, without boasting, that I am striking the right tone with the people here and cannot deny that they are very easy and agreeable to get along with socially. It does no harm to put one's nose in the air occasionally or to become quite harsh; but on the whole, if things are otherwise going well, it suits the character of the people here better if one is friendly and easy-going than if one is *always* stiff and tight-lipped. I am telling you all this at the risk of boring you. But I am doing so in order to have you tell me frankly whether you agree with my views or whether I should alter them in any way. [...]

Farewell, dear old Holstein.
In deep and loving friendship
Your Hugo. [...]

¹ No reply from Holstein has been found.

488. Paul von Hatzfeldt to Holstein

Sunday, 11 October 1895

Dear friend,

Enclosed I am sending you the desired copy.[1] Before the arrival of your letter I had confirmed the receipt of Swaine's[2] letter by telegraph and thanked him for it. To write to him in addition would only be useful if through his mediation I could also send a letter for Sal[isbury] about the impression his statement made on me, or rather, on the Wilhelmstrasse. Think it over, and if necessary let me know *what* I should write.

With respect to the apparent concern of Sal. that we are demanding too much in Africa, or more than he can give, I would remark that according to what Kayser told me recently, we would be content with much less in the hinterland of Togo than we had demanded from Kimberley. He wanted to send word to me in London as to what our minimum demands would be. This would mean that the possibility of an understanding on this point is not completely out of the question.[3]

At the moment I do not believe in the idea that Salisbury is trying to get out of the situation by allowing a general free-for-all. In England people don't reckon ahead so far. But to be sure, Sal. would be happy if the Russians got as deeply involved as possible in China and thereby took the pressure off him in the Mediterranean.[4]

What worries Sal. most about us is his fear that we have made firm commitments to the Russians, that we want to give them Constantinople, etc., and that we are therefore not available for any other policy. You know that I think we should preserve our freedom of action until we can see *which* side offers us the greater security and the greater advantage. But if we openly begin to run after the Russians, we force the English to try to run even faster. [...]

In old friendship

PH [...]

ENCLOSURE

Leopold Swaine to Paul von Hatzfeldt
Copy

Berlin, 4 October 1895

SECRET!

Your Excellency

Permit me herewith to inform you very confidentially that I gave Lord Salisbury a 'hint' about the last part of our most recent conversation. His reply is as follows:[5]

---

[1] See Enclosure.
[2] Leopold Swaine. British Colonel; Military Attaché in Berlin, 1882–9, 1891–6.
[3] Hatzfeldt refers to negotiations between Britain and Germany to reach a territorial agreement over the Togo hinterland, particularly with regard to French expansion in the African interior. The negotiations broke down when the Germans felt Britain was chiefly anxious to stop French expansion around the source of the Nile, and wished to compensate France in West Africa.
[4] See p. 532, note 3.   [5] The quotation of Salisbury's reply is in English in the original.

'He is quite mistaken in thinking that there is any change or uncertainty in our foreign policy. We are just where we were in 1892. If he traces any uncertainty in my action, I should impute it to the fact that I inherit from my predecessor one or two jobs which I do not quite fancy, and which I dare say I am awkward in handling. Africa is and will remain a stumbling block to both Powers. Giving up a portion of not very valuable territory recently acquired seems to Governments a small thing : but it involves the means of living to a certain number of traders, who will raise a fearful outcry if they think their Government is deserting them. I dare say the Germans feel the same difficulty : and it is very hard to come to terms. We must continue the struggle as good humouredly as we may.'

With best wishes, Your Excellency's very devoted

Swaine

489. Bernhard von Bülow to Holstein

Milan, 12 October 1895

Dear Holstein,

[...] As for our attitude towards England, I hope that I have not acted *sutor ultra crepidam* but in agreement with you and according to your intentions by writing to Philipp E[ulenburg] from Venice roughly as follows : In my opinion England would only be a reliable ally for us in peacetime and would only draw her sword in the event of an attack on ourselves or the Triple Alliance if we left her in no doubt that we would quite simply abandon her to her fate unless she concluded a formal alliance with us. I did not think that England was on the verge of collapse or that the English would throw in the towel after their first set-back. The intrinsic power and the resources of the country were in my opinion too vast for that to happen, and there was still too much courage and cockiness in the individual Briton. But I did think that England would only bestir herself when she felt the fire burning her fingernails. And finally it seemed to me that nothing better could really happen to England than to be awakened from the lethargy in which she had been stagnating for the past eighty years by a few kicks delivered by the Russians and the French. If the bull were simply allowed to gather fat without any healthy exercise, its agility and powers of resistance would of course decline; but once properly shaken up, it might again become its former fighting self. [...]

Your very devoted

B.

490. Holstein to Bernhard von Bülow

Copy

23 October 1895

Dear Bülow,

The telegram from H.M. to the Chancellor[1] seemed to me sufficiently important to justify sending the courier.

[1] Of 20 October 1895. (*Grosse Politik*, vol. X, no. 2437, pp. 76–8.)

Kaiserin Friedrich, who almost never talks politics with the Kaiser, has—probably on instructions from England—drawn his attention to the need to put an end to the Turkish mess. They [the English] were trying this route after the probings of Salisbury with Hatzfeldt and H.M. brought no result.

The Kaiser saw through the game and shrugged it off. But the conclusions that he drew show that he is not *au courant* of the actual situation.

'If Russia and England reach an understanding over Egypt and the Dardanelles so that the one gets this and the other that, where does that leave *us*?' asks H.M., and wonders how this dreaded agreement can be prevented.

In reality such an agreement, if it were achieved, would be highly desirable for Germany, because it would drive a wide wedge between France and Russia. But precisely for that reason, because Russian recognition of England's position in Egypt would be equivalent to the end of the Franco-Russian entente, there is *very* little prospect that this plan, which is undoubtedly a cardinal point in Salisbury's programme, will become a reality.

So why should *we* get involved in trying to prevent it? Whether it becomes a reality or not, this plan holds no dangers for us. But there is *serious* danger for Germany in H.M.'s intended anti-English attitude and mistrustful opposition of England, which, in view of the apparent *Russian-French-German* agreement on Mediterranean questions, might so soften up England and Italy that the former would give up Egypt and the Mediterranean, and the latter give up the Triple Alliance. And that just at the moment when Italy, most probably after previous understanding with London, is making this brilliant move in Abyssinia![1] For the first time since there has been an Eritrea I am glad about Italian activity there because thereby—if all goes well—the Russo-Abyssinian delusions of grandeur will be exposed to the world for what they are.[2] For Russia, this complete ignoring of Russian threats on the part of the Italians is a slap in the face. For that reason I also ask the question: 'How will Russia (and hence also France) react? Will they really keep quiet about Abyssinia?' Radolin has been instructed to keep us informed about the attitude of the Russian Press.

I have no real doubt that that haughty and pretentious Lobanov is wondering whether he should risk a harsh word. And in this, too, our attitude may be decisive in encouraging Lobanov to threaten Italy. Then of course Crispi will turn to us and ask: 'What are you doing? Are you allowing Italy to be threatened?' And if we give an elusive reply, the Triple Alliance goes up in smoke.

[1] Since early October 1895, Italy had resumed her military offensive against Abyssinia.

[2] In January 1895, the former Archbishop and Metropolitan of Moscow, Leontiev, led a 'scientific' expedition to Abyssinia. The Italians regarded the expedition as part of a Franco-Russian intrigue to encourage Abyssinia's hostile attitude towards Italy. (See *Grosse Politik*, vol. VIII, p. 376, note *.) On 12 July the Tsar and Tsarina of Russia received a special envoy of the Negus of Abyssinia, who brought the Tsar letters from the Negus and from the Metropolitan of Abyssinia as well as the Order of Solomon, first class. (See Francesco Crispi, *La Prima Guerra d'Africa* (Milan, 1914), pp. 355, 362–6.)

Whereas on the other hand I am convinced that Lobanov and France will not dare to budge as long as they are not certain of our—I wouldn't like to say cowardice, but a nuance milder; and as long as we simply stand by without feeling the need to put in our word everywhere. The policy of Louis XIV: 'not a shot without my permission' is not exactly the principle that will set Germany on the right track. We would do better to attend to Goethe and allow everyone else free play 'far away in Turkey'.

491. Bernhard von Bülow to Holstein

Rome, 24 October 1895

Dear Holstein,

I will await the arrival of the material promised me before I write in detail about the first point you were good enough to mention in your letter of the 19th of this month.[1] Meanwhile only a word to tell you that I completely agree with your views. We would in my opinion risk the dissolution of the Triple Alliance if we gave Russia the opportunity to *use us* to intimidate England and drive away Italy. What I wrote to Eul[enburg] from Venice (and to you from Milan) about our attitude towards England[2] was written out of anxiety lest the pessimism of Sullivan[3] should induce the responsible office to shoulder English burdens. But it would obviously be quite as wrong to discourage England as to allow ourselves to be exploited by her, for we want to and must *encourage* her. We cannot leave John Bull in any doubt that we will not jump into the sea in his place to salvage the pearl of his world status from the briney deep. But neither should we allow him to fear that once he had made up his mind to swim we would not come to his aid when others were trying to pinch his legs and push him under. Although I agree with your desire to avoid a clash and especially single combat with the northern bear if at all possible, we cannot sacrifice *our* alliances—or even the possibility of further alliances—to a Russia that clings to France. Schweinitz told Giers in the spring of 1887: 'As long as you flirt with France, we would be fools to sacrifice our good relations with anyone for your sake, be it even Monaco.'[4] Giers smilingly replied: 'I understand.'[4] Although I don't like to use formulae in politics, still it seems to me in view of the present international situation that the desirable attitude for us can be summarised in the few words: wait and see, polite reserve, no definite engagemennt with anyone in the Near East, and no definite quarrels with anyone. I will wait before writing in greater detail and more precisely to you— and Eul.—until I am more *au courant* thanks to your kindness. I am sending to-day the report I wrote the day before yesterday about my first

[1] Not found.
[2] Letter of 12 October 1895.
[3] Not identified.
[4] In French in the original.

talk with Crispi, so that it doesn't become rancid.[1] In this report I was obliged to bring out that Crispi, on his own initiative, particularly stressed the fact that in his opinion it was impossible for England to give up Constantinople to the Russians, that he was opposed to such an eventuality, and that he wanted good relations with England. I have not yet seen Blanc, he is in Florence. [...]

With warm good wishes, in haste
Always your sincerely devoted
B.

492. Philipp zu Eulenburg to Holstein

Liebenberg, 28 October 1895
Dictated at half past one at night!

I used a report from Bülow in which he discussed the attitude of Crispi, who very decidedly declared he would never agree to the Russian seizure of Constantinople,[2] as the basis for several talks with His Majesty concerning the position that he, or rather Germany, is at the moment taking towards England.

I said that English policy, in holding to its old traditions, had recognised in Italy a pawn to pull its chestnuts out of the fire. By making an alliance with Italy, England would pull the Triple Alliance into Balkan and Mediterranean questions. If we stand by the Triple Alliance and at the same time follow a policy that stirs up the Italians and encourages them to take extreme decisions, then England will have calculated correctly; but if we don't want to be involved in Balkan questions and break with Italy, then we will be furthering the policy of our opponents, Russia and France.

There is no doubt that the Italians have heard about the Malet 'incident'[3] (I have never referred to this matter to H.M. as anything but an 'incident', *a description he accepted without comment*) and that this must have created the impression in Italy that at the moment we are inclining more towards Russia, which must have aroused alarm. If we intend to hold to the Triple Alliance and prevent Italy from becoming alarmed, then Italy must be made to realise that after the Malet incident had been settled, that is, after His Majesty had replied to this imper-

---

[1] According to Bülow's report of 22 October, Crispi had informed him that if England opposed a Russian move against Constantinople—and in his opinion this could be counted on with certainty—Italy would have to stand by England. If only for this reason he 'placed the greatest importance—and as Italian Minister he had to place the greatest importance—on the closest possible relations between Germany and England'. (From the Foreign Ministry files.)

[2] See note 1.

[3] On 14 October Sir Edward Malet had informed Marschall that there was only one dark spot in the otherwise friendly relations between Germany and England, and that was that the Germans were encouraging the Boers in their inimical attitude towards England in the Transvaal. This created an impossible situation for England, Malet continued, and if this German policy concerning the Transvaal continued it might lead to serious consequences. (*Grosse Politik*, vol. XI, no. 2578, pp. 5–7.) Hatzfeldt was informed on 29 October that the Kaiser had regarded Malet's remarks about the Transvaal as a virtual ultimatum. (*Grosse Politik*, vol. XI, nos. 2581, pp. 12–13.)

tinence with the requisite energy, we had returned completely to our former position and we would continue to stand by this position; in other words, that we stand firmly by the terms of the Treaty of Berlin. His Majesty is convinced of the necessity of handling the matter in this way and has complete confidence in the skill of Bernhard Bülow to straighten out our difficult relations with Italy. His Majesty fully approves that instructions along these lines be sent—which does not mean that His Majesty is not still very indignant about Malet's behaviour.

I don't think it will be impossible to persuade His Majesty to say a friendly word to England, which of course, if we want to bring about a clash between England and Russia, would be the only correct thing to do.

I will work on it.

Greetings
PE.

493. Philipp zu Eulenburg to Holstein

L[iebenberg], 29 October [1895], noon

I have just heard His Maj. express the opinion that he would not regard the Malet incident about the Transvaal as settled until he had been informed officially by some suitable person (unfortunately the new Ambassador won't be here for another six weeks) that Lord Salisbury does *not* share Malet's views. (To arrange this would be the task of the Foreign Ministry.)[1]

In greatest haste
Your
PE.

494. Bernhard von Bülow to Holstein

Rome, 30 October 1895

Dear Holstein,

[...] I agree completely with your opinion that an agreement between Russia and England whereby the former received a free hand in the Near East, the latter recognition for its position in Egypt, could only be welcomed by us, because such an arrangement would disturb the Franco-Russian relationship which since 1886 has rested like a dead weight on Europe. If the Russians received Constantinople but the English took the Dardanelles, this in my opinion should not make us sorry either, because this proximity of the Whale and the Bear might soon lead to a fight between the two of them. But the Russians will hardly agree to such a proposal, because Tsarigrad would be of no use to them without the Dardanelles. *Ce serait le cas de dire:* what good is a boat without any water? Nor is it probable that the Russians, with the French falcon in the hand (or on the string), will exchange it for the English bittern in the bush which alternates its singing with abuse.

---

[1] Hatzfeldt telegraphed the desired statement from Salisbury on 1 November. (*Grosse Politik*, vol. XI, no. 2582, pp. 13–14.)

I completely agree with your opinion that for the time being we have no business butting into projects like this Anglo-Russian private partitioning.

But do you think on the other hand that Russia will really succeed in pushing France into the line of fire against any opponent other than ourselves—even against hated Albion? I would be inclined to doubt it. The French want to save their strength (and probably Russia's as well) for us, because they are still far more anti-German than anti-English or anti-Italian. [...]

You also seem to be right in thinking that we should safeguard the Triple Alliance the more carefully because the French and Russians will neglect no opportunity for breaking it up. The French seem to be playing the role of the raging and howling wind in dealing with the Italian wayfarer, whereas the Russians recently seem to have taken over that of the flattering sunshine. At any rate the French seem to be making themselves more disagreeable than ever in the Abyssinian question (Djibouti),[1] whereas the Russians have superficially given in (sentencing of Leontiev,[2] article in the St Petersburg *Börsenzeitung*[3]). I too am of the opinion that the Russians, unlike the French, don't want a war with us *a priori* and *principaliter*, but Lobanov would like to restore Russia to the position she occupied under Nicholas I. French and Russians agree in the desire to restore the status quo ante '66. Like yourself and Eul[enburg], I not only don't want a war against Russia but I want the best possible relations with her. For that very reason I fear that we might make the Russians suspicious by excessively great and frequent offers. If we hold open the door too wide for them in the Near and Far East, they might think there was a trap behind that door into which we would not be sorry to see them fall. Although I may frequently have erred in my judgment about the Russian situation during my assignment to St Petersburg, these errors at least gave me the insight that while one certainly shouldn't annoy the Russians, neither should one make excessively demonstrative advances towards them nor trust them even to the extent that would be correct and proper under some circumstances in dealing with others.

Finally, though I won't deny that the monarchic solidarity of interest between Russia and Germany is a big card in our game, I still believe that we should not allow ourselves exaggerated hopes in this regard. The conservative Russians consider Russia to be so totally different from the West that they don't particularly fear the spread of revolution to their side of the Russian border; and in fact the Pugachev disturbances,[4] the Decembrists,[5] Herzen's Kolokol,[6] and nihilism, have sprung

[1] The Italians believed that France was permitting arms intended for the Abyssinian armies to pass through Djibouti. (Crispi, *Prima Guerra d'Africa*, pp. 347–50.)

[2] See p. 549, note 2.

[3] Not found.

[4] A large scale revolt of peasants and Cossacks during the reign of Catherine II.

[5] A rebellion of December 1825, due in part to the uncertainty about the succession to the imperial crown after the death of Alexander I.

[6] The weekly journal *Kolokol*, edited by the Russian romantic and revolutionary agitator Alexander Herzen.

from internal Russian sources, whereas the great French Revolution, 1830, 1848, the Paris Commune, had no effect whatever on Russia. The Red Russians are happy about every advance of the republican idea in Europe. Neither the one nor the other hold fast to principle so far as alliances are concerned.

I am writing to-day to Eul., in particular to point out to him (absolutely along your lines of thought) how much the present European situation seems to me to demand caution, freedom of action, and reserve. If the sea rises elsewhere, if the Russians and the English are obliged to wear themselves down fighting storms and waves, it would be all the better for us to have solid ground under our feet. In this assumption—that we should calmly stay in the background—I am really more pleased than not to hear of trouble in the Far, Middle, or Near East, which diverts the attention of Europe from ourselves, the Rhine, and the differences about Alsace-Lorraine where the French would like to stir things up, and like Goethe and yourself, I feel that not only on Sundays and holidays but on all the days of the week there is nothing more pleasant than having other people fighting each other far away in Turkey. [...]

With renewed thanks and warmest greetings and good wishes, always in truest devotion.

Your
B.

495. Paul von Hatzfeldt to Holstein

30 October 1895

Dear friend!

I have nothing new to write to-day because I am not seeing Salisbury until Friday, and I think I should desist from mere reflexions about the situation as long as I cannot calculate what effect they will have on H.M. My two telegrams[1] don't seem to have had a bad effect, on the whole, because the long telegram to Rome[2] which was communicated to me was certainly based on them in part. Even on this point I won't be able to see until Friday whether Salisbury will hold to this course or whether Swaine's report[3] will have frightened him off. I am sure you will agree

[1] In telegrams of 24 and 25 October, Hatzfeldt reported that Salisbury had assured him he had received no significant report from Malet for about six weeks, and that Malet had received no instructions to make the statements which had so angered the Kaiser. (See p. 551, note 3; *Grosse Politik*, vol. X, no. 2441, p. 81, and vol. XI, no. 2580, p. 12.)

[2] On 27 October Hohenlohe sent a dispatch to Rome and London which considerably toned down the anti-English sentiments the Kaiser had expressed to Colonel Swaine on 24 October (see below, note 3) as a result of Malet's statements. (*Grosse Politik*, vol. XI, pp. 10–11, note *.)

[3] In his report of a talk with Swaine on 24 October, the Kaiser wrote: 'It is impossible to reconcile the interests of my country with all the moods of English policy or to react to the vague hints and enigmatic claims of English statesmen. This attitude on the part of England virtually compels me to make common cause with France and Russia, both of which have approximately a million men on my frontiers ready to break in, while England does not even give me kind words.

'I concluded the conversation with the earnest warning that England could only escape from her present total isolation, which was the result of her "policy of selfishness and bullying", by uncompromisingly siding openly with the Triple Alliance or against it. The former

with me that even though Salisbury has to some extent agreed to go along, I should not press him but let him come to me in so far as possible.

With respect to the Dardanelles question I should mention by the way that if Salisbury should bring up the subject it would for the time being cause me no embarrassment. As you may remember or if necessary check in the files, I have told Salisbury for years that our attitude in this question was, as a result of earlier events, a different one from that of England and the Powers friendly to her, and that consequently we would have to stay in the background in this matter. He acknowledged this at the time, and I would be able to refer back to this. The whole business would of course become much more difficult if the Russians, with their typical discretion, were to inform the English that we had just opened up prospects to them in this sphere.

This lack of clarity may yet lead to great difficulties for us here. Take for instance the not very likely but still possible case that Salisbury says to me one day: 'Good, I am prepared to make a secret treaty with the Triple Alliance in which the latter guarantees to oppose a Russian advance against Constantinople and the Dardanelles.' The reply would, as things stand, not be an easy one. [...]

I am of course very pleased about the telegram to Rome, which did not go off a moment too soon, it seems to me. But I fear that this won't be enough in the long run to hold the Italians to the straight and narrow path if they are not convinced soon that our relations to England, on whose friendship they place the highest value, will at least be restored to normal.

I would incidentally be very happy if your belief that Lobanov intends to take a strong line about Abyssinia proves to be correct. When I hinted to Salisbury that I would not be surprised by such an eventuality, I found him completely incredulous. He assumes that Russia will not lift her little finger for Abyssinia, or rather for French interests there. If this should happen after all, it would make the seriousness of the situation more obvious to him and perhaps persuade him to establish closer relations with Italy.

Farewell for to-day, dear friend. After my next conversation with Salisbury I hope to be able to tell you more.

With warmest greetings
Your
PHatzfeldt [...]

496. Holstein to Hugo von Radolin[1]

30 October 1895

Dear Radolin,

[...] Our attitude towards European politics is simple and clear:
would require a form such as was customary among continental Powers, i.e. signed and sealed guarantees. The Colonel seemed to be profoundly disturbed and moved.' Swaine informed the Kaiser on 20 December that his report of their conversation of 24 October had been printed and circulated to all the members of the Cabinet. One member had written to him: 'It is the most important document you have ever sent to us from Berlin.' (*Grosse Politik*, vol. XI, no. 2579, pp. 8–11.)

[1] From the Radolin Papers.

as long as Russia and France form one bloc, we have the greater obligation of preserving the European balance and herewith the peace of Europe by maintaining an attitude of reserve in the first instance, but if necessary to see to it that this bloc does not overwhelm weaker blocs or isolated Powers. Otherwise we ourselves would in the end be *à la merci* of the Franco-Russians. You must always bear this principle in mind but never express it openly. H.M. is at the moment moved primarily by anger about a piece of personal tactlessness made by Malet at the last minute, after he had for eleven years succeeded, not altogether unskilfully, in concealing his personal inadequacy by discussing politics as little as possible.

On the other hand, H.M.'s impressions of Franco-Russian intentions which he gained after the return of Colonel Moltke[1] are very dangerous. H.M. made remarks to the effect that the Tsar did not seem to be informed, that Lobanov might be up to all sorts of tricks. [...]

With best wishes

Your H.

497. Paul von Hatzfeldt to Holstein

10 November 1895

Dear friend!

Many thanks for your letter and the enclosure which interested me greatly. According to my observations, the English and the Austrians have recently formed a decidedly closer understanding, and I have the impression, whatever Szögyényi may say, that Vienna has by no means given up the effort to form a league against a possible Russian advance on Constantinople. Here, as in Vienna, they are probably convinced that nothing could be done about a *fait accompli*, that is, once the Russians had occupied Constantinople, which is what H.M. has repeatedly told Kaiser Franz Joseph. For that very reason both parties are trying to anticipate such an eventuality and are quietly hoping that we will not be ill-disposed, just as they hope that we would not leave Austria in the lurch in case Austria got into trouble about the whole business.

Deym, who came to see me yesterday and who is not, as you know, any great light, talked the entire time about the secret treaty between England and Austria,[2] *for which we two, but especially I, were godparents*, and he said it was a great advantage that Salisbury had now stated in Vienna that he regarded himself bound by it, as Goluchowski told Prince Hohenlohe orally, if I am not mistaken. When I remarked that my godchild, so far as I could remember, had after all contained very little, Deym denied this vigorously and pointed out that two important points had been gained thereby: first, that neither party would take anything for itself in the Near East, and second, that Salisbury had undertaken, in case Russia should proceed against *Constantinople* or

---

[1] See above, no. 487.

[2] Deym was referring to the Second Mediterranean Agreement of 12 December 1887. (See *Grosse Politik*, vol. IV, no. 940, pp. 393–4.)

Bulgaria, to reach an understanding at once with Austria about further steps that might be necessary. Deym concluded from this that a further agreement might be made at any time. But when I asked him if he had any basis for his belief that Salisbury would do so at this time, he replied—perhaps to avoid having me see all his cards—that he did not wish to propose such a thing in order that Salisbury should bring it up.

I will only report officially about these remarks of Deym if you ask me to do so by telegram, because I am not certain what impression they would make on H.M., and whether they might not lead him to curtail these Austrian efforts with another bucket of cold water. In my opinion it can only be useful if Vienna and London reach as close an official understanding as possible, which would leave the possibility open to us *de choisir notre parti* if this should ever prove necessary. There is of course another question, and about this I very much want to hear your opinion, as to what I am to do in case the Austrians actually decide to make definite proposals here about the interpretation and extension of the previous agreement, and demand that I, in view of my godparent-hood of the latter, support them in this new endeavour. If I should hear nothing from you on the subject and the case should arise, I would reply that I could not become involved without special instructions and that I was also of the opinion that it was not for us to express our attitude on the question until the two most interested parties had reached an understanding. Incidentally, they are apparently afraid in Vienna that Turkey might throw herself into the arms of the Russians, and that the latter might proceed on the basis of a treaty with the legal owners. Deym confirmed that this possibility also seriously worried Salisbury. You will remember that I once pointed out this possibility to him. If things develop along these lines, which I do not think is impossible, then I don't believe they will go to war here because public opinion would not be behind it. In that case Vienna too would of course merely sulk in silence.[1] [...]

With best wishes
Your
PHatzfeldt [...]

498. Anton von Saurma to Holstein

Tarabya, 10 November 1895

Dear Holstein,

As I cannot express myself so freely in official reports as I would like, I will do so in this private letter.

The Sultan is half insane at the moment. He is crushing everything around him he considers dangerous to his person. He knows about the hatred that exists against him everywhere, and everywhere suspects treason. The number of prisoners who disappear in Yildiz[2] is greater than people believe. The butcheries in Armenia are said to have taken

---

[1] See *Grosse Politik*, vol. X, chapter LXII B.
[2] Yildiz was one of the residences of the Sultan.

place for the most part at his direct orders. This explains the barbaric participation of the troops in them. Some of my colleagues believe that there is a danger that some day the Sultan, if too closely threatened by his subjects, may divert the popular anger against himself by inciting the masses against the Christians. I share this opinion because I consider him to be a thoroughly evil and dangerous person. At present he is surrounded by a low riffraff of advisers, who are also up to no good.

Tewfik Pasha, whom I have come to know well, seems to be one of the few decent people here at present. I am convinced, however, that he will have no influence whatever on the Sultan. He only listens to the advice of evil rascals.

As to the idea of the Foreign Ministry of possibly sending ships to protect our subjects,[1] you have my reports.[2] I should like to add that it would seem to be even more useful if, instead of big ships, which could after all only be sent after time-consuming and perhaps difficult negotiations among the Powers on this side of the Straits, we sent a small armed vessel (which was often done formerly). This would provide us with a little more power if the need for it should arise. [...][3]

499. Paul von Hatzfeldt to Holstein

14 November 1895

Dear friend,

I think that we now have to reckon with two facts: first, that Lord Salisbury is apparently determined to get rid of the present Sultan in one way or another; and second, that Austria will make desperate efforts to secure some kind of common action before Constantinople which might be regarded as a sort of guarantee against unilateral action on the part of the Russians.[4]

I see nothing dangerous for us in this effort of Goluchowski, because he, as you will see from my to-day's telegram about Deym's talk with Salisbury,[5] is proceeding with commendable caution and is apparently anxious to get the English to take the initiative in making proposals. If this doesn't succeed, as seems probable from Salisbury's reply, the Austrians will still be able to change their course if we make such a change seem reasonable to them.

By and large the danger in the present situation does not lie in the inclinations of particular Powers—not even in Russia's, which in my

---

[1] In fact, the Germans were trying to prevent the Italian and Austrian fleets from joining Britain in demonstrations before Constantinople until they were certain of Britain's intentions. (*Grosse Politik*, vol. X, nos. 2502–7, pp. 169–74.)

[2] Saurma's reports were filled with warnings about possible insurrections in Turkey which might lead to grave dangers for the Christians. (See *Grosse Politik*, vol. X, nos. 2450–1, pp. 96–7.)

[3] The end of the letter is missing.

[4] Eulenburg's report of 11 November on Goluchowski's proposal for a naval demonstration by the Powers against Turkey (*Grosse Politik*, vol. X, no. 2505, pp. 172–3) was received in London on 14 November. (From the Foreign Ministry files.)

[5] The reference is to a talk of 12 November. Hatzfeldt's report on this conversation of 14 November (in the London Embassy files) had already been covered by Eulenburg's report of 13 November. (*Grosse Politik*, vol. X, no. 2508, pp. 174–5.)

opinion is not yet ready and regards the present crisis as premature—but above all in the absolutely overwhelming and positively insane hatred that Lord Salisbury feels for the Sultan. Should the latter not be deposed by his own people, which I think is more likely, there are still ways and means for Salisbury to hasten this eventuality. If the Sultan now returns an unsatisfactory reply, or if massacres should take place in Constantinople, the Ambassadors need only declare to the Porte, at the initiative of England, that the Powers can no longer negotiate with *this* Sultan and that, if they are not given satisfaction in a certain length of time, they will secure justice of their own accord. Such a statement would in my opinion be enough to secure the deposition of the Sultan in twenty-four hours, but it might also lead to a complete anarchy which could only be overcome by absolute unity and complete *désinteressement* among the Powers. One might well ask what prospect there would be of that.

I permit myself no opinion as to whether it was right to tell Austria now that, even though the ships of all the Powers should gather before Constantinople, we would not take part with a single vessel.[1] Should a massacre take place there, our public opinion will hardly be satisfied if we do not do as much as other Powers for our threatened citizens. But even apart from that it is difficult to answer the question of whether we are doing the right thing in telling the Austrians at this time that we won't participate in anything, which would discourage them completely. Naturally I assume that *all* Powers, including Russia, will take part in the demonstration, and in this case I can see no reason why we should not participate or why this would even seem advisable. Russia herself would then desire our participation.

Belatedly, many thanks for your last letter and the copies of the report and letter of Philipp Eulenburg.[2] He is, I hope, too clever not to realise that we would be working against our own interest in depending on the Court party in Vienna and in making their game easier for them.[3] Nor do I think that with all his talent he will have an easy time convincing Count Goluchowski or the Kaiser of the need to divide up Turkey to the advantage of Russia simply because we want to be on good terms with the latter. They will at most realise that they will be powerless to deal with a *fait accompli* if we leave them in the lurch. But they must also realise if they give any thought to the matter that in the final analysis, that is, if it were a question of the existence of Austria, we could not leave them in the lurch because the existence of Austria is and will remain of greatest importance to us. Even if we wanted to by-pass this consideration, this would obviously only be conceivable if we were offered a full equivalent for the possible loss of Austria, and this

---

[1] This was done in a telegram to Vienna of 12 November. (*Grosse Politik*, vol. X, no. 2507, pp. 173–4.)

[2] Holstein had sent Eulenburg's report of 8 November and his private letter to Marschall of 9 November (*Grosse Politik*, vol. X, nos. 2497–8, pp. 157–60) to Hatzfeldt on 10 November. (From the London Embassy files.)

[3] In his letter to Marschall of 9 November (see note 2 above) Eulenburg said he had observed that among Court and Parliamentary circles in Vienna the opinion was gaining ground that Austria should reach an understanding with Russia.

could only consist of a binding guarantee on the part of Russia to remain completely neutral in the event of a conflict between ourselves and France. I have heard of no such guarantee, and as long as we don't have it we cannot permit the collapse of Austria.

As things stand, I was of course very much in agreement with your instruction to Rome.[1] But there too great caution is indicated if we don't want to frighten the Italians. Bülow's report of the 12th of this month[2] which arrived to-day already shows that Blanc's inclination to listen to our advice and to co-operate with us may have its limits. The remark at the end about his emphatic desire to do everything possible to avoid opposing our intentions is surely specific enough for anyone who knows how to read between the lines.

For my part I am refraining from taking any initiative whatever here. This can perhaps change only if Salisbury, in the event of a serious crisis, finds the courage to make definite proposals, always assuming that we have not meanwhile committed ourselves elsewhere in a way that makes it impossible for us to change our course.

With best wishes
Your PHatzfeldt.

500. Bogdan von Hutten-Czapski[3] to Holstein

Kassel, 15 November 1895

My dear Baron,

I was very sorry not to have seen you yesterday at the Ministry, despite repeated efforts.

First I would like to tell you how glad I was that the last visit of the Kaiser to the Prince ended satisfactorily so far as matters of foreign policy were concerned.[4] Unfortunately one cannot say the same of domestic affairs. Our 'defenceless ancestors' are still alive, and the poor soldiers will continue in future to be sentenced behind closed doors.[5]

I spent the evening before last alone with Bronsart.[6] He complained

---

[1] In a telegram to Bülow of 10 November, Hohenlohe said: 'I think I am in agreement with Your Excellency in asking you to point out to Baron Blanc that he can best secure those concessions from England (which he thinks he should demand in the interests of Italy's strategic position and in view of the critical position of England) by showing good will in general but by avoiding engaging himself too far at the beginning, especially before England has defined her own policy.' (*Grosse Politik*, vol. X, no. 2503, pp. 170–1.)

[2] Hatzfeldt refers to Bülow's telegram of 11 November (*Grosse Politik*, vol. X, no. 2504, pp. 171–2), sent to London on 12 November. (From the London Embassy files.)

[3] Bogdan, Count von Hutten-Czapski. Attached to the German Embassy in Paris, 1882–3; Aide-de-Camp of the Governor of Alsace-Lorraine, 1884–5; Brigade Adjutant in Hannover, 1885–8; Squadron Commander in Kassel, 1888–96; Castellan of Posen; Member of the Prussian Upper House; unofficial aide and adviser of Prince Hohenlohe.

[4] On 13 November the Kaiser had a long conversation with Hohenlohe and Marschall about Balkan questions and Germany's relations with Austria. (See Hohenlohe, *Denkwürdigkeiten der Reichskanzlerzeit*, pp. 120–2, 125–6.)

[5] Hutten-Czapski refers to the practice in the German army of the secret court-martial and other provisions of the military penal code that had recently come under severe criticism. Hohenlohe was working on a reform of the military penal code which was long delayed because of the opposition of the Kaiser. There is no mention of this problem in Hohenlohe's record of his conversation with the Kaiser. (See above, note 7.)

[6] Walter Bronsart von Schellendorf. Prussian Minister of War, 1893–6. (See Hutten-Czapski, *Sechzig Jahre Politik und Gesellschaft* (Berlin, 1936), vol. I, pp. 284–5.)

bitterly about the daily interference of H.M. in official matters, especially in armament questions which involved the senseless expenditure of large sums; irresponsible advisers always had some new invention on tap that caught the fancy of the Kaiser and brought disorder into the administration; Hahnke's influence in military and Lucanus' influence in political affairs made the routine transaction of official business impossible, etc. Bronsart was above all angry that the Kaiser had Hahnke put him 'on the carpet' and gave him a fairly severe calling down on account of the Munich article.[1] In the past two years I have witnessed many fights between the Kaiser and Bronsart, but have never seen the latter so wrought up. As I heard from the Chancellor, the Kaiser too is very irritated. This mood, or rather this bad mood, the importance of the problems at issue, and the volatile character of the participants arouses fears about a catastrophe; this would be all the more unfortunate because Bronsart is very well liked in the Reichstag, and above all he would fall as the protagonist of a reform that is popular in the whole Reich, which in turn would significantly increase the difficulties of the Government.

Bronsart thinks the Kaiser will give in on the ancestors question. He is furious with Köller[2] and assumes that the latter was the only one in the Ministry to vote against public courts-martial in order to avoid being involved in a possible crisis and in order to pose as the champion of military traditions. Then Bronsart began to talk about the article, said it originated in a Ministry and was intended to damage the Chancellor and himself in the eyes of H.M., but that he would find the author. I think the War Minister's suspicions are correct, but doubt whether the search for 'Mr Unknown' will have any results that will make it possible to proceed against K[öller]. Much as I am in general convinced that the personnel of the Ministry should be tampered with as little as possible, I would nevertheless be very happy indeed if this *enfant terrible*, who has already been so tactless in the Reichstag and who now seems to want to win recognition from the Kaiser at the expense of his colleagues, could be removed on the ground of some personal neglect of duty. It would be good if you could hear an account of the Wednesday meeting of the Ministry of State from someone who was there; the Prince and Marschall were not present when the incident took place; Bötticher, however, was. [...]

In grateful admiration I remain
Your most devoted
Hutten-Czapski

---

[1] The *Münchener Neuesten Nachrichten* had reported that the Prussian Ministry of State had decided to present the Kaiser with the draft of an order providing for a limited public form of Prussian military court-martial proceedings. The article stated further that the Prussian Minister of War would make his remaining in office dependent on whether the Kaiser accepted the measure. (See Hohenlohe, *Denkwürdigkeiten der Reichskanzlerzeit*, p. 123, note 2.)

[2] Ernst Matthias von Köller. Under State Secretary for Alsace-Lorraine, 1889–94; Prussian Minister of the Interior, October 1894–December 1895; Head of the Administration of Schleswig-Holstein, 1897–1901; State Secretary for Alsace-Lorraine, 1901–8.

501. Holstein to Hugo von Radolin[1]

16 November [1895]

Dear Radolin,

Enclosed is a copy of a letter received to-day from Saurma,[2] for your information.

H.M. is beginning to be quite angry with the Tsar because of the repeated cool rebuffs. I don't know the details, but can pretty well reconstruct the matter from the general picture. H.M. would like to restore the Holy Alliance, but Lobanov, who runs the Tsar, won't desert France. H.M. is convinced of *this*: that we must preserve the Triple Alliance as long as the Franco-Russian liaison continues.

Our Kaiser was very irritated for instance when in reply to his telegraphic proposal for an agreement *à deux* about the present Turkish difficulties,[3] the Tsar referred him very briefly and coolly to the Ambassadors of the Powers in Constantinople.[4]

And tell me. Have you ever heard that the Tsar drank? I heard a rumour to that effect in a roundabout way from Paris.

During the past week I have been almost more busy than ever before in my life. So excuse me if I close.

If I were you I would say nothing about the Imperial anger over here. H.M. will do enough of that himself. He treated Grand Duke Vladimir miserably, always answered in German to his French, etc.[5]

With best wishes and respects to your two ladies, warm greetings from

Your old Holstein

502. Hugo von Radolin to Holstein

St Petersburg, 19 November 1895. Evening.

My dear friend,

An unexpected opportunity has given me the chance to write you a few words *in confidence*, unfortunately only briefly because there is not much time. Many thanks for your letter of the 16th.[6]

I am beside myself about Saurma's letter of which you sent me a copy.[7] He is writing irresponsible nonsense, he is not judging from personal knowledge, but is only writing the nonsense he gets from tendentious sources. He probably attended Currie's school and has allowed himself to be stirred up by him. The Ambassadors with *one* exception seem to have lost their heads. But the expression is wrong, because they have *no heads* to lose. [...]

I most deeply regret that S. had made an impression on H.M. with his hateful reports and is the indirect instigator of telegrams like the one communicated to me.[8] I deplore the latter most terribly, and also the reply to it[9] which might have been expected. I can see that this last

---

[1] From the Radolin Papers. [2] Of 10 November. See above.
[3] Telegram of 8 November. (*Grosse Politik*, vol. X, no. 2452, p. 98.)
[4] Telegram of 9 November. (*Grosse Politik*, vol. X, no. 2453, p. 98.)
[5] The Grand Duke was in Berlin at the beginning of October.
[6] See above. [7] Of 10 November. See above.
[8] See note 3. [9] See note 4.

must have caused resentment, but I don't really see what else could have been said. The Franco-Russian understanding is a *factum* that must be taken into consideration, and an *entente à deux* is impossible without the third Power. Things would not be different if another Minister had been in Lob[anov's] place; Fr. is at the moment too important to R. for financial reasons to be dropped. One must take into account the fact that there are eight billions of French money in Russia and that Russia would be in uncanny difficulties if Fr. withdrew and threw the money on the market. In France the disillusionment about *Russia's friendship*, which has as yet profited her nothing and which can profit her nothing, will come of its own accord. [...]

I think (this is my personal opinion) and *to my regret* I am of the same opinion as Lob., that the Goluchowski proposal[1] is impractical; because if one proceeds from the incredible idea of *forcing* the Dardanelles, this would inevitably *mettre le feu aux quatre coins du monde*. First of all, the ships would always *come too late* to rescue foreigners from a massacre in Constantinople, which would break out spontaneously. (But I of course think such a thing is ABSOLUTELY out of the question and is merely the imagination of the fearful Ambassadors) and what should the fleets do in the Golden Horn after that? Would they be able to suppress an uprising in the interior of Asia Minor, for instance in Diarbekr? That would require an army of several hundred thousand men and a fortnight's march! Or should Russia undertake this occupation? Russia will decline with thanks; because the fruit of which they are certain is *not yet* ripe, and I therefore understand very well that the Russians have no desire whatever to embark on a project that will be of benefit only to the English, *perhaps*, because even *that* is *problematical*. The English have after all no intention of hanging on to Constantinople. So why should they go there? If they want anything in Syria or Arabia or the Persian Gulf, then they can direct their attention *there*. The Turks must regard every naval demonstration before Constantinople as hostile, whereas the *insurgents* in Asia Minor or possibly in Macedonia would regard it as a support of their *aspirations*. In this way the efforts of any government in Constantinople would be restricted and the suppression of the insurgents be made more difficult. Under such circumstances I can imagine that it will be difficult to introduce reforms. The Sultan may be quite glad to see the reforms frustrated, but the Powers that take part in the demonstration will thus be supporting the *intentions* of the Sultan.

The Goluchowski project is the product of the clever mind of Calice.[2] Even the Austrian here[3] thinks so, and recognises the wording from the report of the Imp[erial] Amb[assador]. The Englishman here,[4] a

[1] See p. 558, note 4.

[2] Heinrich, Baron von Calice. Austro-Hungarian Ambassador in Constantinople, 1880–1906.

[3] Franz von Paula, Prince von und zu Liechtenstein. Austro-Hungarian Ambassador in St Petersburg, 1894–9.

[4] Sir Nicholas O'Connor. British Ambassador in St Petersburg, 1895–8, in Constantinople, 1898–1906.

sensible man, acknowledges confidentially that England's action is going a bit too far and that it contradicts to some extent the words of Salisbury. But I still think the English will not go as far as seemed likely at first.

Be that as it may, I completely share your opinion and that of another person you mentioned to me that we must absolutely and with all our strength hold the Triple Alliance together as long as the other bloc of F. and R. *exists*. The restoration of the Holy Alliance would of course be a pleasant dream that may some day be realised, but I don't know whether *one* of the three limbs necessary for the Holy Alliance won't sooner or later become a dead branch. If it bears many 'bright fruits' like the one who recently exhibited his experience as *doyen* in Constantinople,[1] then this possibility may occur even sooner than might be expected.

We must reckon with the given factors and accept people as they are. In this way we even get along with our dear friends.

Excuse this long expectoration. I had to do it because the unfounded inflammatory articles—or reports—of S. made me very angry. I repeat that he doesn't *know* Constantinople and judges the situation falsely. I only hope that I am not wrong. His judgment of the Sultan, whom I after all know *very* well, is absolutely wrong. He has many shortcomings, we are all aware of them and I reported enough about them, but I do not think that his position is in danger, and his chief mistake is that he sacrifices much that might be of benefit to his empire for his personal security. But he is neither an evil nor a dangerous person. He wants to do everything alone and be an autocrat. Now that he has seen where the government of Abdul Aziz[2] with Midhat[3] and the English parliamentarians has led, I cannot blame him. And I can also understand—no matter how regrettable it may be—why he exiled Kiamil Pasha,[4] who wanted to emancipate himself from the palace and threatened to become a second Midhat. I know Rifaat Pasha[5] quite well, by the way. He is very energetic and earned his spurs in Albania where he vigorously suppressed Albanian banditry by ruthless hangings. This appointment would really mean that the Sultan intends to put down the revolt energetically. The Sultan is actually in a difficult position. He is supposed to introduce reforms, which between ourselves will *never* satisfy the Armenians simply because they want independence. (The reforms that are to be introduced and which, rationally speaking, should satisfy the Armenians, will not be welcome for the simple reason that they will rob them of every excuse to voice further complaints.) The Sultan, then, is supposed to introduce reforms and treat the Armenians well. On the other hand the Armenians are engaged in a

---

[1] Calice.   [2] Sultan of Turkey, 1861–76.
[3] Midhat Pasha, the dominant figure in the Ministry that came to power in Turkey in May 1876. Midhat, an ardent reformer, deposed Abdul Aziz on 30 May and proclaimed his nephew, Murad V, as Sultan. Murad was deposed on 31 August of that same year on the grounds of insanity. Abdul Hamid II, the new Sultan, dismissed Midhat Pasha on 5 February 1877 and banished him in 1881.
[4] Turkish Grand Vizier, 1885–91, 1895, 1908–9, 1912–13.
[5] Turkish Grand Vizier, 1895–1901.

revolt that must after all be suppressed. If now the Sultan resorts to arms and proceeds energetically against the rebels, the cry will again immediately be raised that the Turkish troops are behaving cruelly towards the rebels. That is a *cercle vicieux* from which it is impossible to escape. Here incidentally everyone is agreed that the Armenians are to blame for everything and that for two years they have put the patience of the Turks to the most severe test. I cannot blame the Moslems for having at last hurled themselves on these horrible Armenians and committed a few excesses. That the Sultan consented to these and indirectly at least approved the brutal conduct of the Turkish troops— that is an infamous lie which was circulating when I was in Constantinople but which no one any longer believed. Now naive S. comes along and spreads this nonsense. Unfortunately nobody in Const. writes me any interesting political news and I don't know the latest, but I don't doubt for a moment that what I am saying is true. If Count Hatzfeldt were to read my letter he would, with his knowledge of Turkey, certainly agree with me. He esteems the Sultan just as I do, and I am sorry that the Ambassador is presenting him in such a poor light. He is *sincerely* devoted to us and we can only *lose* by a change. But enough of that. I am observing with great satisfaction that WE are now very highly regarded here, one can even notice it in the Press. The Russians realise just as much as the English how IMPORTANT it is for the one or the other to have *Germany* on *her* side. I think we might ask *a very high price for our friendship*, and am certain that any price would gladly be paid. This is not suitable for a *report*, but I cannot *refrain* from bringing this earnestly to *your* attention by informing you of the prevailing sentiment here at the moment about this matter. I think the Russians would regard it as a terrible blow if we were to draw away from them. [...]

The news that No. *1*[1] here drinks is a false scent. He had been confused with his brother,[2] who drank a great deal and thereby brought himself closer to the grave. The latter in fact has lived a dissolute life in every respect and is by no means agreeable. He is expected to die soon. I only hear good reports about No. *1*. The only thing I regret is that he cuts himself off and sees only Lob. and Witte, who don't like each other. People think that this cutting-himself-off will cease after the coronation. I am glad to see how warm the relationship is between the imperial couple. That will at any rate lower the influence of the Dowager. [...]

Your faithful
Hugo [...]

503. Paul von Hatzfeldt to Holstein

23 November 1895

Dear friend,

Salisbury is now vegetating in the country and will hardly return to town before Wednesday.

---

[1] Tsar Nicholas II.   [2] Grand Duke Michael.

Deym, who was just here to see me, expressed *complete* confidence in Salisbury, who would agree to anything proposed in Vienna. This conviction is obviously the reason why Vienna attaches no importance to demanding an interpretation of the Nine Points[1] from the people here. Whether an Italian request will carry enough weight here without Austrian support seems doubtful to me. Naturally I too will push as hard as I can if necessary but—if we don't trust Salisbury, he doesn't trust us very much now either. At the end of our last conversation he said: 'You will remember that I always said I would next find you in the arms of Russia.' I: 'Not yet, and that depends a great deal on you.' He: 'Yes, a little.' I: 'No, a great deal', and with that we parted.[2]

While Deym was with me to-day, Courcel arrived and used the opportunity to inform him confidentially of the French reply to the Goluchowski proposal,[3] which is quite courteous. Courcel observed that Paris would have been happy to go along with the Austrians if they had not immediately put *les points sur les i* and spoken about possible cannon balls. If they had merely raised the point about the Ambassadors reaching agreement about possible steps to be taken, this would have been enough and Paris would have agreed.

In spite of that, and although failure was to be expected in St Petersburg and Paris, the Austrian initiative was a *good* idea and we can only hope that Vienna will *stay* on this course. It is much easier for Salisbury to cover himself *here* behind Austrian proposals and one may hope, if he is sincere, that he will agree to everything from that quarter.

Of course *we* must also reckon with the possibility that he is *not* sincere, or that he may not be able to do what he wants to do. But that won't hurt *us* if we *under all circumstances* hold firmly to the policy of not committing ourselves definitively to *anybody*, neither to the Russians nor to the English. If the crisis comes and our hands are free, we will be in a position to make our choice and *pose our conditions*.

Probably nothing will now come of the Togo business. Sanderson was deeply depressed when I told him that, as I predicted, I would be unable to change one iota on the Volta rectification.[4] He said they would be *glad* to do us this favour and urgently wanted the agreement with us, but that he could not deceive himself that it would be impossible for the Government to bring this before Parliament now.

With best wishes
Your
PH.

[1] The German Ambassadors in Vienna and London had been instructed on 14 November to work for an understanding between Britain, Italy and Austria along the lines of the Nine Points Convention—the Second Mediterranean Agreement of 12 December 1887. (*Grosse Politik*, vol. X, no. 2541, pp. 202–3.) On 20 November Marschall telegraphed to Bülow: 'To define England's position, it would be a good idea if Vienna and Rome were to agree to propose in London that a more precise interpretation of the "Nine Points" in their present form be arranged, with the proviso that the latter could be converted into a formal treaty as soon as a crisis in the Near East appeared to be imminent.' (*Grosse Politik*, vol. X, no. 2546, p. 207.)

[2] The conversation is recorded in French in the original.

[3] *Documents diplomatiques français*, Première Série, vol. XII, no. 207, pp. 299–300.

[4] See above, p. 547, note 3.

504. Paul von Hatzfeldt to Holstein

27 November 1895

Dear friend,

The latest Russian manoeuvre, i.e. the 'respite' to be given the Porte with respect to the second *stationaire* seems to have been successful to the extent that the Sultan is apparently again wavering.[1] For Austria the thing is a direct slap in the face, because this was the only point left over from the Goluchowski programme and Lobanov specifically accepted this point. If the anger in Vienna can be measured by that of Deym, it cannot be inconsiderable.

Deym seemed almost more annoyed about the unsatisfactory reply he received this afternoon from Salisbury to the question of what was to happen now.[2] I was not in the least surprised by this answer because as you know I am convinced that Salisbury can take no initiative whatever and wants to let Austria take the lead. If the Austrians don't want to do this, they have only two ways of putting an end to this game: either they propose a specific programme here and make it evident that they regard its acceptance as a token of England's sincerity, and that they will adjust their own future policy accordingly; or they too will sit quiet and explain this by saying that they neither can nor wish to go further than England feels is indicated in her own interests.

I will not report on my own brief talk with Salisbury this afternoon because we had nothing new to say to each other. You may perhaps be interested in one point which I will therefore mention here. I succeeded in directing the conversation to the newspapers and jokingly made the remark that they had no plans or ulterior ideas that were not dictated to them by some other authority. In doing so I let fall the word 'Congress' which some paper had mentioned, and Salisbury then said very definitely: 'Conferences and Congresses are no good unless everyone agrees in advance about what they are to accomplish.'[3] (In other words, exactly what I predicted in my last letter—or was it a telegram—to you, if I am not mistaken.) Salisbury then said further: 'I don't know at all why people ascribe all sorts of mysterious projects to me. I am completely innocent, and have in this case only one idea and that is *to get myself out of a nasty impasse.*'[3] We were then agreed that things would probably stay quiet through the winter. When I added the question: 'What will become of your *impasse* in the spring if at that time things break loose all over in the Turkish Empire, where people are now stoking the fires—that is, if in addition to Armenia, we also have Macedonia, Crete, Arabia, perhaps Albania, etc.?' he replied: 'In that case the impasse will become a bog.'[3]

Sometimes I almost think that he himself doesn't know what he wants

[1] On 26 November the Russians informed the Germans that 'the Sultan had appealed directly to the Tsar of Russia with the request that he use his influence with the Powers to abandon the idea of sending the second *stationaire*'. (*Grosse Politik*, vol. X, no. 2534, p. 195.)

[2] According to a telegram from Hatzfeldt of the same day, Salisbury had stated he did not know what could be done about the Near Eastern question if the Powers failed to agree. (From the Foreign Ministry files.)

[3] In French in the original.

or what he should do. But on one point he is, I think, clear, and that is that he will do nothing as long as he possibly can.

With best wishes
Your
PHatzfeldt [...]

505. Holstein to Bernhard von Bülow[1]

TELEGRAM

Berlin, 29 November 1895

Private. Top Secret.
With reference to to-day's letter.[2]

Chancellor crisis becoming acute because the Kaiser shows little tendency to dismiss Köller.[3] The Chancellor, who just read me his resignation,[4] will first discuss the matter with the other Ministers, with the exception of War and the Interior, all of whom incidentally have already individually stated that they were against Köller.

I have just informed Philipp Eulenburg, who is in Meran, Upper Mais, Leichthof, about the crisis by telegram so that he cannot later accuse me of having left him without information at the decisive moment.[5]

Holstein

506. Philipp zu Eulenburg to Holstein

Meran, 29 November 1895, Evening.

Dear friend,

I have *just* finished the letter to H.M. which I wrote immediately after decoding your telegram.[6] The letter describes a change of Chancellors as an *impossibility*, because Europe would not understand it and the Kaiser would completely discredit himself. I added: the moment would then come for which Friedrichsruh has been lying in wait with eager anticipation; H.M. will have to accept a Chancellor appointed there, whether his name be Waldersee, Schweinitz, or anything else.

About Köller I wrote *quite honestly* that H.M. was wrong about him. But I also said that H.M. could later revert to him if he should find it necessary.

I am disturbed but by no means without hope—only I wish both Bronsart *and* Köller would go. That will have to be arranged. But how? This I cannot visualise from here.

I was properly terrified by your reply!! I had not heard a *single* word from Berlin about the affair, and was suddenly overwhelmed with terror.

[1] From the Bülow Papers. Only a typewritten copy of this document was available to the editors.
[2] Not found.
[3] To ingratiate himself with the Kaiser, Köller had made himself the advocate of imperial measures in the Ministry of State. (See above, Hutten-Czapski's letter of 15 November.) On 28 November Hohenlohe told the Kaiser that it was no longer possible for the other Ministers to work with Köller. The Kaiser categorically refused to dismiss Köller saying that he was the only man on whom he could rely 'when the time came to use force'. (Hohenlohe, *Denkwürdigkeiten der Reichskanzlerzeit*, p. 126.)
[4] *Ibid.*, pp. 126–7.   [5] See Haller, *Eulenburg*, p. 167.   [6] See Haller, *Eulenburg*, p. 167.

That's why I telegraphed—but you can imagine how I felt at this surprise.

Good night. I *can't* do anything more.

Your faithful
PE [...]

507. Holstein to Hugo von Radolin[1]

Berlin, 4 December 1895

Dear Radolin,

[...] We are going through a Ministerial crisis the details of which I don't know but which seems to be very serious. As things stand, I think that Hohenlohe and Marschall will stay together and go together. I will then do the same. For me it makes no great difference because I don't have much longer anyway on account of my eyes.

That you considered me as a godparent for your little daughter[2] pleased me greatly, but I hope you will not misunderstand me if I gratefully decline.

First of all, I haven't had much luck in life and so might perhaps not bring the child much luck.

Second, I think that in view of the acute situation existing to-day the clergy prefers Catholics as godparents[3]—except, of course, for people in exceptionally high positions.

So once again many thanks. It is enough for me that you and the Princess had the intention.

Your old friend
H. [...]

508. Philipp zu Eulenburg to Holstein[4]

Vienna, 7 December 1895

My dear friend,

Those were and are very pleasant days indeed!—yet again.

That you still have any nerves left is one of the biggest riddles in my experience. I feel myself flagging, *especially* when my heart and the feeling of friendship are so severely taxed. This was the case in Breslau.[5]

I happen to love H.M. personally very much, and to see a person suffer deeply whom one has taken to one's heart—that is not my strong point. Nor your's—for beneath your facade of the hard statesman 'glow the flames of *true* humanity'.

At any rate, H.M. really suffered *deeply* and my meeting with him bore the character of the heart outpourings of a tormented spirit. That is

---

[1] From the Radolin Papers.

[2] A daughter, Elizabeth, was born to Radolin and his second wife Johanna, née von Oppersdorff, on 17 November 1895.

[3] Prince Radolin was a Roman Catholic.

[4] Partly printed in Haller, *Eulenburg*, pp. 169–71.

[5] Eulenburg had gone to Breslau to discuss the ministerial crisis with the Kaiser. (Haller, *Eulenburg*, pp. 168–9.)

why I so *urgently* asked the Prince[1] to take into account this feeling of our suffering King, and I am glad that the dear old gentleman and that you too understand me perfectly.

The *form* of how satisfaction is to be rendered doesn't really matter. The form I suggested was not mine, by the way, but that of His Imperial Majesty. If it was modified, that is his affair.[2] I even had to fight because H.M. at first wanted the resignation to be made *public*. I dissuaded him from that—but I agreed to the rest from conviction because one cannot after all force one's King, who gave in on the matter, to *suffer* in addition! Also with regard to the relationship between himself and the Ministry, which was severely strained, I thought it advisable to offer H.M. a proof of human feeling.

I thank you warmly for your detailed reports. These gave me the opportunity to see the situation as a whole and to avoid mistakes. The *centre* of my activity had to be to reconcile the Kaiser and Chancellor. In my letters to both—in addition to my personal intercourse with H.M. in Breslau—I gave advice that will I hope be followed.[3] It was based on my knowledge of both personalities. I don't have any copies. Things were in such a rush that I hardly had time to read over what I had written.

The thing I consider most important at the moment—I wrote and telegraphed to Hohenlohe about it[4]—is to avoid the impression that the Ministry wants *to exploit its victory*. If *that* happens, then the situation is hopeless.

As H.M. is absolutely convinced that he had *overstepped the limits* of what a self-confident Prussian King may do, and has shown by that how impossible he regards a change of Chancellors, his feelings must be spared in this respect as much as possible. *If this is done*, then everything can be arranged because we know how much H.M. wants to keep Hohenlohe as Chancellor. The Ministry must be made to *realise* that H.M. only gave in *for the sake of the Chancellor*. They must be made to see that *for this reason* an audience of the Chancellor is enough to eliminate this or that undesirable element.

But to make this situation possible it is important that H.M. should never feel he is being overridden by the entire Ministry of State, but only that he is facing *the definite firm will of the Chancellor, man to man*. The Chancellor can no longer tell him: 'I am here as the representative of the Ministry of State which has inexorably decided the following, etc.', but, 'it is my fixed opinion that, etc.' The latter form—used in the kindly manner of the Prince—leads to the same result and *spares the King of Prussia*.

[1] In a letter of 6 December. (Hohenlohe, *Denkwürdigkeiten der Reichskanzlerzeit*, pp. 137–8.)

[2] To save face in agreeing to the dismissal of Köller, the Kaiser had suggested that the entire Ministry resign; he would then accept the resignation of Köller. The next day he decided against this method, and instead granted Köller a long leave of absence. (Hohenlohe, *Denkwürdigkeiten der Reichskanzlerzeit*, pp. 132–4.) Köller resigned on 8 December 1895.

[3] See p. 569, note 5; for Eulenburg's letter to the Kaiser of 6 December, see Haller, *Eulenburg*, pp. 189–90.

[4] Hohenlohe, *Denkwürdigkeiten der Reichskanzlerzeit*, pp. 136–8.

I believe you will concede that I am right and hope that the Prince will decide to assume this role.

Now as to the question of Köller's replacement, I of course followed Hohenlohe's wishes exclusively and exactly. I am only very irritated that I had to propose Posadowsky[1] in Breslau and then suddenly heard that Studt[2] was the candidate of the Chancellor.

It is obvious that my proposal concerning Studt would make a flat impression after I had fired all my ammunition in favour of Posadowsky! —and I certainly won't pass on the threat that 'the Ministry of State makes this an ultimatum'.

From the preceding you will surely agree to that. In having been completely loyal in these questions and proposals and having stood by the position held by yourself and Hohenlohe, I feel I deserve all the more credit because with respect to the candidacy of Lucanus I do not agree *at all* with your—or rather the Ministry's—view. Of course I *took* care and *will* take care not to say a word about it.

Why don't you want to make Lucanus a Minister?

If this subaltern creature becomes a Minister, he will above all try to *consolidate* his position. The example of Köller will show him that even the confidence of the Kaiser is not enough to hold him if it brings him into conflict with the rest of the Ministry. Smooth and subservient, he will try to eliminate the suspicion his colleagues feel for him.

It is possible that he may try to exploit his personal relationship with H.M.—but certainly only with the greatest caution, because, as I said, he above all wants to consolidate his position. He had a light stroke in Wiesbaden, is no longer young. He will be more reluctant than anyone else to risk his salary as Minister. It is probable that, farther removed from the person of H.M., his influence will pale before that of the new Chief of Cabinet. And in the job itself I think he would run himself to death. He is a cautious and not a strong character. H.M. will soon be *disillusioned* in him. Then there will be difficulties and he will disappear from the scene. But, as I said, you and Hohenlohe don't want him, so the game is called off.

Addio—the post is leaving

Your faithful
PE

509. Philipp zu Eulenburg to Holstein

Vienna, 13 December 1895

Dear friend,

I would like to add these remarks to supplement my to-day's report

---

[1] Arthur, Count von Posadowsky-Wehner. State Secretary of the Reich Treasury, 1893–7; State Secretary of the Reich Bureau of the Interior and Prussian Minister of State, 1 July 1897–1907.

[2] Konrad von Studt. Head of the Administration in Königsberg, 1882–7; Under State Secretary for Alsace-Lorraine, 1887–9; Head of the Administration in Westphalia, 1889–99; Prussian Minister of Education, 1899–1907.

which is arriving by pouch and deals with the three-cornered agreements of '87.[1]

The report may possibly create the impression that it contradicts dispatch no. 939 of 2 December.[2]

That isn't the case, however. I quite realise that I shouldn't propose or press the question of a renewed understanding among the three Powers. *But I must see to it at least that Austria and Italy don't fall out over this question.*

For *that* reason I thought it very necessary indeed *to whet Goluchowski's appetite* (but on a completely *personal* basis). I think I have succeeded in this to some extent. I won't do more, of course.

This antipathy towards unfortunate Italy is a problem here! It will be difficult ever to overcome it. Naturally the antipathy is always particularly obvious 'when the little fellow gets pretentious'. In this respect Kálnoky and Goluchowski, otherwise so different, resemble one another.

Warmest good wishes!

Your faithful
PE

The Chancellor wrote me a really profoundly moving letter! What a *blessing* that we have him. I will go on fighting for him to the last drop of my blood.

510. Philipp zu Eulenburg to Holstein[3]

Vienna, 14 December 1895

Maddeningly enough, I left my letter yesterday in my brief-case. So I will send it to-day. Well, you will have imagined how things are.

It is lucky that we have Nigra here. He must be kept here till his last breath. A man in whom the present regime has real confidence is the only person to save the situation.

Nothing shows through officially (although Nigra has told me often enough: *on nous déteste ici*), but it is incredible how much anger and fury the decisive people here have stored up in their hearts. The insane policy of the Pope[4] with all its inconveniences is at the moment a sort of corrective—but only a weak one.

The activity of Blanc always brings the anger to the surface, and you can't imagine how much trouble I sometimes have holding our beloved allies together. Now we are again in this phase. Please leave me my freedom of action in this respect. I am hewing sharply to the line to avoid creating the illusion that we are getting 'active'.

[1] Eulenburg had reported that Blanc had made proposals in Vienna with the aim of expanding the Anglo-Austrian-Italian agreements of 1887. To overcome Goluchowski's scepticism, Eulenburg had pointed out that England's isolation might induce Salisbury 'to make more binding commitments than he had been willing to make formerly'. Goluchowski said he would discuss the matter with Deym after the latter had felt out the terrain in London. (From the Foreign Ministry files.)
[2] *Grosse Politik*, vol. X, no. 2553, pp. 214-15.
[3] Partly printed in Haller, *Eulenburg*, p. 145.
[4] In trying to win the support of the Austro-Hungarian Government against the Italian monarchy in the Rome question.

Things will be difficult when the time draws near to renew the treaty with Italy. Everything will then depend on the conjunctures of the moment. Kálnoky would have deserted—directly to Russia and France. Goluchowski won't do so. It would require a quite unprecedented wooing on the part of Lobanov, with *the most far-reaching guarantees*— and I don't believe this will happen. [...]

With best wishes
Your faithful
PE

511. Holstein to Bernhard von Bülow[1]

TELEGRAM

Berlin, 18 December 1895

Private

Contrary to the tradition that Ministers who have resigned do not engage in public polemics, Herr von Köller immediately opened his campaign against the Ministry of State, especially against Bötticher and Baron Marschall von Bieberstein, in the organ of the Union of Landowners and other Fronde newspapers, whereas the Minister of War has vanished from sight. In addition, a remark of Herr von Köller is circulating in Conservative circles to the effect that last Saturday he told the Kaiser that His Majesty was being lied to and deceived by the Ministry of State. Tomorrow there is a meeting of the Ministry. A row not unlikely, because the Kaiser has been stirred up *by* Köller, the Ministry has been stirred up *against* him. Prince Hohenlohe just told me of his determination to declare himself on this occasion to be at one with Bötticher and Baron Marschall von Bieberstein. Nor did the Prince fail to notice that the imperial visit to Friedrichsruh[2] took place without his previous knowledge and that the Kaiser has subsequently not used this occasion to speak with the Chancellor. Bötticher wants to resign, the Prince however told him that the time and the occasion were not suitable for an individual resignation.

A more barefaced misrepresentation of the real facts of the Köller crisis than occurred at this time has probably rarely happened before. The false account would long since have been destroyed if Bronsart von Schellendorf and General von Plessen, who *alone* started the ball rolling, had not wanted to stay out of the business at any price, which is what they should have done.[3] [*sic*] But then one shouldn't be surprised if a crisis occurs. A new Chancellor would have to appear before the world as the continuation of the Köller tradition. A Chancellor with calm judgment, such as the Kaiser may even have had in mind, would not accept under these circumstances, so the Kaiser would have to resort to a

---

[1] From the Bülow Papers. Only a typewritten copy of this document was available to the editors.

[2] The Kaiser visited Prince Bismarck in Friedrichsruh on 16 December on his return from a visit to Kiel.

[3] Köller had informed Plessen and Hahnke of how the members of the Ministry of State had voted on the question of the reform of the military court-martial. Bronsart heard about Köller's indiscretion and brought the matter before a meeting of the Ministry. (Hohenlohe, *Denkwürdigkeiten der Reichskanzlerzeit*, p. 125.)

coup d'état Chancellor who would come into power with a programme of violating Parliament—and, if necessary, the Kaiser. This is my prophecy and this is why I am issuing a warning. I am sending the identical telegram to Philipp, Count zu Eulenburg.[1]

Holstein

512. Philipp zu Eulenburg to Holstein

Vienna, 19 December 1895

My dear friend,

I am not being paradoxical when I tell you that your kind letter in which you purport to find a divergence in our points of view gave me *unspeakable* pleasure.[2] I am of course certain that our views don't differ nearly so much as you perhaps assume—but what pleases me is the kind and friendly manner in which you speak of this fact, which would be sufficient to provoke a complete break among other people!

It is this fact that gives me pleasure! A golden proof of your attachment to me, your loyal feelings, *which can no longer be changed* by certain differences of opinion or methods of action.

I thank you from *the bottom of my heart* for this proof! You know of course *how* attached I am to you, how close I feel to you personally, how I reckon your friendship among my most precious possessions. For that reason don't laugh about this outbreak of happiness and about this turn which my reply took, which may at first have seemed surprising!

You already measure me with other standards than you use for your other friends—so put this outburst down to my particular account!

When we see each other again, we will have to talk about this crisis affair which was interesting in many respects. It would be too much to undertake a written explanation. But everything can certainly be made to work out all right.

Therefore, let us continue to work loyally together shoulder to shoulder. It is very necessary and important; and to me it is obvious that our falling out would cost the Hohenlohe regime its life.

In old loyalty
Your
PE.

513. Philipp zu Eulenburg to Holstein

Vienna, 19 December 1895

My dear friend,

I wrote via this dispatch bag to the Chancellor and reassured him with respect to Friedrichsruh.[3]

But I can assure you most definitely of the following:

---

[1] See Haller, *Eulenburg*, p. 190.

[2] Holstein had written on 17 December: 'I regard myself as a royalist, to be sure, but I am not in favour of complete submission to every idea of His Majesty to the extent that you are. As I know how honest you are, I don't reproach you and sincerely hope that some day you won't reproach yourself when you see what all this is leading to.' (Haller, *Eulenburg*, p. 190.)

[3] See Haller, *Eulenburg*, p. 191; Hohenlohe, *Denkwürdigkeiten der Reichskanzlerzeit*, pp. 142–4.

(1) *After* a visit to Friedrichsruh H.M. will fearfully avoid undertaking any personnel changes in the Ministry.

(2) He still holds to the very definite and unalterable viewpoint of not yielding to pressure from Friedrichsruh—not even to create the *appearance* of doing so; therefore

(3) even if he were tempted to drop Marschall or Bötticher, there would be no question of doing so *now*.

(4) Personnel was *certainly* not discussed in Friedrichsruh—perhaps the Near East. H.M. will talk about that with Hohenlohe too.

(5) H.M. is holding *so firmly* to Hohenlohe that if the latter declares energetically that he needs Marschall, H.M. will *not* drop him. H.M. knows this so well, by the way, that he will oppose point-blank even stronger attacks for ousting Marschall than have been mounted heretofore.

(6) I share your view about Bronsart. I had a very poor opinion of him even before you arrived at this view.

(7) H.M. thinks *even less* of him, than we do, but will *be careful* not to touch him because he knows that the skilfully introduced military courts-martial question affects the Chancellor. H.M. would like to get rid of B., the sooner the better.

. . . . . .

That, my dear friend, is the present situation, as I see it through my eyeglasses—and the glasses are exceedingly well focused.

I earnestly request you not to worry yourself when there is really no serious reason to do so. You need your nerves, and *we* need them too.

I of course feel it is necessary, in view of the incredible perfidy of Köller, to call a halt. But in general—and especially after the visit to Friedrichsruh—the situation is not in any way so out of joint to give grounds for concern.

Now specifically as to our friend Waldersee, it is ABSOLUTELY OUT OF THE QUESTION that H.M. has ideas about making him Chancellor. H.M. won't use a general again, *pro primo*,—and then he has found so many hairs in this Waldersee soup which has been offered him *ad nauseam* that he has his belly full of them.

No, Hohenlohe *stays* and is the *only one* on whom H.M. *wants* to count and *can* count. That is *absolutely certain*. It is only a question of stiffening and strengthening the relationship between them. *I am doing all I can in that regard*. The relationship received a mild shock in the Köller crisis, but H.M.'s *terror* of another crisis is so incredibly great that Hohenlohe's position has thereby gained quite special new strength.

Now addio—the post is leaving

Your faithful
PE

514. Holstein to Hugo von Radolin[1]

21 December 1895

Dear friend,

I can only hastily wish you and yours a happy holiday; because I *can't* do anything more.

[1] From the Radolin Papers.

Our attitude towards England is at the moment mistrustful; for we don't want a war, but we suspect that England is planning a big war not only for herself—this idea we would tolerate—but one that would involve Austria and Italy, in other words something that would seriously endanger our own after-dinner nap. That the latter have consistently rejected recent English proposals was our doing.[1]

I think that Salisbury is untruthful, and remember that Mrs Julia[2] said this about him.

If Russia is cautious in pressing towards the Mediterranean, *si elle y met des ménagements*, we will undoubtedly succeed in restraining Austria, despite the howls of Hungary, and also Italy. As long as these two are out of it and not in danger of being demolished, we can be indifferent to everything else. Marschall to-day told the English Ambassador: 'Even if another hundred thousand Armenians are killed, their death still concerns us less than that of two hundred thousand Germans.'

You can use all the above as topics of conversation with Lobanov.

Please lay my respects at the feet of your ladies

Your tired old
Holstein

515. Holstein to Philipp zu Eulenburg[3]

Copy

Berlin, 21 December 1895

Dear friend,

I am utterly crushed by yesterday's conversation between H.M. and Swaine.[4] H.M. said things that might create a great threat of war for us. H.M. said that England should have forced the Dardanelles, he, H.M., would in that case have seen to it that Austria and Italy joined England. What happens now if Salisbury, whom H.M. has deeply offended, communicated the contents of that conversation to St Petersburg? Then the Russians will know that the German Kaiser is endeavouring to incite Europe against Russia as an *agent provocateur*. Nothing would be more likely than that Lobanov should say to the Tsar: 'Your Majesty must, together with France, first settle accounts with Germany. The other questions will later be easy to solve.' This danger is all the greater because it will never come into the open, but will quietly creep up on us.

From the experiences we have had already, it is unfortunately

---

[1] Holstein refers to the idea of closer political co-operation between Austria-Hungary, Italy, and Britain, especially in the Near East. (See *Grosse Politik*, vol. X, no. 2473, pp. 121–2.) On 20 December Marschall telegraphed to Eulenburg: 'We can only regard with satisfaction the fact that Count Goluchowski, on the basis of our representations and perhaps too as a result of his own most recent experiences, is showing no inclination of allowing himself to be pressed into the forefront by England.' (*Grosse Politik*, vol. X, no. 2565, pp. 237–8.)

[2] Mrs Julia Tyrrell, Radolin's British sister-in-law by his first marriage.

[3] Partly printed in Rogge, *Friedrich von Holstein*, pp. 175–7. See Rogge's comments on the Haller version of the document. (*Eulenburg*, pp. 191–2.)

[4] *Grosse Politik*, vol. X, nos. 2572, pp. 251–5.

established that H.M., for all his ability, has been denied the gift of political tact. Initiative without tact is like a flood without dikes. Consider whether you should counsel H.M., or whether Hohenlohe should do something.[1] Otherwise Kaiser and Reich will rush into the abyss; I am reminded of Henneberg's 'The Pursuit of Pleasure'.

I didn't see Hohenlohe again, and could in any case only have advised him to bestir himself.

It has been about a year, my dear Eulenburg, since I wrote you a letter in which I expressed my fears about what now seems to be coming to pass.[2]

To-day I warn you again. See to it that world history does not some day picture you as the evil spirit who was at the side of the imperial traveller when he chose the false path.

I don't want to say by this that you should do everything by yourself. Take counsel with Hohenlohe. Bernhard Bülow, too, once he has seen the danger, will surely be prepared to counter it skilfully by suitable reports.

In Hohenlohe's great compliance lies the overwhelming danger for the Kaiser, for it will actually strengthen his arbitrary tendencies. Hohenlohe should *never* have permitted an incursion into his sphere of authority such as this imperial conversation with Swaine. By swallowing it, he tempts the Kaiser to do more of the same; this can *only* lead to a crack-up. In that case it would be better if we—Hohenlohe, Marschall and I—resigned at once. This would at any rate be a lesson for the Kaiser, because a more submissive Chancellor than Hohenlohe he will never get again, not even if he takes Schweinitz, with Monts or Raschdau as State Secretary.

When you deal with Hohenlohe, *you* must make a new man of him, *you* must advise him that in certain unavoidable circumstances he must play the *Chancellor of the Reich* in dealing with the Kaiser. In reality the old gentleman now behaves as though he were the second High Chamberlain of the family. Or—you tell me—*who* should advise the Kaiser during these *very* serious times? An aide-de-camp perhaps? Or are you still of the opinion that the Sovereign alone, in solitary grandeur, should be allowed to decide all questions through some Higher Wisdom?

Domestic politics make more noise, but the other is much more dangerous. The fact that H.M. is now mixing into that, fresh from the smoking room, may have consequences which will astound both him and yourself. For that reason I am more discouraged to-day than I have ever been in my worst periods.

My warm thanks for the friendly feelings you expressed again yesterday. You know that I believe that as a character you have the best intentions in everything.

But consider that fate has conferred upon you a sphere of activity in

---

[1] Holstein urged Hohenlohe to write the Kaiser a severe letter warning him of the dangers of meddling in the foreign policy of the Reich. (Hohenlohe, *Denkwürdigkeiten der Reichskanzlerzeit*, p. 146.)

[2] Of 24 December 1894. See above.

which it is not enough to say: *optima voluisse sat est*. Considerably more is expected of you. You yourself should not do everything. Simply use the leverage of your friends and followers. You yourself will easily see what is to be done as soon as you discard that false axiom that 'the King can do no wrong!' This saying, consider it well, was invented in a country in which the king is powerless. Power and responsibility cannot be separated.

May your Christmas holiday at least be happy on the family side.

Your old friend
Holstein

516. Philipp zu Eulenburg to Holstein[1]

Vienna, 30 December 1895

Dear friend,

During the past few days I have had too much excitement on account of the Chancellor to be able to write anything sensible.

I have had additional explanations about your wishes and thoughts from B. Bülow.[2] I concede that you are right. Something must be done —but at the moment it is *most* difficult because the Köller crisis is still so much in the forefront of H.M.'s mind, and renewed *pressure* on the part of Hohenlohe would very soon bring the present regime to an end. None of us want that—especially as your ideas can be realised by other means.

A letter of Hohenlohe's from Vienna would create the irretrievable impression that there is a *conspiracy*. H.M. is so sensitive to such things that the facts of the situation would cause him to overlook the content of the letter. Therefore it is only possible for Hohenlohe to raise his objections personally in Potsdam on the basis of the documents, while I do what I can here in writing (on the basis of the Swaine conversation, which H.M. had telegraphed to me). This will not fail in its effect!

As for the idea of having definite days for an audience, we must hold firmly to having an audience *once* a week (this can also be made *definite*).

A specific day is dangerous. Because postponements would *always* be necessary—H.M. isn't at home every day!—and this in turn would give grounds for complaints. We would always be hearing: 'To-day is the Tuesday when the Chancellor is supposed to have his audience—of course H.M. has gone off.' I would like to see that avoided. But one day in the week—any day—would be a good thing and can be arranged.

Frankly, I regard another question as *more important*. The clearing-up of the Köller crisis. Marschall *must* be protected; that is a main point and I will do *everything* to arrange it. The really disgusting slander-methods of Köller must in some way be radically cleared up. I thought of sending H.M. the minutes of the meetings. If you think of any other way, please let me know *at once*. I hope that Marschall's promised letter will bring me good material.

Finally, one more thing. Bülow has released such a fireworks of ideas

---

[1] Partly printed in Haller, *Eulenburg*, pp. 198-9.   [2] See *Ibid.*, pp. 192-8.

on the present situation and methods for easing the difficulties that I think it would be in the interests of us all to see him. I must visit my mother in Meran early in January because she is unwell. And I would like to ask him to meet me there. It is about half-way. Naturally avoiding publicity as much as possible. I talked about it to the Chancellor, who was very much in favour.

But now addio for to-day. My guests are about to arrive. I am giving a gala banquet of thirty persons for the Prince, with Goluchowski, Badeni,[1] etc. I don't know whether he is pleased—but it is necessary to show our beloved old Prince the greatest possible honour.

I hope to have time to write you tomorrow about politics here.

Your faithful old
PE.

517. Philipp zu Eulenburg to Holstein

Vienna, 31 December 1895

Dear friend,

In greatest haste I am copying the most important parts of the letter to H.M. for you which I am just sending off with the dispatch bag! Excuse the poor handwriting![2] . . . These are certain questions of greatest political significance in which Your Maj. has recently been taking an interest which all have the aspect—that is, have been given the aspect—they now bear. Your Maj. has always been so gracious in listening to me, even if it was something unpleasant, that in this case too I have to hope that I won't arouse anger, but that my intentions will be correctly understood! By this I mean the danger that lies in personal decisions which have been taken in political matters without the knowledge and independently of the Foreign Ministry. This can lead to the situation we have at times observed while hunting: a keeper has found the track of a fox who is killing his pheasants. He sees him *at last*; after vast efforts he gets him within range. On the same evening the master of the hunt goes out, he too knows about the fox, and goes in the general direction of where he has been. Then he suddenly comes upon him: the fox scents danger—and disappears. Master and keeper say oh! and the hunt is spoiled for weeks, if not ruined altogether! I need hardly say more. But I am now and then disturbed that neither the game preserve nor the huntsman profit by such foxhunts! The only remedy I know of is *close* collaboration with the Chancellor and State Secretary and an audience that takes place *once a week*; in view of the seriousness of the situation this would seem to be an almost *imperative* necessity for Your Maj.!

One thing that struck the Prince here rather forcefully was the fact that Kaiser Franz Joseph and Goluchowski hold and strongly emphasise

---

[1] Kasimir Felix, Count von Badeni. Austro-Hungarian Minister-President and Minister of the Interior, 1895–7.

[2] The sections copied by Eulenburg for Holstein are not in the version of the letter to the Kaiser printed by Haller, *Eulenburg*, pp. 199–200.

the old viewpoint, namely that if the Russians go to Constantinople, Austria goes to war.[1]

I told the Prince in strict confidence and repeat my opinion here that this can be explained in the following way:

Your Maj. expressed the view to Szögyényi and me (on the last occasion during our long talk in the New Palace[2]) that Constantinople in the hands of the Russians represented *no* danger and that one had to get accustomed to the idea of compensations. The *energy* with which Your Maj. expressed his idea, which Szögyényi will in duty bound have reported—perhaps supplemented by perfidious gossip from St Petersburg to the effect that Your Maj. had offered the Dardanelles to the Russians—has created the idea here that Germany's inclination to give Const. to the Russians would receive a check if Austria seriously represented this question as a *noli me tangere*.

Now that the Chief of the General Staff and the Minister-President are opposed to this somewhat intransigent attitude of Goluchowski (as I have learned in STRICT SECRECY), the Austrians will *not* resort to force at the decisive moment; but there is a further explanation for the attitude of Goluchowski if one bears in mind *how greatly* a Polish Count must abhor a far-reaching agreement between Your Maj. and Tsar Nicholas over the Dardanelles.

Proceeding from this fact I am permitting myself to express the humble request that, in view of this situation, Your Maj. does *not revert* to the Constantinople question. We now know, thanks to the attitude of Beck, that the Austrians will *not* fight. That is really all we needed to know. To press further and to lean further on the clerical party (which does *not* like us and which wants an understanding with Russia *à tout prix*) might *ruin* Goluchowski's position after all—and this, with the eventual return of Kálnoky, would hurt us badly. The Constantinople question is acute enough as it is! If Your Maj. reverts to the subject often in Russia, the Russians will at once and without hesitation make capital out of it in any way they see fit: first of all by telling Austria and England, to stir them up against us and to isolate us; and if *that* should succeed—if in the end England, isolated and weak militarily, should reach an understanding with Russia—well, then *we* would be in the position of isolation, and what would happen then, in view of the friendly feelings with which we are everywhere regarded, must be realistically considered....

. . . . . .

Unfortunately I broke my typewriter. Please excuse this terrible scrawl.

PLEASE RETURN THIS COPY! [...]

Your faithful old
PE [...]

---

[1] See *Grosse Politik*, vol. X, no. 2497, pp. 157–9.
[2] See Hohenlohe, *Denkwürdigkeiten der Reichskanzlerzeit*, pp. 117–19.

1896

518. Philipp zu Eulenburg to Holstein

Vienna, 2 January 1896

Secret

Dear friend,

Perhaps Hohenlohe has spoken to you about the attitude of Austria in the event of an occupation of the Dardanelles by Russia. He has also perhaps told you what I think, and about my experience in this question.[1]

Nevertheless I am anxious that you and Herr von Marschall should hear directly from me on the subject for it is too important. Only I do not want what I have done to be committed to official files and records— and therefore ask you to keep everything absolutely secret; I would otherwise find myself in a difficult position.

I was not at all pleased by the very categorical declaration by Goluchowski and the Kaiser that the occupation of Constantinople or the Dardanelles by Russia would be regarded as a *casus belli*. Just as little in fact as by an *understanding* between Austria and Russia—at our expense. I thought over what could be done and hit upon Beck, with whom I had by chance made friends in earlier days.[2] The result of my absolutely secret talks with him, in which I did not leave him in any doubt that Austria definitely could not count on us if she should start an affair with Russia on the Bosphorus, was that Beck had several *completely secret* and very urgent audiences of the Kaiser. Beck left him in no doubt that Austria alone—that is to say without us—was in no position to make war on Russia and that Constantinople was not worth such a risk. A few days ago (shortly before Hohenlohe's arrival), after taking great precautionary measures and on condition that we kept the matter absolutely secret, Beck made some disclosures to me from which I must *conclude with certainty* that he had convinced the Kaiser of the impossibility of a war of this kind, and had also persuaded Goluchowski *not* to take so definite a stand in the future. 'They had changed their minds— convinced that certain things were impossible.'

At the same time I brought up this dangerous topic with Badeni (with whom I am on very friendly terms) in confidential discussions, and found that he too knew about the affair and agreed with *Beck*. He asked me to be quite *convinced* that Goluchowski had 'changed' in the last few days.

I must conclude from all this that discussions have taken place in the

[1] See Hohenlohe, *Denkwürdigkeiten der Reichskanzlerzeit*, pp. 145–7.
[2] See Haller, *Eulenburg*, p. 147.

Palace in the course of which Beck's views gained the day with Badeni's support, but that Goluchowski for opportunistic reasons (especially in order to paralyse possible excessive steps by our Most Gracious Sovereign) will adhere officially to his old standpoint.

I think this change in the situation is a good one because Goluchowski —and also Badeni—, with their Polish nationality and sympathies, provide an indispensible brake against an *understanding* with Russia.

I have spoken about this in the letter I wrote to H.M. the day before yesterday, and have added some reflections which will I hope meet with your approval[1] [...].

I hope I will soon get information about our attitude in the Transvaal Question.[2] There is lightning everywhere, just like a summer storm!

With kindest regards and the most heartfelt wishes for a happy New Year.

Your faithful
PEulenburg.

519. Bernhard von Bülow to Holstein

Rome, 3 January 1896

Dear Holstein,

First of all and once again, all good wishes for the New Year. I sincerely hope that we will continue to send each other many New Year wishes—you from the Wilhelmstrasse, I from the Capitol. Anyone who, day in day out, can carry such a load of work as you do without breaking—I really don't understand how you find time even for the instructions that I have received during the last three months—will never go lame under the pressure of work. Even when you are now and then forced to spare your physical vision, your mental eye sees further and more penetratingly than ever before. Bitter impressions and experiences have not been—and are not—spared you, to be sure, but this is the lot of all men of great character. I can only repeat what I wrote to a mutual friend of ours three years ago: foreign affairs would lose their greatest attraction for me if you were no longer to read my reports. I feel this even more strongly to-day than at that time.

Our poor Phili wrote to me on the 29th of last month in low spirits.[3] It will be all the more useful therefore if I see him.[4] I at once telegraphed to you the essence of his reply which reached me on the 1st of this month. In three successive letters to him at the close of last year I presented our views on the situation and its dangers in such detail and so earnestly, using so many contemporary political examples and

---

[1] See above, Eulenburg's letter to Holstein of 30 December 1895.

[2] After a period of acute tension in the relations between Britain and the Transvaal, Dr Leander Starr Jameson, Administrator of Rhodesia for the British South Africa Company, led an armed raid against Johannesburg on 29 December 1895 in an attempt to start a rebellion against Boer domination in the Transvaal. On 1 January 1896 his troops were defeated by the Boers at Krügersdorp.

[3] See Haller, *Eulenburg*, pp. 196–8.

[4] In Meran. See above, Eulenburg's letter of 30 December 1895, and below, Bülow's letter of 16 January 1896.

historical analogies, that there is hardly anything new left for me to say.[1] But it is true that far more can be explained—and refuted—orally than in writing.

Your extremely interesting memorandum of New Year's Day[2] arrived yesterday afternoon and I answered it by telegram yesterday evening.[3] The move in question seems to me not only brilliantly conceived, but thoroughly right and practical from the standpoint of the entire European situation. I could not however conceal what in my opinion would be the great difficulty of winning over Crispi to this idea, nor the possible dangers inherent in it for Italy's international position and the relationship between Italy and ourselves.

Though I am not overburdened, I am so deluged with work that I cannot write as fully as I would like. With this tumult (and hurry) I must ask to be forgiven for using a pencil. Once again most sincere thanks for your very kindly and informative letters, as also for the confidence revealed in these letters and in yesterday's inquiry. You know that I endeavour to earn this trust fully and completely. On one point only I am not in agreement with you. I will not under any circumstances be State Secretary, not merely because this would lower my chances for the highest post, which I desire still less. I believe that intelligence and common sense are revealed above all in an exact knowledge of oneself and one's limitations. Now I am convinced that (*vanité à part!!*) I am a good ambassador, and consequently I am glad to be an ambassador. I am, however, not suited for the central position. Quite apart from all personal considerations (many of them important and deeply rooted), I have no desire to come to Berlin in any position and under any circumstances except for a few days in summer in order to talk and lunch with you. My views and intentions in this regard are unalterable and steadfast, they have long been known to Philipp Eu., but I will again consider with him how every danger from the given quarter[4] can best be prevented.

I leave tomorrow evening,[5] telling everybody that I am going to visit my brother in Lugano. [...]

Once again the very best wishes, ever in most faithful devotion

Your B.

[1] For two of Bülow's letters to Eulenburg see Haller, *Eulenburg*, pp. 195–6.
[2] Holstein had suggested the possibility of a Continental League against England. 'Italy is despised by England because the latter is convinced that Italy will be compelled to assist her militarily the moment England needs her. If Italy, as Blanc threatens, goes over *alone* to the Franco-Russians, she will be at their mercy because she is alone and weak. What would be the situation, however, if Germany, after her experiences with regard to the Transvaal, Volta frontier, etc., went over *with* Italy to the Franco-Russian side?' (*Grosse Politik*, vol. XI, no. 2640, pp. 67–9.)
[3] Bülow telegraphed: 'I think that Baron Blanc could be won over to the idea of a temporary and clearly defined League against England if it were specifically presented to him as a passing phase only, whereby the Triple Alliance intended to ensure the effective co-operation of an Albion finally brought to its senses for the decisive struggles of the future. According to the impressions I have gained so far, Crispi will find it far more difficult to adapt himself to such ideas. [...] He will ask himself further whether even an isolated England did not have it in her power to make even greater difficulties for Italy in Eritrea than France is doing at present.' (*Grosse Politik*, vol. XI, no. 2642, pp. 72–3.)
[4] The Kaiser, who wanted to make Bülow State Secretary in the Foreign Ministry.
[5] In order to see Eulenburg.

520. Holstein to Hugo von Radolin[1]

Berlin, 10 January 1896

Dear Radolin,

In the next few days a small White Book will be published about the Transvaal[2] from which I think the Foreign Ministry comes out quite well.

We have intervened in favour of the status quo. The status quo has been maintained. Should the Boers demand something more than the status quo, that is their affair, we are then confronted with a *novum* and are not tied in any way but have a free hand for our further course of action. Please play on this theme with your accustomed virtuosity with Prince Lobanov, *provided he begins* to speak of the Transvaal. If not, leave the question untouched. It accords with our whole attitude in the matter that we do not take any initiative towards the Powers who have so far not been involved in it, because we do not want either to push ourselves forward unnecessarily nor to ask for assistance which we do not need.

That is also the reason why none of our embassies, except London, has received anything about the Transvaal. When our ambassadors are without instructions it is the best proof that they are not instructed to approach other Powers for support.[3]

If Lobanov does talk about it, everything he says will greatly interest us here, not only about the Transvaal but also in regard to possible conclusions to be drawn as to Russia's attitude to subsequent eventualities. [...]

Your
Holstein [...]

521. Georg zu Münster to Holstein

Paris, 13 January 1896

Very confidential and private
My dear Herr von Holstein,

I deeply regret not being able to come to Berlin, particularly because I would dearly have liked to talk over the present world situation with you.[4] You being a cautious fellow will not write to me what you really

---

[1] From the Radolin Papers.

[2] See *Weissbuch vorgelegt dem Reichstage in der 4. Session der 9. Legislatur Periode—Aktenstücke, betreffend die Südafrikanische Republik* (Berlin, 1896).

[3] See, however, the Kaiser's letter to the Tsar of 2 January 1896 in which he wrote: 'Now suddenly the Transvaal Republic has been attacked in a most foul way as it seems not without Englands knowledge. I have used very severe language in London, and have opened communications with Paris for common defence of our endangered interests, as French and German colonists have immediately joined hands of their own accord to help the outraged boers. I hope you will also kindly consider the question, as it is one of principle of upholding treaties once concluded. I hope that all will come right, but come what may, I never shall allow the British to stamp out the Transvaal!' (*Briefe Wilhelms II. an den Zaren*, pp. 300–1; see also *Grosse Politik*, vol. XI, chapter LXIII.)

[4] Münster refers in particular to the international repercussions, especially in England, of the telegram sent by the Kaiser on 3 January 1896 to President Krüger congratulating him on the defeat of the Jameson Raid. (See above, p. 582, note 2, and *Memoirs*, pp. 160–3, 185.)

think about it, but you would have told me in conversation. I have for a long time past foreseen the coming of the present situation; for I saw how, ever since the beginning of the unfortunate colonial policy which B[ismarck] began against his own convictions and supported in order to gain (or rather to retain) personal popularity, an anti-English campaign has been carried on with stupidity and ill-will. At the outset England tolerated a great deal, but by slow degrees there arose in England an anti-German party, and those colonialists who pursued an imperialist policy were accorded more and more freedom of action. For the English, this expansionist drive made sense, because they could defend their colonies in case of need and would at the same time be enlarging their trade relations. The contrary is the case with us. We could *never* defend our colonies in the event of war, and overseas trade has *injured* rather than benefited our colonies. But the most tragic result is the mistrust and hatred that has grown up between the two great civilised states of Europe. I knew and felt for a long time that this existed latently—the Embassy in London simply does not understand England. Our Kaiser only saw the surface of things, sand is always thrown in his eyes when he comes on a visit; this is how I explain how H.M. sent the telegram, without realising in advance that it was a match to set fire to an accumulation of inflammatory material; I do not believe that it will really come to war. I hope not. God preserve us from that. The Queen and the men in control are too level-headed for that. But if a political [...][1] were at the head of affairs, then the nation in its present temper would follow him. But even without war the political and commercial damage is very great and cannot be estimated. The English Admiralty has used the pretext to strengthen and to arm the fleet to an enormous extent. That is done less against us than against America, for the conflict can break out at any moment;[2] the Eastern Question may also require ships in the spring.

Here *they are rejoicing*. The Press is cautious; but I take it for granted that they are secretly agitating against us in London. As the situation demands, and for the Kaiser's sake, I am very cautious.

But I can see from many signs that the French are trying to get closer to England. A war with America, which Lord Dufferin still believes is a possibility, would in the present very tense situation not be a bad thing for us in many ways.

If that does not come, and if an understanding is reached with the Transvaal, then there will certainly be complications in the Near East in the spring. [...]

As always yours sincerely
Münster.

[1] One word illegible.
[2] Britain and the United States were involved in a serious dispute over the boundary between Venezuela and British Guiana. The affair was settled by arbitration in February 1897.

522. Holstein to Paul von Hatzfeldt[1]

TELEGRAM

Berlin, 16 January 1896

Private

[...] Great pressure is now being brought to bear on the Kaiser regarding an alleged English plan for a landing in Delagoa Bay. A large demand for additional funds for the navy, which Prince Hohenlohe will not introduce because it has no prospect of passing, is to-day being used as a lever to overthrow the Prince, just as was the Anti-Revolutionary Law in Caprivi's time.[2]

I am also afraid that if the Kaiser is not pacified about Delagoa by the day after tomorrow, he will deliver an extemporaneous speech to the Members of the Reichstag of 1871 that could have serious consequences.[3]

I would like a reassuring paragraph about Delagoa to appear by tomorrow at the latest in one of the principal English newspapers, or to have the Ambassador here say something or Lord Salisbury say something to you.[4]

Holstein

523. Bernhard von Bülow to Holstein

Rome, 16 January 1896

Dear Holstein,

[...] My stay in Meran lasted longer than I had intended, since I found Eulenburg so exhausted that—especially for the first few days—I could hardly talk politics and was indeed somewhat anxious about him. Less on account of his bronchial catarrh than by reason of his general exhaustion. He was hardly able to leave his bed, the least exertion tired him. E. has such a wiry constitution, thank goodness, that we do not need to be seriously disturbed about him. The doctor who was treating him assured me that heart and lungs are quite all right. At all events E. certainly needed careful treatment.

I am now very glad by the way that I did not allow the long journey to prevent me from seeing E. The hints which you recently gave me regarding the danger threatening me from Berlin[5] appear to have a more serious background than I had assumed. I was therefore doubly fortunate to have talked things over thoroughly with E., from whom I learned that he had already set things in motion to remove this danger from me. He especially assured me that he had done everything—and would continue to do everything—to support Marschall. Eulenburg also repeated to me that H.M. undoubtedly wanted to retain Hohenlohe,

---

[1] From the London Embassy files.
[2] See Hohenlohe, *Denkwürdigkeiten der Reichskanzlerzeit*, pp. 152–3.
[3] On the occasion of the 25th anniversary of the foundation of the German Reich.
[4] Hatzfeldt telegraphed on 17 January: 'Lord Salisbury assures me that the rumours regarding a prospective landing of troops in Delagoa Bay are completely unfounded. [...] In addition there was the fact that Delagoa Bay belonged to a friendly independent Power which would hardly agree to a landing.' To this the Kaiser made the marginal comment: '*All bosh.*' (From the Foreign Ministry files.)
[5] That Bülow was to be made State Secretary in the Foreign Ministry.

but he thinks nevertheless, in view of the present situation and the impression left by the Köller-crisis, which still rankles, that Hohenlohe in his own interests (and therefore in our interests) would do best to handle H.M. with a certain degree of caution. My total impression was that though many black clouds still hang above the horizon, the sky will again become clear and that lightning will not strike, especially if we take care not to do anything that would cause the storm to break. [...]

With best wishes, in most faithful devotion

Ever your
B.

524. Philipp zu Eulenburg to Holstein

Meran, 19 January 1896

Dear friend,

[...] Like yourself, I heard confidentially from Hohenlohe that Bülow is under consideration for the State Secretaryship. From the manner in which I immediately went to work in support of Marschall you will have sensed what my views are on the matter, which can be explained quite simply by the fact that I cannot allow our friend to be placed in a position he so dislikes without using all my ability and influence to prevent it. Bülow, to whom you seem to have given a hint about the danger threatening him, fully agrees with me and *urgently* asked me to go on working in this sense.

I close these lines, which I am sending from Munich by the dispatch bag, with the most sincere good wishes and in the hope that I will hear from you soon,—for I long to do so.

Your old, somewhat weak,
PEulenburg.

I wrote to H.M. in the above sense—namely, that Marschall is indispensable for Hohenlohe during this session and any change would make the worst impression.

E.

525. Philipp zu Eulenburg to Holstein[1]

Vienna, 31 January 1896

Dear friend,

[...] To-day I have at last roused myself and written the enclosed letter to H.M.[2] which I ask you to return to me at your convenience. Being bound by promises, I could not let the matter go through official channels. The original letter will certainly be given by H.M. to the Chancellor. You will see from it how things look here. Our attitude to

---

[1] Published in part by Haller, *Eulenburg*, pp. 201–2.
[2] Of 31 January. (*Grosse Politik*, vol. XI, no. 2670, pp. 109–12.)

England inwardly frightens and worries the people here. But that will pass; this will not be the case with the feeling of which Beck speaks, namely that the people here do not really know what to make of us. For on the one hand we look benevolently on the *accord à trois*,[1] on the other hand we are still on the very worst terms with London. I candidly admit to you that I myself no longer quite definitely know the path along which I should tread after having read Marschall's memorandum about his conversation with Szögyényi.[2] I have indeed never encouraged Goluchowski to renew or to extend the *accord à trois* and have only observed the benevolent attitude indicated to me.

Now Marschall broaches the idea that the entry of the Russians into the Mediterranean would also have advantageous results for Austria.[3]

That may in fact be so. I think so too. But Austria is bowled over by the idea, because our patronage of the *accord à trois* really implied that we were in agreement with the resistance of the three Powers to the advance of Russia into the Mediterranean. We have not yet abandoned the policy that the most favourable situation for us would be a war between England and Russia, and for that reason we supported *whatever* might lead to England's going to war. I therefore fail to see to what extent a renewal and strengthening of the *accord à trois* can be of value to us? If England commits herself to *start* [a war], she will only do so after the conclusion of a binding *obligation* on the part of Austria and Italy to follow her. I am worried in this connection that she will soon leave the two Powers that will be fighting on land in the lurch, and go home with her fleet. But if *no* agreement is concluded, and instead Austria and Russia come to an understanding over their attitude to the Balkan States (ONLY over that—for it would be impossible to reach an understanding over anything else), then England would be obliged even sooner to take action *all on her own*, while Italy could be won over to this local agreement on the grounds that Austria would then not lay hands on Albania. No matter what happens on this question, I consider one thing indispensable: that Beck is left in no doubt that we will *not* intervene if the Austrians want to go to war because the Russians march into Constantinople. The fact that the Chief of the General Staff is left in a state of uncertainty about a matter of such importance is due either to a bad conscience because they are thinking of making war over Beck's head, or that they are not taking the matter altogether seriously. I think the latter is the case. At all events it is necessary in view of the new project of the *accord à trois* to put a damper on.

[1] Between Britain, Austria-Hungary and Italy.
[2] Memorandum of 22 January. (*Grosse Politik*, vol. XIIi, nos. 2885, 2914, pp. 4–6, 47–8.)
[3] In his memorandum of 22 January Marschall wrote: 'I summed up the tendency of my explanations up to that point as follows: that the Powers should avoid everything which could hasten the downfall of Turkey; but that if the progress of disintegration could not be arrested, one should if possible let the Balkan peoples fight among themselves and allow Russia to go unhindered into the Mediterranean, because Russia would thereby become inconvenient not only to her old enemy England but also to her present friend France. The acute points of controversy would be further removed from the frontiers of Germany and Austria-Hungary, while the rival Empires would have an equal, if not greater, interest than they have to-day not to incur the displeasure of the powerful Austro-German group.'

Please let me know how I am to deal with the question—'England'—here.[1] You now know my objections and the enclosed letter will strengthen them.

If you want to pursue further the idea of a Russo-Austrian understanding regarding the Balkan States, I must repeat that Kapnist is *obviously* trying to make advances *in this regard*. Goluchowski would do nothing. The Russians only *perhaps*—after a push from us. But do we want to support this idea? [...]

The rumours of Chancellor-crises do not at present alarm me. Despite all H.M.'s nervousness, he is pushing—I assure you of this!—the demands for the navy[2] to such an extent because only by means of shock tactics applied to all branches of the administration is he able to achieve any results at all. H.M. wants a lot, but not the impossible. I know his methods of fighting and his desires.

The congratulatory article in the *Hamburger Nachrichten*[3] was somewhat alarming, but really too transparent to do any damage. The damper with the warning about foreign policy on the grand scale has enlightened H.M. on the subject of the Friedrichsruh confederacy.

I only hope one thing: that Hohenlohe does not lose his nerve. If the old Prince remains calm and *slowly* accustoms the world and H.M. to his gradual retirement in some years, then a change will be effected that will enable you peacefully to continue your *indispensable* services to the state. If, however, the Prince suddenly and categorically demands the acceptance of his resignation by H.M., then we can experience surprises. Nevertheless I do not *now* believe it will be Loë, might indeed guarantee that he will not be the one. Hinzpeter[4] says a lot for which he cannot answer and likes to pose as being well-informed. There is also no question of my cousin.[5] But, as I said, anything *sudden* is to be avoided—on the part of the Chancellor. For *H.M.* will not part with him.

---

[1] In order to prevent England from misrepresenting the German position, Hohenlohe requested the Kaiser in a letter of 2 February to allow him to instruct Eulenburg to reply to all enquiries regarding Germany's possible attitude in the event of a Russian action in the Straits to the effect that if Austria-Hungary became involved in war with Russia on that account she would be acting on her own responsibility, but that Germany would not permit Austria-Hungary's position as a Great Power to be seriously threatened. (*Grosse Politik*, vol. XI, no. 2671, pp. 112–14.)

[2] Holstein had written to Eulenburg on 25 January that the Kaiser was in a state of pathological excitement. He was demanding vast appropriations for the fleet—his estimates ranged from 100 to 300 million—and he believed that by dissolving the Reichstag he could easily find people 'who could arrange it'. Holstein predicted that the next Reichstag would not accede to the Kaiser's demands and that the German Princes would not support him in a *coup d'état*. 'All this makes for an uncanny impression of excessive haste,' Holstein wrote. 'The Kaiser's nerves have never been stimulated by anything so much as by the temptations of the great fleet programme.' (From the Eulenburg Papers.)

[3] For the Kaiser's birthday. The Bismarck-inspired article praised the Kaiser and deplored that his initiative was being hampered by his Ministers. (Hohenlohe, *Denkwürdigkeiten der Reichskanzlerzeit*, p. 163.)

[4] Georg Ernst Hinzpeter. Tutor to Prince Wilhelm (Kaiser Wilhelm II), 1866–77.

[5] Holstein had telegraphed to Eulenburg on 27 January that Hinzpeter was saying Hohenlohe's position was shaky, and that the Kaiser was thinking of Botho Eulenburg as Minister-President of Prussia and of General von Loë or one of the Princes of the Reich as Chancellor. (Haller, *Eulenburg*, p. 201.)

That is enough for to-day. I am dead-tired! I really cannot think as yet of travelling to Berlin. I must first be all right again.

Your faithful
PE.

526. Bernhard von Bülow to Holstein

Rome, 31 January 1896

Dear Holstein,

The very informative contents of the last dispatch bag were not only of greatest interest to me but also furnished me with first-rate arguments for my discussions with Blanc, Crispi, and Nigra, about which I have permitted myself to report by telegram.[1]

At the moment Blanc is rather sceptical about the renewal of the 1887 Agreement. But like Crispi he hopes that in the long run England will not tolerate Russian preponderance on the Golden Horn, and that out of this there will come the duel between the whale and the bear that both Crispi and Blanc *in petto* long for. I emphasise here daily that the only correct attitude for Italy in the present European situation is a prudent, reserved, and calm attitude of wait-and-see.

Best thanks for your kind lines of the 23rd of the month. But I was very distressed to hear that you feel tired. A really dreadful burden of work must rest upon you for you to feel it, and you must really feel tired to admit it. For you are not a man to complain. Take care of yourself for your own sake, for us, and for the cause for which you work. I am disquieted by what you write to me about the naval question.[2] I envisage the threatening sand-banks and reefs, but still hold to the firm hope that thanks to Hohenlohe's patience and foresight a conflict (and especially a conflict with H.M.) will be avoided, while on the other hand I know that since our meeting in Meran Philipp E. will try even harder than formerly to forestall a crisis. Demands for ships (within limits) have the advantage that no one could present them better in Parliament than Marschall, and they also give him the opportunity of displaying his outstanding ability and usefulness. I hope that I shall soon hear that there is no longer any ground for anxiety.

With many kind regards from my ladies, and the sincerest good wishes from all of us, in loyal friendship and devotion.

Your
B.

527. Philipp zu Eulenburg to Holstein[3]

Vienna, 7 February 1896

Dear friend,

You have *very* seldom written me such an irritable and unfriendly letter.[4] But the fact that you still write to me at all shows that you are not completely withdrawing the hand of friendship from me. And

---

[1] On 27 January. (*Grosse Politik*, vol. XI, no. 2662, pp. 97–8.)
[2] See above, p. 589, note 2.　　[3] Published in part by Haller, *Eulenburg*, p. 202.
[4] Not found in the Eulenburg Papers.

therefore I hold on to the nail of the little finger of the left hand that is still left in my grasp, because I believe that it is better for *us all* if I do not provoke a row—also it goes against the grain to quarrel with an *old trusted* friend and one to whom I have *so much to be thankful for*.

The unjust reproach hurts less than the censure which we deserve. What would you have said if I had written to you when you were still feeling very unwell at home after your operation: 'You seem to be having a very good time in Berlin—go on amusing yourself.' You would have thought that less than friendly. Well, when I am badly run down by this infamous influenza and still endeavour by exerting all my energy to do my work and to fulfil my social obligations because I think it useful, you will then certainly be able to imagine how 'amusements' affect me at present!—and the effect of the biting scorn of a friend whom I hold dear. Perhaps I have done wrong not to take the long leave I had in mind and go to Liebenberg, something I discuss daily with my wife. *It means far more to me than my friends think*, to whom the abandonment of power, influence, great position seems like madness. Well, I have *always* belonged among these madmen, and in that I have never changed.

But enough of this. Since you never say anything unintentionally, *you* must have known why you wanted to cause me pain. It is completely incomprehensible to *me*.

As far as the factual reproaches in your letter are concerned, you have indeed a right to 'scold' me. But I ask you to reflect very seriously upon the following:

I remain firmly convinced that we can approve a great war which is begun by England and in which others follow suit. But we *absolutely cannot* approve if Austria begins it and is afterwards flatly deserted by England. I do not like the *accord à trois at present* because (1) our relations with England, (2) the strengthening of Russia in the Balkans by the events in Bulgaria,[1] make Austria VERY susceptible to English advice. I tell you that we must watch our step; otherwise something stupid will ultimately happen and we will be left to clean up. I am not supposed to speak about the *accord à trois* and I avoid it. Nor about Constantinople. A few days ago I did briefly mention the subject of the passage through the Dardanelles on the basis of the memorandum about the conversation between Szögyényi and Marschall[2] (which bears *your* style!), and because Goluchowski invariably discusses with me precisely what Szögyényi has heard in Berlin. I am therefore supposed to keep silent in the presence of danger.

That is why I spoke to the *wholly trustworthy* Beck.[3] He, as an old friend of my family, is absolutely safe—but also safe in the sense that as an opponent of agreements with the English he is not in touch with Goluchowski. It now seems to me very urgently necessary to keep Austria from making *silly* agreements with England. Since the method

[1] The willingness of Prince Ferdinand of Bulgaria to have his son, Boris, baptised in the Orthodox Faith helped to bring about a reconciliation between Russia and Bulgaria in February 1896.

[2] See above, p. 588, notes 2 and 3.

[3] On 30 January. (*Grosse Politik*, vol. XI, no. 2670, pp. 109–12.)

proposed does not suit you, I would be grateful for another proposal. The matter has become—as I said—far more acute owing to events in Bulgaria.

I frankly admit to you that to me the *sole correct* basis for the further handling of the Near Eastern Question seems to be the content of the conversation between Szögyényi and Marschall.

I am at present very much opposed to the *accord à trois*. For that reason I indeed hope that nothing comes of it—nevertheless, anger as strong as that now displayed against Russia by the rather easily roused Goluchowski can make for surprises for us which may upset the views presented by Marschall.

I will say nothing about Rumania. I may have made a false parallel between the Dardanelles and the Dobruja:[1] it does not in any way alter my opinion that I consider the linking of such exposed tiny states to the Triple Alliance *highly* undesirable if we follow our former policy. Of what use is Austria's sincere intention of remaining quiet in the event of Balkan quarrels if Rumania becomes involved?

I would be grateful to you if you will let me know your opinion as to how I can emphasise Marschall's points of view here, and what I can do to ease Goluchowski's irritation, which could become dangerous in the *accord à trois*?

Finally one more remark. Please do not forget that with the exception of congratulatory letters and letters of thanks, as well as such letters which contain matters of a *purely* personal friendly nature, I have *without exception* and in *the most loyal way* communicated to you political matters that have reached H.M. through me. I will not depart from this practice because I *feel* myself at one with you. But I would not like my loyalty to be made distasteful to me.

I *am sincere* in my endeavours, and a loyal friend. You will therefore understand the wish that I should not be ill-treated by my friends.

Your old and faithful friend
PE [...]

528. Holstein to Philipp zu Eulenburg[2]

Copy

Berlin, 9 February 1896

Dear friend,

I got your letter three hours ago. I am replying to it in the peace of the evening at home.

At the moment we are both irritated over the use of this or that phraseology. If it were nothing more one could settle the matter by saying in all sincerity 'it was not meant unkindly'. Unfortunately that is not the case.

---

[1] Eulenburg wrote to the Kaiser on 31 January that Kaiser Franz Joseph should not be left in doubt that Germany could not consider a Russian occupation of Constantinople as a *casus foederis* any more than the entry of the Russians into the Dobruja. (*Grosse Politik*, vol. XI, no. 2670, pp. 109–12.)

[2] Published in part in Haller, *Eulenburg*, pp. 202–3.

The difference—I would not like to say the cleavage—is based on the most profound differences in outlook. You instinctively incline to an autocratic regime no matter whether it be Russian patriarchal or *despotisme éclairé* on the French model. I am in favour of a moderate use of a practicable system of constitutional co-operative government which, with the exception of St Petersburg and Constantinople, is in operation in the rest of the European and civilised world. My opinion is, I know, unfashionable at the Court here. 'A strong Government which can manage without the Reichstag' is Admiral von Senden's ideal, and not his alone. You also belong, perhaps without knowing it, to those who believe that every political, military, and legal question is best decided directly by the Kaiser. The old English Cavaliers held similar beliefs, although they did not go so far, and were the object of my unbounded admiration in my youth. To be sure they first ruined the Stuarts, and then they died or ruined themselves in misery and want; but from an ethical standpoint they remain disinterested types of superb chivalry.

I am not so chivalrous, I am for the possible, and since it seems to me that a 'Government without a Reichstag' is at present impossible in Germany, I would prefer that political relations between this Kaiser and this Reichstag were not made impossible for this Chancellor so long as he does not believe he can get a better Reichstag. The fact that the Chancellor is brought closer to his end by each individual incident whereby the Kaiser is put into the position of having to take a decision *before* the Chancellor, or of having to decide *without* or *against* him, surely needs no proof. You are thinking of resigning, a feeling which I share under the existing circumstances. You are doing so because you are afraid you cannot achieve your ideal. I, because I am afraid that something will be achieved which is not my ideal, and that is a political Jena for the Kaiser—the very thing which we have tried for six long years to save him from. After Hohenlohe—if he is sacrificed between now and the next few months to a mood, or let us call it movement—we will get the Dissolution Chancellor, and if the elections, as is probable, go against the Government, he will be followed by the coup d'état Chancellor. Since the German Princes, as you know better than I, will not take part in an action directed against the Reich, the Kaiser will then be confronted with the choice between the Monts Programme[1] (war against Bavaria, etc.) and—Jena, that is to say, beating a retreat. In a sense one can say that the advance on Jena has already begun, since from what I hear opinion in the imperial entourage daily grows stronger in favour of a coup d'état against the Reich; that miserable Lucanus is the only one who may perhaps have civilised scruples, although he grabs what he can for himself without regard for the Chancellor and the Ministers.

I can do nothing about all this, won't complain any more since it

---

[1] See Monts' letter to Tschirschky of 7 January 1896 (*Erinnerungen und Gedanken des Botschafters Anton Graf Monts*, edited by K. F. Nowak and F. Thimme (Berlin, 1932), pp. 401–4) and Eulenburg's letter to Hohenlohe of 8 February (*Denkwürdigkeiten der Reichskanzlerzeit*, pp. 167–9).

does not help, but will just look on as long as Hohenlohe and Marschall are content to stay on—it will hardly be for very long.

As to *foreign affairs* in particular, go on talking to Goluchowski—who gives me the impression of a mediocre afternoon preacher—about everything but the one point of *when* the *casus foederis* comes into force in the event that Austria acts *outside* the framework of the Triple Alliance, that is if, for example, she attacks Russia over the Straits.

If it becomes a matter of life and death for the Austrians, we will have to intervene with or without a treaty; but as to *when* we feel the psychological moment has come is our secret, and through this uncertainty we oblige the Austrians to think well in advance about what they do.

Moreover it is downright impudent for Goluchowski to go on treating the Bulgarians badly and to talk of not allowing himself to be treated in such a manner after Kálnoky coolly looked on while Stambulov was gradually hounded to death.[1] If the Vienna Cabinet had wanted to maintain itself in Bulgaria it should have supported Stambulov. Goluchowski may thank Burian and Kálnoky. I suspect that tomorrow something will be said officially to you about this.

Goodnight. It is 12:45.

Your—notwithstanding everything—very faithful

H.

Schlieffen described Beck as a 'cunning man with small abilities'.

529. Philipp zu Eulenburg to Holstein

19 February [1896]

Dear friend,

Only a word of thanks for your letter.[2]

[...] I am beginning—although very slowly—to get better.

The fact that I know I am again in agreement with you has helped not a little in this respect.

You have no idea how dependent I am upon your opinions!

Never forget how intimate the personal bond is which unites us. For that to be possible it is necessary to have a certain—I would almost say feminine—sensitiveness that is peculiar to us both.

Adieu. More tomorrow.

Your faithful old

PE.

530. Philipp zu Eulenburg to Holstein

Vienna, 29 February 1896

Dear friend,

[...] Quite frankly I was not pleased with the Chancellor's political

---

[1] Stambulov was dismissed on 12 June 1894, partly because Prince Ferdinand wished to pave the way for a reconciliation with Russia, partly because Macedonian groups were dissatisfied with his cautious policy.

[2] Of 17 February. (See Haller, *Eulenburg*, pp. 205–6.)

mood while in Vienna.[1] I draw the conclusion from a mass of details that it would be good if I were sometime to discuss with H.M. the ultimate consequences of Hohenlohe's resignation. [...]

I am unable to judge what goes on in the Ministry. I have heard nothing special but I must ask you to attend very specially to one point:

If anybody wants to bring about Hohenlohe's downfall, he only needs to bring up the question of the reform of the military courts-martial.[2]

I have lately heard with real *alarm* of Bronsart's new effort.[3] It is impossible for Hohenlohe to vote *against* the Bill. If it could be passed he would acquire vast prestige—but unfortunately it is merely an issue to which he would be sacrificed.

I make no secret of the fact that after what happened in Bavaria[4] I am rather against than for the Bill—but I maintain an attitude of complete reserve in the matter as being a purely military affair. I have also never spoken to H.M. about it in any definite way.

But from the Kaiser's attitude, from his remark 'that he had half ruined his army with the two years service and *under no circumstances* could he now be induced to ruin it *completely*', I know definitely that this question *can only* be handled *dilatorily* since H.M. will naturally avoid letting Bronsart resign over this question.

I can only *urgently* advise that in this situation the matter should be treated wholly as *noli me tangere*—if there is any desire to keep Hohenlohe. Over *this* question the Kaiser would *part* with the Chancellor —I know that for certain.

You can judge from this what impression it makes on me when rumours reach me that there was a quarrel with Bronsart!

I am getting better slowly. But *very* slowly. I am still only half of what I was before the influenza. I hope the poison is now slowly going out of the body.

In old friendship
Your PE.

---

[1] Prince Hohenlohe had visited Vienna for the funeral of his youngest brother Konstantin, who had died on 13 February 1896.

[2] The introduction of public trials for military courts-martial when these did not involve purely military matters. Bronsart, the Minister of War, wanted the reform included in a Bill to be submitted to the Reichstag, and had brought up the question in the previous August and again in January 1896, when he had a serious quarrel with the Kaiser on the subject. (Waldersee, *Denkwürdigkeiten*, vol. II, pp. 360, 363–4; Hohenlohe, *Denkwürdigkeiten der Reichskanzlerzeit*, p. 151.) On 1 February 1896 Hohenlohe wrote in his diary: 'Then Holstein arrived and now speaks of the necessity of compelling the Kaiser to approve the Military Penal Law as proposed by Bronsart. I haven't the slightest intention of provoking another conflict.' (Hohenlohe, *Denkwürdigkeiten der Reichskanzlerzeit*, p. 164.) On 28 February Hohenlohe wrote: 'H[olstein]'s proposal is aimed at taking advantage of the present situation in order to coerce H.M. by confronting him with a demand on the part of the entire Ministry of State that the Military Penal Law, including public trials [for courts-martial] be submitted to the Reichstag. At the moment, H. thinks H.M. will not be able to withstand the pressure of the Ministry and will give way; and thereby my position would become so strong that they would not dare simply show me the door, as was contemplated.' (Hohenlohe, *Denkwürdigkeiten der Reichskanzlerzeit*, p. 181.)

[3] In the military courts-martial question.

[4] The system of public courts-martial had already been introduced into Bavaria.

531. Georg zu Münster to Holstein

Paris, 9 March 1896

Very confidential
My dear Herr von Holstein,

Many thanks for your letter which is filled with well-meant but completely unfounded attacks.

I am as always extremely well-informed and if I have not much to report that is due to conditions here. I describe these conditions in my to-day's dispatch.[1]

As to Egypt I always pay attention to this important matter, both here and to a large extent in England where I still learn a good deal.[2]

If Salisbury assured Hatzfeldt that no overtures have been made to him from the French regarding Egypt, then our good old friend has probably not held entirely to the truth.[3] Courcel thought for a moment that he could do business with Salisbury and that a *modus vivendi* would be found. For the moment, however, Courcel seems to understand that Salisbury could not make any concession to him in this question, even if he personally wanted to. Because of the defeat of the Italians,[4] Egypt has become still more important for the English, and notwithstanding their flirting with France they do not think of evacuation.

That the Russians have given Hanotaux a statement that Russia does not intend to penetrate the Mediterranean, I simply don't believe. Nor would a declaration of this kind mean much because whenever it suited it would not be observed.

When I wrote that I could only discuss high explosives with Berthelot,[5] it was not intended as a joke but only to indicate that the old man is an absolute nonentity in foreign affairs. I did not want to warm over the outworn witticism about the *Ministre étranger aux affaires*.

I hope to be in Berlin on 19 March and greatly look forward to being able to greet you there soon.

With friendly feelings, as always yours sincerely
Münster.

532. Paul von Hatzfeldt to Holstein

London, 15 March 1896

Dear friend,

Thank you for your last letter, despite the fact that its contents were

---

[1] In his dispatch about the internal state of France, Münster emphasised the weak position of the Bourgeois Cabinet and the mounting demoralisation of the civil and judicial administration. In a second dispatch on the same day Münster made it clear that the existing Franco-Russian policy would be continued and that Berthelot was very much under the influence of Russia. (From the Foreign Ministry files.)

[2] Münster refers to rumours of an Anglo-French rapprochement over Egypt and an English evacuation of Egypt.

[3] See *Grosse Politik*, vol. XI, nos. 2681–95, pp. 135–51.

[4] The disastrous defeat of the Italians by the Ethiopians at the battle of Adua on 1 March 1896.

[5] Marcelin Berthelot. French chemist; Foreign Minister in the Bourgeois Cabinet, 1 November 1895–28 March 1896.

not very pleasant; as usual I am following your advice by sending via to-day's dispatch bag a fairly large bouquet of my ideas in official form.[1]

What you tell me about H.M. does not surprise me. Only I would prefer to ascribe the feeling to motives other than certain subterranean activities. Although I have stayed quiet, or perhaps just because I have done so, H.M. has got the feeling that I have not hailed all that has happened with sufficient enthusiasm. Secondly, H.M. is annoyed because I have never made use of his repeated permission to write to him direct. I do not need to explain more closely why I have not done so. In the first place it does not accord with my way of doing business to make policy behind the Chancellor's back if I am not certain about his opinion on the matters in question. Furthermore, although I can keep quiet and blindly carry out what I am told to do, I cannot express specific agreement when it would not correspond with my convictions to do so. And in case I had wanted to write, it would hardly have been possible to conceal my own views on certain matters.

You will remember that last autumn the whole correspondence between the Foreign Ministry and myself over the most important questions was carried on by pages-long telegrams, and nobody took exception because I did not at the same time write long reports about the same subjects which would obviously have been out of date when they arrived. And why this should now be a cause for complaint when the situation ever since the Transvaal Question has been such that I must maintain complete reserve, I fail to understand. Nor is it correct to say that I have used only Salisbury and Courcel as sources of information. Both Deym and Ferrero were prepared to report everything to me and have honestly done so. To-day I still regard talks with Courcel as useful because it is always a good thing to have connections in the enemy camp—unless they want to compare me with Herbert Bismarck and Shuvalov and say that although I don't get drunk quicker than Courcel he would nevertheless be able to draw me out because he was more clever.

You used to agree with me that a lot of things happen here which are in no way suitable for official reports. One such instance has just occurred here and I would sooner have my hand cut off than make it the subject of an official report. This refers to the long conversation between H.M. and Sir Frank Lascelles,[2] and as I had to agree to keep the matter secret, I can tell you only in the strictest confidence about the effect produced by this conversation. It literally horrified Salisbury, who had just begun once again to become more candid and more confidential, because he saw herein proof that he would again be con-

[1] See *Grosse Politik*, vol. XI. nos. 2639, 2699, 2818, pp. 61–3, 153–4, 291–3.
[2] A conversation which took place between Wilhelm II and Sir Frank Lascelles on the evening of 3 March when the news reached Berlin of Italy's defeat at the Battle of Adua. The Kaiser pointed out that France and Russia were fighting Italy in Abyssinia in order to cut England's route to India—a step in Russia's campaign to destroy Austria-Hungary and England. According to Lascelles's report of the conversation, the Kaiser said he expected 'that England would join the Triple Alliance or at all events come to Italy's help in her hard-pressed situation'. (*Grosse Politik*, vol. XI, no. 2771, pp. 236–7; see also Hohenlohe's report on the Kaiser's account of the conversation, *ibid.*, no. 2770, pp. 235–6.)

fronted with all sorts of demands and that he could not hope for a calmer conduct of policy on our part. I had considerable trouble in getting him to speak about it at all, and I only succeeded after giving him an assurance that I would not write about it. His final remark was: '*Je vous avoue que cette agitation croissante m'inquiète vivement.*' Naturally I at once sensed a greater reserve on his part in discussing political questions which I have since only with difficulty been able to overcome to some extent.

If we have decided to leave England completely out of the game for the future and to engage ourselves elsewhere, then it naturally can be a matter of indifference to us what humour he is in. But so long as that is not the case it will in my humble opinion be my task to cultivate relations here so that the way to an understanding over the questions in which we have a common interest remains open for the future. You can believe me that Salisbury is in no way a supporter of 'splendid isolation', and that he does not lose sight of the possibility that England and Germany may one day come together over the bridge Austria-Italy. Finally, to revert again to my personal affair, I was reminded of poor Caprivi. At that time underhanded intrigues against me would have been hopeless, for he would have explained to H.M. that I must have good reasons for my actions and that he could not dispense with my services. If to-day the Chancellor and the Foreign Ministry do not stand so solidly behind me as was then the case, the result of the underhanded activity can indeed be quite different. I had nevertheless thought the services which I have rendered and the unqualified recognition of them which has been accorded to me up to the most recent times would have protected me against a momentary ill-humour.

Good-bye for to-day, dear friend, and let me hear from you soon.

With kindest regards
Your
PHatzfeldt.

533. Bernhard von Bülow to Holstein

Rome, 19 March 1896

Dear Holstein,

[...] In the last few days I have received two letters from Philipp E[ulenburg] that depressed me. Our internal situation is so unpleasant! And what difficulties you have to contend with! A bright spot in Eulenburg's letters was his unreserved friendship and love for you, his boundless admiration for your political ability, and the fact that he is more than ever convinced of your complete irreplaceability.[1] But now as before he preaches waiting, tacking about, and caution, because the consequences of a blow-up would be incalculable. I do not need to tell you that for objective and personal reasons I will do everything that lies in my power to prevent a change. After two years' work in Rome and some successes, it is admittedly a bitter feeling to say to oneself that if

---

[1] Eulenburg's letters to Bülow as printed by Haller (*Eulenburg*, pp. 207–8) hardly convey this impression.

my position here became unstable, Engelbrecht might move into the Caffarelli.[1] On the subject of the immeasurable dangers of an 'Aide-de-Camp Government' Eulenburg thinks as we do. [...]

Your sincerely devoted B.

534. Georg zu Münster to Holstein

Paris, 19 March 1896

Confidential and holograph

My dear Herr von Holstein,

[...] There is no longer any possibility of an Anglo-Russo-French entente which was contemplated by many politicians inimical to us. The party in England led by Chamberlain which is opposed to evacuating Egypt made very clever use of the situation to put a spoke in the wheel.[2] It was high time, because Salisbury was already very wobbly. Nothing better could have happened for us, and it both alters and improves the situation, which could have been unpleasant if the English had allowed their excited feelings[3] to seduce them into coming to an understanding with France.

The English action is of a purely political nature, and for the English in Egypt signifies the *noli me tangere*. Military authorities in England, and especially Lord Wolseley whom I myself know very well and about whose views a mutual friend recently informed me, had great misgivings about a large-scale expedition to Khartoum and even to Darfur. He gladly gave his approval to the present expedition for political reasons, but had strongly advised them to proceed cautiously and for the time being to reoccupy only the very fertile Dongola valley on behalf of Egypt, but not to go any further. He regards this expedition as a means to strengthen English rule in Egypt. If the Italians can hold Kassala the English will only be glad.

The French are very angry because they had really thought they could draw England into the Franco-Russian net. They think they were duped, and vain people like the French pardon that least of all.

For the moment this has drawn the Russians and the French closer together again, but this does not mean much because the French dance to the Russian tune anyway, and will continue to dance until the Russians come too close for comfort in the Mediterranean. Mohrenheim has again been very busy and helped to see to it that the Russians immediately rejected the English proposal regarding the money in the Egyptian Reserve Fund even before the French enquiry reached St Petersburg.

Why is there still a Wilhelmstrasse if official business is to be divided up among the Aides-de-Camp?[4]

---

[1] The German Embassy in Rome.

[2] On 12 March the British Government decided to send an expedition up the Nile valley to occupy Dongola in order to protect the Nile on the east after the Italian collapse in Abyssinia. (See Salisbury's explanatory telegram to Lascelles of 15 March, *Grosse Politik*, vol. XI, no. 2698, pp. 152–3, and Hatzfeldt's dispatch of 15 March, *ibid.*, no. 2699, pp. 153–4.)

[3] Since the Krüger Telegram affair.

[4] See below, Holstein's letter to Radolin of 22 March 1896.

One of the greatest qualities of old Kaiser Wilhelm was that he never interfered in the spheres of action and authority of the individual State Ministries and officials! [...]

Sincerely yours
Münster

535. Paul von Hatzfeldt to Holstein

London, 21 March 1896

Dear friend,

I have little to add to my to-day's dispatch about Egypt.[1] Salisbury admitted to me to-day that for a moment he had believed in serious difficulties with Paris, but now these were a thing of the past. He was in the best of spirits and seemed not to have a care in the world. Moreover he is quite calmly going away for three weeks, though some people closest to him in the conduct of affairs are this time shaking their heads doubtfully over his departure.

The point which concerns us is obviously whether even now an understanding with France is still possible and whether Courcel brought any kind of proposals with him.[2] To all appearances this is not the case. I surely do not need to say that I will keep this point clearly in view.

My greatest desire is that Salisbury will not be successful in his intention to keep the expedition within moderate bounds, and that events and the insistence of the soldiers will force him to engage himself more deeply than he wishes. The more this happens the greater in all probability will be the estrangement from France. It is a pity that the coronation in Moscow is not yet over. If that were over France would perhaps be successful in inducing Russia to take part now in joint action against England.

Radolin's report that the Russian Press has been instructed to advocate that Italy leave the Triple Alliance and join France seems to me very valuable and significant.[3] If that succeeds we will soon be taught that nothing remains for us but to go with Russia through thick and thin without expecting any special gratitude for doing so.

I would like to draw special attention to the fact that with Salisbury's departure affairs will as usual come to an almost complete standstill and the majority of the foreign representatives will probably vanish. If you think that there would be no objection to my getting away too for a fortnight, I would be grateful for a telegraphic hint.

As a curiosity and insight into the Italian character let me tell you *in confidence* that Ferrero is exhibiting enormous pleasure here over the fall of Crispi and Co.,[4] although he was allegedly an intimate friend of Blanc. I was assured that he told someone yesterday: *'Puisqu'ils sont partis je puis le dire, c'étaient des canailles.'*

[1] *Grosse Politik*, vol. XI, no. 2715, p. 169.
[2] Courcel, who had been on leave, returned to London because of the Egyptian situation. (See *Grosse Politik*, vol. XI, no. 2708, pp. 162–3.)
[3] Radolin had reported this by telegram on 14 March. (From the Foreign Ministry files.)
[4] The Crispi Cabinet had fallen on 4 March as a result of the Italian defeat at Adua.

It is time for the courier to leave and I must therefore bid you farewell.
With kindest regards
Your
PHatzfeldt. [...]

536. Holstein to Hugo von Radolin[1]

Berlin, 22 March 1896

Dear Ambassador,

[...] Our foreign policy is going well. As you see from Metternich's very interesting dispatch,[2] the Egyptian campaign is the work of Cromer.[3] The Italians were probably nothing more than a pretext for it. The real motive was undoubtedly the thought that this would prevent all further *evacuation projects*.

As you have seen from instruction no. 128[4] we would also have made the best of the evacuation of Egypt. But foreign policy certainly is made *easier* for us if Egypt is *not* evacuated. The most cheated person at the moment seems to be our cunning friend Courcel. In his insinuating way he had made use of the amazement of the English over H.M.'s telegram to President Krüger in order to negotiate about the evacuation of Egypt and friendship with France. *That* negotiations were in progress we know positively.[5]

The Triple Alliance has been strengthened by this action; its position as the central group between the Franco-Russian group and the English is now more advantageous than ever.

Internal conditions, especially at Court, are less pleasant. The Cabinets and Aides-de-Camp are becoming more and more an organised secondary Government. The Aides-de-Camp have actually been assigned to various departments: Count Moltke, Austria and Germany; Colonel [...],[6] Russia; Colonel Arnim, Alsace-Lorraine and England; Colonel Engelbrecht, Italy; Colonel Scheele, African Colonies, etc.

So far I have met with no restraints in foreign policy. On the contrary, H.M. always praises. If this situation changes I will leave. But the Chancellor, Marschall, and other Ministers often have things made more difficult for them by the Camarilla. That will last for a limited time, not for very long. One cannot suddenly turn back world history 150 years. The Press and the Reichstag are beginning little by little to show concern about the concept of a Camarilla. If this should some day erupt, H.M. will have to sacrifice the Camarilla—at least its present excresences. For in this question he has neither the Reichstag nor the electorate nor the German Princes behind him. But before this ever happens I shall long since have taken my departure.

[1] From the Radolin Papers.
[2] *Grosse Politik*, vol. XI, no. 2709, pp. 163–4.
[3] Evelyn Baring, Earl of Cromer. British Consul-General in Cairo, 1883–1907. Cromer was the chief representative of the British Government in Egypt and as such was the actual ruler of the country.
[4] Of 24 February. (*Grosse Politik*, vol. XI, no. 2689, pp. 140–2.)
[5] See *Grosse Politik*, vol. XI, nos. 2681, 2687, 2689, pp. 139, 140–2.
[6] Name illegible.

Ad vocem Rothstein.[1] Precisely the same plan has already been presented here by another semi-official Russian Jew, Raffallovich. The Russians would quite simply like to obtain control of Italian finances *through us*. Do not let Rothstein realise that we have seen through him, but simply keep to the content of the official answer which you will receive tomorrow.

Your report about the Russians working for the separation of Italy from the Triple Alliance was very interesting.[2] They won't succeed in this so quickly. The *échec* suffered by the Italians and the consequent Anglo-Egyptian action served actually to rejuvenate the Triple Alliance.

Remember me to your ladies.
Kindest regards
Your H.

537. Alfred von Kiderlen-Wächter to Holstein

Between Genoa and Naples,[3]
Wednesday, 25 March [1896]

Dear Holstein,

Up to now nothing remarkable has happened, except that in a long tunnel just before Genoa our Carpenter brake broke so that the train suddenly stopped and we had to stay there for about twenty minutes. After the damage had been repaired and we had set off again the brake once more broke, so that in order to avoid dashing into the sea we steamed into Genoa at a walking-pace. [...]

During the journey H.M. gave a great political lecture *coram publico* on the subject of the vast Mohammedan movement which was developing, etc., and which the English, by aiding and abetting the Sheik in Medina, would some day seek to exploit against the Russians. Quite right here and there, but somewhat exaggerated.

In regard to England H.M. said he had not believed that the English would be so thoroughly taken in when he advised them to go to Dongola. He had, however, never said such rude things to an ambassador about his own country as he had to Lascelles,[4] who seems to have reported it pretty accurately!

Cowes actually seems to have been given up, and as compensation we are going for *six* weeks to Norway! [...]

H.M. is in general in a good humour. Up to the present he has talked chiefly about the navy—also to me! That is, I had to tell him a great

---

[1] In a dispatch of 16 March and in a private letter to Hohenlohe on the following day, Radolin reported that Rothstein had expressed his willingness to take over the task of reorganising the Italian finances. In a dispatch of 23 March Radolin was told that as long as the Italian Government did not ask for Germany's mediation, Germany could not express any opinion on the question. (From the Foreign Ministry files.)

[2] See p. 600, note 3.

[3] Kiderlen-Wächter had accompanied the Kaiser on a trip to Italy. The imperial party left Germany on 23 March, arrived in Genoa on the 24th and in Naples on the 25th. At the beginning of April the Kaiser travelled to Sicily, and from 11–13 April he visited the King of Italy in Venice.

[4] See p. 597, note 2.

deal more about the Imperial Yacht *Standard*. He has just received a plan from a certain Captain Diedrichs for building an armoured vessel in a new style—obviously commissioned work! Entirely in accordance with H.M.'s ideas, with particularly powerful armament which is H.M.'s hobby-horse. How the Reichstag will rejoice, and Hollmann, who already had so much trouble in talking H.M. out of his last idea, will be happier still. That last idea of the Kaiser's was very lovely, only it could not float. [...]

Greet the boys of the Foreign Ministry for me and let me hear something some time.

Yours
Kiderlen.

538. Bernhard von Bülow to Holstein

Rome, 3 April 1896

Dear Holstein,

As I telegraphed to you the morning of the day before yesterday, I would sum up my general impressions from Naples to the effect that the maintenance of the status quo seems to me not only possible but also probable. In repeated and exhaustive conversations, H.M. spoke to me of the Chancellor solely in terms of warmhearted sympathy; he said nothing against Marschall. What H.M. told me particularly about foreign policy—his views and intentions—is identical with our standpoint. H.M. praised the conduct of the Foreign Ministry, especially in the Transvaal affair. That there will nevertheless be friction in future obviously lies in the nature of things. Nor will I deny that in the event of a row anything may happen. But I think that what in my opinion must remain our chief aim—no changes between the Wilhelmstrasse and the Tiergarten—can be achieved by cautious manoeuvering. [...] If you agree, I would like to travel to Venice as early as the 7th or 8th of this month in order to talk things over with Philipp E[ulenburg] before H.M. arrives. Perhaps it would be useful if before the *entrevue* I once again told Philipp E. everything I wrote to him before my departure for Naples on the subject of our internal situation and its dangers. [...]

Yours
B.

539. Holstein to Hugo von Radolin[1]

8 April 1896

Dear Radolin,

[...] No complications will arise over the Egyptian Question unless Chamberlain indulges in some manifest tactlessness in South Africa which would compel Germany to side once again with France and Russia to save face. Besides, I am fed up with the whole of South Africa because we have nothing to gain there under any circumstances. We cannot after all squat down at Lourenco Marques, right between the English and the

---
[1] From the Radolin Papers.

French. Lourenco Marques is the chief export harbour for Madagascar. But the question of spheres of interest takes second place in comparison with the indecently impudent behaviour of the English towards us. If Chamberlain continues to behave in this way—*l'affaire se gâtera*. [...]

Your
H.

540. Bernhard von Bülow to Holstein

Rome, 17 April 1896

Dear Holstein,

Just returned here to-day from Venice. Although suffering from a bad cold and somewhat tired—what a rush! and how insupportable I would find such a rush in the long run—I would like to complete my other reports[1] from the City on the Lagoons with the following :

All-in-all my impressions in Venice, too, were favourable. [...]

I had an opportunity in Venice to discuss our situation very thoroughly with Philipp E[ulenburg]. I steadfastly maintained that all other considerations must be subordinated to preventing a change in the influential posts. If we were not always in agreement as to the means, complete agreement existed between us as to the aim. [...]

I was glad that H.M. spoke of Münster in the most appreciative manner, and he specially praised his *bon sens* and how well he handled the French. Hatzfeldt and Radolin were also praised. This time H.M. did not mention Radowitz. H.M. did not let fall a word to me about the Köller affair, not even by way of suggestion. Philipp E. and Kiderlen seem nevertheless to think that the impression made by this affair can only be overcome in the course of time. You can be assured that Philipp E. does everything to support Marschall, whose outstanding parliamentary ability and successes have incidentally also impressed H.M.'s entourage. H.M. frequently spoke in a friendly way about Marschall—for example when I brought up his admirable behaviour in the Transvaal affair—and in front of me he said nothing against the State Secretary. [...]

Your
B.

541. Holstein to Bernhard von Bülow[2]

Berlin, 22 April 1896

Dear Bülow,

[...] Notwithstanding this observation[3] the attitude of Russia to-day fills me with less anxiety than six months ago. The aggressive and swaggering attitude which England has adopted since the New Year—

---

[1] See *Grosse Politik*, vol. XI, no. 2784, pp. 246–7.

[2] From the Bülow Papers. Only a typewritten copy of the document was available to the editors.

[3] In the unprinted part of this letter, Holstein said he believed that Russia was trying to sow discord between the German Governments, especially between Prussia and Bavaria.

unfortunately in the first instance against ourselves—its enormous naval armaments, are not calculated to make the Russians think of joining with France to-day or in the near future in reorganising Germany, a concept that under other circumstances might appeal to them. Because such a war, which would naturally not be a short one, would give England *ipso facto* the position of arbitrator of the old world. This prospect is so imminent that probably even Lobanov sees it. I say this because I am beginning to believe that he is not very perceptive. Nor do I think he is practical; he pursues too many goals simultaneously. At one and the same time he is trying, as I told you at the outset, to stir up the German Governments against each other, to rearrange the Bulgarian Church Question to the disadvantage of Bulgaria, and finally, to guide the French in the Egyptian Question more sharply than they appear willing to accept. He ran aground with his first two efforts and only succeeded in making Berlin as well as Sofia suspicious of him. Let us now wait and see how successful he will be in Paris. The Kronstadt alliance[1] up to now has not fulfilled the expectations of either party. The French wanted to make use of Russia *against us* whilst the Russians may well have flattered themselves with the hope of exploiting their French vassal *permanently* not only against us but especially against England.

Have you noticed that the Mediterranean Question, which is after all a vital question for France, has never been seriously discussed from the Franco-Russian standpoint in recent years—that is to say during the Franco-Russian era? In this time have you ever heard or read a declaration from an authoritative French source that Russia's control of the Dardanelles would be a matter of indifference for France? As far as I can remember I have never seen any such declaration. The more talkative the English were, the more close-mouthed were the French in regard to their own interests in this question. I would assume therefore that France's leading politicians and journalists had so arranged their programme that they would first revise the Peace of Frankfurt in conjunction with Russia, and reserve the settlement of the Mediterranean Question, that is to say the restoration of French hegemony in the Mediterranean, for later.

But now the Franco-Russian war against Germany has been put off; indeed it seems further away to-day than it did a year ago because of the aggravated state of Anglo-Russian relations. During the first months of this year, on the other hand, when our Kaiser's telegram to President Krüger caused a paroxysm of anger [in England], Courcel believed in the possibility of an Anglo-German war and assured the leading Englishmen that in that case they could be certain of the support of France: for France had only one enemy and that was Germany. The possibility of being able to use England as an ally for the *revanche*, of which nobody thought a few years ago, now seemed to the prominent French politicians to be a fact with which one could reckon in certain circumstances. This prospect will make the French even less inclined

[1] The Franco-Russian Alliance.

than they were already to allow themselves to be used against England for Russian ends. Various signs point to the fact that to-day men like Courcel, probably also Hanotaux, but certainly Goluchowski are wondering whether the restoration of the old Crimean War line-up would not in the long run be more useful than the present grouping of states for the achievement of their various particular aims. I do not need to tell you that for us the Crimean War line-up would be more uncomfortable and leave us less room for the play of diplomacy than does the present division of Europe into Triple Alliance, Franco-Russian and England groups. Once France and England line up on the basis of an *entente cordiale*, then Italy and Austria will automatically follow suit. But for our reassurance it can be said that an understanding between France and England would be more difficult to-day than it was 43 years ago: the points of friction between France and England have since then been substantially broadened.

But I would rather not continue to indulge in prophecies to-day. Let us first observe with what degree of energy France will follow Russia's lead in the Egyptian Question. From that all kinds of conclusions can then be drawn.

Always yours
Holstein

542. Georg zu Münster to Holstein

Paris, 25 April 1896

My dear Herr von Holstein,

Your friendly lines interested me greatly.[1]

As far as Hanotaux's views on the Straits Question are concerned, he sees the danger which it will have for France after the experiences he had in Constantinople. Nevertheless he still believes in the assurances which Lobanov gave him that Russia's eyes are solely directed towards Eastern Asia, that Russia desires the continued existence of present-day Turkey, and that she will not raise the Straits Question. I have frequently spoken about it with him recently, and though he was reserved he did tell me repeatedly: *la question des détroits nous touche de trop près et j'espère toujours que la Russia n'y touchera pas, car cela pourrait devenir trop gros pour nous.*

He is not so blind about Russia as are the majority of Frenchmen, he pursues a Russian policy because on account of public opinion here he can do nothing else, and (I have often noticed this) he is deeply concerned that England and Russia might yet reach an understanding with us.

As to Egypt, Russia is pushing the French further than they would like to go.[2] Russia only does this in order to make France and England

---

[1] Of 23 April. (*Grosse Politik*, vol. XI, no. 2848, pp. 342–4.)

[2] France and Russia had refused to sanction the British request to use £500,000 from the Egyptian Treasury Reserve Fund to finance the Dongola expedition. (See *Grosse Politik*, vol. XI, no. 2720, pp. 173–4.)

thoroughly hostile to each other—and that for the moment she has achieved. [...]

Good-bye. In the greatest friendship as always
Münster.

543. Paul von Hatzfeldt to Holstein

London, 28 April 1896

Dear friend,

[...] With respect to the question you have raised as to whether Salisbury was ever serious about the negotiations over the evacuation of Egypt, I share neither Münster's opinion nor that of Metternich. Münster's supposition that Salisbury is pro-French[1] is incorrect if only because he has no political sympathies whatever and in this respect is as cold as a dog's nose. He cares for neither the French nor ourselves but exclusively for English interests, especially his own, that is to say his Party and its maintenance in power. Metternich's opinion that Salisbury only wants to frighten us[2] is in my opinion also incorrect because it is not the whole story. He may have regarded this as a secondary aim, but his principal object *at that time*, when, no matter how laughable it sounds, it was believed here that we would go to war, was to make sure whether he could protect his flank through an understanding with France. Since then he has seen that he must pay too high a price for this understanding, and has admitted this to me occasionally in completely confidential conversations. Hence the sudden desire to serve the Italians by means of the Dongola expedition without any regard for the irritation of the French and Russians over this decision which is certainly to be expected. So far as I have been able to discover since my return, no change has taken place here in this regard. Count Deym, who has followed events with great attention, assured me just now in the most definite way that although Salisbury expects some kind of move by the French and Russians, who have not yet done anything, he faces it with great equanimity. Salisbury had expressed himself to Deym on this matter to the effect that the French and Russians could at most propose a conference at which neither England nor—it was to be hoped—Austria *and her friends* would appear. The Russians and the French could then hold a conference among themselves if they liked which would of course have no importance whatever.

It is open to question whether this opinion is correct and whether the Russians and French are not up to something else. But it can at all events be assumed that both have not done anything yet, and that the English Government, which is counting on the continued goodwill of the Triple Alliance, has not yet thought of making concessions to the French in Egypt.

By the way, I do not think that Cromer started the idea of the

---

[1] This idea was expressed in an unprinted portion of Münster's letter to Holstein of 25 April. See above.

[2] This idea was expressed in a letter to Holstein of 16 April 1896. Not printed.

Dongola expedition.[1] He always used to be opposed to it because of his fear that it would again disrupt his beloved Egyptian finances. He only gave his consent when he saw that they were determined on it here for political reasons. [...]

Nobody has so far asked my opinion about the Cowes question.[2] What I think about it will certainly not be doubtful to you. Feeling here has undoubtedly improved, but for all that it is still not friendly. 'To preach common sense' to these people is in my opinion quite useless at present because of their political ignorance. Even if we may assume that the high society assembled in Cowes and even the local population will behave politely, there is always the *possibility* that some agitators *from here* will go there and, with the freedom of movement which the public enjoys in Cowes, will find an opportunity of provoking an unpleasant incident which would also be very unwelcome to this Government.

I ask that these remarks be regarded as confidential, since as I said I have not been asked and I don't want to expose myself to the reproach that my opinion was not demanded. I enclose an anonymous letter that came to-day and which—whatever may have been the writer's object— does not depict the situation incorrectly.[3] [...]

With kindest regards
Yours
PHatzfeldt

544. Philipp zu Eulenburg to Holstein[4]

Vienna, 30 April 1896

Dear friend,

Your letter[5] gave me great and sincere pleasure. It made me feel distinctly how near you are to me inwardly and how fine is your understanding of my personality. That affords me great comfort for you know how I admire you!

The advice you gave me to let the matter of H.M.'s visit to Hungary rest is certainly right—at all events very pleasant for me since a second Kaiser visit with everything connected with it is unthinkable![6]

After what you told me before my departure from Berlin, I cannot wonder that you maintain complete silence about the seemingly very wretched progress of internal affairs.

Since I hear *nothing* from other sources I am forced to rely on newspaper reports for putting two and two together.

---

[1] See above, Holstein's letter to Radolin of 23 March 1896, and Metternich's dispatch of 12 March. (*Grosse Politik*, vol. XI, no. 2709, pp. 163–4.)

[2] The possibility of Wilhelm II attending the Cowes Regatta.

[3] The letter contained a warning that English public opinion was still too incensed over the Krüger Telegram for it to be wise for the Kaiser to come to Cowes that year.

[4] Printed in part in Haller, *Eulenburg*, p. 209.

[5] A letter of 21 April in which Holstein praised a children's story Eulenburg had written. (From the Eulenburg Papers.)

[6] In a letter to Holstein of 20 April Eulenburg wondered what he should do about Wilhelm II's decision not to go to Hungary as he had planned, because the Hungarians had awaited his visit for a long time.

Naturally I would not dream of intervening in matters in which I would prefer not to interfere *unless I am requested to do so*. I have dealt quite enough throughout the years at the cost of my nerves with things that fundamentally did not concern me!

I therefore do not have the least desire to intervene unless the usefulness of my doing so is proved to me by a *competent* authority.

Isolated as I am, I was of course considerably surprised by the hints in the newspapers, which were probably sent to me at your suggestion, that as an *opponent* of the public military courts-martial, I was being considered for the post of Chancellor. In view of my *absolute reserve* in this question (I have and always will emphasise that I *could* not express an opinion because I could not judge whether it was good or bad and because the matter did not concern me in any way), I am completely in the dark as to who could have spoken about my 'opposition'. If you find out something about it, please let me know your conjectures.

H.M.'s return to Potsdam has *suddenly* made it necessary for me to reply *immediately* to a very excited communication from H.M. which makes it seem to me that a row is not impossible.[1] The reply will go by courier, who will also bring this letter to you. I have no time to make a copy of the letter, in which I have asked H.M. to handle the question as *calmly as possible*, and if there is an interpellation in the Reichstag, to calm people by a statement that the opinion of the army has been requested. I don't know whether this was the right thing to do because I have been left totally without information about developments. I can therefore only express myself in very general terms since what matters to me above all is to do *no harm* and to let things take their course *independently of me*.

I arrive in Pest (Hotel Royal) tomorrow where I must remain until the evening of the 7th in the midst of noisy and horrible festivities.[2]

I am taking the small code with me (1702).

With kindest regards
Your old friend
PEulenburg

545. Philipp zu Eulenburg to Holstein

Pest, 3 May 1896

Dear friend,

I have used your long letter *almost verbatim*.[3] That is the best explanation. I *also* wrote about Marschall's audience—but the details you gave me are indeed almost sufficient.

I have already warned H.M. against *hasty* decisions. I have now repeated this warning. I have also recommended the 'compromise' which we formerly agreed upon, but for the present I do not anticipate

---

[1] Over the military courts-martial question.
[2] For the celebration of the millenium of the Hungarian Kingdom.
[3] A letter of 1 May dealing with agitation in the Press over the reform of the military penal code. On this same day Holstein sent five letters and telegrams to Eulenburg. (From the Eulenburg Papers.)

any success with it. Above all I warned him not to irritate Bronsart too much because he would make a row just for revenge.

All this is very pleasant in the middle of such a *série* of social engagements that I never get out of my golden coat and gala carriage!

I am sitting now in full uniform and have finished the endless letter to H.M.—it is time for Church!

Your
PE [...]

546. Holstein to Philipp zu Eulenburg

Copy

Berlin, 5 May 1896

Dear friend,

The present crisis did not come as a surprise. For some time past one could see it coming. Since I know how painfully it affects you each time His Majesty's actions are the subject of criticism I kept silent. But now that you have voluntarily taken your old post in the hour of danger I consider it necessary to inform you about the general situation which I have hitherto not done. Apart from the military courts-martial question, differences of opinion have existed for a long time over many other questions. Two of these are connected with the Protectorate, while the third is the question of the Lippe inheritance.

In South Africa there is unrest not only with regard to the English but also on the frontier of German territory. The officials in the South-West Africa colony have consequently long been demanding, first, an additional force of some hundreds of infantry who can ride, and second, the right to introduce compulsory military service among the Reich nationals who live there and who are mostly of military age. As to the demand for a strengthening of the garrison, the Chancellor, Marschall, Hollmann, the Admiral-in-Chief,[1] I, and the Minister of War, were unanimously of the opinion that in accordance with the colonial officials' proposal, the commanding officer in South-West Africa[2] should receive the desired number as quickly as possible, composed of volunteers from the entire army. Only Senden was in favour of despatching a battalion of marines into the deserts of Damara, notwithstanding the fact that no troops have had less training in riding, and—His Majesty supported Senden. This created a good deal of trouble, and it was only yesterday morning that His Majesty approved of Marschall's proposal that the colonial officials' request should be fulfilled—that is, by sending out a corps of mounted infantry volunteers. A second difficulty arose in the meantime in that the Military Cabinet objected to the introduction of compulsory military service and to the employment of officers *on the active list* in the Protectorate. Colonel Arnim told Director Kayser that the Military Cabinet finally agreed to both questions on the condition that the commanding officer of the troops there would no longer be

[1] Wilhelm von Knorr.
[2] Major Theodor Leutwein. Commander of the Forces in German South-West Africa, 1894–5; Governor, 1895–1904.

subordinate to the Governor. These two questions also gave rise to all sorts of difficulties. At an audience of His Majesty at which Hohenlohe, Marschall, Kayser, Hahnke, Bronsart, and Senden were present, Hahnke showed himself as often before to be more conciliatory than Senden. The Minister for War spoke 'for-two'—to use Marschall's expression. His Majesty has now at last approved conscription. The officers must resign temporarily from the regular army, but retain the right of reappointment. Although the latter point has not yet been made quite clear, it certainly will be.

I now come to the Lippe question, with which you are very familiar.[1] The latest phase in this was that His Majesty had approved that the Chancellor should try to obtain the consent of the parties to the dispute and the Bundesrat to submit the case to a court of arbitration. After lengthy negotiations and many difficulties, all parties at last agreed that the King of Saxony should be the arbitrator and that he should be assisted by some Counsellors of the Supreme Court. This result was communicated to His Majesty at the Wartburg where he had nobody except Raschdau as 'expert' adviser. The Kaiser returned the very detailed memorandum to Hohenlohe with a most ungracious marginal comment: H.M. disapproved the steps that had been taken and especially disapproved of his not having been asked; he claimed the right to be the chairman of the court of arbitration himself or to name the chairman, for example the Chancellor.[2]

When this unsatisfactory decision arrived on the 23rd of last month, the Chancellor was still very unwell (only since yesterday has he been somewhat better). He consulted with Marschall and myself and said with a determination that he seldom shows: 'With the best will in the world I cannot do the gentleman *this* favour.' He afterwards sent to the Kaiser in Dresden on the afternoon of the 23rd a long telegram in which he cited documents to show that the Chancellor had been empowered by His Majesty to do all that he had done; further he declared that he must abide by his standpoint since the exercise of the functions of arbitrer by His Majesty was absolutely unfeasible; and finally, he urgently asked the Kaiser to do nothing that could appear as a disavowal of the Chancellor's work.

[1] On 20 March 1895 Prince Woldemar of Lippe-Detmold died childless. His brother Alexander was an imbecile and therefore the appointment of a Regent became necessary. Immediately after Prince Woldemar's death, a decree of 15 October 1890 was published which named Prince Adolf zu Schaumburg-Lippe, a brother-in-law of the Kaiser, as Regent, and he took over the office on 21 March 1895. The Counts of Lippe-Biesterfeld and Weissenfeld, who were paternally related to the House of Lippe-Detmold, contested the legality of the Regency, as did the Lippe Diet. On 5 July 1895 the Lippe Government requested the Bundesrat to lay the issue before the German Supreme Court. Many of the German ruling Princes raised objections on principle to this course. On 1 February 1896 the Bundesrat requested the Chancellor to arrange for a court of arbitration to decide the issue. (See Hohenlohe, *Denkwürdigkeiten der Reichskanzlerzeit*, pp. 213–14.)

[2] According to Hohenlohe's diary, the Kaiser's message 'there is only one arbitrator in the Reich and that is the Kaiser' was first communicated to him orally by Lucanus on 22 April. Hohenlohe wrote a justification of his actions in a memorandum to the Kaiser on the same day. On this the Kaiser wrote the marginal comment of 23 April to which Holstein refers. Hohenlohe replied with a further vindication. (See Hohenlohe, *Denkwürdigkeiten der Reichskanzlerzeit*, pp. 214–15.)

After that the Kaiser said nothing, and we awaited in understandable suspense for news as to whether he discussed the Lippe question in Dresden and whether he did disavow the Chancellor. According to reliable information His Majesty has in the meantime, in reply to the question of the King of Saxony on the subject, answered only: he did not know how it stood at the moment,—but he did then add: 'The natural thing would of course be for Adolf to remain in Detmold.'

His Majesty—perhaps to some degree to the astonishment of the Head of the House of Wettin[1]—then mentioned the possibility of an Altenburg succession question, and in that connection remarked: 'The natural thing would be for a son of Prince Albrecht to come to Altenburg.'[2]

In the above you have nothing more than a cut and dried picture of the complicated relationship in which the three factors—Kaiser, entourage, Government—stand to each other. The Kaiser still has, at least up till now, the unfortunate habit of talking all the more rapidly and incautiously the more a matter interests him. Hence it happens that he has generally already committed himself, or at least that the entourage persuades him that he has already committed himself, even before the responsible advisers, or the experts, have been able to submit their opinion to him. Thus there arises—for example in the Lippe question—the chief difficulty that the Kaiser has not sufficiently concealed his personal opinion from various potentates, and Marschall has a hard time finding any kind of pretext to cover this weakness of the All-Highest.

Observations of this phenomenon, which is unfortunately not an isolated case but only one of a whole succession, leads with mathematical precision to the attitude which *every* Government must adopt towards this Kaiser—primarily for his own sake: in cases of precipitate actions by the Kaiser which were encouraged by his entourage and which could not be prevented, it must be the task of the Government to give them the best possible interpretation and to correct them. For this the English expression is so fitting: *a thankless task*. But no Minister who has a sense of duty towards the Monarch and the Reich dare shrink from this task. Take the concrete instance that the Government gave way to the Kaiser's inclination to dispose of Lippe, Altenburg, and other *Federal* districts of the present German Reich just as Charlemagne disposed of vacant fiefs—to what would this sort of thing lead? I doubt whether the Kaiser knows that the German Princes to-day are his *allies*, whereas the German Princes in Charlemagne's time were his *vassals*. Prince Bismarck saw the task of the Reich Government as that of serving as a support to the Federal Princes against the radical elements in the individual States. But if the instincts of our present Kaiser were translated into action, the feeling of security within the Reich on the part of the individual Federal Princes would be wholly lost.

The chief danger in the life of Kaiser Wilhelm II is that he is and

---

[1] The King of Saxony.
[2] Ernst I, Duke of Sachsen-Altenburg, 1853–1908, was succeeded by his nephew Ernst II, 1908–18.

remains absolutely unconscious of the effect which his speeches and actions have upon Princes, public men, and the masses. The life work of every Government of Wilhelm II must be to counter this danger and as far as possible to nullify these effects. A task which soon wears one out. The motto of the penny candles *lucendo consumor* will also remain the motto of Wilhelm II Governments until *he himself* understands how greatly he dissipates his own and the imperial authority by this manner of governing. It is to be hoped that when understanding comes it will still do some good and that it will not already be too late.

547. Philipp zu Eulenburg to Holstein

Vienna, 7 May 1896

Dear friend,

I have been thinking for hours to-day about what can be done and have finally hit upon the idea of informing *H.M.* once again about the notion of a 'presidential motion' which Hohenlohe also proposed.[1] Hence the official courier. For I was not yet satisfied with my ideas at the time the dispatch bag left.

I have not recommended that the Chancellor raise this question with H.M. because the Chancellor might meet with a refusal.[2] H.M. can bring the matter up.

I admit that I have *little* hope that the matter will be settled in this way. I have seen no signs *whatever* to show that H.M. has abandoned his original viewpoint—and the presidential motion does after all mean the abandonment of the public trial in principle.

You will not doubt that I am fully aware of the consequences of a rejection of the proposal.

Well, we have done what we could and are not responsible for the consequences!

There is however one thing I would again like to mention to you. If an interpellation is made in the Reichstag, or the Diet, then we must have an answer ready, and this can only be: 'The fifteen Corps Commanders have been asked for their opinion on this important military matter and they have been ordered to have their answers *definitely ready in the autumn* (better still, name the month!). Thereupon H.M. will give his decision.'

If a definite deadline is given, Bronsart will remain and public excitement will die down.

That is a *postponement* which I described *as such* in a letter to H.M., in which I also referred to the *pressing necessity* of *definitely setting a deadline*.

The latter is indeed only a respite. H.M. must know that as well as you and I.

[1] Prince Alexander zu Hohenlohe had written to Eulenburg: 'He [the Chancellor] thought the question might be solved if the Kaiser permitted the reform of the military courts-martial as now drafted by the Ministry of State to be introduced into the Bundesrat as a presidential motion.' (Hohenlohe, *Denkwürdigkeiten der Reichskanzlerzeit*, p. 219.)

[2] See Eulenburg's letter to Prince Alexander of 7 May. (*Ibid.*, pp. 219–20.)

I am glad that despite all this worry about the situation, dear friend, that we are once again of one mind! How could it be otherwise?

Thanks for your very detailed letters of the 5th[1] and 6th.[2]

The Lippe question is very serious!

Your
Very tired
PE.

Postscript

I am going with H.M. to Prökelwitz on the 15th. It is to be hoped that things remain quiet until then—especially while I am there!

I have *no desire whatever* to have people think I have given advice of any kind in this question!

[I] must also go to Liebenberg one or two days beforehand.

P.E.

548. Philipp zu Eulenburg to Holstein

Prökelwitz, 17 May 1896

Dear friend,

I have really nothing to write to you about. The telegram tells you everything.[3]

I am depressed. It is as I told you in Berlin—as I told you nearly a year ago; in *this* question everything is futile. Many things have contributed to make H.M. absolutely intractable on this question. That cannot be altered.

Whom have we to thank for blowing up this question which need not have been brought up at all?

It will depend *solely* upon Hohenlohe. According to the way he decides it the future will **take** shape.

Your faithful old
PE.

One thing more: During yesterday's conversation H.M. said verbatim: 'They have even tried to arouse my suspicions against good old Holstein, as though he were one of the people who wanted to make trouble for me with the Minister of War. I issued a *sharp* reprimand.'

---

[1] See above.

[2] In his letter to Eulenburg of 6 May, Holstein despaired of the usefulness of their joint efforts, and thought that perhaps only bitter experience could make the Kaiser see reason. (From the Eulenburg Papers.)

[3] Eulenburg refers to a telegram he sent to Hohenlohe on the morning of 17 May on the Kaiser's behalf in which strong objection was raised to Hohenlohe's proposed reply to an interpellation in the Reichstag on military courts-martial reform. 'The Kaiser definitely counts on an evasive statement which does not identify Your Highness with the Minister of War's extreme wishes. The avoidance of a crisis depends, as I must in all conscience and in duty bound tell you, exclusively on Your Highness.' Eulenburg's telegram crossed with a telegram from Hohenlohe in which the Chancellor sent the Kaiser the latest draft of his Reichstag statement. In the evening of 17 May the Kaiser telegraphed his approval of Hohenlohe's statement but at the same time he changed its content and reworded it entirely. (See Hohenlohe, *Denkwürdigkeiten der Reichskanzlerzeit*, pp. 224–8, and Eulenburg's letter to Hohenlohe of 18 May, pp. 229–30.)

549. Philipp zu Eulenburg to Holstein

Prökelwitz, 19 May 1896

Dear friend,

I had the right presentiment when I came here. I am again the one who stands in the fire—and in what a fire!

The work has seldom been so heavy. I knew exactly with what question I would have to deal!

Now do not be annoyed if you get the impression that I am not doing the right thing. I am doing all I can from the *most profound conviction* that we *cannot dispense* with the venerated Prince and *must* retain him.

Therefore please help me—especially with Alexander Hohenlohe, who is now inclined to advise his father to leave—to convince the Prince that now that the statement has been made there is no reason for a row.[1] It was certainly born with convulsions—but now it is *there*.[2]

I imagine that Hohenlohe will show you my letter of to-day.[3] I also wrote Alexander H.[4] to ask him to pacify his father. We definitely need that.

In haste and frightfully tired.

Your faithful and grateful old

PE. [...]

550. Holstein to Hugo von Radolin[5]

21 May 1896

Dear friend,

We have turned down the Russian proposal concerning joint action against England.[6] Our motivation has been drafted with all possible consideration for the Russians.[7] It is an extension of the dispatch of 20 January[8] which you received and which already stated that the evident

---

[1] On 18 May Hohenlohe declared in the Reichstag that the drafting of a new military penal code had begun. 'So much of the draft has now been prepared that I can entertain the definite hope of being able to lay it before the legislatures of the Reich in the coming autumn. With the exception of special points which the military establishments will require, the code will be drawn up according to the principles of modern legal opinion.' (See Hohenlohe, *Denkwürdigkeiten der Reichskanzlerzeit*, pp. 228–9.)

[2] Eulenburg telegraphed to Hohenlohe on 18 May: 'His Majesty had hoped that Your Highness would follow more closely in to-day's statement the wording which His Majesty had edited after mature consideration.' On the 19th Hohenlohe replied: 'I could not follow the wording of the Imperial instruction exactly since the situation did not permit entering into details. I am not a chancellery official, but Chancellor, and must know what it is necessary for me to say.' (Hohenlohe, *Denkwürdigkeiten der Reichskanzlerzeit*, pp. 229 and 231.)

[3] Eulenburg wrote: 'He [the Kaiser] realises very well that Your Highness' statement saved the situation but thinks—I can sense it!—that the army will now count on a concession and is afraid of the *couleur* of Hahnke. The excitement has died down. The mood is again good and lively.' (*Ibid.*, pp. 231–2.)

[4] *Ibid.*, p. 232.

[5] From the Radolin Papers.

[6] Russia used the announcement that England intended to replace the Egyptian garrison at Suakim with Indian troops to ask Germany on 15 May whether it was not necessary '*de formuler des réserves visant les modifications apportées par la mesure précitée au status quo dans la Mer Rouge*'. (*Grosse Politik*, vol. XI, no. 2734, Enclosure, pp. 187–8.)

[7] *Grosse Politik*, vol. XI, no. 2735, pp. 188–90.

[8] Should read: of 19 January. (*Grosse Politik*, vol. XI, no. 2651, pp. 82–3.)

symptoms of enmity in France necessitated the greatest caution on our part.

I suspect that Lobanov will not be exactly in a good humour as a result of the refusal. I would therefore advise you not to start the subject but to wait until he raises it. Meanwhile thoroughly memorise the dispatch[1] and the memorandum by Marschall[2] so that you will have an answer ready. [...]

The French want to use the Russians *only* for the revision of the Treaty of Frankfurt. The Russians who, even if they wanted to, cannot dissipate their strength against us on account of their strained relations with England, are striving for a joint action against England. They will certainly cater to the French in Moscow in every way in order to put them into a good humour. Nevertheless I am very doubtful as to *how far* the French will join them in opposition to England in the Egyptian Question. We are for the present simply observing what is going on. We must also not wholly forget that it has not been quite three months since *The Times* and *Daily Telegraph* advised the Russians, French, and Italians to work together for the revision of the Peace of Frankfurt. The French will not want to bite England any more than the Russians at that time wanted to bite us.

To give the Black Eagle to Lobanov after he has all along been so rude to you would be the surest way to make your position there difficult. Hohenlohe and Marschall are of the same opinion. Only see to it that Prince Heinrich does not make a suggestion to this effect.

Goodbye for to-day. Have fun and—don't get angry!

Bear in mind that you should treat Witte well. Can't you do him some favour socially?

Kindest regards
H.

551. Paul von Hatzfeldt to Holstein

London, 22 May 1896

Dear friend,

I had already decided to send off the courier this evening when I received this afternoon the order to send him. He is bringing you some reports but nothing much that is new because there is nothing new. If one goes to the Foreign Office or meets English statesmen elsewhere, one gets the impression that Europe is living in a state of profound peace and that there is not a cloud on the horizon out of which a thunderstorm could develop within the next fifty years. Even interest in the Transvaal, although it is still being stirred up by some newspapers, is beginning to evaporate. There is only a single word with which one can rouse every Englishman out of his calm and that is the name Lobanov. If one mentions this name one's interlocutor starts and asks 'why in the world should this man be so hostile to us?' But they do not on that account think any more seriously about the future, and take it for granted that

---

[1] See p. 615, note 7.   [2] Of 15 May. (*Grosse Politik*, vol. XI, no. 2734, pp. 185–7.)

Salisbury will find some means of safeguarding English interests and avoiding a war.

Things will probably go on like this here until the storm breaks one day they must decide what to do. In my opinion, as you know, we must calmly await this moment and then see what is most advantageous for us. We have all the more reason to wait because not only Salisbury but other outstanding members of this Cabinet undoubtedly have a secret desire to come to an understanding with Austria and Italy and to seek our friendship.

It is to be hoped that by that time the uproar over the Transvaal, which is now already dying down, will be completely at an end. Salisbury himself has already reached the stage of making jokes about it. When I recently expressed my astonishment that Chamberlain had published the telegram from Krüger in which in conclusion Krüger expressed his thanks for the enquiry about Mrs Krüger—which was very likely ironical—Salisbury laughed heartily and said not without satisfaction: 'What do you expect? Chamberlain has no sense of the ridiculous. And perhaps ridicule is not fatal in Birmingham as it is in France.'[1]

In discussing the indiscretions in the Italian Green Books[2] he several times paid tribute to our own inviolable discretion and remarked: 'It is for that reason that I tell you confidential matters which I would tell no one else, and I will continue to do so when the occasion offers, which it may well do in the future.'[1]

It will probably never be definitely known whether he was really ready at one time to close with the French. As you will see from my to-day's report[3] even Courcel now contests it. At all events one can probably take for granted that he found a hair in the ointment and that he will not try again very soon unless he is compelled to do so by ourselves or by outside circumstances. [...]

With kindest regards
Yours
P Hatzfeldt.

552. Bernhard von Bülow to Holstein

Rome, 12 June 1896

Dear Holstein,

[...] If despite the heat and fatigue of the journey I am going to Vienna for some days, I am doing so because our domestic situation is unhappily too confused and unstable for me to be able to discuss it fully with Philipp E[ulenburg] in writing, and it would certainly be useful to discuss the matter thoroughly with our friend before he starts off on his Norwegian trip.[4] I agree with you in following the viewpoint which

[1] In French in the original.
[2] Hatzfeldt refers to two Italian Green Books, *Camera dei Deputati XXIII and XXIII bis, Documenti Diplomatici, Avvenimenti d'Africa,* (*Gennaio 1895–Marzo 1896*), (Rome 1896), which were submitted to the Italian Chamber of Deputies on 27 April 1896.
[3] *Grosse Politik*, vol. XI, no. 2739, pp. 195–8.
[4] Eulenburg was to accompany the Kaiser on his journey to the Norwegian fiords on 1 July.

Taine formulated in the words: '*En faits d'histoire il vaut mieux continuer que recommencer.*' Obviously I will bear in mind that we must above all avoid anything which could expose E. to the danger of wearing out his influence or anything that could weaken his position in any way. I know too well how valuable—or rather, how irreplaceable—his influence is for the good cause. [...]

Yours
B.

553. Philipp zu Eulenburg to Holstein

Vienna, 21 June 1896

Dear friend,

I have been made excessively happy by your letter which is filled with such a warm feeling of friendship! A thousand thanks!

My telegram defines my attitude to Prince Ludwig's journey to Canossa.[1]

I am more preoccupied with Bronsart's request to resign.[2] H.M. will show little inclination to keep him after the approval of the four battalions,[3] and therefore there rises on the horizon the figure of a War Minister who will fight against public trials in the new military courts-martial procedure. That lies in the nature of things.

Since Hohenlohe is much inclined to join his fate to that of Bronsart and since Bronsart, if he so desired, could create a devilish strong smell in the Press and revive the whole question of the public courts-martial, this might well lead to the general crack-up that has been prevented with so much difficulty.

It is therefore a question of *separating* Hohenlohe and Marschall from Bronsart in regard to the publicity question before the matter of Bronsart's resignation becomes acute. As to the 'how' your head is better than mine at devising schemes that might lead to a beneficial result. At all events we can discuss that in Berlin.

I think that in this lies the key to the situation. [...]

Bülow sends his best regards. We think of you incessantly and wish you were with us. He returns to Rome in two to three days.

Your old faithful
PE

[1] At a garden party for the Germans who had come to Moscow for the coronation of Nicholas II, the Vice-President of the German Reich Association in Moscow, Camesasca, proposed a toast to Prince Heinrich, the Kaiser's brother, in which he spoke of Prince Heinrich and the German Princes who had come 'in his suite'. Thereupon Prince Ludwig of Bavaria (the later King Ludwig III) said: 'We are not vassals but allies of the German Kaiser.' In order to put an end to the lively comment provoked by this incident, a Bavarian *Reichsrat*, Count Konrad Preysing, proposed that Prince Ludwig should visit the Kaiser before returning to Bavaria, and that he himself should accompany the Prince on this 'journey to Canossa'. (See Hohenlohe, *Denkwürdigkeiten der Reichskanzlerzeit*, pp. 236–7.)

[2] On 17 June the Minister of War informed Alexander zu Hohenlohe in the Reichstag of his resolve to submit his resignation to the Kaiser at the end of the current session. (*Ibid.*, pp. 235–6.)

[3] On 16 June the Reichstag passed the third reading of a bill to alter the peace strength of the army which provided that two of every fourth (half-strength) battalion should be amalgamated to form a full-strength battalion, and that this battalion should be brought up to a strength of 500 men by small transfers of men from the first three battalions.

554. Philipp zu Eulenburg to Holstein

Odda, 5 July 1896

Dear friend,

During my travels I will make notes—quite informally—for you. This takes the least time.

Be so good as to keep them for me and to give them to me when we meet again in Berlin. I can then go over them and see whether I need any of them or not.

Enclosed a few such pages which will prove to you how affectionately I think of you!

In old friendship
Your
PE.

ENCLOSURE I
Talks with the Kaiser

Kristiansand, 2 July 1896

The Kaiser told me he has sent a long telegram to the Chancellor about the reception of Prince Ludwig of Bavaria.[1] He had the impression that the Prince most certainly did not come to excuse himself but with the intention of defending the standpoint he had taken up in Moscow. For that reason H.M. had emphasised in 'very clear' words to the Prince the Kaiser's rights and the duties of the German Princes. H.M. repeated to me the wording of his telegram and maintained that he was convinced his words had made an impression upon the Prince. I expressed the view that the very touchy and resentful Wittelsbacher must unquestionably have been 'impressed' by the Imperial words, but that he probably regarded it chiefly in the nature of a rebuke, which would simply widen the gulf that unhappily existed. The Kaiser said that he could not do anything about it. But he would never hesitate energetically to champion the German standpoint. If Bavaria were to force things to a struggle between the Houses of Wittelsbach and Hohenzollern he would take up the challenge. But he doubted very much that Bavaria would push matters so far. The utter stupidity of the Bavarian Government after the speech in Moscow led to the conclusion that they would think ten times before embarking on a struggle which could only be to Bavaria's detriment.

The *anger* of the German Princes over the Prince's conduct gave him the firm conviction that he had acted rightly in reading the Prince a serious lesson. At the consecration of the memorial on the Kyffhäuser,[2] the Princes who were present gave frank expression to their anger. (In Oldenburg, I too heard expressions of anger on the part of the Grand Duke and the Hereditary Grand Duke.)

A remark made by Prince Heinrich to General von Plessen and Marshal of the Court von Lyncker in Wilhelmshaven contrasts sharply with the anger of the German Princes. The Prince told these gentle-

---

[1] On 30 June. (Hohenlohe, *Denkwürdigkeiten der Reichskanzlerzeit*, pp. 238–40.)
[2] The consecration of the memorial to Kaiser Wilhelm I took place on 18 June.

men: 'Prince Ludwig was completely within his rights. The Princes did not have to put up with anything from the Kaiser and had a perfect right to their own independence. The whole "German Rubbish-heap" would not hold together much longer anyway.'

I am wondering whether it is not necessary to inform H.M. of such a remark for purposes of reprimand. It is very close indeed to rebellion in one's own house!

There was a special reason why H.M. did not receive Count Preysing.[1] When I asked about it the Kaiser said: I do not receive a man who has openly lied to me.

It occurred to me that this remark referred to the last dissolution of the Reichstag on account of the Army Bill. On that occasion Preysing out of regard for his electors had voted against the Bill despite a promise he had made to H.M.

In view of this it would have been better if, as I advised at the time, the Preysing Expedition had not taken place at all. I proposed that the Kaiser receive Preysing at the Chancellor's suggestion, but this met with no success because of H.M.'s opinion of the Count.

ENCLOSURE II
Conversation with the Kaiser

Copy

Odda, Hardanger, 5 July 1896

Secret

The reform of the military courts-martial procedure is still the insurmountable difficulty. The Kaiser will not give way, and after receiving agreement from the most widely differing quarters is more firmly fixed than ever in his opinion. He said that an opinion on this question prepared three to four weeks ago by the present Minister of War and found in the War Ministry files pronounced in the most decided way against public procedure; all the generals holding commands were also opposed to publicity.

H.M. believes that this opinion of Bronsart's destroys his case. I allowed myself to contradict.

The Kaiser is also thinking that in view of these facts the Chancellor will be able all the more easily to come to the decision to make good the wrong he committed by delivering that statement to the Reichstag in May. The text was not the one drawn up by H.M. It was made to appear as though H.M. too had now agreed to public procedure. The Chancellor has not, however, actually promised the public procedure, so that by making a concession to the Kaiser, he can make good the wrong he committed.

I told H.M. that the Chancellor held firmly to his opinion, and the Kaiser replied with obvious irritation but also with very marked energy: 'You will never convert me to another view. I hold inexorably to my opinion and must therefore take upon myself all possible con-

---

[1] Konrad, Count von Preysing-Lichtenegg-Moos. Member of the Reichstag (Centre Party), 1871–93.

sequences. That this may result in a change of Chancellors fills me with extreme concern—but even this I *must* take upon myself. I would despise myself if I were to sacrifice my convictions on this question.'

I have the impression that this standpoint will have to be reckoned with, and I see hardly any possibility for a peaceful solution.

The resignation of the Minister of War has not yet reached H.M. Yet it is said to have been mailed.

The Military Cabinet, represented by Arnim, is pressing for H.M.'s acceptance of the resignation.

By August we will probably find ourselves in a crisis.

555. Alfred von Kiderlen-Wächter to Holstein

Odda, 5 July 1896

Dear Holstein,

Rotenhan will have shown you—or will show you—my two secret reports.[1] For your benefit I would like to add: Eulenburg realises that in the autumn the question: either public procedure or a change of Chancellors, must be decided. I found him fairly resigned. He talked remarkably calmly about the possibility, even probability, of a crisis, and surprised me with the remark that it would also be a great initial drawback for Hohenlohe's successor to take up office under the auspice of a refusal of public procedure.

I hear from the Kaiser's entourage that H.M. has recently often praised Botho [Eulenburg] and has referred to his opinion on a wide variety of questions.

I refrain from all conclusions—we will both continue to watch. I will tell you everything I hear.

Yours
Kiderlen.

556. Bernhard von Bülow to Holstein

Rome, 7 July 1896

Dear Holstein,

[...] I did not telegraph you about my meeting with Philipp E[ulenburg] because I knew that you yourself would be talking to him twenty-four hours after our meeting. According to my impression E. regards the present position as a not untenable but certainly a precarious one which can be maintained only with great care. He apparently considers Hohenlohe's weariness of office on the one hand and H.M.'s antagonism towards Marschall on the other as the two major difficulties in the situation.[2] While E. will do all he can to take care of Hohenlohe,

[1] Not found.

[2] Hohenlohe wrote in his diary on 1 July that Lucanus had told him the Kaiser was contemplating further changes in the Ministry. 'He [the Kaiser] will get rid of Marschall, against whom he is embittered on account of his handling of the Lippe Succession Question. Lucanus says the Kaiser took offence because Marschall had told him the affair did not concern H.M.! He does not want to keep Bötticher any longer either; but that can wait a while. When I asked him whom H.M. wanted in Marschall's place he said: Bülow. As to myself, Lucanus thinks the Kaiser will not let the "Uncle" depart. He also wants to keep the Minister of War.' (Hohenlohe, *Denkwürdigkeiten der Reichskanzlerzeit*, p. 240.)

he also hopes that the friends and family of the Chancellor will make it clear to him how essential it is that he hold out for the good cause. *Quoad* Marschall, E. felt that the only hope for his remaining longer in office would be for him to separate his fate from that of Bronsart on the courts-martial reform question and to support H.M.'s standpoint. If Marschall were willing to be somewhat accommodating on this question, the present system could last for a long time. Otherwise, according to E., the door would be wide open to every possibility and danger. I have discussed the situation with E. solely from the factual standpoint.[1] As to what concerns me personally, I still hope and believe that even in the event of a change I will be able to avoid Berlin, where I do not want to go under any circumstances and in any capacity. [...]

With kindest regards and wishes

Always in faithful friendship and devotion

Your

B.

557. Holstein to Alfred von Kiderlen-Wächter

Copy

Berlin, 10 July 1896

Dear Kiderlen,

I am utterly amazed by your communication to Rotenhan yesterday.[2] I think that there must be some mystification somewhere. Before he parts with the present Chancellor, the Kaiser should obtain the WRITTEN agreement of Saxony, Bavaria, and Württemberg to stand by the Kaiser *to the end* in the conflict which would then be unavoidable, and to collaborate in everything. For merely to approve the *first* dissolution of the Reichstag and then to say no to the second would simply be drawing the Kaiser into the struggle under false pretences and then leaving him in the lurch. The temptation to behave in such a way would, however, be very great because those Princes who later used their influence to 'moderate'—that is what it would be called—would acquire immense popularity overnight, even outside their own territories. I can believe that the House of Wittelsbach in particular would be overjoyed at the chance to get quits for the Canossa journey to Kiel.

[1] In a letter to Eulenburg on 10 July, Holstein quoted verbatim the above letter from Bülow, from 'According to my impression' to 'factual standpoint'. Holstein's letter to Eulenburg continues: 'To this I have briefly replied in cipher as follows: "The Chancellor is not weary of office, will resign only if he is compelled. This compulsion exists if the Minister of War goes before the military courts-martial question is settled. In that case Marschall would also have to go. In my opinion this would mean the creation of the very situation which the Kaiser cannot allow until he has the *written* statement of the principal German Princes in his pocket that they will support him through thick and thin. Otherwise, that is if, after the conflict has begun, a number of Princes with Bavaria at their head refuse to follow him in dissolutions or any other moves against Parliament, the Kaiser will find himself in a serious position because the power of the Princes would be augmented by that of all the Opposition parties. Am I mistaken if I take it for granted that the House of Wittelsbach would gladly avail itself of such a good opportunity for paying him back for the Canossa journey to Kiel? The Kaiser can hardly fail to recognise this danger if it is brought to his notice." This, my dear E[ulenburg], is the heart and soul of the whole matter, because it is here a question of the preservation or weakening of the imperial authority. All the other questions—for example ministerial appointments—are of secondary importance.'

[2] Not found.

In view of the serious consequences which would result from a capitulation to Parliament and to the Princes coquetting with Parliament, H.M. should assure himself in *writing* of the loyalty of these Princes before he enters the lists; for *verba volant*. The memory is sometimes weak and also the man.

The whole affair seems to me sinister; I refer to the campaign for a dissolution on account of the military courts-martial question and the naval programme.[1] Both would be very bad slogans for new elections. But to-day everyone knows that it turns on these two questions. Practically every day some paper or other says something about it. And now Hollmann and Lieber and another Deputy—I read about it this morning—are even inspecting the harbours. A very useful matter, undoubtedly, but naturally it will be impossible to avoid comment.

So, as I already said: campaign for dissolution dangerous if the Opposition can use 'courts-martial' and 'fleet programme' as slogans in the next elections. It would be a challenge to fate *unless* one had the *definite assurances* that the greater Princes, especially Bavaria, were ready to go along *to the end*.

After a long interval of quiet, personal attacks are starting again. Eulenburg, you and I are again being torn to pieces; a concentrated fire is being directed particularly against Bötticher and Marschall as servants of the Centre and Centre candidates. The 'shameless manipulation of the provisions' of the Civil Code[2] is once again being brought up, etc., etc. *Hamburger Nachrichten, Berliner and Leipziger Neueste Nachrichten, Hannoverscher Kurier, Zukunft*—all are up in arms. Obviously they know that a psychological moment is approaching.[3]

558. Philipp zu Eulenburg to Holstein

Mariefiord (Sognefiord), 12 July 1896

Absolutely secret
Only for you!
Dear friend,

Enclosed some more notes which may interest you.[4]

After a conversation yesterday with H.M. I regard the existing system as 'done for'. It is impossible to tell whether new forms will develop under Hohenlohe or whether there will be a Chancellor crisis.

The unremitting agitation against Marschall has aroused what appears to me to be such insurmountable dislike against him on the part of H.M. that any possible or useful collaboration is thereby precluded. Unfortunately M. also lacks the talent for making friends among H.M.'s entourage. I have followed your friendly advice and despite the lost

[1] Holstein refers to the Kaiser's personal projects for the fleet. No bill for large-scale naval construction had as yet been introduced in the Reichstag.
[2] The civil code, which passed its third reading in the Reichstag on 1 July 1896, was now being severely criticised on the grounds that it had been rushed through the Reichstag at the Kaiser's request without giving the Reichstag time to make a careful study of its provisions.
[3] Kiderlen replied on 12 July: 'Best thanks for your interesting letter. I have informed H.M. of its contents.'
[4] Not found.

ground have not become involved in differences with H.M. I have often enough given proof of my good will—and even now I did not conceal my honest opinion. To go any further however appears to me quite *hopeless*.

I consider that in these circumstances two things are urgently necessary in the Kaiser's interest and in our own.

(1) To do everything possible to prevent any changes from taking place during the journey or too quickly after the journey. Quite frankly I would prefer not to appear as the instigator and be made answerable for everything that happens. Included under this heading is the *very cautious* handling of the Press in case there should be rumours about a crisis.

(2) In view of the fact that our mutual friend[1] is coming more and more into the foreground and may soon find himself in the position of not *being able* to refuse, we must do all we can to hold off the storm which would force him into the Chancellorship on the platform of *opposing* public procedure in the reform of the military penal code. That would put him into a virtually untenable situation, and we must do everything to smooth the *entrée* for him if the occasion arises. The possibility of his refusing if the storm were too violent is virtually out of the question. He will accept under all circumstances if H.M. makes an *urgent request*. We would all do so. It is not impossible on the other hand that in the event of a negative reply from our friend, H.M. out of ill-humour would suddenly appoint Wald[ersee] or would turn to Botho E[ulenburg].

I think I can take it for granted that Marschall will under no circumstances simply be dismissed but will receive an embassy.

I write all this to you soberly and clearly as I view the situation. I assure you that in this connection I have put all pessimism to one side. But I *cannot* write otherwise. At all events I do not want to abandon the thing as so completely hopeless that afterwards—if any kind of change takes place—our friend's situation would be quite untenable. I want to avoid everything that might heighten the difficulties and to save what is to be saved. For that reason I am writing to you *immediately* after forming my impressions, and count on your loyal friendship.

Yours—if not completely without hope but
still somewhat depressed—
PE.

Kiderlen knows nothing of all this.

559. Holstein to Philipp zu Eulenburg
Copy

Berlin, 14 July 1896

Dear friend,

The present situation as you have depicted it in your memorandum

[1] Bernhard von Bülow.

of the 5th[1] has an unmistakeable resemblance to that of two years ago and fills me with serious apprehension, all the more so since I feel myself helpless. I realise that I cannot speak with authority to the members of the Ministry of State, because they are in the position to make me conscious of the fact that I do not know the inside story—the discussions, declarations, and decisions within the Ministry on which the present state of affairs has gradually been built up. An attempt on my part to bring my influence to bear anywhere is hopeless. I know this is so because I made various attempts in the form of questions as to whether this or that was absolutely necessary.

I am convinced of one thing, namely, that with the exception of Bronsart, whose intentions and plans I do not know, not one of the Ministers would gladly leave office on that account. If they nevertheless identify their fate with that of Bronsart, then they are under the subjective impression of something unavoidable. Both attitudes apply especially to Marschall, who from the beginning was mistrustful of Bronsart, but who to-day, I think, is under the impression that the Ministry is bound to follow this particular course.

I sometimes ask whether the continual discussion and thinking about the military courts-martial problem has not magnified it to an extent which bears no sort of relation to its intrinsic importance. However I am not a competent judge and only arrived at this idea because of your latest communication, from which I unhappily see I must reckon on a change of Chancellors as something which can hardly be avoided. This change will be accompanied by other political problems and slogans which, as I recently wrote, will probably result in a grave conflict between Kaiser and Reich. It is incumbent on you as the friend and confidant of the Kaiser to see to it that before be begins this conflict the Kaiser *first of all secures in an absolutely binding form the unconditional political support of the chief German Princes*, and in such a way that afterwards they really cannot retreat without dishonour. I insist upon this all the more strongly because, owing to the fearful nature of all these gentlemen—apart from other motives that might influence *Bavaria*—I suspect that the whole crowd would be inclined to call a halt immediately after the first step and leave the Kaiser to his own devices.

Is it such an impractical idea if I propose that you ask the Kaiser to give you a secret mission after the Norwegian trip to explore the terrain in Dresden, Munich, and Stuttgart, and if the feeling is favourable, to let you obtain the definite agreement of the three rulers in categorical form and in writing? Another *modus procedendi* would be that you first only explore the terrain and allow other Imperial agents to get the 'agreements' in question. The latter would perhaps be better. Nobody would notice your journeys because of your easy mobility and your many-sided relations with all German capitals.

The Kaiser is too eminent a person to be able to risk putting a direct question to these three rulers when there is the possibility of receiving from one or other a *refus* or an evasive answer unless the terrain has

---

[1] See above.

been previously explored. But if you have sounded them out in advance and found their attitude to be at least not unfavourable, then in my opinion there is no ground for hesitation and the effect of the action would only be increased if His Majesty himself *pops the question*[1] in regard to the 'agreements'. Without these H.M. should not depart from his previous peaceful course, which is after all not so worn that it won't be possible to continue along it for some time to come.

You would be mistaken if after what I have said you were to take it for granted that I regard the possibility of vigorous action in domestic problems as out of the question and that I would like to avoid it at all costs. By no means. Nevertheless I firmly believe that such an action only promises success if the definite support of the leading German Princes is fully guaranteed. It would also be an advantage if a popular slogan could be found for the Kaiser's cause.

I can say no more, dear friend. In the foregoing you have the result of many hours of solitary reflection which I believe is free from personal considerations.

560. Karl von Lindenau[2] to Holstein

14 July 1896

Dear Herr Holstein,

[...] I don't know whether Eulenburg has perhaps already made detailed proposals to the Chancellor for a compromise with the Kaiser over the courts-martial procedure, because the Prince has up to now not spoken to me about Eulenburg's letter to him, although it might have been a good idea to do so. But even if E. should already have attempted to talk the Prince into making certain concessions, I do not believe that His Highness would now be prepared to make the Kaiser (through Eulenburg) any promises whatever in the matter; for the Chancellor's repeated and definite statements of yesterday and to-day may be summed up as follows:

That the Chancellor regards himself as 'bound' both by his statement in the Reichstag[3] and especially by the former decision of the Ministry of State,[4] and therefore for the time being and until the usual time for the entire Ministry of State to reassemble, he sees *no reason* to negotiate at all over the question of the military courts-martial procedure. [...]

With renewed thanks for your letter and enclosures, and with kindest regards

Always yours very sincerely
Lindenau.

[1] In English in the original.
[2] Temporary Assistant in the Foreign Ministry, 1891–4; *Vortragender Legationsrat*, 1894–1906. From 1895 Lindenau was attached to the Chancellor's staff.
[3] See above, p. 615, note 1.
[4] See Hohenlohe, *Denkwürdigkeiten der Reichskanzlerzeit*, p. 224.

561. Note by Philipp zu Eulenburg[1]

At sea. Sognefiord, 15 July 1896

Conversation with H.M.

I told the Kaiser that a change of War Ministers and the crisis which would arise out of it could easily lead to a dissolution of the Reichstag. The reform of the military penal code perhaps already furnished occasion for it. For that reason it was of the greatest importance to be exactly informed about the views and intentions of the Federal Princes in regard to this question. I no longer remembered exactly how the King of Saxony stood on this matter, for instance.

The Kaiser said he had alluded to it when talking with the King of Saxony, because the Minister of War had said that King Albert had spoken to him in an affirmative sense about it. The King had replied that it was not he but Bronsart who had raised the subject. He, the King, shared Bronsart's view, but he did not regard the question as of much importance. It was important above all to know *what* the Kaiser thought about it and what Prussia intended to do. He did not have the slightest doubt that he would share the Kaiser's opinion.

The attitude of the Grand Duke of Baden, which I assumed was known, was only mentioned by H.M. in saying that the old gentleman will certainly not abandon his liberal traditions in this matter but that the Baden delegation was too small to participate fully in such an affair.

My remark that despite the opposition of Princes Leopold and Arnulf, the Bavarian Government would not let the opportunity go by of making common and very troublesome cause with the Liberals and Nationalists, who are *for* public procedure, and the Particularists, who want to trip up Prussia, met with a pretty cool reception from the Kaiser: 'I have seventeen army corps and am therefore the master of the situation.' When I pointed out the effect of a penal reform without public procedure upon the Reichstag, H.M. said: 'The reform will not get beyond the Bundesrat.'

562. Karl von Lindenau to Holstein

16 July 1896

Dear Herr von Holstein,

[...] On the issue of the military courts-martial, there is no question that basically the Prince holds the views which were recently summed up for you.[2] I am also *certain* that he definitely wants Bronsart to remain because, no matter what happens to the Bill, he considers him best qualified to bring it before the Reichstag. I had better not go any further with my positive assertions at this time; but even if Czapski in his to-day's letter[3] (about which I have just heard) has written you the

[1] Sent to Holstein by Eulenburg on 16 July.
[2] See above, Lindenau's letter to Holstein of 14 July.
[3] Hutten-Czapski wrote: 'It seems to me that a certain amount of pressure is being used to induce the Chancellor to lay before the Bundesrat a military penal code without public procedure. I have expressed my conviction, in reply to a direct request for my opinion, that such a step would be impossible in view of the entire political past of the Chancellor.'

exact opposite, I still have the impression that the mere presence of Czapski—with whom the Prince is accustomed to discuss the military and other details of the question—means that now or at least soon (that is, before the negotiations with H.M.) the Prince will imperceptibly be brought closer to the idea of a compromise.

Czapski of course spends the whole day with the Prince.[1] You will no doubt laugh—but I must confess that for me this would be a somewhat singular relationship in the long run. Nevertheless I will not take offence for the present.

With kindest regards
Always your devoted
Lindenau.

563. Holstein to Philipp zu Eulenburg

TELEGRAM

B[erlin], 17 July 1896

For Count Eulenburg. *Private.*
With reference to my letter of the 14th of this month,[2] I may ask that you present my humble request to His Majesty not to accept the resignation of the Minister of War now, and that everything possible be done to avoid what could lead to a crisis in the near future. Letter follows.

Holstein.

564. Holstein to Philipp zu Eulenburg

Copy

Berlin, 18 July 1896

Dear Eulenburg,

I think it is possible that in order to spare me you have not shown my letters to H.M. I foresee a great catastrophe, however, and for the sake of my conscience I want you to submit to His Maj. the letter of the 14th and the one enclosed here.[3] I need not then reproach myself no matter what happens.

You know well on what personal terms I am with Marschall. But that does not prevent me from recognising his great qualities as a parliamentarian. It is very much a matter of secondary importance whether a Minister is *amiable* and *likeable*.

One thing, dear friend, I admire in you: the way in which you shake off all arguments that do not appeal to you. Or do you think that I am talking utter nonsense? Well, you will live long enough to find out about that for yourself. At all events I ask that both these letters be submitted to His Majesty. I shall then have done the utmost I can do. You yourself once advised years ago that in a critical moment I should

---

[1] See Hohenlohe, *Denkwürdigkeiten der Reichskanzlerzeit*, p. 243 et seq.
[2] See above. [3] See Enclosure.

make my opinion known to His Majesty. Since then of course a few more years have passed in which I have been intrigued against with His Majesty.

Kindest regards
H.

ENCLOSURE

Holstein to Philipp zu Eulenburg
Copy

Berlin, 18 July 1896

Dear friend,

Your last letter saying that we are faced with a Chancellor crisis on account of the military courts-martial question and the fleet programme was nothing new to me, as you will have seen from my last letters; especially the letter of the 14th. If after an unusually successful parliamentary session the two chief participants—the Chancellor and Marschall—are nevertheless still in danger of falling, then the cause of this danger is not a secret to any politically-minded man in the German Reich. It would therefore be hopeless to expect that, if the two were actually dropped, the Press could be deluded as to the true reason for it. The conflict with the Reichstag would then be unavoidable; I at least, fail to see how it could be avoided. It was for this reason that I have urged and continue to urge that the Kaiser does not take that weighty step before he has definitely assured himself of the support of Saxony, Bavaria, and Württemberg for the duration of the conflict. If the Kaiser provokes the conflict without being quite certain of these three rulers, then he will meet with a political defeat whose consequences will be felt during his entire reign. In the event of the absence of that prerequisite, I am so firmly convinced of a disastrous result that I would still be relatively glad if I learned that Botho Eulenburg or Waldersee were appointed to Hohenlohe's post. In this way Bernhard Bülow would be spared for the period of pacification and restoration after the catastrophe. Now he would use himself up in a few months.

In the event that the rulers of the three kingdoms do *not* have the intention of fighting the parliamentary conflict to the end at the Kaiser's side, it is of the greatest importance for His Majesty to know this *beforehand*. No conscientious politician could in that eventuality advise the Kaiser otherwise than that he retain Marschall in his present post. For nobody will achieve so much as Marschall for the Kaiser with this Reichstag. H.M. will not easily find a second Minister with such oratorical gifts.

Therefore: either a *definite* statement by Dresden, Munich, Stuttgart. Even then the conflict would be dangerous on account of the unpopular slogans, but would be conceivable.

Or retain Hohenlohe and Marschall and continue working with the present Reichstag.

Tertium non datur, or rather the third would mean a political defeat, a political Jena.

565. Philipp zu Eulenburg to Holstein

Trondheim, 19 July 1896

Dear friend,

I do not think that the crisis will become acute for the present. If only because I put it to H.M. that the rumours about a 'conspiracy during the Norwegian voyage' would throw the most peculiar light upon himself and the state of dependency in which he seemed to exist.

After that the dismissal of the Minister of War was *postponed*. I cannot believe that it has been given up.

I fully agree with your statements of the 14th; namely, in case the change should actually lead to a struggle with the Reichstag. But I still do not consider that as definite. It would surely depend on *how* the reconstruction of the Government were carried out.

Your remark that 'perhaps the military courts-martial reform has been too much exaggerated' comes under this head. I have long had the feeling that that Bronsart has hoaxed us all by a grandiose juggling act.

But by that I *by no means* intend to say that there is no danger in the whole situation! Oh no! This is *very* clear to me—all the more clear the more I recognise that an impulsive nature takes surprisingly quick decisions that are not foreseeable in advance.

I will keep you *au courant* as far as it is possible for me to do so.

Your faithful old
PE.

566. Philipp zu Eulenburg to Holstein

Molde Fiord, 23 July 1896

Secret!
Dear friend,

I cannot write to-day because this morning I had an endless discussion with H.M. which obliges me to write to the Chancellor.[1]

I will only tell you this much: that my explanation was *very* effective and that the situation—at least momentarily—has improved.

H.M. is *deeply* conscious of the fact that the Chancellor's resignation will have grave consequences. For that reason the idea of dismissing Bronsart and Marschall is laid aside for the present.

Ways are being sought of modifying this *unfortunate* penal reform. What will be the result? I do not know.

In great haste
Your
PE.[2]

567. Holstein to Karl von Lindenau

Copy

Berlin, 24 July 1896

Dear Lindenau,

Please destroy the enclosed private telegram from Eulenburg[3] in

---

[1] See Haller, *Eulenburg*, pp. 211–13.

[2] Eulenburg telegraphed the same day: 'Thorough discussion on basis of letters received. As a result situation certainly calmer but a definite clarification still not achieved.'

[3] Of 23 July. (See above, note 2.)

accordance with regulations, after you have submitted it to the Prince. The wording leaves it uncertain as to whether E. submitted my two letters[1] to the Kaiser as I asked him to do or only made use of their contents. I suspect the latter. [...]

I do not know if the method of action I proposed is welcome to our friend E., and therefore I am also not certain whether he submitted my letters. But his telegram, together with the latest Lippe telegrams which have arrived from the North, nevertheless give the impression that feelings up there have gradually become less pathological.[2] I no longer believe in a row overnight, but deduce from the various Imperial pronouncements the intention of saving up some crucial questions—business or personal—for the next *verbal* discussion with the Chancellor in the hope of being able to bowl him over with his innate *suada* aided by some dramatic gestures. I imagine that any such discussion with the Kaiser must be very embarrassing for *anyone who wants to be polite* for the simple reason that H.M. can come closer to the limits of parliamentary freedom of speech than another mortal. For this reason I think it right if all questions now pending were dealt with by the Chancellor either *per procura* or in writing. The effects of the moment do not play the same role as in verbal discussions—that is, there is one less risk.

In this connection I should not omit another question, namely that of the Chancellor's place of residence. The fact that the Prince spends his entire holidays outside the Reich, either in Austria or in Russia, is widely commented upon, and at a time when important questions are in the balance it might even be exploited in Imperial circles to the Prince's disadvantage. I would therefore urgently desire that during the period of the critical decisions—that is up to the end of August or into the first days of September—the Prince would stay somewhere in Southern Germany. The place must also be chosen so that Kaiser and Chancellor do not travel past one another in their journeys. A harmless three weeks' cure somewhere would surely provide a suitable motive. I can understand that this idea is not very pleasant, but nevertheless I would most strongly advise His Highness and all those close to him to carry it out, because in my opinion the discomfort of this small *déplacement* is negligible in comparison with the annoyances and drawbacks of all kinds which might be avoided or at least greatly lessened by this expedient.

568. Bernhard von Bülow to Holstein

Rome, 24 July 1896

Dear Holstein,

I have again written to Philipp E[ulenburg] by to-day's courier—I have not heard from him for some time—and once more sincerely impressed upon him the dangers of taking any action in internal affairs

---

[1] Of 14 and 18 July. See above.

[2] Kiderlen reported on 21 July that the Kaiser, despite his scruples, had said he was ready to sign the arbitral agreement. (See above, Holstein's letter to Eulenburg of 5 May 1896.) (From the Foreign Ministry files.)

without the support of the three kingdoms, and on the other hand, of the dangers of a crisis in the central governmental post. I still believe that despite everything it will be possible to avoid a row if the military courts-martial reform *de part et d'autre* is not taken too seriously and if all other considerations are subordinated to the chief aim—to keep Hohenlohe in office. At all events my conscience is clear for I have done *all* that lay in my power to prevent change and crisis. If contrary to hopes (and in so far as I can judge, contrary to expectations) a sudden change should occur after all, I would then even prefer solutions of which I did not really approve to a reorganisation in which I would be called upon to take part. I have left no doubt at all in Philipp E.'s mind that under no circumstances and *in no post whatever* will I come to Berlin. [...]

With best wishes, as ever in faithful friendship and devotion,

Your B.[1]

569. Paul von Hatzfeldt to Holstein

25 July 1896

Dear friend,

I await with anxiety the result of your communication to Vienna from which it seems to me everything will now depend.[2] If Goluchowski acts, then one can probably count on the agreement of France and Italy, and I imagine that Lobanov will be grateful to us if we provide him with the means to overtrump the Empress Mother and to convince his Imperial Master of the necessity of collaboration. In that case England would also join, and then, as Salisbury himself says, it will be child's play to force the Cretans and the Greeks to give in.[3] If all this is unsuccessful, then in my opinion the wretched farce in Constantinople with its little household remedies must come to an end at least so far as we are concerned. Whether in this case Crete in itself will lead to an outbreak of the Eastern Question is doubtful, and Salisbury does not think so. Instead we will have Macedonian and other pleasures which will be all the more difficult to deal with now that Europe has so openly revealed her weakness. If all that happens—which I would profoundly deplore— then above all we must not have any hand in it. The Russians, English, French, and also the Italians, can quarrel over the scraps. If the affair subsequently takes on the inevitable European character, we will have our hands free and can throw the whole weight of our power into the scales on whichever side offers us the greatest security and the greatest

---

[1] With the exception of a single letter of 26 September 1897, there are no further letters from Bülow to Holstein in the Holstein Papers until June 1898.

[2] In February 1896 revolts against Turkish rule broke out in Crete supported by the Greeks who wanted to annex the island. In a private telegram of 24 July Holstein had asked Hatzfeldt whether he now believed the time had come to raise the question in Vienna as to the policy to be adopted in regard to conditions in Crete. (See *Grosse Politik*, vol. XIIi, no. 3032, pp. 180–1.) Hatzfeldt replied affirmatively to this question in a telegram of the same day. (From the London Embassy files.) On 25 July Austria proposed that if Greek support for the Cretan rebellion did not stop, the Powers should consider a blockade of the Cretan coast. (See *Grosse Politik*, vol. XIIi, no. 3034, pp. 181–3.)

[3] See *Grosse Politik*, vol. XIIi, no. 3036, pp. 184–7.

advantages. Please keep me *au courant* of how things are and what you want so that I can perhaps intervene here without loss of time. It seems to me that we two will still achieve something together; above all, therefore, you must not desert the ship.

With kindest regards
Yours
P. Hatzfeldt.

570. Philipp zu Eulenburg to Holstein

26 July 1896

Dear friend,

Enclosed the *brouillon*, s.p.r., to a small *aide mémoire*[1] that I gave H.M. after I had talked for about an hour with him about it.

The effect was profound—for ever since he has looked at the question from this point of view and will take every decision from this angle.

Unfortunately I must acknowledge at the same time that his attitude towards the military courts-martial reform has *not* changed in principle, he will therefore *not* give way.

I assure you, dear friend, that for my part everything possible was done—but that all that can now be done is to separate Hohenlohe from Bronsart and that we must *work to that end*. H.M. has all sorts of ideas on this subject and is very conciliatory in all sorts of ways—thinks however that he will injure the Crown if he gives way.

Thoughts about the serious consequences have had the effect of postponing everything.

H.M. will therefore not undertake a conflict without being fully aware of what he is doing.

We travel home direct. I am very glad because I am tired and washed out!

Your old friend
PE.

571. Chlodwig zu Hohenlohe to Holstein

Alt-Aussee, 27 July 1896

My dear Baron,

Lindenau has informed me of your letters and memoranda, and I will not delay in telling you that so far as political questions are concerned, especially the military courts-martial procedure and the impossibility of abandoning the public hearing of cases, I am in agreement with you. I likewise regard the removal of Bronsart and Marschall as disastrous. I will categorically tell this to Eulenburg, who according to the enclosed telegram will arrive here during the next few days.[2] It is quite likely,

---

[1] Not found.

[2] On 26 July the Kaiser telegraphed to Hohenlohe from Soeholt: 'I have resolved to return some days earlier than I intended and to go to Wilhelmshöhe. Philipp Eulenburg will accompany me and travel by way of Kassel direct to Aussee in order to discuss the situation with you on the basis of the last letter he wrote to you at my command.'

as you say, that they 'want to pull the teeth of the last statesman of the great era'.[1] It is a mystery to me why Marschall should suddenly be dismissed even if he has earned the displeasure of H.M. by his handling of the Lippe affair. I do *not* however agree with you regarding your proposal to abandon the journey to Werki;[2] for postponement until the end of August would be equivalent to abandonment since the Russian Tsar arrives in Berlin at the beginning or middle of September. It is surely Czapski's idea that a holiday outside Germany would be a black mark against me in the eyes of the public. If all Ministers spend their holidays in Switzerland, the Chancellor may certainly stay in neighbouring Styria. It is simply impossible to postpone the date of the journey to Werki. I have most injuriously neglected my private affairs in my absorption in business of state. I cannot ruin myself completely for the sake of the imperial service. [...]

Moreover, a decision in the affair will be made *now*, for Eulenburg will have been sent to me by the Kaiser for this purpose and will arrive here in a few days.

With kindest regards,
Your most devoted
CHohenlohe.

572. Holstein to Karl von Lindenau

Copy

Berlin, 27 July 1896

Dear Lindenau,

The news which to-day's courier is bringing you establishes what I have been thinking for weeks and have expressed here to my most intimate acquaintances: the events of the last few days were not free from pathological features. I would like to emphasise, however, without dwelling unnecessarily on this sad subject, that even more than formerly it is of paramount importance to uphold the personality and the *prestige* of the Chancellor as the *fixed point* around which the whole conception of the Reich and its supporters can come together. Now more than ever everything must be avoided that might tend to detract from the political personality of the Chancellor. This also involves the Chancellor's remaining quite firm in the military courts-martial affair. The fact that the Chancellor is seeking a solution that could also satisfy the Imperial entourage does all honour to the amiability and noblemindedness of Prince Hohenlohe. Nevertheless this object—the satisfaction of the 'entourage'—would not be achieved without injury to the political personality of the Prince. And this, for reasons on which I need not

---

[1] In a second letter to Lindenau on 24 July Holstein had written: 'I would like to remark in this connection [a proposal for mediation in the military courts-martial question] that as we all know His Majesty was often close to surrender, but that time and again he saw reason to hope that the Chancellor for his part would finally give way, and this caused him to snap back again. [...] Who knows whether many of those who are advising the Kaiser to drive Prince Hohenlohe into a corner are not motivated by the idea of "pulling the teeth" of this last statesman of the great era.'

[2] See above, Holstein's letter to Lindenau of 24 July.

elaborate, is to-day even more than a month ago an indispensable, almost irreplaceable, political working capital for the German Reich, if only because in the event of a crisis the German nation would certainly think twice before according anyone else the degree of confidence which the Prince has earned for himself by long years of successful work in responsible positions. What would the situation be if this trust in the Chancellor and his general staff were lacking at critical moments? Hence, *censeo* that His Highness should above all and for the good of the Reich seek to maintain *his* position undiminished for himself and the German people, and that he should therefore not permit his statement in the Reichstag—that 'the Military Penal Bill will accord with modern ideas'—to be interpreted by Hahnke and his comrades in such a manner as to afford scope for scornful comments.

It is clear from the enclosed letter from Eulenburg of the 23rd that, although they were probably not submitted to the Kaiser, my letters of the 14th and 18th were for the most part turned to account in dealing with H.M. and that they did some good. The crisis is over, and therefore I am sending you the text of those letters to-day for your retrospective information. The cold factual objectivity of the style, which will perhaps at first reading surprise you, was adopted by me as precisely the most effective means of producing an impression, and I now believe that it proved its value. That the tone of unconcern was for outward appearances only can be seen by the fact that at the beginning of the crisis I wrote at once—not to Eulenburg but to Bülow—that in case Prince Hohenlohe and Marschall should resign over the present conflict, I would resign with them.

What can one call the temperamental remarks that have reached us here from the *Hohenzollern* in regard to the Lippe case, Bronsart, Marschall, and the fleet programme? 'Hysterical moods' is perhaps the appropriate description. As a physiological [*sic*] observer the Prince will long ago have known that such moods can *only* be handled with quiet firmness.

The only conceivable concession in the penal reform question would in my opinion be if the Prince expressed himself ready to let Bronsart go *after* the Kaiser had expressed his agreement *in writing* to accept a reasonable penal reform. But of what use is this concession to the Prince? For behind the relatively unimportant penal reform, which has been blown up artificially by Hahnke and his friends, there towers the enormous budget for the limitless fleet programme which the Kaiser told Philipp Eulenburg barely a fortnight ago would never be abandoned. I do not take this 'never' too seriously, no more so than the 'never' that was previously hurled against the two-year military service. The Kaiser is simply trying to see how far he can go. The important role played to-day by Prince Hohenlohe is embarrassing and must therefore be diminished. This diminution will take place as soon as the Prince departs from the standpoint of his latest parliamentary declaration and *coram publico* capitulates to the 'entourage'. From that day onwards Prince Hohenlohe will cease to represent anything firm and definite, and from that day onwards the Kaiser can get rid of him without fearing public indignation. The explanation for his resignation that 'the old gentleman is no longer capable of conducting affairs'—an explanation for which the Press of the Fronde is already trying to prepare the public —would *then* be accepted by public opinion, even though reluctantly; *to-day it would not be.* In a word—*the Prince risks far less both for his historical as for his official reputation if he declares 'here I stand, I can do no other, I have made as many concessions as I could', than if he risks descending still further down the slippery slope of appeasement.* The more decisively he talks to H.M., the more cautious H.M. will be.

All unbalanced persons are like that!

With kindest regards H.

I regret the intimidatory role which P.E. has played in recent days. Perhaps he had in mind the role of Puss in Boots. A fairy-tale, however, is out of place in world history.

573. Holstein to Karl von Lindenau

Copy

Berlin, 29 July 1896

Dear Lindenau,

Czapski to-day sent me a letter to the Chancellor[1] which you must know about, according to the cover-letter which I enclose.[2] It appears from this that word was sent out from the *Hohenzollern* that the premature return was for the purpose of settling the Bronsart affair. The object of this move was twofold: to spread alarm in advance about the deadly seriousness of the Imperial intentions, and to conceal the *true* reason for that return. Therefore despite this announcement and despite Philipp Eulenburg's journey to the Chancellor, I am for the time being holding to my opinion that the crisis is not acute. Eulenburg's journey even affords a good diplomatic opportunity which the Chancellor should not fail to exploit. Ph. E. has a holy terror that his name will be connected with Chancellor and Ministerial crises. He has recently— very recently—repeatedly stated this verbally and in writing, and if there should be any serious question of Prince Hohenlohe's departure he will certainly try to arrange the matter so that six to eight—or even a mere four—weeks go by before the catastrophe actually occurs. In view of P.E.'s frame of mind it is up to the Chancellor *de brusquer les choses*. I think it might be done in this way: after their first greeting the Chancellor asks laughingly: 'Well, so you are bringing me the silken cord.' P.E. swears the contrary, protests the Kaiser's good intentions as well as his own. The Chancellor thereupon says quietly and earnestly: 'Yes. But I must tell you that if you are instructed to inform me that my remaining in office depends upon the introduction of a Military Penal Code Bill excluding public procedure, I would regard this a *consilium abeundi* and my resignation would go from Alt-Aussee to H.M. at the same time as yourself.' I am convinced that P.E.'s fear of his own person

[1] Not found.   [2] Not printed.

being involved is the sole, but also effective, means the Chancellor has of bringing P.E. over to his side and of making him the advocate of his views with the Kaiser. This of course only applies if E. has reason to fear an *immediate* crisis. He would regard a crisis next month with cold objectivity.

This plan of action accords with my view that P.E.'s journey to Aussee is more useful to the Chancellor than a less noticeable meeting somewhere else or even in Berlin. P.E. knows that when he travels to Aussee to the Chancellor directly after the Norwegian trip he will have the eyes of all Germany upon him. It would therefore not surprise me if the proposal for a meeting elsewhere than in Aussee had been raised by P.E. himself, because in these matters he is as clever as a person [*sic*]. I repeat my urgent advice that in case Prince Hohenlohe has already made some other arrangement with P.E. that he send him a telegram saying he is sorry, but on account of indisposition, great heat, etc.—a reason can always be found if one wants one—he has to ask P.E. to come to Aussee.

Another question to be considered is whether the Chancellor should telegraph to His Majesty to Wilhelmshöhe—it would be too late for Kiel—to the effect that he requested His Majesty to postpone sending Count P.E. until His Majesty had read a letter from the Chancellor that was already on its way. I enclose the outline of the main points of such a letter merely to show what I have in mind and not to relieve His Highness of a stylistic performance in which, as I have long known, he is a master.[1]

I am confident that by taking this course—telegram and letter, instead of a discussion with P.E.—the Kaiser will get the impression that the Chancellor is in earnest and that he cannot be bluffed. On the other hand, however, after prolonged reflection I still incline to the opinion that the pressure that can be brought to bear on P.E., and through him in turn on H.M. as soon as P.E. sees that he will inevitably be identified with the present Chancellor crisis, is a trump that one should not leave unplayed. I therefore think that the right thing to do would be to receive P.E. in *Aussee* and then after the discussion to send a letter in the indicated sense to the Kaiser as a *résumé* of the discussion in order to define His Highness' standpoint. This should be done because I am doubtful whether P.E. on his own initiative would ever inform the Kaiser of the idea of using him, P.E., for an exploratory mission to the three Courts which would have little prospect of success. The following ideas could in my opinion also be effectively used in the discussion with P.E.

'The Kaiser's primary prerequisite for great accomplishments, especially in *domestic affairs*, is the confidence of the broad masses of the people. The Germans being as they are, he can only win this confidence by a composed and dignified behaviour. His great restlessness, which as Count P.E. knows better than anyone, is supposed to be occasioned chiefly by mental instability, has for years made the Kaiser

[1] See Enclosure.

an object of mistrust among all German philistines and among other circles as well. Some four or five years ago, in discussing the case of Kaiser Friedrich, the well-known specialist for diseases of the larynx, Dr Semon of London, described the restlessness of the present Kaiser as the precisely definable first stage of a psychiatric condition, but one which in the beginning should be considered and treated from the physiological rather than from the psychological standpoint. The statement was made to an outstanding German specialist and is authentic. Four or five years ago and even later the question caused much anxiety because people were reminded of Kaiser Friedrich on the one hand, and of Kaiser Wilhelm's ear trouble on the other. It was only when year after year went by without any reappearance of the ear trouble that people were reassured, but not wholly, especially in South Germany. Count E. knows that better than anybody. If at this moment a change of Chancellors were to take place for a reason like the one which has gradually been made to seem plausible to the Kaiser by certain persons in his entourage, but which would not be understood by the country at large, then perhaps the question would again arise: "Isn't there perhaps something pathological about all this?" This is something Count E. should think over. The Kaiser's superb state of health happily affords the best refutation of such suspicions and prevents them from becoming firmly rooted; but even so, if they only brush the surface of people's minds they paralyse in a marked manner that aspect of the Kaiser's power that is built up on the confidence of the people. Nothing should therefore be recommended more urgently to those who have influence on the Kaiser than that they devote themselves to guarding the Kaiser from actions and pronouncements which tend to undermine his position more or less slowly, but nonetheless surely, because they make him appear to the people as *indiscreet* and *restless*.'

In short, the Chancellor should indicate to Count E. as His Majesty's confidant that a sick Kaiser must be more circumspect than a healthy one, since otherwise *the idea of placing him under guardianship* would be mooted in some corner of the Reich at the first opportunity, and the thought would never die out. The Prince will not be able to say this *crûment*, if only because P.E. *allegedly* knows nothing about the Kaiser's illness. I myself believe that H.M. will have told P.E. about it and therefore the Prince's broad hints will make P.E. think about this matter and open a new line of thought.

If P.E. should confidentially inform the Chancellor of the illness in the course of conversation, the latter would then be in a position to point out frankly and unequivocally that the rule of the Kaiser, both with regard to the German Princes and the German people, would be made much more difficult if the existence of this illness became known, and that this should be a warning to the Kaiser to be careful.

Prince Hohenlohe is the only man who as Chancellor can say this, because people know that he neither clings to office nor exploits it to satisfy a love of power. No one is so free from suspicion as he. The task of using this advantage for the good of the Fatherland in the present critical moment by speaking frankly and freely is one that I permit myself to designate as a duty of the Prince.

ENCLOSURE

When I stated in the Reichstag that the Military Courts-Martial Bill would accord with modern ideas, the German people as well as I myself believed that this moderate statement did not conflict with the intentions of Your Majesty. If therefore a Bill providing for restricted public procedure is submitted to the Reichstag in the autumn, the public will simply regard this as a confirmation of the Imperial will.

If on the other hand it becomes known that Your Majesty has decided not to agree to public procedure, this would immediately make it impossible for me to remain any longer in office. As the faithful servant of Your Majesty, however, I have the task of drawing the Imperial attention to the consequences which my departure would have under the present circumstances. Even if I used some indifferent matter as the motive for my resignation, public opinion would regard the military courts-martial question and the so-called great fleet programme as the real reason. I believe that a conflict between Your Majesty and the Reichstag would then be inevitable, and must unfortunately add that this would begin under the worst possible conditions for Your Majesty. Should Your Majesty nevertheless be determined to take this path, I would urgently advise that a binding agreement be reached *ad hoc* with the three German Kingdoms by which they would engage themselves to stand by Your Majesty until the end of this conflict. I would regard Ambassador Count Eulenburg as the most suitable person to arrange this agreement. For, apart from his personal qualities, there is hardly anyone who is more familiar with the intentions of Your Majesty.

Until this treaty with the three Kingdoms is concluded—I will not mention the Grand Duke of Baden, because despite occasional misunderstandings he would always stand by Your Majesty in the critical moment—I would regard the initiation of a conflict with the Reichstag as disastrous for the power and prestige of Your Majesty, and can therefore not avoid submitting my humble advice to Your Majesty that for the present you desist from those plans that would perforce compel me to abandon my responsible office.

574. Karl von Lindenau to Holstein

Alt-Aussee, 31 July 1896

Dear Herr von Holstein,

Your last two gratefully received consignments—the letter with four enclosures[1] (Eulenburg's letter of the 23rd and three letters to Eu. of the 14th and 18th), and your long letter[2] which arrived via the next courier with the draft of a letter to H.M. and two letters from Czapski,—are still on the Prince's desk, where they are undoubtedly making their

[1] Of 27 July. See above.   [2] Of 29 July. See above.

influence felt because he looks at the letters *every day*. Especially what you wrote about Eulenburg's reluctance to be connected with a ministerial crisis at once greatly appealed to His Highness. He is completely of your opinion that he should not neglect the opportunity that this offers him and is constantly trying to find a way in which he can best take advantage of it. I have no doubt that he will succeed in impressing Eulenburg in the manner you advise.

The consignment of the 30th which has just arrived—including Eulenburg's letters of the 26th[1] (with enclosure) and a memorandum about Kayser[2]—I will submit to the Chancellor tomorrow morning, Saturday, and will simply record my thanks at this time.

Eu. telegraphed that he would arrive here on Monday afternoon around six o'clock.

How completely the views of the *Princess* accord with your own you will see from the following two remarks which the Prince communicated to me *in confidence* and which I would specifically like to ask you not to repeat to others, at least not *verbatim*—naturally with the exception of Herr von Rotenhan and possibly others of the inner circle—namely:

(1) 'You shouldn't allow yourself to be *discredited* by the *caprices* of the Emperor,' and

(2) (with reference to the question of a possible resignation, even if only for future consideration): 'You must not simply resign, you must make him *dismiss* you.'[3]

With kindest regards
Your devoted
Lindenau

575. Holstein to Karl von Lindenau

Copy

Berlin, 1 August 1896

Dear Lindenau,

[...] This letter will reach you shortly before the arrival of Ph. E[ulenburg]. I have nothing new to say about *this* portentous conversation, but would like to summarise in a few sentences what I have already said:

In my opinion P.E. and perhaps H.M. too would like to use intimidation but neither wants a blow-up. This is also indicated by the effort that is being made to suppress the silly statements which H.M. may have made about Bronsart.

I do not believe, therefore, that the Chancellor will risk much if he stands firm; on the contrary, I believe that he will be acting correctly if he shows he is conscious of being in a sound position. I would be dubious about whether to stand firm or to make concessions if we were dealing with a single isolated question. But this is precisely not the case. If the Chancellor shows through the military courts-martial question

---

[1] See above. Only one letter by Eulenburg of 26 July has been found. [2] Not found.
[3] Both statements of Princess Hohenlohe are in French in the original.

that *in the end* he will give way to constant pressure, he will be laying the basis for an insupportable future during the remainder of his tenure of office, because he will then be under constant pressure over the fleet question. He will make the move easy for himself if he says now: 'I cannot depart from the statement I made in the Reichstag.' If I were the Chancellor, I would not sacrifice the Minister of War either.

In P.E.'s memorandum for the Kaiser, of which I sent you a copy the day before yesterday, there is no mention whatever that *P.E.* intends to sound out the three courts of Dresden, Munich, and Stuttgart— which was to have been expected. If may therefore be assumed that this task, which can only end with a *reductio ad absurdum*, is to be assigned to the Chancellor, or rather the Foreign Ministry. Of course His Highness would have to refuse *avec la dernière énergie*, with the thoroughly logical reason that this sounding-out could only be undertaken by someone in whose skill and zeal the Kaiser had the same kind of confidence as he had in Eulenburg. In case the effort led to totally or partially unfavourable results, a possibility that must after all be reckoned with, the Kaiser must at all events be convinced that nothing had been wanting so far as the negotiator was concerned and that everything possible had been done. In no one, however, would H.M. have the same degree of confidence that he felt in Eulenburg. In addition, it would be better to have this mission undertaken by a distinguished visitor on holiday rather than by an officially accredited emissary. In my opinion these two arguments are irrefutable.

I still think it would be useful if the Chancellor were to write the Kaiser a letter after his conversation with P.E. in which that conversation was summarised, especially the point of view of His Highness.

The illness of the Kaiser, by its injurious effect on the imperial power, makes the process of governing more difficult both for himself and for the Chancellor. No matter how hard one tries to suppress the significance of the symptoms of illness—surely no one can believe that this can be kept quiet indefinitely—the news that the illness has reappeared after lying quiescent for several years will make a profound impression, even though the German Press observes the greatest reserve. Throughout the Reich there will be a general feeling of uncertainty, which may lead to disintegration and revolution if it is allowed to develop. In view of all this the Chancellor believes it to be his duty to tell the Kaiser with absolute firmness:

not: 'I will resign as soon as I have in some way incurred the displeasure of Your Maj.';

but: '*I regard it as my duty towards Your Majesty and towards the Fatherland to remain at my post, but under conditions that correspond to the interests of the Monarchy, namely that I remain at the head of a Cabinet capable of dealing with the problems brought before it in the interests of the Crown and the country. If H.M. wishes otherwise he must specifically dismiss me.*'

And with that, to stand firm, to concede *nothing*. To state this point of view unreservedly in the letter to H.M. as well. He will *not* give

Prince Chlodwig Hohenlohe his walking papers on account of the Military Courts-Martial Bill.

> Now, from the heart,
> Tally ho!
> Holstein.

576. Philipp zu Eulenburg to Holstein

TELEGRAM

Alt-Aussee, 4 August 1896, 12:00 noon
Arrival: 2:25 p.m.

Private. *Top Secret*

Situation is very serious. Kaiser definitely intends to introduce military courts-martial reform and to put it into operation in Prussia if the Bundesrat or Reichstag reject it. Public procedure remains *irrevocably* excluded, however. If Chancellor agrees to this, Marschall stays. If Chancellor refuses to agree, the crisis will have begun. I succeeded in definitely eliminating Bernhard von Bülow's candidacy. A radical change in the system to be expected for certain. Count Waldersee, Botho Eulenburg, or Miquel as successors.

Urgently request that you advise Chancellor to agree IMMEDIATELY in view of dangers involved. Refusal of public procedure is *matter of honour* for H.M. Reform on basis of modern principles will *nevertheless* remain.

If Prince Hohenlohe stays, I too will make the personal sacrifice and come to Berlin in the post previously discussed.[1]

Letter follows.

Eulenburg[2]

577. Holstein to Philipp zu Eulenburg

DRAFT TELEGRAM

Berlin, 4 August 1896, 4:30 p.m.

Private

If, as I see from your telegram, Prince Hohenlohe does not believe it possible honourably to renounce public procedure in the military courts-martial *altogether*, I am not in a position to persuade him to do so because on that he alone is competent.

I would not advise that you yourself now accept the position in Berlin. Your[3] connection with the present crisis would only increase the difficulties of the next regime, which will in any case end in short order in defeat for itself and for the Crown.

Among the candidates for the Chancellorship, Waldersee is perhaps the only one who might be able to survive.

---

[1] In his talk with Hohenlohe in Alt-Aussee, Eulenburg mentioned his willingness to accept the post of Minister of the Royal Household. (See Hohenlohe, *Denkwürdigkeiten der Reichskanzlerzeit*, pp. 253–4.)

[2] At 5 p.m. on 4 August Holstein telegraphed to Lindenau: 'Private. Suggest informing me about situation there to rectify other information.'

[3] At this point in his draft Holstein crossed out the words 'most deplorable'.

The entire present turmoil gives the impression of unstrung nerves. Things will hardly go on much longer like that.

Holstein.

578. Holstein to Paul von Hatzfeldt
Copy

Berlin, 4 August 1896

Dear friend,

Your interesting letters deserve a more detailed answer than they are receiving at present.[1] That does not depend on us, however, but on the attitude of H.M. who, according to a private communication from Kiderlen,[2] stated frankly a few days ago that he would let a crisis in the Near East take its course if it should develop, and would not even do anything to prevent it. Kiderlen, who as an old specialist in the Near East would surely have been able to point out the dangers to the general peace which such a crisis would entail, apparently did not want to burn his fingers but instead observed a diplomatic silence and turned to us with the request for arguments to refute H.M.

I cannot say that this news astonished me. H.M., who was most incensed with the Sultan because of the Armenian horrors and through Saurma's reports, has been wondering ever since the Cretan crisis began how to bring about the union of Crete and Greece. Furthermore, some Princes returning from Moscow told H.M. that Tsar Nicholas had told the Crown Prince of Greece: 'If you want to take it (Crete), I have no objections.'

The report to the Kaiser in which we requested imperial approval for our participation in the blockade was therefore very carefully worded to prevent an imperial refusal.[3] Since we could expect that H.M. would as usual not want to send a ship, the report spoke only of 'consent to', not 'participation in' the blockade. It turned out as we had expected. H.M. agreed to the 'consent' but had no ship available.[4]

Now that England has for her part rejected the blockade idea,[5] it is useless to raise the question with H.M. of participating in a blockade of Crete by the Continental Powers. Nor do I think that Goluchowski will carry on with his proposal contrary to the intentions of England. For the time being he is still trying to persuade the English to agree to the blockade if the Powers join in offering the Cretans all sorts of guarantees and perhaps even their autonomy.[6] I would not advise you, dear friend, to take any further part in these steps of the Austrians. Salisbury has obviously *son siège tout fait*. Lascelles informed us here yesterday after

---

[1] Apart from Hatzfeldt's letter to Holstein of 25 July (see above), no other letters from Hatzfeldt on foreign policy during this period were found in the Holstein Papers. On 22 July Hatzfeldt had commented on Holstein's efforts in the domestic crisis.
[2] Not found.
[3] Report of 27 July. (*Grosse Politik*, vol. XIIi, no. 3035, pp. 183–4.)
[4] See *Grosse Politik*, vol. XIIi, no. 3037, p. 187.
[5] See *Grosse Politik*, vol. XIIi, nos. 3040–1, pp. 189–91.
[6] See *Grosse Politik*, vol. XIIi, no. 3044, pp. 192–3.

receiving a telegraphic instruction that Salisbury must have been misunderstood if we had ever assumed that England would participate in a blockade. Rotenhan did not make an official note of this statement because we have meanwhile been sufficiently informed about England's attitude. This, however, would make it appear that Goluchowski's efforts to change England's mind will be in vain.

When Salisbury brought up the idea of giving Italy some mandate,[1] he was probably thinking less of a simple coastal defence than of the actual establishment of the Italians in Crete. That would have left only Albania to shut up the clamour of the Greeks of the Kingdom; in short, it was the old partition scheme of last year with slight variations. And precisely in this I see the danger for the European position: among the Great Powers there is one that wants war as such, that is a continental war, in order in the meanwhile to establish herself comfortably in Egypt and South Africa. The best way to have met this danger would surely have been to have restored the status quo in Crete, perhaps with certain new guarantees. This possibility is probably out of the question now, because not only England but also Russia and Germany—for dynastic reasons—are opposed to it and the Greeks of course have long known how the wind is blowing.

Next to maintaining an improved status quo, the least dangerous thing to do from the point of view of the peace of Europe would probably be the assignment of Crete to Greece, as you already recently mentioned.[2] Even after the addition of Crete, Greece would still be so small that every European Great Power would, I should think, be ashamed to demand compensation for itself on this account. So the danger probably does not lie in the lusts of the Great Powers but in the effect which this first amputation would have on the Bulgars, Serbs, and Armenians, behind whom there would presumably be English agitators and English money.

At any rate *we* should *not* make this proposal for handing over Crete to Greece, at least not officially, for three reasons:

because of the moral responsibility for the doubtful final outcome;

because of the dynastic relationship, which would give occasion to cast an unfavourable light on our operations; and

because of the German creditors of Greece, who would raise a tremendous howl in the Press if we did the Greeks such an enormous favour gratuitously, that is, in such a way that there would be nothing in it for the creditors.

Or do you think it possible that one could get something for the creditors out of it?

So for the time being it seems to me that our role should be to stay completely in the background as long as there is no unity between the Continental Powers and England. Meanwhile you of course know the

---

[1] See Hatzfeldt's dispatch about his conversation with Salisbury on 24 July. (*Grosse Politik*, vol. XIIi, no. 3036, pp. 184–7.)

[2] In a private telegram to Holstein of 18 July. (*Grosse Politik*, vol. XIIi, no. 3032, pp. 180–1.)

significance the Wilhelmstrasse attaches to your views. So if you are of a different opinion, please say so.[1]

579. Chlodwig zu Hohenlohe to Holstein[2]

Alt-Aussee, 5 August 1896

My dear Baron,

Well, Philipp Eulenburg was here and left again to-day.[3] Although I will be in Berlin in a few days, I nevertheless want to tell you something about our conversations via the courier who leaves tomorrow morning. After we had met I immediately tried to obtain clarification about the prevalent trends of thought in Wilhelmshöhe by saying: 'So you bring me the silken cord.' But instead of protestingly dismissing my remark he said: 'I would not exactly say that.' The situation was then clear to me. They had in fact snugly discussed the question of a successor in Wilhelmshöhe. Waldersee, Miquel, Botho Eulenburg, but *not* B. von Bülow, were mentioned. H.M. will leave him out of consideration because the regime which follows mine will only end in failure and they would rather not waste Bülow. Since the Kaiser does not seriously believe that I would give way, and since he will not give way, the given result is a change of Chancellors. And H.M. wants to settle that before the next session of the Reichstag.

I have provisionally told Eulenburg I would see whether a way out could still be found and would remain as long as H.M. did not dismiss me. The idea that an understanding could be reached between H.M. and myself by making the Minister of War an acting Aide-de-Camp, and by introducing the courts-martial reform in Prussia if the Bundesrat failed to accept it because it did not include public procedure, was for me unacceptable since I must stand or fall on the question of public procedure.

Eulenburg—I think—wants me to stay on but only on the understanding that I bow to the imperial will. That I will not do.

With friendly greetings,
Yours very sincerely
CHohenlohe.

I have just received a telegram summoning me to Wilhelmshöhe.

580. Karl von Lindenau to Holstein

Alt-Aussee, 5 August 1896

Dear Holstein,

The Chancellor was at first *most painfully* disturbed by Eulenburg's

---

[1] Hatzfeldt replied in a private telegram of 7 August: 'Letter received and completely agree with your views. If the situation as depicted in Kiderlen's letter had been known earlier, it would probably have been advisable at the time to follow another course and we must now at all events adjust ourselves accordingly, that is, to remain aloof from everything about which all the Powers are not in agreement. At the same time we could, without making a proposal, let it be understood privately that we too would raise no objection to the cession [of Crete] to Greece if that were desired by everyone else.' (From the London Embassy files.)

[2] Printed in part in Hohenlohe, *Denkwürdigkeiten der Reichskanzlerzeit*, pp. 250–1.

[3] See *ibid.*, pp. 249–50; Haller, *Eulenburg*, p. 213.

manner here, and had already drawn up a letter in which he expressed to you his conviction that E., wholly of *his own* initiative, was now working directly *against* him and wanted to have him removed. His Highness subsequently moderated this opinion, which probably went too far, and is now I think perhaps going too far in the opposite direction —possibly because he does not want to acknowledge *how* much he was upset by Eulenburg at first. The Princess of course was unable to restrain herself from making some very sweeping remarks to Eulenburg, so that E. felt himself called upon to defend himself from the insinuation that *he* sought the Chancellorship. In short E. is *furious* with the Princess. His Highness had instructed me to accompany E. to-day on his return to the railway station (he himself called for him and if his impressions had been more favourable would certainly have accompanied him again to the station). I then told him, as the conversation turned in this direction, that it was after all entirely in the Kaiser's interest to retain the Chancellor. He at once replied, apparently quite sincerely: 'Yes. During these days here I have continually received long telegrams from the Kaiser which he himself put into cipher and which showed me how important this is to him.' I got the impression from this—from the tone of voice and otherwise—that E. went further or at least was inclined to go further than H.M. himself. In all this I was not able to judge whether E. was being deceived by the Kaiser in that the Kaiser made him think he wanted to act more vigorously than he really intended or whether E. was acting vigorously on his own initiative and had to be restrained by the Kaiser. In this connection your recent remark came vividly to my mind: that you now often no longer knew what was H.M. and what was Phil. Eul. Incidentally E. asked me to tell you that he left to-day more satisfied and more hopeful than he had thought possible yesterday, because the Prince told him to-day, very casually to be sure, that he hoped he had found a way out. As a precaution I arranged with His Highness—if I may use that expression— that the remark he made yesterday to E.: 'he hoped to find a way out or was trying to find one' was to be considered the *authentic* version, and not the remark 'he hoped (believed) that he *had* found it'; His Highness will therefore not acknowledge this last version.

The journey to Wilhelmshöhe is obviously something arranged by E. with H.M. If there is anybody *else* behind it, it could only be Czapski (Kassel).[1] E. did not say a word about the matter here (nor did he say anything about the contents of his yesterday's report to the Kaiser!)—but the Prince was in no doubt from the wording of the invitation that he must go, and that he must in fact go on the way to Berlin, not go to Berlin first, because he thinks the Kaiser's distrust would otherwise be too greatly aroused; besides he feels confident of not allowing anything to be extorted from him.

Since I will probably soon be seeing Prince Alexander, you will agree to my having refrained from returning many documents. I will

[1] Count Bogdan von Hutten-Czapski was squadron commander in the 14th Hussars at Kassel, 1886–96.

in any case probably be returning with the Chancellor to Berlin (since it does not now seem possible that I will be able to go on leave from Munich) and I will then give you many further details verbally. But I am counting DEFINITELY—*and in this I appeal specifically to you!*—that the Foreign Ministry will then allow me to take my this year's leave which has already been approved! The time spent here was not *in the least degree* a rest—in fact I need it more *urgently* than ever.

With kindest regards
Yours sincerely
Lindenau.

I just wrote in the same sense to Herr von Rotenhan.

581. Alfred von Kiderlen-Wächter to Philipp zu Eulenburg[1]
Copy

Wilhelmshöhe, 10 August 1896

Dear friend!

I am taking advantage of the courier you sent to H.M. to write you a few words. One doesn't get much opportunity to write here—despite all the idling! Court life simply takes up a lot of time!

You have probably been informed about the visit of the Chancellor and its result.[2] It is not a matter for rejoicing! Who will now take over the succession?

That Hohenlohe separated the personal and the factual issue and at once conceded the dismissal of the War Minister to H.M. without a crisis was in my opinion very correct. I only fear one thing in this connection, and that is that H.M. will think he is now clear of the factual issue as well. In that he would be deceiving himself very badly. Unfortunately he is strengthened in this opinion by Lucanus, for instance, and by other members of the entourage. I would not like to bear the responsibility for this! For Hohenlohe has after all stated *specifically* that in spite of Bronsart's departure he intended to wait for the opinion of the commanding generals; if they decide *in favour* of public procedure and this is *put into practice* he will remain. Otherwise he will *go*. He said that clearly and plainly, and now Lucanus says the question must be immaterial to the Chancellor since it is 'military', and that he will stay on under all circumstances; such a thing is really incomprehensible! Of course that will once again give H.M. quite wrong ideas, and if Hohenlohe leaves after the absolutely predictable decision of the generals, H.M. will be in a far more embarrassing position than if he were informed now about the possibility of Hohenlohe's departure. I see no possibility of his staying on. The result of the *commissioned* work of the generals is obvious! You need only think of the way the question was put.

---

[1] In a letter to Holstein of 10 August Kiderlen wrote: 'Enclosed is a copy of a letter to Phili; you will observe that it does not express my innermost thoughts but is calculated to appeal to Phili's feelings [Gemüt].'
[2] See Hohenlohe, *Denkwürdigkeiten der Reichskanzlerzeit*, pp. 251–2.

'A bill has been submitted to me concerning a reform of the courts-martial procedure. It contains

'(1) Oral proceedings.
'(2) Independent courts.
'(3) Separation of prosecution and defense.
'(4) No public proceedings.

'*I am inclined to accept this draft.*'

And then a request for an independent judgment!!!

That is after all absolutely ludicrous.

If this farce isn't changed, the reply of the generals will be certain and therewith Hohenlohe's resignation as well.

I don't regret the departure of the War Minister in itself, only that of course only made the situation more pointed. For precisely at this time Hohenlohe cannot allow it to be said that Bronsart stood or fell by his convictions, and that the Chancellor sacrificed them.

The idea (probably Hahnke's?) to make Bronsart an Aide-de-Camp is really very naive!

Surely that would deceive no one about the real situation! One should never believe that others are so very stupid.

Much will depend on who becomes Bronsart's successor; the best would probably be Bülow[1] who would stand by the Chancellor and be able to act as go-between. But Hahnke doesn't want him *merely* because he is afraid people might say that he had pushed out Bronsart in order to put his brother-in-law in his place! To such personal considerations the interests of the Kaiser and the state are sacrificed! The storm will at all events be a fine one. The *Berliner Neuesten Nachrichten* has already provided a foretaste. Hohenlohe could not remain without Bronsart, who is the 'staunchest' Minister against Social Democracy! Your 'mission' to Aussee is also being kindly commemorated.

Well, we can't do anything about it—so *tant pis*. I assume that despite an unfortunate experience we will get a military Chancellor; a civilian would be unable to defend the denial of public procedure without very quickly making a fiasco of it. But who is it to be?

My kind regards
Kiderlen

582. Holstein to Alfred von Kiderlen-Wächter

Copy

Berlin, 13 August 1896

Dear Kiderlen,

I have to justify a long silence, and can only do so with the truthful statement that gradually I am no longer able to tell the difference between my right hand and my left. That is, what is means and what is end, who is the driver and who is being driven. The Chancellor declares that he can't do anything else, that he is holding firmly to public procedure 'in principle'. In reality, after his last far-reaching mediation

---

[1] Adolf von Bülow. Aide-de-Camp to the Kaiser.

proposal (whereby the presiding magistrate of the court is empowered on every occasion to exclude the public if he considers this desirable) so little remains of the principle that this little remainder cannot be made the reason for a Chancellor crisis and would at most be an excuse. And so I ask myself the question: what is the *real* reason? This summer Senden said in England, as I am reliably informed, that the great fleet programme must be pushed through and that the Kaiser intended to push it through. Hohenlohe, however, was too old for this sort of thing, and therefore the Kaiser was often talking about bringing in new blood. Senden's hearers thought this referred to Bernhard Bülow; he, however, if I can consider his words as the expression of his thoughts, regards the present situation and even more the immediate future with such intensive distrust that his reluctance to take a position in Berlin will be almost impossible to overcome.

There are people here who think that August Eulenburg is working secretly but with the greatest determination to bring about a crisis. And in fact I hardly think that Philipp would have taken the position he does to-day—or which he at any rate held a few days ago—without the constant pressure of kindred spirits. When he first told me about the possibility of a crisis—only an account of the military courts-martial, of course, and without even alluding to the fleet idea—I wrote him quite objectively and impersonally the same thing you did, namely that the Kaiser, if he removed Hohenlohe and thus intended to consider the use of force as a possible means of government, would first have to secure the adherence of the three German Kingdoms in binding form for the full duration of the conflict.[1] Then he would at least have a *chance* to get out of the business unscathed; without this precondition he would have no prospect of a satisfactory result because the three monarchs would leave him in the lurch the moment he was well bogged down.

This idea was surely simple enough; how little it was understood, however, can be seen from the fact that when the Chancellor was in Wilhelmshöhe he was told that in the event of a Chancellor-crisis they would sound out Dresden, Munich and Stuttgart *immediately* afterwards! Precisely *then* it would be too late, because as things stand now Hohenlohe's successor would be suspected of being the tool of the imperial entourage, and would therefore, especially if he then championed the views of the entourage concerning the military courts-martial and the fleet programme, have the Reichstag irretrievably against him. If the three Kingdoms were not firmly committed to vote for the tenth as well as for the first dissolution of the Reichstag, they would place themselves on the 'side of the Constitution' as soon as things began to ferment in their own countries, and the Kaiser would experience a political Jena —unless he wanted to repeat the drama of 1866 with Russia and France in the wings. This danger is very close, but they *refuse* to see it; it is that that leaves me bewildered. As I said, I am utterly confused.

The day after tomorrow, or Sunday at the latest, I am going on leave and will travel about a little without a fixed address. If something big

---

[1] See above, Holstein's letter to Eulenburg of 14 July 1896.

happens in the meantime, I will after all hear about it through the Press.
With kindest regards
Yours
Holstein.

583. Holstein to Philipp zu Eulenburg[1]
Copy

Berlin, 13 August 1896

Dear friend,

Enclosed I am sending you with best thanks everything I received from you s.p.r. I am tired and want to go into the hills for a few weeks to walk on familiar paths, and will therefore have no address for the time being. Further discussion of the situation between ourselves would serve no purpose, for you are pursuing your own course on which I can no longer find my way. I no longer see what is means and what is end, who is driver and who is being driven. What remains of the famous 'public procedure' after the last proposal of the Chancellor is really only a shadow and cannot be made a reason—can hardly be made an *excuse*—for a Chancellor crisis. The Chancellor himself seems to be of the opinion that it is perhaps not a matter of the public procedure at all. In Karlsbad General Werder is supposed to have told everyone who would listen that H.M. was being pressured by his entourage to eliminate Prince Hohenlohe.

I see only one thing clearly in this whole mess, namely that *you* are busily trying to increase the number and the bitterness of your enemies.

You will see from the enclosure[2] that the Bismarck Press considers the moment favourable for a row precisely because the Kaiser would thereby be placed in the type of dangerous dilemma from which *we* have tried to preserve him for six years! The enclosed article is already the third which states that the crisis is unavoidable. The *Berliner Neuesten Nachrichten* seized on another aspect of the situation by being the first to publish the news of your journey to Aussee. Shared roles. Farewell.

In old friendship
Holstein

584. Philipp zu Eulenburg to Holstein

Hubertusstock, 6 October 1896

Dear friend,

My *warmest* thanks for your kind letter!

You wrote to me in the tone that is the foundation of our understanding—that which has been our bond through all political storms and always will be.

I will never lose the man and the friend in you, though I may lose the politician for days or weeks; even then it is always through some misunderstanding! Because a single conversation will always bring us back together again!

[1] Published in part in Haller, *Eulenburg*, p. 214.   [2] Not found.

I am *much* looking forward to seeing you soon again. Presumably in about a week. Here things are going very well with respect to the Chancellor and Marschall. Yesterday I had a very serious discussion with Lucanus. We will get through the winter all right. I am not troubling myself to look further. We will simply have to do our best to remove combustible material. [...]

I saw Bernhard B[ülow] several times in Austria. He is a faithful friend of yours, and you would have enjoyed being with us doing some mountain climbing together.

You have such a delicate instinct: I think your inner self will acknowledge that I am right when I tell you how glad we would have been to have had you with us!

Your faithful old
PEulenburg.

585. Philipp zu Eulenburg to Holstein

Liebenberg, 21 October 1896

Dear friend,

[...] From your kind letter of yesterday it appears that you believe in a *desire* on my part to come to Berlin. Oh no, dear friend! May God preserve me from all the storms I would have to weather—and from all the additional troubles this would bring into my life! I only showed a certain interest in Hohenlohe—last summer.[1] Because at that time I was convinced that he needed me and I wanted to help him. You know me well enough to realise that I place personal considerations in the background. But now I think that all is going well for the Prince—and therefore I have exhibited less interest and have also honestly said that I would *prefer* to stay in Vienna. So if you are well-disposed towards me, please simply leave me there. [...]

If it suits you I will appear at 12:30 on the 23rd, and would be glad to lunch with you somewhere *tête-à-tête*.

I have a *great deal* to tell you.

Your faithful old
PE [...]

586. Holstein to Philipp zu Eulenburg[2]

Berlin, 24 November 1896

Dear friend,

I did not really intend to bother you about what seems to be happening here. But with your last friendly lines before me I would have to regard it as a poor reply to your faithful and comradely sentiments if I did not keep you informed at a time like the present.

The barometer indicates an approaching storm. The public suspects nothing simply because the causes which public opinion would regard as justifying a Chancellor crisis are not present. On the contrary, on the

---

[1] See above, p. 672, note 1.
[2] From the papers of Baroness von der Heydt. Only a typewritten copy of this document was available to the editors.

terribly difficult interpellation of Hompesch[1] in the Reichstag Hohenlohe and Marschall have achieved a success which, according to the unanimous opinion of the Press both at home and abroad, has given the Government a stronger position in the country and Parliament than at any time since the spring of 1890.[2]

The quarter where the storm is brewing—you probably have a presentiment of it—is the New Palace. People are agitating around the Kaiser as never before. It is the same old agitation which began with Köller's dismissal and is based on the contention that Marschall, i.e. the Foreign Ministry, brought about the fall of that most incapable of all Ministers of the Interior by Press intrigues. But when Marschall two months ago, whether by a lucky chance or more probably as the result of the increasing impudence of his opponents, got on the track of that conspiracy in the Press of which Herr von Tausch formed the focal point, and when he took the matter to court, the previous leaders of the Fronde movement obviously believed that the time had come to put a quick end to the present regime at any price, because the said Tausch, who in all probability was the centre for carrying out all the plots spun out against the New Course during the past six years, could not be allowed to fall without exposing people to the danger that he might 'talk'.[3]

So the Kaiser was informed that the co-defendent *Strassburger Zeitung* was the only newspaper which had taken a stand against the articles inspired by the 'parallel government', in other words, which had championed the imperial prerogatives. The Kaiser actually expressed these views in very strong marginal comments and may well have thought that criminal proceedings had thereby been avoided. But since the false report which started the legal proceedings was a serious insult to Marschall's honour—*he* is supposed to have named August Eulenburg

[1] Alfred, Count von Hompesch-Rurich. Member of the Reichstag (Centre Party).

[2] On 24 October the *Hamburger Nachrichten*, a Bismarck newspaper, revealed the existence of the secret treaty of 18 June 1887 (the German Reinsurance Treaty with Russia). On 16 November Hompesch asked in the Reichstag whether such a treaty had existed, why it had not been renewed and what effect the revelation would have on Germany's international position. Hohenlohe and Marschall replied on the same day. Marschall evaded a detailed reply to the interpellation by pleading that he could not reveal diplomatic secrets. He defended German diplomacy before 1890 against the accusation of duplicity and German diplomacy after 1890 against the charge of having abandoned valuable guarantees of security. (*Stenographische Berichte über die Verhandlungen des Reichstags*, 1895–97, vol. V, pp. 3262 et seq.)

[3] In September 1896 the Tsar visited Breslau to attend the Grand Manoeuvres. At a dinner on 5 September the Tsar replied to a toast of friendship proposed by the Kaiser by saying that he had the same feelings '*que votre Majesté*'. A reporter for the Wolff news agency reported the Tsar as saying: '*que feu mon père*' (i.e. the notoriously anti-German Alexander III), and this version appeared in several newspapers before the correct official report came to hand. On 28 September a newly-founded journal, *Die Welt am Montag*, published an article which ascribed the false report to English influences and to Count August zu Eulenburg. In reply to a *dementi* by the Wolff Bureau, a further article was published on 4 October which virtually named Marschall as the source of this information. Marschall thereupon instructed the Public Prosecutor to institute legal proceedings against *Die Welt am Montag* for libel. At the public trial in December 1896 the author of the article was discovered to be a nineteen-year-old journalist named Leckert, but it was also revealed that behind Leckert stood a certain Lützow, a police agent, and that behind Lützow was Tausch, a Chief Inspector of the Berlin police. (See Hohenlohe, *Denkwürdigkeiten der Reichskanzlerzeit*, pp. 269, 286–8.)

as the originator of that falsified account of the Tsar's toast and to have broadcast this information to the world—it was quite impossible for Marschall or for the Government to drop the case. In case of possible accidents, Marschall has even instituted private criminal proceedings on his own behalf in addition to the proceedings instituted by the Chancellor because, as he says, one cannot back down on affairs of honour.

I don't know what details the preliminary investigation has brought to light. I have only heard that Tausch will be exposed; he is said to have a presentiment of this and to be absolutely beside himself. He is of course playing every trump against his former employers to make them use their influence with the Kaiser in the only way that can do him any good, i.e., to quash the criminal proceedings or overthrow the Government. Among those who 'work' particularly regularly with Tausch is Waldersee.[1] It can therefore be assumed that he will use his entire and very considerable skill to persuade the Kaiser, when the latter spends the entire afternoon with him tomorrow, to 'defend his rights energetically', i.e., to remove Hohenlohe and Marschall.

Another weapon being used against Hohenlohe is the incompetence of the present Minister of War.[2] The latter, to be sure, was selected against the Chancellor rather than by him, but Hohenlohe had already discovered that the Aides-de-Camp are abusing him like a lot of sparrows for failing to make good the incompetence and military ignorance of the War Minister in the Reichstag.

The ultimate intentions of His Majesty can be seen from the following: On Thursday the Minister of War came to the Reichstag and said first to Bötticher and then to Prince Hohenlohe that he, Gossler, had received an order from H.M. to bring about a conflict with the Reichstag. Gossler said the same thing in confidence to Count Mirbach,[3] who replied, horrified: 'You won't have a single member of our Party behind you if you do.' Mirbach, who probably hates us all *tutti quanti*, naturally didn't say this out of friendship for the Government but because he knows that a conflict, or rather a dissolution, would under the present circumstances lead to quite terrible new elections. Gossler then informed the Chancellor that out of consideration for his wishes he would not deliver a provocative speech. I suspect, however, that Mirbach's statement had most to do with this decision.

There are several indications, about which I can say nothing more definite, that make me suspect—and not me alone—that strong influences are at work on the Kaiser to make Botho Eulenburg Chancellor. Radowitz and Raschdau would then probably come into consideration as State Secretary and Under State Secretary. The conduct of the latter towards the present Chancellor is that of a man who knows he has support. I can't prove it, but it is nevertheless plausible to connect the recently much-discussed audience of Bronsart with the Kaiser with the

[1] See Waldersee, *Denkwürdigkeiten*, vol. II, pp. 378 *et seq.*
[2] Heinrich von Gossler. Prussian Lieutenant-General; Prussian Minister for War, 1896–1903.
[3] Julius, Count von Mirbach-Sorquitten. Member of the Reichstag, 1878–81, 1886–98; Leader of the Conservative Party in the Reichstag; Member of the Prussian House of Lords.

mobilisation against Hohenlohe and Marschall. The general, whose feelings towards the Kaiser we know, will nevertheless at the advice of our enemies and in order to whitewash himself request an audience and will on that occasion once again give the Kaiser the assurance he loves to hear that it was not he who was to blame for the attack on Köller, but that this came from quite another quarter.[1]

That is the situation. There is furious agitation around the Kaiser to force things to a crisis *immediately*, for the reasons mentioned above. He is unfortunately in a mood to be susceptible to agitators, and above all he has no idea of the dangers to which he will expose himself if he pushes matters to a crisis at this time. Whereas Mirbach, who can't wait to get rid of us, brusquely told the War Minister in reply to the imperial order to initiate a conflict: 'We won't take part in that.' H.M. thinks a dissolution of the Reichstag is the simplest thing in the world. Last week he telegraphed to the Chancellor: 'If it is true, as I have read in the *Post*, that an interpellation is to be introduced in the Reichstag to restrict my right of amnesty in duelling matters, I will regard that as a personal attack against myself and will reply by a dissolution of the Reichstag.' The Chancellor soothingly replied that the Reichstag was not even empowered to discuss the right of amnesty because that right was one of the *royal* prerogatives.

Three days later another telegram: in case the President of the Reichstag ever again had the impudence to call a Minister to order, His Majesty would deal with the President in the way he saw fit. The Chancellor replied on the basis of the official records that the call to order agreed upon in such cases was: 'If the previous speaker were a Member of the House I would call him to order,' and that it had been repeatedly used in this form during the Bismarckian period since the year 1873, and that Prince Bismarck had never objected to it, presumably because this formula contained the specific acknowledgment that the right of the President to call to order did not extend to the Government bench.

The realisation that the Kaiser is blindly running into dangers the extent of which—indeed, the existence of which—he is hardly aware is the motive that makes me ask you if you can think of any means of influencing him before it is too late, i.e. without delay. If the Kaiser orders a dissolution now he will be backed by no one but a few individuals *rari nantes in gurgite vasto*. The entire people, all branches, all classes, all shades of opinion, will be against him and will *vote* against him. People will vote for socialism, for liberal demagogy, for the Centre, and for Bismarck. Read the debates of the Hompesch interpellation. The speakers of the four groups of the Right, Mirbach, Kardorff,[2] Paasche,[3]

---

[1] According to Waldersee, Bronsart's audience with the Kaiser did not pass off well. The Kaiser was very cold. (See Waldersee, *Denkwürdigkeiten*, vol. II, p. 376.)

[2] Wilhelm von Kardorff. Member of the Reichstag, 1868–1906; co-founder and leader of the Conservative, subsequently the Free Conservative German Reich Party (the 'Bismarck Party').

[3] Dr Hermann Paasche. Member of the Reichstag (National Liberal Party), 1881–4, 1893–1918; Member of the Prussian Chamber of Deputies, 1893–1908.

Liebermann von Sonnenberg,[1] said nothing else than: 'What Bismarck did must be right, otherwise he would not have done it.' And each time this idea was greeted with cheers by the Right. Not because there were no intelligent people among them who could not privately distinguish right from wrong, but they too cried 'Bravo' because they knew that the patriotic voters demanded it of them, and that they demanded it all the more if they believed Bismarck was opposing the Kaiser. Because the German voter no longer understands the Kaiser and therefore has no confidence in him. The phrase current among all Parties in the Reichstag: 'That the behaviour of the Kaiser can only be explained pathologically', is taking effect quietly but devastatingly, like a miasma. For the time being this feeling is not being expressed openly because the present Government, i.e. Hohenlohe and Marschall, have won a position for themselves, people have confidence in them and regard them as security against the imperial nervousness. But if the present Government disappears, we will experience something to reckon with.

Incidentally, how brilliantly Bismarck is informed about everything the Kaiser does and thinks; recently he has talked constantly of the reappearance of English influences at our Court. I previously thought this was all propaganda without any real foundation. But behold! About four days ago Richthofen[2] suddenly returned from the New Palace with the news that the Kaiser had told him: 'Bismarck conceived of our entire colonial policy only to drive a wedge between ourselves and England on account of the "English influences" . . . so use the money the Reichstag gives you for East Africa. Nothing will come of South-west Africa in any case. We will have to sell that at a good price to England one of these days.'

When Richthofen told me this I felt I had received a blow on the head, because I realised that Bismarck had not been shooting into the air after all. But what do *you* think the German people will say if the news leaks out that the Kaiser is talking about abandoning an area which we have already fought to preserve, for which German blood has flowed in battle, for which a whole series of military orders have already been granted? All that is most dismal.

Marschall is sending you a memorandum about his talk to-day with Lascelles,[3] together with a telegram the Kaiser sent about a fortnight ago to the Chancellor.[4] Compare the two and you will realise fully and

[1] Member of the Reichstag since 1890. Co-founder and leader of the antisemitic German Social [Deutsch-Sozialer] Party.

[2] Oswald, Baron von Richthofen. Director of the Colonial Division of the Foreign Ministry, 1896–7; Under State Secretary, 1897–1900; State Secretary, 1900–6.

[3] Lascelles informed Marschall of his conversation with the Kaiser on the occasion of the Kaiserin Friedrich's birthday: 'His Majesty the Kaiser saw in the rejection of the French proposal for a reform of the Turkish finances an opportunity for weakening the hitherto existing Franco-Russian intimacy. It was obvious that Russia wished to reserve a completely free hand for herself with regard to impending events in Constantinople. At the same time the situation in Russia gave cause for anxiety. Although inspired by the best intentions, Tsar Nicholas was completely spineless and was constantly vacillating.' (*Grosse Politik*, vol. XI, no. 2881, p. 385; vol. XIII, no. 3399, pp. 7–8.)

[4] This was a telegram of 12 November in which the Kaiser informed the Chancellor of a conversation with the Grand Duke Vladimir. In discussing the Armenian Question the

completely that a great state cannot be ruled in this way, and that a great people will not be ruled in this way.

All the foregoing is first of all only for your information, for there is almost nothing that can be passed on. In particular never mention the name of Lascelles. But set your inventive mind to work as to how we can counteract this concentric activity of Waldersee, Bronsart, and the other followers of Bismarck who are trying to lure the Kaiser on to the thin ice of a policy of conflict. But whatever is done must be done soon. At all events you will be able to warn in all truthfulness not only of the existence but also of the growth of the Bismarck cult which threatens to monopolise everything that might be left over of the four groups of the Right—Conservatives, Reich Party, National Liberals, and Anti-Semites—after the elections, which may be imminent.

Your faithful but very depressed
Holstein.

587. Holstein to Philipp zu Eulenburg

Copy

Berlin, 30 November 1896

Dear friend,

This letter[1] was a great and courageous action, carried out with that ingenious skill which is your secret. You say dejectedly that the time will come when this means too will fail. *That* time will then also be the beginning of bitter experiences and humiliations for the Kaiser—and unfortunately for the German Reich too, perhaps. That day will come, of course, but as patriotic royalists we will try to put it off as long as possible.

A man in a high position who may know what he is talking about told the Chancellor the day before yesterday that the Kaiser could not get accustomed to the idea that his power was restricted by the Reichstag. The idea of ruling without the Reichstag never left his mind, and was encouraged by one sector of his entourage. The Kaiser intended, in agreement with the German Princes, to dissolve the Reichstag, and if necessary to do so an indefinite number of times. If the Reichstag membership nevertheless grew worse instead of better, he intended—to alter the Constitution independently of the Reichstag, especially the electoral law. The Kaiser knew that at the moment he could not count on any of the older politicians for this policy of coercion, not on you either, and he was not even sure of Waldersee (who may be distasteful to him for other reasons as well). The Kaiser was therefore nursing the

---

Kaiser had explained that only the fact that the Continental Powers held firmly together had prevented 'grave disasters', and he had expressed the hope that in the future too no Great Power would use its army to serve English interests. (From the Foreign Ministry files.)

[1] Eulenburg's letter to the Kaiser of 26 November which he wrote on the basis of Holstein's letter of 24 November. (See above.) 'It would not be wise to move either against the Reichstag or the Hohenlohe Ministry while the Reichstag is in session, and not afterwards either,' Eulenburg wrote. 'The German people would no longer understand Your Majesty.' (Haller, *Eulenburg*, pp. 214–15.)

idea of summoning a younger officer to undertake this task, whom he would previously pledge to go through thick and thin with his Kaiser.

The man who supplied this information is absolutely trustworthy and clear-headed, with reliable sources of information at his disposal. I therefore assume that this information is correct. From this it is easy to see the obvious task of every sensible adviser of the Kaiser: it is necessary to tell the Kaiser again and again that the prerequisite of every dangerous undertaking like the one he is planning must be the agreement of the German Princes. Young military climbers and enthusiasts who pledge themselves to support him in anything, even if it means going to the scaffold, and even if they aren't made Chancellor in the process—these he will find in abundance. But as things stand to-day and with the unfortunately diminished confidence in his person, he will have to look a long time for German Princes who will commit themselves and their subjects in this manner. *And herein—we can say this candidly among ourselves—lies the best protection of the German people against imperial phantasies.*

I agree with you that the domestic situation *may* change in such a way as to compel the Government to adopt extraordinary measures in defence of the social order. But this necessity does not exist to-day. The Reichstag has proved itself far more competent than one could have expected immediately after the elections. It has opened the most varied sources of revenue, and neither the army nor the navy has a right to complain about it. A demand for about 200 million for new artillery is pending, and nobody seriously doubts that this will be granted. In view of this gigantic additional burden, though one which is vital for the Reich, the navy will simply have to accept the fact that cuts will be made in its demand for 70 million. The amount of these cuts will be in direct relationship with the bitterness which the constant insolent public pronouncements of Senden are arousing *crescendo* in all political and parliamentary circles. Even the Conservatives are stating that one won't be able to grant more than half of the demands made by the navy. And two days ago someone in the right wing of the National Liberal Party told Captain Borckenhagen, the Chief of Staff of the Commanding Admiral, that nobody could be astonished if the Reichstag looked upon the naval demands with suspicion when it heard the doctrine preached by authoritative people, especially by Admiral Senden, that our navy had to be made ready for a war with England.

I have no doubts that the cuts in the navy's demands will once again make for a temporarily sultry atmosphere, despite the winter weather. Nothing can be done about that, however. No amount of persuasion would be able to remove the suspicion awakened in the Reichstag by statements emanating from Court, not to mention the speeches of Senden. Nor is H.M. always fortunate in what he says. When Prince Arenberg,[1] a Reichstag Deputy, did the honours for the Kaiser at the Colonial Exposition last summer, H.M. suddenly exclaimed at a place where there were stakes before the house of a negro king with skulls on

[1] Franz Ludwig, Prinz von Arenberg. Member of the Reichstag (Centre Party).

them: 'If only I could see the Reichstag strung up like that.' That is hardly diplomatic. *On ne prend pas des mouches avec du vinaigre.*

The way to deal with the Reichstag and the question of a conflict can be summed up in saying that the Kaiser, before he lifts a foot to take the first step, must receive the unqualified assurance, in black and white and with the personal signature of the people concerned, that the German Princes will promise him their unreserved political and military support to the end in the fight against Parliament. It can be foreseen that this assurance will be denied him as long as the domestic affairs do not get any worse than they are to-day. But the enquiry and the negative result will be useful for the political orientation of the All-Gracious Lord. It would be a practical experience which could have no dangerous consequences either for him or for the Reich. At most the Princes will wonder about the nature of the question, but they are already wondering about a good many things, just as we do.

That the German Princes feel no fundamental ill-will towards the concept of the Reich can be seen from a letter I received yesterday from Monts.[1] You will remember that I told you that the question of military sashes and cockades had been clumsily handled and that the sash question was quite hopeless, whereas there was some prospect of getting the cockades if the matter were handled properly. My information was the product of discussions between Marschall and Lerchenfeld. I think that Marschall also talked with Hohenthal.[2] Shortly afterwards the War Minister raised the question of cockades without the sashes, and now Monts writes on the 28th: 'Please treat as absolutely confidential for the present. I have heard that the Regent to-day gave his consent to the use of the German cockade for all officers of the [Bavarian] army.' If I stress the secret but effective role that the diplomatic element played in securing this valuable concession, it is in order to return to the idea I brought up with you orally that the Kaiser should treat Lerchenfeld a little better, i.e., not so demonstratively badly as he has done in recent years. H.M. would thereby make it decidedly easier for himself and for his organs of government to realise objectives within Germany than by abusing people in public, threats, and pounding his fist on the table.

Here ends that part of my letter which might perhaps afford you some occasion to bring your influence to bear on H.M. There are in my opinion perhaps two points which it would be useful not to forget. *First* the absolute necessity for the Kaiser to secure the co-operation of the German Princes in binding written agreements before embarking on the struggle with Parliament; the Kaiser even needs this agreement for a dissolution of the Reichstag, because this requires a majority in the Bundesrat; there are fifty-eight votes in the Bundesrat, however, and Prussia only has seventeen. *Second* it would be a good thing if the

---

[1] Not found. To commemorate the 100th birthday of Kaiser Wilhelm I (22 June 1897), the Kaiser wanted to introduce a red, white and black cockade for the entire German army. The agreement of Bavaria was obtained only after difficult negotiations.

[2] Wilhelm, Count von Hohenthal und Bergen. Saxon Minister to Berlin, 1885–1906.

Kaiser became aware or bore in mind that Senden's boastful provocations are very largely to blame for slowing up the development of the navy in so far as the financial co-operation of the Reichstag is concerned.

What follows is intended solely for your information.

Yesterday at the audience of the Chancellor, with Marschall and Hollmann, to discuss means for acquiring a naval base in China,[1] the Kaiser also requested Senden, Plessen, and Villaume to be present. The discussion ended with a long speech by the Kaiser in which he said that he would not send Colonel Liebert[2] to China on the one hand, and on the other that he would not seize some Chinese island because we had to keep our hands free for eventualities closer to home. He had received a letter from the Tsar of Russia—which he would afterwards show to Hohenlohe and Marschall—from which he assumed that Russia intended to embark on an aggressive policy. We would therefore have to make ready, etc. etc. Incidentally, he failed to show the letter to Hohenlohe and Marschall afterwards, perhaps because it occurred to him that they were both praised in it. They already know that he told the English Ambassador so.[3]

If I were compelled to formulate my opinion briefly about the present position of Germany with respect to the other European Powers, I would say that I hoped that confidence in the integrity and calm and consistent policy of the Hohenlohe regime would succeed in neutralising to a large extent the serious consequences which would otherwise be unavoidable owing to the contradictory tactics employed by the Kaiser towards sovereigns who talk frankly with one another as relatives despite the conflict of interest among their peoples.

As your friend, however, I cannot advise you to raise this question of the blunders in *foreign* affairs with H.M. because this would wound the imperial self-esteem too severely. It would only make him furiously angry, even if one hinted ever so gently that even the most stupid of that whole porphyrogenital society, whom he regards not without justification as far beneath him intellectually, see through him and ridicule him. A typical example was the remark made by that silly Princess of Wales: 'Yes, isn't he a fool.'[4] So, as I said, my advice would be to keep hands off that subject. My advice is the same with respect to summoning members of the Imperial Household or of the bureaux to the audiences of the Chancellor, although this procedure is somewhat infuriating. Since not one of these officials hardly ever opens his mouth, the purpose of their presence can only be to degrade the

[1] See *Grosse Politik*, vol. XIVi, no. 3670, p. 47, note *; Hohenlohe, *Denkwürdigkeiten der Reichskanzlerzeit*, pp. 279–82.

[2] Eduard von Liebert. Regimental Commander, but for the most part in German East Africa and China; Governor of German East Africa, 1897–1900; Member of the Reichstag (Radical Party), 1907–13. Liebert was to have borne the insignia of the Order of the Black Eagle to the Emperor of China.

[3] Lascelles informed Marschall that the Kaiser had briefly mentioned the interpellation in the Reichstag in their conversation of 21 November: 'They had all talked around the subject, and only Eugen Richter, whom he [the Kaiser] otherwise detests, had hit the nail on the head and said openly what everybody thought and felt.' (*Grosse Politik*, vol. XIII, no. 3399, pp. 7–8.)

[4] In English in the original.

position of the Chancellor. But in my opinion nobody can do anything about improving that situation except the Chancellor himself. It would be of great value to *me* to hear your opinion on this point and how it might be dealt with.

I forgot above to mention at the right place that the Chancellor sends you his warmest thanks for your letter to the Kaiser which His Highness read with lively expressions of approval.[1] [...]

588.   Holstein to Hugo von Radolin[2]

10 December 1896

Dear friend,

Marschall's long audience to-day with H.M. about the law suit went off satisfactorily.[3] The Kaiser assured His Excellency of his complete confidence. I am glad, because it is known that there was a vast amount of agitation against Marschall on the part of the entourage, especially by Senden and Plessen. He has gradually won himself a significant position by his outstanding talents as a speaker.

The statement in to-day's *Reichsanzeiger* is the result of M.'s audience.[4]

After the revelations about the secret treaty, the Kaiser wrote to the Tsar that he hoped their relations would remain the same.[5] The Tsar sent a friendly reply and made some very appreciative comments about the statements of Hoh[enlohe] and Marsch[all]. But surely I wrote you all that already?? One grows old.

As to the Near East, we are at the moment waiting to see what will happen. I dictated the conversation I had yesterday with Lanza[6] to Mumm.[7] You will get the memorandum either to-day or tomorrow in code.

Osten-Sacken hasn't put in an appearance at the Ministry for weeks. Reason unknown; we will have to bear with it.[8]

To-day somebody told me who had heard it from Septi Reuss (*retour de* Friedrichsruh) that Prince Bismarck really seemed to believe that the Tsar had intended to visit him but that he had been prevented from doing so by our Kaiser.

What can be the truth of the matter? The Kaiser—ours—swears

---

[1] Eulenburg replied on 3 December: 'Only *one* word more to tell you how pleased I am that you are satisfied with me. That makes me completely HAPPY!'

[2] From the Radolin Papers.

[3] See Hohenlohe, *Denkwürdigkeiten der Reichskanzlerzeit*, p. 288, note 1.

[4] The following statement appeared in the *Reichsanzeiger* of 10 December: 'We are empowered to make the statement that the intrigues directed against highly placed personages have already been the subject of discussion at the Crown Council held in Hubertusstock on the 7th of October. On its being reported that it had been established that the author of the well-known article in *Die Welt am Montag* was von Lützow, an agent of the political police, His Majesty the Kaiser ordered that the affair should be strictly investigated and cleared up in every particular.'

[5] Letter of 12 November 1896. (*Briefe Wilhelms II. an den Zaren*, pp. 303–4.)

[6] Carlo, Count di Lanza-Busia. Italian Ambassador in Berlin, 1892–1907.

[7] See *Grosse Politik*, vol. XIIi, no. 3076, p. 232.

[8] See Hohenlohe, *Denkwürdigkeiten der Reichskanzlerzeit*, p. 286, note 2.

up and down that he knows nothing about it.[1] The thing is also doubtful in itself; for the Russians after all need France, first for financial reasons and secondly against England. Nothing the Tsar could have done, however, could have thrown more cold water on French enthusiasm than a visit to Friedrichsruh. But—can it be that *Shuvalov* gave birth to this idea of a visit, or that he passed it on? *That* I might perhaps believe. But I could also imagine that this idea would not thrive in the soil of the Russian Court at the present time. Bismarck, however, being as suspicious as he is, now thinks that our Kaiser put a stop to the business.

Perhaps by chance you will hear something. The matter is not suitable for asking questions.

I cannot help telling you that H.M. read your long amusing gossip-report out loud at supper with obvious satisfaction—but to the dissatisfaction of Her M.

With kindest regards
Your old
Holstein

589. Paul von Hatzfeldt to Holstein

London, 10 December 1896

Dear friend,

I received your detailed and most interesting though hardly gratifying letter, and cannot thank you and Baron Marschall enough for sending me this information.

I am in complete agreement, and like you I deplore the vacillations in question about which nothing can be done unfortunately and which must obviously do us great damage. That those insinuations about colonies won't bear much fruit here can be seen by the fact that Salisbury, although he mentioned the report from Lascelles, didn't say a single word to me about the matter.[2] This proves that either he doesn't believe in our sincerity or that he places no value on the colonies we want to give him. Perhaps he also takes it for granted that in the course of events they will some day fall into England's lap of their own accord. This in itself is bad enough, but the main problem is that our public had not been told anything about this imperial idea because, as you rightly assume, the impression created by such information would be profound and extremely unfavourable. The political oscillations are almost worse so far as the impression created abroad is concerned, for they destroy the last remnant of confidence people felt in us. With respect to England, to be sure, our alliance possibilities won't get any worse because the

---

[1] See the Kaiser's letter to Hohenlohe of [3 November 1896]. (Hohenlohe, *Denkwürdigkeiten der Reichskanzlerzeit*, p. 271.)

[2] In his report of his conversation with the Kaiser (see p. 655, note 3) Lascelles said: 'Turning to the colonial question, His Majesty the Kaiser observed that he had come to the conclusion that Germany was unable to develop all her colonies, and that it would be better to restrict oneself to *one* and to abandon the others. An agreement with England on this matter would be easy to achieve in the event that the latter would concede Germany a coaling-station elsewhere.'

English seem resolved in any case to abstain from any alliance with us. Nor does she need such an alliance if she is resolved, as she seems to be, not to create any serious difficulties for the Russians in the East.

As you have written me nothing more about Amoy, I assume and hope that the idea has been abandoned, at least for the present.[1] The assumption that the English would agree to our seizure of territory there and would depart with their ships the moment we appeared is in my opinion absolutely without foundation. They are in the worst possible frame of mind towards us here and there is no reason whatever to believe that they will take pleasure in conceding us a substantial gain in China. I of course fully share your opinion that the present moment is least suitable for a sensational action on the part of Germany in China. Furthermore, I think there are only two ways by which we can get anything in China: either by a friendly agreement with the Chinese in the manner that Marschall has already initiated with Li Hung-chang,[2] or through the mediation of the Russians, who have the power to do so but who would also probably demand that we pay a high price for it. [...]

With kindest regards
Your
PHatzfeldt [...]

590. Holstein to Philipp zu Eulenburg[3]

Berlin, 12 December 1896

Dear friend,

I don't usually read the *Kladderadatsch* because what good does it do to make oneself angry? To-day however I went through it carefully for strategic reasons and recommend that you do the same. You will observe that at the moment the people behind the *Kladderadatsch* feel that *you* are very much in the way. The most important thing in my opinion is the poem 'The Broom' ['Der Kehraus'] on the first page, especially the last verse, because this shows how much that whole group loathes the *public nature* [of the Tausch case].[4] They clamoured for it at the time because they knew better than anyone that we could not take the matter to court.[5] Now they have their wish and are furious.

---

[1] Amoy was one of the Chinese ports under consideration for seizure by the Germans. (See Klehmet's memorandum of 28 November 1896, *Grosse Politik*, vol. XIVi, no. 3669. pp. 43–6.) The Kaiser appears to have decided against Amoy, because on 30 November he instructed Admiral Knorr to draw up a plan for the seizure of Kiaochow. (*Grosse Politik*, vol. XIVi, p. 47, note *; see also *Memoirs*, pp. 179–81.)

[2] See Marschall's memorandum of 19 June 1896. (*Grosse Politik*, vol. XIVi, no. 3663, pp. 27–34.)

[3] From the Papers of Baroness von der Heydt. Only a typewritten copy of this document was available to the editors.

[4] See p. 652, note 3. The issue of the *Kladderadatsch* to which Holstein refers was that of 13 December 1896 which contained a number of attacks on Eulenburg based chiefly on his alleged connection with Tausch. The last verse of the poem 'Der Kehraus' expressed regret that so much dirty linen had been washed in public, and maintained that this had not been necessary in order to clean up the political police.

[5] Holstein refers to the attacks of the *Kladderadatsch* upon himself, Eulenburg, and Kiderlen-Wächter in 1894. (See p. 456, note 4.)

Marschall's audience[1] went off better than I had expected. I would assume from what Marschall told me about it that *this* business hasn't left any stings in H.M. After the first audience of three-quarters of an hour, the Kaiser said to Marschall: 'I must say that at times I felt that things weren't being done according to the old Prussian tradition, but meanwhile the Minister of the Interior and the Head of the Police have assured me that you kept them informed at all stages of the proceedings so that they were always in a position to be able to raise a protest. It is also evident that a mere disciplinary action would not have been adequate to deal with such a deeply-rooted business as this.' In reply to Marschall's question, H.M. assured him of his complete confidence and approved that the *Reichsanzeiger* should announce that H.M. had ordered a thorough clarification of the entire business as early as the beginning of October at the meeting of the Crown Council at Hubertusstock.[2]

Yesterday a member of the Upper House told me that he had heard from Court circles that H.M. had said he had to admit that after Marschall's report he saw the whole matter in quite a different light.

Marschall has been in bed for two days. Stomach cramps. He should be all right again the day after tomorrow, and he will be needed in order to answer all sorts of questions about legal proceedings in the Reichstag.

Septi[3] and his wife together with Lichnowsky had luncheon with the Kaiser the day before yesterday. The latter talked for some time aside with Septi. Lichnowsky found out later that their conversation dealt with the Eastern Question. His Majesty confided all sorts of things to Septi about his Eastern policy which might better have been left unsaid in the case of this interlocutor. When Lichnowsky spoke with the Reusses about the Hamburg revelations[4] and their injurious effect in Vienna and Pest, the Princess pounded on the table and denied that they were injurious. When L. remarked that so far as he could see the revelations had benefited only the Kaiser and Marschall, she exclaimed: 'Of course. It was precisely the Kaiser whom Prince Bismarck wished to benefit.' Further Septi said in part to L. and in part to Szögyényi: that Prince Bismarck was firmly convinced that the Tsar of Russia had wanted to visit him and that he had been prevented from doing so in Breslau. He, the Prince, knew that during the Kaiser's trip to Kiel a telegram had been sent from a station along the way saying that the arrival in Kiel would take place a few hours earlier than had originally been arranged. (This would indicate another indiscretion of some kind, it seems to me.) According to Reuss, Prince Bismarck has been unusually depressed and melancholy for several months and to have sought solace in wine until Schweninger recently put a categorical stop to it—or tried to. Perhaps the beginning of this depression coincides with the collapse of Shuvalov.

It is characteristic of Prince Bismarck to seek external diversions when

[1] See p. 660, note 3.   [2] See p. 660, note 4.
[3] Prince Heinrich VII (Septimus) Reuss.   [4] See p. 652, note 2.

he is in this kind of mood. As we can see, he is occupied at the moment with the Italo-Russian Reinsurance Treaty, and there will probably be a good deal more to come. Although I'm not a prophet, I would suspect from what I am able to observe that a change is taking place in the attitude of the general public. People still admire Prince Bismarck as before, but they no longer accept as gospel everything reported in the Bismarck Press. The *National Zeitung*, for instance, is beginning to be quite sarcastic.

So much for that. The conversations of the Kaiser with foreign ambassadors are not bearing good fruit, as one might have expected. Lord Salisbury is extremely annoyed about the accusation that England played a part in the strike in Hamburg—and he is showing it.[1]

Eisendecher reported to-day that Senden wrote him at the order of the Kaiser to come to Berlin to confer with an Englishman named Allan (presumably a ship builder). It of course didn't occur to Senden to inform the Chancellor.

As for the Eastern Question, it is significant that whereas the English and the Russians seem to be drawing closer together on the question of 'coercive measures', Hanotaux informed the English Ambassador that France could not promise her participation for any kind of coercive measures.[2] At the moment there is friction between Hanotaux and the Russians on account of wounded personal vanity. This situation will stand the English in good stead in the *Egyptian* question.

With kindest regards
Your
Holstein.[3]

591. Paul von Hatzfeldt to Holstein

London, 28 December 1896

Dear friend,

[...] Deym still maintains that Salisbury's only interest in the whole Conference[4] and its results is to be able to use it in a Blue Book to prove that he had done everything he could. He was utterly indifferent as to whether or not any real reforms were secured. Deym also tried very hard to convince me that Salisbury, although he did not say so openly,

---

[1] German newspapers had accused English agitators of fomenting a strike of the Hamburg dock labourers at the end of November 1896. The Kaiser asked the English Government to issue an official denial of the German newspaper reports so as not to increase anti-English feeling in Germany. Salisbury said in reply: 'The imputation is so devoid of foundation that an official denial would be received with ridicule.' (*Grosse Politik*, vol. XIII, no. 3400, pp. 8–9.)

[2] See *Grosse Politik*, vol. XIIi, no. 3081, pp. 237–8; *Documents Diplomatiques Français*, Première Série, vol. XIII, no. 39, pp. 69–72.

[3] Eulenburg replied on 14 December: 'The *Kladderadatsch* is unbelievable! I see from this (and from many other symptoms!) *how* angry they are in certain circles that I came out of the Tausch affair without difficulty. I think that there are few people in Germany who are so hated as I am—and it seems to me that they might instead be a little grateful to me!'

[4] The Conference of Ambassadors of the Great Powers which met in Constantinople to discuss the question of Turkish reforms. (See Hatzfeldt's dispatch of 22 December, *Grosse Politik*, vol. XIIi, no. 3086, pp. 241–3.)

was still determined to oppose every Russian advance towards the Dardanelles. I replied that I did not think so and was on the contrary convinced that if it came to a show-down he would say: '*Messieurs les Autrichiens, tirez les premiers!*' Thereupon Deym became somewhat thoughtful and admitted that this was still a somewhat obscure point. [...]

Good-bye and with best wishes for the New Year

Always yours
Hatzfeldt.

WITHDRAWN
AUGSBURG COLLEGE & SEMINARY
George Sverdrup Library
MINNEAPOLIS 4, MINNESOTA